INTRODUCTION TO THE World OF Communication

REVISED FIRST EDITION

EDITED WITH INTRODUCTIONS TO THE READINGS BY

TAMMY R. VIGIL

cognella™
San Diego, CA

Bassim Hamadeh, CEO and Publisher
Christopher Foster, General Vice President
Michael Simpson, Vice President of Acquisitions
Jessica Knott, Managing Editor
Kevin Fahey, Cognella Marketing Manager
Jess Busch, Senior Graphic Designer
John Remington, Acquisitions Editor
Jamie Giganti, Project Editor
Luiz Ferreira and Brian Fahey, Licensing Associates

First published in the United States of America in 2013 by Cognella, Inc.

Printed in the United States of America

ISBN: 978-1-62131-060-0 (pbk) / 978-1-62131-061-7 (pf)

www.cognella.com 800.200.3908

Contents

Introduction

By Tammy R. Vigil

Welcome to the world of communication. While this welcome is somewhat belated—because humans are active participants in a communicative world for the better part of their existence—the decision to study communication actively in a systematic way marks a new and exciting moment in anyone's relationship, to both the general act of communicating and the various specific communication career fields. No matter if approaching this study with an eye toward academic enlightenment or with a focus on professional preparation and development, anyone studying communication will find that it is a field with unexpected challenges and opportunities at every turn. This text is intended as an overview and introduction to the discipline and its corresponding professions.

The Communication Tradition

There is a common misperception that the study of communication is a relatively young discipline. While it is true the study of mass communication and the development of communication departments, schools and colleges have a relatively short history—beginning mostly in the early 20th century and initially housed in departments such as English, Psychology, and Auditory Sciences—the systematic study of communication as a human action actually dates back beyond the ancient Greek and Roman philosophers. As explained in the chapter titled "Human Communication Theory and Research: Traditions and Models" in this text, some of the world's oldest writings contain lessons in communicating effectively. The study of communication is, in fact, among the oldest and most developed academic pursuits.

The long, rich history of the study of communication has always included the intertwining of intellectual examination with practical application. Whether novices, dilettantes, or experts, scholars of communication generally approach their studies with the aim of improving their own communication skills, the skills of others, or both. For most, this means acquiring a better understanding of some aspect of communication in order to develop suggestions for more effective strategies, to sharpen or expand existing skills, or to chronicle best practices. This is true from the first tomes written centuries ago to modern texts such as this one.

One of the most famous and enduring communication handbooks is *On Rhetoric* written by Aristotle during the 4th century B.C.E. Aristotle's three-book text examines "all the available means of influence."[*] It outlines the ways in which humans appeal to one another in order to alter each other's attitudes, beliefs, and/or behaviors. While

---

[*]   Aristotle. *On Rhetoric*, trans. George A. Kennedy. New York: Oxford University Press, 1991.

providing a codification of influences in the form of artistic (author-constructed) and inartistic (external evidence-based) proofs, *On Rhetoric* also provides ample instances of influential appeals, explains the reasons for their effectiveness, and delineates guidelines for successfully using such appeals. This application-oriented approach stems from Aristotle's fascination with communication as a practical aspect of society.[†] His intertwined theories on ethics and communication are secularly based and are intended to help readers apply specific principles in different situations in order to increase the likelihood of a successful communication outcome. Aristotle takes great care to explain both the underlying principles of what makes communication effective and to give suggestions for how a speaker might improve specific skills. Aristotle's concern is with the proper use of communication skills, not just increasing overall effectiveness. In both *On Rhetoric* and a separate book, *Nicomachean Ethics*, Aristotle outlines proper and improper uses of effective communication skills. Like any responsible communication scholar, Aristotle encourages effective and ethically responsible application of communicative skills.

Aristotle laid the foundation for the now long-standing tradition of blending both descriptive and prescriptive interests via the study of communication. The blend of intellectual examination, ethical consideration, and practical application has always been (and continues to be) essential in the exploration of communication.

Any effective textbook on communication should constantly blend explanations of "what" and "why" with instructions on "how to." All major schools and colleges of communication offer a mix of courses that combine theory and research with professional development and skill building. This is because communication is such an essential part of human existence. All human interactions, be they personal, social, or professional, casual or formal, intentional or unintentional, critical or superficial, successful or unsuccessful, are

only possible via communication. Unfortunately, in spite of the vital nature of communication in a social world, communication as an academic discipline is often misunderstood and misjudged.

Communication: The Misunderstood Discipline

Anyone who studies the field of communication for any length of time quickly discovers that a variety of misconceptions and erroneous judgments regarding the study of communication exists. It is not unusual for parents, grandparents, and others to wonder what it really means to be a communication major. For many individuals, the act of communicating seems so natural and common that the idea of studying it seems either unusual or unnecessary. This often leads to another misperception: that a major in communication is not "real," but an easy pursuit lacking rigor or intensity. These perspectives are usually based on a lack of information and a series of stereotypes associated with the discipline.

Majoring in any aspect of communication is not for the faint of heart. Similar in professional focus to the study of business, medicine, or law, the study of communication can prepare any student for a series of specific careers requiring dedicated skills and knowledge sets. Contrary to mistaken assumptions, the study of communication can be a very challenging professional endeavor. It requires students to be broadly educated within the liberal arts, in addition to engaging in professional training and development, because a successful communicator must know more than simply the most effective means of communicating and how to apply them. An effective communication professional must have an understanding of the specific topic information for the context in which he or she will be working (e.g., political reporters must know politics, a PR specialist working for an environmental organization must have some understanding of environmental sciences, a documentary filmmaker must know something about whatever he or she is documenting). Also, because creating

---

[†]   Aristotle. *On Rhetoric*, trans. George A. Kennedy. New York: Oxford University Press, 1991.

messages for an audience requires knowledge of the physical and social environment the audience resides in, as well as an understanding of the audience, a student of communication would be wise to establish a broad understanding of the world that provides both content and context for the messages he or she will be creating. This means that a well-educated communicator needs some understanding of human psychological and sociological processes. Also, communication specialists increasingly need to understand developing technologies and their impact and uses in contemporary communication environments.

A good communicator is someone who has something to say that is interesting, important, and informed. No matter the particular career, a student of communication is best served by an understanding of history, sociology, politics, science, psychology, art, and other areas that enrich the communicator's understanding of the world in which he or she operates. Knowing simply how to run a camera does not make someone an effective filmmaker; knowing how to create a storyboard does not make someone an effective advertiser; knowing how to talk on camera does not make someone an effective broadcast journalist. It takes a broader interest and understanding of the world at large to be an effective communicator in any industry.

Unlike its professional counterparts, communication is often devalued because of its common nature. People assume that because we all communicate, the study of this daily activity is unnecessary. While it is true that individuals are socialized into communication (i.e., you learn to communicate by being around people who are communicating), this does not invalidate the study of this action. The shared nature of communication makes its study an essential academic and professional pursuit. The importance of communication to our civilization and civility increases this importance.

Effective communication is the foundation for a civil society. Communication, whether verbal, written, nonverbal, interpersonal, small group, mass mediated, via social networks or face-to-face, is the only portal for civilized interaction among individuals. Communication facilitates relationships between interdependent entities. Communication allows for the existence of social contracts and bonds. Communication is the only medium for healthy debate and discussion. Therefore, the study of communication is not only an academically important field; it is essential for human social growth and productivity.

The importance of communication extends beyond the boundaries of its own academic walls. Without communication, there are no other disciplines. It is not possible to teach one another any subject absent communication. There are no books to read, no lectures to give, no mentoring to be had. Without communication, businesses cannot function. Without communication, laws cannot be expressed, interpreted, enforced, or questioned. Without communication, there is no history to be learned or learned from. Politics and political science are entirely based on human interactions, or put another way, politics does not exist without communication. All of the *-ologies* (biology, psychology, theology) cannot exist without communication, because the "study of" any subject requires interpretation, understanding, labeling—all based on the development of shared meaning, a meaning shared through communication.

With a better understanding of communication fundamentals, businesses can be more successful, medical professionals can exchange ideas and better interact with patients, political messages can be more effective and more effectively critiqued. Through communication, engineering innovations are more effectively disseminated. Improved communication leads to improved teaching, learning, and mentoring. Understanding communication principles allows for more effective relationship development and conflict resolution. Improving communication is a means for enhancing a democratic society, because through effective communication, it is possible to transmit information, engage in useful debate, encourage the thoughtful exchange of ideas, critique the powerful, and empower the oppressed.

While it is true that communication can be used for ill as well as for good, a good communicator is an ethical communicator. It is good communication that combats the unethical, unscrupulous communication that can hinder the development of a good society. Communication is vital to human society, and well-educated communicators can make great contributions to the world.

A Well-Educated Communicator

The most basic forms of communication do not take much formal study or training. Yet simply practicing the act without thoughtful introspection and assessment limits the growth one might have in improving his or her skills and knowledge. It is always possible to improve communication through systematic study and training. A thoughtful and well-educated student of communication must have a philosophical as well as practical understanding of the art and craft of communicating. Therefore, a well-educated student of communication must understand:

… the human nature of communication. The individual influence on all acts of communication opens each message to varying interpretations, resulting in more—or less—effective communication.

… the symbolic nature of all communication. Knowing that communication is a human action, and the means by which we communicate are human constructs, allows communicators the ability to embrace the creative opportunities in the art of communicating.

… the power of symbols to unite, divide, and shape one's interpretation of the world. A healthy respect for the immense power of symbols is necessary for students to learn to use symbols ethically and responsibly.

… the multifaceted nature of symbols provides educated communicators with multiple methods for conveying meaning. Understanding differences in audiences, goals, and various communication strategies makes students more agile in message creation and adaptation in order to increase the likelihood of successfully and ethically conveying meaning.

… the influence of communication technologies on individuals and society. Changes in communication technologies necessarily influence the personal and professional interactions of all communicators. These changes also affect societies in various ways. It is essential for a well-educated communicator to consider these impacts in a meaningful way.

… the variety of career opportunities available to an effective communicator. As stated earlier, the tradition of communication is both academic and applied. A well-educated student of communication must consider the professional trades specific to communication, and communication's impact on other professions.

… the intertwined nature of communication careers. It is impossible to point to a single communication career that stands alone without influence from or influence on other career fields. It is important for students to understand this mingled discipline in order to prepare effectively for a successful career.

This text is designed to provide readers with an initial introduction to each of the ideas stated above. Each chapter has been selected for its ability to start the reader down the pathway to becoming a well-educated communicator. This overview will serve the reader well in a continued progression through the systematic study of a particular area of communication.

The World of Communication: An Overview

The chapters in this book are arranged in order to provide a logical introduction to communication for someone seeking a well-rounded approach. The first portion is dedicated to understanding key elements of communicative acts. These concepts and ideas transcend any particular area of study or prospective career path, and are applicable in a multitude of contexts. The second portion of this text is designed to stimulate conversation and consideration of the impact of various media.

By understanding the historic transitions and changes in society brought forth by ever evolving communication technology, students become better prepared to be at the vanguard of communication evolution as technologies continue to emerge and converge. This leads to the third portion of the text, the focus on communication professions. The chapters in this section are intended to provide an overview of three broad areas of communication professions: the audio/visual arts of film and television; the informative/critical nature of journalism; and the strategic/persuasive processes of public relations and advertising.

Section One of the book begins with a very basic introductory chapter aimed at helping set the parameters of the study of communication. "Human Communication: What and Why," by Ronald Adler, George Rodman and Carrie Hutchinson provides insight into the very basics about communication, including what communication is and is not, misunderstandings and myths of communication, and why miscommunication occurs so often.

Chapter 2, "Language," also by Adler, Rodman and Hutchinson explores one of the most commonly considered parts of communication: the spoken or written word. Because it is the mode of communication most frequently identified as an area of emphasis, it makes sense to start here. However, because language is only one of several ways to communicate, Chapter 3 covers "Nonverbal Communication." This chapter, by Walid Afifi, expands the parameters of influence and exchange by including physical, visual, and nonlinguistic auditory cues as valuable and influential means of communicating.

The fourth chapter expands further the basic concepts of communication by examining the individual influence on meaning construction. "Viewers Making Meaning," by Marita Sturken and Lisa Cartwright, approaches communication from the perspective of visual literacy. By discussing the influences and interpretations of visual communication, Sturken and Cartwright drive readers to think about the varied nature of symbols and the human nature of communication.

"On Writing Well," by Brian Carroll, is the fifth chapter. It focuses on the elements of creating an effective written message in a digital age. The essential elements of good writing are the essential elements of effective communication placed in a particular context and medium. This chapter will help readers improve specific writing skills and think more broadly about effective message construction.

Chapter 6, "Human Communication Theory and Research: Traditions and Models," by Virginia Richmond and James McCroskey, reviews the ways in which scholars have examined and explained communication over centuries of study. This chapter provides insights into our broader understanding of the field as well as some of the challenges faced by students of such a broad and important discipline.

The seventh chapter, "Communication Ethics," by Donald K. Wright, outlines key ethical considerations that effective communicators must make. Wright offers an outline of ethical traditions and approaches to ethical decision making, and encourages readers to appreciate more fully the challenges and need for a guiding communication ethic.

Chapter 8, "Communication Law and Regulation in the Digital Age," by John Pavlik and Shawn McIntosh, examines the history of communication law and contemporary laws of particular concern to communication professionals. Some of the many ideas covered include slander and libel, obscenity laws, FCC powers, the Sullivan Rule, net neutrality, and other key concepts in communication law.

The ninth chapter signals a shift from generally applicable concepts to a focus on mass communication and communication technologies. Chapter 9, "Shaping the American Mass Media: A Brief Overview," was written by mass communication studies icon Melvin L. DeFleur. This chapter outlines the development of mass communication technologies and systems. DeFleur's historical perspective provides readers with a deep understanding of the influences mass media have had on the development of American society.

Chapter 10, aptly titled "Understanding Mass Media and the Importance of Media Literacy," addresses the ways media impact communication. In this chapter, Joseph Turow revisits some key concepts covered in the first chapter and places them in the context of mass media. Moving beyond a simple review and application, Turow also discusses the impact of mass media on society and individuals. The chapter ends with an informative discussion about media literacy—what it means, how it is attained, and why it is vital in an age dominated by mediated communication forums.

In Chapter 11, "Cyberspace, Digital Media, and the Internet," Jason Whittaker provides a useful overview of evolving communication technologies. Rather than trying to address the most current evolution of technology, a task that is nearly impossible in any textbook format, Whittaker emphasizes an understanding of the emergence of technologies from a historical and developmental perspective. The focus on cyberspace invites readers to consider the larger web of communication technologies that include and extend beyond the Internet.

Chapter 12 "Making Relationships Work," may initially seem out of place in a section dedicated to mass and mediated communication. However, as one reads the chapter, it becomes clear that while relational communication is traditionally considered personal and dyadic, today's world of mediated interpersonal communication is dominated by technology and mediation. In this chapter, J. Dan Rothwell guides readers through the complex arena of interpersonal relationships, beginning with traditional approaches to relationship building, maintenance, and dissolution, and quickly moves to a valuable discussion of the impact of emerging technologies on relationships of various sorts. As such, it is ideally situated as a follow-up to readings on mass communication and evolving communication technologies.

Beginning with Chapter 13, "An Overview of the TV Industry," the text turns toward the communication professions. This chapter provides insights on basic elements of television from a professional perspective. In it, Martie Cook outlines the business side of television, the ever changing nature of the industry, and the impact of technology on television content and business. This chapter has practical advice for anyone interested in entering the TV industry.

Chapter 14 focuses on film. While less industry-oriented than the previous chapter, "Introduction to Film Studies," by Amy Villarejo, provides readers with an overview of the cinema, including a brief history of film and film production, an understanding of the breadth of film genres, and insight into the concept of stardom as it relates to film. The chapter encourages readers to consider whether or not there is a difference between cinema, film, and movies.

"Journalism," by John Pavlik and Shawn McIntosh, is the title and subject of Chapter 15. This chapter provides a summary of the history of journalism and its development into what we now know as the "fourth estate." It examines the impact of new technologies on news gathering and reporting, including the 24/7 news cycle, nontraditional news sources, and personalization. In addition to discussing convergent journalism, the chapter also addresses enduring concepts related to the field, such as the tension between privacy rights and the public's right to know. The chapter also covers the business of journalism.

Chapter 16, "The Practice of Public Relations," by Shannon Bowen, Brad Rawlins, and Thomas Martin, examines some of the basic elements of PR. The chapter begins with an outline of the different types of public relations efforts that exist, and provides examples of each. Building on this foundation, the authors present readers with basic concepts related to the various PR areas such as issue management, strategy building, corporate responsibility, and activism.

This text concludes with the chapter "What Is Advertising?" by Kathleen Hall Jamieson and Karlyn Kohrs Campbell. This chapter blends a practical description of key advertising concepts related to both traditional and nontraditional advertising strategies with a critical assessment of the impact of advertising on society. It also briefly addresses the important relationship between advertising and news.

This text is designed to help students begin a serious study of communication by providing a foundational overview. This resource is not meant to present a comprehensive understanding of all aspects of the discipline as a whole, or any individual career field. In order to get the most out of this book, readers must put in some time and effort to understand the text for what it is, and to go beyond the boundaries of these pages for a more complete understanding.

Getting the Most Out of *Introduction to the World of Communication*

This text, an edited selection of readings from a variety of sources, provides readers with many advantages over introductory textbooks by single authors. The writings included here have been selected from dozens of options, each with its own strengths and weaknesses, and each with a different focal point in the world of communication. The advantage of an edited volume such as this is that readers get a wider view of the field and diverse interpretations of the discipline. The authors of the various chapters have different educational and professional backgrounds. Therefore, readers get multiple perspectives on the discipline from individuals with different areas of specialization. Such an approach encourages readers to develop their own perspectives on the various components and careers in communication, and invites further investigation of the field.

An edited volume such as this is also advantageous in that it allows for a new formulation of content that some may find unusual—but highly useful—when first approaching the field of communication. Traditional approaches to an introduction to communication generally fall along two lines: the "communication studies" side (frequently called "speech com") that focuses on the day-to-day communication components such as interpersonal communication, small group communication, and public speaking; and "mass communication," which explains the influence of mass media and outlines career

fields in communication. This text combines the two approaches in order to give readers a quality overview of both avenues, and to empower readers with a basic knowledge of the fundamentals of everyday communication, a grasp of the development and impact of communication media, and an understanding of fundamental communication career paths. The goal of this text is to provide the foundation necessary for the reader to become a well-educated communicator.

While there are many advantages to creating and using an edited textbook like this one, there are a few disadvantages as well. Some drawbacks include an occasionally disjointed feel to the text and periodic awkward references to other content. Authors have somewhat distinct voices, meaning that each chapter offers its own tone, vocabulary, and reading comprehension level. Adjusting to these differences should not be difficult, but can be a bit off-putting to a reader at times. Additionally, there are sometimes references within a chapter to contents of the source from which the chapter was originally housed. Those chapter references are not accurate for this text. However, the original source for each chapter of this text is cited at the base of the first page of the chapter. Therefore, the reader can look up additional information if a topic seems particularly interesting.

In order to capitalize on the advantages and limit the disadvantages of using this edited textbook, try the following recommendations:

- Read each chapter carefully and fully. Analyze the content while focusing on what you can learn from each author on each topic.
- Keep a reading journal. Make entries for each chapter that include paraphrased summaries of important concepts and personalized examples that illustrate salient points. Include personal responses to the content: Does the content ring true? Was something particularly insightful or confusing?
- Take advantage of communication technologies to supplement the readings. Feel free to look up concepts, models, and

examples through various search engines. Getting different illustrations of ideas may help make the concepts more memorable and applicable. Also, looking up examples referenced in the chapters will help enhance their informative value.

- Keep a list of key vocabulary words. Mapping together related terms from different chapters will help emphasize the interrelated nature of the concepts and reinforce the importance of oft-repeated ideas.
- Make use of discussion questions and suggested exercises when they are offered. These are designed to increase knowledge and skill.

While these recommendations may seem time consuming, remember that the study of communication is a serious academic and professional pursuit. Learning it properly requires considerable personal investment. The more a reader puts into the study of communication, the more he or she will get out of it.

Summary

The study of communication is an important pursuit grounded in a long and storied history. As both an academic field and an area of professional study, communication intertwines theoretical understanding, practical application, and ethical consideration. It is essential that a well-educated communicator take seriously the power and potential of the art of communication while understanding the larger context in which communication occurs. For this reason, it is necessary that students of communication embrace the responsibility to establish a strong knowledge base in liberal arts, a solid understanding of the fundamentals of communication, and adaptable skill sets appropriate for an ever changing communication environment.

1. Human Communication

What and Why

by Ronald B. Adler and George Rodman

As with any new area of study, it is best to begin by defining the essential elements of the field. Adler, Rodnam & Hutchinson do just that in the following pages. This chapter outlines the foundational elements of communication from a perspective that transcends any particular career field or communication medium. The following pages explain communication as a process—a complex, interactive activity dependent on both senders and receivers for effective exchange. The models provided here encourage readers to visualize the processes by which we build shared meanings and to understand the multiple variables that influence every communicative act. The discussion of common misconceptions about communication reinforces the reader's understanding of the complexity of the process and myriad challenges facing communicators.

Readers should remember that this chapter comes from a different textbook. All references to future chapters are to the original text from which this chapter is drawn. These references do not correspond to the current text. However, if the reader would like to know more about the particular topics covered in this text, there are several recommended texts listed under "Notes" at the end of this chapter. They are helpful and insightful resources.

Communication Defined

Because this is a book about communication, it makes sense to begin by defining that term. This isn't as simple as it might seem because people use the term in a variety of ways that are only vaguely related:

- A dog scratches at the back door, signaling its desire to be let out of the house.
- Data flows from one computer database to another in a cascade of electronic impulses.
- Strangers who live thousands of miles apart spot each other's postings on a social networking website, and they become friends through conversations via e-mail, text messaging, and instant messaging.
- Locals approach a group of confused-looking people who seem to be from out of town and ask if they can help.
- In her sermon, a religious leader encourages the congregation to get more involved in the community.

There is clearly some relationship among uses of the term such as these, but we need to narrow our focus before going on. A look at the table of contents of this book shows that it obviously doesn't deal with animals. Neither is it about Holy Communion, the bestowing of a material thing, or many of the other subjects mentioned in the *Oxford English Dictionary's* 1,200-word definition of *communication*.

What, then, are we talking about when we use the term *communication?* As the reading on this page shows, there is no single, universally accepted usage. This isn't the place to explore the differences between these conceptions or to defend one against the others. What we need is a working definition that will help us in our study.

As its title suggests, this is a book about understanding human communication—so we'll start by explaining what it means to study communication that is unique to members of our species. For our purposes we'll define human communication as the process of creating meaning through symbolic interaction. Examining this definition reveals some important characteristics of human communication.

Communication Is a Process

We often talk about communication as if it occurred in discrete, individual acts such as one person's utterance or a conversation. In fact, communication is a continuous, ongoing process. Consider, for example, a friend's compliment about your appearance. Your interpretation of those words will depend on a long series of experiences stretching far back in time: How have others judged your appearance? How do you feel about your looks? How honest has your friend been in the past? How have you been feeling about one another recently? All this history will help shape your response to the friend's remark. In turn, the words you speak and the way you say them will shape the way your friend behaves toward you and others—both in this situation and in the future.

This simple example shows that it's inaccurate to talk about "acts" of communication as if they occurred in isolation. To put it differently, communication isn't a series of incidents pasted together like photographs in a scrapbook; instead, it is more like a motion picture in which the meaning comes from the unfolding of an interrelated series of images. The fact that communication is a process is reflected in the transactional model introduced later in this chapter.

Communication Is Symbolic

Symbols are used to represent things, processes, ideas, or events in ways that make communication possible. Chapter 4 discusses the nature of symbols in more detail, but this idea is so important that it needs an introduction now. The most significant feature of symbols is their arbitrary nature. For example, there's no logical reason why the letters in the word *book* should stand for the object you're reading now. Speakers of Spanish call it a *libro,* and Germans call it a *Buch.* Even in English, another term would work just as well as long as everyone agreed to use it in the same way. We overcome the arbitrary nature of symbols by linguistic rules and customs. Effective communication depends on agreement among people about these rules. This is easiest to see when we observe people who don't follow linguistic conventions. For example, recall how unusual the speech of children and nonnative speakers of a language often sounds.

Animals don't use symbols in the varied and complex ways that humans do. There's nothing symbolic about a dog scratching at the door to be let out; there is a natural connection between the door and the dog's goal. By contrast, the words in the human utterance "Open the door!" are only arbitrarily related to the request they represent

Symbolic communication allows people to think or talk about the past (while cats have no concept of their ancestors from a century ago), explain the present (a trout can't warn its companions about its close call with a fishing hook), and speculate about the future (a crow has no awareness of the year 2025, let alone tomorrow).

Like words, some nonverbal behavior can have symbolic meaning. For example, to most North Americans, nodding your head up and down means "yes" (although this meaning isn't universal). But even more than words, many nonverbal behaviors are ambiguous. Does a frown signify anger or unhappiness? Does a hug stand for a friendly greeting or a symbol of the hugger's romantic interest in you? One can't always be sure. Well discuss the ambiguous nature of nonverbal communication in Chapter 6.

Types of Communication

Within the domain of human interaction, there are several types of communication. Each occurs in a different context. Despite the features they all share, each has its own focus on characteristics.

Intrapersonal Communication

By definition, **intrapersonal communication** means "communicating with oneself."[1] You can tune into one way that each of us communicates internally by listening to the little voice that lives in your mind. Take a moment and listen to what it is saying. Try it now, before reading on. Did you hear it? It may have been saying something like "What little voice? I don't have any little voice!" This voice is the "sound" of your thinking.

We don't always think in verbal terms, but whether the process is apparent or not, the way we mentally process information influences our interaction with others. Even though intrapersonal communication doesn't include other people directly, it does affect almost every type of interaction. You can understand the role of intrapersonal communication by imagining your thoughts in each of the following situations.

- You are planning to approach a stranger whom you would like to get to know better.
- You pause a minute and look at the audience before beginning a ten-minute speech.
- The boss yawns while you are asking for a raise.
- A friend seems irritated lately, and you're not sure whether you are responsible.

The way you handle all of these situations would depend on the intrapersonal communication that precedes or accompanies your overt behavior. Much of Chapter 3 deals with the perception process in everyday situations, and part of Chapter 13 focuses on the intrapersonal communication that can minimize anxiety when you deliver a speech.

Dyadic/Interpersonal Communication

Social scientists call two persons interacting a **dyad,** and they often use the term **dyadic communication** to describe this type of communication. Dyadic communication can occur in person or via mediated channels that include telephone, e-mail, text messaging, instant messages, and social networking websites.

Dyads are the most common type of personal communication. One study revealed that college students spend almost half of their total communication time interacting with one other person.[2]

Observation in a variety of settings ranging from playgrounds to train depots and shopping malls shows that most communication is dyadic in nature.[3] Even communication within larger groups (think of classrooms, parties, and families as examples) consists of multiple, often shifting dyadic encounters.

Dyadic interaction is sometimes considered identical to **interpersonal communication**, but as Chapter 7 explains, not all two-person interaction can be considered interpersonal in the fullest sense of the word. In fact, you will learn that the qualities that characterize interpersonal communication aren't limited to twosomes. They can be present in threesomes or even in small groups.

Small Group Communication

In **small group communication** every person can participate actively with the other members. Small groups are a common fixture of everyday life. Your family is a group. So are an athletic team, a group of coworkers in several time zones connected in cyberspace, and several students working on a class project.

Whether small groups meet in person or via mediated channels, they possess characteristics that are not present in a dyad. For instance, in a group, the majority of members can put pressure on those in the minority to conform, either consciously or unconsciously, but in a dyad no such pressures exist. Conformity pressures can also be comforting, leading group members to take risks that they would not dare if they were alone or in a dyad. With their greater size, groups also have the ability to be more creative than dyads. Finally, communication in groups is affected strongly by the type of leader who is in a position of authority. Groups are such an important communication setting that Chapters 9 and 10 focus exclusively on them.

Public Communication

Public communication occurs when a group becomes too large for all members to contribute. One characteristic of public communication is an unequal amount of speaking. One or more people are likely to deliver their remarks to the remaining members, who act as an audience. This leads to a second characteristic of public settings: limited verbal feedback. The audience isn't able to talk back in a two-way conversation the way they might in a dyadic or small group setting. This doesn't mean that speakers operate in a vacuum when delivering their remarks. Audiences often have a chance to ask questions and offer brief comments, and their nonverbal reactions offer a wide range of dues about their reception of the speaker's remarks.

Public speakers usually have a greater chance to plan and structure their remarks than do communicators in smaller settings. For this reason, several chapters of this book describe the steps you can take to prepare and deliver an effective speech.

Mass Communication

Mass communication consists of messages that are transmitted to large, widespread audiences via electronic and print media: newspapers, magazines, television, radio, blogs, websites, and so on. As you can see in the Mass Communication section of the *Understanding Human Communication* website, mass communication differs from the interpersonal, small group, and public varieties in several ways. First, most mass messages are aimed at a large audience without any personal contact between sender and receivers. Second, many of the messages sent via mass communication channels are developed, or at least financed, by large organizations. In this sense, mass communication is far less personal and more of a product than the other types we have examined so far. Finally, mass communication is often controlled by many gatekeepers who determine what messages will be delivered to consumers, how they will be constructed, and when they will be delivered. Sponsors (whether corporate or governmental), editors, producers, reporters, and executives all have the power to influence mass messages in ways that don't affect most other types. While blogs have given ordinary people the chance to reach enormous audiences, the bulk of mass messages are still controlled by corporate and governmental sources. Because of these and other unique characteristics, the study of mass communication raises special issues and deserves special treatment.

Functions of Communication

Now that we have a working understanding of the term *communication,* it is important to discuss why we will spend so much time exploring this subject. Perhaps the strongest argument for studying communication is its central role in our lives. The amount of time we spend communicating is staggering. In one study, researchers measured the amount of time a sample group of college students spent on various activities.[4] They found that the subjects spent an average of over 61 percent of their waking hours engaged in some form communication. Whatever one's occupation, the results of such a study would not be too different. Most of us are surrounded by others, trying to understand them and hoping that they understand us: family, friends, coworkers, teachers, and strangers.

There's a good reason why we speak, listen, read, and write so much: Communication satisfies many of our needs.

Physical Needs

Communication is so important that it is necessary for physical health. In fact, evidence suggests that an absence of satisfying communication can even jeopardize life itself. Medical researchers have identified a wide range of hazards that result from a lack of close relationships.[5] For instance:

- People who lack strong relationships have two to three times the risk of early death, regardless of whether they smoke, drink alcoholic beverages, or exercise regularly.
- Terminal cancer strikes socially isolated people more often than those who have close personal relationships.
- Divorced, separated, and widowed people are five to ten times more likely to need

hospitalization for mental problems than their married counterparts.
- Pregnant women under stress and without supportive relationships have three times more complications than pregnant women who suffer from the same stress but have strong social support.
- Socially isolated people are four times more susceptible to the common cold than those who have active social networks.[6]

Studies indicate that social isolation is a major risk factor contributing to coronary disease, comparable to physiological factors such as diet, cigarette smoking, obesity, and lack of physical activity.[7]

Research like this demonstrates the importance of having satisfying personal relationships. Remember: Not everyone needs the same amount of contact, and the quality of communication is almost certainly as important as the quantity. The important point here is that personal communication is essential for our well-being. To paraphrase an old song, "people who need people" aren't "the luckiest people in the world," they're the *only* people!

Identity Needs

Communication does more than enable us to survive. It is the way—indeed, the only way—we learn who we are. As you'll read in Chapter 3, our sense of identity comes from the way we interact with other people. Are we smart or stupid, attractive or ugly, skillful or inept? The answers to these questions don't come from looking in the mirror. We decide who we are based on how others react to us.

Deprived of communication with others, we would have no sense of identity. This fact is illustrated by the case of the famous "Wild Boy of Aveyron," who spent his early childhood without any apparent human contact. The boy was discovered in January 1800 while digging for vegetables in a French village garden.[8] He showed no behaviors one would expect in a social human. The boy could not speak but uttered only weird cries. More significant than this absence of social skills was his lack of any identity as a human being. As author Roger Shattuck put it, "The boy had no human sense of being in the world. He had no sense of himself as a person related to other persons."[9] Only after the influence of a loving "mother" did the boy begin to behave—and, we can imagine, think of himself as a human. Contemporary stories support the essential role that communication plays in shaping identity. In 1970, authorities discovered a twelve-year-old girl (whom they called "Genie") who had spent virtually all her life in an otherwise empty, darkened bedroom with almost no human contact. The child could not speak and had no sense of herself as a person until she was removed from her family and "nourished" by a team of caregivers.[10]

Like Genie and the boy of Aveyron, each of us enters world with little or no sense of identity. We gain an idea of who we are from the ways others define us. As Chapter 3 of others continues throughout life. Chapter 3 also explains how we use communication to manage the way others view us.

Social Needs

Besides helping to define who we are, communication provides a vital link with others. Researchers and theorists have identified a range of social needs we satisfy by communicating: pleasure (e.g., "because it's fun," "to have a good time"); affection (e.g., "to help others," "to let others know I care"); inclusion (e.g., "because I need someone to talk to or be with," "because it makes me less lonely"); escape (e.g., "to put off doing something I should be doing"); relaxation (e.g., "because it allows me to unwind"); and control (e.g., "because I want some on to do something for me." "to get something I don't have").[11]

As you look at this list of social needs for communicating, imagine how empty your life would be if these needs weren't satisfied. Then notice that it would be impossible to fulfill them without communicating with others. Because relationships with others are so vital, some theorists have gone as far as to argue that communication is the primary goal of human existence. Anthropologist Walter Goldschmidt terms the drive for meeting social needs as the "human career."[12]

Practical Needs

We shouldn't overlook the everyday, important functions that communication serves. Communication is the tool that lets us tell the hair stylist to take just a little off the sides, direct the doctor to where it hurts, and inform the plumber that the broken pipe needs attention *now!*

Beyond these obvious needs, a wealth of research demonstrates that communication is an important key to effectiveness in a variety of everyday setting. For example, a survey of over four hundred employers identified "communication skills" as the top characteristic that employers seek in job candidates.[13] It was rated as more important than technical competence, work experience, or academic background. In another survey, over 90 percent of the personnel officials at five hundred U.S. businesses stated that increased communication skills are needed for success in the twenty-first century.[14]

Communication is just as important outside of work. College roommates who are both willing and able to communicate effectively report higher satisfaction with one another than do those who lack these characteristics.[15] Married couples who were identified as effective communicators reported happier relationships than did less skillful husbands and wives.[16] In school, the grade point averages of college students were related positively to their communication competence.[17] In "getting acquainted" situations, communication competence played a major role in whether a person was judged physically attractive, socially desirable, and good at the task of getting acquainted.[18]

Modeling Communication

So far we have introduced a basic definition of *communication* and seen the functions it performs. This information is useful, but it only begins to describe the process we will be examining throughout this book. One way to understand more about what it means to communicate is to look at some models that describe what happens when two or more people interact. As you will see, over the last half century scholars have developed an increasingly accurate and sophisticated view of this process.

A Linear Model

Until about fifty years ago, researchers viewed communication as something that one person "does" to another.[19] In this **linear communication model,** communication is like giving an injection: a **sender encodes** ideas and feelings into some sort of **message** and then conveys them to a **receiver** who **decodes** them. (Figure 1–1)

One important element of the linear model is the communication channel—the method by which a message is conveyed between people. For most people, face-to-face contact is the most familiar and obvious channel. Writing is another channel. In addition to these long-used forms, **mediated communication** channels include telephone, e-mail, instant messaging faxes, voice mail, and even videoconferencing. (The word *mediated* reflects the fact that these messages are conveyed through some sort of communication medium.)

The channel you choose can make a big difference in the effect of a message. For example, a typewritten love letter probably wouldn't have the same effect as a handwritten note or card. Likewise, ending a relationship by sending a text message to your lover's cell phone would make a very different statement than delivering the bad news in person.

The linear model also introduces the concept of **noise**—a term used by social scientists to describe any forces that interfere with effective communication. Noise can occur at every stage of the communication process. Three types of noise can disrupt communication—external, physiological, and psychological. *External noise* (also called "physical") includes those factors outside the receiver that make it difficult to hear, as well as many other kinds of distractions. For instance, too much cigarette smoke in a crowded room might make it hard for you to pay attention to another person, and sitting in the rear of an auditorium might make a speaker's remarks unclear. External noise can disrupt communication almost anywhere in our model—in the sender, channel, message, or receiver. *Physiological noise* involves biological factors in the receiver or sender that interfere with accurate reception: illness, fatigue, and so on. *Psychological noise* refers to forces within a communicator that interfere with the ability to express or understand a message accurately. For instance, an outdoors person might exaggerate the size and number of the fish he caught in order to convince himself and others of his talents. In the same way, a student might become so upset upon learning that she failed a test that she would be unable (perhaps *unwilling* is a better word) to understand dearly where she went wrong.

A linear model shows that communicators often occupy different **environments**—fields of experience that help them understand others' behavior. In communication terminology, *environment* refers not only to a physical location but also to the personal experiences and cultural backgrounds that participants bring to a conversation.

Consider just some of the factors that might contribute to different environments:

- A might belong to one ethnic group and B to another;
- A might be rich and B poor;
- A might be in a rush and B have nowhere to go;
- A might have lived a long, eventful life, and B might be young and inexperienced;
- A might be passionately concerned with the subject and B indifferent to it.

Notice how the model in Figure 1.1 shows that the environments of A and B overlap. This area represents the background that the communicators must have in common. As the shared environment becomes smaller, communication becomes more difficult. Consider a few examples in which different perspectives can make understanding difficult:

- Bosses who have trouble understanding the perspective of their employees will be less effective managers, and workers who do not appreciate the challenges of being a boss are more likely to be uncooperative (and probably less suitable for advancement).
- Parents who have trouble recalling their youth are likely to clash with their children, who have never known and may not appreciate the responsibility that comes with parenting.
- Members of a dominant culture who have never experienced how it feels to be "different" may not appreciate the concerns of people from nondominant cocultures, whose own perspectives make it hard to understand the cultural blindness of the majority.

Differing environments make understanding others challenging but certainly not impossible. Hard work and many of the skills described in this book provide ways to bridge the gap that separates all of us to a greater or lesser degree. For now, recognizing the challenge that comes from dissimilar environments is a good start. You can't solve a problem until you recognize that it exists.

A Transactional Model

Despite its simplicity, the linear model doesn't do a very good job of representing the way most communication operates. The transactional communication model in Figure 1–2 presents a more accurate picture in several respects.

Simultaneous Sending and Receiving Although some types of mass communication do flow in a one-way, linear manner, most types of personal communication are two-way exchanges.[20] The **transactional model** reflects the fact that we usually send and receive messages simultaneously. The roles of sender and receiver that seemed separate in the linear model are now superimposed and redefined as those of "communicators." This new term reflects the fact that at a given moment we are capable of receiving, decoding, and responding to another person's behavior, while at the same time that other person is receiving and responding to ours.

Consider, for instance, the significance of a friend's yawn as you describe your romantic problems. Or imagine the blush you may see as you tell one of your raunchier jokes to a new acquaintance. Nonverbal behaviors like these show that most face-to-face communication is a two-way affair. The discernible response of a receiver to a sender's message is called **feedback**. Not all feedback is nonverbal, of course. Sometimes it is oral, as when you ask an instructor questions about an upcoming test or volunteer your opinion of a friend's new haircut. In other cases it is written, as when you answer the questions on a midterm exam or respond to a letter from a friend. Figure 1–2 makes the importance of feedback clear. It shows that most communication is, indeed, a two-way affair.

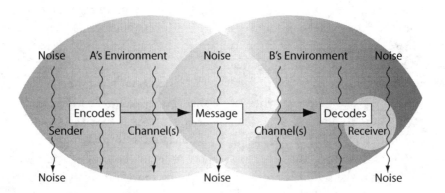

Figure 1. Linear Communication Model

Some forms of mediated communication like e-mail and text messaging don't appear to be simultaneous. Even here, though, the process is more complicated than the linear model suggests. For example, if you've ever waited impatiently for the response to a text message or instant message, you understand that even a nonresponse can have symbolic meaning. Is the unresponsive recipient busy? Thoughtful? Offended? Indifferent? Whether or not your interpretation is accurate, the silence is a form of communication.

Another weakness of the traditional linear model is the questionable assumption that all communication involves encoding. We certainly do choose symbols to convey most verbal messages. But what about the many nonverbal cues that occur whether or not people speak: facial expressions, gestures, postures, vocal tones, and so on? Cues like these clearly do offer information about others, although they are often unconscious, and thus don't involve encoding. For this reason, the transactional model replaces the term *encodes* with the broader term *responds,* because it describes both intentional and unintentional actions that can be observed and interpreted.[21]

Communication Is Fluid, Not Static It's difficult to isolate a discrete "act" of communication from the events that precede and follow it. The way a friend or family member reacts to a sarcastic remark you make will probably depend on the way you have related to one another in the past; likewise, the way you'll act toward each other in the future depends on the outcome of this conversation.

Communication Is Relational, Not Individual The transactional model shows that communication isn't something we do to others; rather, it is something we do with them. In this sense, communication is rather like dancing—at least the kind of dancing we do with partners. Like dancing, communication depends on the involvement of a partner. And like good dancing, successful communication isn't something that depends just on the skill of one person. A great dancer who doesn't consider and adapt to the skill level of his or her partner can make both people look bad. In communication and dancing, even two talented partners don't guarantee success. When two talented dancers perform with-out coordinating their movements, the results feel bad to the dancers and look foolish to an audience. Finally, relational communication—like dancing—is a unique creation that arises out of the way in which the partners interact. The way you dance probably varies from one partner to another because of its cooperative, transactional nature. Likewise, the way you communicate almost certainly varies with different partners. Psychologist Kenneth Gergen captures the relational nature of communication well when he points out how our success depends on interaction with others. As he says, "… one cannot be 'attractive' without others who are attracted, a 'leader' without others willing to follow, or a 'loving person' without others to affirm with appreciation."[22]

Because communication is transactional, it's often a mistake to suggest that just one person is responsible for a relationship. Consider the accompanying cartoon. Both Cathy and Irving had good intentions, and both probably could have handled the situation better. As the humorous outcome shows, trying to pin the blame for a disappointing outcome on one person or the other is fruitless and counterproductive. It would have been far better to ask, "How did we handle this situation poorly, and what can we do to make it better?"

The transactional nature of communication shows up in school, where teachers and students influence one another's behavior. For example, teachers who regard some students negatively may treat them with subtle or overt disfavor. As a result, these students are likely to react to their teachers' behavior negatively, which reinforces the teachers' original attitudes and expectations.[23] It isn't necessary to resolve the "who started it" issue here to recognize that the behaviors of teachers and students are part of a transactional relationship.

The transactional character of communication also figures dramatically in relationships between parents and their children. We normally think of "good parenting" in terms of how well children turn out. But research suggests that the

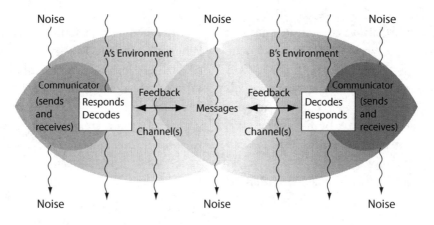

Figure 2. Transactional Communication Model

quality of interaction between parents and children is a two-way affair, that children influence parents just as much as the other way around.[24] For example, children who engage in what social scientists call "problematic behavior" evoke more high-control responses from their parents than do cooperative children. By contrast, youngsters with mild temperaments are less likely to provoke coercive reactions by their parents than are more aggressive children. Parents with low self-esteem tend to send more messages that weaken the self-esteem of their children, who in turn are likely to act in ways that make the parents feel even worse about themselves. Thus, a mutually reinforcing cycle arises in which parents and children shape one another's feelings and behavior. In cases like this it's at least difficult and probably impossible to identify who is the "sender" and who is the "receiver" of messages. It's more accurate to acknowledge that parents and children—just like husbands and wives, bosses and employees, teachers and students, or any other people who communicate with one another—act in ways that mutually influence one another.

By now you can see that a transactional model of communication should be more like a motion picture film than a gallery of still photographs. Although Figure 1–2 does a fair job of picturing the phenomenon we call communication, an animated version in which the environments, communicators, and messages constantly change would be an even better way of capturing the process.

Communication Competence: What Makes an Effective Communicator?

It's easy to recognize good communicators, and even easier to spot poor ones. But what are the characteristics that distinguish effective communicators from their less successful counterparts? Answering this question has been one of the leading challenges for communication scholars.[25] Although all the answers aren't yet in, research has identified a great deal of important and useful information about communication competence.

Communication Competence Defined

While scholars are still working to clarify the nature of **communication competence,** most would agree that effective communication involves achieving one's goals in a manner that, ideally, maintains or enhances the relationship in which it occurs.[26] This definition suggests several important characteristics of communication competence.

There Is No "Ideal" Way to Communicate Your own experience shows that a variety of communication styles can be effective. Some very successful people are serious, whereas others use humor, some are gregarious, whereas others are quiet; and some are straightforward, whereas others hint diplomatically. Just as there are many kinds of beautiful music and art, there are many kinds of competent communication.

The type of communication that succeeds in one situation might be a colossal blunder in another. The joking insults you routinely trade with a friend might be insensitive and discouraging if he or she had just suffered a personal setback The language you use with your peers might offend a family member, and last Saturday night's romantic approach would probably be out of place at work on Monday morning. For this reason, being a competent communicator requires flexibility in understanding what approach is likely to work best in a given situation.[27]

Competence Is Situational Because competent behavior varies so much from one situation and person to another, it's a mistake to think that communication competence is a trait that a person either possesses or lacks. It's more accurate to talk about *degrees* or *areas* of competence.[28] You and the people you know are probably quite competent in some areas and less so in others. You might deal quite skillfully with peers, for example, but feel clumsy interacting with people much older or younger, wealthier or poorer, or more or less attractive than yourself. In fact, your competence with one person may vary from one situation to another. This means that it's an overgeneralization to say, in a moment of distress, "I'm a terrible communicator!" It would be more accurate to say, "I didn't handle this situation very well, even though I'm better in others."

Competence Is Relational Because communication is transactional, something we do with others rather than to them, behavior that is competent in one relationship isn't necessarily competent in others.

A fascinating study on relational satisfaction illustrates that what constitutes satisfying communication varies from one relationship to another.[29] Researchers Brent Burleson and Wendy Sampter hypothesized that people with sophisticated communication skills (such as managing conflict well, giving ego-support to others, and providing comfort to relational partners) would be better at maintaining friendships than would be less skilled communicators. To their surprise, the results did not support this hypothesis. In fact, friendships were most satisfying when partners possessed matching skill levels. Apparently, relational satisfaction arises in part when our style matches those of the people with whom we interact.

The same principle holds true in the case of jealousy. Researchers have uncovered a variety of ways by which people deal with jealousy in their relationships.[30] The ways included keeping closer tabs on the partner, acting indifferent, decreasing affection, talking the matter over, and acting angry. The researchers found that no type of behavior was effective or ineffective in every relationship. They concluded that approaches that work with some people would be harmful to others. Findings like these demonstrate that competence arises out of developing ways of interacting that work for you and for other people involved.[31]

Competence Can Be Learned To some degree, biology is destiny when it comes to communication style.[32] Studies of identical and fraternal twins suggest that traits including sociability, anger, and relaxation seem to be partially a function of our genetic makeup. Fortunately, biology isn't the only factor that shapes how we communicate: Communication is a set of skills that anyone can learn. As children grow; their ability to communicate effectively develops. For example, older children can produce more sophisticated persuasive attempts than can younger ones.[33] Along with maturity, systematic education (such as the class in which you are now enrolled) can boost communicative competence. Even a modest amount of training can produce dramatic results. After only thirty minutes of instruction, one group of observers became significantly more effective in detecting deception in interviews.[34] One study revealed that college students' communication competence increases over their undergraduate studies.[35] Even without systematic training, it's possible to develop communication skills through the processes of trial-and-error and observation. We learn from our own successes and failures, as well as from observing other models—both positive and negative.

Characteristics of Competent Communicators

Although competent communication varies from one situation to another, scholars have identified several common denominators that characterize effective communication in most contexts.

A Wide Range of Behaviors Effective communicators are able to choose their actions from a wide range of behaviors. To understand the importance of having a large communication repertoire, imagine that someone you know repeatedly tells jokes—perhaps discriminatory ones—that you find offensive. You could respond to these jokes in a number of ways. You could:

- Say nothing, figuring that the risks of bringing the subject up would be greater than the benefits.
- Ask a third party to say something to the joke teller about the offensiveness of the jokes.
- Hint at your discomfort, hoping that your friend would get the point.
- Joke about your friend's insensitivity, counting on humor to soften the blow of your criticism.
- Express your discomfort in a straightforward way, asking your friend to stop telling the offensive jokes, at least around you.
- Simply demand that your friend stop.

With this choice of responses at your disposal (and you can probably think of others as well), you could pick the one that had the best chance of success. But if you were able to use only one or two of these responses when raising a delicate issue—always keeping quiet or always hinting, for example—your chances of success would be much smaller. Indeed, many poor communicators are easy to spot by their limited range of responses. Some are chronic jokers. Others are always belligerent. Still others are quiet in almost every situation. Like a piano player who knows only one tune or a chef who can prepare only a few dishes, these people are forced to rely on a small range of responses again and again, whether or not they are successful.

Ability to Choose the Most Appropriate Behavior Simply possessing a large array of communication skills isn't a guarantee of effectiveness. It's also necessary to know which of these skills will work best in a particular situation. Choosing the best way to send a message is rather like choosing a gift. What is appropriate for one person won't be appropriate for another one at all. This ability to choose the best approach is essential because a response that works well in one setting would flop miserably in another one.

Although it's impossible to say precisely how to act in every situation, there are at least three factors to consider when you are deciding which response to choose: the context, your goal, and, the other person.

Skill at Performing Behaviors After you have chosen the most appropriate way to communicate, it's still necessary to perform the required skills effectively. There is a big difference between knowing about a skill and being able to put it into practice. Simply being aware of alternatives isn't much help, unless you can skillfully put these alternatives to work.

Just reading about communication skills in the following chapters won't guarantee that you can start using them flawlessly. As with any other skills—playing a musical instrument or learning a sport, for example—the road to competence in communication is not a short one. You can expect that your first efforts at communicating differently will be awkward. After some practice you will become more skillful, although you will still have to think about the new way of speaking or listening. Finally, after repeating the new skill again and again, you will find you can perform it without conscious thought.

Empathy/Perspective Taking People have the best chance of developing an effective message when they understand the other person's point of view. And because others aren't always good at expressing their thoughts and feelings clearly, the ability to imagine how an issue might look from the other's point of view is an important skill. The value of taking the other's perspective suggests one reason why listening is so important. Not only does it help us understand others, it also gives us information to develop strategies about how to best influence them. Because empathy is such an important element of communicative competence, much of Chapter 5 is devoted to this topic.

Cognitive Complexity Cognitive complexity is the ability to construct a variety of frameworks for viewing an issue. Cognitive complexity is an ingredient of communication competence because it allows us to make sense of people using a variety of perspectives. For instance, imagine that a longtime friend seems to be angry with you. One possible explanation is that your friend is offended by something you've done. Another possibility is that something upsetting has happened in another part of your fiend's life. Or perhaps nothing at all is wrong, and you're just being overly sensitive. Researchers have found that the ability to analyze the behavior of others in a variety of ways leads to greater "conversational sensitivity," increasing the chances of acting in ways that will produce satisfying results.[36]

Self-Monitoring Psychologists use the term *self monitoring* to describe the process of paying dose attention to one's behavior and using these observations to shape the way one behaves. Self-monitors are able to separate a part of their consciousness and observe their behavior from a detached viewpoint, making observations such as:

> *"I'm making a fool out of myself."*
> *"I'd better speak up now."*
> *"This approach is working well. I'll keep it up."*

Chapter 3 explains how too much self monitoring can be problematic Still, people who are aware of their behavior and the impression it makes are more skillful communicators than people who are low self-monitors.[37] For example, they are more accurate in judging others' emotional states, better at remembering information about others, less shy, and more assertive. By contrast, low self-monitors aren't even able to recognize their incompetence. (Calvin, in the nearby cartoon, does a nice job of illustrating this problem.) One study revealed that poor communicators were blissfully ignorant of their shortcomings and more likely to overestimate their skill than were better communicators.[38] For example, experimental subjects who scored in the lowest quartile on joke-telling skill were more likely than their funnier counterparts to grossly overestimate their sense of humor.

Commitment to the Relationship One feature that distinguishes effective communication in almost any context is commitment. People who seem to care about the relationship communicate better than those who don't.[39] This concern shows up in commitment to the other person and to the message you are expressing.

Clarifying Misconceptions About Communication

Having spent time talking about what communication is, we ought to also identify some things it is not.[40] Recognizing some misconceptions is important, not only because they ought to be avoided by anyone knowledgeable about the subject, but also because following them can get you into trouble.

Communication Does Not Always Require Complete Understanding

Most people operate on the implicit but flawed assumption that the goal of all communication is to maximize understanding between communicators. Although some understanding is necessary for us to comprehend one another's thoughts, there are some types of communication in which understanding as we usually conceive it isn't the primary goal.[41] Consider, for example:

- *Social rituals.* "How's it going?" you ask. "Great," the other person replies. The primary goal in exchanges like these is mutual acknowledgment: There's obviously no serious attempt to exchange information.
- *Many attempts to influence others.* A quick analysis of most television commercials shows that they are aimed at persuading viewers to buy products, not to understand

the content of the commercial. In the same way, many of our attempts at persuading another to act as we want don't involve a desire to get the other person to understand what we want—just to comply with our wishes.

- *Deliberate ambiguity and deception.* When you decline an unwanted invitation by saying "I can't make it," you probably want to create the impression that the decision is really beyond your control. (If your goal was to be perfectly clear, you might say, "I don't want to get together. In fact, I'd rather do almost anything than accept your invitation.") As Chapters 4 and 7 explain in detail, we often equivocate precisely because we want to obscure our true thoughts and feelings.

- *Coordinated action.* Examples are conversations where satisfaction doesn't depend on full understanding. The term **coordination** has been used to describe situations in which participants interact smoothly, with a high degree of satisfaction but without necessarily understanding one another well.[42] Coordination without understanding can be satisfying in far more important situations. Consider the words "I love you." This is a phrase that can have many meanings: Among other things, it can mean "I admire you," "I feel great affection for you," "I desire you," "I am grateful to you," "I feel guilty," "I want you to be faithful to me," or even "I hope *you* love *me*."[43] It's not hard to picture a situation in which partners gain great satisfaction—even over a lifetime—without completely understanding that the mutual love they profess actually is quite different for each of them. The cartoon on this page reflects the fact that better understanding can sometimes lead to less satisfaction. "You mean you mostly love me because I've been there for you? Hey, a *dog* is there for you!"

Communication Will Not Solve All Problems

"If I could just communicate better …" is the sad refrain of many unhappy people who believe that if they could just express themselves better, their relationships would improve. Though this is sometimes true, it's an exaggeration to say that communicating—even communicating clearly—is a guaranteed panacea.

Communication Isn't Always a Good Thing

For most people, belief in the value of communication rates somewhere close to parenthood in their hierarchy of important values. In truth, communication is neither good nor bad in itself. Rather, its value comes from the way it is used. In this sense, communication is similar to fire: Flames in the fireplace on a cold night keep you warm and create a cozy atmosphere, but the same flames can kill if they spread into the room. Communication can be a tool for expressing warm feelings and useful facts, but under different circumstances the same words and actions can cause both physical and emotional pain.

Meanings Rest in People, Not Words

It's a mistake to think that, just because you use a word in one way, others will do so, too.[44] Sometimes differing interpretations of symbols are easily caught, as when we might first take the statement "He's loaded" to mean the subject has had too much to drink, only to find out that he is quite wealthy, in other cases, however, the ambiguity of words and nonverbal behaviors isn't so apparent, and thus has more far-reaching consequences. Remember, for instance, a time when someone said to you, "I'll be honest," and only later did you learn that those words did precisely the opposite act. In Chapter 4 you'll read a great deal more about the problems that come from mistakenly assuming that meanings rest in words.

Communication Is Not Simple

Most people assume that communication is an aptitude that people develop without the need for training—rather like breathing. After all, we've been swapping ideas with one another since early childhood, and there are lots of people who communicate pretty well without ever having had a class on the subject. Though this picture of communication as a natural ability seems accurate, it's actually a gross oversimplification.[45]

Many people do learn to communicate skillfully because they have been exposed to models of such behavior by those around them. This principle of modeling explains why children who grow up in homes with stable relationships between family members have a greater chance of developing such relationships themselves. But even the best communicators aren't perfect: They often suffer the frustration of being unable to get a message across effectively, and they frequently misunderstand others. Furthermore, even the most successful people you know probably can identify ways in which their relationships could profit from better communication. These facts show that communication skills are rather like athletic ability: Even the most inept of us can learn to be more effective with training and practice, and those who are talented can always become better.

More Communication Isn't Always Better

Although it's certainly true that not communicating enough is a mistake, there are also situations when *too much* communication is a mistake. The "@Work" box on page 24 illustrates how technology contributes to information overload. Sometimes excessive communication simply is unproductive, as when we "talk a problem to death," going over the same ground again and again without making any headway. And there are times when communicating too much can actually aggravate a problem. We've all had the experience of "talking ourselves into a hole"—making a bad situation worse by pursuing it too far. As two noted communication scholars put it, more and more negative communication merely leads to more and more negative results."[46]

There are even times when *no* communication is the best course. Any good salesperson will tell you that it's often best to stop talking and let the customer think about the product. And when two people are angry and hurt, they may say things

they don't mean and will later regret. At times like these it's probably best to spend a little time cooling off, thinking about what to say and how to say it.

One key to successful communication, then, is to share an *adequate* amount of information in a *skillful* manner. Teaching you how to decide what information is adequate and what constitutes skillful behavior is one major goal of this book.

Summary

This chapter began by defining Communication as it will be examined in *Understanding Human Communication:* the process of creating meaning through symbolic interaction.

It introduced several communication contexts that will be covered in the rest of the book: intrapersonal, dyadic, small group, public, and mass. The chapter also identified several types of needs that communication satisfies: physical, identity, social, and practical.

A linear and a transactional communication model were developed, demonstrating the superiority of the transactional model in representing the process-oriented nature of human interaction.

The chapter went on to explore the difference between effective and ineffective exchanges by discussing communication competence, showing that there is no single correct way to behave, that competence is situational and relational in nature, and that it can be learned. Competent communicators were described as being able to choose and perform appropriately from a wide range of behaviors, as well as being cognitively complex self-monitors who can take the perspective of others and who have commitment to important relationships. After spending most of the chapter talking about what communication is, the chapter concluded by discussing what it is not by refuting several common misconceptions. It demonstrated that communication doesn't always require complete understanding and that it is not always a good thing that will solve every problem, It showed that more communication is not always better; that meanings are in people, not in words; and that communication is neither simple nor easy.

Notes

1. For an in-depth look at this topic, see S. B. Cunningham, "Intra- personal Communication: A Review and Critique" in S. Deetz, ed., Communication Yearbook 15 (Newbury Park, CA: Sage, 1992).

2. L. Wheeler and J. Nelek, "Sex Differences in Social Participation." Journal of Personality and Social Psychology 35 (1977): 742-754.

3. J. John, "The Distribution of Free-Forming Small Group Size." American Sociological Review 18 (1953): 569-570.

4. R. Verderber, A. Elder, and E. Weiler, "A Study of Communication Time Usage among College Students" (unpublished study, University of Cincinnati, 1976).

5. For a summary of the link between social support and health, see S. Duck, "Staying Healthy... with a Little Help from Our Friends?" in Human Relationships, 2nd ed. (Newbury Park, CA: Sage, 1992).

6. S. Cohen, W. J. Doyle, D. P. Skoner, B. S. Rabin, and J. M. Gwaltney, "Social Ties and Susceptibility to the Common Cold." Journal of the American Medical Association 277 (1997): 1940-1944.

7. Three articles in Journal of the American Medical Association 267 (January 22/29, 1992) focus on the link between psychosocial influences and coronary heart disease: R. B. Case, A. J. Moss, N. Case, M. McDermott, and S. Eberly, "Living Alone after Myocardial Infarction" (pp. 515-519); R. B. Williams, J. C. Barefoot, R. M. Calif, T. L. Haney, W. B. Saunders, D. B. Pryon, M. A. Hlatky, I. C. Siegler, and D. B. Mark, "Prognostic Importance of Social and Economic Resources among Medically Treated Patients with Angiographically Documented Coronary Artery Disease" (pp. 520-524); and R. Ruberman, "Psychosocial Influences on Mortality of Patients with Coronary Heart Disease" (pp. 559-560).

8. J. Stewart, Bridges, Not Walls: A Book about Interpersonal Communication, 9th ed. (New York: McGraw-Hill, 2004), p. 11.

9. R. Shattuck, The Forbidden Experiment: The Story of the Wild Boy of Aveyron (New York: Farrar, Straus & Giroux, 1980), p. 37.

10. For a fascinating account of Genie's story, see R. Rymer, Genie: An Abused Child's Flight from Silence (New York: HarperCollins, 1993). Linguist Susan Curtiss provides a more specialized account of the case in her book Genie: A Psycholinguistic Study of a Modern-Day "Wild Child" (San Diego: Academic Press, 1977).

11. R. B. Rubin, E. M. Perse, and C. A. Barbato, "Conceptualization and Measurement of Interpersonal Communication Motives." Human Communication Research 14 (1988): 602-628.

12. W. Goldschmidt, The Human Career: The Self in the Symbolic World (Cambridge, MA: Basil Blackmun, 1990).

13. Job Outlook 2004, National Association of Colleges and Employers. Report at http://www.jobweb.com/joboutlook/2004outlook/.

14. M. S. Peterson, "Personnel Interviewers' Perceptions of the Importance and Adequacy of Applicants' Communication Skills." Communication Education 46 (1997): 287-291.

15. M. W. Martin and C. M. Anderson, "Roommate Similarity: Are Roommates Who Are Similar in Their Communication Traits More Satisfied?" Communication Research Reports 12 (1995): 46- 52.

16. E. Kirchler, "Marital Happiness and Interaction in Everyday Surroundings: A Time-Sample Diary Approach for Couples." Journal of Social and Personal Relationships 5 (1988): 375-382.

17. R. B. Rubin and E. E. Graham, "Communication Correlates of College Success: An Exploratory Investigation." Communication Education 37 (1988): 14-27.

18. R. L. Duran and L. Kelly, "The Influence of Communicative Competence on Perceived Task, Social and Physical Attraction." Communication Quarterly 36 (1988): 41-49.

19. C. E. Shannon and W. Weaver, The Mathematical Theory of Communication (Urbana: University of Illinois Press, 1949).

20. See, for example, M. Dunne and S. H. Ng, "Simultaneous Speech in Small Group Conversation: All-Together-Now and One-at-a-Time?" Journal of Language and Social Psychology 13 (1994): 45-71.

21. The issue of intentionality has been a matter of debate by communication theorists. For a sample of the arguments on both sides, see J. O. Greene, ed., Message Production: Advances in Communication Theory (New York: Erlbaum, 1997); M. T. Motley, "On Whether One Can(not) Communicate: An Examination via Traditional Communication Postulates." Western Journal of Speech Communication 54 (1990): 1-20; J. B. Bavelas, "Behaving and Communicating: A Reply to Motley." Western Journal of Speech Communication 54 (1990): 593-602; and J. Stewart, "A Postmodern Look at Traditional Communication Postulates." Western Journal of Speech Communication 55 (1991): 354-379.

22. K. J. Gergen, The Saturated Self: Dilemmas of Identity in Contemporary Life (New York: Basic Books, 1991), p. 158.

23. T. P. Mottet and V. P. Richmond, "Student Nonverbal Communication and Its Influence on Teachers and Teaching: A Review of Literature," in J. L. Chesebro and J. C. McCroskey, eds., Communication for Teachers (Needham Heights, MA: Allyn & Bacon, 2001).

24. M. Dainton and L. Stafford, "The Dark Side of' Normal Family Interaction," in B. H. Spitzberg and W. R. Cupach, eds., The Dark Side of Interpersonal Communication (Hillsdale, NJ: Erlbaum, 1993).

25. For a thorough review of this topic, see B. H. Spitzberg and W. R. Cupach, Handbook of Interpersonal Competence Research (New York: Springer-Verlag, 1989).

26. See J. M. Wiemann, J. Takai, LI. Ota, and M. Wiemann, "A Relational Model of Communication Competence," in B. Kovacic, ed., Emerging Theories of Human Communication (Albany: SUNY Press, 1997). These goals, and the strategies used to achieve them, needn't be conscious. See G. M. Fitzsimons and J. A. Bargh, "Thinking of You: Nonconscious Pursuit of Interpersonal Goals Associated with Relationship Partners." Journal of Personality and Social Psychology 84 (2003): 148-164.

27. For a review of the research citing the importance of flexibility, see M. M. Martin and C. M. Anderson, 'The Cognitive Flexibility Scale: Three Validity Studies." Communication Reports 11 (1998): 1-9.

28. For a discussion of the trait versus state assessments of communication, see D. A. Infante, A. S. Rancer, and D. F. Womack, Building Communication Theory, 3rd ed. (Prospect Heights, IL: Waveland Press, 1996), pp. 159-160. For a specific discussion of trait versus state definitions of communication competence, see W. R. Cupach and B. H. Spitzberg, "Trait versus State: A Comparison of Dispositional and Situational Measures of Interpersonal Communication Competence." Western Journal of Speech Communication 47 (1983): 364-379.

29. B.R. Burleson and W. Samter, "A Social Skills Approach to Relationship Maintenance," in D. Canary and L. Stafford, eds., Communication and Relationship Maintenance (San Diego: Academic Press, 1994), p. 12.

30. L. K. Guerrero, P. A. Andersen, P. F. Jorgensen, B. H. Spitzberg, and S. V. Eloy. "Coping with the Green-Eyed Monster: Conceptualizing and Measuring Communicative Responses to Romantic Jealousy." Western Journal of Communication 59 (1995): 270-304.

31. See B. J. O'Keefe, "The Logic of Message Design: Individual Differences in Reasoning about Communication." Communication Monographs 55 (1988): 80-103.

32. See, for example, A. D. Heisel, J. C. McCroskey, and V. P. Richmond, "Testing Theoretical Relationships and Nonrelationships of Genetically-Based Predictors: Getting Started with Communibiology." Communication Research Reports 16 (1999): 1-9; and J. C. McCroskey and K. J. Beatty, "The Communibiological Perspective: Implications for Communication in Instruction." Communication Education 49 (2000): 1-6.

33. S. L. Kline and B. L. Clinton, "Developments in Children's Persuasive Message Practices." Communication Education 47 (1998): 120- 136.

34. M. A. de Turck and G. R. Miller, "Training Observers to Detect Deception: Effects of Self-Monitoring and Rehearsal." Human Communication Research 16 (1990): 603-620.

35. R. B. Rubin, E. E. Graham, and J. T. Mignerey, "A Longitudinal Study of College Students'

Communication Competence." Communication Education 39 (1990): 1-14.

36. See, for example, R. Martin, "Relational Cognition Complexity and Relational Communication in Personal Relationships." Communication Monographs 59 (1992): 150-163; D. W. Stacks and M. A. Murphy, "Conversational Sensitivity: Further Validation and Extension." Communication Reports 6 (1993): 18-24; and A. L. Vangelisti and S. M. Draughton, "The Nature and Correlates of Conversational Sensitivity." Human Communication Research 14 (1987): 167-202.

37. Research summarized in D. E. Hamachek, Encounters with the Self 2nd ed. (Fort Worth, TX: Holt, Rinehart and Winston, 1987), p. 8. See also J. A. Daly, A. L. Vangelisti, and S. M. Daughton, "The Nature and Correlates of Conversational Sensitivity," in M. V. Redmond, ed., Interpersonal Communication: Readings in Theory and Research (Fort Worth, TX: Harcourt Brace, 1995).

38. D. A. Dunning and J. Kruger, Journal of Personality and Social Psychology (December 1999).

39. Adapted from the work of R. P. Hart as reported by M. L. Knapp in Interpersonal Communication and Human Relationships (Boston: Allyn & Bacon, 1984), pp. 342-344. See also R. P. Hart and D. M. Burks, "Rhetorical Sensitivity and Social Interaction." Speech Monographs 39 (1972): 75-91; and R. P. Hart, R. E. Carlson, and W. F. Eadie, "Attitudes toward Communication and the Assessment of Rhetorical Sensitivity." Communication Monographs 47 (1980): 1-22.

40. Adapted from J. C. McCroskey and L. R. Wheeless, Introduction to Human Communication (Boston: Allyn & Bacon, 1976), pp. 3-10.

41. J.L. Smith, W. Ickes, and S. Hodges (eds.), Managing Interpersonal Sensitivity: Knowing When—and When Not—to Understand Others (Hauppauge, NY: Nova Science Publishers, 2010).

42. W.B. Pearce and K. A. Pearce, "Extending the Theory of the Coordinated Management of Meaning (CMM) through a Community Dialogue Process." Communication Theory 10 (2000): 405-423. See also E.M. Griffin, A First Look at Communication Theory, 5th ed. (New York: McGraw-Hill, 2003), pp. 66-81.

43. J.A.M. Meerloo, Conversation and Communication (Madison, CT: International Universities Press, 1952), p. 91.

44. For a detailed rationale of the position argued in this section, see G.H. Stamp and M.L. Knapp, "The Construct of Intent in Interpersonal Communication." Quarterly Journal of Speech 76 (1990): 282-299. See also J. Stewart, "A Postmodern Look at Traditional Communication Postulates." Western Journal of Speech Communication 55 (1991): 354-379.

45. For a thorough discussion of communication difficulties, see N. Coupland, H. Giles, and J.M. Wiemann, eds., "Miscommunication" and Problematic Talk (Newbury Park, CA: Sage, 1991).

46. J.C. McCroskey and L.R. Wheeless, Introduction to Human Communication (Boston: Allyn & Bacon, 1976), p. 5.

2. Language

by Ronald B. Adler and George Rodman

Language is usually one of the first things a person thinks about when he or she hears the word "communication." Whether on a page, on a screen, or verbally extended, words are fundamental tools for the transmission of information and exchange of ideas or feelings. We rely so heavily on words that we frequently translate our experiences into words in order to "make sense" of them. This chapter provides an overview of the nature and power of words and the larger, cultural context for words—language. By learning about the symbolic nature of language, readers should gain a respect for the power of language. An important lesson of this chapter is that language is a human construct that simultaneously exerts immense influence over users while giving them the power to build, shape, create, and recreate the world around them.

Upon completing this chapter, readers should take a moment to reflect on their use of language. What patterns emerge in the linguistic choices made on a daily basis? How do these choices reflect the attitudes and experiences of the reader? How might a change in language choices result in a change of experience and attitude? The more someone reflects on his or her own word choice, the more he or she understands the influence and revelatory nature of language.

At one time or another, every one of us has suffered the limits and traps of language. Even though we are using familiar words, it's clear that we often don't use them in ways that allow us to communicate smoothly with one another.

In the following pages we will explore the nature of linguistic communication. By the time you have finished reading this chapter, you will better appreciate the complexity of language, its power to shape our perceptions of people and events, and its potential for incomplete and inaccurate communication. Perhaps more importantly, you will be better equipped to use the tool of language more skillfully to improve your everyday interaction.

The Nature of Language

Humans speak about ten thousand dialects.[1] Although most of these sound different from one another, all possess the same characteristics of **language:** a collection of symbols governed by rules and used to convey messages between individuals. A closer look at this definition can explain how language operates and suggest how we can use it more effectively.

Language Is Symbolic

There's nothing natural about calling your loyal four-footed companion a "dog" or the object you're reading right now a "book." These words, like virtually all language, are **symbols**—arbitrary constructions that represent a communicator's thoughts. Not all linguistic symbols are spoken or written words. Sign language, as "spoken" by most deaf people, is symbolic in nature and not the pantomime it might seem to nonsigners. There are literally hundreds of different sign languages spoken around the world that represent the same ideas differently.[2] These distinct languages include American Sign Language, British Sign Language, French Sign Language, Danish Sign Language, Chinese Sign Language—even Australian Aboriginal and Mayan sign languages.

Symbols are more than just labels: They are the way we experience the world. You can prove this by trying a simple experiment.[3] Work up some saliva in your mouth, and then spit it into a glass. Take a good look and then drink it up. Most people find this process mildly disgusting. But ask yourself why this is so. After all, we swallow our own saliva all the time. The answer arises out of the symbolic labels we use. After the saliva is in the glass, we call it *spit* and think of it in a different way. In other words, our reaction is to the name, not the thing.

The naming process operates in virtually every situation. How you react to a stranger will depend on the symbols you use to categorize him or her: gay (or straight), religious (or not), attractive (or unattractive), and so on.

Meanings Are in People, Not Words

Ask a dozen people what the same symbol means, and you are likely to get twelve different answers. Does an American flag bring up associations of patriots giving their lives for their country? Fourth of July parades? Cultural imperialism? How about a cross:

What does it represent? The message of Jesus Christ? Firelit rallies of Ku Klux Klansmen? Your childhood Sunday school? The necklace your sister always wears?

As with physical symbols, the place to look for meaning in language isn't in the words themselves but rather in the way people make sense of them. One unfortunate example of this fact occurred in Washington D.C., when the newly appointed city ombudsman used the word "niggardly" to describe an approach to budgeting.[4] Some African American critics accused him of uttering an unforgivable racial slur. His defenders pointed out that the word, which means "miserly," is derived from Scandinavian languages and that it has no link to the racial slur it resembles. Even though the criticisms eventually died away, they illustrate that, correct or not, the meanings people associate with words have far more significance than do their dictionary definitions.

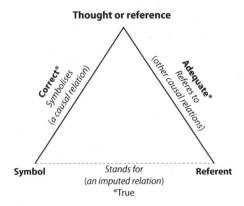

Figure 1. Ogden and Richard's Triangle of Meaning

Linguistic theorists C.K. Ogden and I.A. Richards illustrated the fact that meanings are social constructions in their well-known "triangle of meaning" (Figure 1).[5] This model shows that there is only an indirect relationship—indicated by a broken line—between a word and the thing it claims to represent. Some of these "things" or referents do not exist in the physical world. For instance, some referents are mythical (such as unicorns), some are no longer tangible (such as Elvis, if he really is dead), and others are abstract ideas (such as "love").

Problems arise when people mistakenly assume that others use words in the same way they do. It's possible to have an argument about *feminism* without ever realizing that you and the other person are using the word to represent entirely different things. The same goes for *environmentalism, Republicans, rock music,* and thousands upon thousands of other symbols. Words don't mean; people do—and often in widely different ways.

Despite the potential for linguistic problems, the situation isn't hopeless. We do, after all, communicate with one another reasonably well most of the time. And with enough effort, we can clear up most of the misunderstandings that do occur. The key to more accurate use of language is to avoid assuming that others interpret words the same way we do. In truth, successful communication occurs when we negotiate the meaning of a statement.[6] As one French proverb puts it, "The spoken word belongs half to the one who speaks it and half to the one who hears."

Language Is Rule Governed

Languages contain several types of rules. **Phonological rules** govern how words sound when pronounced. For instance, the words *champagne, double,* and *occasion* are spelled identically in French and English, but all are pronounced differently. Nonnative speakers learning English are plagued by inconsistent phonological rules, as a few examples illustrate:

> He could lead if he would get the lead out.
> A farm can produce produce.
> The dump was so full it had to refuse refuse.
> The present is a good time to present the present.
> I did not object to the object.
> The bandage was wound around the wound.
> I shed a tear when I saw the tear in my clothes.

Phonological rules aren't the only ones that govern the way we use language to communicate. **Syntactic rules** govern the structure of language—the way symbols can be arranged. For example, correct English syntax requires that every word contain at least one vowel and prohibits sentences such as "Have you the cookies brought?", which is a perfectly acceptable word order in German. Although most of us aren't able to describe the syntactic rules that govern our language, it's easy to recognize their existence by noting how odd a statement that violates them appears.

Technology has spawned subversions of English with their own syntactic rules.[7] For example, users of instant messaging on the Internet have devised a streamlined version of English that speeds up typing in real-time communication (although it probably makes teachers of composition grind their teeth in anguish):

> A: Hey
> B: r u @ home?

A: ys
B: k I'm getting offline now
A: y
B: cuz i need to study for finals u can call me tho bye
A: TTYL

Semantic rules deal with the meaning of specific words. Semantic rules are what make it possible for us to agree that "bikes" are for riding and "books" are for reading; they also help us to know whom we will and won't encounter when we open doors marked "men" or "women." Without semantic rules, communication would be impossible, because each of us would be using symbols in unique ways, unintelligible to one another.

Semantic misunderstandings occur when words can be interpreted in more than one way, as the following humorous notices prove:

> The peacemaking meeting scheduled for today has been canceled due to a conflict. For those of you who have children and don't know it, we have a nursery downstairs.

> The ladies of the Church have cast off clothing of every kind. They may be seen in the basement on Friday afternoon.

> Sunday's sermon topic will be "What Is Hell?" Come early and listen to our choir practice.

Pragmatic rules govern how people use language in everyday interaction, which communication theorists have characterized as a series of *speech acts*.[8] Consider the example of a male boss saying "You look very pretty today" to a female employee. It's easy to imagine how the subordinate might be offended by a comment that her boss considered an innocent remark. Scholars of language have pointed out several levels at which the rules each person uses can differ. You can understand these levels by imagining how they would operate in our example:

Each person's self-concept
Boss: Views himself as a nice guy.
Subordinate: Determined to succeed on her own merits, and not her appearance.

The episode in which the comment occurs
Boss: Casual remark at the start of the workday.
Employee: A possible come-on?
Perceived relationship
Boss: Views employees like members of the family.
Employee: Depends on boss's goodwill for advancement.

Cultural background
Boss: Member of generation in which comments about appearance were common.
Employee: Member of generation sensitive to sexual harassment.

As this example shows, pragmatic rules don't involve semantic issues, since the words themselves are usually understood well by almost everybody. Instead, they involve how those words are understood and used.

The Power of Language

On the most obvious level, language allows us to satisfy basic functions such as describing ideas, making requests, and solving problems. But beyond these functions, the way we use language also influences others and reflects our attitudes in more subtle ways, which we will examine now.

Language Shapes Attitudes

The power of language to shape ideas has been recognized throughout history. The first chapters of the Bible report that Adam's dominion over animals was demonstrated by his being given the power to give them names.[9] As we will now see, our speech—sometimes consciously and sometimes not—shapes others' values, attitudes, and beliefs in a variety of ways.

Naming "What's in a name?" Juliet asked rhetorically. If Romeo had been a social scientist, he would have answered, "A great deal." Research has demonstrated that names are more than just a simple means of identification: They shape the way others think of us, the way we view ourselves, and the way we act.

At the most fundamental level, some research suggests that even the phonetic sound of a person's name affects the way we regard him or her, at least when we don't have other information available. One study revealed that reasonably accurate predictions about who will win an election can be made on the basis of some phonetic features of the candidates' surnames.[10] Names that were simple, easily pronounced, and rhythmic were judged more favorably than ones that lack these qualities. For example, in one series of local elections, the winning candidates had names that resonated with voters: Sanders beat Pekelis, Rielly defeated Dellwo, Grady outpolled Schumacher, Combs trounced Bernsdorf, and Golden prevailed over Nuffer. Names don't guarantee victory, but in seventy-eight elections, forty-eight outcomes supported the value of having an appealing name.

Names are one way to shape and reinforce a child's personal identity. Naming a baby after a family member (e.g., "Junior" or "Trey") can create a connection between the youngster and his or her namesake. Name choice can also be a powerful way to make a statement about cultural identity. For example, in recent decades a large percentage of names given to African American babies have been distinctively black.[11] In California, over 40 percent of black girls born in a single year had names that not a single white baby born in the entire state was given. Researchers suggest that distinctive names like these are a symbol of solidarity with the African American community. Conversely, choosing a less distinctive name can be a way of integrating the baby into the majority culture. Whether common or unusual, the impact of names recedes after communicators become more familiar with one another.[12]

Choosing a newborn's name can be especially challenging for people from nondominant cultures with different languages. One writer from India describes the problem he and his wife faced when considering names for their first child:

> How will the child's foreign name sound to American ears? (That test ruled out Shiva, my family deity; a Jewish friend put her foot down.) Will it provoke bullies to beat him up on the school playground? (That was the end of Karan, the name of a warrior from the Mahabharata, the Hindu epic. A boy called "Karen" wouldn't stand a chance.) Will it be as euphonic in New York as it is in New Delhi? (That was how Sameer failed to get off the ground. "Like a bagel with a schmear!" said one ruthless well-wisher.)[16]

First names aren't the only linguistic elements that may shape attitudes about men and women.

Credibility Scholarly speaking is a good example of how speech style influences perception. We refer to what has been called the Dr. Fox hypothesis.[17] "An apparently legitimate speaker who utters an unintelligible message will be judged competent by an audience in the speaker's area of apparent expertise." The Dr. Fox hypothesis got its name from one Dr. Myron L. Fox, who delivered a talk followed by a half-hour discussion on "Mathematical Game Theory as Applied to Physical Education." The audience included psychiatrists, psychologists, social workers, and educators. Questionnaires collected after the session revealed that these educated listeners found the lecture clear and stimulating.

Despite his warm reception by this learned audience, Fox was a complete fraud. He was a professional actor whom researchers had coached to deliver a lecture of double-talk—a patchwork of information from a *Scientific American* article mixed with jokes, non-sequiturs, contradictory statements, and meaningless references to unrelated topics. When wrapped in a linguistic package of high-level professional jargon, however, the meaningless gobbledygook was judged as important information. In other words, Fox's audience reaction was based more on the credibility that arose from his use of impressive-sounding language than from the ideas he expressed.

The same principle seems to hold for academic writing.[18] A group of thirty-two management professors rated material according to its complexity rather than its content. When a message about consumer behavior was loaded with unnecessary words and long, complex sentences, the professors rated it highly. When the same message was translated into more readable English, with shorter words and clearer sentences, the professors judged the same research as less competent.

Status In the classic musical *My Fair Lady,* professor Henry Higgins transformed Eliza Doolittle from a lowly flower girl into a high-society woman by replacing her Cockney accent with an upper-crust speaking style. Decades of research have demonstrated that the power of speech to influence status is a fact.[19] Several factors combine to create positive or negative impressions: accent, choice of words, speech rate, and even the apparent age of a speaker. In most cases, speakers of standard dialect are rated higher than nonstandard speakers in a variety of ways: They are viewed as more competent and more self-confident, and the content of their messages is rated more favorably. The unwillingness or inability of a communicator to use the standard dialect fluently can have serious consequences. For instance, speakers of Black English, a distinctive dialect with its own accent, grammar, syntax, and semantic rules, are rated as less intelligent, professional, capable, socially acceptable, and employable by speakers of standard English.[20]

Sexism and Racism By now it should be clear that the power of language to shape attitudes goes beyond individual cases and influences how we perceive entire groups of people. For example, Casey Miller and Kate Swift argue that incorrect use of the pronoun *he* to refer to both men and women can have damaging results.

> On the television screen, a teacher of first-graders who has just won a national award is describing her way of teaching, "You take each child where you find him," she says. "You watch to

see what he's interested in, and then you build on his interests."

> A five-year-old looking at the program asks her mother, "Do only boys go to that school?"

> "No," her mother begins, "she's talking about girls too, but—"

> But what? The teacher being interviewed on television is speaking correct English. What can the mother tell her daughter about why a child, in any generalization, is always he rather than she? How does a five-year-old comprehend the generic personal pronoun?[21]

It's usually easy to use nonsexist language. For example, the term *mankind* may be replaced by *humanity, human beings, human race,* or *people; man-made* may be replaced by *artificial, manufactured,* and *synthetic; manpower* maybe replaced by *human power, workers,* and *workforce;* and *manhood* may be replaced by *adulthood.*

The use of labels for racist purposes has a long and ugly past. Names have been used throughout history to stigmatize groups that other groups have disapproved of.[22] By using derogatory terms to label some people, the out-group is set apart and pictured in an unfavorable light. Diane Mader provides several examples of this:

> We can see the process of stigmatization in Nazi Germany when Jewish people became vermin, in the United States when African Americans became "niggers" and chattel, in the military when the Vietnam-era enemy became "gooks."[23]

The power of racist language to shape attitudes is difficult to avoid, even when it is obviously offensive. In one study, experimental subjects who heard a derogatory label used against a member of a minority group expressed annoyance at this sort of slur, but despite their disapproval, the negative emotional terms did have an impact.[24] Not only did the unwitting subjects rate the minority individual's competence lower when that person performed poorly, but also they found fault with others who associated socially with the minority person—even members of the subject's own ethnic group.

Language Reflects Attitudes

Besides shaping the way we view ourselves and others, language reflects our attitudes. Feelings of control, attraction, commitment, responsibility—all these and more are reflected in the way we use language.

Power Communication researchers have identified a number of language patterns that add to, or detract from, a speaker's ability to influence others, as well as reflecting how a speaker feels about his or her degree of control over a situation.[25] Table 1 summarizes some of these findings by listing several types of "powerless" language.

You can see the difference between powerful language and powerless language by comparing the following statements:

> "Excuse me, sir, I hate to say this, but I … uh … I guess I won't be able to turn in the assignment on time, I had a personal emergency and … well …, it was just impossible to finish it by today. I'll have it in your mailbox on Monday, okay?"

> "I won't be able to turn in the assignment on time. I had a personal emergency, and it was impossible to finish it by today. I'll have it in your mailbox on Monday."

Even a single type of powerless speech mannerism, such as hedges, appears to make a person appear less authoritative or socially attractive.[26] By contrast, speakers whose talk is free of powerless mannerisms are rated as more competent, dynamic, and attractive than speakers who sound powerless.[27] In employment interviews, powerful speech results in more positive attributions of competence and employability than powerless speech.[28]

Despite the potential drawbacks of powerless speech, don't assume that the best goal is always to sound as powerful as you can. Along with gaining compliance, another conversational goal is often building a supportive, friendly relationship, and sharing power with the other person can help you in this regard. For this reason, many everyday statements will contain a mixture of powerful speech and powerless speech.[29] Our student-teacher example illustrates how this combination of powerless mannerisms and powerful mannerisms can help the student get what she wants while staying on good terms with the professor:

> "Excuse me, Professor Rodman. I want you to know that I won't be able to turn in the assignment on time. I had a personal emergency, and it was impossible to finish it by today. I'll definitely have it in your mailbox on Monday."

Whether or not the professor finds the excuse acceptable, it's clear that this last statement combines the best features of powerful speech and powerless speech: a combination of self-assurance and goodwill.

Simply counting the number of powerful or powerless statements won't always reveal who has the most control in a relationship. Social rules often mask the real distribution of power. Sociolinguist Deborah Tannen describes how politeness can be a face-saving way of delivering an order:

> "I hear myself giving instructions to my assistants without actually issuing orders: 'Maybe it would be a good idea to …;' 'It would be great if you could …' all the while knowing that I expect them to do what I've asked right away … This rarely creates problems, though, because the people who work for me know that there is only one reason I mention tasks—because I want them done. I *like* giving instructions in this way; it appeals to my sense of what it

means to be a good person … taking others' feelings into account."[30]

As this quote suggests, high-status speakers often realize that politeness is an effective way to get their needs met while protecting the face of the less powerful person. The importance of achieving both content goals and relational goals helps explain why a mixture of powerful speech and polite speech is usually most effective.[31] Of course, if the other person misinterprets politeness for weakness, it may be necessary to shift to a more powerful speaking style.

Powerful speech that gets the desired results in mainstream North American and European culture doesn't succeed everywhere with everyone.[32]In Japan, saving face for others is an important goal, so communicators there tend to speak in ambiguous terms and use hedge words and qualifiers. In most Japanese sentences the verb comes at the end of the sentence so the "action" part of the statement can be postponed. Traditional Mexican culture, with its strong emphasis on cooperation, makes a priority of using language to create harmony in interpersonal relationships, rather than taking a firm or oppositional stance. In order to make others feel more at ease, Korean culture represents yet another group of people that prefers "indirect" (for example, "perhaps," "could be") to "direct" speech.

Affiliation Power isn't the only way language reflects the status of relationships. Language can also be away of building and demonstrating solidarity with others. An impressive body of research has demonstrated that communicators who want to show affiliation with one another adapt their speech in a variety of ways, including their choice of vocabulary, rate of talking, number and placement of pauses, and level of politeness.[33] On an individual level, close friends and lovers often develop special terms that serve as a way of signifying their relationship.[34] Using the same vocabulary sets these people apart from others, reminding themselves and the rest of the world of their relationship. The same process works among members of larger groups, ranging from street gangs to military personnel. Communication

researchers call this linguistic accommodation **convergence.**

Communicators can experience convergence in cyberspace as well as in face-to-face interactions. Members of online communities often develop a shared language and conversational style, and their affiliation with each other can be seen in increased uses of the pronoun "we."[35] On a larger scale, IM and e-mail users create and use shortcuts that mark them as Internet-savvy. If you know what ROTFL, IMHO, and JK mean, you're probably part of that group. (For the uninitiated, those acronyms mean "Rolling on the floor laughing," "In my humble opinion," and "Just kidding.") Interestingly, instant-messagers may find that their cyberlanguage creeps into everyday conversations.[36] (Have you ever said "LOL" instead of the words "laughing out loud"—or instead of actually laughing out loud?)

When two or more people feel equally positive about one another, their linguistic convergence will be mutual. But when communicators want or need the approval of others they often adapt their speech to suit the others' style, trying to say the "right thing" or speak in a way that will help them fit in. We see this process when immigrants who want to gain the rewards of material success in a new culture strive to master the prevalent language. Likewise, employees who seek advancement tend to speak more like their superiors: Supervisors adopt the speech style of managers, and managers converge toward their bosses.

The principle of speech accommodation works in reverse, too. Communicators who want to set themselves apart from others adopt the strategy of **divergence,** speaking in a way that emphasizes their difference from others. For example, members of an ethnic group, even though fluent in the dominant language, might use their own dialect as a way of showing solidarity with one another— a sort of "us against them" strategy. Divergence also operates in other settings. A physician or attorney, for example, who wants to establish credibility with his or her client might speak formally and use professional jargon to create a sense of distance. The implicit message here is "I'm different (and more knowledgeable) than you."

TABLE 1. Powerless Language

TYPE OF USAGE	EXAMPLE
Hedges	"I'm kinda disappointed …"
	"I think we should …"
	"I guess I'd like to …"
Hesitations	"Uh, can I have a minute of your time?"
	"Well, we could try this idea …"
	"I wish you would—er—try to be on time."
Intensifiers	"So that's how I feel …"
	"I'm not very hungry."
Polite forms	"Excuse me, sir …"
Tag questions	"It's about time we got started, isn't it?"
	"Don't you think we should give it another try"?
Disclaimers	"I probably shouldn't say this, but …"
	"I'm not really sure, but …"

Convergence and divergence aren't the only ways to express affiliation. **Linguistic intergroup bias** reflects whether or not we regard others as part of our in-group. Researchers have discovered a tendency to describe the *positive* behaviors of others with whom we identify as personality traits.[37] A positive bias leads us to describe in-group members in favorable terms and out-group members negatively. For example, if an in-group member gives money to a homeless person, we are likely to describe her behavior as a positive personality trait: "Sue is a generous person." If an out-group member (someone with whom we don't identify) gives the same homeless person some money, we are likely to describe her behavior as a discrete behavior. "Sue gave away money."

The same in-group preferences are revealed when we describe undesirable behaviors. If an in-group member behaves poorly, we are likely to describe the behavior using a concrete descriptive action verb, such as "John cheated in the game." In contrast, if the person we are describing is an out-group member, we are more likely to use general disposition adjectives such as "John is a cheater." These selective language choices are so subtle and subconscious that when asked, people being studied report that there were no differences in the way they described in-group versus out-group members' behavior. We tend to believe we are less biased than we are, but our language reveals the truth about our preferences.

Attraction and Interest Social customs discourage us from expressing like or dislike in many situations. Only a clod would respond to the question "What do you think of the cake I baked for you?" by saying, "It's terrible." Bashful or cautious suitors might not admit their attraction to a potential partner. Even when people are reluctant to speak candidly, the language they use can suggest their degree of interest and attraction toward a person, object, or idea. Morton Weiner and Albert Mehrabian outline a number of linguistic clues that reveal these attitudes.[38]

- **Demonstrative pronoun choice.** *These* people want our help (positive) versus *Those* people want our help (less positive).
- **Negation.** It's *good* (positive) versus It's *not bad* (less positive).
- **Sequential placement.** Dick and Jane (Dick is more important) versus Jane and Dick (Jane is more important). However, sequential placement isn't always significant You may put "toilet bowl cleaner" at the top of your shopping list simply because it's closer to the market door than is champagne.

Responsibility In addition to suggesting liking and importance, language can reveal the speaker's willingness to accept responsibility for a message.

- **"It" versus "I" statements.** *It's* not finished (less responsible) versus *I* didn't finish it (more responsible).
- **"You" versus "I" statements.** Sometimes *you* make me angry (less responsible) versus Sometimes *I* get angry when you do that (more responsible). "I" statements are more likely to generate positive reactions from others as compared to accusatory ones [39]
- **"But" statements.** It's a good idea, *but* it won't work. You're really terrific, *but* I think we ought to spend less time together. (*But* cancels everything that went before the word.)
- **Questions versus statements.** Do you think we ought to do that? (less responsible) versus I don't think we ought to do that (more responsible).

Troublesome Language

Besides being a blessing that enables us to live together, language can be something of a curse. We have all known the frustration of being misunderstood, and most of us have been baffled by another person's overreaction to an innocent comment. In the following pages we will look at several kinds of troublesome language, with the goal of helping you communicate in a way that makes matters better instead of worse.

The Language of Misunderstandings

The most obvious kind of language problems are semantic: We simply don't understand others completely or accurately. Most misunderstandings arise from some common problems that are easily remedied—after you recognize them.

Equivocal Language *Equivocal words* have more than one correct dictionary definition. Some equivocal misunderstandings are simple, at least after they are exposed. A nurse once told her patient that he "wouldn't be needing" the materials he requested from home. He interpreted the statement to mean he was near death when the nurse meant he would be going home soon. A colleague of ours mistakenly sent some confidential materials to the wrong person after his boss told him to "send them to Richard" without specifying which Richard. Some equivocal misunderstandings can be embarrassing, as one woman recalls:

> In the fourth grade the teacher asked the class what a period was. I raised my hand and shared everything I had learned about girls' getting their period. But he was talking about the dot at the end of a sentence. Oops![40]

Equivocal misunderstandings can have serious consequences. Equivocation at least partially explains why men may sometimes persist in attempts to become physically intimate when women have expressed unwillingness to do so.[41] Interviews and focus groups with college students revealed that women often use ambiguous phrases to say "no" to a man's sexual advances: "I'm confused about this." "I'm not sure that we're ready for this yet." Are you sure you want to do this?" "Let's be friends" and even "That tickles." (The researchers found that women were most likely to use less direct phrases when they hoped to see or date the man again. When they wanted to cut off the relationship, they were more likely to give a direct response.) Whereas women viewed indirect statements as equivalent to saying "no," men were more likely to interpret them as less clear-cut requests to stop. As the researchers put it, "male/female misunderstandings are not so much a matter of males hearing resistance messages as 'go,' but rather their not hearing them as 'stop.'" Under the law, "no" means precisely that, and anyone who argues otherwise can be in for serious legal problems.

Relative Words *Relative words* gain their meaning by comparison. For example, is the school you attend large or small? This depends on what you compare it to: Alongside a campus like UCLA, with an enrollment of over thirty thousand students, it probably looks small, but compared to a smaller institution, it might seem quite large. In the same way, relative words like *fast* and *slow, smart* and *stupid, short* and *long* depend for their meaning on what they're compared to. (The "large" size can of olives is the smallest you can buy; the larger ones are "giant," "colossal," and "supercolossal.")

Some relative words are so common that we mistakenly assume that they have a clear meaning. For instance, if a new acquaintance says "I'll call you soon," when can you expect to hear from him or her? In one study, graduate students were asked to assign numerical values to terms such as *doubtful, toss-up, likely, probable, good chance,* and unlikely.[42] There was a tremendous variation in the meaning of most of these terms. For example, the responses for *possible* ranged from 0 to 99 percent. *Good chance* meant between 35 and 90 percent, whereas *unlikely* fell between 0 and 40 percent.

Using relative words without explaining them can lead to communication problems. Have you ever responded to someone's question about the weather by saying it was warm, only to find out that what was warm to you was cold to the other person? Or have you followed a friend's advice and gone to a "cheap" restaurant, only to find that it was twice as expensive as you expected? Have you been disappointed to learn that classes you've heard were "easy" turned out to be hard, that journeys you were told would be "short" were long, that "unusual" ideas were really quite ordinary? The problem in each case came from failing to anchor the relative word used to a more precisely measurable word.

Slang and Jargon *Slang* is language used by a group of people whose members belong to a similar coculture or other group. Some slang is related to specialized interests and activities. For instance, cyclists who talk about "bonking" are referring to running out of energy. Rapsters know that "bling" refers to jewelry and a "whip" is a nice-looking car.

Other slang consists of *regionalisms*—terms that are understood by people who live in one geographic area but that are incomprehensible to outsiders. This sort of use illustrates how slang

defines insiders and outsiders, creating a sense of identity and solidarity.[43] Residents of the fiftieth U.S. state know that when a fellow Alaskan says, "I'm going outside," he or she is leaving the state. In the East End of London, Cockney dialect uses rhyming words as substitutes for everyday expressions: "bacon and eggs" for "legs," and "Barney Rubble" for "trouble." This sort of use also illustrates how slang can be used to identify insiders and outsiders: With enough shared rhyming, slang users could talk about outsiders without the clueless outsiders knowing that they were the subject of conversation ("Lovely set of bacons, eh?" "Stay away from him. He's Barney.").

Slang can also be age related. Most college students know that drinkers wearing "beer goggles" have consumed enough alcohol that they find almost everyone of the opposite—or sometimes the same—sex attractive. At some schools, a "monkey" is the "other" woman or man in a boyfriend's or girlfriend's life: "I've heard Mitch is cheating on me. When I find his monkey, I'm gonna do her up!"[44]

Almost everyone uses some sort of **jargon:** the specialized vocabulary that functions as a kind of shorthand for people with common backgrounds and experience. Skateboarders have their own language to describe maneuvers: "ollie," "grind," and "shove it." Some jargon consists of *acronyms*—initials of terms that are combined to form a word. Stock traders refer to the NASDAQ (pronounced "naz-dak") securities index, and military people label failure to serve at one's post as being AWOL (absent without leave). The digital age has spawned- its own vocabulary of jargon. For instance, computer users know that "viruses" are malicious programs that migrate from one computer to another, wreaking havoc. Likewise, "cookies" are tiny files that remote observers can use to monitor a user's computer habits. Some jargon goes beyond being descriptive and conveys attitudes. For example, cynics in the high-tech world sometimes refer to being fired from a job as being "uninstalled." They talk dismissively about the nonvirtual world as the "carbon community" and of books and newspapers as "treeware." Some technical support staffers talk of "banana problems," meaning those that could be figured out by monkeys, as in "This is a two-banana problem at worst."[45]

Jargon can be a valuable kind of shorthand for people who understand its use. The trauma team in a hospital, emergency room can save time, and possibly lives, by speaking in shorthand, referring to "GSWs" (gunshot wounds), "chem 7" lab tests, and so on, but the same specialized vocabulary that works so well among insiders can mystify and confuse family members of the patient, who don't understand the jargon. The same sort of misunderstandings can arise in less critical settings when insiders use their own language with people who don't share the same vocabulary. Jeffrey Katzman of the William Morris Agency's Hollywood office experienced this sort of problem when he met with members of a Silicon Valley computer firm to discuss a joint project.

> When he used the phrase "in development," he meant a project that was as yet merely an idea. When the techies used it, on the other hand, they meant designing a specific game or program. Ultimately, says Katzman, he had to bring in a blackboard and literally define his terms. "It was like when the Japanese first came to Hollywood," he recalls. "They had to use interpreters, and we did too."[46]

Overly Abstract Language Most objects, events, and ideas can be described with varying degrees of specificity. Consider the material you are reading. You could call it:

A book
A textbook
A communication textbook
Understanding Human Communication
[This chapter] of *Understanding Human Communication*
[This page] of Chapter 4 of *Understanding Human Communication*

In each case your description would be more and more specific Semanticist S.I. Hayakawa created an **abstraction ladder** to describe this process.[47] This ladder consists of a number of descriptions of the same thing. Lower items focus specifically on the person, object, or event, whereas higher terms are generalizations that include the subject as a member of a larger class. To talk about "college," for example, is more abstract than to talk about a particular school. Likewise, referring to "women" is more abstract than referring to "feminists," or more specifically naming feminist organizations or even specific members who belong to them.

Higher-level abstractions are a useful tool, because without them language would be too cumbersome to be useful. It's faster, easier, and more useful to talk about Europe than to list all of the countries on that continent. In the same way, using relatively abstract terms like *friendly* or *smart* can make it easier to describe people than listing their specific actions.

Abstract language—speech that refers to events or objects only vaguely—serves a second, less obvious function. At times it allows us to avoid confrontations by deliberately being unclear.[48] Suppose, for example, your boss is enthusiastic about a new approach to doing business that you think is a terrible idea. Telling the truth might seem too risky, but lying—saying "I think it's a great idea"—wouldn't feel right either. In situations like this an abstract answer can hint at your true belief without a direct confrontation: "I don't know … It's sure unusual … It might work." The same sort of abstract language can help you avoid embarrassing friends who ask for your opinion with questions like "What do you think of my new haircut?" An abstract response, like, "It's really different!" may be easier for you to deliver—and for your friend to receive—than the dear, brutal truth: "It's really ugly!" We will have more to say about this linguistic strategy of equivocation later in this chapter.

Although vagueness does have its uses, highly abstract language can cause several types of problems. The first is *stereotyping*. Consider claims like "All whites are bigots," "Men don't

TABLE 2. Abstract and Behavioral Descriptions

| | | Behavioral Description | | | |
	Abstract Description	Who Is Involved	In What Circumstances	Specific Behaviors	Remarks
Problem	I talk too much.	People I find	When I want them to like me	I talk (mostly about myself) instead of giving them a chance to speak or asking about their lives.	Behavirol description more clearly identifies behaviors to change.
Goal	I want to be more constructive.	My roommate	When we talk about household duties	Instead of finding fault with her ideas, suggest alternatives that might work.	Behavioral description clearly outlines how to act; abstract description doesn't
Appreciation	"You've really been helpful lately."	(Deliver to fellow workers)	"When I've had to take time off work because of personal problems."	"You took my shifts Without-complaining."	Give both abstract and behavioral descriptions for best results
Request	"Clean up your act!"	(Deliver to target person)	"When we're around my family."	"Please don't tell jokes that involve sex."	Behavioral description specifies desired behavior.

care about relationships," "The police are a bunch of goons," or "Professors around here care more about their research than they do about students." Each of these claims ignores the very important fact that abstract descriptions are almost always too general, that they say more than we really mean.

Besides creating stereotypical attitudes, abstract language can lead to the problem of *confusing others*. Imagine the lack of understanding that results from imprecise language in situations like this:

A: We never do anything that's fun anymore.
B: What do you mean?
A: We used to do lots of unusual things, but now it's the same old stuff, over and over.
B: But last week we went on that camping trip, and tomorrow were going to that party where

we'll meet all sorts of new people. Those are new things.
A. That's not what I mean. I'm talking about really unusual stuff.
B: (*becoming confused and a little impatient*) Like what? Taking hard drugs or going over Niagara Falls in a barrel?
A: Don't be stupid. All I'm saying is that we're in a rut. We should be living more exciting lives.
B: Well, I don't know what you want.

The best way to avoid this sort of overly abstract language is to use **behavioral descriptions** instead. (See Table 2.) Behavioral descriptions move down the abstraction ladder to identify the specific, observable phenomenon being discussed. A thorough description should answer three questions:

1. **Who Is Involved?** Are you speaking for just yourself or for others as well? Are you talking about a group of people ("the neighbors," "women") or specific individuals ("the people next door with the barking dog," "Lola and Lizzie")?

2. **In What Circumstances Does the Behavior Occur?** Where does it occur: everywhere or in specific places (at parties, at work, in public)? When does it occur: When you're tired or when a certain subject comes up? The behavior you are describing probably doesn't occur all the time. In order to be understood, you need to pin down what circumstances set this situation apart from other ones.

3. **What Behaviors Are Involved?** Though terms such as *more cooperative* and *helpful* might sound like concrete descriptions of behavior, they are usually too vague to do a clear job of explaining what's on your mind. Behaviors must be *observable*, ideally both to you and to others. For instance, moving down the abstraction ladder from the relatively vague term *helpful*, you might come to behaviors such as *does the dishes every other day, volunteers to help me with my studies*, or *fixes dinner once or twice a week without being asked*. It's easy to see that terms like these are easier for both you and others to understand than are more vague abstractions.

Behavioral descriptions can improve communication in a wide range of situations, as Table 2 illustrates. Research also supports the value of specific language. One study found that well-adjusted couples had just as many conflicts as poorly adjusted couples, but the way the well-adjusted couples handled their problems was significantly different. Instead of blaming one another, the well-adjusted couples expressed their complaints in behavioral terms.[49] For instance, instead of saying "You're a slob," an enlightened partner might say, "I wish you wouldn't leave your dishes in the sink."

Disruptive Language

Not all linguistic problems come from misunderstandings. Sometimes people understand one another perfectly and still end up in conflict. Of course, not all disagreements can, or should be, avoided. But eliminating three bad linguistic habits from your communication repertoire can minimize the kind of clashes that don't need to happen, allowing you to save your energy for the unavoidable and important struggles.

Confusing Facts and Opinions Factual statements are claims that can be verified as true or false. By contrast, **opinion statements** are based on the speaker's beliefs. Unlike matters of fact, they can never be proved or disproved. Consider a few examples of the difference between factual statements and opinion statements:

FACT	OPINION
It rains more in Seattle than in Portland.	The climate in Portland is better than in Seattle.
Kareem Abdul Jabbar is the all-time leading scorer in the National Basketball Association.	Kareem is the greatest basketball player in the history of the game.
Per capita income in the United States is higher than in several other countries.	The United States is not the best model of economic success in the world.

When factual statements and opinion statements are set side by side like this, the difference between them is clear. In everyday conversation, we often present our opinions as if they were facts, and in doing so we invite an unnecessary argument. For example:

"That was a dumb thing to say!"
"Spending that much on [   ] is a waste of money!"
"You can't get a fair shake in this country unless you're a white male."

Notice how much less antagonistic each statement would be if it were prefaced by a qualifier like "In my opinion …" or "It seems to me …"

Confusing Facts and Inferences Labeling your opinions can go a long way toward relational harmony, but developing this habit won't solve all linguistic problems. Difficulties also arise when we confuse factual statements with **inferential statements**—conclusions arrived at from an interpretation of evidence. Consider a few examples:

FACT	INFERENCE
He hit a lamppost while driving down the street.	He was daydreaming when he hit the lamppost.
You interrupted me before I finished what I was saying.	You don't care about what I have to say.
You haven't paid your share of the rent on time for the past three months.	You're trying to weasel out of your responsibilities.
I haven't gotten a raise in almost a year.	The boss is exploiting me.

There's nothing wrong with making inferences as long as you identify them as such: "She stomped out and slammed the door. It looked to me as if she were furious." The danger comes when we confuse inferences with facts and make them sound like the absolute truth.

One way to avoid fact-inference confusion is to use the perception-checking skill described in Chapter 3 to test the accuracy of your inferences. Recall that a perception check has three parts: a description of the behavior being discussed, your interpretation of that behavior, and a request for verification. For instance, instead of saying, "Why are you laughing at me?" you could say, "When you laugh like that [*description of behavior*], I get the idea you think something I did was stupid [*interpretation*]. Are you laughing at me [*question*]?"

Emotive Language Emotive language contains words that sound as if they're describing something when they are really announcing the speaker's attitude toward something. Do you like that old picture frame? If so, you would probably call it "an antique," but if you think its ugly, you would likely describe it as "a piece of junk." Emotive words may sound like statements of fact but are always opinions.

Barbra Streisand pointed out how some people use emotive language to stigmatize behavior in women that they admire in men:

A man is commanding—a woman is demanding.
A man is forceful—a woman is pushy.
A man is uncompromising—a woman is a ball-breaker.
A man is a perfectionist—a woman's a pain in the ass.
He's assertive—she's aggressive.
He strategizes—she manipulates.
He shows leadership—she's controlling
He's committed—she's obsessed.
He's persevering—she's relentless.
He stick to his guns—she's stubborn.
If a man wants to get it right, he's looked up to and respected.
If a woman wants to get it right, she's difficult and impossible.[50]

Problems occur when people use emotive words without labeling them as such. You might, for instance, have a long and bitter argument with a friend about whether a third person was "assertive" or "obnoxious," when a more accurate and peaceable way to handle the issue would be to acknowledge that one of you approves of the behavior and the other doesn't.

Evasive Language

None of the troublesome language habits we have described so far is a deliberate strategy to mislead or antagonize others. Now, however, we'll consider euphemisms and equivocations, two types of language that speakers use by design to avoid communicating clearly. Although both of these have some very legitimate uses, they also can lead to frustration and confusion.

Euphemisms A **euphemism** (from the Greek word meaning "to use words of good omen") is a pleasant term substituted for a more direct but potentially less pleasant one. We are using euphemisms when we say "restroom" instead of "toilet" or "full-figured" instead of "overweight." There certainly are cases where the euphemistic pulling of linguistic punches can be face-saving. It's probably more constructive to question a possible "statistical misrepresentation" than to call someone a liar, for example. Likewise, it may be less disquieting to some to refer to people as "senior citizens" than "old."

Like many businesses, the airline industry uses euphemisms to avoid upsetting already nervous flyers.[51] For example, rather than saying "turbulence," pilots and flight attendants use the less frightening term "bumpy air." Likewise, they refer to thunderstorms as "rain showers," and fog as "mist" or "haze." And savvy flight personnel never use the words "your final destination."

Despite their occasional advantages, many euphemisms are not worth the effort it takes to create them. Some are pretentious and confusing, such as a middle school's labeling of hallways as "behavior transition corridors." Other euphemisms are downright deceptive, such as the U.S. Senate's labeling of a $23,200 pay raise as a "pay equalization concept."

Equivocation It's 8:15 P.M., and you are already a half-hour late for your dinner reservation at the fanciest restaurant in town. Your partner has finally finished dressing and confronts you with the question "How do I look?" To tell the truth, you hate your partner's outfit. You don't want to lie, but on the other hand you don't want to be hurtful. Just as important, you don't want to lose your table by waiting around for your date to choose something else to wear. You think for a moment and then reply, "You look amazing. I've never seen an outfit like that before. Where did you get it?"

Your response in this situation was an **equivocation**—a deliberately vague statement that can be interpreted in more than one way. Earlier in this chapter we talked about how unintentional equivocation can lead to misunderstandings. But our discussion here focuses on *intentionally ambiguous speech* that is used to avoid lying on one hand and telling a painful truth on the other. Equivocations have several advantages.[52] They spare the receiver from the embarrassment that might come from a completely truthful answer, and it can be easier for the sender to equivocate than to suffer the discomfort of being honest.

As with euphemisms, high-level abstractions, and many other types of communication, it's impossible to say that equivocation is always helpful or harmful. As you learned in Chapter 1, competent communication behavior is situational. Your success in relating to others will depend on your ability to analyze yourself, the other person, and the situation when deciding whether to be equivocal or direct.

Gender and Language

So far we have discussed language use as if it were identical for both sexes. Some theorists and researchers, though, have argued that there are significant differences between the way men and women speak, whereas others have argued that any differences are not significant.[53] What are the similarities and differences between male and female language use?

Content

The first research on the influence of gender on conversational topics was conducted over seventy years ago. Despite the changes in male and female roles since then, the results of more recent studies are remarkably similar.[54] In these studies, women and men ranging in age from seventeen to eighty described the range of topics each discussed with friends of the same sex. Certain topics were common to both sexes: Work, movies, and television proved to be frequent for both groups. Both men and women reserved discussions of sex and sexuality for members of the same gender.

The differences between men and women were more striking than the similarities, however. Female friends spent much more time discussing personal and domestic subjects, relationship problems, family, health and reproductive matters, weight, food and clothing, men, and other women. Men, on the other hand, were more likely to discuss music, current events, sports, business, and other men. Both men and women were equally likely to discuss personal appearance, sex, and dating in same-sex conversations. True to one common stereotype, women were more likely to gossip about close friends and family. By contrast, men spent more time gossiping about sports figures and media personalities. Women's gossip was no more derogatory than men's.

These differences can lead to frustration when men and women try to converse with one another. Researchers report that *trivial* is the word often used by both sexes to describe topics discussed by the opposite sex.

Reasons for Communicating

Research shows that the notion that men and women communicate in dramatically different ways is exaggerated. Both men and women, at least in the dominant cultures of the United States and Canada, use language to build and maintain social relationships.[55] How men and women accomplish these goals is often different, though. Although most communicators try to make their interaction enjoyable, men are more likely than women to emphasize making conversation fun. Their discussions involve a greater amount of joking and good-natured teasing. By contrast, women's conversations focus more frequently on feelings, relationships, and personal problems. In fact, communication researcher Julia Wood flatly states that "for women, talk is the essence of relationships."[56] When a group of women was surveyed to find out what kinds of satisfaction they gained from talking with their friends, the most common theme mentioned was a feeling of empathy—"To know you're not alone," as some put it.[57] Whereas men commonly described same-sex conversations as something

they liked, women characterized their woman-to-woman talks as a kind of contact they needed. The greater frequency of female conversations reflects their importance. Nearly 50 percent of the women surveyed said they called friends at least once a week just to talk, whereas less than half as many men did so. In fact, 40 percent of the men surveyed reported that they never called another man just to talk.

Because women use conversation to pursue social needs, female speech typically contains statements showing support for the other person, demonstrations of equality, and efforts to keep the conversation going. With these goals, it's not surprising that traditionally female speech often contains statements of sympathy and empathy: "I've felt just like that myself," "The same thing happened to me!" Women are also inclined to ask lots of questions that invite the other person to share information: "How did you feel about that?" "What did you do next?" The importance of nurturing a relationship also explains why female speech is often somewhat powerless and tentative. Saying, "This is just my opinion …" is less likely to put off a conversational partner than a more definite "Here's what I think …"

Men's speech is often driven by quite different goals than women's. Men are more likely to use language to accomplish the job at hand than to nourish relationships. This explains why men are less likely than women to disclose their vulnerabilities, which would be a sign of weakness. When someone else is sharing a problem, instead of empathizing, men are prone to offer advice: "That's nothing to worry about …" or "Here's what you need to do …" Besides taking care of business, men are more likely than women to use conversations to exert control, preserve their independence, and enhance their status. This explains why men are more prone to dominate conversations and one-up their partners. Men interrupt their conversational partners to assert their own experiences or point of view. (Women interrupt too, but they usually do so to offer support: quite a different goal.) Just because male talk is competitive doesn't mean it's not enjoyable. Men often regard talk as a kind of game: When researchers asked men what they liked best about their all-male talk, the most frequent answer was its ease.[58] Another common theme was appreciation of the practical value of conversation: new ways to solve problems. Men also mentioned enjoying the humor and rapid pace that characterized their all-male conversations.

Conversational Style

Some scholarship shows little difference between the ways men and women converse. For example, the popular myth that women are more talkative than men may not be accurate. Researchers found that men and women speak roughly the same number of words per day.[59]

On the other hand, there are ways in which women do behave differently in conversations than do men.[60] For example, women ask more questions in mixed-sex conversations than do men-nearly three times as many, according to one study. Other research has revealed that in mixed-sex conversations, men interrupt women far more than the other way around. Some theorists have argued that differences like these result in women's speech that is less powerful and more emotional than men's. Research has supported these theories—at least in some cases. Even when clues about the speakers' sex were edited out, raters found clear differences between transcripts of male speech and female speech. In one study women's talk was judged more aesthetic, whereas men's talk was seen as more dynamic, aggressive, and strong. In another, male job applicants were rated more fluent, active, confident, and effective than female applicants.

Some gender differences also exist in mediated communication. For example, instant messages written by women tend to be more expressive than ones composed by men.[61] They are more likely to contain laughter ("hehe") emoticons (smiley faces), emphasis (italics, boldface, repeated letters), and adjectives. However, there are no significant gender differences in a number of other variables—such as questions, words per turn, and hedges.

Given these differences, it's easy to wonder how men and women manage communicate with one another at all. One reason why cross-sex conversations do run smoothly is because women accommodate to the topics men raise. Both men and women regard topics introduced by women as tentative, whereas topics that men introduce are more likely to be pursued. Thus, women seem to grease the wheels of conversation by doing more work than men in maintaining conversations. A complementary difference between men and women also promotes cross-sex conversations: Men are more likely to talk about themselves with women than with other men, and because women are willing to adapt to this topic, conversations are likely to run smoothly, if one-sidedly.

An accommodating style isn't always a disadvantage for women. One study revealed that women who spoke tentatively were actually more influential with men than those who used more powerful speech.[62] On the other hand, this tentative style was less effective in persuading women. (Language use had no effect on men's persuasiveness.) This research suggests that women who are willing and able to be flexible in their approach can persuade both other women and men—as long as they are not dealing with a mixed-sex audience.

Nongender Variables

Despite the differences in the ways men and women speak, the link between gender and language use isn't as clear-cut as it might seem. Research reviews have found that the ways women and men communicate are much more similar than different. For example, one analysis of over twelve hundred research studies found that only 1 percent of variance in communication behavior resulted from sex difference.[63] There is no significant difference between male speech and female speech in areas such as use of profanity, use of qualifiers such as "I guess" or "This is just my opinion," tag questions, and vocal fluency.[64] Some on-the-job research shows that male and female supervisors in similar positions behave the same way and are equally effective. In light of the considerable similarities between the sexes and the relatively minor differences, some communication scholars suggest that the "men are from Mars, women are from Venus" claim should be replaced by the metaphor that "men are from North Dakota, women are from South Dakota." [65]

A growing body of research explains some of the apparent contradictions between the similarities and differences between male speech and female speech. They have revealed other factors that influence language use as much or more than does gender. For example, social philosophy plays a role. Feminist wives talk longer than their partners, whereas nonfeminist wives speak less than their husbands. Orientation toward problem solving also plays a role in conversational style. The cooperative or competitive orientations of speakers have more influence on how they interact than does their gender.

The speaker's occupation and social role also influence speaking style. For example, male day-care teachers' speech to their students resembles the language of female teachers more closely than it resembles the language of fathers at home. Overall, doctors interrupt their patients more often than the reverse, although male patients do interrupt female physicians more often than their male counterparts. At work, task differences exert more powerful effects on whether speakers use gender-inclusive language (such as "he or she" instead of just "he") than does biological sex. [66] A close study of trial transcripts showed that the speaker's experience on the witness stand and occupation had more to do with language use than did gender. If women generally use "powerless" language, this may possibly reflect their historical social role in society at large. As the balance of power grows more equal between men and women, we can expect many linguistic differences to shrink.

Another powerful force that influences the way individual men and women speak is their sex role—the social orientation that governs behavior—rather than their biological gender. Researchers have identified three sex roles: masculine, feminine, and androgynous. These sex roles don't always line up neatly with gender.

There are "masculine" females, "feminine" males, and androgynous communicators who combine traditionally masculine and feminine characteristics.

Research shows that linguistic differences are often a function of these sex roles more than the speaker's biological sex. Masculine sex-role communicators—whether male or female—use more dominant language than either feminine or androgynous speakers. Feminine speakers have the most submissive speaking style, whereas androgynous speakers fall between these extremes. When two masculine communicators are in a conversation, they often engage in a one-up battle for dominance, responding to the other's bid for control with a counterattempt to dominate the relationship. Feminine sex-role speakers are less predictable. They use dominance, submission, and equivalent behavior in an almost random fashion. Androgynous individuals are more predictable: They most frequently meet another's bid for dominance with a symmetrical attempt at control, but then move quickly toward an equivalent relationship.

All this information suggests that, when it comes to communicating, "masculinity" and "femininity" are culturally recognized sex roles, not biological traits. Research suggests that neither a stereotypically male style nor female style is the best choice. For example, one study showed that a "mixed-gender strategy" that balanced the stereotypically male task-oriented approach with the stereotypically female relationship-oriented approach received the highest marks by both male and female respondents. [67] As opportunities for men and women become more equal, we can expect that the differences between male and female use of language will become smaller.

Culture and Language

Anyone who has tried to translate ideas from one language to another knows that communication across cultures can be a challenge. [68]

Even choosing the right words during translation won't guarantee that nonnative speakers will use an unfamiliar language correctly. For example, Japanese insurance companies warn their policyholders who are visiting the United States to avoid their cultural tendency to say "excuse me" or "I'm sorry" if they are involved in a traffic accident.[69] In Japan, apologizing is a traditional way to express goodwill and maintain social harmony, even if the person offering the apology is not at fault. But in the United States, an apology can be taken as an admission of guilt and may result in Japanese tourists' being held accountable for accidents for which they may not be responsible.

Difficult as it may be, translation is only a small part of the communication challenges facing members of different cultures. Differences in the way language is used and the very worldview that a language creates make communicating across cultures a challenging task.

Verbal Communication Styles

Using language is more than just choosing a particular group of words to convey an idea. Each language has its own unique style that distinguishes it from others. And when a communicator tries to use the verbal style from one culture in a different one, problems are likely to arise.[70]

Direct-Indirect As you read in Chapter 2, one way in which verbal styles vary is in their *directness*. You'll recall that low-context cultures use language primarily to express thoughts, feelings, and ideas as clearly and logically as possible. By contrast, high-context cultures value language as a way to maintain social harmony. Rather than upset others by speaking clearly, communicators in these cultures learn to discover meaning from the context in which a message is delivered: the nonverbal behaviors of the speaker, the history of the relationship, and the general social rules that govern interaction between people.

The clash between cultural norms of directness and indirectness can aggravate problems in cross-cultural situations such as encounters between straight-talking low-context Israelis, who value speaking directly, and Arabs, whose high-context

culture stresses smooth interaction. It's easy to imagine how the clash of culture stresses smooth interaction. It's easy to imagine how the clash of cultural styles could lead to misunderstandings and conflicts between Israelis and their Palestinian neighbors. Israelis could view their Arab counterparts as evasive, whereas the Palestinian neighbors could view their Arab counterparts as evasive, whereas the Palestinians could perceive the Israelis as insensitive and blunt.

Even within a single country, subcultures can have different notions about the value of direct speech. For example, Puerto Rican language style resembles high-context Japanese or Korean more that low-context English.[71] As a group, Puerto Ricans value social harmony and avoid confrontation, which leads them to systematically speak in an indirect way to avoid giving offense.[72] Researchers Laura Leets and Howard Giles suggest that the traditional Asian tendency to favor high-context messages explains the difference: Adept at recognizing hints and nonverbal cues, high-context communicators are more sensitive to messages that are overlooked by people from cultural groups that rely more heavily on unambiguous, explicit low-context messages.

It's worth noting that even generally straight-talking residents of the United States raised in the low-context Euro-American tradition often rely on context to make their point. When you decline an unwanted invitation by saying "I can't make it," it's likely that both you and the other person know that the choice of attending isn't really beyond your control. If your goal was to be perfectly clear, you might say, "I don't want to get together."

Elaborate-Succinct Another way in which language style can vary across cultures is in terms of whether they are elaborate or succinct. Speakers of Arabic, for instance, commonly use language that is much more rich and expressive than most communicators who use English. Strong assertions and exaggerations that would sound ridiculous in English are a common feature of Arabic. This contrast in linguistic style can lead to misunderstandings between people from different backgrounds. As one observer put it,

…[A]n Arab feels compelled to overassert in almost all types of communication because others expect him [or her] to. If an Arab says exactly what he [or she] means without the expected assertion, other Arabs may still think that he [or she] means the opposite. For example, a simple "no" to a host's requests to eat more or drink more will not suffice. To convey the meaning that he [or she] is actually full, the guest must keep repeating "no" several times, coupling it with an oath such as "By God" or "I swear to God."[73]

Succinctness is most extreme in cultures where silence is valued. In many American Indian cultures, for example, the favored way to handle ambiguous social situations is to remain quiet.[74] When you contrast this silent style to the talkativeness common in mainstream American cultures when people first meet, it's easy to imagine how the first encounter between an Apache or Navajo and a white person might feel uncomfortable to both people.

Formal-Informal Along with differences such as directness-indirectness and elaborate-succinct styles, a third way languages differ from one culture to another involves formality and informality. The approach that characterizes relationships in countries like the United States, Canada, and Australia is quite different from the great concern for using proper speech in many parts of Asia and Africa. Formality isn't so much a matter of using correct grammar as of defining social position.

In Korea, for example, the language reflects the Confucian system of relational hierarchies.[75] It has special vocabularies for different sexes, for different levels of social status, for different degrees of intimacy, and for different types of social occasions. For example, there are different degrees of formality for speaking with old friends, nonacquaintances whose background one knows, and complete strangers. One sign of being a learned person in Korea is the ability to use language that recognizes these relational distinctions. When you contrast these sorts of distinctions with the casual friendliness many North Americans use even when talking with complete strangers, it's easy to see how a Korean might view communicators in the United States as boorish and how an American might view Koreans as stiff and unfriendly.

Language and Worldview

Different linguistic styles are important, but there may be even more fundamental differences that separate speakers of various languages. For almost 150 years, some theorists have put forth the notion of **linguistic relativism**: the notion that the worldview of a culture is shaped and reflected by the language its members speak.[76] The best-known example of linguistic relativism is the notion that Eskimos have a large number of words (estimated from seventeen to one hundred) for what we simply call "snow." Different terms are used to describe conditions like a driving blizzard, crusty ice, and light powder. This example suggests how linguistic relativism operates. The need to survive in an Arctic environment led Eskimos to make distinctions that would be unimportant to residents of warmer environments, and after the language makes these distinctions, speakers are more likely to see the world in ways that match the broader vocabulary.

Even though there is some doubt that Eskimos really do have one hundred words for snow,[77] other examples do seem to support the principle of linguistic relativism.[78] For instance, bilingual speakers seem to think differently when they change languages. In one study, French Americans were asked to interpret a series of pictures. When they spoke in French, their descriptions were far more romantic and emotional than when they used English to describe the same kind of pictures. Likewise, when students in Hong Kong were asked to complete a values test, they expressed more traditional Chinese values when they answered in Cantonese than when they answered in English. In Israel, both Arab and Jewish students saw bigger distinctions between their group and "outsiders" when using their native language than when they used English, a neutral tongue. Examples like these show the power of language to shape cultural identity—sometimes for better and sometimes for worse.

Linguistic influences start early in life. English-speaking parents often label the mischievous pranks of their children as "bad," implying that there is something immoral about acting wild. "Be good!" they are inclined to say. On the other hand, French parents are more likely to say *Sois sage!*—"Be wise." The linguistic implication is that misbehaving is an act of foolishness. Swedes would correct the same action with the words "*Var snoll*"—"Be friendly, be kind." By contrast, German adults would use the command "*Sei artig!*"—literally, "Be of your own kind"—in other words, get back in step, conform to your role as a child.[79]

The best-known declaration of linguistic relativism is the **Sapir-Whorf hypothesis**, formulated by Benjamin Whorf, an amateur linguist, and anthropologist Edward Sapir.[80] Following Sapir's theoretical work, Whorf found that the language spoken by the Hopi represents a view of reality that is dramatically different from more familiar tongues. For example, the Hopi language makes no distinction between nouns and verbs. Therefore, the people who speak it describe the entire world as being constantly in process. Whereas we use nouns to characterize people or objects as being fixed or constant, the Hopi view them more as verbs, constantly changing. In this sense our language represents much of the world rather like a snapshot camera, whereas Hopi reflects, a worldview more like video.

Although the Sapir-Whorf hypothesis originally focused on foreign languages, Neil Postman illustrates the principle with an example closer to home. He describes a hypothetical culture where physicians identify patients they treat as "doing" arthritis and other diseases instead of "having" them and where criminals are diagnosed as "having" cases of criminality instead of "being" criminals.[81]

The implications of such a linguistic difference are profound. We believe that characteristics people "have"—what they "are"—are beyond their control, whereas they are responsible for what they "do." If we changed our view of what people "have" and what they "do," our attitudes would most likely change as well. Postman illustrates the consequences of this linguistic difference as applied to education:

> In schools, for instance, we find that tests are given to determine how smart someone is or, more precisely, how much smartness someone "has." If one child scores a 138, and another a 106, the first is thought to "have" more smartness than the other. But this seems to me a strange conception—every bit as strange as "doing" arthritis or "having" criminality. I do not know anyone who has smartness. The people I know sometimes do smart things (as far as I can judge) and sometimes do stupid things—depending on what circumstances they are in, and how much they know about a situation, and how interested they are. "Smartness," so it seems to me, is a specific performance, done in a particular set of circumstances. It is not something you are or have in measurable quantities. What I am driving at is this: All language is metaphorical, and often in the subtlest ways. In the simplest sentence, sometimes in the simplest word, we do more than merely express ourselves. We construct reality along certain lines. We make the world according to our own imagery.[82]

Subtle changes like this illustrate the theme of this chapter: that language is a powerful force for shaping our thoughts, and our relationship with others.

Notes

1. W.S.Y. Wang, "Language and Derivative Systems," in W.S.Y. Wang, ed., *Human Communication: Language and Its Psychobiological Basis* (San Francisco: Freeman, 1982), p. 36.

2. O. Sacks, *Seeing Voices: A Journey into the World of the Deaf* (Berkeley: University of California Press, 1989), p. 17.

3. Adapted from J. O'Brien and P. Kollock, *The Production of Reality*, 3rd ed. (Thousand Oaks, CA: Pine Forge Press, 2001), p. 66.

4. M. Henneberger, "Misunderstanding of Word Embarrasses Washington's New Mayor." *New York Times* (January 29, 1999). Online at http://www.nyt.com

5. C.K. Ogden and I.A. Richards, *The Meaning of Meaning* (New York: Harcourt Brace, 1923), p. 11.

6. S. Duck, "Maintenance as a Shared Meaning System," in D. J. Caharg and L. Stafford, eds., *Communication and Relational Maintenance* (San Diego: Academic Press, 1993).

7. D. Crystal, *Language and the Internet* (Cambridge, England: Cambridge University Press, 2001).

8. W. B. Pearce and V. Cronen, *Communication, Action, and Meaning* (New York: Praeger, 1980). See also J. K. Barge, "Articulating CMM as a Practical Theory." *Human Systems: The Journal of Systemic Consultation and Management* 15 (2004): 193-204, and E. M. Griffin, *A First Look at Communication Theory*, 6th ed. (New York: McGraw-Hill, 2006).

9. Genesis 2:19. This biblical reference was noted by D.C. Mader, "The Politically Correct Textbook: Trends in Publishers' Guidelines for the Representation of Marginalized Groups." Paper presented at the annual convention of the Eastern Communication Association, Portland, ME, May 1992.

10. G.W. Smith, "The Political Impact of Name Sounds." *Communication Monographs* 65 (1998): 154-172.

11. R.G. Fryer and S.D. Levitt, "The Causes and Consequences of Distinctively Black Names." *Quarterly Journal of Economics* 119 (2004): 767-805.

12. C.A. VanLear, "Testing a Cyclical Model of Communicative Openness in Relationship Development." *Communication Monographs* 58 (1991): 337-361.

13. J.L. Cotton, B.S. O'Neill, and A. Griffin, "The 'Name Game': Affective and Hiring Reactions to First Names." *Journal of Managerial Psychology* 23(2008): 18-39.

14. J.L. Brunning, N.K. Polinko, J.I. Zerbst, and J.T. Buckingham, "The Effect on Expected Job Success of the Connotative Meanings of Names and Nicknames." *Journal of Social Psychology* 140 (2000), 197-201.

15. B. Coffey and P. A. McLaughlin, "Do Masculine Names Help Female Lawyers Become Judges? Evidence from South Carolina." *American Law and Economics Review* 11 (2009): 112-133.

16. T. Varadarajan, "Big Names, Big Battles." *New York Times* (July 26, 1999). Online at http://aolsvc.aol.com/computercenter/internet/index,adp.

17. D.H. Naftulin, J.E. Ware Jr., and F.A. Donnelly, "The Doctor Fox Lecture: A Paradigm of Educational Seduction." *Journal of Medical Education* 48 (July 1973): 630-635. See also C. T. Cory, ed., "Bafflegab Pays." *Psychology Today* 13 (May 1980): 12, and H. W. Marsh and J. E. Ware Jr., "Effects of Expressiveness, Content Coverage, and Incentive on Multidimensional Student Rating Scales: New Interpretations of the 'Dr. Fox' Effect." *Journal of Educational Psychology* 74 (1982): 126-134.

18. J.S. Armstrong, "Unintelligible Management Research and Academic Prestige." *Interfaces* 10 (1980): 80-86.

19. For a summary of research on this subject, see J.J. Bradac, "Language Attitudes and Impression Formation," in H. Giles and W. P. Robinson, eds., *The Handbook of Language and Social Psychology* (Chichester, England: Wiley, 1990), pp. 387-412.

20. H. Giles and P.F. Poseland, *Speech Style and Social Evaluation* (New York: Academic Press, 1975).

21. C. Miller and K. Swift, *Words and Women* (New York: HarperCollins, 1991) p. 27.

22. For a discussion of racist language, see H.A. Bosmajian, *The Language of Oppression* (Lanham, MD: University Press of America, 1983).

23. Mader, "The Politically Correct Textbook" p. 5.

24. S.L. Kirkland, J. Greenberg, and T. Pysczynski, "Further Evidence of the Deleterious Effects of Overheard Derogatory Ethnic Labels: Derogation Beyond the Target." *Personality and Social Psychology Bulletin* 12 (1987): 216-227.

25. For a review of the relationship between power and language, see J. Liska, "Dominance-Seeking Language Strategies: Please Eat the Floor, Dogbreath, or I'll Rip Your Lungs Out, O.K.?"

in S.A. Deetz, ed., *Communication Yearbook 15* (Newbury Park, CA: Sage, 1992). See also N.A. Burrell and R.J. Koper, "The Efficacy of Powerful/ Powerless Language on Persuasiveness/Credibility: A Meta-Analytic Review," in R.W. Preiss and M. Allen, eds., *Prospects and Precautions in the Use of Meta-Analysis* (Dubuque, LA: Brown & Benchmark, 1994).

26. L.A. Hosman, "The Evaluative Consequences of Hedges, Hesitations, and Intensifies: Powerful and Powerless Speech Styles." *Human Communication Research* 15 (1989): 383-406. L.A. Hosman and S.A. Siltanen, "Powerful and Powerless Language Forms: Their Consequences for Impression Formation, Attribu-tions of Control of Self and Control of Others, Cognitive Responses, and Message Memory." *Journal of Language and Social Psychology*, 25 (2006): 33-46.

27. S.H. Ng and J.J. Bradac, *Power in Language: Verbal Communication and Social Influence* (Newbury Park, CA: Sage, 1993). See also S.A. Reid and S.H. Ng, "Language, Power, and Intergroup Relations." *Journal of Social Issues* 55 (1999): 119-139.

28. S. Parton, S. A. Siltanen, L. A. Hosman, and J. Langenderfer, "Employment Interview Outcomes and Speech Style Effects." *Journal of Language and Social Psychology* 21 (2002): 144-161.

29. A. El-Alayli, C. J. Myers, T. L. Petersen, and A. L. Lystad, " 'I Don't Mean to Sound Arrogant, but...': The Effects of Using Disclaimers on Person Perception." *Personality and Social Psychology Bulletin* 34, 130-143.

30. D. Tannen, *Talking from 9 to 5* (New York: Morrow, 1994), p. 101.

31. D. Geddes, "Sex Roles in Management: The Impact of Varying Power of Speech Style on Union Members' Perception of Satisfaction and Effectiveness." *Journal of Psychology* 126 (1992): 589- 607.

32. L. A. Samovar and R. E. Porter, *Communication Between Cultures*, 3rd ed. (Belmont, CA: Wadsworth FTP, 1998), pp. 58-59.

33. H. Giles, J. Coupland, and N. Coupland, eds., *Contexts of Accommodation: Developments in Applied Sociolinguistics* (Cambridge, England: Cambridge University Press, 1991).

34. See, for example, R. A. Bell and J. G. Healey, "Idiomatic Communication and Interpersonal Solidarity in Friends' Relational Cultures." *Human Communication Research* 18 (1992): 307-335, and R. A. Bell, N. Buerkel-Rothfuss, and K. E. Gore, "Did You Bring the Yarmulke for the Cabbage Patch Kid?: The Idiomatic Com-munication of Young Lovers." *Human Communication Research* 14 (1987): 47-67.

35. J. Cassell and D. Tversky, "The Language of Online Intercultural Community Formation." *Journal of Computer-Mediated Communication* 10 (2005): Article 2.

36. "OMG: IM Slang Is Invading Everyday English." NPR Weekend Edition, February 18, 2006. Online at http://www.npr.org/templates/story/story.php/ storyId=5221618.

37. A. Maass, D. Salvi, L. Arcuri, and G.R. Semin, "Language Use in Intergroup Context." *Journal of Personality and Social Psychology* 51 (1989): 981-993.

38. M. Wiener and A. Mehrabian, *A Language within Language* (New York: Appleton-Century-Crofts, 1968).

39. E.S. Kubanyu, D.C. Richard, G.B. Bower, and M.Y. Muraoka, "Impact of Assertive and Accusatory Communication of Distress and Anger: A Verbal Component Analysis." *Aggressive Behavior* 18 (1992): 337-347.

40. T.L. Scott, "Teens Before Their Time." *Time* (November 27, 2000): 22.

41. M.T. Motley and H.M. Reeder, "Unwanted Escalation of Sexual Intimacy: Male and Female Perceptions of Connotations and Relational Consequences of Resistance Messages." *Communication Monographs* 62 (1995): 356-382.

42. T. Wallstein, "Measuring the Vague Meanings of Probability Terms." *Journal of Experimental Psychology: General* 115 (1986): 348-365.

43. T. Labov, "Social and Language Boundaries Among Adolescents." *American Speech* 4 (1992): 339-366.

44. UCLA Slang. Retrieved October 24, 2001, from http://www.cs.rpi.edu/'vkennyz/doc/humor/slang. humor.

45. M. Kakutani, "Computer Slang Scoffs at Wetware." *Santa Barbara News-Press* (July 2, 2000): Dl.

46. M. Myer and C. Fleming, "Silicon Screenings." *Newsweek* (August 15, 1994): 63.

47. S.I. Hayakawa, *Language in Thought and Action* (New York: Harcourt Brace, 1964).

48. E.M. Eisenberg, "Ambiguity as Strategy in Organizational Communication." *Communication Monographs* 51 (1984): 227-242, and E.M. Eisenberg and M.G. Witten, "Reconsidering Openness in Organizational Communication." *Academy of Management Review* 12 (1987): 418-426.

49. J.K. Alberts, "An Analysis of Couples' Conversational Complaints." *Communication Monographs* 55 (1988): 184-197.

50. B. Streisand, Crystal Award speech delivered at the Crystal Awards, Women in Film luncheon, 1992.

51. B. Morrison, "What You Won't Hear the Pilot Say." *USA Today* (September 26, 2000): Al.

52. E.M. Eisenberg, ed., *Strategic Ambiguities: Essays on Communication, Organization and Identity* (Thousand Oaks, CA: Sage, 2007).

53. For detailed discussions of the relationship between gender and communication, see D.J. Canary and T.M. Emmers-Sommer, *Sex and Gender Differences in Personal Relationships* (New York: Guilford, 1997); J. Wood, *Gendered Lives: Communication, Gender, and Culture* (Belmont, CA: Wadsworth, 1994); and J.C. Pearson, *Gender and Communication*, 2nd ed. (Madison, WI: Brown & Benchmark, 1994).

54. See, for example, A. Haas and M.A. Sherman, "Reported Topics of Conversation Among Same-Sex Adults." *Communication Quarterly* 30 (1982): 332-342.

55. R.A. Clark, "A Comparison of Topics and Objectives in a Cross Section of Young Men's and Women's Everyday Conversations," in D.J. Canary and K. Dindia, eds., *Sex Differences and Similarities in Communication: Critical Essays and Empirical Investigations of Sex and Gender in Interaction* (Mahwah, NJ: Erlbaum, 1998).

56. J.T. Wood, *Gendered Lives: Communication, Gender, and Culture*, 4th ed. (Belmont, CA: Wadsworth, 2001), p. 141.

57. M.A. Sherman and A. Haas, "Man to Man, Woman to Woman." *Psychology Today* 17 (June 1984): 72-73.

58. A. Haas and M.A. Sherman, "Conversational Topic as a Function of Role and Gender." *Psychological Reports* 51 (1982): 453-454.

59. M.R. Mehl, S. Vazire, N. Ranrirez-Esparza, R.B. Slatcher, and J.W. Pennebaker, "Are Women Really More Talkative Than Men?" *Science* 317 (July 2007): 82.

60. For a summary of research on the difference between male and female conversational behavior, see H. Giles and R. L. Street Jr., "Communication Characteristics and Behavior," in M.L. Knapp and G.R. Miller, eds., *Handbook of Interpersonal Communication* (Beverly Hills, CA: Sage, 1985): 205-261, and A. Kohn, "Girl Talk, Guy Talk," *Psychology Today* 22 (February 1988): 65-66.

61. A.B. Fox, D. Bukatko, M. Hallahan, and M. Crawford, "The Medium Makes a Difference: Gender Similarities and Differences in Instant Messaging." *Journal of Language and Social Psychology* 26 (2007): 389-397.

62. L.L. Carli, "Gender, Language, and Influence." *Journal of Personality and Social Psychology* 59 (1990): 941-951.

63. D.J. Canary and K.S. Hause, "Is There Any Reason to Research Sex Differences in Communication?" *Communication Quarterly* 41 (1993): 129-144.

64. C.J. Zahn, "The Bases for Differing Evaluations of Male and Female Speech: Evidence from Ratings of Transcribed Conversation." *Communication Monographs* 56 (1989): 59-74. See also L.M. Grob, R.A. Meyers, and R. Schuh, "Powerful? Powerless Language Use in Group Interactions: Sex Differences or Similarities?" *Communication Quarterly* 45 (1997): 282-303.

65. J.T. Wood and K. Dindia, "What's the Difference? A Dialogue About Differences and Similarities Between Women and Men," in D.J. Canary and K. Dindia, eds., *Sex Differences and Similarities in Communication: Critical Essays and Empirical Investigations of Sex and Gender in Interaction* (Mahwah, NJ: Erlbaum, 1998).

66. D.L. Rubin, K. Greene, and D. Schneider, "Adopting Gender-Inclusive Language Reforms: Diachronic and Synchronic Variation." *Journal of Language and Social Psychology* 13 (1994): 91- 114.

67. D.S. Geddes, "Sex Roles in Management: The Impact of Varying Power of Speech Style on

Union Members' Perception of Satisfaction and Effectiveness." *Journal of Psychology* 126 (1992): 589- 607.

68. For a thorough discussion of the challenges involved in translation from one language to another, see L.A. Samovar, R.E. Porter, and E.R. McDaniel, *Communication Between Cultures*, 7th ed. (Boston: Cengage, 2010), pp. 149-154.

69. N. Sugimoto, "'Excuse Me' and 'I'm Sorry': Apologetic Behaviors of Americans and Japanese." Paper presented at the Conference on Communication in Japan and the United States, California State University, Fullerton, CA, March 1991.

70. A summary of how verbal style varies across cultures can be found in Chapter 5 of W.B. Gudykunst and S. Ting-Toomey, *Culture and Interpersonal Communication* (Newbury Park, CA: Sage, 1988).

71. M. Morris, *Saying and Meaning in Puerto Rico: Some Problems in the Ethnology of Discourse* (Oxford, England: Pergamon, 1981).

72. L. Leets and H. Giles, "Words as Weapons—When Do They Wound?" *Human Communication Research* 24 (1997): 260-301, and L. Leets, "When Words Wound: Another Look at Racist Speech." Paper presented at the annual conference of the International Communication Association, San Francisco, May 1999.

73. A. Almaney and A. Alwan, *Communicating with the Arabs* (Prospect Heights, IL: Waveland, 1982).

74. K. Basso, "To Give Up on Words: Silence in Western Apache Culture." *Southern Journal of Anthropology* 26 (1970): 213-230.

75. J. Yum, "The Practice of Uye-ri in Interpersonal Relationships in Korea," in D. Kincaid, ed., *Communication Theory from Eastern and Western Perspectives* (New York: Academic Press, 1987).

76. For a summary of scholarship supporting the notion of linguistic determinism, see L. Boroditsky, "Lost in Translation." *Wall Street Journal Online* (July 23, 2010). Retrieved August 11, 2010 from http://online.wsj.com/article/NA_WSJ_PUB: SB1 0001424052748703467304575383131592767868. html.

77. L. Martin and G. Pullum, *The Great Eskimo Vocabulary Hoax* (Chicago: University of Chicago Press, 1991).

78. H. Giles and A. Franklyn-Stokes, "Communicator Characteristics," in M.K. Asante and W.B. Gudykunst, eds., *Handbook of International and Intercultural Communication* (Newbury Park, CA: Sage, 1989).

79. L. Sinclair, "A Word in Your Ear," in *Ways of Mankind* (Boston: Beacon Press, 1954).

80. B. Whorf, "The Relation of Habitual Thought and Behavior to Language," in J.B. Carrol, ed., *Language, Thought, and Reality* (Cambridge, MA: MIT Press, 1956). See also Harry Hoijer, "The Sapir-Whorf Hypothesis," in Larry A. Samovar and Richard E. Porter, eds., *Intercultural Communication: A Reader*, 7th ed. (Belmont, CA: Wadsworth, 1994), pp. 194-200.

81. N. Postman, *Crazy Talk, Stupid Talk* (New York: Delta, 1976), p. 122.

82. Ibid., pp. 123-124.

3. Nonverbal Communication

by Walid A. Afifi

Language is not the only tool of communication. Nonverbal communication is a broad category of communication that encompasses the many ways that movement, space, vocal inflection, and other nonverbal elements influence, and in many cases become, the messages we send. This chapter provides a foundational explanation of different types of nonverbal codes and corresponding examples of each, thus demonstrating the wealth of information individuals often exchange without uttering a single word. This overview provides readers with an understanding of how to better interpret and encode nonverbal messages.

The information contained in this chapter is of use to all individuals seeking a career in a communication industry. While the explanations are often general and usually situated in an interpersonal context, the elements presented are easily applicable in myriad settings. From a journalist using nonverbal cues to set an interviewee at ease to an advertiser designing an ad layout to portray a particular visual message to a filmmaker wanting to make a scene "ring true," the use of nonverbal cues plays an essential part in every communication career. Producers of aural and visual messages should have a fundamental understanding of haptics, kinesics, proxemics, and vocalics to enable them to make the most effective messages possible. Upon completion of this chapter, readers should consider the ways multiple media messages rely on nonverbal communication to convey a particular message and encourage a specific interpretation of reality.

Sayings that attest to the importance of nonverbal communication in our lives vary from "A picture is a worth 1,000 words" to "Appearances are deceiving." But what are we talking about when discussing nonverbal elements of communication? Many people think of "body language" when discussing nonverbal messages. However, thinking of nonverbal only as body language ignores several important elements. For our purposes, nonverbal communication will be defined as "those behaviors other than words themselves that form a socially shared coding system" (Burgoon, 1994, p. 231). Two primary aspects of this definition are worth noting: First, it includes a wide variety of behaviors besides "body language." Second, it assumes people recognize the meaning of these behaviors within their social or cultural setting. These two aspects of nonverbal will become very clear by the end of this selection.

Scholars often claim that nonverbal messages are more important than verbal ones (see Burgoon, Buller, & Woodall, 1996). Their claim is based on several arguments. First, studies suggest that nonverbal messages make up a majority of the meaning of a message (see Andersen, 1999). Think of the times you've watched people from a distance, not being able to hear what they're saying but being able to see them. Based only on their nonverbal messages, you are able to understand a lot about their relationship and their interaction. You may be able to determine whether they are friends or dating partners, whether they are having a pleasant or unpleasant interaction, and whether they are in a hurry or not; all these interpretations occur without hearing a word. Although the importance of nonverbal messages for the meaning of an interaction varies, they play at least some role in every interaction. Second, nonverbal communication is omnipresent. In other words, every communication act includes a nonverbal component; nonverbal behavior is part of every communicative message. From how we say something to what we do and how we look when saying it, nonverbal messages are constant influences on our interpretation of what others are communicating to us. Third, there are nonverbal

signals that are understood cross-culturally. Unlike verbal messages, which carry meaning strictly within the relevant language culture, nonverbal messages can be used as a communication tool among individuals from vastly different language cultures. For example, individuals from a wide variety of cultures recognize smiles to indicate happiness or recognize hunger from the act of putting fingers to your mouth. Finally, nonverbal messages are trusted over verbal messages when those two channels of information conflict. Because we (somewhat erroneously) believe that nonverbal actions are more subconscious than verbal messages, we tend to believe the nonverbal over the verbal. All these arguments for the importance of nonverbal messages will be defended by the end of this selection.

In part because nonverbal behaviors are an important aspect of every communication message, this selection will be organized somewhat differently than some others in this book. Rather than focus on one theory or one concept, the primary goal of this selection is to make you aware of the many aspects of our behavior that fall under the rubric of nonverbal communication. As part of that goal, several theories will be briefly reviewed when they seem to apply particularly well to a type or function of nonverbal behavior. However, it is important to keep in mind that all theories described in this book are behaviorally represented through nonverbal messages; the theories noted in this selection are simply a small sampling of the many theories that could be used as illustrations of nonverbal messages "in action."

The selection is divided into roughly two sections. The first section overviews the various types of nonverbal messages (i.e., codes), starting with body movements (i.e., kinesics) and ending with physical aspects of the environment that affect behavior (i.e., artifacts). You should have a good sense for the breadth and importance of nonverbal communication by the end of that section. The next part of the selection overviews the ways we use nonverbal messages (i.e., functions). Nonverbal messages can be used to accomplish a wide variety of outcomes, from allowing the smooth flow of an interaction to deceiving others.

Theories will be applied throughout the selection but will be concentrated in the discussion of functions.

NONVERBAL CODES

As noted earlier, nonverbal behaviors include a lot more than "body language." Although scholars disagree on the exact number, there are seven codes (or categories) of nonverbal behavior that will be reviewed in this selection: kinesics, haptics, proxemics, physical appearance, vocalics, chronemics, and artifacts. I will define each code in turn and discuss some of the associated behaviors.

Kinesics

What do you think of when you ponder nonverbal behavior? If you're like many people who have not studied nonverbal communication, you think of gestures, body movements, eye contact and the like. In other words, you think of only one of the seven codes that exist to describe nonverbal behavior. The kinesic code includes almost all behaviors that most people believe make up nonverbal ways of expression, including gestures, eye contact, and body position. Burgoon et al. (1996) defined kinesics as referring to "all forms of body movement, excluding physical contact with another" (p. 41). As you can imagine, these movements number in the hundreds of thousands, but there are classifications of kinesic activity that help us better place the movements into discrete categories. Perhaps the most, widely used is Ekman and Friesen's (1969) distinction among emblems, illustrators, regulators, affect displays, and adaptors. This typology describes kinesic behaviors according to their intended purpose.

Emblems are body movements that carry meaning in and of themselves. Emblems stand alone, without verbal accompaniment, and still convey a clear message to the recipients. Common examples of emblems include a thumbs-up gesture, "flipping someone the bird," using the thumb and index finger to signal "OK," and moving two fingers across your throat to signal someone to stop. In fact, sports are often an arena where celebratory emblems are displayed or become a part of our cultural fabric. An example is the "raise the roof" signal, an emblem signaling celebration that quickly caught on among sports players and is now understood relatively widely in this culture. The historical development of emblem form and meaning is fascinating and varies dramatically from culture to culture. Certain cultures (e.g., Italy, France, Egypt) rely on emblems for the delivery of meaning much more so than other cultures, but all cultures include emblems as part of their communication channel.

Unlike emblems, *illustrators* do not carry meaning without verbal accompaniment. Instead, illustrators are body movements that help receivers interpret and better attend to what is being said verbally. The sort of "nonsense" hand gestures that often accompany a person's speech, especially when speaking publicly, are one form of illustrators. Yet these "nonsense" gestures actually serve important functions: They help focus the receiver's attention on what is being said, they help the sender emphasize a part of his or her speech, they help the sender clarify what is being said, and so on. A father who scolds his child may accentuate the seriousness of the message by waving a finger in the youngster's face, or a traveler may clarify a description of her lost luggage by drawing a "picture" of its shape in the air as she describes it; these are simply two examples of how we use illustrators to assist the verbal component.

Regulators are body movements that are employed to help guide conversations. They may be used to help signal a desire to speak, or a desire not to be called on, or to communicate to the speaker that you are or are not listening. Perhaps the most common example of a regulator is the head nod. We consistently use head nods during conversation to signal to speakers that we are listening, a sign that encourages them to continue. Other behaviors that function as regulators of our conversation include maintaining eye contact, turning our bodies toward or away from the speaker, and looking at our watch.

Adaptors are body movements that "satisfy physical or psychological needs" (Burgoon et al., 1996, p. 42). These movements are rarely intended to communicate anything, but they are good signals of the sender's physiological and psychological state. There are three categories of adaptors: self-adaptors, alter-directed adaptors, and object adaptors. *Self*-adaptors are movements that people direct toward themselves or their bodies; examples include biting fingernails, sucking on a thumb, repeatedly tapping a foot, adjusting a collar, and vigorously rubbing an arm to increase warmth. *Alter-directed* adaptors include the same sorts of behaviors found among self-adaptors except that they are movements people direct to the bodies of others; examples include scratching a friend's back itch, caressing a partner's hair, adjusting a partner's collar, or dusting off a friend's rarely worn jacket. Alter-directed adaptors often signal to the target person or to the audience the level of attachment between the individuals in the exchange. *Object* adaptors are movements that involve attention to an object; common examples include biting on a pen, holding a (sometimes unlit) cigar, or circling the edge of a cup with a finger.

Finally, *affect* displays are body movements that express emotion without the use of touch. Like emblems, affect displays often do not require verbal accompaniment for understanding. In fact, several studies have shown that people across cultures understand certain nonverbal facial expressions as reflective of particular emotions (see Ekman & Oster, 1979; Izard, 1977). By manipulating three facial regions (the eyes and eyelids, the eyebrows and forehead, and the mouth and cheeks), people can create affect displays that are recognizable world wide. For example, sadness is expressed by somewhat constricting the eyes and forehead region, while flattening the cheeks and displaying a slight downward curvature of the mouth.

Although Ekman and Friesen's category system captures most gestural movements, it doesn't describe all kinesic behaviors. Perhaps most importantly, it gives short shrift to the types and functions of eye contact. A popular saying exults that "the eyes are the window to the soul." Research on eye behavior supports these beliefs. Eye contact has been shown to vary dramatically in form and to differ significantly in function (for review, see Gramet, 1983). It clearly occupies a central place as a channel for message transmission and will emerge in studies reviewed throughout the selection.

One concept that captures several aspects of our kinesic activity and has received considerable research attention is *immediacy*. Included as part of the cluster of immediacy behaviors are the kinesic behaviors of eye contact, body orientation (i.e., the degree to which the interactant's body is oriented toward or away from the other), body lean (i.e., the degree to which the person's body is leaning forward or back), head nods, interpersonal distance (part of the proxemic code), and touch (part of the haptic code). Together, this set of behaviors communicates the degree to which an individual is involved in the interaction. Studies have shown that changes in immediacy behavior strongly affect the outcome of interactions, from having important consequences for the success of job interviews to influencing the attentiveness of patients during interactions with physicians (Buller & Street, 1992; Forbes & Jackson, 1980).

Haptics

A second general category of nonverbal behavior is labeled haptics and refers to all aspects of touch. Perhaps no other code has stronger communicative potential than does touch. Research has shown that individuals place considerable weight on the meaning of touch and that touch has important developmental benefits (see Jones & Yarbrough, 1985). In fact, several studies have found that the absence of touch from parents has serious consequences for children's growth (for review, see Montagu, 1978). Close, physical contact with the caregiver seems to give children the critical sense of protection and security that cannot be attained in other ways. As such, it is not surprising that holding babies is often the behavior that can best calm them and that physicians spend some time explaining baby-holding techniques to new parents.

Touch does not only play an important role during early childhood, it is a critical part of our life as we age as well (see Barnard & Brazelton, 1990). Indeed, the elderly may be most affected by the harmful consequences of touch deprivation (see Montagu, 1978). When lifelong partners pass away, the elderly often lose the one source of affectionate touch on which they have relied for much of their lives. Although certain associations (e.g., long-time neighbors, family members) may help alleviate some potential for loneliness, it is unlikely that their needs for touch will be fully satisfied by these connections.

As with kinesics, haptic behaviors may be classified in multiple ways, some focused on type and others focused on function. Among the type of haptics discussed, scholars have distinguished between the form of touch and its qualities. On the one hand, the form of the touch sends an important communicative message. For example, we could easily separate nuzzles from kisses, rubs from hugs, pokes from hits, pushes from punches, and so on. In fact, Morris (1971) observed 457 different types of touch that seemed to signal the presence of a relationship between the parties. He then categorized the touches into 14 categories of what he labeled tie signs. Among these tie signs are hand-holding, patting, arm-linking, several types of embraces, and kissing. Afifi and Johnson (1999) compared dating partners and male–female friends in their use of these tie signs in college bars. Interestingly, they found more similarities than differences in the frequency that the tie signs were used across the two relationship types. Specifically, all types of tie signs were used in both dating relationships and friendships. However, daters were more likely than friends to lean against one another, use shoulder and waist embraces, and to kiss. Given the relative similarity between daters and friends of the opposite sex in their use of tie signs in bars, it is no wonder that young adults often report confusion about the status of their cross-sex friendships (see Monsour, 2002). Although not assessed by Afifi and Johnson, qualities of

the touch, such as the duration and intensity (e.g., amount of pressure) undoubtedly play an important role in their meaning. Both friends and daters may exchange kisses, but a "peck" is different from a longer and more intense kiss. Similarly, a hug can differ dramatically in duration and intensity, aspects that are much more meaningful than simply recognizing that a hug occurred. In other words, both the type of touch and its characteristics serve to define its meaning and affect its outcome.

A final way that touches have been categorized is by their intended purpose. Heslin (as cited in Andersen, 1999) differentiated between five purposes of touch, each increasing in intimacy.

Functional/professional touches have a specific task-related purpose. They are considered the least intimate forms of touch. Although the type and quality of touch may be considered intimate in other contexts, the receiver of the touch recognizes the function of the touch as being necessary for the task at hand. For example, physicians sometimes touch us in highly intimate areas, but the touch is not considered an intimate one because its function is recognized as being part of the required task of health maintenance. The next function of touch is labeled

Social/polite and is characterized by relatively formal touches that accompany greetings and departures. A common example of social/polite touches is the handshake. Although other cultures utilize more intimate sorts of greetings (e.g., kisses), the context again defines the otherwise intimate touch as functioning as a polite expression rather than an intimate one.

Friendship/warmth touches are the sort typically exchanged between friends. The formality of social/polite touches is gone and replaced with qualities of touch that signal increased bondedness. Examples of friendship/warmth touches include partial embraces, full embraces, and pats.

Love/intimacy touches function to signal elevated closeness and are less likely to be enacted publicly. Touches such as a kiss or a prolonged embrace may serve the love/intimacy function. Finally, touches that function to increase sexual arousal are the most intimate types of touch. The sort of touch that occurs during sexual activity is the most common example of this function. In sum, rather than consider touches as differing by type, this category scheme focuses on their function. The same type of touch (e.g., a backrub) may serve a functional/professional purpose when conducted by a masseuse or sports therapist but act to increase sexual arousal when conducted by a romantic partner. Unfortunately, the existing categorization schemes do not adequately capture the many types of more harmful touches or the more negative purposes of touch (e.g., to harm, to intimidate).

Proxemics

The proxemic category of nonverbal behavior captures the way we use space. From analyses of overpopulation in certain nations, to the impact of small dorm room space, to overcrowding in prisons, studies consistently show harmful, effects of limited space. Although cultures differ dramatically in the amount of space that is typically given, we are all born with at least minimum needs for space. Threatening those space needs, especially for prolonged periods, produces high stress that, in turn, affects our psyche and behavior dramatically (see Edwards, Fuller, Vorakitphokatorn, & Sermsri, 1994). It is not surprising then, that confinement in a very small and dark room is commonly used as a method of torture (www.amnesty.org) and that such torture has devastating psychological impact. Indeed, Lester (1990) found an increase in suicide rates associated with overcrowding in prisons. Donoghue (1992) reported overcrowding as a factor contributing to stress among teenagers in the Virgin Islands. Curiously, he noted that sexual activity (sometimes leading to pregnancy) was one of consequences. Also, Gress and Heft (1998) showed that, the number of roommates in college dorms negatively affected the residents both emotionally and behaviorally. One way in which this need for space is expressed is through our behavior around territories.

Territories are physically fixed areas that one or more individuals defend as their own (Altman, 1975). To maintain the spatial needs provided by these territories, we set up markers so that others know the territory's boundaries (Buslig, 1999). For example, students may put books on the seat next to them to ensure that the seat is not taken, or spread their belongings across a wide area of a table to indicate the area as their own. Fences around property, "Keep Away" and "Do Not Disturb" signs, and markers around beach blankets are other common examples of signaling territory. Interestingly, locations where space is limited are particularly prone to markers of territory. Roommates often send very clear signals about the boundaries of their territory by hanging unique posters or signs that mark the area as their own. The importance of these territories to our well-being is evident in the way individuals react to their violation. Intrusions into territory have been shown to produce elevated stress, and behavioral responses varying from withdrawal to confrontation (for review, see Lyman & Scott, 1967).

Unlike territories, which are fixed physical entities, *personal space* is a proxemic-based need that moves along with the individual. It is an "invisible bubble" that expands and shrinks according to context, but follows each individual, protecting him or her from physical threats (Hall, 1966). Violation of that personal space bubble produces responses similar to those found for the violation of territory. In North America, typical personal space has a circumference of approximately 3 ft., but the size of that space varies dramatically and is influenced by a variety of factors, from the target of your conversation to its location (see Burgoon et al., 1996). For example, you would likely feel much more uncomfortable standing 2 ft. away from someone in a relatively empty elevator than in a crowded elevator. We recognize that certain contexts necessitate the temporary violation of our personal space, but we also keenly anticipate extracting ourselves from that context and restoring the security that comes with maintaining those personal space needs. A behavior that is commonly used both to violate personal space and restore it is eye contact. Have you ever felt that your personal space has been violated by someone simply staring at you, even from a distance? Many people report such a sensation. Have you ever looked away from someone who got too close physically? That sort of behavior is a common response to the violation of personal space in elevators, for example (see Rivano-Fischer, 1988).

Physical Appearance

The physical appearance category of nonverbal behavior includes all aspects related to the way we look, from our body type, to body adornments (e.g., tattoos, rings), to what we wear. Perhaps no other category of nonverbal behavior has a stronger effect on initial impressions than our physical appearance. The two general types of physical appearance that will be addressed in this selection are body type and attire.

Researchers have identified three general body types: ectomorphs, mesomorphs, and endomorphs (see Burgoon et al., 1996). *Ectomorphic* bodies are characterized by thin bone structures and lean bodies, *mesomorphic* bodies have strong bone structures, are typically muscular and athletic, and *endomorphic* bodies have large bone structures, and are typically heavy-set and somewhat rounded. An individual's body type is partly based on genetic elements such as bone structures and partly based on other elements such as diet and levels of activity. Regardless of the source of one's body structure or the degree to which it has any actual effect on behavior, research has clearly shown that people have strong impressions of others based on their body type. Specifically, ectomorphs are perceived to be timid, clumsy, and anxious, but also intelligent; mesomorphs are seen as outgoing, social, and strong; and endomorphs are considered lazy, jolly, and relatively unintelligent (Burgoon et al., 1996). Some factors may affect these perceptions. For example, women ectomorphs and male mesomorphs may be perceived more favorably than their other-sex counterparts. Unfortunately, research has not sufficiently addressed these possibilities. However, one pattern that has been well documented is that, regardless of actual body size, women are more likely than men to perceive their bodies negatively (for review, see Cash & Pruzinsky, 1990). Such "body image disturbances" have devastating consequences, affecting self-esteem, leading to eating disorders, and even increasing suicide rates (e.g., Phillips, 1999; Stice, Hayward, Cameron, Killen, & Taylor, 2000). Why do many women have such dislike for their bodies? Although the answer to this question is not at all simple, it is undoubtedly based, at least in part, on a cultural obsession with images of overly thin women (see Botta, 1999).

However, body shape is not the only aspect of physical appearance that has been shown to affect people's perceptions of us. Another strong influence on perceptions is height. Taller men and women are more likely to be seen as competent, dominant, and intelligent (see Boyson, Pryor, & Butler, 1999). Interestingly, however, the advantage of height does not extend to perceptions of women's attractiveness. Instead, shorter women are perceived as more attractive and date more frequently than taller women (Sheppard & Strathman, 1989). Men and women who fall well above or below this preferred standard encounter lifelong difficulties, including a diminished likelihood of relational success and struggles with perceptions of credibility across a wide range of evaluative contexts (see Martel & Biller, 1987). To combat these perceptions, short people sometimes change their environment to hide their height. For example, Robert Reich, who served on three presidential administrations and is under 5 ft. tall, would speak behind a podium and use a step stool, making media viewers unaware of his short stature.

One explanation for the strong perceptions associated with body type and height comes from Evolutionary Theory. Evolutionary theorists (otherwise called sociobiologists) argue that our attraction to others is based in large part on our perceptions of their genetic makeup (see Buss, 1994). They suggest that, much like other mammals, the strongest members of our species receive the greatest attention and are considered the most attractive. For us, signs of health, wealth, and intelligence are the primary determinants of "strength." As such, it is not surprising to these scholars that people's body type (which may be associated with health) and height (which often translates to physical superiority) affect their life success.

Finally, the clothes we wear are a part of our physical appearance that also affects people's perceptions of us. The clothes we wear strongly influence perceptions of credibility, status, attractiveness, competence, and likability (e.g., Kaiser, 1997). This should come as no surprise to anyone who has seen students proudly display their *Abercrombie & Fitch* shirts, observed the respect often afforded to those wearing their military uniforms, or shook their head in frustration at someone who leaves for an interview in completely disheveled clothes. Indeed, individuals wearing formal clothes are seen as more credible and more persuasive than those wearing informal clothes, affecting their success across a range of interaction contexts, from job interviews to dates. Other aspects of physical appearance that relate to people's judgments include tattoos, rings, and hair styles. In sum, studies unequivocally demonstrate that physical appearance, both things under individuals' control (e.g., attire) and those not (e.g., height), strongly influence perceptions.

Vocalics

Vocalics, a category that people sometimes have difficulty recognizing as a nonverbal component, reflect all aspects of the voice, including loudness, pitch, accent, rate of speech, length of pauses between speech, and tone, among many others. Vocalic elements carry much of the meaning of a message and communicate a lot about the sender. Its importance can be reflected by a simple exercise. Try saying the same words (e.g., "Come over here") with slightly different vocalic qualities. Depending on how we say these words, we could communicate anger, passion, sadness, love, or a variety of other emotions. Indeed, studies have shown that we make relatively accurate judgments about a person's sex, age, height, and cultural background based on vocal cues alone (see Argyle, 1988). Like many of the codes discussed so far, vocalic elements also affect perceptions of attractiveness and competence (Semic, 1999). Deeper voices among men, like that of Barry White for example, are considered sexual and romantic, whereas high-pitched voices among men are considered feminine and weak. Other vocal qualities such as accent and speech rate are also associated with intelligence. For example, certain accents (e.g., British accents) may be considered sophisticated whereas others may not (e.g., thick Boston accents). This difference in the attractiveness of accents is illustrated in the movie *My Fair Lady* which is based on the premise that individuals sometimes must change their accent to affect judgments of their credibility.

One theory that has been applied to understand vocalic shifts is Communication Accommodation Theory (CAA, see chap. 16, this volume). Central to CAA is the belief that we converge our speech toward the style of individuals with whom we want to be associated and diverge away from that of individuals with whom we do not want association (see Giles, Mulac, Bradac, & Johnson, 1987). Examples of this behavior can be found across a wide range of contexts, including interactions between individuals of different ages (e.g., adults and the elderly), individuals from different cultures, individuals with different levels of status, even individuals of different sexes (see Gallois, Giles, Jones, Cargile, & Ota, 1995). So, if you were from the eastern United States and were to spend considerable time in the South, you would likely develop somewhat of a Southern accent, at least when around your friends from the South. That accent accommodation is a way of signaling connectedness with the South. Not surprisingly, the degree to which you are willing to accommodate others in your language has also been shown to significantly affect their perceptions of you. Failure to accommodate your vocalic patterns to others implicitly signals to them that you are not interested in joining their cultural group. On the other hand, a willingness to accommodate communicates attraction.

Chronemics and Artifacts

Chronemics and artifacts are the last two categories of nonverbal behavior that we will discuss in this selection. Rarely considered when discussing nonverbal messages, these codes nevertheless play a strong role in our interactions. The chronemic code captures our use and perception of time, including (among other things) our perception of the "appropriate" duration of an event, the number of things we do at once, the importance of punctuality, our use of time in our language, and the desired sequencing of events (Andersen, 1999). The North American culture is preoccupied with the notion of time; life is fast-paced and individuals are seemingly always struggling against time constraints. Two hours seems to be the maximum time that one expects to allot for entertainment or food events; movies are typically 2 hr or less, plays may go 3 hr but will have a prolonged recess to affect the perception of time, and guests often start getting anxious when meals take longer than 2 hr. Other countries differ dramatically from this North American norm. Although we rarely think of these time norms, they become very evident when we visit other countries. For example, Mediterranean countries often take 3 to 4 hr for a meal, making it as much as a social event as it is time for nourishment. This selection will focus on three chronemic elements: duration, punctuality, and the distinction between polychronism and monochronism.

The expectations surrounding event duration are captured in part by the example provided previously. For every event or interaction, we have culturally and socially based expectations about its duration (Gonzalez & Zimbardo, 1999). Whether it be the amount of time a professor spends in an office meeting with a student, the amount of time set aside for a lunch date, or the amount of time before contact is made following a successful first date, these expectations strongly affect our perceptions of others' competence or attractiveness. Imagine if you had strong expectations that someone not call you back until 2 or 3 days after a first date but the person calls you within minutes after dropping you off. That violation of your chronemic expectations would undoubtedly affect your perceptions of him or her. In a similar vein, perceptions associated with punctuality vary according to the context and have important consequences. Punctuality is held with relatively high esteem in the North American culture, especially for more formal engagements. Arriving late to an interview, even if 5 min, is considered inexcusable, but 5 min late for a lunch date may be acceptable. However, even informal occasions have relatively strict punctuality expectations; arriving 30 min late for a lunch date is not appropriate, for example. In other cultures, however, there is a recognition that the time set for an appointment is rarely adhered to, and expectations are that the appointment may begin 30 to 45 min following the originally set appointment time. Failing to meet these culturally and contextually driven expectations have important implications for assessments of individuals (see Burgoon & Hale, 1988).

A final concept related to chronemics that will be considered in this selection is the distinction between polychronism and monochronism (Hall & Hall 1999). Polychronism reflects the act of doing multiple activities at once, whereas monochronism characterizes a focus on one activity at a time. For example, interacting with someone while you are cleaning your apartment, or watching TV while talking to someone reflects polychronistic behavior. Although sometimes necessary, such behavior is often considered a reflection of (dis) interest in the conversation. Of course, certain careers (e.g., secretarial work, CEOs) require that individuals are adept at polychronistic activity, and some cultures consider polychronism a sign of importance, so monochronism is not universally preferred.

The final nonverbal code is *artifacts,* a category that includes "the physical objects and environmental attributes that communicate directly, define the communication context, or guide social behavior in some way" (Burgoon et al., 1996, p. 109). Hall (1966) classified artifacts into two main types: fixed-feature elements and semifixed-feature elements. Fixed features include aspects of our surroundings that are not easily movable and are unlikely to change. Among these features is the structure of our surroundings, including the architectural style, the number and size of windows, and the amount of space available. Studies have shown that such architectural features directly impact the sort of communication that occurs (see Sundstrom, Bell, Busby, & Asmus, 1996). For instance, people who work in small cubicles are much less productive and less satisfied than people who work in their own office space, especially when the office space includes windows. Semifixed features are defined as aspects of our surroundings that are somewhat easily movable. Examples include rugs, paintings, wall color, the amount of lighting, and the temperature, among others. Considerable evidence suggests that these features also strongly affect both psychological health and communication outcome (for review; see Sundstrom et al., 1996). For example, research has shown that the semifixed aspects of a hospital affect the speed of patient recovery (Gross, Sasson, Zarhy, & Zohar, 1998).

In sum, nonverbal messages affect our interactions in hundreds of ways, from movement in our face, to our body posture, our gestures, the space between us, the ways we touch, the intonations in our voice, the way we use time, and the surroundings in which we find ourselves. Together, these nonverbal features inescapably guide the way we act and the outcome of our interactions. However, noting the population of nonverbal message types is only part of the equation. Each of these nonverbal behaviors can serve a variety of functions or purposes.

FUNCTIONS OF NONVERBAL CODES

There are three assumptions about nonverbal behavior that shape the research reviewed in the remainder of this selection (for review, see Cappella & Street, 1985). First, all behavior is motivated by particular goals. In other words, all behavior is functional in some way. You gesture to someone with a specific purpose in mind, you look at someone to get his attention, you touch someone to let her know you're here, you yell at someone to communicate your anger,

and so on. Second, each function or purpose can be achieved in multiple ways. For instance, you are not limited to only one way that you can show affection to people. You may hug them, kiss them, hold their hand, or take them out to a fancy restaurant. The third assumption related to this perspective on nonverbal messages is that a single behavior can serve multiple functions. For example, a hug can show someone you care, while simultaneously signaling to others that you and the recipient of the hug are in a committed relationship. These three assumptions are an inherent part of almost all studies of nonverbal communication and guide our understanding of nonverbal messages and their use.

Although scholars disagree on the exact number of functions served by nonverbal behaviors, there are six functions that seem to emerge in most discussions on this issue and that will be highlighted in this selection. These six functions are (a) structuring and regulating interaction, (b) creating and managing identities, (c) communicating emotions, (d) defining and managing relationships, (e) influencing others, and (f) deceiving others.

Structuring and Regulating Interaction

Each of the nonverbal codes serves to shape the quality of the interactions in which we find ourselves. By so doing, they structure and regulate these encounters. For example, Robinson's (1998) analysis of physician–patient interaction reveals the way in which the kinesic behaviors of eye gaze and body orientation signal to patients the physician's willingness to begin the interaction. Patients learn to stay silent until the physician kinesically signals that he or she is ready to start the interaction. Indeed, as noted earlier, many studies of immediacy reach similar conclusions, with varying levels of nonverbal involvement strongly affecting the quality of the interaction. Research on our use of vocalics also demonstrates the many ways that we nonverbally structure interactions. Conversations are typically considered a series of turns at talk. Each turn is requested, given, and ended in subtle, but clearly understood, nonverbal ways. For example, turns at talk are requested by such behaviors as establishing eye contact with the speaker, abruptly and noticeably inhaling a short breath, and starting to gesture toward the speaker (Wiemann & Knapp, 1975). In contrast, we communicate that our turn is ending by subtly changing the rhythm, loudness, and pitch of our voice (Boomer, 1978). In another interesting study on the potential of nonverbal message to structure interactions, Eaves and Leathers (1991) compared the physical layouts of McDonald's and Burger King to determine whether they affected interactions. Their study demonstrated that customers at McDonalds showed considerably higher levels of nonverbal involvement than did Burger King customers. Given these differences within two relatively similar fast-food chains, you can imagine how more noticeable differences in the level of restaurant formality affect our interactions.

One of the clearest signs that nonverbal behavior serves to structure the flow of interactions comes from examining how people adapt behavior during interaction. Indeed, a long history of research has shown that we react and adapt to one another's nonverbal expressions during interaction (for review, see Burgoon, Stem, & Dillman, 1995). Interaction Adaptation Theory (Burgoon, Stern, & Dillman, 1995) argues that people carry certain nonverbal needs for affiliation, recognize societal expectations for levels of affiliation, and have preferences for particular levels of affiliation from each interaction partner. The levels of these components differ in each context. For example, you may be upset one day and feel the *need* for some autonomy. You *expect* your roommate to greet you and welcome you home. But, your *preference* is that your roommate not interact with you at all for the next few hours. The combination of these three elements produces what is called the *Interaction Position*, a concept that reflects the amount of distance you anticipate from your roommate. The argument in this theory is that your needs and preferences act together with your general social expectations to affect what behavior you anticipate from your interaction partner (i.e., the interaction position, the IP). In the previous example, the IP may be

that your roommate will greet you but recognize your mood and give you some space. This IP is then compared to the actual behavior you receive (A). The theory argues that the comparison between your IP and the A determines how you will nonverbally adapt. If the actual behavior (i.e., the A) is better than you anticipated (i.e., the IP) you will converge toward the person's behavior, but if the actual behavior is worse than you anticipated, you will diverge away from that behavior. This "dance" is perhaps the greatest example of the effect of nonverbal behavior on the structure of interactions.

Creating and Managing Identities and Impressions

Another general function of nonverbal messages is to communicate to others the groups to which we belong and to convey particular impressions of ourselves to others. I will review two theoretical frameworks that apply this function. Social Identity Theory (Tajfel & Turner, 1979) focuses on our identity as group members, whereas theoretical work on self-presentation (e.g., Goffman, 1959) focuses on our identity as individuals. Together, these theories help explain the way in which we use nonverbal behavior to achieve the function of creating and managing identities and impressions.

Communicating Group Identities

The main premise of Social Identity Theory is that we develop and maintain our self-concept in large part from the social groups with which we affiliate or to which we belong (e.g., ethnicity, sports team, club membership, department, organizational unit). The importance of these group memberships vary according to context (e.g., the importance of your status as a member of a particular fraternity decreases when with your parents), but each group has specific ways through which membership is communicated to others. So, when group membership becomes relevant, we act in ways that convey to others that we are a part of that group, while also letting people who are not in that group become more aware of their out-group status. Not surprisingly, the primary method of communicating these group memberships is nonverbal.

Take membership in a high school clique, for example. Members of a particular clique are likely to dress in relatively similar ways (physical appearance), and often have specific gestures they use to greet one another or that they use during conversation (kinesics). Individuals can indicate group membership by standing close to one another or by sitting next to each other at the lunch table (proxemics). Group members may spend a significant portion of their day with others in their clique (chronemics), place indicators of affiliation (signs, letters, etc.) on their lockers (artifacts), and may whisper to one another in the presence of an outgroup member (vocalics). Given the importance of group membership (Worschel & Austin, 1986), it is not surprising that we go to such lengths to identify with groups that we consider enhancing to our self concept.

It is also the case that we distance ourselves nonverbally from groups with which we want to remain independent. A look around college campuses shows a lot of the ways that people accomplish this distancing. Individuals often make little effort to include members of ethnic groups other than their own in their conversations. Eder's (1985) study of behavior among midadolescent females showed that group members communicated distance from group outsiders by avoiding interaction, body contact, or eye contact with nonmembers. Although these are examples of interpersonal ways in which we send group-related identity messages, there are ways in which societies or cultures communicate outgroup status to entire groups. Certainly laws discriminating against where particular cultural groups can gather—let alone eat, sit, or stand— are examples of such societal messages that become translated through nonverbal means. Everything from kinesics gestures (e.g., lack of eye contact) to proxemic decisions (e.g., maintaining large distances) to artifacts (e.g., signs indicating that entrance is prohibited to certain groups) communicate exclusion. For example,

laws prohibiting the homeless from loitering in certain parks or communities are violations of public territorial rights that reflect one of many ways through which the homeless are shown their status as a societal "outgroup."

Communicating Individual Identities

Besides communicating our identity as members of particular groups, we also send nonverbal messages that are intended to convey our individual identities. Several theories have been advanced to capture this aspect of our behavior. The labels of these frameworks include Politeness Theory (Brown & Levinson, 1987), the Theory of Self-Identification (Schlenker, Britt, & Pennington, 1996), and Facework (Tracy, 1990). Within each of these theories are such concepts as self presentation, impression management, and identity management. In general, they all refer to the idea that we are motivated by a desire to maintain a positive impression of ourselves in the eyes of others. In other words, we generally want others to see us in a positive light. DePaulo (1992) defined *self-presentation* as "a matter of regulating one's own behavior to create a particular impression on others, of communicating a particular image of oneself to others, or of showing oneself to be a particular kind of person" (p. 205). For many reasons, we often manage our impression in front of others nonverbally (see DePaulo, 1992). For example, Albas and Albas (1988) examined ways in which students reacted after receiving graded exams. They found that individuals who received good grades smiled (kinesics), displayed an open body posture (kinesics), and left their exams open with the grade showing, whereas those who received poor grades displayed a closed body posture (kinesics) and left immediately following the class (chronemics).

The use of nonverbal methods to manage impressions is obviously not limited to students' reactions to exam scores; evidence for other applications can be found across a whole host of contexts. Daly, Hogg, Sacks, Smith, and Zimring (1983) reported that people in early stages of relationships spend more time adjusting their clothes, fixing their hair, and attending to their physical appearance than those in later stages. In a similar vein, Montepare and Vega (1988) showed that women's vocalic cues communicated greater approachability and sincerity, among other characteristics, when talking over the phone with men with whom they had an intimate relationship, as compared to those with whom they had no relationship. Finally, Blanck, Rosenthal, and Cordell (1985) reported that judges were more likely to display nonverbal cues associated with warmth, professionalism, and fairness when facing older, more educated jurors than younger, less educated jurors. In sum, the function of creating and managing identities is a common purpose of our nonverbal activity and involves actions from all codes.

Communicating Emotions

Another common purpose of nonverbal behavior is to communicate emotion. In fact, as noted earlier, the majority of emotion messages are communicated through facial cues (i.e., kinesically). Particularly impressive is the evidence that some of these expressions are recognized cross-culturally. The argument underlying the Universality Hypothesis on emotion expression is that humans are innately equipped to decode certain expressions of emotion (for review, see Ekman, 1978), leading to cross-cultural recognition of these emotions. Initially, several studies supported that claim (e.g., Ekman, 1973; Izard, 1977). However, when researchers improved their studies, they found dramatic differences in individuals' nonverbal responses. To reconcile the differences in the research and to help account for both cultural-specific and universal patterns of expression, Ekman and colleagues developed the Neurocultural Theory of emotion expression (Ekman & Friesen, 1969). The theory argues that there is an element of biological innateness in our expression of emotion that accounts for the consistency across cultures in recognition of emotion expressions. For example, an experience of joy produces an upward curvature of the mouth and lips. However, differences in actual expression of emotion occur across cultures due to (a) cultural differences in the association between events and the experience of particular emotions and (b) culturally learned and context-based rules about the appropriateness of expressing particular emotions (labeled *display rules*). The first of these two factors makes sense once you consider the way that cultures shapes the emotions we experience (for review, see Nussbaum, 2000). For instance, some cultures emphasize individuality and are likely to encourage intense emotional responses to events that threaten individuality, whereas other cultures emphasize the collective and are likely to shape emotional responses accordingly. In other words, the same events are unlikely to produce the same emotions across cultures. However, researchers have devoted much more energy toward understanding the second of these factors: display rules. *Display rules* are defined as "socially learned habits regarding the control of facial appearance that act to intensify, deintensify, mask, or qualify a universal expression of emotion depending on the social circumstance" (Kupperbusch et al., 1999, p. 21).

Studies have shown that infants' emotional expressions abide by cultural, gender, and familial display rules before their first birthday (e.g., Malatesta & Haviland, 1982). These rules are communicated by parents from infancy but reinforced throughout life by the media, family members, peers, and even strangers. Common examples of these display rules are those generally discouraging overt public displays of affection, or those directing people on appropriate methods of emotional expression in movie theatres, funeral homes, classrooms, concerts, and so on. Display rules also direct people regarding the appropriateness of emotion expression in close relationships. Considerable evidence demonstrates that "negative" emotions (e.g., anger, jealousy) are considered inappropriate to express in early stages of relationships (for review, see Aune, 1997). Moreover, studies show the way that these display rules affect our expression of emotion even in our most intimate relationships. For example, Cloven and Roloff (1994) found that one fifth of relational irritations were not expressed in couples at the most advanced relational stages, and Aune, Buller, and Aune (1996) found that positive emotions were considered more appropriate to express than negative emotions, regardless of relationship stage.

Defining and Managing Relationships

Another important function of nonverbal messages is to help people negotiate and express the quality or status of the relationship they have with others. These relational messages vary along five dimensions (see Burgoon & Hale, 1987). Labeled the topoi (themes) of relational communication, the five dimensions along which nonverbal messages can differentially communicate relational qualities are (a) the amount of dominance, (b) the level of intimacy, (c) the degree of composure or arousal, (d) the level of formality, and (e) the degree to which the interaction is focused on task or social elements. Evidence associated with how each of these dimensions is communicated nonverbally will be briefly summarized.

Dominance

Nonverbal messages help indicate the degree to which one member of the interaction is powerful, dominant, and controlling. The way in which men and women communicate power nonverbally has been examined frequently, most notably by Henley (1977). Behavior from each nonverbal code can be applied to study how dominance is conveyed (see Burgoon et al., 1996). For example, people communicate dominance by refusing to engage in eye contact (kinesics), by initiating touch (haptics), by arriving late for a meeting (chronemics), by having access to large office space or by displaying awards (artifacts), by demanding large personal space needs or unilaterally changing the amount of space between themselves and their interactants (proxemics), by speaking loudly and in a lower pitch (vocalics), and by emphasizing their body size or dressing in formal attire (physical appearance).

Intimacy

Nonverbal messages help communicate the amount of affection, inclusion, involvement, depth, trust, and similarity there is between interactants. As noted earlier in this selection, several studies have shown the benefits of expressing nonverbal involvement in interactions. Displays such as gestural activity, direct body orientation, forward body lean, and close (but socially acceptable) conversational distance increase the success of job interviews, increase liking, and produce perceptions of personality warmth (Burgoon et al., 1996). Whereas expressing involvement is one method of communicating relational intimacy and interest, more intimate messages are communicated in other ways, such as the use of tie signs and an increase in the frequency and intimacy of touch. Interestingly, the eyes are often the best indicator of attraction (Grumet, 1983). Establishing eye contact is typically the first way individuals communicate attraction and people who are attracted to one another look into each other's eyes more than others do. Also, our pupils involuntarily increase in size when we are talking to someone to whom we are attracted, a fact that, in turn, subconsciously seems to make us more attractive to others (Hess, 1975). In sum, the nonverbal methods for communicating intimacy are numerous.

Composure and Arousal

The degree to which individuals are relaxed and calm in an interaction has also been shown to communicate qualities of their relationship. As a general rule, people in close relationships are more likely to be relaxed around one another than acquaintances. In fact, people sometimes manipulate their levels of composure to send messages about their comfort in the interaction or the relationship. For example, job candidates or people on first dates usually do their best to hide the amount of anxiety being felt in part because they want to show a level of relational comfort. In other words, we make efforts to appear composed in certain situations precisely because we know what anxiety communicates about relationships.

Formality

Another way in which individuals can communicate qualities of the relationship is through the degree of casualness conveyed in their nonverbal behavior. Although relatively few studies have examined it, the level of formality, like other dimensions of relationship quality, can be communicated in many different ways. Three common methods of indicating the formality of the relationship are through the formality of the attire, through kinesic rigidity, and through conversational distance (Burgoon, 1991; Burgoon et al., 1996). The more casual the clothing, the more relaxed the body posture, the more frequent the hand gesturing, and the greater the distance between interactants, the greater the perception that the interaction is an informal one. Not surprisingly, studies have shown that the likelihood of communicating formality differs across status and that these differences affect people's perceptions. For example, Lamude and Scudder (1991) reported that upper-level managers are more likely to be formal than lower- or middle-level managers. Interestingly, research has also shown that college teachers are perceived as more effective when they dress informally (Butler, & Roesel, 1991; Lukavski, Butler, & Harden, 1995), whereas physicians and interview candidates are perceived as less effective when behaving or dressing informally (Burgoon et al., 1987; Gifford, Ng, & Wilkinson, 1985).

Task or Social Orientation

Nonverbal messages reflecting the degree to which the interaction is one focused on a task constitute the final dimension through which people communicate qualities of their relationships nonverbally. This dimension is typically communicated through the chronemic code and, again, the desirability of communicating a focus on task is strongly affected by context. On the one hand, managers who focus on task, to the exclusion of relational maintenance behaviors, receive the lowest ratings of satisfaction by subordinates (Lamude, Daniels, & Smilowitz, 1995). On the other hand, teachers whose in-class behavior focuses on task produce better student outcomes (Harris, Rosenthal, & Snodgrass, 1986). In general, the communication of a task orientation has been shown to convey lower levels of relational connectedness than socially oriented messages (Burgoon & Hale, 1987).

Influencing Others

A long history of research has examined the methods we use to attempt to change someone's attitudes or behavior or to strengthen already established attitudes or behaviors (see O'Keefe, 1990). In general studies find that we are most influenced by people who we find attractive (i.e., likeable), credible, or powerful (see O'Keefe, 1990).

Social Attractiveness or Liking

Scholars have shown many ways in which individuals can increase their attractiveness to others. For example, studies demonstrate that establishing eye contact increases the likelihood of influencing others in a wide variety of situations including persuading strangers to give a dime for a phone call, donate to a charity, take pamphlets, or pick up a hitchhiker (for review, see Segrin, 1999). Also, light touching is linked to bigger tips, an increase in petition signings, and a greater willingness to sign up for volunteer work (e.g., Goldman, Kiyohara, & Pfannensteil, 1985). Physical appearance cues also strongly affect perceived attractiveness and the potential to influence others. In one study, a confederate gave the same speech to two different audiences but varied her physical appearance through differences in the messiness of her hair and the fit of her clothes (Mills & Aronson, 1965). Results showed that she was more convincing when she was dressed more neatly. In a similar vein, physically attractive political candidates are more likely to get elected for office and physically attractive defendants are less likely to be found guilty (Mazzella & Feingold, 1994; Sigelman, Thomas, Sigelman, & Ribich, 1986). However, other studies suggest that the advantage of physical attractiveness depends at least somewhat on context. Juhnke, Barmann, Cunningham, and Smith (1987) found that strangers were more willing to give detailed directions to college students who were poorly dressed and asking about the location of a lower status location (i.e., a thrift shop) than students who were well dressed or asking for directions to a higher status location (e.g., the Gap). In sum, physical appearance has repeatedly been shown to be a nonverbal signal that functions to increase or decrease the success of social influence attempts.

Credibility

Besides physical attractiveness, research has shown that our perceptions of someone's credibility affect the degree to which they influence us. The notion of credibility refers to "the judgments made by a perceiver (e.g., a message recipient) concerning the believability of a communicator" (O'Keefe, 1990, pp. 130–131). Kinesic behaviors that are related to perceptions of credibility include eye contact, moderate amounts of gesturing, use of supportive head nods, facial expressiveness, and moderately forward leans, all indicators of conversational immediacy (see Burgoon, Birk, & Pfau, 1990). For example, Badzinski and Pettus (1994) showed that jurors determined a judge's credibility by attending to his or her kinesic behavior. Equipped with this knowledge, many lawyers approach the bench of jurors during opening and closing remarks, establish eye contact with each juror, and use other kinesic behaviors that are known to increase credibility ratings.

Besides kinesic elements, vocalic cues also affect perceptions of credibility. Among the most common findings is that nonfluencies in speech strongly decrease credibility ratings and the potential for successful persuasion. Nonfluencies include pauses in speech (e.g., "Auh," "Aummm"), repetition of "nonsense" words (e.g. "like"), and difficulty in articulation (O'Keefe, 1990). Besides the absence of nonfluencies, credible speakers use

more varied intonation, speak more loudly and with more intensity, and talk faster (see Burgoon et al., 1996). But perhaps no other nonverbal code has received more attention for its effect on perceptions of credibility than physical appearance. For example, studies have shown that women who have specific eye shapes, short hair, appear older (although not elderly), wear a moderate amount of makeup, and are conservatively dressed were rated as more credible than their counterparts (Dellinger & Williams, 1997; Rosenberg, Kahn. & Tran, 1991). The final aspect known to increase persuadability is the perceived power of the speaker.

Power

Power will be defined in this selection as a perception that the speaker holds a position of authority. Like most assessments, this perception of authority is primarily established through nonverbal means. Again, perhaps the most common method of affecting perceptions of power is through physical appearance. Attire and physical size go a long way toward establishing a speaker's authority. For example, individuals wearing suits or uniforms, and those standing tall, as opposed to those with a slumped posture, are immediately afforded greater perceptions of power than their counterparts (see Andersen & Bowman, 1999). An extreme example of the effect of physical appearance on the success of influence came from Milgram's (1974) research program on obedience. In his studies, he showed that individuals dressed in lab coats were able to convince research participants to administer what participants believed to be fatal levels of electric shock to others. The result of Milgram's research program starkly demonstrated the degree to which people will obey others who they perceive to hold power positions, a perception primarily guided by nonverbal cues.

Deceiving Others

The last purpose of nonverbal messages that will be reviewed in this selection is to deceive others. Deception is defined as "a message knowingly transmitted by a sender to foster a false belief or conclusion by a receiver" (Buller & Burgoon, 1996, p. 205). Although people assume that most interactions involve truth-telling, some studies suggest that a majority actually involve some element of deception (e.g., O'Hair & Cody, 1994). So, how is it that we get away with so much deception and when is it that we're likely to be caught? The answer to both questions lies in our manipulation of nonverbal behavior.

Interpersonal Deception Theory (Buller & Burgoon, 1996) is a framework that, combines several perspectives to help explain the process of deception in interactions. Although the theory is quite complex, it relies primarily on the idea that deception is an interactive activity and that its detection is a process affected by the behavior of both sender and receiver, as well as contextual and relational factors. In other words, whether you are successful at lying is partly based on your nonverbal cues, but it is also affected by the receiver's behavior, the relationship you have with him or her, and the context surrounding the interaction, among other elements. Given the emphasis of this selection, I will focus on the nonverbal behaviors that have been shown to affect the success of the deceiver.

Research suggests that successful liars are those who maintain eye contact, display a forward body lean, smile, and orient their bodies toward the other person (for review, see Buller & Burgoon, 1994). That is, people who can display elevated levels of immediacy are more likely to get away with a lie (Burgoon, Buller, Dillman, & Walther. 1995). Burgoon and colleagues offer at least two explanations for this finding. First, the high immediacy by receivers may produce an adaptational response by the deceiver—increased immediacy. That response, in turn, makes the deceiver appear honest. So, the receiver's immediacy "pulls" the liar into that behavioral pattern and causes him or her look more honest. Another possibility is that the receiver's immediacy makes the deceiver feel better about the success of his or her deception and lessens the anxiety cues that often "leak" from deceivers. In addition to the previously noted cues, successful liars display vocalic fluency and kinesic composure, while also being generally expressive nonverbally and avoiding extended pause rates during conversation. In contrast, unsuccessful liars "leak" their anxiety nonverbally through heightened pitch, greater nonfluencies, negative expressions, nervous behaviors, and generally lowered immediacy levels (for review, see Burgoon, Buller, & Guerrero, 1995).

Although the research on deception is vast and includes much more detailed analysis of factors affecting deception success and failure, among other aspects of the deception episode, the previously noted cues seem to capture some of the essential elements of deceiver behavior.

CONCLUSION

The research reviewed in this selection leaves no doubt as to the impact of nonverbal messages on our lives. To summarize, nonverbal actions are often considered more important than verbal messages for determining message meaning. One reason for their importance is that they are omnipresent—an inherent part of every communication act. Indeed, there are seven codes of nonverbal behavior that could be simultaneously sending messages. For example, one could be communicating attraction by dressing nicely (physical appearance), maintaining eye contact (kinesics), interacting at a close distance (proxemics), lightly touching the other (haptics), varying vocal intonation (vocalics), extending the conversation (chronemics), and setting up the interaction to be in an intimate setting (artifacts). Relatedly, many of these cues could be serving multiple functions, from interaction management to emotion expression to relational management to influence. As such, it is important to keep nonverbal behaviors in mind when assessing the application of all communication theories; they undoubtedly play a critical role in explaining interaction outcomes.

ADDITIONAL READING

Given the breadth of the research on nonverbal communication, it is difficult to summarize the literature well. Nevertheless, there are very good texts available. Textbooks that do an exceptional job of summarizing the research in the area include Burgoon et al. (1996) and Andersen (1999). Another resource for interested readers is Guerrero, DeVito, and Hecht (1999), an edited volume that includes excellent readings from across the spectrum of nonverbal research, each written by some of the best scholars in the area.

Recommended readings within specific areas of nonverbal messages include Burgoon, Stern, et al. (1995) for nonverbal adaptation, DePaulo (1992) for research on nonverbal self-presentation strategies, and Henley (1977) for an extended discussion of dominance and sex differences in the use of touch.

REFERENCES

Afifi, W. A., & Johnson, M. L. (1999). The use and interpretation of tie signs in a public setting: Relationship and sex differences. *Journal of Social and Personal Relationships, 16,* 9–38.

Albas. D., & Albas. C. (1988). Acers and bombers: Post-exam impression management strategies of students. *Symbolic Interaction, 2,* 289–302.

Altman, I. (1975). *The environment and social behavior.* Monterey, CA: Brooks/Cole.

Andersen, P. A. (1999). *Nonverbal communication: Forms and functions.* Mountain View, CA: Mayfield.

Andersen, P. A., & Bowman, L. L. (1999). Positions of power: Nonverbal influence in organizational communication. In L. K. Guerrero, J. A. DeVito, & M. L. Hecht (Eds.), *The nonverbal communication reader: Classic and contemporary readings* (2nd ed., pp. 317–334). Prospect Heights, IL: Waveland.

Argyle, M. (1988). *Bodily communication* (2nd ed.). London: Methuen.

Aune, K. S. (1997). Self and partner perceptions of the appropriateness of emotions. *Communication Reports, 10,* 133–142.

Aune. K. S., Buller, D. B., & Aune, R. K. (1996). Display rule development in romantic relationships: Emotion management and perceived appropriateness of emotions across relationship stages. *Human Communication Research, 23,* 115–145.

Badzinski, D. M., & Pettus, A. B. (1994). Nonverbal involvement and sex: Effects on jury decision making. *Journal of Applied Communication Research, 22,* 309–321.

Barnard, K. E. & Brazelton, T. B. (Eds.). (1990). *Touch: The foundation of experience.* Madison, CT: International Universities Press.

Blanck, P. D., Rosenthal, R., & Cordell, L. H. (1985). The appearance of justice: Judges' verbal and nonverbal behavior in criminal jury trials. *Stanford Law Review, 38,* 89–164.

Botta. R. A. (1999). Televised images and adolescent girls' body image disturbance. *Journal of Communication, 49,* 22–41.

Boomer, D. S. (1978). The phonemic clause: Speech unit in human communication. In A. W. Siegman & S. Feldstein (Eds.), *Nonverbal behavior and communication* (pp. 245–262). Hillsdale, NJ: Lawrence Erlbaum Associates, Inc.

Boyson. A. R., Pryor, B., & Butler, J. (1999). Height as power in women. *North American Journal of Psychology, 1,* 109–114.

Brown, P., & Levinson, S. (1987). *Universals in language usage: Politeness phenomena.* Cambridge, England: Cambridge University Press.

Buller, D. B., & Burgoon, J. K. (1994). Deception: Strategic and nonstrategic communication. In J. A. Daly & J. M. Wiemann (Eds.), *Strategic interpersonal communication* (pp. 191–223). Hillsdale, NJ: Lawrence Erlbaum Associates, Inc.

Buller, D. B., & Burgoon. J. K. (1996). Interpersonal Deception Theory. *Communication Theory, 6,* 203–242.

Buller, D. B., & Street, R. L., Jr. (1992). Physician-patient relationships. In R. S. Feldman (Ed.), *Applications of nonverbal theories and research* (pp. 119–141). Hillsdale, NJ: Lawrence Erlbaum Associates, Inc.

Burgoon, J. K. (1991). Relational messages interpretations of touch, conversational distance, and posture. *Journal of Nonverbal Behavior, 15,* 233–259.

Burgoon, J. K. (1994). Nonverbal signals. In M. L. Knapp & G. R. Miller (Eds.), *Handbook of inter-*

personal communication (2nd ed., pp. 229–285). Thousand Oaks, CA: Sage.

Burgoon, J. K., Birk, T., & Pfau, M. (1990). Nonverbal behaviors, persuasion, and credibility. *Human Communication Research, 17,* 140–169.

Burgoon, J. K., Buller, D. B., Dillman, L., & Walther, J. B. (1995). Interpersonal deception: IV. Effects of suspicion on perceived communication and non-verbal behavior dynamics. *Human Communication Research, 22,* 163–196.

Burgoon, J. K., Buller, D. B., & Guerrero, L. K. (1995). Interpersonal deception: IX. Effects of social skill and nonverbal communication on deception success and detection accuracy. *Journal of Language and Social Psychology, 14,* 289–311.

Burgoon, J. K., Buller, D. B., & Woodall, W. G. (1996). *Nonverbal communication: The unspoken dialogue* (2nd ed.). New York: McGraw-Hill.

Burgoon, J. K., & Hale, J. L. (1987). Validation and measurement of the fundamental themes of relational communication. *Communication Monographs, 54,* 19–41.

Burgoon, J. K., & Hale, J. L. (1988). Nonverbal expectancy violations: Model elaboration and application to immediacy behaviors. *Communication Monographs, 55,* 58–79.

Burgoon, J. K., Pfau, M., Parrott, R., Birk, T., Coker, R., & Burgoon, M. (1987). Relational communication, satisfaction, compliance-gaining strategies, and compliance in communication between physicians and patients. *Communication Monographs, 54,* 307–324.

Burgoon, J. K., Stern, L. A., & Dillman, L. (1995). *Interpersonal adaptation: Dyadic interaction patterns.* Cambridge, England: Cambridge University Press.

Buslig, A. L. S. (1999). 'Stop' signs: Regulating privacy with environmental features. In L. K. Guerrero, J. A. DeVito. & M. L. Hecht (Eds.), *The nonverbal communication reader: Classic and contemporary readings* (2nd ed., pp. 241–249). Prospect Heights, IL: Waveland.

Buss, D. M. (1994). *The evolution of desire.* New York: Basic Books.

Butler, S., & Roesel, K. (1991). Students perceptions of male teachers: Effects of teachers' dress and students' characteristics. *Perceptual and Motor Skills, 73,* 943–951.

Cappella, J. N., & Street, R. L. (1985). A functional approach to the structure of communicative behavior. In R. L. Street & J. N. Cappelia (Eds.), *Sequence and pattern in communicative behavior* (pp. 1–29). London: Edward Arnold.

Cash. T. E, & Pruzinsky, T. (Eds.). (1990). *Body images: Development, deviance, and change.* New York: Guilford.

Cloven, D. H., & Roloff, M. E. (1994). A developmental model of decisions to withhold relational irritations in romantic relationships. *Personal Relationships, 1,* 143–164.

Daly, J. A., Hogg, E., Sacks, D., Smith, M., & Zimring, L. (1983). Sex and relationship affect social self-grooming. *Journal of Nonverbal Behavior, 7,* 183–189.

Dellinger, K., & Williams, C. L. (1997). Makeup at work: Negotiating appearance rules in the workplace. *Gender and Society, 11,* 151–177.

DePaulo, B. M. (1992). Nonverbal behavior and self-presentation. *Psychological Bulletin, 111,* 203–243.

Donoghue, E. (1992). Sociopsychological correlates of teenage pregnancy in the United States Virgin Islands. *International Journal of Mental Health, 21,* 39–49.

Eaves, M. H., & Leathers, D. G. (1991). Context as communication: McDonald's vs. Burger King. *Journal of Applied Communication, 19,* 263–289.

Eder, D. (1985). The cycle of popularity: Interpersonal relations among female adolescents. *Sociology of Education, 58,* 154–165.

Edwards, J. N., Fuller, T. D., Vorakitphokatorn, S., & Sermsri, S. (1994). *Household crowding and its consequences.* Boulder, CO: Westview.

Ekman, P. (1973). *Darwin and facial expression: A century of research in review.* New York: Academic.

Ekman, P. (1978). Facial expression. In A. W. Siegman & S. Feldstein (Eds.). *Nonverbal behavior and communication* (pp. 96–116). Hillsdale, NJ: Lawrence Erlbaum Associates, Inc.

Ekman, P., & Friesen, W. V. (1969). The repertoire of nonverbal behavior: Categories, origins, usage, and coding. *Semiotica, 1,* 49–98.

Ekman, P., & Oster, H. (1979). Facial expression of emotion. *Annual Review of Psychology, 30,* 527–554.

Forbes, R. J., & Jackson, P. R. (1980). Nonverbal behavior and the outcome of selection interviews. *Journal of Occupational Psychology, 53,* 67–72.

Gallois, C., Giles, E. L., Jones, E., Cargile, A. C., & Ota, H. (1995). Accommodating intercultural encounters: Elaborations and extensions. *International and Intercultural Communication Annual, 19,* 115–147.

Gifford, R., Ng, C. R., Wilkinson, M. (1985). Nonverbal cues in the employment interview: Links between applicant qualities and interviewer judgments. *Journal of Applied Psychology, 70,* 729–736.

Giles, H., Mulac, A., Bradac, J. J., & Johnson, P. (1987). Speech Accommodation Theory: The first decade and beyond. In M. McLaughlin (Ed.), *Communication Yearbook* (Vol. 10, pp. 13–48). Newbury Park, CA: Sage.

Goffman, E. (1959). *The presentation of self in everyday life.* Garden City. NY: Doubleday.

Goldman, M., Kiyohara, O., & Pfannensteil, D. A. (1985). Interpersonal touch, social labeling, and the foot-in-the-door effect. *Journal of Social Psychology, 125,* 143–147.

Gonzalez, A., & Zimbardo. P. G. (1999). Time in perspective. In L. K. Guerrero. J. A. DeVito, & M. L. Hecht (Eds.), *The nonverbal communication reader: Classic and contemporary readings* (2nd ed., pp. 227–236). Prospect Heights, IL: Waveland.

Gress, J. E., & Heft, H. (1998). Do territorial actions attenuate the effects of high density? A field study. In J. Sanford & B. R. Connell (Eds.), *People, places, and public policy* (pp. 47–52). Edmond, OK: Environmental Design Research Association.

Gross, R., Sasson, Y., Zarhy, M., & Zohar, J. (1998). Healing environment in psychiatric hospitals. *General Hospital Psychiatry, 20,* 108–114.

Grumet, G. W. (1983). Eye contact: The core of interpersonal relatedness. *Psychiatry, 48,* 172–180.

Guerrero, L. K., Devito, J. A., & Hecht, M. L. (Eds.). (1999). *The nonverbal communication reader: Classic and contemporary readings* (2nd ed.). Prospect Heights, IL: Waveland.

Hall, E. T. (1966). *The hidden dimension* (2nd ed.). Garden City, NY: Anchor/Doubleday.

Hall E. T., & Hall. M. R. (1999). Monochrome and polychrome time. In L. K. Guerrero, J. A. DeVito, & M. L. Hecht (Eds.), *The nonverbal communication reader: Classic and contemporary readings* (2nd ed., pp. 237–240). Prospect Heights. IL: Waveland.

Harris, M. J., Rosenthal, R., & Snodgrass, S. E. (1986). The effects of teacher expectations, gender, and behavior on pupil academic performance and self-concept. *Journal of Educational Research, 79,* 173–179.

Henley, N. M. (1977). *Body politics: Power, sex, and nonverbal communication.* Englewood Cliffs, NJ: Prentice-Hall.

Hess, E. H. (1975). The role of pupil size in communication. *Scientific American, 233,* 110–119.

Izard, C. E. (1977). *Human emotions.* New York: Plenum.

Jones, S. E., & Yarbrough, A. E. (1985). A naturalistic study of the meanings of touch. *Communication Monographs, 52,* 19–56.

Juhnke, R., Barmann, B., Cunningham, M., & Smith, E. (1987). Effects of attractiveness and nature of request on helping behavior. *Journal of Social Psychology, 127,* 317–322.

Kaiser, S. B. (1997). *The social psychology of clothing: Symbolic appearances in context* (2nd ed.). New York: Fairchild.

Kupperbusch, C, Matsumoto. D., Kooken, K., Loewinger, S., Uchida, H., Wilson-Cohn, C., et al. (1999). Cultural influences on nonverbal expressions of emotion. In P. Philippot, R. S. Feldman. & E. J. Coats (Eds.), *The social context of nonverbal behavior* (pp. 17–44). Cambridge, England: Cambridge University Press.

Lamude, K. G., Daniels, T. D., & Smilowitz, M. (1995). Subordinates' satisfaction with communication and managers' relational messages. *Perceptual and Motor Skills, 81,* 467–471.

Lamude, K. G., & Scudder, J. (1991). Hierarchical levels and type of relational messages. *Communication Research Reports, 8,* 149–157.

Lester, D. (1990). Overcrowding in prisons and rates of suicide and homicide. *Perceptual and Motor Skills, 71,* 274.

Lukavsky. J., Butler, S., & Harden, A. J. (1995). Perceptions of an instructor: Dress and students' characteristics. *Perceptual and Motor Skills, 81,* 231–240.

Lyman, S. M., & Scott, M. B. (1967), Territoriality: A neglected sociological dimension. *Social Problems, 15,* 236–249.

Malatesta, C. Z., & Haviland, J. M. (1982). Learning display rules: The socialization of emotion expression in infancy. *Child Development, 53,* 991–1003.

Martel, L. F., & Biller, H. B. (1987). *Stature and stigma: The biopsychosocial development of short males.* Lexington, MA: Lexington.

Mazzella, R., & Feingold, A. (1994). The effects of physical attractiveness, race, socioeconomic status, and gender of defendants and victims on judgments of mock jurors: A meta-analysis. *Journal of Applied Social Psychology, 24,* 1315–1344.

Milgram, S. (1974). *Obedience to authority: An experimental view.* New York: Harper & Row.

Mills, J., & Aronson, E. (1965). Opinion change as a function of the communicator's attractiveness and desire to influence. *Journal of Personality and Social Psychology, 1,* 74–77.

Monsour, M. (2002). *Women and men as friends: Relationships across the life span in the 21st century.* Mahwah, NJ: Lawrence Erlbaum Associates, Inc.

Montagu, A. (1978). *Touching: The human significance of the skin* (2nd ed.). New York: Harper & Row.

Montepare, J. M., & Vega, C. (1988). Women's vocal reactions to intimate and casual male friends. *Personality and Social Psychology, 14,* 103–113.

Morris, D. (1971). *Intimate behavior.* New York: Random House.

Nussbaum, M. C. (2000). Emotions and social norms. In L. P. Nucci & G. B. Saxe (Eds.), *Culture, thought, and development* (pp. 41–63). Mahwah, NJ: Lawrence Erlbaum Associates, Inc.

O'Hair, H. D., & Cody, M. J. (1994). Deception. In W. R. Cupach & B. H. Spitzberg (Eds.), *The dark side of interpersonal communication* (pp. 181–214). Hillsdale, NJ: Lawrence Erlbaum Associates, Inc.

O'Keefe, D. J. (1990). *Persuasion: Theory and research.* Newbury Park, CA: Sage.

Phillips, K. A. (1999). Body dysmorphic disorder and depression: Theoretical considerations and treatment strategies. *Psychiatric Quarterly, 70,* 313–331.

Rivano-Fischer, M. (1988). Micro territorial behavior in public transport vehicles: A field study on a bus route. *Psychological Research Bulletin, 28,* 18.

Robinson, J. D. (1998). Getting down to business: Talk, gaze, and body orientation during openings of doctor–patient consultations. *Human Communication Research, 25,* 97–123.

Rosenberg, S. W., Kahn. S., & Tran, T. (1991). Creating a political image: Shaping appearance and manipulating the vote. *Political Behavior, 13,* 345–367.

Schlenker, B. R., Britt, T. W., & Pennington, J. (1996). Impression regulation and management: Highlights of a theory of self-identification. In R. M. Sorrentino & E. T. Higgins (Eds.), *Handbook of motivation and cognition: The interpersonal context* (Vol. 3, pp. 118–147). New York: Guilford.

Segrin, C. (1999). The influence of nonverbal behaviors in compliance-gaining processes. In L. K. Guerrero, J. A. DeVito, & M. L. Hecht (Eds.), *The nonverbal communication reader: Classic and contemporary readings* (2nd ed., pp. 335–346). Prospect Heights, IL: Waveland.

Semic, B. (1999). Vocal attractiveness: What sounds beautiful is good. In L. K. Guerrero, J. A. DeVito, & M. L. Hecht (Eds.), *The nonverbal communication reader: Classic and contemporary readings* (2nd ed., pp. 149–155). Prospect Heights, IL: Waveland.

Sheppard, J. A., & Strathman, A. J. (1989). Attractiveness and height: The role of stature in dating preference, frequency of dating, and perceptions of attractiveness. *Personality and Social Psychology Bulletin, 15,* 617–627.

Sigelman, C. K., Thomas, D. B., Sigelman, L., & Ribich, F. D. (1986). Gender, physical attractiveness, and electability: An experimental investigation of voter biases. *Journal of Applied Social Psychology, 16,* 229–248.

Stice, E., Hayward, C., Cameron, R. P., Killen. J. D., & Taylor, C. B. (2000). Body-image and eating disturbances predict onset of depression among female adolescents: A longitudinal study. *Journal of Abnormal Psychology, 109,* 438–444.

Sundstrom, E., Bell, P. A., Busby, P. L., & Asmus, C. (1996). Environmental psychology 1989–1994. *Annual Review of Psychology 47,* 482–512,

Tajfel, H., & Turner, J. C. (1979). An integrative theory of group conflict. In W. G. Austin & S. Worchel (Eds.), *The social psychology of intergroup relations* (pp. 33–47). Monterey, CA: Brooks-Cole.

Tracy. K. (1990). The many faces of facework. In H. Giles & W. P. Robinson (Eds.), *Handbook of language and social psychology* (pp. 209–226). Chichester, England: John Wiley & Sons.

Wiemann. J. M., & Knapp, M. L. (1975). Turn-taking in conversation. *Journal of Communication, 25,* 75–92.

Worschel, S., & Austin, W. G. (Eds.). (1986). *The social psychology of intergroup relations.* Chicago: Nelson Hall.

4. Viewers Make Meaning

by Marita Sturken and Lisa Cartwright

By this point in the text, readers should understand that communication occurs through human-made symbols, both verbal and nonverbal, that are arbitrary in nature. This is an important point because it helps students of communication to understand why multiple interpretations of the same message are not only possible but inevitable. This chapter addresses the variations in making meaning by addressing fundamental elements of visual literacy. The study of visual culture is important to communication because so much of contemporary communication is visual. This chapter provides insight into the influences various media have on allowing and encouraging audience members to engage in making meaning. It also provides an excellent vocabulary for intelligently discussing the impact of visual culture on our daily experiences.

This chapter challenges the reader in a number of ways. First, it invites the reader to consider elements of culture and engage in cultural critique in a manner unfamiliar to most novices in the field. The reader should actively engage the ideas of critique in order to develop a strong sense of visual literacy and efficacy in a visual world. The second challenge is a vocabulary that may be unfamiliar to the reader. Concepts such as interpellation, bricolage, and counter-bricolage are informative and important, and should be applied to the reader's common experience to truly be understood. Finally, the chapter is challenging because it lacks images—it is heavily word-laden for a visual literacy chapter. Because the chapter points to the accessibility of images in the digital age, it is important for readers to use their skills as information consumers to locate examples from this chapter. Using search engines to access visual examples such as Wilson's Guarded View (1991) and Duchamp's Fountain (1917) will enhance the experience of the chapter and help prove the overarching point made about the amount of access we have to so many visual images.

Images generate meanings, yet the meanings of a work of art, a photograph, or a media text do not, strictly speaking, lie in the work itself, where they were placed by the producer waiting for viewers to find them. Rather, meanings are produced through the complex negotiations that make up the social process and practices through which we produce and interpret images. In the process of making, interpreting, and using images, meanings change. The production of meaning involves at least three elements besides the image itself and its producer: (1) the codes and conventions that structure the image and that cannot be separated from the content of the image; (2) the viewers and how they interpret or experience the image; and (3) the contexts in which an image is exhibited and viewed. Although we can say that images have what we call dominant or primary meanings, they are interpreted and used by viewers in ways that do not strictly conform to these meanings.

Throughout this book, we discuss the *viewer* more than the *audience*. A viewer is, in the most basic sense of the term, an individual who looks. An audience is a collective of lookers. In focusing on the viewer, we are concerned with the activity of the individual as a social category that emerges through practices of looking. Viewing involves a set of relational social practices. These practices occur not simply between individual human subjects who look and are looked at but among people, objects, and technologies in the world. Viewing, even for the individual subject, is a multimodal activity. The elements that come into play when we look may include not only images but also other images with which they are displayed or published, our own bodies, other bodies, built and natural objects and entities, and the institutions and social contexts in which we engage in looking. Viewing is a relational and social practice whether one looks in private or in public and whether the image is personal (a photograph of a loved one, for example), context-specific (a scientific image used as an information source in a laboratory), or public (a news photograph).

By looking at the *viewer*, we can understand certain aspects of practices of looking that cannot be captured by examining the concept of the audience, an entity into which producers hope to mold viewers as consumers.[1] The term *interpellation* is an important aspect of this point. To interpellate, in the traditional usage of this concept, is to interrupt a procedure in order to question someone or something formally, as in a legal or governmental setting (in a Parliamentary procedure, for example). The term was adapted by political and media theorists in the 1970s who made the case that *images interpellate viewers*. They used this term, as we do, to describe the way that images and media texts seem to call out to us, catching our attention. Here, we draw on and move beyond the theories of French philosopher Louis Althusser, whose ideas theorists have drawn on to suggest that ideologies "hail" subjects and enlist them as their authors. Images hail viewers as individuals, even when each viewer knows that many people are looking at the same image—that the image was not intended "just for me" but reaches a wider audience. There is an interesting paradox inherent in this experience: for viewer interpellation by an image to be effective, the viewer must implicitly understand himself or herself as being a member of a social group that shares codes and conventions through which the image becomes meaningful. I may feel that an image apprehends or touches me personally, but it can do so only if I am a member of a group to whom its codes and conventions "speak," even if the image does not "say" the same thing to me as it does to someone else. I do not have to like or appreciate the dominant messages of the image to be interpellated by it or to understand that message. To be interpellated by an image, then, is to know that the image is meant for me to understand, even if I feel that my understanding is unique or goes against the grain of a meaning that seems to have been intended.

Advertising seeks, of course, to interpellate viewer consumers in constructing them within the "you" of the ad. The codes and meanings of an advertisement, for example, might be entirely clear to me, even if I do not share or am opposed to the tastes and values it promotes and even if the ad tries to represent "people like me" in a manner that I feel is "not really me" or is offensive to me. This Olay ad interpellates the viewer with the promise of an idealized future self. The ad uses the "O" of "You" to target the model, who stands in for the consumer and whose transformation is promised. Here, the ad visualizes the "you" that is normally implied within image texts. The message of the image, even if not intended for me, nonetheless draws me in as a spectator, interpellating me, even though I know I am not the person for whom it was meant. Some images strongly interpellate viewers, some do not. But even if the primary or dominant message conveyed by the image is not, strictly speaking, "for me," my experience with the image may be personal in that there are various roles I may occupy in relationship to the image.

In the process of interpellation we are describing, an image or media text can bring out in viewers an experience of being "hailed" in ways that do not always promote a sense of being exactly the subject for whom the message is intended. As John Ellis notes, the term *audience*, a unifying concept that is so important to media marketing experts, does not adequately capture this process. A viewer's direct and complete engagement with the image producers' intended messages may be the goal of the producer, but such an engagement is not really possible. Even the most personal images work this way. I may feel that a photograph of a loved one interpellates, or speaks, to me and only me, but it does so through the photographic codes and conventions of "the personal" that we use to convey such messages. Such photographs can use close-ups to give the sense that the photographed subject looks directly into the viewer's eyes and soul. Romantic photographs of stars coveted by fans use the same conventions and may hail viewers in the same way, inciting romantic fantasies of intimacy. I may be interpellated by such an image, recognizing romantic love as a dominant or intended message that others will "get" without having these feelings invoked in me personally but rather recognizing them as feelings others are likely to have (those who admire the star, for example). I may even feel disgust or contempt for

the intended message. This would be another way of being interpellated by the image.

By focusing on the viewer (and not the audience) throughout this book, we are emphasizing the practices through which images and media texts reach out and touch audience members in ways that engender experiences of individual agency and interpretive autonomy, even in cases in which the image is widely viewed as a shared text with effective dominant meanings with which we may or may not fully engage. For some theorists, the effective delivery of dominant messages is "ideological" in the sense that "individual" felt experience with the image or text is thought to be a false feeling that producers aim to achieve in viewers through marketing strategies that figure out which codes and conventions will most effectively "reach" targeted audiences. In this view, to feel touched by a mass image is to harbor a mistaken understanding of oneself as the individual for whom that image's meaning is *personally* intended. The viewer, in this view, is duped by the image. We understand the process of interpellation to work differently from this. To be interpellated or touched in an individual way as a viewer is a common and all but unavoidable aspect of looking at images and media texts, public and private. But this aspect of practices of looking is neither insidious nor fully controlled by external forces such as advertisers or the media industry. Individual human agency and desire are not wholly controlled by the strategies of industry market experts, and dominant meanings are not the only or the most important ones that we experience. By considering viewers, not audiences, we can describe some of the many ways that viewers make meanings outside the boundaries of producers' intended messages and effects, even as viewers recognize those intended meanings.

Producers' Intended Meanings

Who produces images? The concept of the producer becomes complicated when we consider forms that involve multiple producers, as in the case of a major studio film production or the work of a collective of artists. In film parlance, a producer is a person who identifies financing and oversees the many jobs involved in a production. When the art collective Group Material displayed their public art throughout the streets and subways of New York City in the 1980s, the "producer" widely noted for generating this category or "brand" of work was the collective itself, and not the individual artists who designed each work. In advertising, the term producer could refer to the advertising agency, the lead designer, or the company whose product is represented in the ad. When we use the term *producer*, then, we may be referring to an individual maker (as in the case of one artist who produces a painting), a plurality of creative individuals unified by a shared set of aesthetic strategies of production design and display (the art collective or collaborators creating a work), or a corporate conglomerate engaged in different phases and aspects of an ad. The art collective RTMark plays up the anonymity of the individual artist in the manufacture of goods in postindustrial capitalism by presenting itself as an anonymous artist collective structured like a corporation and using corporate language and investment strategies to make a parodic critique of the mass visual culture of commodity production and branding.

French theorist Roland Barthes, in his classic 1967 essay on "The Death of the Author," was concerned with questions of authority and power between the individual author and readers.[2] We adapt his concept of the author's "death" to consider questions of authority and power as they are enacted between viewers and producers of images and media texts. According to Barthes, the text offers a multidimensional space that the reader deciphers or interprets. There is no ultimate authorial meaning for readers to uncover in the text. The approach to the image that we adopt throughout this book follows a similar logic. Although images and media texts may hold dominant meanings, it is the job of the critical reader not to simply point out dominant meanings for others to see but to show how these meanings are made. The text is also open to meanings and interpretations that exist alongside and even against

these more obvious meanings. Barthes advocated for the work of a critical and analytical reader whose interpretive practices are grounded in the historical contexts and positions from which texts are always read, as a means of showing how the authority of the author as the primary producer of the literary text is in fact a myth. His point was, in part, that texts are produced in the act of reading them and that these acts are performed from the cultural and political perspectives of readers and never fully according to the intentions of the author or producer.

Barthes's idea of critical reading was adapted among critics and theorists writing about images as a means of advocating for critical viewing practices—that is, practices of looking that take into account the authority and power of the historically and culturally situated viewer in the production of meanings. This perspective was especially important at the moment in history at which Barthes wrote, which preceded the era of the 1980s and 1990s, when video and computer hardware and software became widely available to the broad public. Today it goes without saying that consumers can produce their own media images and texts, because the technology to self-produce or to copy and manipulate found images is so widely available. During the time that Barthes's essay first circulated, however, home video and digital production and editing programs were a futuristic fantasy. The idea of the consumer of images as the producer of meaning was quite radical and new in the 1960s and 1970s, but today it is an everyday reality.

The French philosopher Michel Foucault, in his 1979 essay, "What is an Author?," written in response to Barthes's "Death of the Author," argues that the concept of author did not always exist and will probably pass out of relevance but that it is not exactly dead.[3] Foucault uses the concept of an "author function" rather than an "author." We adapt this concept as a means of thinking about the producer function. The producer function is a set of beliefs that lead us to have certain expectations about a work with regard to the status of its producer. The function of the author or producer is linked to the idea that "someone" (an artist, a company) must stand behind any given image. Copyright law is based on the premise that ownership of creative expression can be traced to someone, whether that be an individual or a company that owns the rights to the work. The "producer function" concept helps us to understand that "authorship" derives not just from who created something but often from who owns the rights to something. When we speak of a Nike ad, for example, we attribute the producer function to Nike because the corporation, and not the actual creative director of the ad, is the entity that owns and appears to speak through the work.

Most if not all images have a meaning that is preferred by their producers. Advertisers, for example, conduct audience research to try to ensure that the meanings they want to convey about a particular product are the ones viewers will perceive when they encounter an advertisement for that product. Artists, graphic designers, filmmakers, and other image producers create images with the intent that we read them in a certain way. It is also the case that architects design buildings with the intent that people will engage with and utilize the spaces in particular ways. Analyzing images and built spaces according to what we believe to be the intentions of their producers, however, is rarely a completely useful strategy. We usually have no way to know for certain what a producer, designer, or artist intended his or her image or structure to mean. Furthermore, knowing a producer's intentions often does not tell us much about the image, because intentions may not match up with what viewers actually take away from an image or text. People may experience an image or media text differently from how it is intended to be seen, either because they bring experiences and associations that were not anticipated by its producers or because the meanings they derive are informed by the context in which an image is seen. Context cannot fully be controlled by the producer. For example, we could say that the intentions of the creators of the many advertising images that are on display in an urban context may not necessarily coincide with the ways those images are seen by the many different viewers who encounter them. The visual clutter of the context alone of,

say, a place like Times Square, may affect how viewers interpret these images, as may juxtapositions with other images. Similarly, a video that is uploaded onto YouTube will be instantly linked to many other videos, and how viewers see it can be influenced by the range of videos they see before and after it. Many contemporary images, such as advertisements and television images, are viewed in a huge variety of contexts, each of which may affect their meanings. As visual culture scholar Nicholas Mirzoeff writes, "intervisuality," or the interaction of a variety of modes of visuality, is a key aspect of visual culture; thus any experience of viewing may incorporate different media forms, networks of infrastructure and meaning, and intertextual meanings.[4] Importantly, viewers themselves bring cultural associations that will affect their individual interpretations of an image, as our discussion below will show. This does not mean that viewers wrongly or subjectively interpret images or that images are unsuccessful or fail to persuade viewers when intended and received meanings diverge. Rather, meanings are created in part when, where, and by whom images are consumed, and not only when, where, and by whom they are produced. Simply put, a producer may make an image or media text, but he or she is not in full control of the meanings that are subsequently made through the work.

Although it has always been the case that viewers make different meanings in different cultural contexts, the context of global cultural flows has made this even more true. For example, in 1998, film viewers in China had an unexpected and overwhelmingly positive response to *Titanic*, the 1997 movie directed by James Cameron. According to the *Encyclopaedia Britannica*, in its entry on "cultural globalization," scores of middle-aged Chinese viewers saw the film numerous times and were reduced to tears, prompting a lively street trade in facial tissue outside Shanghai theaters. Sales of posters and the soundtrack were strong, as were video sales, with an estimated 25 million pirated and 300,000 legitimate copies sold. *Titanic* was invested with meanings in China that did not match the meanings produced in the film by its Western viewers, and these meanings were not anticipated by the movie's producers. These meanings were produced by viewers who spontaneously used the text to share emotions about a difficult cultural transition. As the author of the *Britannica* entry writes, "*Titanic* served as a socially acceptable vehicle for the public expression of regret by a generation of aging Chinese revolutionaries who had devoted their lives to building a form of socialism that had long since disappeared."[5] We learn from this example that viewers may make meanings that are not intended or anticipated by its producers, and that viewers are active agents in the production of meaning. Some critics might argue that the movie's marketing to China simply expanded the U.S. movie industry's power and authority and is an example of a kind of cultural imperialism and market domination. The author of the *Encyclopaedia Britannica* entry makes a different case: in fact, the production of meaning was very much in the hands of the viewers, who made the text their own.

Neither interpretation of the movie is more or less accurate than the other. An image creates meaning through its circulation among viewers. Hence, we can say that meanings are not inherent in images. Rather, meanings are the product of a complex social interaction among image, viewers, and context. Dominant meanings—the meanings that tend to predominate within a given culture—emerge out of this complex social interaction and may exist alongside alternative and even opposing meanings.

Aesthetics and Taste

All images are subject to judgments about their qualities (such as beauty or coolness) and their capacity to have an impact on viewers. The criteria used to interpret and give value to images depend on cultural codes, or shared concepts, concerning what makes an image pleasing or unpleasant, shocking or banal, interesting or boring. As we explained earlier, these qualities do not reside in the image or object but depend on the contexts in which it is viewed, on the codes that prevail in a society, and on the viewer who is making that judgment. All viewer interpretations involve two fundamental concepts of value—aesthetics and taste.

When we say that we appreciate something (a work of art, a photograph) for "aesthetic" reasons, we usually imply that the value of the work resides in the pleasure it brings us through its beauty, its style, or the creative and technical virtuosity that went into its production. Aesthetics has traditionally been associated with philosophy, and the arts, and aesthetic objects have stood apart from utilitarian objects. In the twentieth century, the idea of aesthetics steadily moved away from the belief that beauty resides within a particular object or image. By the end of the century, it was widely accepted that aesthetic judgment about what we consider naturally beautiful or universally pleasing is in fact culturally determined. We no longer think of beauty as a universally shared set of qualities. Contemporary concepts of aesthetics emphasize the ways in which the criteria for what is beautiful and what is not are based on taste, which is not innate but rather culturally specific.

Taste, however, is not simply a matter of individual interpretation. Rather, taste is informed by experiences relating to one's class, cultural background, education, and other aspects of identity. This idea was popularized in the late twentieth century by the influential book by the sociologist and philosopher Pierre Bourdieu, *Distinction: A Social Critique of the Judgement of Taste* (1979), which captured the century's changed understanding of taste as something that is always connected to social identity and class status. Bourdieu provided a description of tastes and their origins in patterns of class distinction. Following from Bourdieu, when we speak of taste or say that someone "has taste" we are usually using culturally specific and class-based concepts. When we say that people have "good taste" we may mean that they participate and are educated in middle-class or upper-class notions of what is aesthetically pleasing, whether or not they actually inhabit these class positions. Or we may regard someone as having "good" taste when they have in common with us a particular aesthetic or style that we believe reflects some special, elite knowledge, such as participation in a market that trades in "quality," edgy, or elite products. Taste can be a marker of education and an awareness of elite cultural values, even if one's expression of taste is to stick one's nose up at what is deemed "good" taste. "Bad taste" is sometimes regarded as a product of ignorance of what is deemed "quality" or "tasteful" within a society. Embracing "bad" taste or "artless" taste, on the other hand, can also signify cultural belonging to an educated elite that stands in opposition to the dictates of taste. Taste, in this understanding, is something that can be learned through contact with culture. But it is also something that one can studiously defy. Taste can be exercised and displayed through patterns of consumption and display.

Notions of taste provide the basis for the idea of connoisseurship. The traditional image of a connoisseur evokes a "well-bred" person, a "gentleman" who possesses "good taste" and knows the difference between a good work of art and a bad one and who can afford the "quality" work over the shoddy reproduction. A connoisseur is considered to be more capable than others of passing judgment on the quality of cultural objects. Traditionally "good taste" has been associated with knowledge of "high" culture forms such as fine art, literature, and classical music. Yet what counts as good taste is more complex than this notion of taste suggests. The term *kitsch* formerly referred to images and objects that are trite, cheaply sentimental, and formulaic. Kitsch is associated with mass-produced objects that offer cheap or gaudy versions of classical beauty (plastic reproductions of crystal chandeliers, for example). Cheap tourist trinkets, gift cards embossed with seraphim, paintings on velvet—these are kitsch. Art critic Clement Greenberg wrote a famous essay in 1939, "Avant Garde and Kitsch," in which he argued that unlike avant garde art, kitsch is formulaic, offering cheap and inauthentic emotion to the uneducated masses.[6] In the 1980s the concept of kitsch was newly revived by postmodern artists, architects, and critics interested in defying the austere aesthetics and universalizing values of modern works of art and architecture. Embracing the lowbrow aesthetics of

kitsch and the "bad" design elements of everyday mass culture became a means of defying modernism's tendency toward elite, "high quality" design. Kitsch objects also gained value precisely because they became recognized as iconic of a historical moment in which everyday life was saturated with cheesiness. Certain objects formerly deemed "tasteless" or just silly, the everyday artifacts of the everyday middle-class or working-class consumer, were given new value over time precisely because they had become iconic artifacts of a past era. The educated connoisseur can collect and display these now-valuable artifacts to demonstrate engagement in the culture of lowbrow aesthetics.

The lava lamp is an example of how kitsch can gain value in a second level of meaning. When it was first made in England in the postwar period, the lamp, in which wax floats in strange shapes in oil, was widely regarded as ugly. But in the 1960s, the weird Astro Lamp (in the American market dubbed the Lava Lite) meshed perfectly with the tastes of the psychedelic generation. The light then fell out of fashion again, tumbling back into the obscurity of bad taste such that even thrift shop collectors spurned it. However, with the broad resurgence of interest in 1960s music and visual and clothing styles in the 1990s, the lamp was back in vogue to the delight of the company that bought out the original U.S. manufacturer after the lamp fell out of favor during the 1980s. Now the original lamp goes for over $100 on eBay, and the copy sells for about $20 in retail stores. In contemporary taste cultures, the circulation of objects through categories of taste and the reclassification of objects according to new scales of value show us that hierarchies of taste and beauty are not fixed but are relative to historical and cultural interpretations.

The Most Wanted Paintings on the Web (1995), a Web work by Vitaly Komar and Alex Melamid, artists originally from the former Soviet Union who have worked in the United States since 1978, is an excellent project through which to examine questions about taste in an international context. The artists, who have worked in the medium of painting to parody and critique forms such as Soviet realism, commissioned a professional market survey in which people in the United States and Russia were asked about their recreational preferences, their politics and lifestyles, their knowledge of famous artists and historical figures, and their preferences for or reactions against paintings with angles, curves, brushstrokes, colors, sizes, themes, and styles. Komar and Melamid then tallied and computed the results of the survey, using their findings to arrive at a formula for the creation of paintings showing each country's most and least wanted image. Each painting represents a composite of the dominant answers from each group. These paintings were exhibited under the rubric of "The People's Choice." Both countries disliked abstract images and preferred calm landscapes in which were featured well-known figures. America's "most wanted" painting was calculated to be "dishwasher-sized" and to include a landscape, wild animals, and George Washington, whereas America's "most unwanted" painting was abstract with sharp angles and a thick textured surface.[7] The Russian most wanted painting displays Jesus in a landscape similar to that depicted in America's most wanted. Both paintings utilize a sort of pictorial realism associated with Soviet-era state-mandated form. Komar and Melamid expanded this project into a Web extravaganza for which groups in twelve countries were polled and their preferences analyzed to arrive at digitized renderings of composite paintings for each nation. This Web project is hosted by the Dia Center for the Arts and has as its primary sponsor the Chase Manhattan Bank, an institutional relationship that the artists no doubt find befitting of their ironic message. With a few exceptions, the results of this poll are remarkably consistent, with most countries preferring soft landscapes and pictorial realism over abstract, minimal compositions. Italy's most wanted painting, is, by contrast, more impressionistic, whereas Italy's most unwanted painting features a picture of Elvis and a nude male figure.

One of the chief points of this project is to make a joke about the degree to which the art market is not immune to consumer values and tastes; artists are not unresponsive to the vagaries

of a mass public psychology of taste uninformed by the avant-garde aesthetics represented in some museums and galleries of modern art. In this project, decisions about the making of art are brought down to the level of the Nielsen television poll, turning the revered individual fine art painting into something tacky and generically pleasing. The project is also a pointed critique of the ways in which opinion polls and statistics about collective opinions carry so much weight in contemporary society and in the media, even as it uses those statistics to render its works. This art project posed the question about what art would look like if it were produced by audience ratings and opinion polls. Yet at the same time it is also a visual manifestation of just how shallow opinion polls can be in providing an image of the tastes of viewers, here made into a mockery of the conglomerate concept of "the people."

In *Distinction*, Bourdieu established through extensive survey research that taste is used by individuals to enhance their position within the social order and that distinction is the means through which they establish their taste as different from that of other, lower classes of people. This is not a matter of actual class position based on one's economic status but of cultural capital. "Taste classifies," Bourdieu famously wrote, "and it classifies the classifier. Social subjects, classified by their classifications, distinguish themselves by the distinctions they make, between the beautiful and the ugly, the distinguished and the vulgar, in which their position in the objective classifications is expressed or betrayed."[8] Bourdieu also concluded that taste is learned through exposure to social and cultural institutions that promote certain class-based assumptions about correct taste. So, for instance, institutions such as museums function not only to educate people about the history of art but also to instill in them a broader sense of what is tasteful and what is not, what is valuable and what is not, and what is "real" art and what is not. Through these institutions, people, regardless of their class position, learn to be "discriminating" viewers and consumers of images and objects. That is, they "learn" to rank images and objects according to a system of taste that is deeply steeped in class-based values. Even the collecting of objects "in bad taste" is steeped in elite class values, insofar as one must be educated in the meaning of everyday design and kitsch style to appreciate those aesthetics.

In Bourdieu's theory, all aspects of life are interconnected and unified in what he called a *habitus*—a set of dispositions and preferences we share as social subjects that are related to our class position, education, and social standing. This means that our taste in art is related to our tastes in music, food, fashion, furniture, movies, sports, and leisure activities and is in turn related to our profession, class status, and educational level. Taste may often work to the detriment of people of lower classes because it relegates objects and ways of seeing associated with their lifestyles as less worthy of attention and respect. What is more, the very things deemed tasteful—works of fine art, for example—are often off limits to most consumers.

These distinctions between different kinds of taste cultures have traditionally been understood as the difference between high and low culture. As we noted in the introduction, the most common definition of culture throughout history was the idea of the best of a given culture. However, this definition was highly class-based, with those cultural pursuits of the ruling class seen as high culture and the activities of the working class as low culture. Thus high culture has traditionally meant fine art, classical music, opera, and ballet. Low culture was a term used to refer to comic strips, television, and at least initially, the cinema. However, in the late twentieth century, this division of high and low was heavily criticized, not only because it affirms classist hierarchies but also because it is not an accurate measure of the relationship between the cultural forms people consume and the class positions they occupy. The distinction between fine art and popular culture has been consistently blurred in the art movements of the late twentieth century, from pop art to postmodernism. (We discuss this work in chapters 7 and 8.) In addition, as we have noted, the collection of certain kinds of cultural artifacts, such as kitsch, which are valued now precisely because they once were the expression of the everyday consumer's "bad" taste, blurs distinctions between high and low. Furthermore, analyses of B movies (and other cultural products such as popular romance novels) that were once regarded as low culture have emphasized the impact and value of contemporary popular culture among specific communities and individuals, who interpret these texts to strengthen their communities or to challenge oppression. Comic books and graphic novels, once considered to be for children or the uneducated, are now thought of as mainstream and cutting-edge cultural forms. Animated films are now one of the most popular and lucrative genres of popular film, aimed at all ages. It was once the case that universities did not study forms of popular culture—in British universities, for instance, even the study of the novel (as opposed to poetry) did not begin until the mid-twentieth century, because novels were considered lowbrow. The study of popular culture and visual culture in all its forms is now integral to university and high school curricula because of the now widespread belief that we cannot understand a culture without analyzing its production and consumption of all forms of culture, from high to low.

The model of analysis that Bourdieu used is class-stratified in ways that are specific to what he perceived to be a largely homogeneous native French population when he collected his survey data in the mid-1960s. Both the context in which he asked those questions—that of a postwar pre-May 1968 French society that was significantly class-stratified, with a highly class-based educational system—and the kinds of questions he asked of French bourgeois society are historically and culturally specific. His idea that categories of taste and distinction trickle down from the upper, educated to the lower, less educated classes does not account for the dynamics of taste and judgment in the evaluation of those valued cultural forms that began as the expression of a marginalized culture or class, such as jazz in the 1920s and hip-hop in the 1980s. In the case of forms such as these, taste and distinction can trickle up to more affluent, culturally dominant groups. The same can be said about the graffiti or street art of producers such as Jean-Michel Basquiat, whose graffiti was brought from the streets to the galleries in New York in the 1980s, or Shepard Fairey, the world-renowned street artist, founder of *Swindle* magazine, and designer of the loading screen for Guitar Hero II who stenciled and postered his André the Giant logo in urban public spaces in the 1980s. Fairey's Obey stickers and stencils were designed to get people to think about the messages of images on the street. Yet their meaning was often ambiguous, what Fairey calls an "experiment in phenomenology." His artwork is now copyrighted under the lable "Obey Giant" and an offshoot clothing line for sale in mall skate stores alongside Vans, Diesel, and Stussy. Bourdieu's system does not help us to understand the particular patterns of minority, immigrant, or countercultural values and distinction—for example the patterns of taste

and distinction among those who immigrated to France from Northern and Sub-Saharan Africa in the years following the demise of French colonialism. Our point is not only that cultural values and tastes may trickle up or may develop differently among members of a politically and culturally minoritized diaspora but also that cultural values and tastes are increasingly subject to movement in a variety of directions, as markets diversify in kind laterally, as well as to globalization. In today's culture, images and objects circulate within and across social strata, cultural categories, and geographical distances with speed and ease, such that youth cultures in Central Asia and North America may look very much alike in their clothing choices despite these groups being separated by geographic distances and political differences. The globalization of manga (Japanese comics) is an example of this phenomenon in which taste

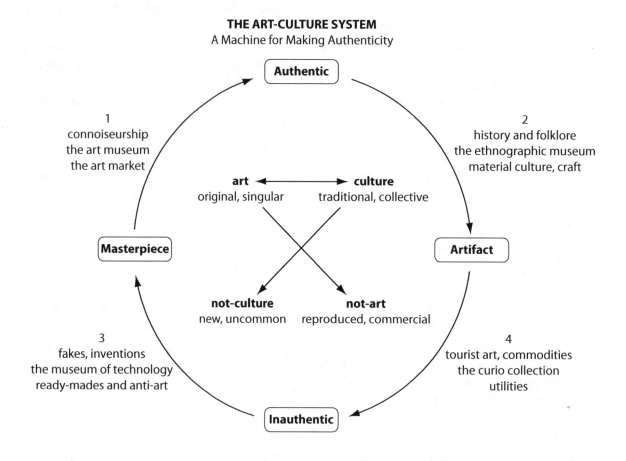

FIGURE 1. The Art-Culture System

and distinction are forged in ways that do not strictly follow Bourdieu's observed patterns of class and cultural influence.

Collecting, Display, and Institutional Critique

As we noted in chapter 1, there are many ways in which the value of a work of art is determined in the art market. One of the key economic and cultural factors in the valuing of art is collecting by art institutions such as museums and by private collectors. Not only does this activity create a market for art, but it also creates a financial context in which work is expected to appreciate in value over time. The collecting of art for economic and cultural capital has a long history. This seventeenth-century painting by David Teniers of Archduke Leopold Wilhelm's collection was one of the first visual catalogings of an art collection. In this image, Teniers imagined the archduke standing among his many paintings as a means to both illustrate the collection and affirm the importance of the archduke's role as collector. The large scale of the painting, in which the figures seem diminutive, affirms the size of the collection. This painting thus functions as an actual catalogue of the archduke's collection, as an affirmation of his taste and role as a connoisseur, and as evidence of the value of his large collection. Ownership is a key factor in establishing value in art. Much of the value of art collections is established through the details of the provenance of artworks, such as the history of who has owned them and when they changed ownership—information that has little to do with the artist or the work's creation.

Collecting always involves the elements of hierarchy and value judgments. The cultural theorist James Clifford has written about how the practices of collecting and exhibiting art and artifacts contributed to the ways viewers make meaning. In a well-known essay on practices of collecting, "On Collecting Art and Culture," Clifford considers the fact of African tribal art, artifacts, and cultural practices when these items and practices are relocated to Western museums, archives, art markets, and discursive systems. He adapts the "semiotic square" (designed by A. J. Greimas) for the purpose of mapping the movement of art and cultural artifacts from one cultural context to another in relationship to changes in their classification and value. Clifford's map of the "art-culture system" allows us to see how the movement of objects through the collecting practices of museums, scholars, and connoisseurs effects transitions in the meaning and value of works from, for example, not-art (such as religious artifacts) to art or from authentic to inauthentic. Clifford describes the collecting process as a machine in which common works of everyday culture are given value as a commodity in the rarified fine art market, trading on the mystified aura of the work as "true" tribal religious artifact.

Although the context in which contemporary art is collected includes dealers, galleries, and art auction houses as the primary arbiters of taste and value, there is also a parallel set of collecting practices in cultural artifacts, the "culture" section of Clifford's chart. These collections are, as his chart indicates, primarily based on notions of cultural authenticity. In the early 1990s, the anthropologists Ilisa Barbash and Lucien Taylor followed Gabai Baaré, a West African merchant who trades in wood carvings produced by members of his village and surrounding communities. In their documentary, *In and Out of Africa* (1992), Barbash and Taylor reveal the complex role played by "insider" figures such as Baaré in the entry of "local" cultural art and artifact to the lucrative global art market. They reveal that Baaré and the artists who produce the reproductions of religious artifacts that he peddles to art galleries in New York's Soho and to tourist emporia alike are neither native nor beholden to the Western value system. They actively engage in the irony of a process in which they recognize that their mythification by Western consumers can bring profit. Their products have, since the era of colonialism, included iconic "Colon" figures, hand-carved parodies of the colonial authorities and the very connoisseurs who covet their "authentic" reproductions of religious iconography produced exclusively for the tourist and art trade market.

Practices of collecting are intricately tied up in practices of exhibition and the valuing of work that comes from display contexts. Thus works of art and cultural artifacts are awarded value when they are purchased by museums and put on display within the institutions that represent art and culture, such as museums and galleries. In these institutional contexts, viewers can engage in a broad array of viewing practices, some in concert with institutional missions such as art pedagogy (by listening to commentaries on audio players offered for rent at the start of an exhibition, for instance) and some in defiance of them (as when we move quickly through an exhibition, skipping over many works within it, or make ironic or critical interpretations of the work on the basis of our taste, politics, or the cultural knowledge we bring to the show that is elided from the safe facts offered in the canned exhibition narrative).

Photographer Thomas Struth took a series of photographs of people viewing art in museums in order to capture the complexity of these kinds of art-viewing practices. These photographs, which are normally displayed within a museum or gallery, give a sense of the varied responses that ordinary people have to art. Struth took these photographs in some of the most famous museums around the world, capturing images of people gazing at, scrutinizing, and walking past famous works of art. In this image, visitors at the Hermitage Museum in St. Petersburg, Russia display a full range of responses to looking at art—turning away, listening to audio commentary without looking at the work, looking at it intently. Struth created these images with a large-format camera and displays them in the form of very large prints, effectively replicating the experience of the viewers they portray when they are exhibited in large museum spaces. These museum photographs give us a sense of the range of responses and expressions of taste that can be found in museums. They also convey, in part through their large size, the sense of presence of the large works of art on exhibition in these spaces. Struth has remarked on how art is fetishized by being exhibited in museums as great masterworks. He suggests that in this process they become dead objects, but that through viewers'

interactions with these works they can regain some of their vitality.[9] At the same time, Struth's images point to the central role that museums play in designating which images and objects are of value in any given society by determining what it is that gets displayed and by creating the conditions (majestic, pristine, grandiose, or gritty) under which works of art are displayed. Our taste is influenced not only by what we are taught to seek out and appreciate but also by how those artworks and objects are publicly exhibited.

In the 1990s, the discipline of museum studies (or museology) became a location of vibrant intellectual critique among visual culture scholars and artists interested in challenging the role of the museum in shaping taste. The systems of value imposed by museums, they held, were a means of protecting, maintaining, and hiding ruling class interests in the art market. Some of these artists began to do work later described as a form of *institutional critique*. This concept draws on writings by Michel Foucault about the function of institutions, such as asylums and prisons, in the production of particular forms of knowledge and states of being. One of the tenets of institutional critique is that institutions historically have provided structures through which power could be enacted without force or explicit directives, but rather through more passive techniques such as education, the cultivation of taste, and the cultivation of daily routines. With this focus on the institution as a structure through which power is enacted in a banal way, social critics of art and artists concerned with dynamics of power in the art market turned to the museum as a site where viewers could be interpellated with messages that reflexively drew attention to the politics of the museum itself. Viewing practices, they realized, could be disrupted as a means of undercutting the smooth trickle of standards of taste from the institution down to the viewing public.

Institutional critique can be traced back to the Dadaist interventions of Marcel Duchamp, the French artist who challenged taste and aesthetics. In the 1910s, Duchamp took a jab at the veneration of art objects with his "readymades," gallery and museum displays composed of mundane everyday objects such as a bicycle wheel. In 1917 Duchamp contributed a urinal, titled *Fountain* and signed with the pseudonym R. Mutt, to a highly publicized painting exhibition he helped to organize. The exhibition's organizers were offended by the piece and its clear message about art's value, taste, and the practices of display; they threw it out of the show Duchamp subsequently became the cause célèbre of Dada, a movement that reflexively poked fun at the conventions of high art and museum display conventions. Dada helped to inspire many movements in art that aimed to critique the art market and its valuing of art for collecting, including political art, guerrilla art, performance art and happenings, and other ephemeral kinds of art that could not be commodified in the form of valued objects.

Many of Duchamp's ideas about disrupting the art system were taken up starting in the 1960s by artists who attempted to examine museums as financial institutions and arbiters of taste. In the late 1960s, the German artist Hans Haacke, working primarily in the United States, made a number of works that famously revived this strategy of leading the viewer to question the museum's role in shaping taste. Haacke's conceptual works included an exposé of the business connections of the trustees of the Guggenheim Museum, the intended site of this work's exhibition in 1971. Although this solo exhibition was canceled by the museum's director, many other of his works of institutional critique were displayed in museums around the world. In the 1990s, artists engaged in institutional critique interrupted viewing practices through strategies that included taking on the role of the curator and reordering or disrupting the logic of display as a means of making obvious, and thereby disrupting, the formerly invisible politics and policies of the institution. To prepare for the installation *Mining the Museum* (1992–1993), the American artist Fred Wilson spent a year in residence at the staid Maryland Historical Society getting to know their collections, their exhibition practices, and the community they served. He then "mined" the museum's collection, resurrecting pieces held in storage and organizing them in a series of juxtapositions with more conventional exhibition objects. With minimal labeling, these displays relied on juxtaposition to make their point about the politics of display, concealment, and assignation of meaning and value in which this museum had engaged. Slave shackles were resurrected from storage and placed alongside a silver tea service that had previously been on display. Wilson gave lectures and tours of his exhibition. By shifting his role from the traditional one of artist as producer to that of artist as curator and docent, Wilson was able to make an intervention in the hidden politics of a museum that had remained entrenched in traditional, "neutral" exhibition practices that included the showing of works of material value (the silver tea service) and the hiding of works that made visible the shameful and ugly aspects of Southern culture and politics.

In another work of institutional critique, *Guarded View* (1991), Wilson displays life-size headless statues of museum guards, forcing viewers to ponder directly those very institutional subjects who are rendered invisible by the dynamics of the gaze at work in the museum. Whereas many of the guards in U.S. art museums are black and Latino, most of the patrons are white. This installation foregrounded the issue of race in relation to labor and marketing practices of museums. These works of figurative sculpture disrupted conventions of viewing by forcing museumgoers to notice the human presence of living guards, the very figures we are likely to ignore when we focus intently on the artworks the museum has displayed for our appreciation and scrutiny. By displaying the "invisible" figure of the guard, Wilson brings to our attention the selectivity of our gaze, which readily excludes notice of these underpaid, low-level employees who have always been fully present in the visual field of the museum gallery.

Cultures of collecting and display have also been radically transformed by the emergence of online collecting and exhibition. Thus many people create online galleries for their own images on photographic websites, artists are increasingly exhibiting and selling their work online, and collecting takes place through such websites as eBay. The critique of institutional power in relation to display has thus been paralleled by the changes taking place in cultural production and technological access. In this sense, the roles of the expert, the author, and the amateur are constantly being disrupted and reconfigured in ways that form a direct lineage back to Duchamp and readymade culture.

Reading Images as Ideological Subjects

As we often accept the idea of good taste unquestioningly, taste can be seen as a logical extension of a culture's ideology. Societies function by naturalizing ideologies, making the complex production of meaning take place so smoothly that it is experienced as a "natural" system of value or belief. As a consequence, it is easier for us to recognize the production of meanings in other times and cultures as ideological than it is to see our own meanings as ideological. Most of the time, our dominant ideologies just look to us like common sense.

Much of the way that ideology is conceived today originates with its formulation in the theories of Karl Marx. Marxism is a theory that analyzes both the role of economics in the progress of history and the ways that capitalism works in terms of class relations. According to Marx, who wrote in the nineteenth century during the rise of industrialism and capitalism in the Western world, those who own the means of production are also in control of the ideas and viewpoints produced and circulated in a society's media venues. Thus, in Marx's terms, the dominant social classes that own or control the newspaper, television, film, and communication industries are able to control the content generated by these media forms. Marx's ideas, and the ideas that they inspired in subsequent theorists, can help us understand how we interpret images as ideological subjects. Marx thought of ideology as a kind of false consciousness that was spread by dominant powers among the masses, who are coerced by those in power to mindlessly buy into the belief systems that allow industrial capitalism to thrive. Marx's idea of false consciousness, which has since been rejected as too simplistic by most contemporary theorists, emphasized the ways that people who are oppressed by a particular economic system, such as capitalism, are encouraged to believe in it anyway. Many now view his concept of ideology as overly totalizing and too focused on a top-down notion of ideology.

There have been at least two significant alterations to the traditional Marxist definition of ideology that have shaped subsequent theories about media culture and looking practices. One change came in the 1960s from Louis Althusser, whom we discussed earlier in relation to the concept of interpellation. He insisted that ideology cannot be dismissed as a simple distortion of the realities of capitalism. Rather, he argued, "ideology represents the imaginary relationship of individuals to their real conditions of existence."[10] Althusser moved the term ideology away from its association with false consciousness. His intervention at the level of thinking of this "imaginary" relationship is crucial to changing concepts of ideology, as it brings in psychological (and psychoanalytic) concepts in understanding what motivates subjects to embrace particular values. For Althusser, ideology does not simply reflect the conditions of the world, whether falsely or not. Rather, it is the case that without ideology we would have no means of thinking about or experiencing that thing we call reality. Ideology is the necessary representational means through which we come to experience and make sense of reality.

Althusser's modifications to the term ideology are crucial to the study of visual culture because they emphasize the importance of representation (and hence images) to all aspects of social life, from the economic to the cultural. By the term *imaginary*, Althusser does not mean false or mistaken ideas. Rather, he draws from psychoanalysis to emphasize that ideology is a set of ideas and beliefs shaped through the unconscious in relationship to other social forces, such as the economy and institutions. By living in society, we live in ideology, and systems of representation are the vehicles of that ideology. Althusser's theories have been especially useful in film studies, in which they helped theorists to analyze how media texts invite people to recognize themselves and identify with a position of authority or omniscience while watching films.

Althusser's concepts of ideology have been influential, but they can be seen as disempowering as well. If we are always already defined as subjects and are interpellated to be who we are, then there is little hope for individuality or social change. In other words, the idea that we are already constructed as subjects does not allow us to feel that we have any agency in our lives. Althusser's concept of interpellation contains within it a restrictive sense of individual agency. Ideologies speak to us and in the process recruit us as "authors"; thus we become/are the subject that we are addressed as. In Althusser's terms, we are not so much unique individuals but rather are "always already" subjects—spoken by the ideological discourses into which we are born and in which are asked to find our place. This means that in his model, the different modalities of interpellation that we described at the beginning of this chapter would not be possible.

It is important for us to think in terms of ideologies, in the plural. The concept of a singular mass ideology makes it difficult to recognize how people in economically and socially disadvantaged positions really do challenge or resist dominant ideology. Long before Althusser, an Italian Marxist, Antonio Gramsci, had already introduced the concept of hegemony in place of the concept of domination in order to help us to think about this kind of resistance. Within visual studies, Gramsci's concept of hegemony has been useful among critics who want to emphasize the role of image consumers in influencing the meanings and uses of popular culture in ways that do not benefit the interests of producers and the media industry. Gramsci wrote mostly during the 1920s and 1930s in Italy, but his ideas became highly influential in the late twentieth century. There are two central aspects to Gramsci's definition of hegemony that concern us: that dominant ideologies are often presented as "common sense" and that dominant ideologies are in tension with other forces and constantly in flux.

The term *hegemony* emphasizes that power is not wielded by one class over another; rather, power is negotiated among all classes of people. Unlike domination, which is won by the ruling class through force, hegemony is enacted through the push and pull among all levels of a society. No single class of people "has" hegemony; rather, hegemony is a state or condition of a culture arrived at through negotiations over meanings, laws, and social relationships. Similarly, no one group of people ultimately "has" power; rather, power is a relationship within which classes of people struggle. One of the most important aspects of hegemony is that these relationships are constantly changing; hence dominant ideologies must constantly be reaffirmed in a culture precisely because people can work against them. This concept also allows counter-hegemonic forces, such as political movements or subversive cultural elements, to emerge and to question the status quo. The concept of hegemony and the related term *negotiation* allow us to acknowledge the role that people may play in challenging the status quo and effecting social change in ways that may not favor the interests of the marketplace.

How can Gramsci's concepts of hegemony and counter-hegemony help us to understand how people create and make meaning of images? In her work, the American artist Barbara Kruger takes "found" photographic images and adds text to give these images ironic meanings. In this example, created in 1981, Kruger took a well-known image of the atomic bomb, changing its meaning by adding text. The image of an atomic bomb indicates a broad set of ideologies, from the spectacle of high technology to anxiety about its tremendous capacity to destroy, that depend on the context in which the image is viewed. It could be argued that the bomb itself and images of it are indicative of a particular set of ideological assumptions that emerged from the Cold War about the rights of nations to build destructive weapons and the so-called need to create more and more destructive weapons in the name of protecting one's county. In the 1940s and 1950s, an image of the bomb was thus likely to uphold many ideas about the primacy of Western science and technology and the role of the United States and the Soviet Union as superpowers. Produced close to the end of the twentieth century, however, this image clearly criticizes the existence of nuclear weapons throughout the world.

Kruger used text in this image to comment on these ideological assumptions about Western science. Who is the "you" of this image? We could say that Kruger is speaking to those with power, perhaps those who helped to create the atomic bomb and those who approved it. But she is also speaking in a larger sense to the "you" of Western science and philosophy that allowed a maniacal idea (bombing people) to acquire the validation of rational science. In this work, the image is awarded new meaning through the bold, accusatory statement spread across it and the red frame placed around it. Here, the text dictates the meaning of the image and provokes the viewer, in often oblique ways, to look at it differently. Kruger's work functions as a counter-hegemonic statement about the dominant ideology of science.

It is important, when thinking about ideologies and how they function, to keep in mind the complicated interactions of powerful systems of belief and the things that very different kinds of viewers bring to their experiences. If we give too much weight to the idea of a dominant ideology, we risk portraying viewers as cultural dupes who can be "force fed" ideas and values. At the same time, if we overemphasize the potential array of interpretations viewers can make of any given image, we can make it seem as if all viewers have the power to interpret images any way they want and that these interpretations will be meaningful in their social world. In this perspective, we would lose any sense of dominant power and its attempt to organize our ways of looking. Meanings of images are created in a complex relationship among producer, viewer, image or text, and social context, and the negotiation of meaning is a key factor in that relationship. Because meanings are produced out of this relationship, there are limits to the interpretive agency of any one member of this group.

Encoding and Decoding

All images are encoded with meanings in their creation and production that is decoded by viewers. In a well-known essay titled "Encoding, Decoding," Stuart Hall has written that there are three positions that viewers can take as decoders of cultural images and artifacts:

1. **Dominant-hegemonic reading.** They can identify with the hegemonic position and receive the dominant message of an image or text (such as a television show) in an unquestioning manner.
2. **Negotiated reading.** They can negotiate an interpretation from the image and its dominant meanings.
3. **Oppositional reading.** Finally, they can take an oppositional position, either by completely disagreeing with the ideological position embodied in an image or rejecting it altogether (for example, by ignoring it).[11]

Viewers who take the dominant-hegemonic position can be said to decode images in a relatively passive manner. But it can be argued that few viewers actually consume images in this manner, because there is no mass culture that can satisfy all viewers' culturally specific experiences, memories, and desires. The second and third positions, negotiation and opposition, are more useful and deserve further explanation.

The term *negotiation* invokes the process of trade. We can think of it as a kind of bargaining over meaning that takes place among viewer, image, and context. We use the term negotiation in a metaphorical sense to say that we often "haggle" with the dominant meanings of an image when we interpret it. The process of deciphering an image always takes place at both the conscious and unconscious levels. It brings into play our own memories, knowledge, and cultural frameworks, as well as the image itself and the dominant meanings that cling to it. Interpretation is thus a mental process of acceptance and rejection of the meanings and associations that adhere to a given image through the force of dominant ideologies.

In this process, viewers actively struggle with dominant meanings, allowing culturally and personally specific meanings to transform and even override the meanings imposed by producers and broader social forces. The term negotiation allows us to see how cultural interpretation is a struggle in which consumers are active meaning-makers and not merely passive recipients in the process of decoding images.

Let's consider how this might work with a particular product of popular culture, such as the *Idol* series. Originally begun as *Pop Idol* in Britain, the *Idol* television program now has versions in more than thirty countries, many of them designated nationally, such as *American Idol, Australian Idol, Deutschland such den Superstar* (Germany), and *Philippine Idol*. What would a dominant reading of the *Idol* series entail, considering that so many local versions exist? The ideological basis of the series, clearly an element in its enormous popularity, is the idea that ordinary people can rise to stardom and celebrity purely on the basis of their talent, which is sometimes presented as "natural" rather than acquired or learned. Watching the show is also about the pleasures (both generous and sadistic) in seeing people succeed, fail, and be subjected to often withering criticism from the panel of expert judges. In those versions of the series that are nationally coded, such as *Australian Idol*, the show also conveys a set of values about national identity, designating the winner as somehow emblematic of national values and taste. Versions, such as *American Idol*, that involve audience voting for contestants embody a set of ideological beliefs about democracy, encouraging the idea that voting in the show (which is usually done as a part of a product placement deal for a particular telephone service) is like voting in political elections. Finally, a dominant reading of the show would be that ordinary people have the same opportunities to be rewarded for their talent as those who have the advantages of wealth and social capital as means to building fame.

The *Idol* programs have been enormously popular and the source of much public discussion and debate. Most viewers watching these shows throughout the world interpret them not with an uncritical dominant reading but in a negotiated reading, agreeing with some elements of the shows' message and critiquing others. The decision in the 2008 season of *American Idol* to include Carly Smithson, the former recipient of a major record label contract under her former name (Carly Hennessy), in the roster of finalists was criticized by viewers who saw the show as a venue for undiscovered talent and not a place for an unsuccessful recording artist to get a second chance. As we discuss in chapter 7, *American Idol* has been ridiculed for its blatant product placement (large Coca-Cola glasses line the judges' table, labels facing the camera). A negotiated reading of the show might see the *Idol* shows as entertainment that offers an image of success that is blatantly obvious to viewers as fantasy, as constructed mythology. An oppositional reading of the shows might interpret reality television programming in general as a means for television industries to create cheap programming without having to pay the high fees of known performers and scriptwriters. Such an oppositional critique might also interpret the show as an example of the myth that everyone has equal opportunity to succeed, when in fact it is fundamental to the structure of capitalism that only a few achieve power, wealth, and fame.

Reception and the Audience

Of the three different modes of engagement with popular culture introduced by Stuart Hall (dominant-hegemonic, negotiated, and oppositional), the category of oppositional readings raises perhaps the most complicated set of questions. Hall's theory has been criticized for reducing what viewers do to three positions, when in fact the viewing practices of most viewers fall along a continuum of negotiated meanings. Nevertheless, it is important to ask: What does it mean to read a television show or a media image in an oppositional way? Does it make any difference that individual viewers may often read against the intended meaning of an image? The lone oppositional reading of a single viewer may mean nothing compared with the popularity of a particular cultural product on the basis of its dominant shared meanings. This consideration raises the important issue of power: Whose readings matter, and how and when do subjugated or minority readings come to matter? There are many ways in which negotiated and oppositional readings of popular culture demonstrate the complicated dance of power relations in contemporary societies, the tension of hegemonic and counter-hegemonic forces.

When we are considering viewer responses to cultural texts, we are looking at the question of reception. Reception theory has for the most part looked at the practices of individual viewers in interpreting and making meaning from watching and consuming cultural products. Entertainment and marketing industries gauge audience responses in many ways. Nielsen audience ratings have historically measured the number of viewers watching television shows (through viewing logs and electronic devices), although these practices are now largely questioned as television viewing has declined. Industries often expend significant amounts of money doing focus-group and marketing research to find out what viewer-consumers think of different shows, advertisements, and products. Marketing research uses an increasingly complex array of techniques, from surveys to consumer-viewer blogging and diaries to consumer-generated videos, as well as significant amounts of quantitative data about viewership and consumer purchases, to attempt to gauge viewer-consumer interest.

Scholarly reception studies differ from audience studies in that they focus on viewers, not audiences. Scholars who undertake reception studies typically rely on ethnographic methods, interviewing actual viewers to try to get a sense of the meaning they take away from a particular cultural product. For instance, in the 1980s, British researcher David Morley used Hall's model of encoding–decoding as a framework for focus group research to study viewers of the BBC television show *Nationwide*; Janice Radway studied women who read romance novels as a kind of "interpretive community" through interviews and participant observation; and Ien Ang used letters from viewers of *Dallas* to explore the meaning of the television show for Dutch viewers.[12]

Most viewer-consumers make meaning from cultural products by watching and interpreting them. Yet, particularly with the advent of a broad array of computer technologies, the Web, iPods, cell phone imaging, and the capacity to easily upload digital and video images to websites such as YouTube, many people have access to the technical means to produce images and cultural products. Nevertheless, the fact remains that the vast amount of cultural production and image production is done through the entertainment and business industries, which are also increasingly skilled in infiltrating amateur media and finding ways to profit from it. We discuss the cultural production of fans and viewers in the next section. Here, we attempt to make clear the complexity of that process of viewing and interpreting.

As we have noted, viewers are not simply passive recipients of the intended message of public images and cultural products such as films and television shows. They have a variety of means by which to engage with images and make meaning from them. This negotiation with popular culture is referred to as "the art of making do," a phrase that implies that although viewers may not be able to change the cultural products they observe, they can "make do" by interpreting, rejecting, or reconfiguring the cultural texts they see. An oppositional reading can take the form of dismissal or rejection—turning off the TV set, declaring boredom, or turning the page. But it can also take the form of making do with, or making a new use for, the objects and artifacts of a culture. As viewers, we can appropriate images and texts (films, television shows, news images, and advertisements), strategically altering their meanings to suit our purposes. As we explained earlier, however, meanings are determined through a complex negotiation among viewers, producers, texts, and contexts. Hence images themselves can be said to resist the oppositional readings that some viewers may wish to confer on them. In other words, meanings that oppose the dominant reading of an image may not "cling" to an image with the same tenacity as meanings that are more in line with dominant ideologies.

The kind of negotiation of meaning that goes on when viewers engage with images can thus be seen as a fluid and complex process. It is for this reason that Hall's tripartite formulation has since begun to seem too reductive and fixed. Reading and viewing can be seen as highly active and individual processes, even as readers and viewers do them within the confines of the dominant meanings of culture. This strategy was famously called *textual poaching* by French literary and cultural theorist Michel de Certeau. Textual poaching was described by de Certeau as inhabiting a text "like a rented apartment."[13] In other words, viewers of popular culture can "inhabit" that text by negotiating meanings through it and creating new cultural products in response to it, making it their own. De Certeau saw reading texts and images as a series of advances and retreats, of tactics and games, through which readers can fragment and reassemble texts with as simple a strategy as a television remote control.

De Certeau saw the relationship of readers/writers and producers/viewers as an ongoing struggle for possession of the text—a struggle over its meaning and potential meanings. This notion operates in opposition to the educational training that teaches readers to search for the author's intended meanings and to leave a text unmarked by their own fingerprints, so to speak. However, this is a process steeped in the unequal power relations that exist between those who produce dominant popular culture and those who consume it. De Certeau defined strategies as the means through which institutions exercise power and set up well-ordered systems that consumers must negotiate (the programming schedule of television, for instance), and he defined tactics as the "hit and run" acts of random engagement by viewers/consumers to usurp these systems, which might include everything from using a remote control to change the "text" of television to creating a website that analyzes a particular film or TV show. De Certeau examined in particular the kinds of tactics used by workers to feel just a small amount of agency during their working day—doing personal activities during work hours, for instance, or even engaging in low-level office sabotage by "helping" office machines to malfunction.

Reading and viewing are thus processes of give and take. One example of negotiated looking is the technique of reading lesbian or gay subtexts in movies that feature gender-bending (bending the traditional codes of gender roles and sexual norms) performances or same-sex friendships. Films starring Marlene Dietrich, a well-known film star of the 1920s and 1930s, for example, have a cult following among lesbian viewers interested in appropriating Dietrich's sometimes gender-bending performances for the underconsidered history of lesbian and gay film culture. In the 1930 film *Morocco*, Dietrich, who was an icon of glamour in her time, dresses in a man's tuxedo and kisses another woman. Her films have been widely noted as depictions that are open for interpretation within the terms of lesbian desire as a queer reading of the films as texts.

Another example of oppositional viewing is the affirmation of qualities within genres previously regarded as exploitative or insulting to a group. The blaxploitation "B movie" film genre, for example, has been widely noted for its negative representations of black culture during the 1970s, with such stereotypes as the black male stud, gangster, and pimp. Yet, more recently, this genre has been revived to emphasize the evidence these films provide of valuable aspects of black culture and talent during the 1970s. Not only did these films star black actors, but they also were the first to include soundtracks that featured black music (funk and soul). Pam Grier, the star of numerous prison dramas and blaxploitation films of the 1970s, such as the *Foxy Brown* (a flim that preceded the contemporary rap performer of this name), reemerged in the cinema in the lead role of *Jackie Brown*, director Quentin Tarantino's 1997 homage to the blaxploitation genre. We can say, then, that this genre has been appropriated, its meanings strategically transformed to create an alternative view of representations of blackness in film.

These forms of making do and appropriation for political empowerment can also be found at the level of language. Social movements sometimes take terms that are derogatory and reuse them in empowering ways. This process is called transcoding. In the 1960s, the phrase "Black is beautiful" was used by the civil rights and black power movements as a means to reappropriate the term black and change its meaning from a negative to positive one. Similarly, in recent decades, the term queer, which was traditionally used to insult gays, has been transcoded as a cultural identity to be embraced and proudly declared.

One of the terms that can help us to understand the kinds of signifying practices that people use to make sense of culture is *bricolage*. Bricolage is a mode of adaptation in which things (mostly commodities) are put to uses for which they were not intended and in ways that dislocate them from their normal or expected context. It derives from a French term used by anthropologist Claude Levi-Strauss to mean "making do," or creatively making use of whatever materials are at hand, and it loosely translates to the idea of do-it-yourself culture. In the late 1970s, cultural theorist Dick Hebdige applied the term *bricolage* to the practices of youth subcultures such as punk, and the way they took ordinary commodities and gave them new stylistic meanings.[14] The use of household safety pins as a form of body decoration by punks in the 1970s is the iconic example of bricolage, in which a safety pin that would have previously signified a simple fastener became recoded as a form of body decoration that signaled a refusal to participate in mainstream (parent) culture and disdain for the norms of everyday consumer culture. Hebdige called these kinds of moves *signifying practices* in order to emphasize that they do not simply borrow commodities from their original context but rather give them new meanings, so that, in the terminology of semiotics, they create new signs.

The concept of bricolage and Hebdige's influential use of it focused on youth subcultures of the 1970s and 1980s and the kinds of fashion, music, and style statements they were making, mostly on the street. Hebdige defined a youth subculture as a group that distinguished itself from mainstream culture through various aspects of its style that are assembled by participants from various "found" items whose meanings are altered. Doc Martens, for example, were originally created in the 1940s as orthopedic shoes and sold in Britain in the 1960s as work boots, but they were appropriated to become key elements in various subcultures from the 1970s onward, such as punk, AIDS activism, neopunk, and grunge. The Carhart brand of denim clothing, also originating as blue-collar work gear, became popular among youths favoring the hip-hop look during the 1990s. Cultural theorist Angela McRobbie has examined the ways in which the "ragmarket" of used clothing, begun in the 1990s, has allowed young people to create new styles by mining styles of the past.[15] McRobbie argues that women have played a central role as both entrepreneurial street sellers and as consumers in fostering complex styles of retro fashion, the appropriation of work clothes, and the use of men's clothing, such as formal dress suits and long underwear (as leggings) to create styles that were then appropriated by mainstream fashion.

The subcultures that Hebdige and other theorists of that time were writing about were mostly white working-class male subcultures, and since that time, subculture style (and analyses of it) has undergone many transformations. For participants in fashion subcultures, the remaking of style through appropriation of historical objects and images can be a political statement about class, ethnic, and cultural identity. Many young people assert their defiance of mainstream culture specifically by developing styles that do not conform to the "good taste" of mainstream culture. Chicano "lowriders," for instance, enact style with their cars, which are named and decorated with paintings of Mexican figures and history, remodeled to both rise up and drive slowly, and refashioned like living spaces. As cultural theorist George Lipsitz notes, the lowrider car defies utilitarianism; it is about cruising for display, codes of ethnic pride, and defying mainstream car culture. He writes, "Low riders are themselves masters of postmodern cultural manipulation. They juxtapose seemingly inappropriate realities—fast cars designed to go slowly, 'improvements' that flaunt their impracticality, like chandeliers instead of overhead lights. They encourage a bi-focal perspective—they are made to be watched but only after adjustments have been made to provide ironic and playful commentary on prevailing standard of automobile design."[16] In remaking these cars so that they defy their design functions and in painting their cars so that they are works of art incorporating meanings from Mexican culture, lowriders produce cultural and political statements in defiance of mainstream Anglo culture. The radical intervention of this culture can be seen in the ways that it has prompted the response of law enforcement, with the creation of laws in the United States that make it illegal to drive too slowly on certain roads after lowriders made it a regular Saturday-night activity to drive at minimal speeds (impeding traffic) down the main streets of certain towns and cities such as Los Angeles. Similarly, skateboard culture, which has at various times intersected with punk culture and hip-hop culture, is associated more broadly with youth and has produced an array of antiskating ordinances restricting its practice in certain locations or the use of metal barriers in public spaces to make it difficult to practice there.

In contemporary urban centers such as New York, Los Angeles, and London, much of fashion is seen as specifically ethnic in its significations, with the prominence of Latino and hip-hop subculture street fashion, such as low-slung chinos, do-rags, platform shoes, gold chains, skull-and-bones insignia, and hoodies filtering out to a range of youth consumers beyond the ethnic groups with which these styles were originally associated. Subculture style is evident not simply in fashion and hairstyles but also in styles of body marking, such as tattoos and piercings, that have become far more mainstream forms of self-expression in Western urban culture in the twenty-first century than they were in the twentieth. The rapid cooptation and marketing of styles signifying resistance makes the idea of individual expression through alternative clothing styles a complicated process for youths committed to independent expression and resistance to the mainstream values promoted through the clothing lines marketed to mall culture and chain stores.

At the same time, the early 2000s saw a notable upsurge of independent retailers specializing in youth-produced independent clothing and retail goods ranging from magazines and toys to housewares and beauty products. Giant Robot is a five-store chain of boutiques launched by *Giant Robot* magazine editors Eric Nakamura and Martin Wong in the late 1990s. It sells indie designer clothing, toys, fine art and art books in the genres of lowbrow, pop surrealism, and Tokyo pop—including the work of Dalek (aka James Marshall), Elizabeth McGrath, Yuko Marada, Marcel Dzama, Tabaimo, and Chiho Aoshima, whose print *The Rebirth of a Snake Woman* depicts the passage of a woman through the digestive tract of a python from which she reemerges anew. The store and magazine take their name from the Giant Robot era of Japanese animated cartoons. Poketo is a Los Angles independent merchandising team that was founded in 2003 by Ted Vatakan and Angie Myung to market the designs of seventy independent contemporary pop artists on affordable necessities such as wallets, bags, T-shirts, plastic (notably dishwasher-safe) dishes, and stationery. The success of these ventures rests not on some hoped-for corporate buyout but on the identification of an alternative global and transcultural youth market that seeks out independent labels and products as a matter of personal aesthetics and a politics of consumptions that favors small business and independent expression.

Distinctions between subculture fashion and mainstream fashion have become increasingly blurred—for instance, in the hip-hop community, a mixing of different styles has become quite common, with traditionally preppy brands, such as Tommy Hilfiger and Polo, becoming popular among hip-hop celebrities and their fans. The wearing of heavy gold chains and of fashions associated with the wealthy preppy classes by many hip-hop performers signified access to the goods and codes of the upper classes. These subcultures do not fit the model of working against consumer culture and mainstream value. Rather, they are complexly appropriative, buying into the system while creating codes of irony through exaggeration of scale that are intended to signify resistance to it. Many hip-hop stars have become fashion designers themselves, creating brands that market a range of styles that would otherwise be coded as upper-class fashion. It is too simple to say that these kinds of moves are "selling out." Rather, they form new kinds of negotiations over cultural forms and power. Such trends call into question simple hierarchies of taste: symbols of upper-class taste are appropriated by subcultures, and subculture styles gain taste and cultural capital and in turn become valuable to monied classes. These kinds of dynamics create new signs, in semiotic terms, for a critique of class status and knowledge. Not only does this demonstrate the degree to which traditional notions of class difference no longer hold in the same way today, but it also shows how cultural capital, in particular the knowledge of culture, has been dramatically reconfigured at a time when knowledge of hip-hop culture, for instance, might be valued across social strata just as knowledge of classical music might be. Cultural capital can trickle up as well as down.

Appropriation and Cultural Production

Thus far, we have been discussing the negotiated process of reading and viewing, yet the negotiation over the meaning of texts can also take the form of cultural production. There is a long history, for instance, of artists appropriating particular texts of art or popular culture in order to make a political statement; of fans of particular shows engaging with those by remaking the texts into new productions, and, increasingly in the context of Web media, of viewer-consumers actively engaging with advertising, popular culture, and news media images by remaking them into new kinds of texts with altered meanings. The term *appropriation* is traditionally defined as taking something for oneself without consent. Cultural appropriation is the process of "borrowing" and changing the meaning of cultural products, slogans, images, or elements of fashion.

Cultural appropriation has been used quite effectively by artists seeking to make a statement that opposes the dominant ideology. Thus an image that appropriates a famous image can have a kind of doubled meaning, building on its reversal of the original that it remakes. This image by photographer Gordon Parks, *Ella Watson* (1942), makes a statement by referring to the well-know 1930 painting *American Gothic*, by Grant Wood, of an American farming couple standing holding a pitchfork before a classic wooden farmhouse. *American Gothic* has been the source of innumerable remakes, many of them humorous commentaries on changing social values in the United States. Parks's image, however, taken before the emergence of the civil rights movement, is a bitter commentary on the discrepancy between the codes of this black woman office cleaner, holding her broom and mop before an American flag, and the puritan codes of Americana in the *American Gothic* icon. Most important, by playing off the well-known codes of the American Gothic image, Parks pointed to the fact that not all Americans were included in its mythic image. As Steven Biel writes, Parks ensured that "the normative whiteness of the now iconic *American Gothic* did not go unrecognized and unchallenged."[17] It is precisely the strategy of appropriation that allows Parks's image to make this larger statement about social exclusion and inequality.

Strategies of appropriation have often been key to political art. A good example is the public art of Gran Fury, an art collective formed in 1987 (named after the Plymouth car then favored by undercover police) that produced posters, performances, installations, and videos alerting people to facts about AIDS and HIV that public health officials refused to publicize. One of their posters advertised a 1988 demonstration, a "kiss in" intended to publicly dispel the myth that kissing transmits the AIDS virus. The phrase "read my lips," which refers to the posters image of two women about to kiss, was appropriated from a much-discussed slogan in the presidential campaign of President George H. W. Bush. His slogan was "read my lips, no new taxes." In "lifting" the phrase "read my lips" and placing it with images about homosexual contact, Gran Fury suggested that the phrase had meanings that Bush and his campaign advisors clearly did not intend. Gran Fury's appropriation gives the poster a biting political humor, making it both a playful twist of words and an accusation at the time against a president who was overtly homophobic and helped to lead a political denial of the seriousness of the AIDS epidemic that had tragic consequences.

These strategies of appropriation in art, which have been integral to various movements of modern art, also emerged as part of fan cultures in the 1980s and 1990s. Before the Web created a forum for the sharing of images and video, fan cultures of certain television shows and series would meet at conventions, rewrite episodes of the shows, and reedit (sometimes crudely on rudimentary video equipment) episodes to change their meaning.[18] Analysis of these fan cultures often used de Certeau's concepts of "textual poaching" to talk about how these viewers remade the shows in order both to change their meaning and to affirm their fan status (as viewers who are authoritative about the show, seeing themselves as more knowing than the producers themselves). Most famous of these 1980s fan cultures was the "slash fiction" culture of fans of the science fiction television series Star Trek, who would rewrite scenes from the show and reedit episodes of the show to depict a romantic and erotic relationship between the characters of Spock and Captain Kirk (the term "slash" connotes the combining of the two characters' names to indicate their pairing, as in Spock/Kirk). These fan cultures expanded into numerous other shows and strategies, though the rereading of screen relationships through new sexual desires is a primary theme. Analysis of this kind of cultural production saw them as emblematic of de Certeau's concept of "poaching" in that they "make do" with the original popular culture texts, yet use them to make new kinds of scenarios that depend on the original texts for their new meanings.

These kinds of fan productions signaled the beginning of what would become a much more significant cultural trend with the rise of Web media that allow Web users to create their own websites, use Web cameras to create streaming video, rework and remake television episodes, ads, and news images, and parody media and popular culture in general. Much of the vast array of cultural production by people who would have traditionally been thought of as "amateurs" is playful and humorous, with little social or political critique. These image cultures circulate largely though social networks in which people recommend videos to their friends via e-mail and social networking sites such as Facebook and in which Web media sites such as YouTube recommend videos to viewers. In these online contexts, users are increasingly deploying images (often uploading images daily from their cell phones) to define their public profiles and construct their identities. These social networks have also become primary resources and outlets for marketers, who are constantly creating new strategies to tap into them, and who use them to target networked, plugged-in youth consumers.

In many ways, the proliferation of digital (moving and still) images on the Web has replaced the role played by images in the street, such as the Gran Fury poster we discussed earlier. As people increasingly upload their personal images onto public websites and use images to define themselves through their Web pages, and as search programs make finding certain kinds of images on the Web easy, the circulation of images on the Web has dramatically accelerated. Yet there remains a street culture of political art in some major cities, and this was clear when an artist or artist collective in New York, going by the pseudonym of Copper Greene waged a guerrilla campaign in 2004 by putting up numerous posters on the street and in the subways that used the well-known iPod campaign to comment on the then-recent revelations of the atrocities committed by U.S. soldiers in Iraq at the Abu Ghraib prison. Copper Greene (which took the pseudonym from the Pentagon, code name for detainee operations in Iraq) managed in this campaign to create a new set of meanings with the most well-known of the Abu Ghraib images, that of a man standing hooded on a box with electrical wires attached to his hands (see fig. 6.17). Reportedly the man had been told that he would be shocked by electricity if he moved or lowered his arms.[19] The posters replaced the iPod slogan "iPod: 10,000 songs in your pocket" with the tagline "iRaq: 10,000 volts in your pocket, guilty or innocent." In placing the posters near and within actual iPod ads, Copper Greene succeeded in subtly getting pedestrians to do double takes and in creating a critique not only of the use of torture in military prisons, but also of advertising culture and consumer culture in general. (We discuss the Abu Ghraib images more fully in chapter 6 and the iPod campaign and culture jams at more length in chapter 7.) Thus the meaning of the work is a demand not only to recognize the Abu Ghraib image as integral to the "home front" of the war but also to make connections between the culture of the Iraq War and consumer culture in the United States. The white wires of the iPod advertising campaign become the electric wires of torture to critique the way in which iPod culture (with headphones that shut us off from the surrounding environments) reflects an insular consumer culture, one that has allowed U.S. citizens to disavow the war and their complicity in it. Copper Greene's campaign affirms that the street remains a site of contested intents and meanings.

It is not incidental to the Copper Greene campaign that it had a second life on the Web after the city and the Metropolitan Transit Authority took down the posters. Photographs of the iRaq/iPod images, some of them showing it inserted into billboards of numerous iPod ads, circulated on the Web, and the poster was eventually included in an art book about the design of dissent.[20] The image thus continued to resonate on the "street" context of the Web, gaining a more global audience just as the Abu Ghraib images themselves circulated out of the control of any of the players in that incident in a very short time.

Reappropriation and Counter-Bricolage

Appropriation is not always an oppositional practice. The study of fan cultures has been critiqued precisely because it is often difficult to ascertain what counts as "resistant" when producers are at the ready to incorporate fan ideas into their product lines and shows. In an age when marketers are actively selling a broad range of brands as hip and cool, the appropriation of alternative cultures and subcultures by mainstream producers and fashion designers has never been more prevalent.[21] Since marketers began to borrow the concepts of the counterculture of the 1960s to sell products as youthful and hip, there has been a constant mining of youth cultures and marginal subcultures for mainstream fashion and other products. (We discuss aspects of the marketing of coolness at more length in chapter 7.) Most obviously, one of the consequences of these kinds of trends is that commodities that had been appropriated by subcultures through bricolage lose their political meaning when they are reappropriated and marketed to the mainstream. The vintage thrift store clothing fashions originally associated with oppositional youth culture were, in turn, reappropriated by the mainstream fashion industry, which capitalized on the market for inexpensive and widely available knockoffs of vintage fashions. Although Doc Martens work boots in the early 1990s might have signaled an association with AIDS activism or the values of neopunk culture, within a few years they had become respectable everyday shoes for a wide range of consumers, bearing no clear political significance beyond being somewhat fashionable. Their revival, along with other punk fashions, in the early 2000s may or may not invoke the legacy of the shoe as a symbol of activism, depending on the wearer's knowledge and interests.

This process of appropriation by mainstream marketers and producers has been termed "counter-bricolage" by Robert Goldman and Stephen Papson.[22] This process, by which the counter-hegemonic bricolage strategies of marginal cultures are reappropriated by mainstream designers and marketers and then parlayed into mainstream designs that signal "coolness," is thus counter to the intent of the bricolage strategy. Of course, as the example of hip-hop makes clear, appropriating strategies works back and forth to the point at which the distinction between the margins and the mainstream is increasingly unclear. For instance, the street style of wearing boxer shorts visibly above one's pants that emerged in the 1990s then produced a fashion trend for designer boxer shorts, in which Calvin Klein and other designers began marketing high-end designer boxer shorts. Calvin Klein marketed this new men's underwear in an ad campaign that borrowed codes from Greco-Roman images of men bonding in homosocial contexts. Similarly, designers use signifiers of hip culture, such as tattoos and body piercings, in fashion photos as a means of creating signs of coolness. In this Juicy Couture ad (fig. 2.20), tattoos, previously a signifier of countercultural status, are appropriated to signify being on the cutting edge of fashion—by a highly mass-marketed brand.

The marketing of the qualities of hipness and cool points to how the class-based categories of high and low culture have been rendered meaningless. The signifiers of youth street culture are marketed to middle- and upper-class consumers so they can look edgy. The signifiers of inner-city ethnic subcultures are marketed to white consumers with the promise of conferring hip insider status. Mainstream culture, through the processes of hegemony and counter-hegemony, is constantly mining the margins of culture for new sources of meaning—and new styles for making money. The culture industries are constantly establishing what is new style by mining the margins, and subcultures on the margins are always reinventing themselves by appropriating from mass culture and from other margins.

What are the consequences of this kind of cultural circulation of meaning? On one hand, we could see this as evidence of the complexity of cultural signs, the way that semiotic meaning can easily be remade, reworked, and reconfigured in new cultural contexts. Yet this also means that important ideals and concepts can become what are known as "free-floating" signifiers, floating through cultural domains with little grounded meaning. Take, for instance, the trend of fashion designers to use particular concepts as brand names, with the creation of brands such as "Theory" and "Ideology." Calling a clothing brand Ideology suggests a use of concept reflexively to

draw our attention to the ways ideology draws us into consumption. But the fact that this message is used by a brand that successfully encourages consumption makes the message benign. Signifiers of cultural critique are emptied of their potential effects as agents of change when they are used by major brands themselves.

Cultural meaning is highly fluid and ever changing, the result of complex interactions among images, producers, cultural products, and readers/viewers/consumers. The meaning of images emerges through these processes of interpretation, engagement, and negotiation. Importantly, this means that culture is not a set of objects that are valued in some way but a set of processes through which meaning is constantly made and remade through the interactions of objects and peoples. We might look to new designers and business owners such as Nakamura and Wong, the entrepreneurs of the Giant Robot magazine and retail store chain, as offering a way of living one's life with everyday art and artifacts designed to intervene in the dynamics of consumption on a small scale for a globalized niche demographic of consumers. This can be seen as a way of making an intervention in the corporate politics of mass media production and in the art market politics of high-culture aesthetic reverence. If in the 1990s institutional critique was expressed in the form of artists such as Fred Wilson, who "mined the museum" to exhibit old work to make new meanings, in the 2000s creative producers such as Nakamura and Wong engage in a new iteration of institutional critique, changing the marketing of "good taste" by creating commercial venues that combine the popular magazine, the fine art gallery, the retail clothing store, the small book merchant, and the kitsch tchotchke shop into one emporium. In doing so, these new entrepreneurs challenge the worn dichotomies of high and low culture, of mainstream and resistant culture, of good and bad taste, making art into an affordable form of everyday consumption for everyday youth culture. They also give the corporate conglomerate a run for the money by turning synergy on its head, maximizing connections across forms and genres on a small and human scale. Their products engage youth in everyday ways in the ideal of being both producers and consumers of culture without apology and in practices of looking that are not reactively resistant but instead are actively productive of new cultural forms that resist corporate and institutional cooptation.

As this chapter has shown, we have moved beyond the moment of the death of the author heralded by Barthes into an era in which we might speak about the death of the producer. The new modes embraced by youth culture consumers are about networks, connections, and aggregation-using websites and social networking to link to their interests and friends, and blogs to create networks about their style choices and social concerns. The viewer or consumer has emerged as the locus of creative production, in the performative guise of the anonymous corporate investment manager, as the example of RTMark illustrates, as a curator who reorders art and artifact to make new meanings, and as the purveyor of small-market lifestyle art for everyday youth who cannot afford "high" art and would not even want it. Just as the identification of the locus of creative production of meaning was, for Barthes, relocated from writer to reader, so it was again relocated, in the late twentieth century, to the less glamorous work of the viewer as manager, marketer, and bricoleur of visual culture's products. The viewer who makes meaning does so not only through describing an experience with images but also through reordering, redisplaying, and reusing images in new and differently meaningful ways in the reordering of everyday life.

Notes

1. See John Ellis, "Channel 4: Working Notes," Screen, 14.6, (1983) 37–51, citation from page 49.

2. Roland Barthes, "The Death of the Author," in Image, Music, Text, trans. Stephen Heath, 142–48 (New York: Hill and Wang. 1978).

3. Michel Foucault, "What is an Author?" trans. Donald F. Bouchard and Sherry Simon, in Language, Counter-Memory, Practice, 124–27 (Ithaca, N. Y.: Cornell University Press, 1977).

4. Nicholas Mirzoeff, "The Subject of Visual Culture," in The Visual Culture Reader 2nd ed., ed. Nicholas Mirzoeff, 3 (New York: Routledge, 2002).

5. Encyclopaedia Britannica Online, s.v. "Globalization, cultural," www.britannica.com/eb/article. 225011 (accessed March 2008).

6. Clement Greenberg, "Avant-Garde and Kitsch," in Clement Greenberg: The Collected Essays and Criticism, Vol. I, Perceptions and Judgments, 1939–1944, ed. John O'Brian, 5–22 (Chicago: University of Chicago Press, [1939] 1986).

7. See JoAnn Wypijewski, ed., Painting by Numbers: Komar and Melamid's Scientific Guide to Art, 6–7 (New York: Farrar, Strauss, & Giroux, 1997).

8. Pierre Bourdieu, Distinction: A Social Critique of the Judgement of Taste, trans. Richard Nice, 6 (Cambridge, Mass.: Harvard University Press, 1984).

9. Phyllis Tuchman, "On Thomas Struth's Museum Photographs,'" Artnet.com, July 8, 2003.

10. Louis Althusser, "Ideology and Ideological State Apparatuses," in Lenin and Philosophy and other Essays, trans. Ben Brewster, 162 (London: Monthly Review Press, 1971).

11. Stuart Hall, "Encoding, Decoding," in The Cultural Studies Reader, ed. Simon During, 90–103 (New York: Routledge,1993).

12. David Morley, The Nationwide Audience (London: British Film institute, 1980) and Television, Audiences, and Cultural Studies (New York: Routledge, 1992); Janice Radway, Reading the Romance: Women, Patriarchy, and Popular Literature (Chapel Hill University of North Carolina Press, [1984] 1991; Ien Ang, Watching Dallas: Soap Opera and the Melodramatic Imagination (London: Methuen, 1985).

13. Michel de Certeau, The Practice of Everyday Life, trans. Steven Rendall, xxi (Berkeley: University of California Press, 1984).

14. Dick Hebdige, "From Culture to Hegemony," in Subculture: The Meaning of Style, 5–19 (New York: Routledge, 1979).

15. Angela McRobbie, "Second-Hand Dresses and the Role of the Ragmarket," in Postmodernism and Popular Culture, 135–54 (New York: Routledge, 199a).

16. George Lipsitz, "Cruising around the Historical Bloc," in The Subcultures Reader, ed. Ken Gelder and Sarah Thornton, 358 (New York: Routledge, 1997),

17. Steven Biel, American Gothic: A Life of America's Most Famous Painting, 115 (New York: Norton, 2005).

18. See, in particular, work by Henry Jenkins and Constance Penley on the television series Star Trek: Henry Jenkins, Textual Poachers: Television Fans and Participatory Culture (New York: Routledge, 1992); and Constance Penley, NASA/Trek: Popular Science and Sex in America (London: Verso, 1997).

19. Devin Zuber, "Flanerie at Ground Zero: Aesthetic Countermemories in Lower Manhattan," American Quarterly 58.2 (June 2006), 283–285.

20. Milton Glaser and Mirko Ilic, eds., The Design of Dissent (Gloucester, Mass.: Rockport Publishers, 2005).

21. See Thomas Frank, The Conquest of Cool: Business Culture, Counterculture, and the Rise of Hip Consumerism (Chicago: University of Chicago Press, 1998).

22. See Robert Goldman and Stephen Papson, "Levi's and the Knowing Wink," Current Perspectives in Social Theory, 11 (1991), 69–95; and Robert Goldman and Stephen Papson, Sign Wars: The Cluttered Landscape of Advertising, 257 (New York: Guilford, 1996).

Further Reading

Althusser, Louis. "Ideology and Ideological State Apparatuses." In Lenin and Philosophy and Other Essays. Translated by Ben Brewster, 127–86. London: Monthly Review Press, 1971.

Bad Object-Choices. How Do I Look? Queer Film and Video. Seattle, Wash.: Bay Press, 1991.

Barthes, Roland. "Death of the Author." In Image, Music, Text. Edited and translated by Stephen Heath, 142–48. New York: Hill and Wang, 1978.

———. The Fashion System. Translated by Matthew Ward and Richard Howard. Berkeley: University of California Press, 1990.

Bourdieu, Pierre. Distinction. A Social Critique of the Judgement of Taste. Translated by Richard Nice. Cambridge, Mass.: Harvard University Press, 1984.

Clifford, James. The Predicament of Culture: Twentieth Century Ethnography, Literature and Art. Cambridge, Mass.: Harvard University Press, 1983.

de Certeau, Michel. The Practice of Everyday Life. Translated by Steven Rendall. Berkeley: University of California Press, 1984.

Doty, Alexander. Making Things Perfectly Queer: Interpreting Mass Culture. Minneapolis: University of Minnesota Press, 1993.

Duncombe, Stephen, ed. Cultural Resistance Reader. London: Verso, 2002.

Eagleton, Terry, ed. Ideology. London: Longman Press, 1994.

Flske, John. Reading Popular Culture. New York: Routledge, 1989.

Frank, Thomas. The Conquest of Cool: Business Culture, Counterculture, and the Rise of Hip Consumerism. Chicago: University of Chicago Press, 1998.

Foucault, Michel. "What Is an Author?" In Language, Counter-Memory, Practice, translated by Donald F. Bouchard and Sherry Simon, 124–27. Ithaca, N. Y.: Cornell University Press, 1977.

Golden, Thelma, ed. Black Male: Representations of Masculinity in Contemporary American Art. New York: Whitney Museum of AmeriCan Art, 1994.

Goldman, Robert, and Stephen Papson. Sign Wars: The Cluttered Landscape of Advertising. New York: Guilford, 1996.

Gramsci, Antonio. Selections from the Prison Notebooks. Translated by Quintin Hoare and Geoffrey Nowell-Smith. New York: International Publishers and London: Lawrence & Wishart, 1971.

Hall, Stuart. "Encoding, Decoding." In The Cultural Studies Reader. Edited by Simon During, 90–103. New York: Routledge, 1993.

——— "The Problem of Ideology: Marxism Without Guarantees." In Stuart Hall: Critical Dialogues in Cultural Studies. Edited by Kuan-Hsing Chen and David Morley, 25–46. New York Routledge, 1996.

——— "Gramsci's Relevance for the Study of Race and Ethnicity." In Stuart Hall: Critical Dialogues *in Cultural Studies*. Edited by Kuan-Hsing Chen and David Morley, 411–40. New York: Routledge, 1996.

Hebdige, Dick. *Subculture: The Meaning of Style*. New York: Routledge, 1979.

Jenkins, Henry. *Textual Poachers: Television Fans and Participatory Culture*. New York: Routledge, 1992.

Klinger, Barbara. *Beyond the Multiplex: Cinema, New Technologies, and the Home*. Berkeley: University of California Press, 2006.

Lipsitz, George. "Cruising around the Historical Bloc: Postmodernism and Popular Music in East Los Angeles." In *The Subcultures Reader*. Edited by Ken Gelder and Sarah Thornton, 350–59. New York: Routledge, 1997.

McRobble, Angela, "Second-Hand Dresses and the Role of the Ragmarket." In *Postmodernism and Popular Culture*, 135–54. New York: Routledge, 1994.

McShine, Kynaston. *The Museum as Muse: Artists Reflect*. New York: Museum of Modern Art, 1999.

Nakamura, Lisa. *Digitizing Race: Visual Cultures of the Internet*. Minneapolis: University of Minnesota Press.

Penley, Constance. *NASA/TREK: Popular Science and Sex in America*. London: Verso, 1997.

Price, Sally. *Primitive Art in Civilized Places*. Chicago: University of Chicago, 1989.

Radway, Janice. *Reading the Romance: Women, Patriarchy, and Popular Culture*. Rev. ed. Chapel Hill: University of North Carolina Press, 1991.

Sconce, Jeffrey. "'Trashing' the Academy: Taste, Excess, and an Emerging Politics of Cinematic Style," *Screen*, 36.4 (Winter 1995) 371–93

Vartanian, Ivan. *Drop Dead Cuts*. San Francisco: Chronicle Books and Tokyo: Coliga Books, 2005. (A catalog of art of the 2000s by ten female painters and illustrators, some of whom were members of the Kaikai Kiki Art Collective of the Tokyo pop artist Takashi Murakami.)

5. On Writing Well

By Brian Carroll

This chapter has a clear, skills-based focus. It is all about getting the reader to think about and improve his or her writing skills. The point of this chapter is for readers to respect the writing process and improve the way they approach writing in order to improve the outcome of their efforts. The chapter begins by providing contextual information on the history of writing and print. This exposition on the tradition of the written word and the attributes of different types of writing offer the reader an understanding of variations in the art and craft of composing a written message based on audience, medium, and purpose.

The reader is encouraged to complete the exercises in this chapter. However, more important than completing each exercise is to understand the intent and purpose of each. The different tasks delineated throughout the chapter are intended to stress different points of improvement and thoughtfulness about writing. It is best not to skim over the exercises, but to consider them as guidelines for enhancing a particular and important communication skill.

I sometimes think that writing is like driving sheep down a road. If there is any gate to the left or right, the readers will most certainly go into it.

—C.S. Lewis, novelist

But words are things, and a small drop of ink falling like dew, upon a thought, produces that which makes thousands, perhaps millions, think …

—Lord Byron, *Don Juan*

If, for a while, the ruse of desire is calculable for the uses of discipline soon the repetition of guilt, justification, pseudo-scientific theories, superstition, spurious authorities, and classifications can be seen as the desperate effort to "normalize" formally the disturbance of a discourse of splitting that violates the rational, enlightened claims of its enunciatory modality.

—Homi K. Bhabha, Professor of English, Harvard University, "Mimicry and Man"

Introduction

Whether a person is writing a news story, novel, letter-to-the-editor or advertising copy, the principles of good writing are the same. Different media place different burdens and responsibilities on writers, but the reason behind writing is always to communicate ideas in your head to an audience through words. Does Professor Homi K. Bhabha's sentence above communicate his ideas clearly? Can you understand what he means by efforts to normalize the disturbance of a discourse of splitting? Perhaps that's why this sentence was awarded second prize in the annual "Bad Writing Contest." Bad writing, like Bhabha's prize-winning example, obfuscates and confuses; it promotes misunderstanding and perhaps even apathy. This chapter provides a foundation for good writing, including sections on grammar, spelling and punctuation, as it aims to help students identify weaknesses in their writing, then to offer help and resources to improve in those weak areas.

The Medium Is the Message: A Brief History of Writing

The writing tools of today—computers and word processing software, primarily—are a far cry from the earliest writing instrument, a caveman's stone. Think for a moment about how the innovation of clay tablets, the first portable writing artifact, changed the written record of human history. Now consider texting, twitter or the phone-enabled mobile Web and the ways these and other Internet-enabled technologies and tools are changing the way people communicate today. The tools that we use *to* communicate affect *how* and *what* we communicate. This book pays special attention to writing in the digital environment, but we will look as far back as the beginning of writing itself for timeless lessons on writing well, whether you're using a stone or a tablet PC.

In approximately 8500 BC, clay tokens were introduced to make and record transactions between people trading goods and services. An alphabet of sorts began to emerge to record what was being traded. A clay cone, for example, represented a small measure of grain. A sphere represented a larger measure. A cylinder signified the transaction of an animal. Writing evolved, therefore, by transferring literal depictions into abstract forms.

The alphabet that we would recognize today was invented around 2000 BC. Jews in Egypt used 27 hieroglyphs to produce this recognizable alphabet, assigning to each of the simple hieroglyphs a sound of speech. This phonetic alphabet led to the Phoenician alphabet, the "great-grandmother" of many Roman letters used today in roughly 100 languages worldwide (Sacks 2003).

At about the same time, papyrus and parchment were introduced as early forms of paper. The Romans wrote on papyrus with reed pens fashioned from the hollow stems of marsh grasses. The reed pen would evolve into the quill pen around AD 700. Though China had wood fiber paper in the 2nd century AD, it would be the late 14th century and the arrival of Gutenberg before paper became widely used in Europe. So what we think of as writing's main use—language communication—was a low priority for a long, long time, in part because literacy remained so rare. Until Gutenberg, there was not much for the average person to read—mainly inscriptions on buildings and coins. When Gutenberg began printing books, scholars estimate that there were only about 30,000 books in all of Europe. Fast forward only 50 years and Europe could count between 10 million and 12 million volumes and witness a rapid increase in literacy. The democratization of knowledge generates along with it advances in literacy.

In 286 BC, Ptolemy I launched an ambitious project to archive all human knowledge. His library in Alexandria, Egypt, housed hundreds of thousands of texts. None survive today. Invaders burned the papyrus scrolls and parchment volumes as furnace fuel in AD 681, so some of history's lessons here should be obvious:

- Make a copy.
- Backup your data.
- Beware of invaders.

Although Korea was first to make multiple copies of a work, Johannes Gutenberg gets most of the credit in histories of printing. In 1436, he invented a printing press with movable, replaceable wood letters. How much Gutenberg knew of the movable type that first had been invented in 11th-century China is not known; it is possible he re-invented it. Regardless, these innovations, which combined to create the printing process and the subsequent proliferation of printing and printed material, also led to a codification of spelling and grammar rules, though centuries would be required to agree on most of the final rules (and we are still arguing, of course).

New communication techniques and technologies rarely eliminate the ones that preceded them, as Henry-Jean Martin pointed out in his *History and Power of Writing* (1994). The new techniques and technologies redistribute labor, however, and they influence how we think. These early tools—pen and paper—facilitated written communication, which, like new communication technologies today, arrived amidst great controversy. Plato and Socrates, for instance, argued in the 4th century BC against the use of writing altogether. Socrates favored learning through face-to-face conversation over anonymous, impersonal writing. Plato feared that writing would destroy memory. After all, why make the effort to remember or, more correctly, to memorize something when it is already written down? In Plato's day, people could memorize tens of thousands of "lines" of poetry, a practice still common in Shakespeare's day many centuries later. Think for a moment: What have you memorized lately? Plato also believed that the writer's ideas in written form would be misunderstood. When communication is spoken, the speaker is present to correct misunderstanding, and the speaker has control over who gets to hear what. If you have ever had an email terribly misunderstood—or read by entirely the wrong person—these ancient concerns might still find sympathy today.

Another ancient Greek, Aristotle, became communication's great hero by defending writing from its early detractors. In perhaps one of the earliest versions of the "if-you-can't-beat-'em, join-'em" argument, Artistotle argued that the best way to protect yourself and your ideas from the harmful effects of writing was to become a better writer yourself. Aristotle also saw the potential of writing as communication, as a means to truth, and therefore a skill everyone should learn. Aristotle believed that with truth at stake, honesty and clarity were paramount in writing. These values perhaps are as important, and just as rare, in the 21st century as they were in the 4th century. Aristotle also was the first to articulate the concept of "audience," which has been variously defined ever since. He instructed rhetoricians to consider the audience before deciding on the message (Vandenberg 1995). This consideration more than any other distinguishes communication from expression for expression's sake, a distinction perhaps best understood by comparing visual communication to art, or journalism to literature.

Printing quickly became crucial to education by making it possible to produce multiple copies of the same text. With the availability of multiple copies, you could distribute the same text to many individuals, allowing readers separated by time and space to refer to the same information. With the advent of the printing press, no longer were people primarily occupied by the task of preserving information in the form of fragile manuscripts that diminished with use.

The book changed the priorities of communication, and the book, like any communication technology, has attributes that define it. These include:

- **Fixity.** The information contained in a given text is fixed by existing in many copies of the same static text.
- **Discreteness.** The text is experienced by itself, in isolation, separated from others. If there is a footnote in a book directing a reader to a reference or source material, the reader has to go get that material, physically, by going to the library or filling out an interlibrary loan request, expending time and perhaps money.
- **Division of labor.** The author or creator and the reader or audience perform distinctly different tasks, and the gulf cannot be crossed. The book is written, published, distributed and then perhaps bought or borrowed and read.
- **Primacy for creativity and originality.** The value set embodied by books does not include collaboration, community or dialogue, values impossible in a medium that requires physical marks and symbols on physical surfaces such as paper.
- **Linearity.** Unless it is a reference book, the work likely is meant to be read from front to back, in sequence, one page at a time. After hundreds of years of familiarity with this linearity, non-linear forms have found it difficult to gain acceptance.

Compare and contrast the book's fixed attributes to Web content, for which all writing and all content development depends on a process of generating lines and lines of computer code. Web pages can be static, or writing on or for the Web can be dynamic, increasing or decreasing in size, changing in font and color and presentation. Web "pages" aren't even pages; what you are actually viewing on screen is a picture of a page.

Web space is non-linear, with changing borders and boundaries. Unlike a book, the Web is scaleable and navigable, a space people move through rather than a series of pages read in a particular order. Online readers can easily subvert planned sequences of "reading" by accessing information in any order they wish (or click). The Web also is networked. Think about how the search function alone has changed use or consumption of Web documents compared to books, with search engines allowing a viewer to navigate directly to page 323 of a document and to begin reading there. Technology changes the way an artifact is used, read, stored, searched, altered and controlled. These changes are not necessarily progress, though often they can be.

The idea that a technology is not inherently good or inherently evil, that its virtues and liabilities evolve as its contexts change, is an important assumption that this book makes, one that underpins many of the book's other assumptions. Though a commonly held view, it is not necessarily true that the book is somehow natural while the Internet is somehow unnatural. Gutenberg's printing press was revolutionary as a technology; the Internet, too, as the product of hundreds of technologies, is revolutionary.

Principles of Good Writing

When asked what he would do first were he given rule over China, Confucius is believed to have said:

> To correct language … If language is not correct, then what is said is not what is meant. If what is said is not what is meant, then what ought to be done remains undone. If this remains undone, morals and art will deteriorate. If morals and art deteriorate, justice will go astray. If justice goes astray, the people will stand about in helpless confusion. Therefore, there must be no

arbitrariness in what is said. This matters about everything.

This section aims to help you better understand the principles of good writing. These principles transcend any particular media, principles important no matter the medium and no matter the audience. Below is a list of some of these fundamentals, realizing that writing is a process of prewriting, writing, editing, revising, editing again, revising again and evaluating. Each fundamental is paired with an exercise or two demonstrating the instructional point being made. The exercises are designed to help you think like a writer. The "want" to write starts now.

Be Brief

I have made this letter longer than usual only because I have not had the time to make it shorter.

—Blaise Pascal,
17th-century philosopher

Writing should be clear and concise. Readers need little reason *not* to read further, and this is especially and painfully true online. Prune your prose.

Exercise 1.1

Here are some samples of cluttered writing. Rewrite the sentences to convey the same meaning, but with fewer words, perhaps using a sentence or phrase you've seen somewhere else.

Example: The essential question that must be answered, that cannot be avoided, is existential, which is, whether or not to even exist.
Solution: To be or not to be, that is the question.

Try these:

- People should not succumb to a fear of anything except being fearful in the first place; and we should stick together on this so we can't be defeated.

- The male gender is so different from the female gender that it is almost as if the two are from completely different planets.
- There were two different footpaths in the forest, one that had been cleared by foot traffic and another that obviously fewer people had used. I decided to take the one that fewer people had used, and it really made a big difference.

Be Precise

When I use a word it means exactly what I say, no more and no less.

—Humpty Dumpty in
Through the Looking-Glass

Use the precise word that your meaning requires, not one that is close or, worse, one that sounds close. A dictionary and thesaurus should never be far away (and online, they never are). Examples:

- "A sense of trust was **induced**"—no, trust is enabled or rewarded or encouraged, it is not induced.
- "Put into **affect**"—no, put it into effect, though A might affect B.
- "She was **surrounded** by messages"—perhaps she was inundated with messages, or drowning in information, but surrounded by a ring of messages? No.
- "He was **anxious** to go to the game"—he was probably eager, not anxious, unless he was playing in the game, in which case it is possible he indeed was anxious, or worried.
- "He watched a **random** TV show"—perhaps he arbitrarily chose a show to watch, but it likely wasn't "random" at all; a broadcaster determined with great precision what to air and when. Random has a specific meaning, which is that each and every unit in a population had an equal statistical chance of being selected.
- "**In lieu** of this new information, we should …"—no, *in light of* the new information … "In lieu of" means "in the absence of."

Exercise 1.2

Write a sentence for each of the words in the pairing of words below. The sentences should illustrate the differences in meaning or nuance in each pairing:

Example:

Deduce: From the blood on the glove, he deduced that the murderer was left-handed.

Infer: By leaving her bloodless glove on the table, she inferred her innocence.

ambiguous	healthy	conscience
ambivalent	healthful	conscious
apprise	disinterested	affect
appraise	uninterested	effect

Be Active

Just do it.
—Ad slogan for Nike

Though there are times when passive voice is appropriate, too much yields writing that is lifeless. Habitually writing in the passive is what we want to avoid. In the passive, which uses a form of the verb to be and a past participle, the subject is acted upon. An example:

- The baseball player fielded the ball (active).
- The ball was fielded by the baseball player (passive).

The second sentence is longer and therefore more difficult to read.

Exercise 1.3

Re-write the following two sentences to make them active and more descriptive.

Example: Exhausted and bleary-eyed, I somehow negotiated the winding staircase, spilling me into my bed. Work would have to wait for a fresh day.

Solution: I was tired, so I finished my work and went up to bed.

- The labour leaders were frustrated by the latest offer which forced them to go through with the strike.
- She walked into the room without saying a word, sat down and looked at me.

Be Imaginative

You have to try very hard not to imagine that the iron horse is a real creature. You hear it breathing when it rests, groaning when it has to leave, and yapping when it's under way ... Along the track it jettisons its dung of burning coals and its urine of boiling water; ... its breath passes over your head in beautiful clouds of white smoke which are torn to shreds on the trackside trees.
—Novelist Victor Hugo,
describing a train

Analogies, similes and metaphors are like sutures and scalpels. In expert hands, they can be transformative. In the hands of quacks, however, somebody is going to get to get hurt, to use a bad though not mixed metaphor.

For the poet Maya Angelou, social changes have appeared "as violent as electrical storms, while others creep slowly like sorghum syrup." For French novelist Colette, the skyscrapers of Paris resembled "a grove of churches, a gothic bouquet, and remind us of that Catholic art that hurled its tapered arrow towards heaven, the steeple, stretching up in aspirations." Dorothy Parker, a riotously funny writer, once declared, "His voice was as intimate as the rustle of sheets." (She also wrote that "brevity is the soul of lingerie.")

Visualize analogies and metaphors when writing them, as well as the images they conjure. Are they apt and effective in conveying their intent? Be warned, however, that mixed metaphors are not only inaccurate, they distract the reader and discredit the writer. "He smelled the jugular." ESPN broadcaster Chris Berman actually said this in 2002 describing a playoff football game. (To hold a broadcaster to the standards of the written word is unfair, but it makes the point about how easily metaphors can go wrong.) In addition, global audiences will have great difficulty with metaphors and analogies. Great care should be exercised when employing them, using them only where they *help* communicate an idea and do not *hinder* understanding, or worse, offend and alienate.

Berman's example points to another danger—clichés. It is easy to settle for a cliché, but doing so is like arriving a day late and a dollar short, like taking candy from a baby, like picking low-hanging fruit. Because at the end of the day, when all is said and done, laziness is perhaps the writer's greatest enemy.

Avoid these clichés *like the plague*:

- last but not least;
- give 110 percent;
- untimely death (think about this one just for a moment);
- brutal rape (what would its opposite be, a friendly rape?);
- few and far between;
- stick to the game plan;
- off the wagon, on the wagon or circling the wagons.

Exercise 1.4

Think of some more clichés—the more the merrier. If you need inspiration, more clichés than you can shake a stick at can be found at the American Copy Editors Socitey Web site, http://www.copydesk.org/words/cliches.htm.

Exercise 1.5

Describe the Internet using analogy in two different sentences, each with a different emphasis in meaning. For attempts at this from the past, think information superhighway, cyberspace or getting a Second Life.

Example: As an information superhighway, the Internet too often resembles a Los Angles cloverleaf during rush hour.

Be Direct

I am hurt. A plague o' both your houses!
I am sped.
　　　—Mercution in *Romeo and Juliet*

Shakespeare knew how to deliver a verbal punch with a stab of brevity. The short sentence can affect emphasis and power in writing. Ernest Hemingway perfected this skill: "*He knew at least twenty good stories … and he had never written one. Why?*" And an example from another rhetorical master, Rev. Dr. Martin Luther King, Jr.: "*This is our hope. This is the faith with which I return to the South to hew out of the mountain of despair a stone of hope.*"

In King's quote, the brief introductory sentence sets up the sentence of normal length following. In Hemingway's, the abrupt question "Why?" adds emphasis to the character's flaw under examination. The short sentence (Hemingway's was one word) also can be used for transition. For Shakespeare, Mercutio's words are his last, like final, choking gasps for air.

Be Consistent

Failing to use parallel structure is one of the most common problems in writing. Here are some examples of this:

Good: One cannot think well, love well, sleep well, if one has not dined well.
Bad: One cannot think well, have love, fall asleep, if dinner was bad.

Good: Jane likes hunting and fishing.
Bad: Jane likes to hunt and fishing.

Sentences should be balanced and faithful to a reader's subconscious expectations in terms of the physical act of reading. Parts of a sentence with coordinating conjunctions (*and, but* or *for, nor, yet, so*), therefore, should be joined in consistent fashion.

Exercise 1.6

Re-write the following sentences to make them parallel in structure.

- Delta promises a bounty of flights that are on time, have convenient connections and offer a well-balanced in-flight meal.
- Heroes in movies are always wealthy, always get the girls, wear high fashion and usually arrive at the scene about two seconds after the bad guy has left.
- Speaking of movies, telephones in movies are always knocked over if they wake up a character, never ring more than three times before getting answered, and get restored by frantically tapping on the cradle and shouting, "Hello? Hello?"

Just as laziness or lack of care prevents good parallel structure, verb tenses should not mysteriously change mid-sentence, nor should the singularity or plurality of subjects or objects being described or discussed.

Be Aware

Here are some common pitfalls you'll want to be sure to avoid when writing:

- **plagiarism**—both intentional and inadvertent; it is almost impossible to over-cite, so when in doubt, cite the source;
- **stereotyping**—"journalists are cynical";
- **oversimplifying**—rarely is a choice either/ or; rarely does a question or issue have only two sides;
- **generalizing**—"All computer users struggle with addiction." Every last one of them? Be wary of *all, none, nobody, always, everything*;
- **jumping to conclusions**—see *generalizing*;
- **faulty logic or circular arguments**—using the Bible, for example, to justify one's Christian faith; however the Bible is fine for explaining Christian faith;
- **overuse of pronouns and articles**—"this," "these," "those," "he" or "she." Which one(s)? Who? What are you talking about? Don't risk confusing the reader.

Be Concise

What difference does it make if you live in a picturesque little outhouse surrounded by 300 feeble minded goats and your faithful dog ... ? The question is: Can you write?

    Ernest Hemingway

Exercise 1.7

Hemingway could write, obviously. He once wrote a short story in six words. "For sale: baby shoes, never worn." He called it his best work. The task in this exercise is to do as Hemingway did, to write a short story in just six words. Here are some examples, from *Wired* magazine's November 2006 issue:

"Failed SAT. Lost scholarship. Invented rocket."—William Shatner

"Computer, did we bring batteries? Computer?"—Eileen Gunn

"Vacuum collision. Orbits diverge. Farewell, Love."—David Brin

"Gown removed carelessly. Head, less so."—Joss Whedon

An Example of Good Writing

To consider how to improve your own writing (and thinking), consider some of the problems in writing George Orwell observed in his essay, "Politics and the English Language," an essay as timely today as the day it was published more than 50 years ago:

- staleness of imagery;
- lack of precision or concreteness;

- use of dying (or dead) metaphors;
- use of "verbal false limbs," such as "render inoperative" or "militate against";
- pretentious diction (words like *phenomenon*, *element*, *individual*);
- use of meaningless words.

Orwell wrote that a scrupulous writer will ask himself at least four questions in every sentence that he writes:

1. What am I trying to say?
2. What words will express it?
3. What image or idiom will make it clearer?
4. Is this image fresh enough to have an effect?

And he will probably ask himself two more:

1. Could I put it more shortly?
2. Have I said anything that is avoidably ugly?

Finally, in cautioning against "prefabricated phrases" and "humbug and vagueness generally," Orwell's essay provides writers with several points of advice:

1. Never use a metaphor, simile, or other figure of speech which you are used to seeing in print.
2. Never use a long word where a short one will do.
3. If it is possible to cut a word out, always cut it out.
4. Never use the passive where you can use the active.
5. Never use a foreign phrase, a scientific word or a jargon word if you can think of an everyday English equivalent.

To Orwell's last point, take a look at a concurring judicial opinion written by Supreme Court Justice Robert H. Jackson in a First Amendment case from 1945, *Thomas v. Collins*. Revel in Jackson's directness, in how accessible the language is compared to the legal jargon that characterizes many if not most court opinions. The case had to do with the constitutionality of a Texas law requiring labor organizers to register with the state before soliciting memberships in a union. From p. 323 of the decision:

As frequently is the case, this controversy is determined as soon as it is decided which of two well established, but at times overlapping, constitutional principles will be applied to it. The State of Texas stands on its well settled right reasonably to regulate the pursuit of a vocation, including—we may assume—the occupation of labor organizer. Thomas, on the other hand, stands on the equally clear proposition that Texas may not interfere with the right of any person peaceably and freely to address a lawful assemblage of workmen intent on considering labor grievances.

Though the one may shade into the other, a rough distinction always exists, I think, which is more shortly illustrated than explained. A state may forbid one without its license to practice law as a vocation, but I think it could not stop an unlicensed person from making a speech about the rights of man or the rights of labor, or any other kind of right, including recommending that his bearers organize to support his views. Likewise, the state may prohibit the pursuit of medicine as an occupation without its license, but if do not think it could make it a crime publicly or privately to speak urging persons to follow or reject any school of medical thought. So the state, to an extent not necessary now to determine, may regulate one who makes a business or a livelihood of soliciting funds or memberships for unions. But I do not think it can prohibit one, even if he is a salaried labor leader, from making an address to a public meeting of workmen, telling them their rights as he sees them and urging them to unite in general or to join a specific union.

This wider range of power over pursuit of a calling than over speech-making is due to the different effects which the two have on interests which the state is empowered to protect. The modern state owes and attempts to perform a duty to protect the public from those who seek for one purpose or another to obtain its money. When one does so through the practice of a calling, the state may have an interest in shielding the public against the untrustworthy, the incompetent, or the irresponsible, or against unauthorized representation of agency. A usual method of performing this function is through a licensing system.

But it cannot be the duty, because it is not the right, of the state to protect the public against false doctrine. The very purpose of the First Amendment is to foreclose public authority from assuming a guardianship of the public mind through regulating the press, speech, and religion. In this field, every person must be his own watchman for truth, because the forefathers did not trust any government to separate the true from the false for us (*West Virginia State Board of Education v. Barnette*, 319 U.S. 624). Nor would I. Very many are the interests which the state may protect against the practice of an occupation, very few are those it may assume to protect against the practice of propagandizing by speech or press. These are thereby left great range of freedom.

This liberty was not protected because the forefathers expected its use would always be agreeable to those in authority, or that its exercise always would be wise, temperate, or useful to society. As I read their intentions, this liberty was protected because they knew of no other way by which free men could conduct representative democracy.

(Opinion available: http://supreme.justia.com/us/323/516/case/html)

The first thing you may notice is how Jackson is present with you through his writing. He is speaking to you, you right there. He isn't "performing," trying to impress you with rhetorical flourishes.

Jackson's intellect as a jurist is on display here, as are his voice and method of thinking. He first identifies what he sees as the core issue. He presents the facts. He identifies the principles by which he will decide. He decides, then he explains in such a way that we non-lawyers can understand him. In short, Jackson says what he means and means what he says. Sherwood Anderson wrote that "the danger lies in the emptiness of so many of the words we use."

Getting Started: Putting Your Ideas in Words

Mindful of how writing has evolved (and why), inspired by Pascal, Hemingway, Shakespeare and Orwell, finally it is time to write. The following steps will help us get started.

A. Get the Idea: Determine Your Purpose

- **Brainstorm:** write down whatever might be related to the task, even if it seems irrelevant at the moment. There is no judgment in brainstorming, which, to use a sailing metaphor, is akin to producing your own wind. As the Latin proverb goes, "If there is no wind, row!" The best way to get some ideas, at least one good idea, is to generate a lot of ideas.
- **Cluster:** similar to brainstorming, this is more for visual people. Put the main idea in the middle of the page, then link related ideas, then related ideas to those related ideas, and so on. The ideas should radiate out from a conceptual center.

- **Free write:** write down the thesis or purpose statement at the top of the page, then write under it all the ideas that flow from that thesis, including sources, questions to pursue and things not to do.

B. Map It Out

- What is the topic?
- What is/are the main point(s)?
- Who is the primary audience? Are there secondary audiences?
- What is the specific purpose of the writing? (What is the goal?)
- What sources will be used?
- What method will be used to gather the information?

A word about audience: There is much more on audience in Chapter 5, but even now it is critical to know who the readers will be or to whom the content is being targeted. This knowledge should influence topic, tone, complexity and a host of other content issues. To help, here are some things to think about adapted from a worksheet put together by long-time literary agent Laurie Rozakis (1997):

1. How old are your readers?
2. What is their gender?
3. How much education do they have?
4. Are they mainly urban, rural or suburban?
5. In which country were they born? How much is known about their culture and heritage?
6. What is their socio-economic status?
7. How much does the audience already know about the topic?
8. How do they feel about the topic? Will they be neutral, oppositional, or will this be more like preaching to the choir?

The answers to all of these questions might not yet be available, which is fine. The point is to consider the readers or users* as completely as possible before writing. (*A better term for readers/users/consumers is desperately needed. Online, we do not merely read. Presumably most of us are not addicted to the Net. And content online is not like a bag of potato chips. What do we call the people who visit our blogs and Web sites and interact with our content? Interactors, perhaps? Hmm …)

C. Outline and Storyboard It

Outlining helped prepare this very section on writing. After answering the basic questions, it makes sense to then organize how the content will be presented to readers. Similar to home-building, the outline or blueprint can be used to organize the work, especially when different pieces of the project are being done at different times by different people. This blueprint can always be changed, and it does not have to be an elaborate outline replete with Roman numerals and series of alphabetized lists. Even a visual map, using circles, for example, might do the trick. Reverse-outlining, or outlining after the piece is written, can also be very useful, revealing structural flaws or a better order for the information.

Before getting to work, writing students are advised to buy or borrow a writing handbook like the one most of us used in English composition as first-year undergraduates. Examples include *The Everyday Writer*, by Andrea A. Lunsford (this book's author's favorite); *The Longman Handbook for Writers and Readers; Rules for Writers*; or *When Words Collide* (Lunsford 2009; Anson and Schwegler 2009; Hacker 2009; Kessler and McDonald 1984). Most every major publisher has one.

D. Revise It. Then Revise It Again

Plan time for revisions. As Hemingway famously said, "All first drafts are [crap]," so give yourself time and room to fail. The only reason for a first draft is to have something to revise. And be tenacious! Editing and revising takes patience and perseverance.

During the revision process, question the decisions you made in writing the first draft. Reconsider, critique and question:

- Your first paragraph. Re-write your first paragraph from an entirely different perspective, sit back and see which beginning you like better. For that alternate beginning, try thinking sideways. In other words, come at the subject from an entirely different angle.

- Your last paragraph. Re-write your last paragraph, your landing, as well.
- The one or two sentences you absolutely love. Highlight these and delete them. Is your writing stronger without your precious darlings there preening for attention? (The lesson here is to remove anything that is merely for effect, to impress, to be admired as witty or clever. Hemingway described prose not as interior decoration but as architecture.)
- Your adjectives. Look for redundancy, for empty descriptives, like "the long hallway" or "the deep, blue ocean."
- Your adverbs. Often one good verb is far better than a verb-adverb combination. Example: "He ran briskly across the field" Try: "He galloped in pursuit." While revising for adverbs, you might also re-consider your verb choices. Highlight all your verbs in one color and all of your adverbs in another. Re-think your choices.
- Clichés. Get rid of them.
- Ambiguity, vagueness, generalities. If you are not quite sure what a passage means, your reader most definitely won't either. Cut it out.

You might also read your piece with the following catalog of common writing problems at hand. The product of years of grading and editing undergraduate student writing, this list, which is in no particular order, will keep your writing out of potholes.

1. "Media" is a plural term. "Medium" is singular. So media are; a medium is. Even senior journalism and mass communication students haplessly struggle with this basic usage.
2. Avoid ethnocentric references such as "we" or "our" or "us" or "our country." It assumes too much, and it communicates exclusivity. Assume as little as possible. Many readers might not consider themselves members of any one person's "us" or "we" or "our." What of immigrants, green card aliens, international students? What does "us" even mean? Be precise instead.
3. Singular-plural agreement is a very common writing problem.
   —*Example 1*: "The government is wrong when they tell us what to do." The government is an "it." People who work for governments are a "they."
   —*Example 2*: "A, B and C are a predictor of future behavior." No, they are predictors. There are three of them.
   —*Example 3*: "The surfer is able to read the article themselves." Word processing makes moving words around so easy—too easy, in fact. Writers oftentimes lose track of agreement with so much cutting and pasting.
4. Beware of imprecise, even reckless use of personal pronouns such as "they," "their," "them" and "it." Often these are used at the sacrifice of clarity. Which "they" is being referenced? Most articles include discussion of more than one group. Which "them"? What "it"? "Their" refers to ownership, but by whom? The writer knows the words' references because they flowed from the writer's head. The reader, however, likely will be confused. A second reading or edit can reveal the vagueness of many of these usages. Night-before or on-deadline writing is notorious for producing this kind of carelessness and imprecision.
5. Use the right word, not just a good word. This was discussed earlier in the chapter.
6. A related issue, imprecision with adjectives. "A lot" ... "more and more" ... "massive amounts" ... "very detrimental" ... "a great deal." None of these suffice. Instead be specific, precise and show supporting evidence for such statements and judgments.
7. Do your part to prevent semi-colon abuse! Semi-colons, colons, commas, hyphens and dashes each have their own specific purposes. A writer's handbook is valuable in figuring

them out. The comma, for example, is "a small crooked point, which in writing followeth some branch of the sentence & in reading warneth us to rest there, & to help our breth a little" (Richard Mukaster, writing in his 1582 volume, *The First Part of the Elementarie*). A common apostrophe problem pits "its" v. "it's." "It's" is a contraction. "Its" is possessive.

8. After beginning a quote, make sure you end it, somewhere, sometime. It is a common mistake to begin a quote but then to forget the close quotes, effectively putting the rest of the treatise into the quotation. This is the writing equivalent of flicking on your turn signal, turning, then leaving it blinking the rest of the way down the highway. Other motorists are laughing at you!

9. A related issue, orphaning quotes. Quotes should all have parents, so be sure to identify this parentage. Orphan quotes are quotations dropped into an article without identification of the speaker or writer or source. There should be a source in the narrative ("said the inspections officer" or "the Civil War historian wrote").

10. Another related issue, stringing quotations together. The writing can quickly become a very thin piece of string merely holding other people's work together. The writer should be providing some pearls as well, which means taking the time to integrate and weave the parts into a coherent, meaningful whole. Rarely is there benefit in merely grafting in quoted material just because it is on topic and seems worded more ably than the writer thinks he or she could pull off him- or herself. Writers should avoid subletting their space to others.

11. Hyphens pull together, like staples; dashes separate. "Twin-engine plane": hyphen, for a compound adjective. "She was—if you can believe this—trying to jump out of the car!": dashes, to separate the parenthetical phrase. In general, dashes should be avoided. They have no agreed upon rules and therefore are or can be a sign of laziness.

12. More editing required. After something has been written, long or short, even a single blog post, walk away. Go to the coffee shop and sip a latte. Go for a jog. Once refreshed, return to the writing and edit. Revise. Re-work. Improve. All good writers do this. Of course, it takes planning.

The Online Effect

Email, texting, social networking, IM and chat arguably are having a corrosive effect on writing. The informality of writing for these online environments is "seeping into … schoolwork," according to a study by the Pew Internet & America Life Project, in partnership with the College Board's National Commission on Writing. Nearly two-thirds of 700 students surveyed acknowledged that their electronic communication style, which primarily is an informal, interpersonal style, found its way into school assignments. About half said they sometimes omitted proper punctuation and capitalization in their schoolwork, while a quarter said they used emoticons. These are alarming trends, calling for more education on the different styles that should be employed for different forms or kinds of communication.

Chapter Assignments

1. Produce a writing sample. The choice of subject is entirely yours. You could, for example, write a short travelogue piece about somewhere you have recently visited. An opinion piece on some question or issue of the day, such as U.S. immigration policy or whether online communication has eroded language skills, also is an option. You could even review a movie, play or book.
Length: about 700 words.
Be sure to include:
(a) a headline summarizing the work;
(b) identification of the audience(s) for whom it is intended;

(c) an abstract (a one- or two-sentence summary of your piece);

(d) a list of key words a search engine might use to find this writing piece online.

2. Students should pair up and work together to improve the writing of one another. This exercise can be extremely valuable, and from both perspectives, that of being critiqued and that of (gently) critiquing. Some might be nervous or uncomfortable critiquing a classmate, especially early in a course, but students should not fret. Be civil and constructive, and demonstrate that you have or are developing a tough skin. Writing improvement demands a great deal of constructive criticism and therefore an increasingly thick skin and short memory. Workshop partners should have at their disposal a writing handbook and this text. It does not matter which handbook; they cover the same general topics. Each student will use the handbook to analyze his or her own writing and that of the assigned workshop partner(s). Length: about 500 words, but this word count is admittedly arbitrary.

Online Resources

Elements of Style (original 1918 ed.) by William Strunk, Jr.

http://www.bartleby.com/141

A free, online edition of the classic guide to writing well.

"More Cliches Than You Can Shake a Stick At"

http://www.copydesk.org/words/cliches.htm

A list of journalistic clichés compiled by Mimi Burkhardt on the Web site for the American Copy Editors Society.

Poynter Institute's Writer's Toolbox

http://poynter.org/subject.asp?id=2

Tips and best practices from, and blogs by, some of Poynter's writing faculty, including Roy Peter Clark and Chip Scanlan.

Purdue University's Online Writing Lab

http://owl.english.purdue.edu/

Style guides, writing and teaching helps, and resources for grammar and writing mechanics.

Sources

Chris M. Anson and Robert Schwegler, *The Longman Handbook for Writers and Readers*, 5th ed. (New York: Longman, 2009).

Jacques Barzun, *Simple & Direct* (New York: Harper & Row, 1984).

Homi K. Bhabha, "Mimicry and Man," in Homi K Bhabha, *The Location of Culture* (New York: Routledge, 2004).

E.L. Callihan, *Grammar for Journalists* (Radnor, PA: Chilton Publishing, 1979).

John Dufresne, *The Lie that Tells a Truth* (New York: Norton, 2003).

Elizabeth Eisenstein, *The Printing Press as an Agent of Change: Communications and Cultural Transformations in Early-Modern Europe* (Cambridge: Cambridge University Press, 1980).

P. Elbow, "Revising with Feedback," in P. Elbow, *Writing with Power* (New York: Oxford University Press, 1981).

Michelle Esktritt, Kang Lee, and Merlin Donald, "The Influence of Symbolic Literacy on Memory: Testing Plato's Hypothesis," *Canadian Journal of Experimental Psychology*, 55 (March 2001): 39–50.

Fred Feller, John R. Bender, Lucinda Davenport, and Michael W. Drager, *Writing for the Media* (Oxford: Oxford University Press, 2001).

Diana Hacker, *Rules for Writers*, 5th ed. (New York: St. Martin's, 2009).

Lauren Kessler and Duncan McDonald, *When Words Collide: A Journalist's Guide to Grammar and Style* (Belmont, CA: Wadsworth Publishing, 1984).

George P. Landow, *Hypertext 2.0* (Baltimore: Johns Hopkins University Press, 1997). Tamar Lewin, "Informal Style of Electronic Messages is Showing Up in Schoolwork, Study Finds," *New York Times*, April 25, 2008: A12.

Gunnar Liestol, Andrew Morrison, and Terje Rasmussen, eds., *Digital Media Revisited* (Cambridge, MA: MIT Press, 2003).

Andrea A. Lunsford, *The Everyday Writer*, 4th ed. (New York. St. Martin's, 2009).

Elizabeth McMahan and Robert Funk, *Here's How to Write Well* (Boston: Allyn and Bacon, 1999).

Henry-Sean Martin, *The History and Power of Writing* (Chicago:University of Chicago Press, 1994).

John Pavlik and Shawn McIntosh, "Convergence and P. Concentration in the Media Industries," *in Living in the Information Age*, Erik P. Bucy, ed. (Beltnor, CA: Wadsworth Publishing, 2005): 67–72.

Laurie Rozakis, *Complete Idiot's Guide to Creative Writing* (New York: Alpha Books, 1997).

David Sacks, *Language Visible. Unraveling the Mystery of the Alphabet from A to Z* (New York: Broadway Books, 2003).

Lynne Truss, *Eats, Shoots & Leaves* (New York: Gotham Books, 2004).

Peter Vandenberg, "Coming to Terms," *English Journal*, 84 (April 1995): 79–80.

Rick Williams and Julianne Newton, *Visual Communication: Integrating Media, Art, and Science* (New York: Lawrence Erlbaum, 2007).

Gary Wolf, "The Great Library of Amazonia," *Wired* magazine, December 2003: 215–21.

6. Human Communication Theory and Research

Traditions and Models

By Virginia P. Richmond and James C. McCrosky

An introduction to the world of communication would not be complete without a chapter outlining the ways people understand and explain communication. This chapter provides a history of the academic study of the field. It also explicates the broad ways we have understood the various types of communication. Finally, it delineates more contemporary approaches to this type of study. The rhetorical and relational approaches give readers a "broad strokes" appreciation for the complexities of the field by demonstrating that differences in interpretation and meaning extend beyond particular messages and include the ways we interpret the entire process of communication.

This chapter is important because it gives readers a sense of the work scholars do to understand the complex world of communication. Students read the work of scholars and are taught best practices based on research in the field. They should understand the long tradition of research and critique that supports the practice of communication.

The study of human communication has a long and distinguished history. We can safely say that, since humankind first acquired the ability to communicate through verbal and nonverbal symbols and norms, people have "studied" communication. Indeed, one advantage we hold over other animals is the ability to communicate abstractions such as time, place, and space as though each was a concrete object. Thus, since the beginning of our time, we have studied human communication—albeit unscientifically at first, but through more formal systems as we came to better understand both the role of communication in society and its role in daily activity. The importance of the study of human communication is found in its inclusion in educational programs since the first formal schooling systems were developed over 5,000 years ago.

In order to understand how human communication is studied today, it is important to appreciate how we got to where we are now. We will not, however, attempt to provide a complete discussion of the history of communication scholarship here. Rather, we will focus on the more important developments and time periods which have impacted the contemporary study of human communication. Our goal is to foster an understanding of how what was done in the past influences what we do today, and most likely will influence what we do in the future.

The importance of communication in human society has been recognized for thousands of years, far longer than we can demonstrate through recorded history. The oldest essay ever discovered, written about 3,000 BC, consists of advice on how to speak effectively. This essay was inscribed on a fragment of parchment addressed to Kagemni, the eldest son of the Pharaoh Huni. Similarly, the oldest extant book is a treatise on effective communication. *The Precepts* was composed in Egypt about 2,675 BC by Ptah-Hotep and written for the guidance of the Pharaoh's son. While these works are significant because they establish that the study of human communication is older than any other area of current academic interest, the actual contribution to current communication theory was minimal.

The study of human communication today can be divided into two major classifications—rhetorical and relational (Shepherd, 1992). The rhetorical communication approach focuses primarily on the study of influence. The function of rhetorical communication is to get others to do what you want or need them to do or think the way you want or need them to think—to persuade them. The relational approach, on the other hand, examines communication from a transactional or co-orientational perspective. That is, two (or more) people coordinate their communication to reach a shared perspective satisfactory to all. Of paramount concern is the relationship between the two people and the perceived well-being of the "other."

These two divergent orientations represent the dominant orientations of Western (individualistic) and Eastern (collectivistic) cultures. At their extremes, the Western (rhetorical) orientation would sacrifice relationships to accomplish influence and the Eastern (relational) orientation would sacrifice the achievement of influence to protect relationships. It is not pragmatic, however, to conceive of these two approaches to the study of human communication as polar opposites. Rather, they represent differences in emphasis. Both are interested in accomplishing objectives and maintaining good relationships through communication. Each, however, emphasizes one objective over the other.

We will examine the influence of both of these orientations toward the study of human communication. The impact of the rhetorical tradition has been the strongest and longest (McCroskey, 1968, 2006), so we will consider it first.

The Rhetorical Tradition

The rhetorical tradition begins some 2,500 years after Kagemni's early writing, during the 5th century BC, at Syracuse, in Sicily. When a democratic regime was established in Syracuse after the overthrow of the tyrant Thrasybulus, its citizens flooded the courts to recover property that had been confiscated during his reign.

The "art of rhetoric" that Corax developed was intended to help ordinary people prove their claims in court. Corax and his student, Tisias, are also generally credited with the authorship of a manual on public speaking, but the work is no longer extant. Although we are not certain of its contents, scholars suggest that it included two items significant to the development of rhetorical theory. The first was a theory of how arguments should be developed from probabilities, a theory more thoroughly developed by Aristotle a century later. Corax and Tisias are also credited with first developing the concept of message organization, what we today call an introduction, a body, and a conclusion.

In Athens, during the 5th century BC, there was a large group of itinerant teachers, known as *sophists,* who established small schools and charged students for attending their lectures on rhetoric, literature, science, and philosophy. Many of these teachers became quite wealthy through their efforts. Protagoras of Abdara, sometimes called the "Father of Debate," was one of the first and most important sophists. His teachings contended that there were two sides to every proposition (a *dialectic)* and that speakers should be able to argue either side of the proposition equally well. This view, commonly accepted by today's teachers of argumentation and debate, provides the foundation in the United States for communication in today's legal and legislative systems, the very basis of democratic government itself.

Aristotle's Rhetoric

Aristotle, in the 3rd century BC, is generally considered the foremost theorist in the history of the study of human communication from the rhetorical perspective. His *Rhetoric,* written in about 330 BC, is the most influential work on the topic. It consists of three books, one primarily concerned with the speaker, another concerned with the audience, and the third with the speech itself.

Book 1 discusses the distinction between rhetorical communication and dialectical communication (the process of inquiry). Aristotle criticized his contemporaries for dwelling upon irrelevant matters in their rhetorical theories rather than concentrating on proofs—particularly enthymemes—or arguments from probabilities. He defined *rhetoric* as "the faculty of discovering in a particular case what are the available means of persuasion." To Aristotle, the means of persuasion were primarily *ethos* (the nature of the source), *pathos* (the emotions of the audience), and *logos* (the nature of the message presented by the source). He focused his concern on three types of speaking: deliberative (speaking in the legislature), forensic (speaking in the law court), and epideictic (speaking in a ceremonial situation). He was concerned with formal public speaking settings and did not address what we would call today "everyday" or "interpersonal" communication.

Within his overall theory of rhetoric, Aristotle included three critical elements. The first was that effective rhetoric is based on argumentation, and that all arguments must be based on *probabilities.* Aristotle held that absolute, verifiable truth is unobtainable in most instances. Therefore, persuasion must be based on what an audience believes to be true. Whereas his teacher, Plato, found this to be a defect in rhetoric and condemned it, Aristotle perceived it simply as a fact, and not a moral issue.

The second essential element in his approach was a conception of the rhetorical communicator's basic task was to *adapt to the audience.* Aristotle believed that you could not persuade a person unless you knew what was likely to persuade that individual. That is, he believed that a knowledge of what we now call "psychology" was essential to effective communication.

These two elements, probability and psychology, led to the third important element in his theory: rhetoric's basic "amorality." Aristotle viewed rhetoric as a tool, one which could be used by anyone—by a good person or a bad one, by a person seeking worthy ends or by one seeking unworthy ends. At the same time, he argued that rhetoric was a self-regulating art. By that he meant the person who is unethical, or who advocates evil, is less likely to be successful than the moral person advocating something good. As justification, he claimed that good and right, by their very nature, are more powerful persuasive tools than their opposites. While acknowledging that evil might win out in the short-run, Aristotle believed that evil would ultimately fail unless people arguing on behalf of good were incompetent rhetorical communicators.

During the Roman period, the 1st century AD, Aristotle's work was known and writers such as Cicero and Quintillion (often called the "greatest orator" and "greatest teacher," respectively) wrote works within the general perspective of his work, although they were not always in agreement with Aristotle's ideas. In general, the Roman period applied the rhetorical theory of the ancient Greeks, and helped to spread its use across the ancient world. There was not a great amount of writing on rhetoric in the Middle Ages. During the Renaissance, however, more attention was directed toward rhetoric, and although Aristotle's works were known to the scholars of the time, most of their writings centered on matters of style rather than the concerns Aristotle had advanced.

During the 18th century writers such as George Campbell and Richard Whately in England resurrected the Aristotelian perspective toward communication and advanced it with their own theories. In the United States, Professor John Quincy Adams (the same John Quincy Adams later to become President of the United States), who held the chair of rhetoric at Harvard University, presented a series of lectures which set forth for the first time in America a thoroughly classical view of rhetoric. This view was extended in the early 20th century by the early writers, such as James Winans, in what became the field of "Speech."

American Rhetorical Study

The first professional organization of people concerned with the study of human communication, now known as the Eastern Communication Association, was formed in 1909 by a group of teachers of public speaking housed mainly in departments of English at Eastern colleges and universities. Five years later, many of these same people joined with people from other parts of the United States to form what is now known as the National Communication Association, a national professional association that was then primarily composed of teachers of public speaking.

The people in these associations were primarily concerned (then and now) with developing greater understanding of how human communication works and how people can be taught to be more effective communicators. Because the political and social systems in American society in the first half of this century were very similar to those of Greece in the time of Aristotle, the Aristotelian rhetorical tradition was an excellent fit to the needs of the scholars of that era. The Aristotelian tradition soon became solidly entrenched as the dominant paradigm for the study of human communication.

During the first half of the 20th century the study of human communication expanded rapidly into what has come to be known as the "Speech" tradition. Academic departments of speech were founded in most major colleges and universities across the United States, particularly in the large Midwestern institutions. The primary emphasis in these programs was the teaching of public speaking and the study of human communication in the Aristotelian rhetorical tradition. Most programs sponsored debating teams, á la Protagoras, and attempts to generate new knowledge about effective rhetoric were centered primarily on rhetorical *criticism* of the addresses of effective, or usually at least famous, public orators.

Although the rhetorical tradition held sway for the most part, departments of speech expanded their attention to include many other aspects of oral communication. Theater and oral reading, voice and diction, speech pathology and audiology, radio and television broadcasting, and film classes all become common. By the middle of the 20th century many of these new offerings had grown into full-blown programs. Many of these speciality areas began leaving the speech departments and forming academic units of their own. Theater and oral reading often joined other fine arts programs. Speech pathology and audiology, often accompanied by voice and diction, usually formed their own unit or joined other allied health programs. Broadcasting frequently joined with journalism, and print-oriented programs in public relations and advertising, to form mass communication programs. Sometimes film studies joined this group as well.

In many cases, departments which began with their focus on public speaking and the rhetorical tradition diversified extensively and split into several academic units. They then came full circle back to the study of public speaking and the rhetorical tradition. These programs continue to have a strong focus on public presentations, argumentation, and persuasion. Whereas, as we discuss more fully later, most of these programs made major changes in their curricula (and their names) in the last half of the 20th century, most continue to include a strong emphasis on work that follows the rhetorical tradition.

Perspectives on the Rhetorical Tradition

In order to understand the nature of the rhetorical approach to the study of human communication, it is useful to gain perspective on the culture in which it originated and where it still thrives. From today's perspective the cultures of ancient Greece and Rome had many positive and many negative characteristics. Despite their interest in philosophy, religion, and the arts and their commitment to a form of democracy, they were harsh cultures. Life expectancies were short, and life was very hard for most people.

These were slave-owning societies in which slaves could be killed or severely punished for even slight offenses against their masters. There was one dominant culture and the rulers of that culture were highly ethnocentric. People of other races and cultures were seen as inferior beings whose lives and well-being were of little value. Women were considered men's property and often treated only slightly better than the slaves. The men of the dominant race and ethnic group totally ruled society. The society was both racist and sexist, and these views were seldom challenged. For all, master and slave, that was just

the way it was. From most people's perspectives, these were *not* the good old days.

The legislative and legal systems of these societies were devoted to the maintenance of the ruling class. It was important that the members of that class could resolve disputes and engage in coordinated action to maintain their power and control over the society. Understanding how to communicate effectively within this small ruling group was critical to one who wished to protect one's own interests or attain higher leadership status. Communication, then, was seen as a strategic tool—one to be used by those in power. The perspective was source-oriented—how a speaker could get an audience to do what he wanted them to do. Communication in the courts and in the legislature was primarily concerned with public speaking, and the effective orator was a much respected and powerful person.

Although we sometimes do not like to acknowledge it, this description of ancient Greece and Rome can be applied to earlier periods of Western culture, including the United States and many other societies of the 17th through 19th centuries. Like many other societies, we were a slave-owning society, one in which women, too, were seen as possessions of men. Our legislative and legal systems were modeled on Greco-Roman, Judea-Christian, Anglo-European tradition. The rhetorical orientation of the Speech Tradition was tailor-made for this society.

The mass communication tradition, like the speech tradition, sprouted from roots in the rhetorical orientation. The predecessors of many of the people working in mass communication today were in departments of journalism and advertising, as well as in speech. Since the beginnings of the study of mass communication focused on public presentation and mass influence, the rhetorical orientation also fit the needs of these early scholars.

The Relational Tradition

The relational tradition is at least as old, and possibly older, than the rhetorical tradition.

However, no serious attention was devoted to this orientation in the United States until the latter half of the 20th century. The foundations of the relational orientation stem from ancient Confucian philosophy. Hence, this orientation is most commonly associated with Eastern thought.

While individualism, competition, and straightforward communication are highly valued in most Western societies, Eastern societies have higher values for congeniality, cooperation, and indirect communication which will protect the "face" of the people interacting. Maintaining valued relationships is generally seen as more important than exerting influence and control over others.

The existence of approaches to communication other than the rhetorical approach was recognized by some scholars in the United States prior the mid-20th century. However, serious attention to the relational orientation did not begin until the 1950s and 1960s. Influential writers such as Robert Oliver (1962) attempted to get the field to pay more attention to the role of culture in communication and how different cultures viewed communication in other parts of the world.

Transitioning to the Relational

A new professional association for communication scholars was founded in 1950, the National Society for the Study of Communication, now known as the International Communication Association. This group was comprised of individuals disillusioned with studying communication exclusively from the rhetorical perspective. Some were general semanticists, others were primarily concerned with communication in organizations, and others in yet more applied communication settings. In the 1960s and 1970s this association attracted many scholars who were interested in interpersonal communication or the effects of mass media, particularly those who wished to study communication employing quantitative or experimental research methodologies.

The social-scientific movement was very important for the development of the study of human communication as it currently exists. Prior to the onset of this movement, most scholarship in this area employed critical or rationalistic approaches. These approaches were seen as appropriate for the study of essentially monological, one-way communication. Their focus was on the message and context as objects of study. As this one-way, hypodermic-needle approach to understanding communication came under increasing criticism both the target of research and the methodologies for research came into question.

The social scientific approach to studying human communication had been employed by some since early in the 20th century. However, it was not until the post–World War II era that the scientific method became the method of choice for a substantial number of communication scholars. It was natural that a different scholarly method would be applied to the same kinds of questions previously asked (how to persuade effectively) and to new questions. This, indeed, was the case. In the 1960s much of the social scientific research focused on the effects of sources and messages in producing persuasive effects. So much so that, when the early books on interpersonal communication were written, there was very little social-scientific research which could be cited in them. By the mid-1970s, however, it was possible to base a book on human communication almost entirely on the social scientific research (McCroskey & Wheeless, 1976).

By the time NSSC became ICA and reached its 25th anniversary, sizeable groups of scholars had formed scholarly interest areas representing organizational communication, interpersonal communication, information systems, mass communication, intercultural communication, instructional communication, health communication, and political communication. Most of these groups also included people from both the rhetorical and the relational traditions.

The quarter-century between 1950 and 1975 represented revolutionary change both in the culture of the United States and in the way people chose to study human communication. The post–World War II and Korean War eras saw dramatic increases in the enrollments of women and members of ethnic and racial minorities in American colleges and universities. Higher education no longer was the domain only of the elite, male, white ruling class.

The civil rights movement of the early 1960s was followed by the women's rights movement of the later 1960s and 1970s. The way people saw themselves relating to others began to change. There were enormous enrollment increases in colleges and universities when the "baby boomers" reached college age, which was exacerbated by rapid acceptance of the goals of the civil rights and women's rights movements.

These new students had different needs and arrived with different perspectives from those of their predecessors. Because colleges were no longer solely focused on educating "tomorrow's leaders," people began to question the extreme emphasis on teaching public speaking over other types of communication. Classes in small-group communication, and research in this area, greatly increased.

A Truly Relational Perspective

A call for more practical and realistic communication courses was heard. The response by the early 1970s was the initiation of new courses with the term "interpersonal" in their titles. Because little research from a relational perspective had been done by that time, the early courses tended to focus on rhetorical and psychological approaches to interpersonal communication. The early texts tended to focus on either humanistic (Giffin & Patton, 1971) or social scientific (McCroskey, Larson, & Knapp, 1971) orientations. A true relational perspective did not appear until later (Knapp, 1984).

Because *speech* was a term used to identify the traditional rhetorical orientation of the people who studied human communication, and the field was changing, people sought ways to change the identity of their field. While public speaking was no longer the sole, or even most important, focus of the field, people outside the field were generally unaware of this fact. At first, it seemed sufficient to simply add "communication" to the names of departments and associations. Soon it became clear that this change was not enough to make

outsiders aware that a major change had been made. Thus, by the mid-1990s the term *speech* had been dropped from the names of almost all scholarly journals in the field, from the names of all the regional and many of the state professional associations, and from the names of most of the departments at major universities. The names generally were changed to "Communication" or "Communication Studies," but some were renamed "Human Communication," "Interpersonal Communication," or "Communication Sciences," although the latter could be confused with some names used by groups concerned with speech pathology and audiology.

Human Communication Today

The study of human communication today is more diversified than ever before in its history. This diversity is reflected in both what is studied and the way that one goes about studying it.

Both the rhetorical and the relational traditions are alive and well and reflected in the chapters that follow. Each chapter outlines current thinking in either what could pass for a subfield (persuasion, intercultural communication, organizational communication), or a topic area (credibility, nonverbal communication), which has been and continues to be a focus of attention for numerous scholars, or an approach that some prefer to take in their study of human communication (cultural, feminist).

Because these chapters speak to the way these subfields, areas, or approaches are examined today, there is no need to go into detail here. Within the limitations of a book this size, it is not possible to fully introduce all of the areas within the human communication side of the field. Thus, we simply mention a few that are important but for which no chapter is included here.

The individual differences approach is one which has been employed by some scholars for the past half century and continues to draw major attention today. This approach looks at how people consistently differ from one another in their communication orientations and behaviors.

Sometimes this approach is referred to as the personality approach (McCroskey & Daly, 1987).

Scholars studying human communication from this approach investigate how different people have different traits or orientations which result in them communicating differently from other people and responding to others' communication differently as well. Two of the major topics within this area are concerns with people's general willingness to communicate with others and the fear or anxiety that people experience when confronted with communication (Daly & McCroskey, 1984).

With the rapid advances in social biology which indicate that personality has a firm genetic base, this area is one in which we can expect major advances in the next two decades. The possibility exists that through genetic engineering we will even be able to alter individuals' patterns of communication behavior that are found dysfunctional in society. Whether we will want to do this, however, is another question.

From the beginning of professional associations in the communication field, a significant number of the members have had a major concern with teaching. Originally that interest was centered on how to teach people to be better communicators. In recent years, this interest in instruction has expanded to a concern with the role of communication in the instructional process generally, not just in teaching communication (McCroskey, 1992). Considerable research in this area (Richmond & McCroskey, 1992) has pointed toward a central position for the study of communication to improve instruction in all disciplines.

Another applied area of communication study is an expansion of the basic interpersonal area. It is the study of communication within the family (Pearson, 1989). Recent research has been able to track the impact of communication between parents and children into the relationships that the younger generation have years later with their significant others. It would appear that understanding the communicative relationships within the family may be key to understanding other relationships people have.

An area which has received considerable attention in recent years is the role of gender in communication (Pearson, 1985). Although research focusing on the impact of biological sex differences on communication has generally found little impact, research on culturally based gender roles has indicated a very large impact. This is an area in which cross-cultural study is particularly useful, for we have learned that gender communication roles are so socialized into people that they are unlikely to recognize they are behaving according to a norm unless they see that there are different norms in other cultures.

A comparatively new approach to the study of communication is the developmental approach (Nussbaum, 1989). This approach examines how communication orientations and behaviors are likely to change during the individual's life span. Of particular interest has been the impact of aging on communication (Nussbaum, Thompson, & Robinson, 1989).

The most recent advance in the study of human communication is the introduction of the new paradigm named "communibiology" (Beatty & McCroskey, 1997, 2001; Beatty, McCroskey, & Heisel, 1998). For the previous history of the study of communication, most scholars assumed that most if not all communication behaviors were learned. Most research relating to the causes of communication behaviors was dominated by this learning paradigm. Near the end of the 20th century, scholars in communication became suspicious of this paradigm. The results of most of the research being reported at that time indicated that learning accounted for very little variance in their data analyses. The question then, was that if learning is not the primary cause of communication orientations or behaviors, what is the real cause(s)? Beatty and McCroskey speculated that some communication behavior may be a manifestation of biological factors. The results of their research supported that view. Genetics was the first biological area that was determined to have a powerful impact on communication orientations and behavior. In particular, genetically based brain systems known to drive human temperament have also been found to predict substantial variance in orientations and behaviors associated with the communication traits of verbal aggression and communication apprehension. More recent research is uncovering other biological factors with similar impact on communication orientations and behaviors, some of which are genetically based and some not.

Summary

Although steeped in tradition, the general trend of scholarship in the human communication side of the field of communication is toward more sophisticated theoretical development. It continues to develop more diverse subareas within each larger area of the field, while grounding itself in research methodologies useful for the specific concerns in the study of communication (rather than borrowing from other fields). Its approach is also increasingly concerned with applied communication research. The study of human communication today is undertaken in a vibrant and forward looking environment, building on firm traditions but diversifying to confront newly learned realities.

References

Beatty, M. J., & McCroskey, J. C. (1997). It's in our nature: Verbal aggressiveness as temperamental expression. *Communication Quarterly, 45,* 446–460.

Beatty, M. J., & McCroskey, J. C. (2001). *The biology of communication: A communibiological perspective.* Cresskill, NJ: Hampton Press.

Beatty, M. J., McCroskey, J. C., & Heisel, A. D. (1998). Communication apprehension as temperamental expression: A communibiological paradigm. *Communication Monographs, 65,* 197–219.

Daly, J. A., & McCroskey, J. C. (1984). *Avoiding communication: Shyness, reticence, and communication apprehension.* Beverly Hills, CA: Sage.

Giffin, K., & Patton, B. R. (1971). *Fundamentals of interpersonal communication.* New York: Harper & Row.

Knapp, M. L. (1984). *Interpersonal communication and human relationships.* Boston, MA: Allyn & Bacon.

McCroskey, J. C. (1968). *An introduction to rhetorical communication.* Englewood Cliffs, NJ: Prentice-Hall.

McCroskey, J. C. (1992). *An introduction to communication in the classroom.* Edina, MN: Burgess International.

McCroskey, J. C. (2006). *An introduction to rhetorical communication* (9th ed.). Boston: Allyn & Bacon.

McCroskey, J. C., & Daly, J. A. (1987). *Personality and interpersonal communication.* Newbury Park, CA: Sage.

McCroskey, J. C., Larson, C. E., & Knapp, M. L. (1971). *An introduction to interpersonal communication.* Englewood Cliffs, NJ: Prentice-Hall.

McCroskey, J. C., & Wheeless, L. R. (1976). *Introduction to human communication.* Boston, MA: Allyn & Bacon.

Nussbaum, J. F. (1989). *Life-span communication: Normative processes.* Hillsdale, NJ: Erlbaum.

Nussbaum, J. F., Thompson, T., & Robinson, J. D. (1989). *Communication and aging.* New York: Harper & Row.

Oliver, R. T. (1962). *Culture and communication: The problem of penetrating national boundaries.* Springfield, IL: National Textbook.

Pearson, J. C. (1985). *Gender and communication.* Dubuque, IA: William C. Brown.

Pearson, J. C. (1989). *Communication in the family: Seeking satisfaction in changing times.* New York: Harper & Row.

Richmond, V. P., & McCroskey, J. C. (1992). *Power in the classroom: Communication, control and concern.* Hillsdale, NJ: Erlbaum.

Shepherd, G. J. (1992). Communication as influence: Definitional exclusion. *Communication Studies, 43,* 203–219.

Suggested Readings

Beatty, M. J., & McCroskey, J. C. (2001). *The biology of communication: A communibiological perspective.* Cresskill, NJ: Hampton Press.

Daly, J. A., & McCroskey, J. C. (1984). *Avoiding communication: Shyness, reticence, and communication apprehension.* Beverly Hills, CA: Sage.

McCroskey, J. C. (2006). *An introduction to rhetorical communication* (9th ed.). Boston: Allyn & Bacon.

McCroskey, J. C., & Daly, J. A. (1987). *Personality and interpersonal communication.* Newbury Park, CA: Sage.

McCroskey, J. C., & Wheeless, L. R. (1976). *Introduction to human communication.* Boston, MA: Allyn & Bacon.

Richmond, V. P., & McCroskey, J. C. (1992). *Power in the classroom: Communication, control and concern.* Hillsdale, NJ: Erlbaum.

7. Communication Ethics

By Donald K. Wright

Popular television shows such as Mad Men, 30 Rock, *and* Scandal *and movies like* Absence of Malice, Wag the Dog, *and* Broadcast News *portray communication professionals in a negative light: news reporters willing to do anything for a juicy story; public relations practitioners lacking any sort of moral compass; advertisers acting in devious and deceptive ways; and film and television professionals being greedy, hyper-competitive egomaniacs. However, the reality is that a good communication professional has a considered and enforced ethical code. It is important that all communication professionals behave ethically because a communicator is judged by his or her credibility, and unethical behavior in any field will result in diminished credibility.*

This chapter summarizes various approaches to communication ethics, including both academic explanations of ethical theories and practical examples of ethics in professional practice. The concepts and practices summarized here are applicable in all communication career fields. Ethics is such an important component of good communication that many of the career-based chapters later in this text also address ethical considerations in the specific communication careers.

Although the study of ethics has been a significant part of social science scholarship for centuries and of communication study for many decades, it is a huge understatement to say the importance of ethics in communication has increased dramatically during the first years of the current century.

There are many reasons for this, including, but not necessarily limited to, serious ethical questions that concern communication scholars and practitioners. Some of these questions center upon the tactics journalists use to get information as the news business has become increasingly competitive in today's era of the non-stop, 24/7 news cycle complete with 24-hour news channels coupled with newspaper and broadcast station websites, not to mention bloggers and others who disseminate information through what have become known as consumer generated information channels. There has been some focus on public relations as this aspect of communication has advanced from merely helping organizations to say things, to providing guidance and counsel regarding what these organizations should do and how they should do it. Advertising, organizational communication and other aspects of the field also have faced their own stream of new ethical questions and concerns.

Philip Meyer (1987), who enjoyed two distinguished professional careers in the communication field—first as a newspaper reporter with *The Miami Herald* and then as a journalism professor at the University of North Carolina–Chapel Hill—called communication ethics "a slippery topic," and likened the assignment of defining ethical behavior to the task of defining art (p. vii).

Ethics—in all aspects of communication study and practice—has attracted a good deal of attention over the past few decades. Many who work in various aspects of communication are bombarded regularly with diverse ethical cues, and too few of these communications practitioners really have developed frameworks for making ethical judgments. This selection explores the concept of ethics from several perspectives, aiming at a *broad* understanding of the pragmatic, the conceptual, and the practical implications of *communication* ethics across disciplinary areas.

The Desire to Be Ethical

The desire for ethical behavior depends entirely upon the actions of individuals and the assumption that these people wish to act responsibly. Goodpaster and Matthews (1989) addressed three important concerns in terms of the ethical *responsibility* of individuals: someone is to blame, something has to be done, and some kind of trustworthiness can be expected.

The first of these affects an individual's action and whether he or she was responsible for the action. The second exists in circumstances in which individuals are responsible for others: lawyers to clients; physicians to patients; or, in the communication context, journalists to their readers, public relations professionals to their organizations and the public, and so on. The third meaning of ethical responsibility focuses on the individual's moral reasoning and the intellectual and emotional processes connected to it. Thus, ethical responsibility rests on the decisions people make regarding who is responsible for acting responsibly. These decisions are influenced by a variety of factors, most of which are often beyond the individual's understanding at the time (the individual is unprepared to deal with them for a variety of reasons, including lack of training in ethical reasoning), deal with a relationship with another person, or other persons, or communication environmental factors. However looked at, communication ethics boils down to making—or not making—a decision.

Ethics and Decision Making

The topic of ethics has attracted a good deal of attention throughout the communication community over the past few decades. Although those working in journalism, advertising, broadcasting, public relations, organizational communication, corporate communications, and communication education are bombarded with many diverse ethical cues, too few really have developed frameworks for making ethical judgments.

Ethics is the division of philosophy that deals with questions of moral behavior. Making ethical decisions in the communication environment is easy when the facts are clear and the choices are black and white. It's a different story when ambiguity clouds the situation along with incomplete information, multiple points of view, and conflicting responsibilities. In such situations, ethical decisions depend on both the decision-making process and on the decision makers—their experience, intelligence, and integrity.

Much of the applied communication and ethics literature centers on the role of the decision maker in ethical behavior. Although communication professionals do not always make decisions, their counsel quite frequently enters that decision-making process. There are circumstances where the decision-making role rests firmly within the communication function. An important aspect of many communication jobs is trying to help management make decisions.

In this process, the ethical question might be whether or not to say something as much as it might be whether or not to do something. Unfortunately, for some it is easy: to say nothing and later blame the unethical results on somebody else's decision. Dick Rosenberg (1991), Chairman of the Bank of America, told an audience of corporate communication professionals that, "We don't shoot people for bringing us bad news; we shoot them for delivering it too late." This view suggests that communications managers who can head off serious problems before they blow up in the company's face, surface in a newspaper's columns, or ruin an individual's reputation are two steps ahead of the game.

George (2007) encourages people to have an "internal compass that guides you successfully through life" (p. xxiii). He says individuals should establish personal ethical boundaries that could become "moral compasses [that] will kick in when you reach your limits and tell you it is time to pull back, even if the personal sacrifices may be significant" (p. 101). George claims that's what Enron executives Kenneth Lay and Jeffrey

Skilling lacked during the crisis that destroyed their company. According to George, a good way to understand individual ethical boundaries is to apply what he calls "the *New York Times* test."

> Before proceeding with any action, ask yourself, "How would I feel if this entire situation, including transcripts of our discussions, was printed on the first page of the *New York Times*?" If your answers are negative, then it is time to rethink your actions; if they are positive, you should feel comfortable proceeding, even if others criticize your actions later. (p. 101)

Outside of individual responsibility, people must assume that they work for somebody who wants to be told the truth. Further, that truth should be respected. Some system of ethics must serve as a cornerstone for any civilized society. Communication cannot be effective without being ethical and socially responsible.

Unfortunately, the people who make the decisions in American business do not always possess responsible moral judgments. Harvard business school professor Kenneth R. Andrews (1989) contends that ethical decisions require three qualities that can be identified and developed by individuals. These are:

1. Competence to recognize ethical issues and to think through the consequences of alternative resolutions.
2. Self-confidence to seek out different points of view and then to decide what is right at a given place and time, in a particular set of relationships and circumstances.
3. "Tough-mindedness," which is the willingness to make decisions when all that needs to be known cannot be known and when the questions that press for answers have no established and incontrovertible solutions. (p. 2)

Some Basic Questions

Most people understand the clear-cut differences in moral choice. They can recognize and decide what is good or evil, right or wrong, honest or dishonest. There is, however, a faulty assumption held by many in our society that communication practitioners can be unethical—as long as they resolve conflicting claims in their own hearts and minds. There are people who often resort to certain rationalizations that appear to justify questionable behavior.

Although ethical decisions are often hard enough to make, there is much more to communication ethics than struggling with the short-range decisions on a case-by-case basis. Ethical communication begins with individuals' capacity for socially constructing a long-range moral realism.

One way or another, most people break some law at least once every day. Those who fall into that category rationalize away some of their illegal (and morally wrong) behavior. The speed limit is 55 miles-per-hour but a person drives at 62 ("everyone's doing it; it would be unsafe to do otherwise"). People jaywalk ("no traffic, why walk to the corner and then back?"). Healthy people sometimes park their cars in places reserved for handicapped drivers. Merely breaking the law, however, is not necessarily equivalent to acting unethically; sometimes adhering to the law can be unethical, as examples of Martin Luther King, Jr. and Mahatma Gandhi illustrate.

Communication scholars often see ethically perplexing situations where deciding who is ethical and who is not might depend more upon individual or organizational beliefs than anything else. Paul (1994) pointed out that although the fast-food industry frequently gets called unethical for producing food that is high in fat and cholesterol and encourages obesity, nobody forces people to eat the products of the fast-food restaurant industry. In recent years, retailers have been accused of being unethical for encouraging the concept of "vanity sizing," which involves changing labels of "extra large" sized clothes to "large" or "medium" so customers will ignore the reality they are gaining weight. As the *New York Times* (2007) pointed out, when controversial nationally syndicated radio "shock-jock" Don Imus was fired for making racially and sexually insulting remarks, some questioned why the exact same words Imus used on the radio are allowed to be broadcast daily as part of the genre known as rap music. Poniewozik (2007) said although "it was clear he [Imus] crossed a line. What's unclear is: Where's the line and who can cross it?" (p. 32). Carr (2007) addressed the Imus situation this way, pointing out that remarks such as those Imus made were much less damaging years ago before new technologies were a factor in the ethics of communication:

> Mr. Imus is an old school radio guy caught in a very modern media paradigm. When he started 30 years ago, if he made the same kind of remark, it would have floated off into the ether—the Federal Communications Commission, if it received complaints, might have taken notice, but few others.

> But radio is now visible—Mr. Imus's show was simulcast on MSNBC, and more to the point, it is downloadable. By Friday, reporters and advocates could click up the remark on the Media Matters for America website, and later YouTube, and see a vicious racial insult that delighted him visibly as it rolled off his tongue. The ether now has a memory.

> Time heals, time forgets, but Mr. Imus was seeking to shore up his career immediately. Mr. Imus never caught a breath because he was in the middle of a 24-hour news cycle that kept him in the crosshairs. It is the kind of media ceremony that generally ends in a human sacrifice. (2007, pp. C1, C5)

Defining the Concept of Ethics

As noted earlier, *ethics* is the branch of philosophy that deals with questions of moral behavior. It is similar to a set of principles or a code of moral conduct (Fink, 1988). The study of ethics can provide the tools for making difficult moral choices. Students of communication do not need to know as much about how to make ethical decisions as they need to possess the knowledge and ability to defend critical judgments on some rational basis. Perhaps more than anything else, they need to recognize ethical problems when they arise.

It is inevitable that conflicts among competing values will emerge in this process. The study of ethics and moral reasoning cannot necessarily resolve such conflicts, but they can provide the tools to make it easier to live with difficult ethical choices. And, cutting through the rhetoric, most—if not all—know when we are ethical and when we are not.

According to ethics scholar Richard Johannesen (1983), ethical situations are multifaceted. They usually arise when a *moral agent* (the one making the ethical decision) commits an *act* (either verbal or nonverbal) within a specific *context* with a particular *motive* directed at an *audience*. Johannesen argues that *each* factor must be taken into account before passing judgment on the outcome of any moral scenario.

As a formal field of inquiry, ethics can be further divided into three related subareas (Callahan, 1988). *Meta-ethics* attempts to assign meanings to the abstract language of moral philosophy. *Normative ethics* provides the foundation for decision making through the development of general rules and principles of moral conduct. *Applied ethics* is concerned with using these theoretical norms to solve real-world ethical problems. Each provides ethics scholars with areas from which to construct ethical frameworks at varying levels of the decision-making process, from the language used in rationalizing an ethical decision to applying an ethical framework in real-world situations.

Why This Concern about Ethics?

Why this concern about communication ethics? One popular answer suggests that Americans have become morally adrift without traditional anchors. We have compromised our individual

ethics so frequently that it sometimes becomes just as easy to compromise our professional ethics.

Followers of Sigmund Freud suggest that the development of moral character and habits of moral thought essentially are complete in early childhood. This Freudian view meets considerable resistance, particularly from Lawrence Kohlberg (1981) and his followers who believe that moral development undergoes significant structural changes well into adulthood.

Despite some huge differences between these two theses, there is strong agreement that moral development is *learned* behavior. The following scenario, filled with communication examples, forces us to think about that:

> A man and a woman take their two children, whose ages are 6 and 13, to a movie. The neighbors think they're great parents. En route to the theatre the man breaks the speed limit, drives through one stoplight after it has turned from green to amber and fails to come to a complete stop at two separate stop signs. He also fails to signal while making turns and changing lanes. Just before purchasing the movie tickets, the woman tells the 13-year-old to claim he is 12, so the parents can pay the less expensive children's ticket rate. After the movie the family eats in a buffet restaurant. The parents ask the 6-year-old to claim she is 5 so they can pay less. What message do these children learn from these examples?

> Does it matter that the man was speeding? Does it matter that there was no other traffic at the intersections where he did not completely stop at the stop signs?

> A week later the 13-year-old is arrested for shoplifting at a local mall. The parents, and the neighbors, wonder why.

Many of these decisions present us with difficulty. Some ethical decisions are simple. Others are more complex. If you support abortion you are a killer of babies; if you oppose abortion you do not respect the rights of women. To attempt to justify a principle morally, belief, attitude, policy, or action is to seek good reasons in support of it. *Good* reasons are reasons you are willing to commend to others rather than simply accept privately.

A large portion of our concern about ethics comes from a realization that possessing a system of ethics is not merely a *sufficient* condition for social intercourse, but is a *necessary* requirement. Ethics is the foundation of advanced civilization, a cornerstone that provides some stability to society's moral expectations. In the communication business it is essential that we enter into agreements with others. As such, we must be able to trust one another to keep those agreements—even if to do so is not always in our best self-interest.

Ethics not only has to be the cornerstone of effective practice of organizational communication, it also must be the cornerstone of any civilization where virtues such as truth, honesty, and integrity are to prevail. A system of ethics is essential for:

1. building trust and cooperation among individuals in society;
2. serving as a moral gatekeeper in apprising society of the relative importance of certain moral values;
3. acting as a moral arbitrator in resolving conflicting claims based on individual self interests; and
4. clarifying for society the competing values and principles inherent in emerging and novel moral dilemmas.

Can Ethics Be Taught?

There are two schools of thought on the question of whether ethics can be taught. One school claims it is a waste of time to study ethics because moral character and habits of moral thought are fully developed even before children begin formal education. Advocates of this position (e.g., Freud, 1923/1961; Simon, 1971) pointed out that

knowledge about ethical principles does not always produce moral behavior. These skeptics also believe that the process of moral development is completed in most people before they are 6 years old. They do not believe the teaching of ethics in public schools is needed, much less at colleges and universities.

The other school of thought views ethics as a subject like history, sociology, chemistry or mathematics. Advocates (e.g., Florman, 1978; Jaska & Pritchard, 1994; Toffler, 1986) argue that ethics has its own sets of standards and rules as well as distinctive methods of problem solving.

The study of ethics comes with its own unique set of problems. More than most academic subjects, ethical viewpoints are shaped and molded through a variety of different aspects of society. A person's individual ethical beliefs are the product of many factors, including family, religion, economic status, environment, age, gender, race, and so forth.

One of the strongest arguments in favor of studying ethics comes from scholars who believe in the process of moral reasoning (e.g., Kohlberg, 1981). These scholars believe ethics involves much more than memorizing a list of ethical principles and view ethics instruction as an important component in moral conduct because it provides information and perspectives that people need to make ethical judgments.

Ethical decisions are not made in a vacuum. Day (1991) pointed out that these decisions involve a variety of considerations which can be grouped into three categories: (1) the situational definition; (2) an analysis of the situation; and (3) the ethical judgment. Advocates of moral reasoning view it as a structured, systematic approach to ethical decision making. It also provides an intellectual means of defending ethical judgments against criticisms. The Hastings Center (1980), a pioneer in ethics education, recommended these five steps be followed in preparing people to be effective in the process of moral reasoning: stimulating the moral imagination, recognizing ethical issues, developing analytical skills, eliciting a sense of moral obligation and personal responsibility, and tolerating disagreement.

Ethical Theories

The study of ethics is certainly not new. In his history of philosophy, Anders Wedberg (1982) traces ethical theories to antiquity, to the ancient Greeks. From these early beginnings can be traced the modern moral questions that contemporary communication researchers and theorists now study.

Classical Ethical Theory

The study of ethics began in ancient Greece with Socrates (c. 470–399 BC), who claimed virtue could be identified and practiced. Plato (c. 428–348 BC), who was his disciple, advocated moral conduct, even in situations when responsible behavior might run counter to societal norms. Plato's student, Aristotle (384–322 BC), argued that moral virtue often required tough choices.

Development of the Judeo-Christian ethic brought forward the concept of "love thy neighbor as thyself," which introduced the importance of a love for God and all other people. In the 18th century, Immanuel Kant (1724–1804), a German philosopher, introduced the *categorical imperative* which was a duty-based moral philosophy. Kant (1785/1982) believed in the duty to tell the truth even if it resulted in harm to others. Partially in response to Kant came the progressive relativism school of thought that believes what is right or good for one is not necessarily right or good for another, even under similar circumstances.

Classical ethical theory views ethical obligation in two different ways. *Teleological ethics* underscores the consequences of an act or decision, whereas *deontological ethics* emphasizes the nature of an act or decision.

The teleological approach deals with two basic approaches, *ethical egoism* and *utilitarianism*. Egoists make decisions based on what result is best for them, whereas utilitarianism attempts to foster whatever is best for the entire society. The tradition of egoism dates to Epicurus (c. 342–271 BC), who advocated people should do those things that would lead to their own satisfaction (Albert, Denise, & Peterfreund, 1980). Writings of more contemporary egoism theorists, such

as Ayn Rand (1964), are much more a blend of reason and justification of self-interest. Jeremy Bentham (1748–1832) is noted as the founder of utilitarianism, a philosophy that endeavors to provide "the greatest happiness for the greatest number" (Christians, Rotzoll, & Fackler, 1987, pp. 12–13). Bentham's "hedonistic calculus" was designed to serve as a manual to direct his followers in taking appropriate actions. Now seen as old-fashioned, the calculus has given way to the broad overview of Bentham's philosophy. The more modern versions of utilitarianism focus on either acts or rules. *Act utilitarianism* places little value in precepts, claiming rules such as "thou shalt not kill," "never lie," and so forth, only provide rough directions for moral and ethical experiences. *Rule utilitarianism,* in contrast, is more concerned with what rule or action, when followed, will maximize the greatest good rather than with what rule or action will result in the greatest good result (Boyce & Jensen, 1978).

In examining the nature of the act in determining the lightness of an action, deontologists believe there are acts that are moral or immoral by their very nature, regardless of consequences or outcome. Immanuel Kant generally is considered the forefather of deontological ethics. He is especially known as the seminal thinker in *pure rule deontology,* by which people follow a rationally derived duty to tell the truth. Another branch of this thinking, known as *pure act deontology,* asserts that because no two circumstances are alike the nature of acts and decisions constantly change (Kant, 1785/1982). As such, act deontologists reject reason as a means to calculate moral conduct and are influenced more by the urgency of the moment and their innate ethical sense. Some deontologists consider not only the nature of an act in determining its lightness, but also its consequences. These people are known as *mixed deontologists* (Lambeth, 1986).

As ethical theory and research developed in the traditional areas of scholarship—philosophy, the classics, and so forth—*moral rules* came to represent the fuel that powered the ethical system. They provided guideposts for resolving ethical dilemmas and posed moral duties on individuals.

In fulfilling moral duties people took into account all parties, including themselves, who may be touched by our ethical decisions.

Moral Reasoning Theories

Four criteria form the basis of any system of ethics. These are shared values, wisdom, justice, and freedom. First of all, an ethical system must have shared values. Before ethical judgments can be made, society must reach agreement on its standards of moral conduct. Second, these standards should be based on reason and experience. They should seek to harmonize people's rights and interests with their obligations to their fellow citizens. Third, a system of ethics should seek justice. There should be no double standard of treatment unless there is an overriding and morally defensible reason to discriminate. Finally, an ethical system should be based on freedom of choice. Moral agents must be free to render ethical judgments without coercion. Only in this way will the individual's ethical level of consciousness be raised.

In the cosmopolitan sense of the terms, ethics and moral values outline the ideals and standards people should live by. However, as those who study ethics quickly realize, no set of principles exists that will solve all ethical dilemmas. Much of the literature involved with communication ethics views ethics with a focus on what too many people refer to as *degrees* of *rightness* and *wrongness*. While ethics certainly deals with truth, fairness, and honesty, in the United States at least, the legal environment has the clear-cut mandate to be concerned with right and wrong.

Differences between *Law* and *Ethics*

The central core of what ethics and morality are all about deals with differences between what is *good* or *bad*. Laws focus on questions of what is *right* or *wrong*. Although it is possible for a law to be bad, something ethically good should always be right. Societies make and change laws, but ethical principles, theoretically at least, remain constant over time.

For example, for decades in the United States certain laws prevented African-Americans and women from voting. Many considered these laws to be bad because they violated a greater good. And, of course, eventually these laws were changed. Although societies can enact these laws, they are not ethical. Most laws, however, are consistent with ethical philosophy. Few would challenge laws that protect members of a society against those who murder, rape, or commit armed robbery. However, laws frequently are challenged by members of society who do not believe the ordinances are good.

Various Sets of Loyalties

The morally and ethically responsible person gives each set of loyalties its share of attention before rendering an ethical determination. For most of us the following categories must be examined: duty to ourselves, duty to one's organization or firm, duty to professional colleagues, and duty to society.

These loyalty sets provide interesting questions for professional communicators. Some newspaper journalists might believe their first duty is to their readers, advertising people could think their first loyalty to clients, public relations professionals might think their first loyalty is to client stockholders. An ethical issue could present itself for communicators if actions that might be moral for one public are unethical for another.

The issue of loyalty and ethics frequently surfaces in the area of religion, especially among fundamentalists. Muslim fundamentalists planned and carried out the horrible terrorist attacks of September 11, 2001 while apparently believing they were performing actions approved by a supreme being. Christian fundamentalists have been accused of bridging unethical territory when they urge believers to rally against what others perceive as the human rights of women seeking abortions and homosexuals seeking a world devoid of prejudice based upon sexual preference.

Issues Involving Communication Ethics Research

Most research involving ethics and responsibility in communication and related disciplines is concerned with problems of justice and duties—that is, *good*, *truth*, and *right*—and with stages of moral judgments and duties. Frankena (1963) claimed the academic study of ethics involves three kinds of normative or moral judgments. These include:

> judgments of moral obligation or deontic judgments, which say a certain action is right or obligatory; judgments of morally good or aretaic judgments, which say that certain people, motives, or character traits are morally good, virtuous; and judgments of nonmoral value in which we evaluate not so much actions and persons but all sorts of other things including experiences, paintings, forms of government, and what not. (p. 147)

The study of ethics in contemporary communication public relations research and practice generally reflects some interpretation or judging of value systems and is representative of much contemporary research. As Wilcox, Ault, and Agee (1986) described it, "a person determines what is right or wrong, fair or unfair, just or unjust. It is expressed through moral behavior in specific situations" (p. 108).

Early work involving communication ethics usually considered the basic human need to function in honest and ethical ways. A good number of these articles also combined ethics and professionalism while some concerned themselves with accreditation and licensing. Writings of Appley (1948), Bateman (1957), Bernays (1979, 1980), and Harlow (1951, 1969) justify this claim. Bateman was one of the first to encourage communication practice to develop a philosophic structure to serve as the source of its ethics. The early works of Carr-Saunders and Wilson (1993) and Flexner (1930) suggest that professions be "guided by altruism." Greenwood (1966) and Liberman (1956) were among the first to mention a code of ethics as part of the criteria which must be satisfied for an "occupation" to be a "profession."

A Divergence of Communications Viewpoints

Ethics in communication can be confusing, especially when scholars and practitioners do not always agree with their colleagues in other segments of the discipline.

Print and broadcast journalists, for example, frequently differ from people who work in public relations. These disagreements can be over simple matters such as whether or not journalists are ethical if they accept free food and beverages at press conferences. They also can entail more complex and serious controversy. For example, some journalists actually believe that anything that happens in public relations is unethical and would deny organizations the right to seek counsel on matters related to public opinion. Izard (1984–1985) reported that many journalists believe some forms of deception are permissible "if the situation demands it and circumstances are right" (p. 8). Some public relations people, on the other hand, point out that the media's agendas often hurt society, even though they might sell publications and attract broadcasting audiences.

Disagreements of this nature were common during the Watergate scandals in the early 1970s. Although journalists praised the work of *Washington Post* reporters Bob Woodward and Carl Bernstein in exposing the misdeeds of big government, many public relations experts questioned the ethics that appeared to permit these journalists to practice deception while seeking information. In academic research, for instance, the ethical perceptions journalists and public relations professionals have for similar situations been found to differ (Ryan & Martinson, 1984).

Codes of Ethics

Any discussion about communication ethics would not be complete without devoting some time to issues such as licensing, accreditation, and codes of ethics. In some ways, ethical research involving these topics has raised more issues than it has resolved. Rarely, if ever, is there total agreement regarding topics such as licensing, accreditation, and codes of ethics.

In all likelihood American communication professionals never will become licensed by the government. One reason for this might be found in the First Amendment. Print and broadcast journalists as well as those who work in public relations, advertising, and organizational communication, hold strong beliefs suggesting free and open communication for all is more important than the restrictions some would face through licensing in any of these areas.

Codes of ethics are fairly commonplace throughout the communication industry. Most communication professional organizations have ethical codes. The most noted of these codes are those of the Society of Professional Journalists, the Public Relations Society of America, the International Public Relations Association, and the International Association of Business Communicators. Such codes represent industry self-regulation in the absence of government restrictions and are controversial to say the least (Bernays, 1979, 1980).

Although many have praised the merits of communication codes of ethics, critics point out these codes usually are unenforceable. They also are dismissed by many as being merely cosmetic (Merrill & O'Dell, 1983). Still, supporters claim the field is better with them than without them. Just as the voluntary nature of codes of ethics makes most of them unenforceable, professional accreditation programs have not made ethical codes any more accountable, and this situation is unlikely to change in Western society.

The fact that there are no legal restrictions on the practice of communication—as there are in law or medicine—poses dilemmas for the communication industry that must be resolved. The problem is that any person—qualified or not—who wants to work in journalism, public relations, broadcasting, advertising, or any other aspect of communication in most Western nations, can do so. Violations of conduct codes have kept a small

minority out of some professional organizations, but codes cannot prevent them from working in the field.

Codes of ethics in communication have some strengths and can be valuable, but their voluntary nature—that is, their inability to be enforced—breeds inherent problems. Most codes of ethics for communication-related associations are filled with meaningless rhetoric, do not accomplish much, and are not taken seriously by most of the people who work in organizational communication. These codes might be able to make ethical behavior less likely because of awareness. With or without professional codes of conduct, most who practice communication will choose to be ethical because they behave ethically themselves and want others to respect them. In light of the voluntary nature of these codes, most communicators are ethical because they want to be, not because they have to be. Some claimed that enforcement of these codes often is infrequent and uneven (e.g., Cutlip, Center, & Broom, 1985). Others pointed out that many communications professionals do not belong to professional associations and note the inability of these organizations to prohibit these nonmember practitioners from violating these codes, even if the organization belongs to or adheres to a professional code of conduct (Grunig & Hunt, 1984).

Is Ethics an Individual Issue?

Our own studies of communicators in a number of contexts—including corporate communications, public relations, broadcasting and journalism—suggest that ethics is an individual issue, claiming it is up to individual practitioners to decide whether or not to be ethical regardless of professional ethical codes (Wright, 1976, 1979, 1982, 1985).

Although not dealing directly with the wide variety of occupational duties in public relations practice—including the four Grunig (1976) models of practice and the Broom-Dozier (Broom & Dozier, 1986) assessment of different practitioner roles—a major assumption of this doctrine of the individual implies press agents could be as ethical as the two-way symmetrical communicators if they had such a desire (see chapter 29). It also would contend that communication managers are not necessarily more ethical than communication technicians. We have suggested many times that public relations and communication never will be any more ethical than the level of basic morality of the people who are in public relations. This is to agree with those who claim the occupational or professional ethics of a person cannot be separated from that individual's personal ethics. Indeed one major sign of ethical and moral maturity, in Kohlberg's (1981) opinion, is the ability to make ethical judgments and formulate moral principles on our own rather than our ability to conform to moral judgments of people around us. Scholars have supported this argument for centuries. Socrates, Plato, and Aristotle all stressed the importance of individual moral convictions in their writings about ethics.

Ethics in Group Decision Making

Most ethical choices center around decision making. Although some decision-making situations in organizational communication involve the individual, most include task-oriented small groups of employees.

Modern-day organizations consider sensitivity to ethical behavior to be a strong leadership attribute. Although management groups are not always able to comprehend the ethical and moral value interpretations of all their decisions, groups try to avoid making unethical decisions. Dennis Gouran (1991) suggested five ideas that help encourage more ethical group decisions:

1. show proper concern for all affected by the group's decision;
2. explore the discussion stage of decision making as responsibly as possible;
3. avoid misrepresenting any position or misusing any information;
4. do not say or do anything that could diminish any group member's sense of self-worth; and,
5. make certain all group members respect each other. (pp. 166–167, 222)

Herbert E. Gulley (1968) provided another set of guidelines for ethical communication in small-group settings. These suggest:

1. communicators have the responsibility for defending the policy decisions of groups in whose deliberations they have participated;
2. communicators must be well informed and accurate;
3. communicators should actively encourage the comments of others and explore all viewpoints;
4. communicators should openly reveal their own biases and identify their sources of information;
5. communicators should neither lie, deceive, fabricate evidence, falsify facts, nor invent information or sources;
6. communicators should not attempt to manipulate group discussions unfairly so that selfish motives are served at the expense of the group; and,
7. communicators should avoid the use of tactics such as name calling, emotionally "loaded" language, guilt-by-association, hasty generalizations, shifting definitions, and oversimplified either-or alternatives. (pp. 334–366)

Examining Communication Ethics Research

The contemporary study of ethics in communication research and practice is fairly young and generally reflects some interpretation or judging. Opinions about ethics and moral values in all aspects of communication vary widely. Some of the early research, particularly in journalism, attempted to determine what was right and what was wrong, fair or unfair, just or unjust. Other research approached the study of ethics through moral behavior in specific situations, much of which also considered the basic human need to function in honest and ethical ways.

Most of the research concerning ethics and communication employs a wide variety of quantitative and qualitative methodologies, traceable to three separate and unique areas: journalism and broadcasting, public relations, and speech communication. These studies include survey research, personal interviews, focus groups, experimental, and critical methods.

Journalism and *broadcasting studies* involving ethics have existed for nearly half a century. The Hutchins Commission report on freedom of the press in 1947 criticized print journalism for its lack of social responsibility (Hocking, 1947). Journalism ethics also concerns the First Amendment, business aspects of the mass media, invasion of privacy, the relationship between reporters and a wide variety of news sources, pornography and allegedly morally offensive material, and a variety of case study reports dealing with examples in many of these topical areas.

Most of these ethical topics are discussed thoroughly in four of the foremost books on the topic of journalism ethics. Rivers and Mathews (1988) provided a fairly thorough clarification of ethical issues combined with specific and practical suggestions for solutions. Their work included journalistic virtues, objectivity, basic news gathering, standards for news reporters, press councils, and media codes of ethics. The book also addresses sexism, investigative reporting, privacy, photojournalism, and freedom of the press. Christians, Flacker, and Rotzoll (1995) devoted several editions of a book that used commentaries and cases taken from actual media experiences to encourage journalists and other media practitioners to think analytically and to improve ethical awareness.

Lambeth (1986) concentrated on outlining the principles journalists should consider in making ethical judgments. His work also attempts to provide direction on to whom, or what, journalists owe professional loyalty—themselves, the public, an employer, or colleagues. Hulteng (1985) used the case study approach to illustrate the problems media practitioners face in making practical applications of ethical principles and moral standards. Meyer's research (1987) involved a large survey of editors, publishers, and reporters and documents ethical confusion

in American journalism during the Watergate and Pentagon Papers controversy. Swain (1978) explored how newspaper reporters handle the delicate questions of ethics that arise repeatedly in their pressured daily routines.

Public Relations ethics research studies began in the 1950s with articles that encouraged public relations to develop a philosophic structure to serve as the source of its ethics. Since then, a number of empirical studies examined various aspects of the public relations process including ethical questions concerning individual practice, dealings with the news media, and the overall improvement of professional working standards.

Ferre and Willihnganz (1991) reported that nearly 300 books or articles had been published on the subject of public relations ethics since 1922, which, since public relations considers itself to be the conscience of corporations and society, is a very low number indeed. Unlike other areas of communication, in which many books were written, Ferre and Willihnganz noted that most of the ethics articles that concern public relations are short essays. The majority also are positive articles, claiming, for the most part, that public relations people believe in honesty, integrity, and in telling the truth.

Public relations ethics receive some coverage, albeit minor, in some of the books concerned mainly with ethics in journalism and mass communication (Christians et al., 1995, pp. 225–262; Day, 1991, pp. 71–75, 89–90, 131, 148–158, 171–174, 273–275, 313–315). Of the many journal articles, Ryan and Martinson's (1984) comparison of differences between journalists and public relations professionals stands alone, as does Kruckeberg's (1989) research on codes of ethics, Pearson's (1989) work on the theory of public relations ethics, and some of Wright's articles involving communicator analysis studies of individual public relations practitioners (Wright, 1979, 1982, 1985, 1989).

Speech Communication ethics research has been conducted from political, human nature, dialogical, and situational perspectives. The literature in this area also lists studies regarding ethics and various aspects of oral communication skills—public speaking, interpersonal, and small-group communication.

Much of the speech communication studies involving ethics explore ethical implications of a wide variety of human communication experiences, both oral and written. One of the most prolific scholars in this area is Richard L. Johannesen, whose work also attempts to provide direction to participants in the communication process and to encourage individuals to develop their own working approach to assessing communication ethics (e.g., Johannesen, 1983). Other leading research in this area includes Nilsen's (1974) efforts to provide a general orientation by which to guide communication conduct, Barnlund's (1962) insistence that all human communication theory must include moral standards specifications, and Miller's (1969) perceptions about ethical implications between communicators and audiences.

Practical Applications of Communication Ethics Research

This section examines two practical applications of communication ethics research. One involves journalism; the other corporate communications. Both of these studies could be adapted to other aspects of communication research.

Sample Journalism Ethics Study

The journalism study involves the moral values of journalists that would be measured via a mail questionnaire sent to a large, random national sample of members of the Society of Professional Journalists.

Assuming a 40 percent return rate for studies of this nature, obtaining 350 usable responses would necessitate an initial mailing of no fewer than 875 questionnaires. If funding was available, 1,000 questionnaires would be mailed. Questionnaires, accompanied by a cover letter from a noted journalist encouraging participation in the study, and a self-addressed and stamped return envelope would be mailed to randomly selected participants. Any questionnaire of this nature would need to be extremely user-friendly and probably no longer than three or four pages to enhance the return rate.

In addition to a small number of basic demographic questions, the questionnaire would concentrate on three areas: perceived moral values of subjects themselves; perceived moral values of subjects' peers; and, subjects' job satisfaction. Questions could be derived from any number of indices and previous research questions measuring these items. Data analysis would compare and contrast scores registered in each of these three areas. If additional funding could be acquired the researcher might wish to test results through five or six focus groups of journalists in various parts of the nation.

Sample Corporation Communication Ethics Study

The corporate communications study is concerned with the impact on corporate public relations professionals of organizational codes of ethics, sometimes known as *corporate vision, values,* or *beliefs statements.* The sample would consist of senior-level corporate public relations executives; the most likely sources for the sample's population would be the directories of the Public Relations Seminar or the Arthur W. Page Society, both populated by senior-level public relations professionals.

Data gathering would consist of two parts. First, the researcher would identify several organizations that have corporate ethical codes, value statements, or similar codes. Ideally these would be Fortune 100 companies and should yield no fewer than five and no more than ten organizations. Public relations practitioners in these organizations would be surveyed in an attempt to measure the perceived impact these organizational behavior codes have on professional behavior in their specific organizations.

Second, public relations executives from other organizations would be surveyed to determine how they perceived the impact of these behavior codes. This external study also would attempt to gather information concerning the impact, if any, on corporate communications and public relations behavior caused through codes of ethics of professional societies such as the Public Relations Society of America and the International Public Relations Association. Data analysis would test for differences between the perceived effectiveness of various aspects of these codes of ethics.

Conclusion

All in all, those who work in various professional aspects of the field of communication have made considerable progress in the direction of more ethical behavior. The field has come a long way, but it still has a long way to go.

When it comes to the bottom line, the final arbiter in separating right from wrong or good from evil in communication is the decision maker. And the authenticity of any decision depends on a universal form of morality. The higher good is purity of motive rather than the good or harm of outcome. The central value in the unwritten contract people make with society is fairness or decision making guided by principles anyone and everyone would agree with.

References

Albert, E. M., Denise, T. C., & Peterfreund, S. (1980). *Great traditions in ethics.* New York: Van Nostrand.

Andrews, K. R. (Ed.). (1989). *Ethics in practice: Managing the moral corporation.* Boston: Harvard Business School Press.

Appley, L. A. (1948). The obligations of a new profession. *Public Relations Journal, 4,* 4–9.

Barnlund, D. C. (1962). Toward a meaning-centered philosophy of communication. *Journal of Communication, 12,* 198.

Bateman, J. C. (1957). The path to professionalism. *Public Relations Journal, 13,* 6–8, 19.

Bernays, E. L. (1979). The case for licensing and registration for public relations. *Public Relations Quarterly, 24,* 26–28.

Bernays, E. L. (1980). Gaining professional status for public relations. *Public Relations Quarterly, 25,* 20.

Boyce, W. D., & Jensen, L. C. (1978). *Moral reasoning.* Lincoln: University of Nebraska Press.

Broom, G. M., & Dozier, D. M. (1986). Advancement for public relations role models. *Public Relations Review, 12,* 37–56.

Callahan, J. C. (Ed.). (1988). *Ethical issues in professional life.* New York: Oxford University Press.

Carr, D. (2007). Flying solo past the point of no return. *New York Times* (April 13), C1 & C5.

Carr-Saunders, A. M., & Wilson, P. A. (1933). *The professions.* Oxford: Clarendon Press.

Christians, C. G., Fackler, M., & Rotzoll, K.B. (1995). *Media ethics: Cases and moral reasoning* (4th ed.). White Plains, NY: Longman.

Christians, C. G., Rotzoll, K.B., & Fackler, M. (1987). *Media ethics: Cases and moral reasoning* (2nd ed.). White Plains, NY: Longman.

Cutlip, S.M., Center, A. H., & Broom, G.M. (1985). *Effective public relations* (6th ed.). Englewood Cliffs, NJ: Prentice-Hall.

Day, L. A. (1991). *Ethics in media communications: Cases and controversies.* Belmont, CA: Wadsworth.

Ferre, J.P., & Willihnganz, S.C. (1991). *Public relations and ethics: A bibliography.* Boston, MA: Hall. Fink, C. C. (1988). *Media ethics: In the newsroom and beyond.* New York: McGraw-Hill.

Flexner, A. (1930). *Universities: American, English, German.* Oxford: Oxford University Press.

Florman, S. (1978, October). Moral blueprints. *Harpers, 31.*

Frankena, W. K. (1963). *Ethics.* Englewood Cliffs, NJ: Prentice-Hall.

Freud, S. (1961). *Civilization and its discontents* (J. Strachey, Ed. & Trans.). New York: Norton. (Original work published 1923).

George, B. (2007). *True north: Discover your authentic leadership.* San Francisco: Jossey-Bass.

Goodpaster, K. E., & Matthews, J. B., Jr. (1989). Can a corporation have a conscience? In K. R. Andrews (Ed.), *Ethics in practice: Managing the moral corporation* (pp. 155–167). Boston: Harvard Business School Press.

Gouran, D. (1991). *Making decisions in groups.* Glenville, IL: Scott Foresman.

Greenwood, E. (1966). The elements of professionalism. In H.M. Vollmer & D. L. Mills (Eds.), *Professionalization* (pp. 9–19). Englewood Cliffs, NJ: Prentice-Hall.

Grunig, J.E. (1976). Organizations and public relations: Testing a communication theory. *Journalism Monographs, 46,* 1–59.

Grunig, J. E., & Hunt, T. (1984). *Managing public relations.* New York: Holt, Rinehart & Winston.

Gulley, H. E. (1968). *Discussion, conference, and group process* (2nd ed.). New York: Holt, Rinehart & Winston.

Harlow, R. F. (1951). A plain lesson we should heed. *Public Relations Journal, 5,* 7–10.

Harlow, R. F. (1969). Is public relations a profession? *Public Relations Quarterly, 14,* 37.

Hastings Center. (1980). *The teaching of ethics in higher education.* Hastings-on-Hudson, NY: Author.

Hocking, W. E. (1947). *Freedom of the press: A framework of principle* (Report from the Commission on Freedom of the Press). Chicago: University of Chicago Press.

Hulteng, J. L. (1985). *The messenger's motives: Ethical problems of the news media* (2nd ed.). Englewood Cliffs, NJ: Prentice-Hall.

Izard, R. S. (1984–1985). *Deception: Some cases rate approval if other methods don't work* (Journalism Ethics Report). Chicago: Society of Professional Journalists.

Jaska, J. A., & Pritchard, M. S. (1994). *Communication ethics: Methods of analysis* (2nd ed.). Belmont, CA: Wadsworth.

Johannesen, R. L. (1983). *Ethics in human communication* (2nd ed.). Prospect Heights, IL: Waveland Press.

Kant, I. (1982). The good will and the categorical imperative. In T. L. Beauchamp (Ed.), *Philosophical ethics: An introduction to moral philosophy* (pp. 3–17). New York: McGraw-Hill. (Original work published 1785)

Kohlberg, L. (1981). *Essays on moral development: Vol. 1. The philosophy of moral development: Moral stages and the idea of justice.* New York: Harper & Row.

Kruckeberg, D. (1989, Summer). The need for an international code of ethics. *Public Relations Review,* 6–18.

Lambeth, E. B. (1986). *Committed journalism: An ethic for the profession.* Bloomington, IN: Indiana University Press.

Liberman, M. (1956). *Education as a profession.* Englewood Cliffs, NJ: Prentice-Hall.

Merrill, J. C., & O'Dell, S. J. (1983). *Philosophy and journalism.* White Plains, NY: Longman.

Meyer, P. (1987). *Ethical journalism.* New York: Longman.

Miller, G. R. (1969). Contributions of communication research to the study of speech. In A. H. Monroe & D. Ehniger (Eds.), *Principles and types of speech communication* (6th brief ed., p. 355). Glenview, IL: Scott, Foresman.

Nilsen, T. R. (1974). *Ethics of speech communication* (2nd ed.). Indianapolis: Bobbs-Merrill. *New York Times.* (2007). The light goes out for Don Imus: CBS radio joins MSNBC in cutting ties to broadcaster. (April 13), p. C1, C5.

Paul, R.N. (1994). Status and outlook of the chain-restaurant industry. *Cornell Hotel & Restaurant Administration Quarterly, 35*(3), 23–27.

Pearson, R. (1989, September 20). Remarks to the San Francisco Academy, San Francisco, CA.

Poniewozik, J. (2007, April 23). Who can say what? *Time,* 32–37.

Rand, A. (1964). *The virtue of selfishness.* New York: New American Library/Signet Books.

Rivers, W. L., & Mathews, C. (1988). *Ethics for the media.* Englewood Cliffs, NJ: Prentice-Hall.

Rosenberg, R. (1991, September 20). *Remarks to the San Francisco Academy.* San Francisco, CA.

Ryan, M., & Martinson, D. L. (1984). Ethical values, the flow of journalistic information, and public relations persons. *Journalism Quarterly, 61,* 27–34.

Simon, S. (1971). Value-clarification vs. indoctrination. *Social Education, 35,* 902.

Swain, B. M. (1978). *Reporters' ethics.* Ames: Iowa University Press.

Toffler, B. (1986). *Tough choices: Managers talk ethics.* New York: Wiley.

Wedberg, A. (1982). *A history of philosophy: Antiquity and the middle ages* (Vol. 1). Oxford: Clarendon Press.

Wilcox, D. L., Ault, P. H., & Agee, W. K. (1986). *Public relations strategies and tactics.* New York: Harper & Row.

Wright, D. K. (1976). Social responsibility in public relations: A multi-step theory. *Public Relations Review, 2,* 24–36.

Wright, D. K. (1979). Professionalism and social responsibility in public relations. *Public Relations Review, 5,* 20–33.

Wright, D. K. (1982). The philosophy of ethical development in public relations. *IPRA Review, 9,* 18–25.

Wright, D. K. (1985). Individual ethics determine public relations practice. *Public Relations Journal, 41,* 38–39.

Wright, D. K. (1989, Summer). Examining ethical and moral values of public relations people. *Public Relations Review,* 19–33.

8. Communication Law and Regulation in the Digital Age

by John Pavlik and Shawn McIntosh

An effective communicator must understand that communication does not occur in a vacuum. As evident from the previous readings in this book, communication is a powerful process that can be deeply influential. Because of the power of communication, it is necessary in a civil society that communication be regulated. Communication laws and regulations exist to protect both creators and consumers of communicative acts. This chapter surveys the complexities of regulating communication in a digital age and in a democratic state. It provides an informative, yet still somewhat cursory, glimpse into the tangled web of laws and industry-driven self-regulation that impacts the work of both professional communicators and the common communicator.

This chapter includes many references to historical events that have influenced the laws and regulations surrounding communication. The reader should not hesitate to investigate further any unfamiliar references. Again, this is an excellent opportunity to exercise the research skills that are invaluable to all communicators. Also, the "Further Reading" list at the end of the chapter provides many excellent ideas for expanding an understanding of communication law and regulation beyond this introduction.

On April 3, 2007, Josh Wolf stepped out of a federal prison in California and into the record books after spending 226 days in jail, the longest any journalist in U.S. history was held for protecting his sources.

There were several ironies with this case, not the least of which was that there were questions about whether Wolf was actually a journalist. A self-described activist, he participated in, videotaped, and blogged about various protests conducted by anarchist or radical-left groups.

In July 2005 he videotaped an anti-G8 demonstration held in San Francisco, posting excerpts of his footage on the local Indymedia site, part of a worldwide network of activists and citizen journalists.

A policeman was injured during the demonstration, and Wolf was subpoenaed by federal authorities to appear before a grand jury and hand over his footage so investigators could determine if any of the protestors could be identified. Wolf refused on First Amendment grounds and was sentenced to jail, then eventually federal prison, as he continued to refuse to surrender his videotapes.

The prosecution claimed that Wolf was not a journalist but an activist who happened to be capturing a public event on tape and thus had no First Amendment protections. Supporters of Wolf claimed that he was acting in a journalistic capacity by his video reporting and blogging and that his imprisonment could have a chilling effect on other journalists who could be threatened by the government.

On the day Wolf was released from prison he posted all his video footage to his blog. After an unsuccessful run for mayor of San Francisco in 2007, in July 2008 he began work as a general-assignment reporter for a local newspaper, the *Palo Alto Daily Post*. The final bits of irony in the case are that he put down his video camera and focused solely on writing for his new job and is doing so for a newspaper that does not even have a website.

Congress shall make no law respecting an establishment of religion, or prohibiting the free exercise thereof, or abridging the freedom of speech, or of the press, or the right of the people peaceably to assemble, and to petition the government for a redress of grievances.

First Amendment to the Constitution of the United States

Although the First Amendment guarantees that Congress shall make no law restricting freedom of speech or of the press, it has been interpreted by the courts, elected officials, and legal scholars to permit some level of regulatory and legal restriction. Some of these laws deal with libel, obscenity, and other media-content matters. Others deal with technical issues related to broadcast station operation, such as to prevent one station from interfering with another's signals, and others pertain to media ownership, intellectual property rights, and fulfilling the requirements of broadcasting licenses.

And of course it is important to remember that the First Amendment is very much an American invention. Most other countries have no such stipulation in their constitutions, which of course has resulted in sometimes vastly different laws and regulations regarding mass communication and journalism.

The Legal Framework

When printing began in Renaissance Europe, political and religious authorities were quick to recognize the power of publishing to spread not only religious teachings but political edicts as well. However, political and religious dissidents found printing presses equally useful in disseminating their views against authority. The tension between government control of the press and using the press as a means to be free of political or religious control continues to this day.

The reasons underlying the value of freedom from governmental control were perhaps best articulated by U.S. president Thomas Jefferson, who said, "information is the currency of democracy." When the first U.S. Congress passed the

Bill of Rights in 1789, there were fewer than three dozen printing presses in the country. Despite this small number, the importance of the press was recognized by the nation's founders. Jefferson said, "Were it left for me to decide whether we should have a government without newspapers, or newspapers without a government, I should not hesitate a moment to prefer the latter."

The press is a critical watchdog of government as well as other of powerful institutions in society, including business. But it is as an unofficial "fourth branch" of government, or **fourth estate**, that the press must be free from government censorship or control.

In societies where government control over the press, or media, is substantial, as in China or other authoritarian countries where journalists must be licensed to operate, the press suffers from an inability to criticize the government, its policies, or its representatives. More often than not, the press becomes a puppet to the government and is used to promote government positions rather than independently evaluate them. In the United States and other democratic societies, the press ideally acts as an independent balance of power to government bodies. However, concentration of ownership, commercialism, and other circumstances can adversely affect the ability of the press to act responsibly or effectively in its role as watchdog of powerful societal institutions. Business interests may sometimes outweigh public interests, for news organizations.

Despite the early constitutional admonitions to protect freedom of speech and press, there have been many attempts by the government at all levels to infringe upon the independence of the press and to censor. In addition, a second problem has plagued the media with regard to acts of general governmental control. This problem is the failure of the government, in each of its three branches, to extend full First Amendment protection to the media in all their forms. Instead, only the print media have received full protection. In *Miami Herald Publishing Co. v. Tornillo* (1974), for instance, the U.S. Supreme Court struck down a Florida statute that required newspapers to give space at no cost to political candidates whose personal or professional character the paper had criticized. However, television and radio stations must provide airtime should the station itself editorially endorse or oppose a candidate.

Radio, television, cinema, and today the Internet have received much less protection than print media, and only through extended legal battles have they won a certain degree of freedom. In fact, during the first half of the twentieth century, cinema was not provided any First Amendment protection. Not until the Supreme Court's 1952 *Miracle* decision (*Joseph Burstyn, Inc. v. Wilson*), when the court ruled that the showing of a film could not be prohibited because a censor deemed it sacrilegious, did any constitutional protection extend to motion pictures.

The historical influences and legal and regulatory decisions on print and electronic media are complex, but they are worth exploring briefly in order to better understand the reasons given for restrictions on media content today.

The Foundations of Freedom of Expression

Governments continue to use many means to control print media. One heavy handed method is to jail journalists and editors, thus not only silencing them but also often having a **chilling effect** on others who maybe tempted to write on similar topics.

However, such tactics can also backfire in that jailed journalists may stoke public anger at the government or damage the government's reputation. More subtle means of control, such as licensing laws for owning a printing press or being a journalist, or special taxes on printing equipment, paper, or ink, have been used in the past. By controlling the materials needed for printing, governments hoped to be able to control the free flow of information. Government censors, or bodies that examine and approve all printed material, have also been used.

Although these measures continue to be used in various countries, it has been harder for governments to control information than in the past. This is partly because vastly more information is available and partly because electronic media, including the Internet, have become important information sources alongside print media.

Though there is still a long way to go, in many countries, to gain freedom of expression, there have been great strides made in many developed countries over the past few hundred years. Today we may look at the strict censorship and licensing laws of seventeenth- and eighteenth-century England and see them as draconian, yet within this period some of England's most noted literary and journalistic voices flourished, such as Jonathan Swift and Samuel Johnson. Nevertheless, it is important to remember that our concept of freedom of expression was not immutable. The notion evolved over time and has largely been influenced by several major court cases that dealt with either national security issues, libel, or censorship.

National Security

In 1798, only a little over a decade since the creation of the Constitution and Bill of Rights, a series of four acts limiting freedom of speech were passed by the U.S. Congress. The **Alien and Sedition Acts** were passed by the Federalist-controlled U.S. Congress as a response to a threat of war with France and were meant to crush the position of the Jeffersonian Republicans, who were sympathetic to France.

Among other things, the acts prohibited **sedition**, meaning spoken or written criticism of the U.S. government, and imposed penalties of a fine or imprisonment upon conviction. With the end of the threat of war, the Sedition Act expired in 1801, but other sedition acts have resurfaced throughout U.S. history, especially during times of war.[1]

Several important legal concepts have developed with court cases that involved issues of national security, one of the main areas where press freedoms are curtailed.

Clear and Present Danger

The most basic restriction is when the speech in question meets both of the following conditions:

(1) it is intended to incite or produce dangerous activity (as with falsely shouting "Fire!" in a crowded theater), and (2) it is likely to succeed in achieving the purported result. This two-part framework is known as the **clear and present danger** test and is subject to the appropriate criminal-law-enforcement authorities and to the judicial system rather than regulatory authorities.

The dear-and-present-danger test emerged from *Schenck v. United States* (1919). In that case, the U.S. Supreme Court unanimously upheld the conviction of Charles T. Schenck for violating the Espionage Act of 1917. Schenck had been distributing handbills urging resistance to U.S. involvement in World War I. He was a Communist but did not commit any violent acts. The Court based its decision on the notion not only that the First Amendment is not absolute, but that in wartime ordinary constitutional rules do not apply.

Prior Restraint

An important ruling came in the 1931 Supreme Court case *Near v. Minnesota*. Minnesota courts had stopped the publication of an anti-Semitic weekly on the basis that it was a "malicious, scandalous and defamatory" periodical in violation of the state's nuisance law. The Supreme Court reversed the decision, saying that **prior restraint**, or the government preventing or blocking the publication, broadcasting, showing, or otherwise distributing of media content, whether in print, over the air, or in movie theaters, must only be used in cases of serious or grave threats to national security.

In 1971, the Supreme Court made another important ruling in this regard in the case of *New York Times Co. v. United States*. In this case, the Supreme Court overturned a lower court ruling that had stopped the Times from publishing "The Pentagon Papers," a top-secret Pentagon study of U.S. involvement in the Vietnam War. The government failed to prove that national security interest outweighed a heavy presumption against prior restraint.

In 1979, a district court stopped *The Progressive* magazine (*U.S. v. Progressive*) from publishing "The H-Bomb Secret." The magazine had obtained its information from publicly available documents, and six months later the court injunction was lifted after others published similar material.

In sum, the courts have ruled that freedom of speech is not an absolute, especially during time of war. There is, however, a strong presumption against permitting the government any form of prior restraint on publication or distribution of speech, and it is incumbent on the government to clearly show that publication poses a clear and present threat to national security. This framework seems especially relevant in the aftermath of the September 11, 2001, terrorist attack on the World Trade Center and Pentagon.

In his book *Mass Media Law*, Don Pember describes a **preferred-position balancing theory** that has particular utility in this regard. According to this theory, a balance must be struck between speech and other rights, but speech is given a preferred position (especially in print media), and limitations on freedom of speech in print are usually illegal. The burden of proof falls on the government to show that some speech or expression of information is harmful to national security; it is not journalists or media organizations that must prove that it is not harmful.

Libel

The foundation for the relationship between freedom of expression and libel in the United States was established in the colonial era. Foremost is the case of John Peter Zenger, a New York printer and journalist who faced a libel suit from the publication of the *New York Weekly Journal*, a political journal opposed to the colonial governor, William Cosby. As publisher of the *Journal*, Zenger was responsible for the articles, which frequently featured scathing attacks on the governor.

In November 1734 Zenger was arrested for libel, and he spent nearly ten months in prison awaiting trial. Zenger's attorney, Andrew Hamilton, requested the jury rule on the veracity of Zenger's printed statements, and in a surprise ruling in August 1735 Zenger was acquitted of libel. This important precedent established the principle of freedom of press in early America and marked a departure from the way much of the world considers libel in the courts, even today. For example, in England someone can successfully be sued for libel even if the statements are true, if the statements damage a person's reputation.

In the United States, libel is a type of defamation, such as a false attack on a person's character, which damages a person's reputation. Libel is different historically from **slander** on the basis that slander involves the spoken word, and libel involves the written word.

With the rise of electronic media in the twentieth century, libel has been extended to broadcasting on television or radio; as well as online communications, even though broadcast media are technically spoken rather than printed.

In the case of *Phipps v. Clark Oil & Ref. Corp.* (1987), the Minnesota court ruled that libel occurs when a publication "tends to injure the plaintiff's reputation and expose the plaintiff to public hatred, contempt, ridicule, or degradation."

New York Times v. Sullivan (1964)

Media historians and legal scholars tend to agree that the most important legal decision to establish a free press in the United States was the 1964 Supreme Court ruling in *New York Times Co. v. Sullivan*.

In 1960, the *New York Times* printed a fund-raising advertisement for the civil rights movement, which contained several minor factual errors. L. B. Sullivan, a Montgomery, Alabama, city commissioner in charge of the police, said that some of the false statements in the advertisement regarding Montgomery police actions defamed him, even though he was not mentioned by name. A jury agreed and awarded him a half million dollars. The *New York Times* appealed the case and it eventually went to the Supreme Court, which overturned the lower court ruling.

The Supreme Court ruled that public figures (defined as publicly prominent) and public officials (defined as public policy makers) may not file suit for libel unless they can prove "actual malice." For nonpublic figures (private citizens), the standard for libel is less stringent, requiring merely that the plaintiff show objectively that a "reasonable person" knew or should have known the defamatory statement was false.

The Court defined "actual malice" in terms of either (1) the intent of the defendant being malicious or (2) the defendant knowing the statement is false but acting with reckless disregard for the truth and publishing it regardless. This is known as the "actual malice" test. The Court ruled that the common law of defamation violated the guarantee of free speech under the First Amendment and that the citizen's right to criticize government officials is too important to be intolerant of speech containing even harmful falsehoods. The result of the ruling has been to maintain a more robust environment for media to publish criticisms of public figures, knowing that they can be found libelous only if they meet the stringent actual-malice test.

Protecting Journalists Against Libel

Most media organizations have libel insurance to protect journalists. Freelance journalists, however, often do not have libel insurance, so the threat of libel can have a serious chilling effect. This is especially true for online journalists and others who operate on a shoestring budget or who are not widely recognized by media organizations as "real" journalists.

Moreover, although there is no prior restraint for libel cases, journalists can be imprisoned for contempt in libel cases or others. Most typically this happens when a journalist is protecting sources (i.e., refusing to disclose their identities), but it can also occur for other reasons, such as failing to release one's notes.

There are at least five steps journalists can take to minimize chances of committing an act of libel:

1. Engage in thorough research, including investigating the facts and maintaining good records, establishing and adhering to written criteria in making decisions about when and what to publish, and using reliable sources.
2. Confirm the identity of the target of your report.
3. Use quotations whenever possible and attribute statements to sources.
4. Report facts only and avoid language that draws conclusions.
5. Avoid bias in reports and strive for balance (i.e., give the different sides in a debate fair play).

Shield Laws

Shield laws are laws intended to protect journalists from legal challenges to their freedom to report the news. Journalists have received neither blanket protection from the Supreme Court nor a federal shield law. Yet thirty-four states have enacted laws to protect journalists from being required to answer every subpoena.[2] In these states, journalists are not required to testify or produce materials obtained from sources in confidence. Most of the other states and territories provide some court protection for journalists, although they have no shield laws.

Without these shield laws, unrestrained legal action might exert a chilling effect on journalists, some suggest, including Reed Hundt, former chairman of the FCC.[3] "Newsgatherers might be less aggressive and cease to pursue confidential sources or information. Whistle-blowers and other sources could be left without any legal protection from discovery," Hundt said.

Evidence suggests that shield laws have limited effectiveness, based on studies done on the number of subpoenas served to journalists in states with shield laws compared to the number in those without. Opponents of shield laws argue that journalists should not be given special protections from answering subpoenas, given how difficult it is to define what a journalist is.

Others worry that trying to explicitly state what defines a journalist could be a first step toward official licensing for journalists, which most news organizations strongly appose as a curtailment of their First Amendment rights.

Censorship

Censorship is the third major dimension of government control over media. It refers to the act of prohibiting certain expression or content. In a sense, it is a form of prior restraint, only rather than prohibiting an entire publication, it targets specific content within that publication, broadcast, film, or website. Censorship is not generally permitted in the United States, although it is routine in some countries, especially ones with authoritarian regimes that prohibit criticism of the government or rulers. In the United States, censorship is most common in two circumstances, (1) during wartime, when content, especially that being reported from the battlefield, is subject to censorship under the principle of national security, and (2) with pornographic or obscene content, which can sometimes include graphic violence or detailed accounts of criminal behavior.

An important censorship case is *Hazelwood School District v. Kuhlmeier* (1988). This case established that not all citizens have the same First Amendment rights. In particular, people still in school, typically but not necessarily those under eighteen, are not afforded full First Amendment protection. In this case, a school principal was permitted to censor school newspaper articles dealing with pregnancy and divorce. The court found that school-sponsored publications are not a public forum and thus may be subject to censorship to protect the young from harm.

Indecent Content

Although not prohibited, **indecent speech** is also subject to federal regulation. Broadcasters may not air indecent speech when children are likely to be in the audience or between 6 a.m. and 10 p.m. This has been called a safe harbor period, and concerned groups sometimes request portrayals of violence or sex to be barred from the time period as well.

Federal law defines indecent speech as "language or material that, in context, depicts or describes, in terms patently offensive as measured by contemporary community standards for the broadcast medium, sexual or excretory organs or activities." Exempted from this definition is profanity that is neither indecent nor obscene. "Damn" is an example of a permitted word. Indecent speech was put to the test in a landmark First Amendment case involving comedian George Carlin.

Carlin recorded before a live California audience a twelve-minute monolog titled "Filthy Words." He opened his routine by contemplating "the words you couldn't say on the public airwaves, the ones you definitely wouldn't say, ever." He then listed those words and repeated them in a variety of contexts. The Supreme Court decision in *Federal Communications Commission v. Pacifica Foundation* (1978) was the basis for subsequent regulations on indecent speech for broadcasters.

Other entertainers have tested and pushed the limits of freedom of speech in the electronic media as well, including radio "shock jock" Howard Stern, whose frequently crude and vulgar on-air commentary before he moved to satellite radio drew criticism not only from citizen groups but from government regulators. In 1995, Infinity Broadcasting Corp. (owned by CBS), the producer and broadcaster of Stern's radio show, agreed to pay $1.7 million without admitting guilt to settle a variety of indecency charges that had been leveled by the FCC since 1989 against Stern, whose comments are frequently sexually graphic.

As part of the **Telecommunications Act of 1996**, the first sweeping federal legislation to rewrite the foundation of communications regulation in the United States since 1834, legislators had sought to curb "indecent" speech online, but the Communications Decency Act (CDA) passed as part of the act was ultimately struck down by the U.S. Supreme Court in *ACLU v. Janet Reno* (1998). The CDA made it illegal to "depict or describe" on the Internet anything considered indecent and made no distinctions between scientific or literary works and pornography. The ACLU filed a lawsuit against the government the same day the Telecommunications Act was passed, and a lower court ruled the CDA unconstitutional, which the Supreme Court affirmed.

In late 2008 and early 2009 Facebook found itself the object of "lactivists" who protested its policy of removing photos of breastfeeding mothers from member pages. Threatened with banishment from Facebook for violating its policy on showing exposed breasts, women created the group "Hey Facebook, breastfeeding is not obscene!" and staged online and offline protests, which quickly grew to the tens of thousands.

The protestors pointed out the hypocrisy of Faceboolds policies, which accept pictures of women in thongs striking sexy poses and couples making out. Despite getting soundly ridiculed in the press and blogosphere, Facebook refused to change its policy.

Obscenity

Pornography, or **obscenity**, is one of the major forms of speech deemed unprotected by the First Amendment, and is subject to censorship by the government. A landmark case in this regard was *Miller v. California* (1973), in which Miller had been convicted in California of mailing unsolicited pornographic brochures. He appealed his conviction on the grounds that it inhibited his right to free speech, but the Court disagreed and outlined three criteria for determining whether content is obscene.

1. An average individual applying contemporary community standards must believe the content, taken as a whole, appeals to prurient interest.
2. The content must show or describe in an offensive manner sexual conduct.
3. The content on the whole must lack serious literary, artistic, political, or scientific value.

Defining obscenity, however, is difficult, and some would say simply that "I know it when I see it (or hear it)."

The digital age has produced unique issues for obscenity cases. One is the ease with which pornography can be distributed across national boundaries. Another is computer-generated pornography in which increasingly realistic images can be created. In April 2002, the Supreme Court reaffirmed that free-speech principles applied online when it struck down provisions in the Child Pornography Prevention Act of 1996, which made it a crime to create, distribute, or possess "virtual" child pornography, or computer-generated images of children in sexual acts (as opposed to images of actual children). Justice Anthony M. Kennedy wrote for the majority, saying the act "prohibits speech that records no crime and creates no victims by its production." Although some justices voted in favor of keeping penalties for computer-generated images, and the government argued that real children could be harmed and exploited if a market for virtual child pornography were sustained, Justice Kennedy said, "The mere tendency of speech to encourage unlawful acts is not a sufficient reason for banning it."[4]

Criticism, Ridicule, or Humor

As objectionable as they may be, stereotypes and other offensive material are protected by the U. S. Constitution. Criticism, ridicule, and jokes about individuals (including government officials), groups, or institutions based on race, religion, gender, national background, or other factors are protected speech, whether in print or electronic media, and may not be regulated by the FCC. In the case of licensed broadcasters, it is incumbent upon station owners and operators to act responsibly in offering programming that meets the needs of the communities they serve.

The following discussion of the origins and evolution of electronic-communications regulations will highlight how the FCC came about, its role, how regulations differ from those of print media, and how they have influenced the programming and communication networks we have today.

The Evolution of Regulating Electronic Media

The origins of U.S. electronic-communications regulations lie in the development of broadcasting in the early part of the twentieth century, starting with radio and later including television. The approach has evolved considerably over the years as a result of changing technical and economic factors surrounding and underpinning those media.

Early Days and the Radio Act of 1912 (1911–1926)

The regulation of broadcasting in the United States has moved through a series of four stages. Prior to 1911, there was no regulatory authority for broadcasting, which at the time meant specifically radio transmissions. The technology of radio was in its infancy, and so little was known about the new medium or its potential that there was little to regulate. Because radio emerged as a vital medium for ships at sea, especially for making distress calls, the Commerce Department's Bureau of Navigation was put in control of radio and made it a legal requirement in the **Radio Act of 1912** that all large ships maintain radio contact with ships or shore stations. Responsibility for radio regulation rested with the Commerce Department until 1927.

During this period, radio broadcasting was done largely by amateur technology enthusiasts. The process of obtaining a frequency on which to broadcast was very informal. As broadcast historian Mark Goodman points out, "By mailing a postcard to Secretary of Commerce Herbert Hoover, anyone with a radio transmitter, ranging from college students experimenting in science classes, to amateur inventors who ordered kits, to newspaper-operated stations, could broadcast on the frequency chosen by Hoover."[5]

By 1926 there were 15,111 amateur radio stations and 536 broadcasting stations in the United States. Despite geographic separation of radio transmitters and various power restrictions on those transmitters, there was a great amount of interference between the different stations' signals. Radio became what historian Erik Barnouw calls "A Tower of Babel," and the need for regulation grew. In the 1920s much public attention became focused on the new medium of radio and how the government was attempting to regulate it.[6]

Increasing Regulation and the Federal Radio Commission (1927–1933)

"The airwaves by 1927 were an open forum for anyone with the expertise and equipment to reach a forum with 25 million listeners," explains Mark Goodman.[7] But the rapid and largely uncontrolled growth of the new medium required a new regulatory structure. The **Radio Act of 1927** was signed into law in February and borrowed from railroad regulations. It said that anyone who owned a radio frequency and radio should operate for the "public convenience, interest, or necessity"—even though it didn't define those terms.[8]

The Federal Radio Commission (FRC) was established by the act. The FRC comprised five politically appointed commissioners and a limited staff whose mandate was to sort out the mess in radio. They revoked the vast majority of radio licenses and instituted a new system that favored fewer, high-powered stations over many, low-powered stations.[9] This change effectively favored radio for big companies over educational institutions or other groups that had small radio stations at the time.

The Communications Act and Spectrum Scarcity (1934–1999)

In 1934, Congress enacted the Communications Act, which became the foundation of communications law for the next sixty-two years. The act was based on the premise established in the Radio Act of 1927 that the airwaves were a public good, a limited natural resource that belonged to the people. Broadcasters were granted licenses to use those airwaves at no cost, but were public trustees and bore a responsibility to use the air-waves in "the public interest, convenience, or necessity." Because of the limited nature of the airwaves, the act established regulations based on the notion of "spectrum scarcity," or limited channel capacity. It was under this model that news, whether profitable or not, came to meet the public service requirements for radio and television broadcasters.

The Communications Act of 1934 established the Federal Communications Commission (FCC), with five political appointees, including one chair, and a series of bureaus, each assigned responsibility for an area of the growing radio industry. The FCC would eventually assume regulatory responsibility for the emerging medium of television as well.

The Telecommunications Act and Its Effects (1996–Present)

The technological transformation of the communication system in the United States and throughout the world, of which the Internet was an important part, was the impetus for Congress enacting the Telecommunications Act of 1996, the first major overhaul of the Communications Act of 1934. The convergence of telecommunications, computing, and traditional media in a digital, networked environment created the need for a basic reconstruction of the regulatory framework for the media of mass communication.

The act introduced that new framework. Although it preserved the requirement to serve in the "public interest, convenience, and necessity," the act's new mandate was to foster competition in the communications marketplace. The preamble of the act states it is intended "[t]o promote competition and reduce regulation in order to secure lower prices and higher quality services for American telecommunications consumers and encourage the rapid deployment of new telecommunications technologies." The motivation for this new mandate was the digital revolution that made the premise of channel scarcity virtually obsolete. The public no longer only had

three or four network channels to watch—it now had broadcasting choices ranging from cable or satellite television to, increasingly, Internet-based programming.

More than one hundred pages in length, the complex Telecommunications Act of 1996 raises a variety of issues that affect not just the structure of the communications industry and how it is regulated, but the nature of programming and production. The act promotes direct competition among all telecommunications providers, including terrestrial broadcasters, direct broadcast satellite providers, mobile communication services, cable providers, and the regional Bell telephone companies. Further, the act specifically targets two forms of programming: violent or sexual programming and interactive services.

Since passage of the act, there has been dramatic growth in the concentration of media ownership. Whether this trend will have the stated desired effect of fostering competition or whether it will simply create powerful media cartels has been a subject of some debate. Another trend has been an increase in alternate media–service providers: cable companies are allowed to provide telephone service, for example, and telephone companies could provide, in theory, programming content.

The act puts no limit on the number of television stations a single person or organization may own in the United States, as long as the combined reach is no more than 35 percent of U.S. households. This also will spur greater concentration of ownership, which has already occurred in the radio industry. As a result of these regulatory, economic, and technological trends, Eli Noam and Robert Freeman point out that the media offer unprecedented programming diversity at the national level and ever-dwindling diversity at the local level.[10]

Because the act eliminates the legal barriers preventing telephone and television companies from competing in the areas of telephone and video services, consumers have seen an increased array of alternative service providers. Similarly, consumers have seen an increase in the range of both phone and video services, such as video-on-demand, voicemail, and call waiting. There have been several attempts in recent years to pass further sweeping legislation that deals with issues such as Net neutrality, voice-over IP (VOIP), and other new technologies that either did not exist or were just emerging in 1996.

Electronic Media Regulation Internationally

Electronic media of course developed differently in various countries throughout the world, and it is impossible to thoroughly cover the historical development within each country or even each region here. However, several general trends and patterns can be explored.

In many countries, the development of radio as mass communication was an extension of the already existing telegraph services, which were generally run by the government. Unlike the United States, where commercial forces tended to dominate, in Europe and European colonies a public service ethos for electronic media was most prevalent. What this meant for the public was a limited number of radio or television networks that were licensed or directly run by the government. Because of the principle of public service, programming content tended to emphasize news, education, and cultural shows rather than pure entertainment.

In the European Union in the last twenty years there has been a steady trend toward privatization and less regulation of the radio and television industries. As a result, more U.S. programming has been licensed by European broadcasters, making shows like *Baywatch* or *The Simpsons* highly popular throughout the world. This trend, although perhaps good from the audience's perspective, as it can now see more types of programming, also raises charges of cultural imperialism. Local broadcasters may too easily choose to simply buy U.S. programming rather than supporting home-grown productions.

Nevertheless, the EU is moving toward more liberalization and privatization, so it is likely that the EU, like the United States, will also see growth in the concentration of media ownership. Asian countries each have their own regulations and laws, but with the exception of Japan, India, the Philippines, and South Korea, most Asian countries have stronger degrees of government control over electronic media than the EU or the United States. For example, it is illegal to own a satellite dish in Malaysia, and countries like Singapore and Indonesia have strict regulations on content, especially criticism of the government.

The Federal Communications Commission (FCC)

The **FCC** is the principal communications regulatory body at the federal level in the United States. Some would say the FCC is also a lightning rod for criticism because of its prominent position on the communications regulatory landscape. Oftentimes, regardless of how the commission rules, some group is left unhappy and frequently is quite vocal in expressing its displeasure.

The principal mandate of the FCC is "regulating interstate and foreign commerce in communication by wire and radio so as to make available, so far as possible, to all the people of the United States a rapid, efficient, nation-wide, and world-wide wire and radio communications service ..." In this sense, the term "radio" is interpreted to include television. The commission is authorized to "make such regulations not inconsistent with law as it may deem necessary to prevent interference between stations and to carry out the provisions of [the] Act." The FCC mandate was reaffirmed under the Telecommunications Act of 1996, which supplanted the 1934 act. The new act added an emphasis on fostering competition in the newly converged digital landscape, in the hopes of both supporting and expanding the communications industry and bringing a greater range of communications services, at an affordable price, to the American public.

The FCC consists of five commissioners appointed by the president, each of whom must be confirmed by the Senate. The commission must include at least two representatives of each of the major parties to help ensure its nonpartisan nature.

Regulating Radio and Television

Among its principal duties, the FCC allocates new broadcast radio and television stations and renews the licenses of existing stations, ensuring that each licensee is complying with the laws mandated by Congress. The FCC does not license TV or radio networks, such as CBS, NBC, ABC, Fox, UPN, WB, or PBS, except when they are owners of stations.

The commission considers two basic sets of factors regarding the allocation of new stations. First, it evaluates the relative needs of communities for additional broadcast outlets. This depends on a variety of considerations, including a community's population and its heterogeneity. Second, the commission considers various engineering standards that eliminate interference between stations.

In fulfilling its duties, the FCC invites public comment on its proposed rules, publishes those rules, and implements them through a set of seven bureaus and eleven offices. The bureaus include the Mass Media Bureau, which regulates radio and television stations (and absorbed the Cable Services Bureau, which had regulated cable television), and the Common Carrier Bureau, which regulates wireline and wireless telephony.

Cable and satellite television are not under the same FCC rules as broadcast stations or those transmitted via terrestrial frequencies. Cable TV and satellite channels are available only to subscribers and have fewer rules to abide by than network broadcasters. Among the most important rules administered by the Cable Services Bureau are the following:

1. Basic service, which is the lowest level of cable service a subscriber can buy. It includes, at a minimum, all over-the-air television broadcast signals carried pursuant to the must-carry requirements of the Communications Act and any public, educational, or government access channels required by the system's franchise agreement.
2. "Must carry," in which every broadcast TV station, whether commercial or noncommercial, is entitled to have its programming carried on any local cable TV system. The station receives no compensation, but its programming is carried via the cable system. A broadcaster may opt instead to grant permission to the cable system to carry the station and receive compensation for the programming. This is called retransmission consent and is available only to commercial TV stations.

Universal Service

An important item for the FCC is the definition of universal service, a long-cherished notion central to the 1934 act. The act does not go so far as to provide a definition of universal service, however. It states, "Universal service is an evolving level of telecommunications services that the commission shall establish periodically under this section." It identifies six principles central to this evolving notion of universal service:

1. Quality services at reasonable and affordable rates
2. Access to advanced telecommunications and information services throughout the United States
3. Access in rural and high-cost areas
4. Equitable and nondiscriminatory contributions to the preservation and advancement of universal service
5. Specific, predictable, and sufficient federal and state mechanisms to preserve and advance universal service
6. Access to advanced telecommunications services in elementary and secondary schools and classrooms, health care providers, and libraries

The outcome of this evolving notion is a new model of universal service. One scenario would include fully interoperable high-bandwidth, two-way communication service—the twenty-first-century equivalent of "plain old telephone service" (POTS) mandated in the 1934 act. This would create a powerful network engine to drive a new information infrastructure linking wired and wireless technologies and empower the development of fully interactive, multimedia communications. An alternative paradigm, however, would simply mandate that all homes have access to at least two communication-service providers capable of delivering both traditional and new media services (including the Internet).

Spectrum Auction

Since 1994, the FCC has held auctions for available electromagnetic spectrum. The auctions are open to any individual or company that makes an upfront payment and that the FCC deems a qualified bidder. Many countries auction spectrum, and the auctions can generate large revenues for the governments. Some critics claim that the spectrum tends to be leased too cheaply, resulting in essentially corporate giveaways, considering the money that the winning bidders make from the spectrum.

The auction in the United States in 2008 drew special attention thanks in part to disagreements and lawsuits among several major telecommunications companies and Google, all bidders for the spectrum. Google requested that the auctioned spectrum be open, meaning that the winning bidder would have to keep the spectrum available to anyone to develop applications and communication tools that could be used by anyone else, along the lines of open-source business models. Google claimed that this would give consumers more choices and spur greater innovation in mobile communication devices.

Open communications like this directly threaten the established business models of telecommunication companies, and Verizon filed a lawsuit against the FCC to stop the open requirement. In the end, Google got two of its four requests, creating a partially open system, and the auction generated close to $20 billion for the government.

The FCC, Station ID, and License Renewal

Each station must air station-identification announcements as it signs on and off each day, and it must air announcements hourly, at what the commission calls a natural programming break. The requirements for station identification foster a certain level of uniformity in programming style in the broadcast media, but they do not mandate that programmers insert station IDs at the top of the hour and at other well-defined intervals.

The FCC licenses stations to operate either as commercial or noncommercial-educational (public) broadcasters for up to eight years, after which the station must renew its license. This is the case for both radio and television broadcasters licensed to transmit their signals via terrestrial frequencies.

At the time of license renewal, a station must meet five basic requirements, primarily that it has served in the public interest and met all legal requirements. A station must also accept and respond to viewer or listener complaints. Audience members, journalists, or anyone else may also review what is called the station's "public inspection file," which contains a variety of information about the station.

FCC Limits on Stations

There are a variety of station activities that are either regulated or prohibited by federal law. Among the regulated activities are station-conducted contests, television games and quiz shows, and the broadcast of telephone calls. When a station hosts a contest, it must fully disclose all terms and rules of the contest, including in any advertising promoting the contest. Stations are required to inform any parties to a phone call before recording it for broadcast, or broadcasting it live, although there are certain exceptions, such as call-in shows, when callers can reasonably be expected to understand their calls may be broadcast.

If a licensee violates the rules, the FCC is authorized to levy a fine or even to revoke a station's license. Among the programming concerns for which the FCC may levy fines or revoke licenses are the airing of obscene or indecent language when children are likely to be viewing, and nudity. The FCC does not advise stations regarding artistic standards, format, or grammar. Stations must rely on their own judgment. Generally, only the stations themselves are responsible for selecting the material they air, including coverage, of local issues, news, public affairs, religion, sports events, and other subjects.

Among the prohibited activities for stations are knowingly broadcasting a hoax, including false information regarding a crime or catastrophe (defined as a disaster), especially when a broadcast might cause public harm. This rule came about largely as a result of the 1938 *War of the Worlds* radio broadcast.

Regulating Content

In addition to the ways content is regulated in electronic media by the FCC and the federal controls over libel, obscenity, and speech that threatens national security, there are at least eight other types of content restrictions in the United States. These are largely, but not entirely, unique to the broadcast media and may involve other agencies besides the FCC. The restrictions are primarily aimed at protecting children, controlling political communication, and limiting commercial speech.

In the cases of libel, copyright, clear and present danger, and obscenity and pornography, the judicial system has authority over broadcast or publication. In the case of false or deceptive advertising, the Federal Trade Commission has primary responsibility, although the Food and Drug Administration (FDA) has authority when food or drugs are involved. Most of the remaining content restrictions are subject to the jurisdiction of the FCC.

Commercial Speech

Commercial speech, including advertising, has generally been afforded less First Amendment protection than other forms of speech, especially political speech or the news. In a landmark decision, the U.S. Supreme Court ruled in 1942 in *Valentine v. Chrestensen* that "purely commercial advertising" was unprotected by the First Amendment. Chrestensen was a businessman who was displaying a World War I–era submarine at a pier in New York City and dispersed leaflets advertising tours of the submarine. The leaflets were becoming litter, and the police commissioner in New York forbade him from distributing them. Even though Chrestensen attempted to subvert the ruling by adding political messages on the opposite side, the city still barred him from distributing his advertising leaflets, and the Supreme Court agreed, giving commercial speech no protection under the First Amendment.

In the 1970s the broad powers granted to government regarding commercial speech were restricted somewhat by cases that allowed some First Amendment protection, although not on par with other forms of speech. In 1976, the Court ruled in *Virginia State Board of Pharmacy v. Virginia Citizens Consumer Council, Inc.,* that speech that does "no more than propose a commercial transaction" is entitled to at least some First Amendment protection. This was in response to a case brought by some citizens' groups in Virginia that wanted to see pharmacies advertise prices of drugs, which the state legislature had prohibited.

In some cases, however, commercial speech has been afforded more protection than one might expect. An interesting example comes from a case involving former New York City mayor Rudolph Giuliani. Giuliani was lampooned in an advertising campaign by *New York* magazine in 1997 on the city buses of New York, which said that the magazine was "possibly the only good thing in New York that Rudy hasn't taken credit for." Giuliani, who had often taken credit for everything from drops in the crime rate to a booming economy, found the ads to be offensive and ordered them removed from the buses. In this case, commercial speech won. Consider the conclusion of United States District Judge Shira Scheindlin, who said, "Who would have dreamed that the mayor would object to more publicity?" She ruled that Giuliani's administration violated the First Amendment when it ordered city buses to remove paid ads.

Tobacco and Alcohol Advertising

Most products can be legally advertised on electronic media under the jurisdiction of the FCC. However, one type of product generally may not be legally advertised by broadcasters: tobacco. Advertising cigarettes, small cigars, smokeless tobacco, or chewing tobacco is prohibited on radio, television, and any other electronic medium regulated by the FCC, such as telephony. It is permissible to advertise smoking accessories, cigars, pipes, pipe tobacco, or cigarette-making machines. There are no federal laws or FCC regulations prohibiting the advertising of alcoholic beverages, such as beer, wine, or liquor, on television and radio.

False Advertising

One other area of commercial speech that is subject to federal regulation is false or deceptive advertising. However, this form of commercial speech is regulated by the Federal Trade Commission (FTC), not the FCC. In the case of food or drug products, the Food and Drug Administration is also involved. It has strict regulations on what can be said on the air in prescription drug commercials, which is why such commercials usually include long lists of possible side effects. Areas of commercial speech that are not regulated or prohibited by any federal law or agency include loud commercials (which the FCC has shown through research are only perceived as louder than programs but actually are not), offensive advertising, and subliminal programming.

In the latter case, the FCC states that use of subliminal messages, which are meant to be perceived only on a subconscious level, is "inconsistent with a station's obligation to serve the public interest." However, it does not officially prohibit subliminal programming. Research does not provide conclusive evidence that subliminal messages are even understood or have an influence on behavior.

Political Speech

Historically, the heart of freedom of expression is in political speech, or speech that deals with the political process, government, elected officials, or elections. Some go so far as to contend that the only speech the founders intended when they wrote the First Amendment was political speech. Political speech is also one area where federal regulations have been most extensive.

Equal-Time Rule

Stations are required to adhere to an **equal-time rule**, outlined in the 1934 Communications Act, which says that broadcasters must give "equal air time" to candidates running in elections. Under this provision, if a station permits a qualified candidate for public office to use its facilities, including commentaries or paid commercials, the station is required to "afford equal opportunities to all other such candidates for that office." Two circumstances are exempted from the equal-time provision: when the candidate appears in a newscast, interview, or documentary and when the candidate appears during on-the-scene coverage of a news event.

Candidate debates have been ruled as "on-the-spot" news coverage and thus are exempt from equal-time–rule provisions. Early in the 2008 election season there was some question whether the town hall forums conducted by McCain and Obama, even before they declared their candidacies, would be considered the same way by the FCC.

The U.S. Supreme Court ruled in 1981 in support of the equal-time rule, saying that it is the right of viewers and listeners, not of broadcasters, that should be considered paramount. It went on to say, "As defined by the FCC and applied here, [it] does not violate the First Amendment rights of broadcasters by unduly circumscribing their editorial discretion, but instead properly balances the First Amendment rights of federal candidates, the public, and broadcasters."

Fairness Doctrine

The equal-time rule is not the same thing as the **Fairness Doctrine**, though it is often confused with it. The equal-time rule deals only with giving political candidates equal time compared to other candidates, with the exceptions noted above. The Fairness Doctrine was much broader in scope, requiring broadcasters to seek out and present all sides of an issue when covering a controversy, allowing people who were personally attacked on-air a chance to respond, and giving candidates airtime to respond to a station's endorsement of another candidate. The Fairness Doctrine, which the FCC had adopted in 1949, was largely discarded in 1987.

In 1969, in *Red Lion Broadcasting Co. v. FCC*, which required Red Lion Broadcasting to provide equal airtime for a politician's response to an attack on him, the Court held that, because of the scarcity of broadcasting frequencies, the government might require a broadcast licensee to share the frequency with others who might not otherwise have a chance to broadcast their views. The Court thus gave the public a right of access "to social, political, esthetic, moral, and other ideas and experiences."

Even after the overturning of the Fairness Doctrine in 1986, two parts of it in particular remained in effect until October 2000, when they too were discarded by the FCC and the decision of a federal court. These were political editorials and personal attacks.

The FCC defined a political editorial as "when a station endorses or opposes a legally qualified candidate(s) during a broadcast of *its own* opinion." It distinguished the opinions of third parties broadcast by the station as "comments" or "commentaries" and thus exempt from these rules. A station had a week to provide other qualified candidates for the same office, or the candidates that were opposed in the editorial, with these three things: (1) notice of the date and time of the editorial, (2) a tape or script of the editorial, and (3) free and comparable airtime in which to respond.

The FCC defined a personal attack as "during the presentation of views on a controversial issue of public importance, someone attacks the honesty, character, integrity, or like personal qualities of an identified person or group." After such an occurrence, the station had one week to provide

the attacked party with the same three things provided candidates opposed in political editorials. Stations were not required to maintain copies of the material they broadcast, with two exceptions: personal attacks and political editorials.

In early October 2000, the FCC suspended these last vestiges of the Fairness Doctrine and a federal court overturned the provision entirely, ruling that the FCC had not demonstrated the value to the public of the doctrine, given the limitation it places on broadcasters' First Amendment rights.

Despite a number of attempts in 2005 and 2008 to resuscitate the Fairness Doctrine with new legislation, mostly by liberals and Democratic politicians who claim the imbalance in conservative versus liberal talk shows on radio and TV skews public debate and perceptions on important issues, such moves are strongly resisted by libertarians and conservatives. The FCC has refrained on the basis that the doctrine never really produced more diversity in programming and that with channel proliferation there is more diversity than could have been hoped for when television was dominated by three major commercial networks.

Children's Programming Protections

Parents, elected officials, and others have long sought to protect children from unwanted or offensive speech and to create a media system that actively nurtures and nourishes children. As such, there has been considerable regulation designed to both protect and promote children's welfare in the context of the media, especially the electronic media. Among the most important pieces of regulation in this regard is the **Children's Television Act**.

The Children's Television Act

The Children's Television Act (CTA) took effect in 1990. It places limits on the amount of commercial content permitted in children's TV programming (including broadcast, satellite, and cable). The act also mandates that each television station provide programming specifically designed to meet the educational and informational needs of children age sixteen and younger. The FCC determination of whether programming meets this criterion is based on four standards:

1. The programming is primarily designed to meet children's educational and informational needs (i.e., it can't be primarily entertainment, such as a cartoon, and have as a by-product some educational value).
2. It is broadcast between 6 a.m. and 10 p.m., hours when children are likely to be viewing.
3. It is scheduled to run regularly each week.
4. It is at least a one-half-hour program.

In addition, commercial stations are required to identify their educational programs for children at the beginning of those programs; they must identify these programs to publishers of program guides as well. Moreover, all programs aimed at children twelve and younger may not contain more than 10.5 minutes of advertising per hour on weekends and 12 minutes on weekdays. The FCC also established that stations that air at least three hours of "core" children's programming a week would be in fulfillment of their obligations under the CTA, "core" being defined primarily in terms of item number one above.

Violent and Sexual Programming: The V-Chip

Violent and sexual programming receives special attention from the FCC because of concern about the implications of such material for young viewers. With the passage of the Telecommunications Act of 1996, the federal government began regulating televised violent content in addition to sexual content, which it already regulated. The act seeks to give parents greater control over their children's viewing of violent and sexual programming. The act begins by summarizing research findings that demonstrate the negative impact of television-violence viewing on children. It notes, "Parents express grave concern over violent and

sexual video programming and strongly support technology that would give them greater control to block video programming in the home that they consider harmful to their children."

In order to give parents control over what kind of programming their children are able to watch, the government mandated that from January 2000 all television sets thirteen inches or larger come equipped with what is called a **V-chip**, or "violence chip." The V-chip is a computer device that enables parents or any other viewer to program a TV set to block access to programs containing violent and sexual content, based on the program rating.

The rating system developed for the V-chip is also called the "TV Parental Guidelines." At the request of the government, the television industry created its own voluntary ratings system and agreed to broadcast signals that contain programming ratings that can be detected by the V-chip. The ratings are shown on the TV screen for the first fifteen seconds of rated programming and permit viewers to use the V-chip to block those programs from their sets. On the basis of the First Amendment, all news programming is exempted from the V-chip.

In the digital age, the V-chip is no longer the only tool at parents' disposal to restrict television viewing among their children. All digital media systems, including digital cable and satellite television, contain software controls that can block individual programs, entire channels, or classes of programs based on their ratings.

TV Parental Guidelines

The new television rating system identifies six categories of programming. The first two refer to programming designed solely for children, and the final one is programming aimed solely at adults. The middle three ratings refer to programming that has not been designed for children, but that may be suitable for some children, and it is up to parents to decide. The rating system is similar to the system developed for motion pictures. Following are the categories and their official definitions.

Programs designed specifically for children:

TV-Y (All Children. This program is designed to be appropriate for all children.) Whether this program is animated or live-action, the themes and elements in it are specifically designed for a very young audience, including children from ages two to six. This program is not expected to frighten younger children.

TV-Y7 (Directed to Older Children. This program is designed for children ages seven and above.) It may be more appropriate for children who have acquired the developmental skills needed to distinguish between make-believe and reality. Themes and elements in this program may include mild fantasy or comedic violence or may frighten children under the age of seven. Programs where fantasy violence may be more intense or more combative than other programs in this category will be designated TV-Y7-FV.

Programs not designed for children, but possibly suitable for audiences including at least older children:

TV-G (General Audience. Most parents would find this program suitable for all ages.) Although this rating does not signify a program designed specifically for children, most parents may let younger children watch this program unattended. It contains little or no violence, no strong language, and little or no sexual dialogue or situations.

TV-PG (Parental Guidance Suggested. This program contains material that parents may find unsuitable for younger children.) Many parents may want to watch it with their younger children. The theme itself may call for parental guidance and/or the program contains one or more of the following: moderate violence (V), some sexual situations (S), infrequent coarse language (L), or some suggestive dialogue (D).

TV-14 (Parents Strongly Cautioned. This program contains some material that many parents would find unsuitable for children under fourteen years of age.) Parents are strongly urged to exercise greater care in monitoring this program and are cautioned against letting children under the age of fourteen watch unattended. This program contains one or more of the following: intense violence (V); intense sexual situations (S); strong, coarse language (L); or intensely suggestive dialogue (D).

Programs designed only for adult audiences:

TV-MA (Mature Audience Only. This program is specifically designed to be viewed by adults and therefore may be unsuitable for children under seventeen.) This program contains one or more of the following: graphic violence (V); explicit sexual activity (S); or crude, indecent language (L).

Intellectual Property Rights

Of significant and growing concern to those in mass communication is protecting their **intellectual property** (IF). IF refers to ideas that have commercial value, such as literary or artistic works, patents, software programs, business methods, and industrial processes, particularly in the form of copyright protection. Copyright law ("copy-right" refers to the legal right to make a copy of a work) is one form of intellectual property rights protection that deals with protecting specific expressions of ideas. The other two main areas of intellectual property law are patents and trademarks.

Patents are intended to protect a specific form of intellectual property known as "inventions." Once granted, a patent prohibits anyone from copying the invention, pattern, or design. Anyone can apply for a patent, as long as the idea is new. **Trademarks** refer to images, designs, logos, or even words or phrases. For example, in March 2004 Donald Trump, host of *The Apprentice* reality TV show, attempted to trademark his phrase "You're Fired!" so it could be sold on clothing and other items. However, the U.S. Patent and Trademark Office turned down his request because it was too similar to another phrase, "You're Hired!", an educational board game that had that phrase trademarked in 1997.

A copyright exists from the moment a work is created in its fixed form, such as being written down or recorded, so simply claiming an idea does not give you a copyright to it. Inserting a © symbol (although in the case of a musical recording the symbol is a P in a circle, but that symbol may be hard to find on your keyboard), along with a date and the name of the copyright owner, also helps show that you are copyrighting a work, but it is not necessary. In the case of a work for hire, the employer generally owns the copyright. A copyright is in effect for the lifetime of the author, plus 70 years, although it may be up to 125 years in the case of a work for hire. The rationale of a copyright is to protect not only the intellectual product but the author/owner's financial interests. In 1989, the United States joined the Berne Convention for the Protection of Literary and Artistic Works, extending copyright protection globally.

Copyright law protects a wide range of expression, primarily the creations of authors or artists. A book or an article is protected by a copyright, not a patent. Included are literary works (including newspapers, books, magazines), musical works, dramatic works, pantomimes and choreographic works, pictorial, graphic, and sculpture works, motion pictures and other audiovisual works, sound recordings, and architectural works. Under the **Digital Millennium Copyright Act**, it extends to digital works as well, including those on the Internet or other online media, because if something exists on hard drive it is considered a fixed form.

Fair Use

Holding a copyright to a work provides the owner an exclusive right to reproduce, distribute (over any media), perform, display, or license that work. There are limited exceptions to the rights under copyright law, including primarily for **fair use** of an expression, such as in a movie or book review where the reviewer might include an excerpt, or in criticism or commentary. In general, there are four factors considered in deciding whether the use of another's copyrighted work is legal under the "fair use" provision of the act:

1. The purpose and nature of the use (i.e., is it purely commercial, educational, or for the news, the latter two of which are generally more likely to qualify)
2. The character of the copyrighted work (some works are inherently more protected; this is a subjective matter determined by the courts)
3. The amount and extent of the excerpt used, in proportion to the copyrighted work in its entirety (this is more qualitatively than quantitatively determined, however, and there are no exact rules on the permissible number of words one may borrow from a text or the amount of video, audio, or image one may excerpt, since even a small clip may represent the most significant creative aspect of the work)
4. The effect of the use on the copyrighted work's market potential (i.e., in dollar terms), especially when the copyrighted work is used as the basis for a derivative work (i.e., a movie based on a book)

The issue of fair use has become a flash point for digital media, especially in relation to content aggregators such as Google News or video search engines. There have been several court cases in the past ten years in which copyright holders have sued content aggregators, claiming copyright infringement. However, if the content aggregator has been able to show that it has sufficiently transformed the content—for example, by making low-resolution thumbnails of images or video clips—and to show that it is not profiting directly from doing so, it has generally won the case. Other aggregators have arrived at licensing agreements with media companies in order to continue to display or aggregate their content. An example is a deal Google struck with Associated Press to aggregate its news stories and keep them on Google News for a limited time.

Legal Issues in the Digital World

The courts and legal system have not been able to keep up with the many changes to mass communication that the Internet and digital media have brought. As a result, cases decided by the courts from the mid-1990s through today can have dramatic effects because they can establish precedent, meaning they become the basis for subsequent court decisions and legislation.

One example of just how far the legal system has had to come occurred in a 2000 ruling against Eric Corley (Emmanuel Goldstein), publisher of *2600: The Hacker Quarterly*. He included links in the online version of the magazine to a site that contained the code to DeCSS, a computer program that opened encrypted DVDs and allowed them to be freely copied. Corley argued that being forced to remove the hyperlinks was an infringement of his First Amendment rights. The court disagreed, saying that a hyperlink was not an example of free speech because it acted as a kind of "mechanism" that allowed users to go to the site. However, posting the URL of a site without it being hyperlinked would still be considered free speech. An appellate court agreed with this decision in May 2001, and Corley decided not to take the case to the Supreme Court.

Because digital media have certain characteristics unlike analog media, there have been a host of new issues raised that our legal system has been ill-equipped to deal with. In some cases the courts are able to rely on existing laws and apply them to digital media, but in other cases the fit has been awkward, at best.

Digital Rights Management

File-sharing and royalty issues related to music, and increasingly video, have been discussed in earlier chapters, and this continues to be one of the main areas of contention in the digital space. Record labels have tried various measures to deter free file sharing, including suing customers and having universities hold seminars for incoming students on the matter, but with little success.

Broadly speaking, **digital rights management**, or DRM, is about finding ways using technology to rein in copyright infringement of digital content. Encryption has had some success,

although, as the DeCSS example demonstrates, it is not foolproof. **Digital watermarks** are a very important part of DRM. Watermarks are computer code (usually invisible, but sometimes visible) inserted into any digital content—images, graphics, audio, video, or even text documents—that authenticates the source of that content. Copyright owners value watermarks because they can protect media assets, or intellectual property, from theft—or at least make them easier to track when they are used illegally.

For example, if a media company sends digital video over the Internet and someone else tries to copy the video and distribute it without obtaining permission, the original copyright holder, an end user, or even an intelligent software agent can examine the content for an embedded digital watermark. If the watermark is present and is that of the original copyright holder, then it can be easily demonstrated that the redistributor is in violation of copyright law. In essence, the digital watermark is analogous to a brand placed on cattle by a rancher in order to deter or catch cattle rustlers.

DRM has faced resistance from some groups, such as the Electronic Frontier Foundation, who claim that media companies are trying to limit the capabilities of new technologies simply to increase their revenues and force media to behave like their analog counterparts. In some cases, new DRM technologies have severely limited use of content, not allowing someone who has purchased a CD to copy songs more than once, for example, or not allowing transfer between different devices. These restrictions have angered consumers and raised serious questions about what exactly a person is "buying" when purchasing a CD and what rights the purchaser has to that content.

Although not DRM per se, companies have also had to learn to manage their online presence through company websites and domain names. Some who did not see the value of the Internet in its early years discovered later that others had already leased their company name as a domain name, usually with the intent to sell it at a higher price, in a practice called **cybersquatting**. The World Intellectual Property Organization (WIPO) handles complaints from parties who claim others are unfairly using their names for personal gain.

WIPO decides on each case and generally applies standards of fair use, although there is no hard-and-fast rule. For example, Fox news personality Bill O'Reilly brought a case to WIPO to acquire www.billorielly.com, The person who had the site was actually named Bill O'Rielly (note the "i" and "e" are reversed in the spelling of his name), yet WIPO ruled in favor of O'Reilly and he got that domain name as well.

Keywords have also come before the courts as contested intellectual property. This has become especially important, as search engines dominate how people find information on the Web. Although keywords have become less important in terms of how search engines find and rank websites, they still play a role and can mislead users.

The courts have generally ruled that as long as a keyword fairly represents the content of a website, it can be used. However, a company cannot put a competitor's name in its keyword list in the hope of drawing people who were searching for the competitor.

Privacy

Privacy issues have become increasingly important on a number of levels with the Internet and digital media. Not only can websites track users in ways that are impossible with analog media, but they can insert code, called a cookie, onto users' computers and track them even after they have left that particular website. Not all cookies track users so relentlessly, however, and in fact cookies are needed to make the Web a more user-friendly environment.

Still, the overuse of cookies can be a problem. Just as a website will add a cookie to your computer, so will advertisers on a website. These **third-party cookies** also track your Web usage and send information directly to the advertisers, who can determine how long you've stayed on a page and where you went afterward.

Content Rights and Responsibilities

Another new area that media companies have had to deal with is the status of user-generated content (UGC). It is virtually impossible for a company to police all the content that is uploaded to the Internet, and the question of who is responsible for the content on a site arises when someone is defamed in a user comment as opposed to something the company itself wrote.

In general, the courts have made a "safe haven" provision for content providers, protecting them to some extent from libel lawsuits as long as they promptly removed the offending content and showed good efforts in preventing such content. Similarly, Internet service providers (ISPs) have been considered largely immune from responsibility for what is sent over their networks, although the threat of a lawsuit can sometimes be enough to get them to remove offending content.

Looking Back and Moving Forward

The Internet has raised a host of legal and regulatory issues regarding media, and the legal system lags generally far behind in dealing with them. The apparently simple question of whether a hyperlink is protected by the First Amendment can generate some complex discussions about the nature of digital media and the online environment. Similarly, the question "Where does publishing occur?" brings up complex legal debate.

The global nature of the Internet also raises questions on which laws should be followed if content that is offensive or illegal in one country can be viewed online. With analog media, the answer was obvious—publishing occurred in the country where the printing press was located. A book might be legally printed in one country but banned in another, thus if a copy was smuggled into the country where it was banned, the person caught with the book would be penalized, not the printer

But on the Internet the question of where something is published is not at all clear. A person may create some banned content in his country for his website, which is hosted by a company in another country, where the content is not banned.

Someone else may come across the content in a third country, where the material is considered harmful, sacrilegious, or defamatory. Several issues are raised in this scenario, including what country's laws will be used if a lawsuit is brought, and what constitutes libel, since it differs from country to country.

A pertinent highly controversial case was settled in December 2002. *Dow, Jones and Co. Inc. v. Gutnick* involved an article in *Barron's* (published by Dow Jones) in October 2000 that mentioned Melbourne businessman Joseph Gutnick several times. He sued for libel and claimed that the case should be heard in Australia, where he was defamed.

Although the number of print copies of *Barron's* sent to Australia was minuscule, the online readership of the magazine was over half a million, and Gutnick claimed that many more people would see the article in Australia than just those who subscribed to the print version. Dow Jones argued that the article was actually published in the United States, where Dow Jones's web servers were located, and thus the case should be heard in the United States (where libel charges are harder to win than in Australia). The Australian High Court agreed with Gutnick, however, and Dow Jones eventually settled with him in 2004.

The case was of serious concern to Internet watchers and media companies because of its potential implications for publishers on the Web. If this case becomes a precedent, then anyone could sue a media company or website according to his or her own country's laws, which may be stricter regarding types of acceptable content than where the material was published. On the other hand, it can be argued that it is not fair to impose another country's views of acceptable free speech simply because it is on the Internet. The question remains open and will likely come up again in the future.

Discussion Questions

1. In light of the terrorist attacks on the World Trade Center and Pentagon on September 11, 2001, do you think the government should have more or less power to exercise prior restraint and block publication or broadcast of material it feels might hurt national security interests? What would some of the effects be, both positive and negative, if the government adopted your opinion?

2. Tobacco and tobacco products cannot be advertised on electronic media such as TV and radio, yet alcohol can. Should similar restrictions be placed on these products on the Internet, or should there be even stronger restrictions?

3. Can traditional standards of what makes a "community" be applied when dealing with Internet obscenity or pornography? If so, what would those criteria be? If not, what standards could be applied?

4. Given the harm that ridicule or stereotyping can cause for the groups being ridiculed, do you think there should be greater legal restrictions on ridicule or offensive stereotypes in the media? Why or why not?

5. Do you think television and movie rating systems are effective in protecting children? Why or why not? Could there be a better system than ratings to protect children from objectionable content?

6. What dangers are there in a media industry that regulates itself or self-censors? Why could self-censorship be a good thing?

7. Put yourself in the role of a young novelist or struggling musician who is trying to make a living writing stories or making music. Would you oppose or support greater government or corporate control on copyright if the technology promised that unauthorized copies of your work could not be circulated?

Notes

1. Dwight L. Teeter Jr. and Don R. Le Due, Law of Mass Communications (Westbury, NY: The Foundation Press, 1992).

2. "How Effective Are Shield Laws?", Agents of Discovery: A Report on the Incidence of Subpoenas Served on the News Media in 1997, Reporters Committee for Freedom of the Press website, http://

www.rcfp.org. Retrieved November 8, 2002, from http://www.rcfp.org/agents/shieldlaws.html.

3. Reed E. Hundt, FCC Chairman, transcript of speech given at the Museum of Television and Radio, New York, New York, June 3, 1997. Retrieved November 8, 2002, from http://www.fcc.gov/Speeches/Hundt/spreh729.txt.

4. Linda Greenhouse, "'Virtual' Child Pornography Ban Overturned," New York Times, April 17, 2002. Retrieved April 17, 2002, from http://www.nytimes.com.

5. Mark Goodman, "The Radio Act of 1927 as a Product of Progressivism," vol. 2, no. 2. Media History Monographs. Retrieved November 8, 2002, from http://www.scripps.ohiou.edu/mediahistory/mhmjour2-2.htm.

6. Erik Barnouw, A Tower of Babel: A History of Broadcasting in the United States, vol. 1 (New York: Oxford University Press, 1966).

7. Mark Goodman, "The Radio Act of 1927 as a Product of Progressivism," vol. 2, no. 2. Media History Monographs. Retrieved November 8, 2002, from http://www.scripps.ohiou.edu/mediahistory/mhmjour2-2.htm.

8. M. S. Mander, "The Public Debate About Broadcasting in the Twenties: An Interpretive History," Journal of Broadcasting 28 (1984): 167-185.

9. Alan B. Albarran and Gregory G. Pitts, The Radio Broadcasting Industry (Boston: Allyn & Bacon, 2001), 27-29.

10. Eli Noam and Robert Freeman, "Global Competition," Television Quarterly (1998) Vol. 29, number 1, 18-23.

Further Reading

Mass Communication Law: In a Nutshell, 6th ed. Juliet Lushbough Dee, Harvey Zuckman (2006) Thomson West.

Freedom for the Thought That We Hate: A Biography of the First Amendment. Anthony Lewis (2008) Basic Books.

The Associated Press Style Book and Briefing on Media Law. Norm Goldstein (2007) Basic Books.

The Journalist's Guide to Media Law: Dealing with Legal and Ethical Issues, 2nd ed. Mark Pearson (2004) Allen & Unwin Academic.

We're All Journalists Now: The Transformation of the Press and Reshaping of the Law in the Internet Age. Scott Gant (2007) Free Press.

Insult to Injury: Libel, Slander and Invasions of Privacy. William Jones (2003) University of Colorado Press.

Rethinking Global Security: Media Popular Culture, and "The War on Terror". Andrew Martin, Patrice Petro, eds. (2006) Rutgers University Press.

Intellectual Property Law and Interactive Media: Free for a Fee. Edward Lee Lamoureux, Steven Baron, Claire Stewart (2009) Peter Lang.

The Future of Ideas: The Fate of the Commons in a Connected World. Lawrence Lessig (2001) Random House.

Remix: Making Art and Commerce Thrive in the Hybrid Economy. Lawrence Lessig (2008) Penguin Press.

9. Shaping the American Mass Media: A Brief Overview

By Melvin L. DeFleur

The ideal way to begin a focused study on mass communication, its technologies and its effects on society and individuals is to examine its history. Written by one of the premiere communication scholars of our time, Dr. Melvin L. DeFleur, this chapter gives readers a broad view of the ways mass media developed in the United States beginning with the pilgrim's landing and continuing through to contemporary America. This historical context highlights the relationship between mass media technologies, communication systems and the continual evolution of society.

Because individuals often do not realize the wealth of factors that influence the development of media systems, a true understanding of the complex relationship between mass media and society requires a purposeful historical review such as this. Throughout this chapter, readers are encouraged to contemplate the reciprocal evolutionary impacts of media and society as they consider each of the historical examples provided. This will help create a proper foundation for understanding current technologies and their impacts. It will also give readers a better appreciation of the complexity of communication systems and the importance of studying mass communication.

To understand the origins of both our contemporary mass media as well as the theories that explain their processes and their influences on their audiences, it is necessary to look back at *where they came from and how they developed*. It does not take any great flight of imagination to realize that the mass communication system we have today is quite different from what we have had in the past. Similarly, it is obvious that our system will continue to develop, and what we have in the future will not be the same as what we now have. For that reason, we begin with a historical overview of how our mass communication system developed within an ever-changing society to produce what we have today.

The American society essentially began in September of 1620, when 101 passengers, along with 48 crew members and a number of chickens and pigs, left Plymouth, England, on the Mayflower. Nearly two months later, they landed on Cape Cod, where they spent another eight weeks before moving to the mainland. There they quickly laid out a road up from the shore and began constructing shelters. Within two years they had a small village of simple homes that they named New Plymouth. The houses they built were small and compactly arranged close together on each side of the road, each with its own garden plot.

The people in the new community worked hard all day, tending gardens and animals, but had very little to do after sunset other than talk with their families and friends. There were religious services on the Sabbath and daily family prayers, but the strict codes of the Pilgrims did not permit frivolous activities. Aside from the family Bible, there was nothing to read in most of the houses. Even if there had been, the majority could neither read nor write. Even for the few who could, it was difficult. After dark, tallow candles, crude lamps, and the fireplace provided barely enough light to move around inside. Thus, by comparison with today, the citizens of New Plymouth led a life almost free of any form of communication other than talking.[1]

The contrast between the availability of mass communications to the people of New Plymouth in the early 1600s and their counterparts in any community in the United States in the 2000s is startling, to say the least. Today, any of us can select from an almost bewildering set of choices among media. Information and news, entertainment, and other content can be delivered instantly to homes via copper wire, optic cable, microwaves, and even satellite transmissions from space. A typical citizen has available, twenty-four hours a day, virtually any form of communication content from gangsta rap and spectator sports to classical music and serious political analysis. He or she can read a book or a magazine, peruse the newspaper, listen to the radio, go to the movies, view a rented film on the home DVD player, check out a sitcom or game show on television, view TV on a cell phone, play games on a computer, log on to the Internet, or exchange text messages with strangers from all parts of the world. Thus, an almost incredible spectrum of mass communication content is instantly available from intensely competing media.

THE RELATIONSHIP BETWEEN MASS MEDIA AND SOCIETY

The American system of mass communication today—its media, those who pay its costs, and the audiences it serves—are embedded in a larger context. They are part of the American society as a whole. That society, as is perfectly obvious, has constantly undergone change. Nowhere is this change more obvious and visible than in the case of our means of communicating. As our opening section indicated, the earliest English colonists in our New World society had virtually nothing we would classify as mass communication. In contrast, today we live in a sea of mediated messages.

This incredible change from what we were to what we are raises a critical question for anyone wanting to understand our contemporary system of mass communications in the United States: How did we get here from there? That is, why do we have the kind of mass communication systems that we do—the most complex in the world? What social and cultural factors within the society shaped their nature? How did they come to be based on such market concepts as free enterprise, competition, the profit motive, and private ownership? Moreover, why is it that our government has such limited control over the content of the media? Other societies do not have identical mass communication systems. Some are similar, but many are very different indeed.

The answer, of course, is that each society's mass communication system is a product of its history and has been shaped by the culture developed by its people over many generations. To be sure, each system at any point in time has been influenced in important ways by existing technologies. However, these technologies are essentially the same from one society to the next. For example, printing presses or television sets operating in, say, China, Cuba, Iceland, Iran, or the United States all use the similar physical principles. The differences between those mass media systems and the one in the United States have come about because each nation has developed uses and controls over the process of mass communication in different ways—within its own set of values, political system, economic institution, and other cultural factors. Therefore, to gain a clear understanding of a specific society's media system, just knowing the technology is not enough. It is essential to understand the social, political, economic, and cultural context within which each nation's media developed and now functions.

Essentially, the critical factors that have most influenced the media in the United States have been the country's basic cultural values. It is these values that have shaped its political and economic systems along with its moral norms and laws. These values are products of our past, and they continue to define our contemporary way of life—including the nature of our mass communication system. In the future these values will continue to determine the characteristics of the system's content, controls, operations, patterns of use, and influences on audiences. For that reason it is essential to understand them, including where they came from. Our system of mass communication will influence your work, your leisure, your ideas, and even your children in the decades ahead.

The basic values of a society are, in turn, a product of its collective historical experience. Clearly, the events of our past, such as the founding of the original colonies, the American Revolution, expansion of the frontier, the Industrial Revolution, population growth, complex patterns of immigration, various wars, legislation, and the development of technology have all had significant influences on each new medium as it was introduced and widely adopted. In a very real sense, then, the development of mass communication in the U.S. has been profoundly influenced by what took place in the American society in years past.

But there is another side to the coin. While the mass media in the United States have been shaped by social and cultural factors, they have, in turn, had a powerful influence on all of us, both individually and socially. There is little doubt that the numbers of people who receive, and are influenced in some way by, mass-communicated information on a daily basis are simply staggering. In fact, the recipients and users of media-provided information include virtually every American, excluding only those too young, too old, or too ill to attend. Their purchasing decisions are shaped in significant ways by a vast advertising industry that supports the media financially. Those decisions, in turn, shape what the manufacturing and service industries can successfully produce and market. In a very real sense, then, the work that Americans perform and the health of their economy are intimately linked to mass communications. Moreover, most forms of recreation enjoyed by citizens are linked to print, film, broadcasting, or computer media in some way. The same is true of political participation. Patterns of voting are shaped to a considerable degree by mass-communicated news and mediated political campaigns. Therefore, the relationship between media and society is a very complex and reciprocal one.

The bottom line is that understanding our contemporary mass media, and how they came to be shaped into their present form, is no idle academic enterprise. It is a key to understanding life in our time and how it will undoubtedly be shaped in the future. Against the background provided by the present chapter, additional ones will provide summaries of various theories that have been advanced to explain their origins, as well as the processes and effects of mass communications as they influence both individuals and society. Without first understanding this background, however, there is no way in which their nature can truly be appreciated.

The purpose of the remainder of the present chapter, then, is to summarize very briefly, and in a general way, the circumstances that shaped our mass communication system into its present form during a span of nearly four hundred years. The chapter not only provides an answer to the question of how we got here from there, but also it provides a foundation for understanding basic aspects of the structure and functioning of our contemporary mass media today and how they are likely to develop in the future. Thus, the overview that follows focuses less on specific media than on features of the American experience that have had consequences for our entire media system. The more detailed events and circumstances that shaped each specific medium will be addressed in subsequent chapters.

THE LEGACY OF THE EARLY PERIOD: THE 1600s

Few media scholars write about the influence of the earliest settlements in North America on our mass communication systems today. In many ways that connection may seem remote. Nevertheless, there is a relationship between the shared values and beliefs that developed in the earliest American colonies and the nature of our contemporary mass communication system. The unique lifestyle that quickly came to characterize those early communities provided the beginnings of the general American culture that we know now. It was within the limits of that culture, as it was developed over succeeding generations, that our present mass media came into existence. Therefore, it is important to understand the origins of the central features of American shared beliefs and values that are relevant to understanding how our modern mass communications systems developed.

The first task in looking briefly at the American colonial experience is to understand the underlying values of our economic system. The second will be to examine the political values that came to characterize Americans as they moved toward a separation from England. A third is to understand the very early role played by newspapers and other forms of print in the process of achieving independence.

Mercantilism: The Importance of Private Enterprise

The early 1600s were an age of mercantilism—a concept that is still with us. It is based on the idea of trade—the ancient idea of buying and selling goods and products to make a profit. A related idea is industrialization—using machines to produce goods to sell. That would come later, beginning about the end of the 1700s. More recently, providing services for fees has also become increasingly important. Together they are the basis of modern capitalism. Thus, capitalism refers to an economic system designed to make profits for those who invest in the means by which goods and services are produced and distributed—or by which some resource is "exploited" (used to produce products to sell).

While traders have been a part of human life for many centuries, the era of mercantilism began to expand and mature about the time of Columbus. European merchants had begun routinely to send ships to foreign lands (mainly India and China) to buy goods that they could sell for a profit when they returned. They bought products that were in high demand, such as spices and silk, that they could easily sell to European markets. Thus, exploration of routes to places where such goods could be bought was critical. Thus, the profit motive was a major factor that motivated Columbus and other early explorers to set sail for the New World.

During the 1600s, after sea routes to the New World were better understood, came an era of colonization of the Americas by a number of European nations. The initial purpose of these settlements was (again) to make profits for those who bankrolled each project. A secondary purpose was to establish global political claims by the monarchies of the time. In North America these were mainly the English, the French, and the Dutch.

At first, the English, like the Spanish farther South, sought gold. They paid lip service to converting the Indians to Christianity. However, the English were about a century late in getting established in the Americas. The only area left that was open to them for settlement was along the Atlantic seaboard north of St. Augustine (in Florida) and to the south of what is now Newfoundland. It soon became apparent that there was little gold to be had in that part of the New World, so investors had to try to make their profits in other ways.

The first successful English settlement in the New World was in Bermuda. It was followed in 1607 by a colony at Jamestown, in what is now Virginia. A third was the one established in 1620 at New Plymouth, in what later became Massachusetts. Within a decade, a number of others were authorized and settled in both Massachusetts and Maryland. By the middle of the 1600s, English settlements were in place all up and down the Atlantic seaboard. Thus, by the end of the seventeenth century, with substantial immigration from England, these became the thirteen original colonies.

As noted, each of the thirteen English colonies started as a commercial undertaking. Groups of "merchant adventurers" sold shares in the enterprise and recruited people to establish a new "plantation." They obtained a charter from a supervising government agency to locate a community in a particular area approved by the Crown. The goal of such a settlement ("plantation") was to exploit some sort of local resource in order to ship products back to England to be sold at a profit. These commodities could be crops, such as tobacco or grain, or whatever was available. In more northern areas, dried and salted fish were particularly profitable. Thus, the practice of risking capital in private enterprises for potential gain

was very much a part of our cultural inheritance from England.

Today, we live in a society characterized by controlled capitalism. It is not the totally unfettered, sink-or-swim capitalism first described in 1776 by Adam Smith in his famous book, *An Inquiry into the Nature and Causes of the Wealth of Nations*. It has long been one in which both local and national governments—whether British or American—have played parts in regulating economic activities. An important lesson is that, from the very beginning, economic considerations have been a primary factor in the movement of populations from the old world to the new. Another important lesson is that the main values underlying our contemporary American economic system began to be set into place with the very first settlements in our part of the New World.

A Commitment to Local and Autonomous Government

Shifting from economic considerations to political factors, it is important to note that a critical early development that would influence our media was the establishment of local systems of laws to provide stable government within each new plantation. It is not difficult to see this situation as laying the foundation for resentment of outside controls. That would develop at a later date, resentment of the faraway government of England. For example, the Mayflower colonists designed their own system of local self-government even before they sighted land. They were supposed to have landed much farther south and be bound by the prior agreements of the Virginia colony. However, during their voyage, ocean currents swept them north to Cape Cod. To avoid anarchy, they decided to design their own rules for living together, and they drafted the Mayflower Compact while still at sea. It set forth rules for orderly collective living.

As early as 1639, three small communities in Massachusetts banded together and prepared a document of Fundamental Orders, which served as a constitution for a Public State or Commonwealth.[2] It made no reference to England whatsoever, and it incorporated almost all of the provisions that would eventually become part of the U.S. Constitution. Thus, the idea of local autonomy, and freedom from big government that was far away, became a part of the colonial culture very early. Later, that idea would play a critical role in shaping our nation's press.

Separating Church and State

While the plantations were funded and organized for a return on investment, those that were initially established in the Massachusetts area had a second important purpose for their members. Those who came to New Plymouth on the Mayflower called themselves "Pilgrims"—which even today means "people who journey to alien lands in search of truth." They saw themselves as seeking religious truth. From the standpoint of the Crown, however, they were little more than troublesome religious radicals. The Crown saw them as "separatists" who had split from the official (Anglican) Church of England. Like many religious sects today, the Pilgrims had rejected the established Church in favor of their own sectarian beliefs. Indeed, because of religious persecution in England, they had fled to Holland earlier and then on to the New World. Many in England said "good riddance."

Others, who were also religious dissidents but still living in England, soon followed to establish a second settlement—the Massachusetts Bay Colony (now Boston). These settlers believed themselves to be "Puritans" because they were intent upon "purifying" the beliefs of the Anglican Church. A main point is that these early New England colonists were determined to be free from religious interference by the state. This concept—the separation of church and state—of course prevailed through subsequent generations and became a critical part of the political culture of the new nation that would emerge.

Individualism: The Frontier Mentality

Other factors shaped the emerging fundamental cultural values of the colonists. For one thing,

they were by no means environmentalists! In front of them was a sea rich with resources and at their backs was a vast continent with unlimited land, forests, minerals, and wild animals. Almost immediately they set about to exploit those assets. They set up fishing and whaling industries. Acre by acre they hacked their way into the forests. They killed the deer and sent the skins to England, along with the furs of other animals that they could trap or obtain in trade from Native Americans. They mined small deposits of iron for export. They burned down the trees to clear fields on which to grow crops. When these lands were exhausted, they simply moved farther inland. It was an economy of exploitation.

More and more people arrived from England. Indeed, the population doubled every generation right up until the time of the American Revolution. As this happened, the pace of destructive activities increased. By the time the United States was established as a new nation with its own Constitution (1787), the deer, furs, and fish from the rivers and streams were greatly diminished in most of the areas east of the Mississippi. As the population had moved westward, the land was denuded. By the mid-1800s, just before the Civil War, there was little virgin forest left from the Atlantic clear to the Missouri River.

This economic system, based on exploitable resources, land exhaustion, and relocation, produced a set of shared cultural beliefs that has often been called a frontier mentality. It was a set of shared beliefs that saw "rugged individuals" pitted against nature—with a justifiable right to subjugate the environment for their own uses. Such individuals not only saw no need for controls by a powerful government, but also they resented attempts by rulers far away to regulate any aspect of their lives. In other societies, the activities of the individual remained under collective control. But in the emerging America, an emphasis on individuality, personal responsibility, and freedom from government interference became an important part of the national culture from the beginning. Such values continue to shape the thinking of many Americans, and they clearly played a part in shaping our contemporary mass communication system as it developed.

Another feature of life in the American colonies was that it lacked the aristocratic system that prevailed in Europe. That was particularly true in the North. In the southern colonies, large land holdings, along with abundant cheap labor, were needed by plantation owners to grow such crops as rice, cotton, and tobacco. Slaves provided the agricultural labor in such settings and a kind of unofficial aristocracy developed based on ownership of both land and slaves. Even so, the majority of the population in southern colonies were poor subsistence farmers who worked the land themselves. In New England, and later elsewhere, most people established small farms or ranches and worked them as a family team.

Generally, then, in the New World, there was more democracy and fewer social distinctions between haves and have nots. There were social class levels, of course, but the rigid and inherited class structure that characterized England never took root in the colonies. This yielded the shared belief that each citizen was just as good as the next—except for black people—and each should have the same rights as the next. These beliefs provided a strong foundation for a sense of equality that would shape the nation's political values during the centuries ahead.

Overview of the Influences of the Early Period

From the above, the influences from the 1600s that would eventually shape our contemporary mass media can be summarized briefly: The conditions of life that the colonists established in the New World were not the same as those that prevailed in the mother country. They brought with them an economic structure that emphasized private ownership, profits, and an almost complete dependence on extracting natural resources. Eventually, this would produce a kind of frontier mentality emphasizing rugged individualism and a distaste for government interference. Life in the new settlements was much less bound by class and social distinctions than was the case in England, leading to greater feelings of political equality.

Moreover, there were far more opportunities for poor people to move up the social ladder—mainly by acquiring land. The early settlers placed great importance on autonomous local government, as opposed to rule by powerful people far away. These were important foundations for a change from monarchy to democracy. Those in the New England area, in particular, insisted on a total separation between church and state, because religion, and the right to worship in their own way, was an important part of their lives.

In many ways, these emphases from the period of early settlement still define some of the most basic values of Americans. We continue to believe in the importance of individual responsibility, political equality, limited government, and local autonomy. Americans still approve of private ownership, the legitimacy of a pursuit of profits, and a separation between government and religion. It was on this cultural foundation that the mass communication system of the nation would eventually develop, and it continues to shape its contemporary nature in important ways.

INFLUENCES OF THE LATER COLONIAL ERA: THE 1700s

Between the end of the 1600s and the late 1700s, the settlements and inhabited areas along the eastern seaboard developed rapidly into thirteen prosperous and successful English colonies with specific geographical boundaries. While there were many similarities among the colonies in their separate governments, there was no overall federation—no central assembly or national legislature that brought the separate colonies together into a single political system. That concept would develop during the 1700s.

Basically, during the 1700s, each colony was politically controlled by the English king and Parliament through a governor. This administrator was sometimes locally elected but always had to be confirmed by the king. Each colony had a local legislative body whose members were chosen by the "freemen." Local towns (townships) elected "selectmen"—which they still do today in many communities in New England. Those allowed to vote were white male property owners. In some cases, they also had to be of the right religion. Those who were elected sometimes appointed other officials, such as assistants to the governor as well as judges. Thus, the basic three-part form of government, executive, legislative, and judicial, was in some respects already a familiar idea by the time that a refined version would be built into the U.S. Constitution of 1787.

By the mid-1700s, the American colonies had become of critical economic importance to England. The British Empire was being established all over the world, and the pattern was much the same in each colonial area. Each was required to send back to England whatever products they could produce for their merchants to sell. In return, English craftsmen and merchants supplied the colonies with processed goods, such as cloth, shoes, tools, or whatever was being produced in the home country. For many years it was a system within which each party prospered. The abundant resources of the American colonies yielded wealth for many locals, while the processed goods from England sold into the colonial market created wealth for the English entrepreneurs. In addition, the colonies benefitted because the powerful English navy and armed forces kept out potential invaders.

Deep Distrust of Big Government

As the 1700s wore on, however, many dissatisfactions with the system developed. Great Britain continued rigidly to control the pattern of commerce between its colonies and the homeland. By the 1760s, a number of serious problems became evident. For one thing, there was a substantial negative balance of trade between England and the colonies. In some ways it was just like our current relationship with countries like Japan and China. The colonists bought goods from England, costing far more in total value than what was earned from the products they sold to the mother country. This created a lopsided flow of money from the colonies to England. This began to produce economic difficulties and great resentment

in the colonies. However, England would not change the rules. It came to be widely believed among the colonists that the far-distant government in London was not sensitive to their needs, was exploiting them economically, and was ruling them with a heavy hand. A particularly sensitive issue was "representation." There were no elected representatives from the colonies in the English Parliament.

Growing Dissatisfaction with England's Controls

As dissatisfaction grew, a number of men joined political groups with names like the Sons of Liberty, or quasi-military militia such as the Minute Men (who pledged to be ready to fight with a minute's notice). These militias thought of themselves as patriots and felt that some day it might be necessary to resist the English government by force of arms. They stockpiled arms and ammunition—which was against the law. Their members met regularly in taverns and other places to discuss ways to resist the government, and they developed networks of spies and messengers to keep themselves informed about the activities of the British armed forces.

The single most galling issue was taxes. England had been almost constantly at war with other European countries—especially with France. These protracted conflicts drained the English treasury, and great debts piled up. Ways had to be found to pay them off. King George and the English Parliament decided that money should be raised by taxing the people in the American colonies. After all, they had protected the colonies for many decades. Thus, a Stamp Act was passed in 1765, requiring a small fee (about a nickel in current terms) for a little imprinted stamp on every official document produced in the colonies. The colonials were outraged, not so much by the size of the fee, but by the principle. It was "taxation without representation." Because of the outcry, the Stamp Act was repealed by the British a year later.

Meanwhile, in 1765 the first step was taken that would lead to a federation of colonies. Nine colonies sent representatives to the American Union—a group that met in New York. There the participants drew up resolutions concerning such issues as inalienable rights, personal liberties, and freedom from taxation (by Britain) without having elected representatives in Parliament. The Parliament back in England, however, insisted that it was in total control and then went on to impose a new series of import taxes on the colonies. One such tax was levied on tea. Hotheads in the colonies—especially in Boston—saw these impositions as a total outrage (again, taxation without representation). Dressed like Native Americans, a small band boarded and burned several ships and threw 26,000 pounds of tea packaged in lead boxes into the bay.

By 1774, a group of self-appointed colonial leaders would form the Continental Congress. That group would unite and guide the colonies through the eight years of war that would soon start. On July 4, 1776, that Congress formally and publically announced political separation from England with the Declaration of Independence. It was a critical step, and the newspapers of the time played a key role in making the document known to the public.

The Role of Newspapers in the Independence Movement

The importance of these various developments for shaping our current media system was that distrust of powerful government became an important element in shaping the role of the press in the American society. It laid the foundation for the role of contemporary journalists as the "watchdogs" of society—calling attention to the transgressions of those in positions of power. Many of the early newspapers publishers risked going to jail by speaking out against the Crown. As England tightened its grip to make sure that the colonies remained under its control, a number of very able writers prepared public statements advocating separation from England, and they did go to jail! It is important to understand that the colonial press became the medium that carried

those messages to an increasingly enthusiastic audience. Using not only newspapers but also other printed tracts and pamphlets, those who spoke out strongly made a convincing case for total independence from England. Their essays and other appeals were widely read. These media played an important part in shaping the thinking of those who saw English rule as repressive. The print media of the time, then, were an important factor in shaping the popular support for political separation from the mother country.

Overview of Influences of the Colonial Era

In summary, the colonial period, before the time of the Revolution, saw the beginnings of the American press. A number of important traditions and features that are retained today, not only by newspapers but also by later media, were established during the period. Clearly, newspapers helped shape and clarify opinion during the time when the colonies were moving toward separation from England. Many provided the means by which important views on various sides of the issue were made available to the population.

Another important tradition was defining the role of the press as the "watchdog" of society. Those who published newspapers saw themselves as totally independent of, and even antagonistic to, government. They saw their mission as keeping an eye on politicians and officials, and their policies, to make sure that power was not being misused. When such abuses were detected, it was the duty of the newspaper, according to this conception, to call public attention to what was going on. Through such disclosures, it was believed, government excesses could be held in check. Today, investigative journalism—which is now an important feature not only of newspapers but also of other media—remains a strong tradition in the American media system.

Newspapers also provided a great deal of useful information of a nonpolitical nature. They published notices of ship arrivals, accounts of events that had occurred in their area, and even some foreign news. This was the beginning of the critical information function that the press (all news media) serves today. During the 1700s, newspapers even provided a certain amount of lighter fare. Often, they contained poems, essays on manners, and other material that was neither news nor political commentary. While these efforts were limited, they foreshadowed the entertainment function of the media that has also become a central feature today.

Overall, then, the 1700s saw not only the remarkable American Revolution and the establishment of the United States as a new and independent nation but also the beginnings of a mass communication system that was a product of the emerging American culture. These features of the mass media of the time were added on to the accepted concept of private ownership and the emphasis on the profit motive that were brought forward from the previous century.

MASS MEDIA IN AN EXPANDING NATION: THE 1800s

By any measure the 1600s and the 1700s were periods of slow but steady change, punctuated with dramatic events, such as American struggle for independence. In contrast, the 1800s saw constant and often rapid change. The term "Industrial Revolution" is used to characterize the transformations of society that began early in the 1800s. However, the people of the time did not realize how rapidly their way of life was being altered. We think of the last half of the 1900s and the early years of the 2000s as a period of social and technological change. Indeed, that is the case, but in many ways the first half of the 1800s was even more dramatic.[3]

As the 1800s began, travel was still a matter of either walking, riding a horse, or bumping along in a wagon or carriage pulled by horses or mules. Sending a message to a loved one, or for business purposes, took weeks or even months—depending on the distance the letter had to be carried. Just five decades later, by mid-century, people were riding on trains that could get up to the astonishing speed of 45 miles an hour. Messages sent by telegraph, along copper wires that connected many distant towns and cities, traveled at a mind-boggling 186,000 miles per second!

Early in the nineteenth century, the boundaries of what is now the United States (mainland) were greatly expanded by acquisition of vast territories from the French as well as from Mexico. Other areas were acquired as well by various means to establish the boundaries of what is now the continental United States. For the most part, those areas were occupied by a few Europeans and by scattered tribes of native people. These Native Americans, in particular, were seen mainly as troublesome barriers to the advance of civilization. Consequently, they were systematically killed off, rounded up, or moved to be confined to reservations.

American leaders of the time developed policies favoring immigration, especially from Europe. The new country needed people—and they came in great waves. To protect against potential foreign incursion, the huge middle and the far western reaches of the country had to have people. It was a land of great natural resources—minerals, forests, and farmland. Continuing the frontier mentality of the first two centuries, the shared belief was that the wilderness had to be tamed and its resources brought under control for economic gain.

The Industrial Revolution and Its Consequences

It was a combination of a new source of brute power, the inventive genius of vigorous people, and the prospect of great economic rewards that drove the ever-increasing pace of the Industrial Revolution. It had begun when the steam engine became a reality.

Steam as a New Source of Power

It is difficult today to understand fully what took place after the steam engine arrived. Until that happened, power was something obtained from wind, water, or muscles—human or animal. Steam engines came into the picture early in the 1800s. By the 1830s, steam was driving early railroads, ships, river boats, and machinery in factories. Some parts of the country made the change more quickly than others. In New England, with poor and rocky soil, a steam-based factory economy came as a blessing. In the South and in the West, where much of the land had yet to be settled, the industrial society developed much more slowly.

Coupling a steam engine to a printing press was only one of many such applications, but it revolutionized the business of publication. It had a profound effect on the nature of newspapers. By 1830, a cylinder-type press became available. It had two big rotors about three feet long and a foot and a half in diameter (rather like a giant version of an old-fashioned washing machine ringer). The rotors were turned by the steam engine. A cast lead "stereotype" was placed over the roller. It contained all the letters and characters for the passages that were to be printed on single big sheets of paper. Such sheets were fed into the rollers. Several pages of a book or magazine could be printed at one time, to be folded and cut after printing.

The power press was a godsend for book publishing, but it was also quickly adapted for newspapers. By 1834, a new kind of newspaper— the "penny" press—would come into existence in New York City. It was the forerunner of the modern mass newspaper. It would never have been possible without the advertising brought by the Industrial Revolution, the power of the steam engine, and the efficiency of the rotary press. As will be made clear, the financial format and content of the penny press was quickly and widely adopted in communities throughout the United States. Within a very short time, the "daily newspaper" became a very different type of publication than those of the colonial press that had preceded it.

Literacy

Another factor that would make it possible for newspapers to serve much larger audiences was a historic change in public education that began during the early 1800s. Horace Mann, an educator and politician in Massachusetts, persuaded the Commonwealth's legislature to establish an innovative system of compulsory (and tax-based) education to ensure that children would be able to read, write, and do basic arithmetic. These skills were seen as important in a democracy and in a part of the nation in which industrial work was becoming more and more important. As public schools became common, increasing levels of literacy greatly expanded the potential market for newspapers.

Advertising

In addition, as industrialization continued, the flow of goods produced in factories produced a growing need for advertising. Newspapers were able to take advantage of steadily increasing revenues from both advertising and subscriptions, which increased their profitability. All of these factors worked together, and the result was a surge of growth in both the number of daily papers being published and the proportion of the population that was able to subscribe to and read them. In fact, as the nation continued to expand, both in terms of territory and population, both the number of newspapers and the size of their audiences increased rapidly.

Revolutions in Transportation

Railroads would not be widely established until the 1840s, and it would be 1874 before the two coasts were linked by rail. Meanwhile, another form of transportation played a key role in the developing nation, and it had a very clear effect on the mass communication industries that would come in the future. At a time before steam, canals were a relatively efficient way to move goods and even people. Because no roads linked regions, boats on rivers and other waterways were the most efficient and most comfortable way to travel. However, rivers and lakes were not conveniently located in places where they were needed, so canals linking them had to be dug to serve as an alternative.

One of the most remarkable construction projects ever undertaken in the early 1800s was the Erie Canal. It was a 363-mile system of ditches and locks, connecting several lakes and rivers, between Albany on the Hudson River on the eastern border of New York and Buffalo and Lake Erie at the western end. Long barges pulled slowly by horses or mules walking on a path beside the waterways could float heavy cargoes and passengers across the entire state. Its importance was that it connected much of what is now the Midwest with New York City and the Atlantic Ocean.

This great new waterway opened the entire Great Lakes area to commerce and settlement. Agricultural products came across the state by canal and then down the Hudson to be shipped from the docks of New York City to foreign markets. Many kinds of finished goods were taken back up the waterways to supply the new communities in the new states surrounding the Great Lakes. Because of the canal, the entire Northwest Territory (Ohio, Indiana, Illinois, Michigan, and Minnesota) became a kind of vast "inland empire," producing products that were sold world wide. New York City became the economic beneficiary of this bounty, and New York State came to call itself the "empire state." (Later, the Empire State Building would be constructed in New York City.) Because of its economic dominance and its large population, New York City became the center of America's emerging media industries.

New Communication Technologies

In 1844, Samuel F.B. Morse sent a telegraph message from Washington, D.C, to Baltimore (a distance of about thirty-five miles). The message moved at the speed of lightening—an astounding 186,000 miles per second. Actually, Morse did not "invent" the telegraph. Other working systems were already in use in Great Britain. However, they were cumbersome and rather unreliable. Morse's system was simple, reliable, and quite easy to use. He also developed a code that remains in use even today. The telegraph was so practical and effective that by the time of the Civil War, an underseas cable was being laid across the Atlantic Ocean. Regular telegraph service with England began in 1866, It was the first step toward a high-speed global communication system.

The telegraph and the transatlantic cable truly opened a new era in communication. Within a few years, newspapers and press associations would establish wire services that would bring reports of important events in both Europe and the United States to many of the nation's newspapers within a much shorter time than had ever before been possible. Other cables soon linked additional continents and countries. By 1874 the telephone would follow, increasing once again the speed at which people could communicate over distance.

In 1839, five years before Morse demonstrated his telegraph, Louis Daguerre and Joseph Niepce showed the world the first photograph. The science of chemistry had advanced to a point where it was possible to make photographs on shining plates of metal with a process that came to be called the "daguerreotype." Although photography did not find its way into newspapers and magazines for several decades, the daguerreotype provided the initial foundation upon which both photojournalism and eventually a great movie industry would be built.

Territorial Expansion

The nation had begun to expand even before the Revolution. Daniel Boone had explored the Kentucky and Tennessee areas as early as 1769, leading a group of settlers from Virginia through the Cumberland Gap (a pass between mountains). He lived to see a million people pour into the new territory. After the nation was founded, other migrants went still farther and took up lands in the Northwest Territory (around the Great Lakes), and new states in the region quickly came into the union.

The nation's new boundaries were growing at an astonishing rate. In 1803, Napoleon Bonaparte was having trouble financing his wars in Europe. Short of cash, he decided to sell off "Le Louisiannne"—vast territories in North America (about a third of the territory in the middle of current U.S. boundaries). This land was claimed and loosely controlled by France. He felt that the land was a drag on his budget and had no future in any case. Little was known about what was there. Some even claimed that prehistoric animals roamed the area. The Americans had proposed to buy only an area around New Orleans (as a means of controlling access to the Mississippi River). But Napoleon said "Take the whole territory or nothing." The result was one of the most spectacular real estate deals in history. The United States paid $15 million for Louisiana—a huge triangular area that stretched west of the Mississippi clear to the Rocky Mountains and north from the Gulf of Mexico to Canada. It cost just under three cents per acre.

A short time later, disputes between Mexico and the United States brought about a war (in 1846). At the time, Mexico was a formidable foe, with an army twice as big as that of the Americans. Nevertheless, the leaders in Washington wanted to take over much of the northern tier of Mexican territories and add them to what is now the continental United States. As a result, President James Polk sent American troops under General Zachary Taylor into Mexico and a force under General Winfield Scott to California. Scott had two young officers with him—Captain Robert E. Lee and Lieutenant Ulysses S. Grant.

The war did not last long. In 1847, U.S. Marines entered Mexico City (The "Halls of Montezuma"), and negotiations were commenced. The conflict was formally concluded in 1848 with the signing of the Treaty of Guadalupe Hidalgo and a payment of $15 million to Mexico. The United States then took over what is now California, New Mexico, and Utah; parts of Arizona, Texas, and Colorado; plus smaller sections of other states. Again, vast territories came under the American flag for about three cents per acre. The continental United States was now an enormous land mass that stretched from the Atlantic to the Pacific and from the Rio Grande on the south to the long border with Canada to the north.

The Mexican war had a strong influence on American newspapers for two reasons. One was that a huge new area eventually came to be settled, and many newspapers were established to serve their growing populations. Another was in the way news was gathered at the scene of an event

and a report sent back to editors. Understandably, the American public was deeply concerned about the battles in Mexico. Many papers had sent correspondents (reporters) into the area to write about the engagements and their outcomes. These reports were taken as quickly as possible to New Orleans, where the copper "lightening lines" were used to transmit the stories by telegraph directly to newsrooms in most of the major cities in the northeast. It was from this arrangement that the Associated Press, the first national wire service, was developed.

Influence of the Civil War

The Civil War began on April 12, 1861, when Confederate cannons bombarded and all but destroyed Fort Sumpter—which was located on a small island in the harbor of Charleston, South Carolina. Although there was only one death (due to an accident), it was a momentous act touching off a great conflict. The war raged on for four years, until April 9, 1865, when Robert E. Lee surrendered to Ulysses S. Grant at Appomattox Courthouse. More than 2.3 million men fought, and more than 600,000 (one out of every four) were killed or died of their wounds or diseases. It remains the greatest number of war deaths ever experienced by the nation in any conflict.

The Civil War understandably created a great demand for news. The papers of the time were able to supply it. The great technological advances in steam-powered printing, electric communication, and swift distribution brought about by the Industrial Revolution had made it possible for virtually every major city to have one or more daily papers. Newspaper readership had increased greatly. During the war years, about four families out of every ten in the nation subscribed to a daily paper. Almost all of the larger papers had one or more reporters observing each battle. News from the conflict was sent via telegraph wire to editors back home, and reports of the victories and losses were provided to the public on a timely basis. Of special interest were the casualty lists for families waiting anxiously at home to hear whether their loved ones had been killed or wounded.

Increased Pace of Urbanization

An important change in the society was the growth of towns and cities. As the 1800s began, the United States was a nation mainly of farmers and ranchers. Only a small proportion of the population lived in cities and towns. However, factories and their related jobs began to draw more and more people to urban communities. That process increased sharply in the upper Midwest as great deposits of iron ore and coal were discovered and exploited to establish iron and steel industries. As the century wore on, the nation was slowly transforming itself into a great industrial power. Large parts of the country remained rural, and agriculture was their major industry. However, more and more people were moving to towns and cities to find employment in the developing manufacturing industries.

The movement of people from farms to cities is called urbanization. This was a constant and accelerating process all during the last half of the 1800s. Rural families moved to the city, and many of the foreigners who arrived from abroad also settled there. Urbanization was important for the development of mass communications because it was far easier for a newspaper or magazine to serve a population concentrated in a city than one thinly scattered on farms.

Consequences of Population Increases and Migrations

Of major significance for the development of newspapers and magazines were massive population movements into and within the United States. As noted, immigration from abroad was encouraged in order to settle the huge land masses acquired from France and Mexico. The pace of immigration increased beginning in the late 1840s, when waves of migrants arrived from Ireland to escape the great potato famine. A factor that greatly encouraged additional immigration was the first Homestead Act. President Lincoln signed the legislation in 1862. It providing for 180 acres of free land for any American citizen—or even a person who declared his or her intention of becoming a citizen—who would agree to establish a farm. This was a remarkable opportunity for many Europeans. No country had ever given away free land! Large numbers of Northern Europeans came to take up farming in the Midwest and on the great plains. Later, millions would arrive from southern and eastern Europe to labor in the new industries. They hoped to escape political turmoil, religious persecution, or grinding poverty in their mother lands.

In all of these areas, communities were established. Some were economic centers for agriculture. Others served mining or industrial economies. Some that were located at points where transportation brought rapidly increasing commerce grew and became cities. In each of these communities, daily and weekly newspapers were needed. The American population was growing rapidly. Free and mandatory public education had been widely adopted, and an increasing number of people could read and write. Conditions were very favorable, in other words, for a considerable growth in newspaper and magazine readership. In 1870, five years after the end of the Civil War, three out of every ten households in the United States subscribed to a daily newspaper. By the end of the nineteenth century, the U.S. Census reported that (on average) there was one newspaper subscription for every household. Saturation had been achieved.

Immigration from abroad was not the only factor promoting growth in newspapers. There was a great movement of population from east to west all during the last half of the 1800s. Even during the 1840s, wagon trains streamed across the prairie, bound for the Oregon Territory. Many families stopped along the way and established farms and communities in the Dakotas or in other parts of what are now the mountain states. When gold was discovered in California in 1848, more than 250,000 people (mainly men) descended on Northern California within a few months.

Meanwhile, as the century was coming to an end, the pace of immigration picked up. Millions of people passed through the great immigration station at Ellis Island. Many stayed in the cities along the eastern seaboard, but others traveled on to join relatives or earlier migrants in the Midwest and elsewhere. At about the same time, in a real sense, the frontier came to an end. Most of our states had already been admitted to the union. However, additional territories and populations came under American control just as the century was ending. In a war with Spain that lasted only ten weeks, Puerto Rico and the Philippines became American overseas possessions. Hawaii and Alaska were taken over at about the same time.

Overview of the Influences of the Nineteenth Century

As the foregoing indicates, the changes that took place during the nineteenth century are truly remarkable. As the period began, the United States was an insignificant country with a population of just over five million people in fifteen states located mainly east of the Mississippi and south of the Ohio. By the end of the century it was a vast country of forty-eight states and other territories, with a population of seventy-six million, many of whom were immigrants from other countries. Its population had begun shifting from farming to urban life. It had impressive industries concentrated in the Northeast, a huge agricultural base in the South, and millions of fertile acres under production in the Midwest. Great advances in technology directly and indirectly related to communication had been achieved at an ever-increasing pace.

As the 1900s were about to begin, people could travel relatively swiftly from the Atlantic to the Pacific by rail or take a swift steam-driven vessel from San Francisco to New York. They could send messages along thousands of miles of telegraph lines and even across the oceans to other countries. They could call on the telephone for business and social reasons, and they could use a small "Kodak" to record family scenes and other activities in still photos. In addition, scientific discoveries had been made, and practical inventions developed, that within two decades would bring

totally new and remarkable mass media—home radio and the motion picture. These media, like magazines and newspapers before them, would also be shaped by the economic, political, and cultural factors that had been brought forward from earlier times.

NEW MEDIA IN AN URBAN-INDUSTRIAL SOCIETY: THE 1900s

The 1900s saw the rise of new media that could not possibly have been imagined by people in the 1600s. All were products of the continuing Industrial Revolution and its scientific counterpart. Black-and-white silent movies, along with home radio, came early in the century. Just after mid-century, television was available in virtually every American home. It was soon followed by the VCR, the DVD, cable systems, direct broadcast satellites, cellular phones, fax, and the computer-based Internet.

As the twentieth century came to a close, the pace of change in new mass communication technologies became almost frantic. Some media were shrinking; others were expanding. Still others were converging. The pace was so fast that it became difficult to predict in a detailed way what people would have available in the early decades of the twenty-first century or, in some cases, even the next month. In spite of this pace, however, the new mass media to come, like what came earlier, will be shaped by the same factors that have operated in the past.

The United States Becomes a Mass Communication Society

One of the first major mass media developments of the 1900s was the rise of a new kind of journalism within the magazine industry. Starting in 1900, an almost endless number of articles were prepared to expose political, economic, and social problems in American life. President Theodore Roosevelt called these writers "muckrakers." He did so because they concentrated on corruption in American politics, ruthlessness in business, and the plight of the poor—rather than championing the remarkable achievements of the American society. However, by the time of World War I, the public was tired of such exposures, and the muckraker era came to an end. Nevertheless, its lasting influence was to ensure the place of investigative journalism in the American press.

The Golden Age of the Print Media

The first World War was of great significance to the ninety-two million people in the United States when it broke out in 1914. However, America did not enter the war actively until 1917. Before it ended, in November of 1918, more than two million young men and a few hundred women went to France. Of the young men who served in the trenches, or in ships in the Atlantic, 130,000 lost their lives. Understandably, the public was horrified—but eager to follow the war news from France. During the period, subscriptions to daily newspapers rose to a historic high. Newspapers were literally in a "golden age"—one that they would never see again. On average, American families subscribed to more than 1.3 daily newspapers. Many families had both a morning and evening paper delivered to their doors, or they bought them from street vendors. The newspaper had a total monopoly on the news because it had no rivals.

Magazines also came into a kind of golden age during the first several decades of the 1900s and especially between 1920 and 1950. Beautifully printed general magazines with slick paper and huge circulations rose to great prominence. They prospered because they were an ideal vehicle for delivering advertising of nationally mass-marketed products. For that purpose, they too had no serious rivals. Millions of subscribers in all parts of the country received their magazines by mail. Such magazines as the *Saturday Evening Post, Colliers,* or *Cosmopolitan* also served the entertainment function by providing collections of short stories, serialized novels, simple analyses of public affairs, recipes, and humor.

American Movies Come to Dominate the World Market

One of the major consequences of World War I for our contemporary media system had to do with global markets for American entertainment products. With France, Germany, and Britain locked in the Great War, motion picture production facilities in Europe were essentially shut down after 1914. American film makers rushed to supply the world market. The silent black-and-white movies of the time used subtitles to tell the ongoing story. Almost any language could be used. Thus, the movies were a flexible product that sold well in every country that had even primitive movie theaters. People in those countries, especially the young, adored them. American films established a world dominance by this means, and they retain that dominance even to this day. Those global distribution systems have now been greatly expanded, and American movies, TV programs, music, video cassettes, and other entertainment products are both loved and hated all over the world.

The motion picture industry matured greatly between the two World Wars. Going to the movies became the recreation of choice for millions of American families as well as for audiences in almost all other countries. The experience was cheap, wholesome, available, and fun. The movies were ideal for dating couples. American kids of the time loved the Saturday matinees with cowboys, comics, and serialized adventures. Many movies attracted the whole family. Mom, pop, and the kids all went together. Attendance in the U.S. rose to record heights between 1930 and 1950, when more than two tickets were sold per family every week. However, that golden age would soon go into serious decline as television became the dominant medium.

Radio as a New Mass Communication Technology

By the beginnings of the 1920s, radio was transformed from a wireless dot-dash telegraph used for commercial, navigational, and governmental purposes into a home medium. Regularly scheduled broadcasts of music, drama, and comedians began early in the 1920s, and in the U.S. the medium quickly turned to advertising as a means of financial support. That had been the solution taken by the popular newspapers nearly a century earlier and by magazines as they developed during the last half of the 1800s. It was the American way—private ownership, profit-oriented, and minimal governmental interference in terms of content. Radio did require certain technical regulation to avoid signal interference, but (except for dirty words) the system essentially retained the freedom of speech that was a deep-seated cultural value.

Television Challenges Other Mass Media

Television was about to become a mass medium in the United States when the Japanese attacked Pearl Harbor. Little was done to develop the medium during the war years. However, when the conflict was over, a number of stations quickly went on the air, and wherever there was a signal to receive, television sets were snapped up by a waiting public. The Federal Communications Commission restrained growth of the medium for four years while developing a plan to avoid signal overlap. Even so, the public could not get enough of television broadcasts.

Television created significant displacements among the other media. It quickly attracted advertising dollars from print and radio, and it took audiences away from the movies. TV inherited radio's financial structure, its relationship with the Federal Communication Commission, much of its programming, and most of its audience. In addition, its advantages as an advertising medium drew dollars away from the general magazines, many of which went out of business. Television's advertising and its news services made inroads into the financial health of newspapers.

New Technologies and Changing Mass Media Systems

After the middle of the twentieth century, the American mass communication system was deeply established in essentially its present form (but without the Internet, which came later). There have been recent changes and additions, but by the late 1950s, television had already become the medium to which most Americans paid close attention. Books retained their niche as a specialized medium for information, education, and entertainment. Movies remained popular, but the numbers paying at the box office were clearly declining. Newspapers were losing readers steadily, and many papers were either going bankrupt or being absorbed into chains to reduce costs. Magazines were hard hit at first but rebounded by becoming increasingly specialized. Few of the older, general, large-circulation magazines survived, and niche publishing had become the pre-dominant mode. Radio rebounded by turning to music, news, and talk-show programming after being nearly put out of business by TV. However, still further changes were coming. They would be based on both satellites and the digital technology of the computer.

The Increasing Importance of Computers

No one quite foresaw the truly remarkable role that computers would play in the media industries. At first, the huge electronic computers, like the ENIAC (more than one hundred feet long) developed for the military during and just after World War II, were seen by the public as scientific curiosities. They were seen as little more than "electronic brains," used by the military and operated by geeky scientists with thick glasses and nerd packs in the pockets of their white coats.

By comparison with today's computers, the early machines were not only huge but very slow. Moreover, they seemed to have little or no significance for ordinary citizens. However, by the mid-1950s it became clear to businesses and government agencies that computers could be used for a great many practical purposes. The card-programmed, mainframe computers of the time were soon in use in every large corporation, educational institution, and government agency. Because of their efficiency, they soon helped to move the United States into the information age.[4] What that means is that, after the middle of the century, more people were manipulating numbers and words than were producing objects with hands and machines. By 1960, the age of the digital, electronic computer had truly arrived, and it would soon change the lives of almost everyone.

The Constant Invention and Replacement of Media

During the 1960s and '70s, using a large mainframe computer was accomplished only by highly trained specialists using arcane commands and programming "languages." Early in the 1980s, however, the small "desktop" machines came onto the market. They were quickly adopted and pressed into use for thousands of different applications. Within a decade, the computer had literally transformed the ways in which business was conducted in almost every walk of life. By 2000, a computer could be found in about four out of every ten American homes, and the rate of adoption was rising rapidly. Currently, millions of people are subscribers to such online services as America Online. The numbers continue to increase every month.

Overview of Factors Influencing Mass Media Development in the 1900s

The above review indicates that, as the twentieth century began, people could subscribe to a sophisticated morning and afternoon daily newspaper or receive many kinds of magazines in the mail. The more affluent could call friends on the telephone (but long-distance was not well developed). People could also send a telegram. However, there were no movie theaters to attend, no radio to hear, and no television to view. Computer networks could not even be imagined. The population of the United States continued to expand rapidly in the early decades (slowing in more recent times) and educational levels increased greatly. These trends provided a larger and more literate market

for print media. As a result, the early part of the century was the "golden age" of print.

The change from agriculture to industry gave people more expendable income on average and more scheduled free time. The result was a corresponding interest and need for diversion and amusement. Entertainment-oriented media developed to meet these needs—the movies, radio, television, and its related systems—and more recently the Internet. By the mid nineteenth century, and in more recent times, the newer media were growing while the older traditional print media began a slow decline in audience share. Among them, only books resisted the trend.

The pace of scientific and technological development was spurred by the increase in the standard of living, brought by the advance of the industrial revolution. The 1900s brought not only dramatic increases in the accomplishments of science but also growth in average family income. People could afford the new gadgets and amusements that were being produced. In addition, two World Wars spurred technology of many kinds. In particular, World War II and the following Cold War stimulated the development of computers. Digital technology, now at the heart of the almost daily media modifications and advances we read about, will bring great changes in our media systems in the twenty-first century.

WHAT LIES AHEAD?

Digital technology, the foundation of computer operations, will continue to bring us new forms of information, advertising, and entertainment. We now enjoy new systems for delivering clearer television signals to our home sets. While all are not technically mass media, constant innovations are bringing Americans and others many kinds of information, services, and entertainment on the Internet and its World Wide Web as well as on hand-held devices, such as cell phones and iPods.

The basic principle that will prevail is that, in a technological society, there is a constant invention, obsolescence, and replacement of media. In an economic system based on capitalism, new products capable of earning profits are constantly being invented, tried, and developed. Many displace older systems that lose profitability. It is a pattern as old as the Industrial Revolution. To illustrate, in the early 1900s a strong ice industry thrived in New England. Big blocks of ice were sawn from frozen lakes to be shipped in the insulated holds of vessels all over the world. When ice-making machines were invented, that industry collapsed, and factories in the area began making and shipping the new machines. Then, the home refrigerator came on the market. Few commercial ice-making machines were needed, and the "iceman" who delivered to homes lost his job.

The same invention/replacement pattern can be seen in media technology. An example is the VCR, which began life as a machine the size of a small piano. At first, it was used by television broadcasters to record and replay their shows. After refinement and standardization, the videocassette tape came into use in the majority of American households for watching movies. It is now almost fully replaced by movies on small discs, which use digital technology and are much more durable and easier to store. At some point, it is likely that our now familiar DVDs will also become obsolete. And so it goes. New technologies come, are widely adopted, and then fall into obsolescence as more effective ones are developed.

It is difficult to specify the exact form of new mass communication systems that will exist in the years ahead. The pace of invention is very fast. Also, the plans and ownership patterns among the major corporations developing such systems undergo change and modification every day. Generally, however, the following seem likely:

1. More and more homes will have large, flat-panel, very clear television screens, high-definition television (HDTV), based on digital technology, has now become the standard. As the 1900s came to an end, it was forecast to quickly replace conventional-format TV, but adaptations to this new technology slowed somewhat as conventional TV pictures got better. Now, however it is clear that digital HDTV broadcasts have arrived. By mid-2009, TV signals received in homes were all in this format, and older TV sets required special "boxes" to transform the signals.

2. Far more channels will be available on our home TV receivers, including the World Wide Web. New ways of delivering digital signals to small satellite dishes and home receivers have rapidly been developed and adopted. Older systems for delivering information by wires and cables may decline. Television and computer reception will converge, allowing Internet communication to use the TV screen.

3. Interactive menus on our TV screens have become the norm, where we click with a pointer and get information similar to the manner in which we can now "jump" from a "button" on a computer screen to another screen. That will continue. The remote control has changed advertising from "in your face" (whether you want it or not) to more voluntary exposure selected by the viewer.

4. There will be a continuing slow decline in the proportion of families who subscribe to traditional print media (newspapers and magazines). However, these will not disappear because they will combine with online delivery of news and other information.

5. The current slow decline in the proportion of people who pay at the box office to go to the movies will continue. The availability of motion pictures on television and computer screens will correspondingly increase. However, financial health and vigor of the movie production (as opposed to the exhibition) industry will increase because of a growing demand for entertainment products, both in the U.S. and abroad, for existing and new media.

6. There will be a continued production and use of traditional printed books. This venerable medium remains vital in the fields of entertainment, education, and many other uses. Contrary to predictions that they would be replaced by computer-based readers that receive text online, this does not appear to be taking place in any real sense. However, electronic forms of books may become more common as the new technologies become cheaper and easier to use.

Notes and References

1. See John E. Ponfret, Founding the American Colonies: 1583-1660 (New York: Harper and Row, 1970).

2. Vincent Wilson, Jr., ed., The Book of Great American Documents (Brookeville, MD: American History Research Associates, 1993).

3. J. C. Furnas, The Americans: A Social History of the United States, 1587-1914 (New York: G.P. Putnam and Sons, 1969).

4. Wilson Dizard, The Coming Information Society (New York: Longman 1990).

10. Understanding Mass Media and the Importance of Media Literacy

by Joseph Turow

This chapter guides the reader through the intriguing maze of mass or mediated communication. It helps relate the basics of communication to a mediated setting. While revisiting key concepts covered in previous chapters, the emphasis of this chapter is on modifications to those concepts that occur when communication becomes mediated and/or mass disseminated. It is an interesting opportunity for readers to both review and expand their understanding of the fundamental concepts.

This chapter also extends beyond basic contextual application of previous concepts. It delves into the impact of mass communication on culture creation and society, as well as its impact on individuals. Of particular interest in this chapter are the discussions of convergence and of media literacy. Again, the reader is reminded that the references in this book to "other chapters" are to the book in which it was originally published. However, if this chapter piques a reader's interest, the course instructor could certainly provide guidance for exploring the topic further.

Y our TV is ringing."
Maybe you saw the Verizon ad that shows a cellphone with a TV attached to it—pointing out that you can talk on the phone and watch TV at the same time, on one piece of equipment. If you saw it, you might have said, "cool," or "I want that," or "what a ridiculous thing to do." But Verizon could have gone further. The ad could have pointed out that some

of the company's cellphones also let you watch movies, play video games, download and listen to music, and read a newspaper or magazine.

It's an exciting time to study mass communication. None of the activities described above could have been attempted on a cellphone (call it a mobile device) just a few years ago. They raise questions about the impact that these and other technologies will have on us, our society, and the content of TV, movies, video games, music, newspapers, magazines, and movie companies. In fact, the transformations are so great that you have the opportunity to know more than conventional experts, to challenge traditional thinking, and to encourage fresh public discussions about media and society.

Consider the mass media menu that Americans have today. Instead of three or four TV channels, most Americans receive more than fifty and a substantial number receive one hundred and fifty and more. Radio in urban areas delivers dozens of stations; satellite radio brings in hundreds more, and music streaming on the Web—sometimes called Internet radio—is carried out by countless broadcast and non-broadcast entities. The advent of home computers, VCRs, CD players, DVDs, and DBS has brought far more channels of sights and sounds into people's lives than ever before. So has the Internet and the World Wide Web, the computer network that Americans use to interact with information, news and entertainment from all over the nation and the world.

Research indicates that Americans typically spend an enormous amount of time with mass media.[1] Think about your own media habits. How close do you come to the average 32 hours a week (about 4.5 hours a day) of television that Americans view on the traditional TV set as well as online? What about radio? Studies suggest that Americans listen to around 15 hours a week of radio in the regular broadcast mode, via satellite channels or from their online feeds. Do you do that, or do you instead listen to recorded music on your iPod or on your MP3 or CD player? Studies show that Americans spend an average of about 3.5 hours a week with recorded music, but college students undoubtedly do more of it.

And what about your time reading books, newspapers and magazines? Data show that on average Americans spend about 8 hours a week with one or another of these, both their printed versions and their websites. Just a few years ago, media such as television, radio, books and newspapers seemed pretty separate. It was clear what content from each medium looked or sounded like, and it would have been foolish to suggest that newspaper articles and television programs would show up on the same channel. Today, with the rise of new computer technologies that we will explain in the coming pages, this "foolishness" is exactly what has happened. The access people have on the Internet to content from different types of media is part of a process called convergence. Convergence takes place when content that has traditionally been confined to one medium appears on multiple media channels.

The media of mass communication, then, are an integral part of our lives, occurring in a wide variety of settings. In this chapter, we will explore and define communication, media, and culture, and we will consider how the relationships among them affect us and the world in which we live. We will also consider why the term mass communication remains relevant in the twenty-first century, contrary to what some writers say. In fact, the changes taking place in the media system actually make a rethought and redefined version of the term more important than ever.

Varieties of Communication

To understand why some writers suggest that the term *mass communication* doesn't connect to what's going on in today's world, we have to look at how the term has traditionally been used. Over the past one hundred years, people who wrote about mass communication tended to relate it to the size of the audience. That made a lot of sense back then. From the mid-nineteenth century onward, new technologies such as high-speed newspaper presses, radio, movies, and television provided access to the huge "masses" of people. Not only were those audiences very large, they were dispersed geographically, quite diverse (that is, made up of different types of people), and typically anonymous to the companies that created the material. The essential reason newspapers, radio, television, and other such media were considered different from other means of communication had to do with the size and composition of the audience.

This perspective on mass communication worked very well until the past couple of decades when the key aspects of the traditional definition of mass communication as reaching huge, diverse groups no longer fit. The reason is that the arrival of media channels—including the growing number of radio and TV stations, the rise of the VCR, the multiplication of cable networks, and the rise of the Web—led to **audience fragmentation**. That is, as people watched or read these new channels, there were fewer people using any one of them. Because these new media channels do not necessarily individually reach large numbers of people—the "masses"—some writers suggested that we can abandon the term *mass communication*.

However, the view in this book is that mass communication is still a critically important part of society. In our view, what really separates mass communication from other forms of communication is not the size of the audience—it can be large or small. Rather, what makes mass communication special is the way the content of the communication message is created.

Mass communication is carried out by organizations working together in industries to produce and circulate a wide range of content—from entertainment to news to educational materials. It is this industrial, **mass production process** that creates the potential for reaching millions, even billions, of diverse, anonymous people at around the same time (say, through televising the Olympic games). And it is the **industrial nature** of the process—for example, the various companies that work together within the television or Internet industries—that makes mass communication different from other forms of communication even when the audience is relatively small and even one-to-one. To help you understand how mass communication relates to other forms of communication, let's take a closer look.

Communication Defined

Different types of communication are a basic feature of human life. In general, the word **communication** refers to people interacting in ways that at least one of the parties involved understands as messages.

What are messages? **Messages** are collections of symbols that appear purposefully organized (meaningful) to those sending or receiving them. Think about the many ways that you signal to others what you want to do or how much you care about them. The signals are often verbal but they can also be through body language. When Jane shouts excitedly to her friend Jack and leaps with joy into his arms after she wins a tennis match, that's a form of communication. It's likely that Jack, whose arms she almost broke, realizes that she wants to tell him something. People who study communication would typically call the interaction just described **interpersonal communication,** a form that involves two or three individuals signaling to each other using their voices, facial and hand gestures, and other signs (even clothes) that they use to convey meaning. When you talk to your parents about your coursework, discuss a recent movie over dinner with friends, or converse with your professor during her office hours, you are participating in the interpersonal form of communication.

Mediated interpersonal communication, which is a specialized type of interpersonal communication, can be described as interpersonal communication that is assisted by a device, such as a pen, a computer, or a telephone. When you write a thank you note to your grandmother, send an email to your graduate teaching assistant, or call a friend on the phone, you are participating in the mediated form of interpersonal communication. In this form of communication, the people you are interacting with can't touch you and you can't touch them. You might even be thousands of miles from each other. The technology—the pen and paper, the computer, the telephone—becomes the vehicle (the medium) that allows you to interact with them.

Communication scholars also differentiate among other forms of communication. Some write about **intrapersonal communication,** which involves an individual "talking" to himself or herself—for example, an internal "conversation" that weighs the pros and cons of a decision.

Other researchers write *about small group communication, organizational communication, or public communication.* Small group communication involves communication among three or more individuals. Think of the deliberations of five friends who get together to plan a ski trip. **Organizational communication** involves the interaction of individuals in a formal working environment. When an executive sends messages down the chain of command, this is a form of organizational communication. **Public communication** involves one person who speaks to a large number of people—for instance, a professor speaking to students, or a candidate for public office talking to a crowd at a rally.

Note that these forms of communication can each take place interpersonally or they can be mediated. A group planning a ski trip can meet face-to-face or can interact through email. The boss could talk to her department heads in her office, or leave a message on their phone mail system. A professor can talk in front of the class, or leave a video of himself or herself for the students to watch.

While the types of communication described above have their differences, they have a central similarity: they involve messages. Seven major elements are involved in every interaction that involves messages. These elements are the source, encoder, transmitter, channel, decoder, receiver, and feedback. Let's take them one at a time.

Source

The source is the originator of the message. The source may be a person (when Jane speaks to Jack), or several people (a choir singing). But the source can also be an organization. For example, suppose you receive a notice in your mailbox from your bank. While individuals who work there created and sent the notice, from your standpoint, "the bank" was the source of the message. The source may or may not have knowledge about the intended receiver of the message, but it does have a thought or idea to transmit to some other person or organization.

Encoding

Encoding is the process by which the source translates the thoughts and ideas so that they can be perceived by the human senses—these are primarily sight and sound, but may also include smell, taste, and touch. A source creates or encodes a message in anticipation of its transmission to a receiver. When the source is an individual, the encoding goes on in the individual's brain. When the source is an organization, encoding takes place when people in the organization create messages.

Transmitting

The transmitter performs the physical activity of actually sending out the message. Picture an employee apologizing to a supervisor for taking an unauthorized day off from work. The employee's vocal cords and face muscles— in fact, his entire body—will be involved in the transmission of the words, tone, and physical movements that the supervisor standing in front of him will understand as meaningful. Now, picture this same employee apologizing to his supervisor, not in person, but over the phone. In this case, a second type of transmitter operates along with the vocal cords. That second transmitter is the telephone, which turns sound waves from the vocal cords into electrical impulses that can travel across the phone lines.

The telephone is an example of a mediating technology, or medium, of communication. A medium is part of a technical system that helps in the transmission, distribution, or reception of messages. It helps communication take place when senders and receivers are not face-to-face. The Internet is an example of a medium, as are the radio, CD, television, and DVD. (Note that the term medium is singular; it refers to one technological vehicle for communication. The plural is media.)

Channel

All communication, whether mediated or not, takes place through channels. Channels are the pathways through which the transmitter sends all features of the message, whether they involve sight, sound, smell, or touch. When a man on the street walks up to you and shouts at you in a way that you can hardly understand, the channel is the air through which the sound waves move from the man's vocal cords. If your roommate yells at you through the phone, two channels are at work: one channel is the air that vibrates the phone mechanism, and the other is the wire through which the electrical impulses move toward you.

Decoding

Before a receiver can hear (and make sense of) a source's message, the transmitted impulses must be converted to signs that the brain can perceive as meaningful. Decoding is the way in which this is done. It is the reverse of the encoding process—it is the process by which the receiver translates the source's thoughts and ideas so that they have meaning.

In the case of the interpersonal communication, the decoder is biological: the brain is the decoder. When the telephone is involved, the electrical impulses that traveled through the phone lines must be decoded into sound waves before they can be decoded by the brain. In fact, all media require this sort of decoding. When you play music on an MP3 player or iPod, it decodes the impulses that have been laid down on the disk so that you can hear the tunes. Similarly, the television is the decoder that takes the electrical impulses from the air or cable and converts them into the programs you watch.

Receiver

As suggested above, the receiver is the person or organization that gets the message. Sometimes the source's message will reach its intended receiver; sometimes it reaches another receiver altogether. But even if someone other than the intended receiver receives the message, communication has still taken place. Say, for example, that you assume that your friend Brad is in the next room and, as a result, you shout your opinion about his new girlfriend, Keiko. Even if it turns out that Brad wasn't in the next room at all and did not hear (receive) the message you sent him, but instead his girlfriend, Keiko, was in the next room, the episode can still be considered interpersonal communication: your message was encoded, transmitted via your vocal cords, sent through the channel of the air, decoded by the receiver (although not the one you intended), and received.

Feedback

Feedback occurs when the receiver responds to the message with what the sender perceives as a message. When Keiko, your friend's girlfriend, tells you, "I never knew you felt that way about me, you jerk," that is feedback. In fact, this sort of feedback continues the interpersonal communication process. Two people continue their communication by continually receiving and responding to each other's messages. The same thing happens with mediated interpersonal communication. The communication "episode"between the two ends when one of them sends no more feedback to the other (the person walks away, the parties hang up the phone).

Feedback doesn't always take place immediately, especially in mediated interpersonal communication. Say you send your friend an email. Keiko reads it, gets embarrassed by something you wrote and decides to write you a reply. You read the note and then, after thinking about it for a day, write back directly to her. Her email and your response are examples of delayed feedback.

Noise

Noise is an environmental, mechanical, and semantic sound in the communication situation that interferes with the delivery of the message. Environmental noise comes from the setting where the source and receiver are communicating. In an interpersonal communication situation, Ahmed, the source, may be at a cricket match trying to talk on the phone, and Sally, the receiver, might be at an auction where people are screaming bids. Mechanical noise comes from the medium through which the communication is taking place. Say there is static on the phone—that would be mechanical noise that would add to the environmental noise. Semantic noise involves language that one or more of the participants doesn't understand. Let's say Ahmed tells Sally that "the bowler attempted a bouncer that turned into a beamer." Even when Ahmed repeats the words three times through the environmental and mechanical noise so that she hears them, Sally has no idea what Ahmed is talking about, since she knows little about the sport of cricket.

From Communication to Mass Communication

One way to understand mass communication is to show its similarities to and differences from other forms of communication. One similarity is that mass communication takes place through media. Small groups can come together in virtual chat rooms that are connected by wired networks, organizations can connect their far-flung employees via video conference facilities that are linked through cables and satellites, and professors who deliver public lectures can record them for projection from a computer server to different classes at different times. In other words, the channels used in mediated forms of interpersonal, group, organizational and public communication are sometimes similar to those used in mass communication.

Yet another similarity between these other forms of communication and mass communication is that we can describe mass communication

using the same terms of source, encoder, transmitter, channel, decoder, receiver, feedback, and noise. But here is also where we begin to see differences. The most important differences relate to the source of the message, its transmitter and the way feedback takes place.

Differences in the Source

In the other forms of communication we've discussed, individuals are the source of the message that scholars study. In mass communication, by contrast, complex organizations, often companies, take responsibility for the activity. The source is an organization such as a company, not a single person.

To get a strong grasp of the difference, think of Jon Stewart delivering his version of the news on Comedy Central's *The Daily Show*. If Jon were in the same room as you telling you about what he just read in the paper, that would be a clear case of interpersonal communication and Stewart would be a source. If your friend were to record that conversation on his video camera and his brother were to watch the video of Jon talking about the news, that is an example of mediated interpersonal communication where Jon is still the source.

The difference between these two examples of the source and Jon's appearance on *The Daily Show* is that behind Stewart is an organization that is creating the news satire for him to present. Sure, Jon is reading the messages, and so it may seem that he should be called "the source." But employees of *The Daily Show* helped him write his script, produced and edited the videos he introduces, and prepared his set for the broadcast. Moreover, the photos and clips he satirizes sometimes come from news firms, such as ABC News. So Jon is really just the most visible representative of an organizational source.

Differences in Transmission

The critical role of organizations in mass communication compared to other communication forms also shows up in the transmission of the message. In interpersonal, small group, and public communication, an individual sender or a committee takes responsibility for transmitting the message—perhaps using microphones when speaking to a crowd or telephones when speaking at a distance. In mass communication, however, transmission is too complex to be accomplished by an individual or even a few people. That is because transmission involves distributing the material to several locations and presenting the material (that is, exhibiting it) at those locations. Instead of a few individuals, a number of organizations (usually large ones) are typically involved in the process.

Think of our *Daily Show* example again. When Jon reads the script on *The Daily Show*, his vocal cords transmit the words into a microphone; the air and electric current are a channel for them. That may seem no different from mediated interpersonal communication, but it is only the beginning. Transmission of Jon on Comedy Central involves a number of further steps. First the show is sent to a satellite company that the network uses to send its programs to cable TV systems around the country. The cable systems, which themselves are complex organizations, receive those messages and send them to "head-end" transmission centers that they own. These centers send out the program through coaxial cables that eventually connect to television sets in locations (homes, bars, hotels) where subscribers have paid to receive the signal. In this way, millions of people around the country can watch *The Daily Show* at the same time.

Of course, individuals do work for production and distribution firms involved in mass communication. Unlike mediated communication activities, though, the creation and transmission of mass media messages—of news articles, television programs and recorded music, for example—are the result of decisions and activities by many people working together in companies that interact with other companies.

Differences in Feedback

The third major difference between mass communication and other communication forms relates to feedback. We can talk about feedback in two ways, (1) whether it is immediate or delayed and (2) whether or not it goes directly to the initial message creator or to someone else who may or may not pass it on to the creator.

In other forms of communication, feedback from the people receiving the message goes directly to the individual who created the message, either immediately (the clapping of an audience in response to a speaker) or in delayed form (your email in response to your mom's email). In mass communication, though, feedback from all the receivers is often impossible because of the number of people involved. (Think of the millions of people watching a TV program.) Even when feedback does happen (for example, when you respond right away by clicking on an Internet ad), the people in the organization who created the message in the first place (in this case the ad creators) will typically not get it. Someone else who is specifically appointed to deal with feedback will generally receive your message.

An indirect approach to audience feedback marks a common difference between mass communication and other forms of communication. In unmediated interpersonal communication, group communication, organizational communication, and public communication, feedback is often both immediate and direct. In mass media organizations, however, feedback is not only often delayed, it is indirect. It is generally routed through layers of the company that deal specifically with "audience" concerns, weighed for its relevance, and only then summarized for the people who sparked the feedback in the first place.

Consider the following comparison: you meet Jon Stewart in a movie line and have a leisurely conversation with him about current events in New York City, where he lives. Jon nods in response to your comments, answers your questions, and parries your criticisms of his positions on the issues. By contrast, a week later you see a satirical piece about New York City on *The Daily Show* that angers you. Moved to complain, you phone Comedy Central in New York to speak to Stewart or a producer. Instead, you get an operator who will politely take down your comments, send you to a voicemail service that will record them, or suggest that you provide feedback through the program's website. If you write to Jon Stewart or one of the show's producers, chances are that staff members whose job it is to summarize complaints for production executives will intercept it. That is typical of mass media organizations. *The Daily Show* gets thousands of letters and emails, and its principals are too busy to attend to all audience letters and phone calls themselves.

Differences in Noise

It's not hard to show how the idea of noise as applied to mass communication can be similar to and different from its use in other communication forms. Remember our example of Ahmed and Sally? If their microphones were not working properly, the television announcers at a cricket match might have the same environmental problems being heard as Ahmed—but by more people. We can apply this situation to mass communication, but put game announcers working for a TV network in the position of Ahmed. Similarly, people at a party where the game is on TV can take Sally's place; they might not be able to hear because of noise in the apartment. Mechanical noise in a mass communication situation can take place in the sending-and-receiving technologies. Breakdowns in cable or satellite receivers, for example, can create mechanical noise problems for large audiences. To complete the comparison, the announcers' use of cricket terms might befuddle some people in the audience just as Ahmed befuddled Sally.

A hypothetical comparison of interpersonal and mass communication might further help explain these differences in sender, transmitter, feedback and noise. Meet Antwaan Andrews, a self-employed independent insurance agent who is working hard to support himself by selling life insurance policies. Using names of potential clients that he received from friends, acquaintances and other clients, Antwaan writes postal or email letters to ten people a night for two months to tell them about his service. He develops his sales pitch himself and tailors it to each person. Each note contains his name, postal address, phone number,

and email address, along with the assurance that he will reply quickly to their messages.

Note that Antwaan's audience—the receivers of his postal letters and email messages—are limited in number by the people he can learn about from others and contact personally. Note, too, that any feedback goes straight to Antwaan. They either speak to him directly or they leave a message on his voicemail or email. (Of course, if a potential client doesn't return his message at all, Antwaan may take that as feedback that the person is not interested in buying life insurance.) One example of unwanted noise might be a problem Antwaan sometimes has with a hum on his answering machine. It's a pain in the neck, he says, but it generally works OK and he doesn't want to spend money for a new one.

Contrast Antwaan's mediated interpersonal work with the mass communication activities of Safety Trust Mutual, one of the insurance companies Antwaan represents. Safety Trust is mounting its own campaign to help agents like Antwaan attract specific groups of clients that they have identified as particularly profitable. In fact, Safety Trust has recently hired an advertising agency and a public relations agency for the express purpose of attracting potential clients who fit the following profile: young parents with a combined income of over $75,000 a year. Members of the advertising and public relations teams have come up with a multimedia marketing plan built around the twin themes of safety and trust. Their plan involves:

- Creating commercials using the two themes and airing them on two or three TV series that rate highly with young married couples
- Creating print ads and buying space for those ads in upscale newspapers and magazines
- Attempting to place Safety Trust's young and photogenic president on NBC's Today Show and ABC's Good Morning America to speak about new government insurance regulations
- Paying a custom-magazine firm to create and mail a glossy new magazine for young, upscale SafetyTrust clients

- Advertising during a VH1 cable series
- Paying an Internet advertising company to send an email ad to 30,000 people, on a list the company bought of individuals who fit the profile and have indicated that they would be interested in learning about how to save money on insurance
- Reworking a website where customers can learn about their plans and send responses to the company

Note that although these messages reach millions of people, getting feedback from them is difficult. Typical feedback would include phone responses to an 800 number in the TV commercials and print ads, but this would probably include only a tiny percentage of the people who saw the messages. SafetyTrust might also pay a company to conduct research to estimate the number of people who viewed the materials and what they thought about them.

These methods would often yield delayed feedback from potential customers. SafetyTrust executives are particularly proud of the plan for the website, because it customizes the message and encourages immediate feedback. The site changes its sales pitch and look based on information that the person types in at the site. For example, whenever a person goes to the company's homepage at www.safetytrust.com, that person is asked a number of questions about age, salary, marital status, and educational background, among other things. Based upon a person's responses to such questions, and a computer program's evaluation of those responses, the person will be able to view a site that is tailored to their replies. This instantaneous response to consumer feedback helps SafetyTrust to best explain its products and sell its services. At the same time, the feedback helps tailor the message so as to minimize semantic noise that might drive some potential customers away.

Additionally, users of the website may choose to email SafetyTrust at any time with questions, concerns, or requests for more information. This feedback doesn't reach a real agent at SafetyTrust. Instead, it is collected and analyzed daily by "consumer response specialists," who may eventually contact people who seem good prospects and refer them to an agent the specialists choose. Their conversations may not be the carefully responsive discussions that individual agents like Antwaan carry out when they call back every person who has left messages on their voicemail services. SafetyTrust finds that its approach is quite efficient, however, since it can quickly weed out people that the company considers too old for its programs or high insurance risks. But just in case a person who comes to the site wants to speak to an agent near his or her home, SafetyTrust has links to those of its agents who have websites. Antwaan is one of these agents with his own content, and he finds that many of the best prospects who come to his home page are referred through the SafetyTrust site.

With his much smaller operation, Antwaan couldn't possibly do what SafetyTrust is doing with its website and feedback from prospective customers. In fact, even if he had thought of all of SafetyTrust's marketing activities, Antwaan could never implement them without adding enormously (and unrealistically) to his staff and overhead costs. After all, SafetyTrust—a large insurance company with millions of dollars in its marketing budget—hired an advertising agency and a public relations agency to help it create its messages to potential customers. It also used large organizations (NBC, ABC, VH1, and an Internet access firm) to help distribute its messages.

The difference between mediated interpersonal and mass communication, then, can be seen as a difference between personal, hand-crafted production on the one hand, and mass production on the other. Put another way, Safety Trust's work is part of an industry process. An industry is a grouping of companies that use technology to work together in a regularized way to produce and distribute goods and services. It is this industrial approach that makes it possible for SafetyTrust to get its messages out to its intended audiences.

Mass Communication Defined

And so we come at last to the definition of mass communication that we have been building: mass communication is the industrialized production and multiple distribution of messages through technological devices. The industrial nature of the process is central to this definition of mass communication.

As the definition suggests, mass communication is carried out by mass media industries. Think, for example, of the movie industry, in which many different companies—from production studios, to film providers, to catering firms—work to make and circulate movies. Mass media are the technological instruments—for example, newsprint, televisions, radios—through which mass communication takes place. Mass media outlets are companies that send out messages via mass media. Magazines and television are mass media; for example, *Time* magazine and the NBC television network are mass media outlets. The term mass media is plural; it refers to more than one technological instrument. The singular version is mass medium.

Media Innovation

Media companies are usually in business to make money from the materials they produce and distribute (which is another way they are different from interpersonal communication activities like gossip among friends or the construction of an Internet site by a class). Because of this focus on making money, media professionals view the programs, articles, and films they create at least partly as commodities, as goods in a real marketplace.

In many ways, the making of mass media commodities is similar to the industrial manufacture of other products like soap, candles, and cars. An important difference between industries making these kinds of products and making media products, however, has to do with the pace of innovation. Innovation means the introduction of something new in a company's products. Companies of all kinds have research and development (R&D) departments that explore new ideas and generate new products and services aimed at helping the firm attract customers in the future. Even so, companies that are not involved in mass communication can allow successful products

to roll off the assembly line unchanged for long stretches of time. For an example, identical bars of Ivory Soap have been rolling off mass-production lines for decades. The manufacturer may make new products with the Ivory name, but an Ivory Soap bar that you bought on Tuesday will be the same as the one you will buy on Friday. But in mass media firms, both the R&D function and the basic production line for the same product must focus on change continually. For example, the *Wall Street Journal* must update its stories or people will stop buying the paper and subscribing to their website; Twentieth Century Fox cannot survive on only one film; executives at the MTV cable network realize that if they run only one music video or one reality program, viewers will catch on and tune out.

This need for constant innovation means constant risk. The next day's issue of a newspaper could turn off many readers. Fox's next film could fail. MTV's lineup of programs could lead people to reach for their remote controls. For this reason, media employees always look for ways to balance the need for continual, rapid innovation with a desire to control risk. As we will see in Chapter 2, they try to lower their chances of failure by relying on themes and plots and people that have done well in the past. The ways in which they solve these problems can influence much of what we see and hear.

Mass Media in our Personal Lives

Mass media materials speak to the most personal parts of our lives. They also connect us to the world beyond our private circumstances. As a result, mass media industries are a major force in society. To understand what this means, we have to dig a bit deeper into how people use the media and what they get out of them.

How People Use the Mass Media

Scholars have found that individuals adapt their use of mass media to their own particular needs.[2] Broadly speaking, we can say that people use the media in four ways: enjoyment, companionship, surveillance, and interpretation. Let's examine these uses one at a time.

Enjoyment

The desire for enjoyment, or personal pleasure, is a basic human urge. Watching a television program, studying the Bible, finishing a newspaper crossword puzzle, even reading an advertisement can bring this kind of gratification to many people.

News stories, daytime soap operas, sports, and primetime dramas can ignite everyday talk with friends, relatives, work colleagues, and even strangers. During the mid-1990s, for example, many local television stations around the United States were advertising their morning talk programs with the phrase "We give you something to talk about." This process of using media content for everyday interpersonal discussions is called using media materials as social currency or coins of exchange. "Did you hear Jay Leno's joke last night?" someone might ask around the water cooler at work. "No, I watched Letterman," might be one reply. That might trigger a chain of comments about TV comedy that bring a number of people into the conversation.

Of course, another way people can bring mass media material into friendly conversation is by experiencing the content together. If you have attended Super Bowl parties, you have an idea of how a televised event can energize friends in ways that have little to do with what is taking place on the screen. In this way, the media provide us with the enjoyment we seek as a basic human need.

Companionship

On a very different note, mass media bring pleasure to the lonely and the alone. A chronically ill hospital patient or a home-bound senior citizen may find companionship by viewing their favorite sports teams on TV, or listening to the music of days gone by on the radio.

Sometimes, media can even draw out people who feel troubled and in need of friends. The term parasocial interaction describes the psychological connections that some media users establish with celebrities they learn about through the mass media. People who are involved in a parasocial interaction typically enjoy a feeling of bonding with those celebrities. You might know someone who gets so involved with media images of rock or rap stars that they sometimes act as if they know them well. In a few publicized cases, this feeling has gotten out of control, leading individuals to stalk, and even harm, the media figures who were the objects of their adulation. In 1999, for example, actor Brad Pitt found himself with an unwanted visitor when a nineteen-year-old woman broke into his home. He was not there at the time, but a caretaker found this self-styled "Number one fan" wearing Pitt's clothes and asleep in his bed.[3]

Surveillance

Using media for surveillance means employing them to learn about what is happening in the world around us. We do this every day, often without realizing it. Do you turn on the radio or TV each morning to find out the weather? Do you check the stock listings to find out how your investments are faring? Have you read classified ads online to look for a job, concert tickets, or previously owned furniture? Have you ever called or logged on to Fandango or Moviefone to find out where and when a film is playing? All these activities are illustrations of using the mass media for surveillance. Of course, our surveillance can be more global. Many people are interested in knowing what is going on in the world beyond their immediate neighborhood. Did the flooding upstate destroy any houses? Will Congress raise taxes? What's going on with the negotiations for peace in the Middle East?

Interpretation

Although surveillance through the mass media satisfies many people, it supplies only part of what they want to know about the world. They also want to find out why things are happening—who or what is the cause—and what to do about them.

When people try to find reasons, they are looking for interpretation.

Many of us turn to the media to learn not just what is going on, but also why and what, if any, actions to take. We may read newspaper editorials to understand the actions of national leaders and come to conclusions about whether or not we agree with these actions. We know that financial magazines such as Money and Barron's are written to appeal to people who want to understand how investment vehicles work and which ones to choose. And we are aware that libraries, bookstores, and some websites (howstuffworks.com comes to mind) specialize in "how to" topics ranging from raising children, to installing a retaining wall, to dying with dignity. Some people who are genuinely confused about some topics find mass media the most useful sources of answers. Pre-teens, for example, may want to understand why women and men behave romantically toward each other but they may feel embarrassed to ask their parents. They may be quite open to different opinions—in *Spiderman*, *Oprah*, Justin Timberlake's music, or *Mad* magazine—about where sexual attraction comes from and what the appropriate behavior is.

But how do people actually use the explanations they get from the mass media? Researchers have found that the credibility people place in the positions that mass media take depends on the extent to which the individuals agree with the values they find in that content.[4] For example, a person who is rooted in a religiously conservative approach to the Bible would not be likely to agree with a nature book that is based on the theory of evolution; a political liberal would probably not be persuaded by the interpretations that politically conservative magazines offer about ways to end poverty. Keep in mind, however, that in these examples, these people would probably not search out such media content to begin with. Unless people have a good reason to confront materials that go against their values (if they will be engaging in a debate on the ideas, for example), most people stay away from media that do not reflect (and reinforce) their own beliefs, values, or interests. And if they do come across materials that go

against their values, they tend to dismiss them as biased.

Multiple Use of Mass Media Content

The example of a pre-teen seeking interpretations of romance from four very different outlets—a movie series, a television talk show, a musical record, and a magazine—raises an important point about the four uses that people make of the mass media: the uses are not linked to any particular medium or genre. If we take television as an example, we might be tempted to suggest that enjoyment comes from certain sitcoms or adventure series, that companionship comes from soap operas, that surveillance is achieved through network and local news programs, and that interpretation can be found in Sunday morning political talk shows such as *Meet the Press*, as well as from daily talk fests such as *Jerry Springer* and *The View*. In fact, we may divide many kinds of content in these ways. Communication researchers point out, however, that individuals can get just about any gratification they are seeking from just about any program—or any kind of mass media materials.[5]

You might find, for example, that you use the *CBS Evening News* for enjoyment, surveillance, and interpretation. Enjoyment might come from the satisfaction of watching reporters' familiar faces day after day (is a little parasocial interaction working here?); surveillance might be satisfied by reports from different parts of the globe; and interpretation might flow from stray comments by the reporters and those they interview about what ought to be done to solve problems.

Mass Media, Culture, and Society

At the same time that mass media are fulfilling private desires for enjoyment, companionship, surveillance, and interpretation, they often lead us to share the materials we are reading and listening to with millions of people. This sharing is made possible, of course, because of the industrial nature of the activity and its technology of production and distribution. When complex organizations comprising of many workers join together to use the latest technology to produce media, those organizations have the potential to distribute the same message to huge numbers of people.

Consider the typical television broadcast of the Grammy Awards, the ceremony in which the recording industry honors its most successful talent. It is transmitted via satellite from Los Angeles to broadcast television production facilities in New York, then distributed "live" to every corner of the United States, as well as to many parts of the world.

Or, consider a typical presidential news conference. It is covered by dozens of newspaper reporters and television and radio news crews. Snippets of the event will commonly end up confronting Americans around the country in many different forms during that day and the next on the national news, on the local news, in the morning paper, and throughout the day on hourly radio news reports.

As a third, and slightly different example, consider a mega-hit film such as one of the *Shrek* movies. Millions of people around the world saw it in theaters within a few months of its release. In addition, word of the movie's popularity sped around the globe as Dreamworks and Universal, its joint domestic distributors, and UIP, its distributor outside the United States, revved up a publicity and advertising machine. It peppered as many media outlets as possible with word of the high-octane action and head-lopping digital effects.

Shrek, the presidential news conference, and the Grammy Awards represent only three examples of activities that happen all the time in industrialized countries such as the United States. Linking large numbers of people to share the same materials virtually instantly has become standard practice for the broadcast television, Internet, radio, cable TV, and satellite television industries. Just as significant is the sharing that takes place relatively more slowly when newspapers, magazines, books, movies, billboards, and other mass media release their messages. Because of mass

media industries and their abilities to mass produce media content, millions of people within the United States and around the world can receive the same messages within a fairly short time. Think about it: here are huge numbers of people who are physically separated from one another, have no obvious relationship with one another, and most often are unknown to one another. Yet on a daily basis they are watching the same news stories, listening to the same music, and reading the same magazine articles.

What is Culture?

We can understand why this large-scale sharing of messages is important by exploring the cultural context in which the mass media operate. Culture is a very broad term. When we use the term *culture*, we are talking about ways of life that are passed on to members of a society through time and that keep the society together. We typically use the word society to refer to large numbers of individuals, groups, and organizations that live in the same general area and consider themselves connected to one another through the sharing of a culture.

What is shared includes learned behaviors, beliefs, and values. A culture lays out guidelines about who belongs to the society and what rules apply to them. It provides guideposts about where and what to learn, where and how to work, how to eat and sleep. It tells us how we should act toward family members, friends, and strangers, and much, much more. In other words, a culture helps us make sense of ourselves and our place in the world.

A culture provides people with ideas about the kinds of arguments concerning particular subjects that are acceptable. In American culture, people would likely feel that on certain topics (vegetarianism, for example), all sorts of positions are acceptable, whereas on other topics (cannibalism, incest) the range of acceptable views is much narrower. Moreover, American culture allows for the existence of groups with habits that many people consider odd and unusual but not threatening to the more general way of life. Such group lifestyles are called subcultures. The Amish of Pennsylvania who live without modern appliances at home represent such a subculture, as do Catholic monks who lead a secluded existence devoted to God.

For small populations living close together, people use interpersonal communication to share an awareness of their culture and to pass on that way of life to the next generation. Consider campers and their counselors coming together in a summer camp as an example of a culture. The counselors establish their leadership over the campers by making sure everyone follows traditional rules. The counselors threaten them with extra chores if they violate rules, and give them rewards when they follow the rules. Traditional camp songs encourage campers to feel good about the camp, to see themselves as connected to each other, and to want to return year after year. Arguments over certain rules—like Friday night lights-out time—may be tolerated, but arguments over other rules (for example, daily bunk inspection) are not. Subcultures considered dangerous aren't tolerated. If campers decide that they wanted to live alone in the woods instead of in the bunks, for example, they would not be allowed to do that and would be punished if they disobeyed.

Mass Communication and Culture

The camp's culture provides the camp society's members with direct evidence of who belongs and what the rules are. In places with large numbers of people—cities or countries, for example—such notions cannot always be understood simply by looking around. The mass media allow us to view clearly the ideas that people have about their broad cultural connections with others, and where they stand in the larger society. When mass media encourage huge numbers of people who are dispersed and unrelated to share the same materials, they are focusing people's attention on what is culturally important to think about and to talk and argue with others about. In other words, mass media create people's common lived experiences, a sense of the common culture and the varieties of subcultures acceptable to it.

The mass media present ideas of the culture in three broad and related ways: (1) They direct people's attention toward codes of acceptable behavior within the society and how to talk about them, (2) they tell people what and who counts in their world and why, and (3) they tell people what others think of them, and what people "like themselves" think of others. Let's look at each of the ways separately.

The Mass Media Direct People's Attention Toward the Codes of Acceptable Behavior Within Society and How to Talk About Them

A culture provides individuals with notions about how to approach the entire spectrum of life's decisions, from waking to sleeping. It also gives people ideas about the arguments concerning all these subjects that are acceptable. If you think about the mass media from this standpoint, you'll realize that this is exactly what they do. Newspapers continually give us a look at how government works, as do Internet sites such as Wonkette and Huffington Post. TV's *CSI* series act out behavior the police consider unacceptable and open up issues where the rules of police and "criminal" behavior are contested or unclear. Magazine articles provide ideas, and a range of arguments, about what looks attractive, and how to act toward the opposite sex. We may personally disagree with many of these ideas. At the same time, we may well realize that these ideas are shared and possibly accepted broadly in society.

These cultural rules and arguments can be found in even the most sensational mass media materials. You may have heard of, or remember, the first trial of O.J. Simpson, the ex-football star and actor accused of murdering his wife and her friend. The criminal prosecution, covered live on Court TV and the Cable News Network (CNN), became *the* media event of the mid-1990s. Although some observers dismissed the trial as sensationalist trash, others pointed out how it paraded for viewers cultural rules and arguments about marriage, race, and violence. Years later, in 2006, anger erupted in many media outlets when

Regan Books announced that it would release a memoir by Simpson that would discuss how he might have killed the two people. Commentators voiced the opinion that such a book was taboo, and public indignation seemed so intense that the book company's owner, News Corporation, decided not to release the title and recalled printed copies from stores.

The Mass Media Tell What and Who Counts in Their World and Why

Mass media tell us who is "famous"—from movie stars to scientists—and give us reasons why. They define the leaders to watch, from the U.S. president to religious ministers. News reports tell us who these people are in "real life." Fictional presentations such as books, movies, and TV dramas may tell us what they (or people like them) do and are like. Many of the presentations are angrily critical or bitingly satirical; American culture allows for this sort of argumentation. Through critical presentations or heroic ones, though, mass media presentations offer members of the society a sense of the qualities that we ought to expect in good leaders.

Fiction often shows us what leaders *ought* to be like—what values count in the society. Actor Denzel Washington excels at playing law enforcement officers who are courageous, smart, loyal, persevering, strong, and handsome; think, for example, of the movies *Déjà Vu* and *Inside Man*. Sometimes, mass media discussions of fiction and nonfiction merge in curious ways. During the election of 2000, for example, several mass media commentators noted that President Bartlett of the then-popular *West Wing* TV drama would be a better choice than any of the real candidates because of his better leadership qualities.

The Mass Media Help People to Understand Themselves and Their Connection With, or Disconnection From Others

Am I leadership material? Am I good-looking? Am I more or less religious than most people?

Is what I like to eat what most people like to eat? Is my apartment as neat as most people's homes? How do I fit into the culture? Mass media allow us, and sometimes even encourage us, to ask questions such as these. When we read newspapers, listen to the radio, or watch TV we can't help but compare ourselves to the portrayals these media present. Sometimes we may shrug the comparisons off with the clear conviction that we simply don't care if we are different from people who are famous or considered "in." Other times we might feel that we ought to be more in tune with what's going on; this may lead us to buy new clothes or adopt a new hair style. Often, we might simply take in ideas of what the world is like outside our direct reach and try to figure out how we fit in.

At the same time that the mass media get us wondering how we fit in, they may also encourage feelings of connection with people whom we have never met. Newscasters, textbooks, and even advertisements tell us that we are part of a nation that extends far beyond what we can see. We may perceive that sense of connection differently depending on our personal interests. We may feel a bond of sympathy with people in a U.S. city that the news shows ravaged by floods. We may feel linked to people thousands of miles away that a website tells us share our political opinions. We may feel camaraderie with Super Bowl viewers around the country, especially those rooting for the team we are supporting.

Similarly, we may feel *dis*connected from people and nations that mass media tell us have belief systems that we do not share. U.S. news and entertainment are filled with portrayals of nations, individuals, and types of individuals who, we are told, do not subscribe to key values of American culture. Labels such as *rogue nation*, *Nazi*, *communists*, *terrorists*, and *Islamic extremists* suggest threats to an American sense of decency. When mass media attach these labels to countries or individuals, we may well see them as enemies of our way of life, unless we have personal reasons not to believe the media portrayals.

Criticisms of Mass Media's Relation to Culture

Some social observers have been critical of the way mass media have used their power as reflectors and creators of culture. One criticism is that mass media present unfortunate prejudices about the world by systematically using **stereotypes**—predictable depictions that reflect (and sometimes create) cultural prejudices—and **political ideologies**—beliefs about who should hold the greatest power within a culture, and why. Another is that mass media detract from the quality of American culture. A third criticism, related to the first two, is that the mass media's cultural presentations encourage political and economic manipulation of their audiences.

Criticisms such as these have made people think deeply about the role that mass media play in American culture. These criticisms do have their weak points. Some might note that it is too simplistic to say that mass media detract from the quality of American culture. Different parts of the U.S. population use the mass media differently and, as a result, may confront different kinds of images. Related to this point is the idea that people bring their own personalities to the materials they read and watch. They are not simply passive recipients of messages. They actively interpret, reshape, and even reject some of them.

Nevertheless, the observations about stereotypes, cultural quality and political ideology should make us think about the power of mass media over our lives. Many people—most people at one time or another—do seem to see the mass media as mirroring parts of the society and the world beyond it, especially parts they do not know first hand. Most people do accept what the mass media tell them in news—and even in entertainment—about what and who counts in their world and why. Many seem to believe that the mass media's codes of acceptable behavior accurately describe large numbers of people, even if the codes don't describe their own norms. And they accept the mass media's images as starting points for understanding where they fit in society in relation to others and their connection with, or disconnection from, others. They may disagree with these images, or think that they shouldn't exist. Nevertheless, the media images serve as starting points for their concerns about, and arguments over, reality. We will have more to say about critical views on the effects of media in Chapter 4.

Media Literacy

It is no exaggeration to say that everyone is influenced in one way or another by mass media messages. Some people, though, have learned how to step back and seriously examine the mass media's role in their lives and in American life. The aim of this book is to help you to be one of those people. The goal is not to make you cynical and distrustful of all mass media. In the vast landscape of the media, there is much to enjoy and appreciate. Instead, the goal is to help you think in an educated manner about the forces that shape the media and your relationships with them so that you will better evaluate what you see and hear. The aim is to help you to be media literate.

There are very practical benefits to being media literate.

- Consider your use of the Internet. Most Americans go online on a regular basis, but research shows that they have little understanding of the privacy policies of the websites they visit. As a media literate person—certainly as someone who has read this book—you would know about website privacy issues and how to take care not to give out private information about yourself.
- Consider your use of the TV set. Do you know that the United States is going through a conversion to digital television that may make your TV obsolete? Did you know that Americans who have the obsolete television sets can apply for government funds to buy a special converter so that they can continue to receive over-the-air TV? As a media literate person, you would understand why all this is happening and how to save money as a result of the government program.

- Consider that you are applying for a job working for a media firm, or a position that requires you to relate to media personnel. The person who interviews you may test your knowledge of the business by using industry terms and discussing new developments. Would you know how to engage in an energetic conversation on the present and future of new and traditional media industries? If you were media literate, you would.

More generally, being media literate can be satisfying and fun. For example, knowing movie history can make watching films fascinating because you will be able to notice historical and technical features of the films that you wouldn't have otherwise noticed. Having a comparative understanding of different forms of news can help you think more clearly about what you can expect from journalism today and how it is changing. Understanding the forces that shape formulas and genres, and the social controversies around stereotyping and violence, can make playing even the most predictable video games and watching even the most hackneyed television shows jumping-off points for thinking critically about yourself in relation to images of others in society. All these and other media activities can also start important conversations between you and your friends about the directions of our culture and your place in it. That, in turn, can help you become a more aware and responsible citizen—parent, voter, worker—in our media-driven society.

Foundations of Media Literacy

When we speak about **literacy**, we mean the ability to effectively comprehend and use messages that are expressed in written or printed symbols, such as letters. When we speak about **media literacy**, however, we mean something broader. To quote the National Leadership Conference on Media Literacy, it is "the ability to access, analyze, evaluate and communicate messages in a variety of forms."[6]

There are many views of exactly what media literacy is and what it can do for people. It seems, however, that most scholars would accept the following six "foundation principles" for teaching people literacy skills.[7] We have already been building these principles in this chapter, so you will be familiar with the ideas behind them.

Principle 1: Media Materials are Constructed

As we already know, when we read newspapers, watch TV, and surf the Web we should continually be aware that what we are seeing and hearing is not any kind of pure reality. Rather, it is a construction—that is, a human creation that presents a kind of script about the culture.

Principle 2: Media Materials are Created and Distributed Within a Commercial Environment

When we try to understand media materials as human-created cultural scripts, we must look at many considerations that surround and affect the humans who are involved in creating and releasing the media materials. We have already noted in this chapter that mass media materials are produced by organizations that exist in a commercial setting. The need to bring in revenues, often to sell advertising, is foremost in the minds of those who manage these organizations. In forthcoming chapters we will elaborate on what this means and how it affects the media products.

Principle 3: Media Materials are Created and Distributed Within a Political Environment

"Political" refers to the way a society is governed. When it comes to mass media, the term refers to a variety of activities. These range from the specific regulations that governments place on mass media, to decisions by courts about what restrictions the government can place on the media, to the struggle by various interest groups to change what media do (often using government leverage). For many media observers, being aware that media operate within a political environment leads to the idea that this environment deeply influences the media content itself. To them, it means being aware that the ideas in the media have political implications—that they are ideological.

Principle 4: Mass Media Present Their Ideas Within Primary Genres of Entertainment, News, Information, Education, and Advertising

Media scholar Patricia Aufterheide and others note that every medium—the television, the movie, the magazine—has its own codes and conventions, its own ways of presenting cultural reality. Although you probably haven't thought about it, it's a good bet that you recognize the differences between the way these media do things. A report of a presidential press conference looks different depending on whether it was written for a newspaper or a magazine, presented on TV as news, described on a website's blog, or put together for the big screen. You probably also recognize, though, that mass media are similar in some of their approaches to presenting the world. The most important commonality is that they organize the world into a number of basic storytelling forms that we recognize as entertainment, news, information, education, and advertising.

Principle 5: People are Active Recipients of Media Messages

As we noted earlier, the process of meaning-making out of media forms consists of an interaction between the reader and the materials. People bring their own personalities to the materials they read and watch. They may get angry at some ideas and reject or change them. We also noted, though, that emphasizing the input of the individual does not take away from the broad social importance of the media. Because so many people share mass media materials, we might expect that large segments of the society see mass media as having cultural importance for the society as a whole. That realization points to the final foundation principle.

Principle 6: Media Representations Play a Role in the Way Society Understands its Reality

People may like what they see about their society or they may complain about it. They may want people to view media images about themselves and others, or they fear that others will be influenced by presentations (for example, stereotypes and violence) in ways that could cause problems. Even with an active audience, then, mass media hold crucial importance for society's visions of itself.

Media Literacy Skills

While it is important to understand the foundational principles of media literacy, there are skills you'll need to acquire if you are to make use of those elements in your daily life. They are presented below, along with some of the questions you should be able to answer if you have those skills:

An Understanding of the Commercial Forces Behind Media Materials

How do firms in various media industries make money? How exactly does advertising fit into that? What role does market research play in the activities of media producers and distributors? How do all these activities influence actual mass media materials and how do I know when they do?

An Awareness of Political Influences That Shape Media Materials

What are current political issues relating to the regulation of media industries? How is the federal government approaching the regulation of new media such as the Internet? What roles do states and local communities play in regulation of the mass media? What are ways to think about the ideological messages in mass media materials?

An Ability to Examine Media Content Systematically for Broadly Cultural as well as Specifically Commercial and Political Meanings

How do we systematically examine news, entertainment, and advertising from various critical perspectives? How, for example, can we see the popularity of the Fox TV show *American Idol* as a reflection of broad trends in American culture? To what extent can we see the show as a product of the network's particular commercial situation within the changing TV industry? And to what extent can we see it as an ideological statement about the American people's readiness to vote when they are enthusiastic about a person or topic?

An Ability to Think Through the Ethical Implications of Media Firms' Activities

How do we explore and analyze the moral dilemmas that might be created as a result of commercial or political pressures that weigh on mass media organizations? Consider sexist and racist gangsta rap as an example. The music can be very profitable. Some observers insist, however, that producing and distributing such music is immoral. Others argue that the music reflects a part of U.S. culture that should not be swept under the rug. What is an executive to do? How should firms systematically think about such issues? How should consumers respond to them?

An Understanding of Research on the Mass Media's Implications for the Individual and Society

What have scholars learned over the years about the effects of violent programming on children? How much do people really learn from news programs? What kinds of conversations do people have about what they watch and read? What can cultural historians tell us about the long-term effects of media such as the book and the television on society?

An Awareness of Ways the Public Can Influence the Production and Distribution of Mass Media Materials

How can a group concerned about certain media images complain effectively about that material? How can the group add its pressures to the many industrial and political pressures on media organizations in ways that will be make its arguments effective? What constitutional and moral issues might be relevant here?

Becoming a Media Literate Person

Once you understand the foundational elements of media literacy, and have developed key media literacy skills, you are on your way to becoming a media literate person. Based on what we have just discussed, you can see that a media literate person is:

- Knowledgeable about the influences that guide media organizations
- Up-to-date on political issues relating to the media
- Sensitive to ways of seeing media content as a means of learning about culture
- Sensitive to the ethical dimensions of media activities
- Knowledgeable about scholarship regarding media effects
- Able to enjoy media materials in a sophisticated manner

Questioning Media Trends

For executives and would-be executives, understanding the strategies of multimedia conglomerates can mean the difference between a successful career and failure. But changes in the media business affect more than just the fortunes of the people who work in the business. For members of the media literate public, the power held by the mass media raises a host of social issues. Here are just a few:

- Do media conglomerates have the ability to control what we receive over a variety of media channels? If so, do they use that ability?
- Are portrayals of sex and violence increasing in the new media environment, as some critics allege? Do media organizations have the power to lower the amount of sex and violence? Would they do it if they could?
- Does the segmentation of audiences by media companies lead to groups that those firms consider more attractive, getting better advertising discounts and greater diversity of content than groups that those firms consider less important? If so, what consequences will that have for social tensions and the ability of parts of society to share ideas with one another?
- What (if anything) should be done about the increasing ability of mass media firms to invade people's privacy by storing information they gain when they interact with them? Should the federal government pass laws that force companies to respect people's privacy, or should we leave it up to corporate self-regulation? What do we know about the history of corporate self-regulation that would lead us to believe that it would or wouldn't work in this situation?
- Should global media companies adapt to the cultural values of the nations in which they work, even if those values infringe upon free press and free speech?

Our exploration of these and related questions will take us into topics that you may not associate with the mass media business—for example, mobile telephones, toys, games, and supermarkets. It will also sometimes take us far beyond the United States, because American mass media companies increasingly operate globally. They influence non-U.S. firms around the world and are influenced by them. As we will see, their activities have sparked controversies in the United States and abroad that will likely intensify as the twenty-first century unfolds.

Notes

1. The data in this paragraph come from Paul Verna, "Recorded Music: Digital Falls Short," *Emarketer Report*, February 2007.
2. See Elihu Katz, Jay Blumler, and Michael Gurvitch, *Uses of Mass Communication by the Individual* (Beverly Hills: Sage Publications, 1974).
3. John Harlow, "Brad and Jennifer Marry Among Friends at Sunset," *Sunday Times* (London), July 30, 2000, via LexisNexis.
4. For a summary of this work, see Lawrence Grossberg, Ellen Wartella, and D. Charles Whitney (eds), *MediaMaking* (Thousand Oaks, CA: Sage Publications, 2005), pp. 277-297.
5. See Elihu Katz, Jay Blumler, and Michael Gurvitch, *Uses of Mass Communication by the Individual* (Beverly Hills: Sage Publications, 1974).
6. Quoted in UCLA Graduate School of Education & Information Studies, "Literacies at the End of the Twentieth Century" (2000), page 5.
7. Sources consulted for these ideas include the following: Rene Hobbes, "The Seven Great Debates in the Media Literacy Movement," which can be found at http://interact.uoregon.edu/MediaLit/FA/mlhobbs/hbindex.html; Robert Kubey (ed.) *Media Literacy in an Information Age* (New Brunswick, NJ: Transaction Publishers, 1997); Ladislau Semali, *Literacy in Multimedia America* (New York: Falmer Press, 2000); Len Masterman, *Teaching the Media* (London: Comedia, 1985); Chris M. Worsnop, "20 Important Reasons to Study the Media," which can be found at http://interact.uoregon.edu/MediaLit/FA/articles/worsnop/cwindex.html; and Patricia Aufterheide, "Media Literacy: A Report of the National Leadership Conference on Media Literacy" (Washington, DC: Aspen Institute, 1992).

11. Cyberspace, Digital Media and the Internet

by Jason Whittaker

This chapter provides an introductory overview of the broad complexities of cyberspace and its impact on communication. The historical context provided in this chapter encourages readers to understand that the development of current communication technologies began long ago. While the fast-paced development of applications and tools for communicating is fascinating, placing such evolution in the context of the broader history of communication makes it more relevant and encourages deeper thinking on the impacts today's technologies will have on the future. This long view of communication technologies provides a solid foundation of essential information that students can build upon through their daily interaction with developing technologies.

This chapter is particularly helpful in reminding readers that dominant technologies do not always remain so. Therefore, readers should understand the technologies as they have emerged and transformed as a means of developing the skills necessary to decipher the potential uses of new technologies that are constantly emerging. There are many additional chapters in other texts (including the text this chapter was selected from) that provide more detailed information, both historical and technical in focus, for those interested in exploring this idea further.

What is Cyberspace?

When asked to define cyberspace, most people will probably envisage a personal computer connected to the Internet. Important as both these technologies are to our concept of cyberspace, it is clear that such elements constitute only a very small part of the wider political, social, economic, cultural and financial networks that constitute what we can call *cyberspace*. Cyberspace is not merely hardware, but a series of symbolic definitions, or 'tropes' as David Bell (2001) refers to them, that constitute a network of ideas as much as the communication of bits.

Imagine the following: a technologically savvy female student is speaking to a friend on her mobile phone while drawing money from a cash machine. Both the money and the conversation share a common purpose—visiting the cinema to watch a Hollywood blockbuster—but while the woman knows which film she wishes to watch (she has, after all, read a number of previews recommending the movie), she is not sure what time it is playing. Her friend has just checked listings for the nearby multiplex online and reminded her that she also needs to contact customer services for the company that made her MP3 player, which has developed a fault. She could send them an email, but as they have a 24-hour helpline it will probably be simpler to phone.

Cyberspace is one name for the technological glue that binds many of these elements together. Telephone masts and satellite connect the voice communication between the two friends, while similar networks link the woman to databases that hold details on her finances (including potential information on spending activities and personal financial ratings if she uses debit and credit cards to make purchases). Movie magic is not something particularly new to the age of cyberspace, but the film she wishes to see is of a kind that regularly uses digital effects to fill in details for the camera—special effects, furthermore, that often do not wish to draw attention to their own pyrotechnics but instead pass themselves off as reflections of the real world. As a young woman, she has grown up in a school environment where information and communication technology (ICT) is increasingly the norm for delivering many parts of education, and her music player will have probably been constructed in southeast Asia—probably China or Taiwan—while there is a good chance that the call centre which handles her request is based in India. Finally, while her friend could easily check the local newspaper for film times, this is the sort of information that indicates the commonplace, even banal, uses to which the Internet is put on a daily basis.

It is now possible to travel to more parts of the world than ever before, a world in which trade is increasingly globalised and, more than ever, dependent on services and information as much as on the trade of material goods. And while we tend to still think of books, films and photographs as *things*, information technology—in particular the Internet—is transforming our view of communications into texts and images that can be more easily downloaded as mutable bits rather than immutable atoms.

The term 'cyberspace' was invented by William Gibson in his cyberpunk novel, *Neuromancer*:

> The matrix has its roots in primitive arcade games ...in early graphics programs and military experimentation with cranial jacks. ... Cyberspace. A consensual hallucination experienced daily by billions of legitimate operators, in every nation, by children being taught mathematical concepts. ... A graphic representation of data abstracted from the banks of every computer in the human system. Unthinkable complexity. Lines of light ranged in the nonspace of the mind, clusters and constellations of data. Like city lights, receding. (1984: 67)

Part of the success of Gibson's novel lay in the fact that he was able to provide expression to the emerging technologies (personal computers, the Internet, computer graphics and virtual reality) that were beginning to capture the popular imagination. Gibson, as poetic futurologist of cyberspace, provided a vision of the matrix that was much more than the bare technical bones of the putative Internet: for him, cyberspace is technical complexity—computer-generated graphical representations of data that are transferred across networks—but is also framed by psychology, epistemology, juridical and social systems. It is taught to children, a 'consensual hallucination' shared by users defined by their relation to legitimate (and also, the source of many of Gibson's plots, criminal) sources of power. Such power can be political, military and commercial, the huge transnational conglomerates that fill the backgrounds of his novels.

As Katherine Hayles (1996) points out, Gibson's vision of cyberspace did not spring out of nothing, but emerged from technical and social innovations that changed our worldview in the 1980s and 1990s, some of the consequences of which will be explored in this book. Outside science fiction, then, we encounter cyberspace most obviously when we use the Internet from a personal computer or, increasingly, a handheld device or our television sets. It integrates with older communication technologies, such as the telephone, and draws on theoretical conceptions of information and space that have enabled such things as communication and representation to be digitised and networked. We participate in cyberspace when we talk across a GSM phone network, change channels on a digital television set, or access our finances from an ATM. In its widest sense, then, cyberspace is space transformed by networks of information and communication. As Dodge and Kitchin (2001: 1) point out:

> At present, cyberspace does not consist of one homogeneous space; it is a myriad of rapidly expanding cyberspaces, each providing a different form of digital interaction and communication. In general, these spaces can be categorised into those existing within

the technologies of the Internet, those within virtual reality, and conventional telecommunications such as the phone and the fax, although because there is a rapid convergence of technologies new hybrid spaces are emerging.

Margaret Wertheim, in *The Pearly Gates of Cyberspace* (1999), draws attention to the fact that the human conception of space has not been fixed throughout history. The world of the Middle Ages, at the centre of the universe and connected to higher spiritual spheres or planes, was transformed by a series of revolutions from the Renaissance on due to discoveries in the solar system as well as transformations of perception and perspective. From the sixteenth century, we have become used to changing discernments of our psychological, philosophical and scientific world, but, suggests Wertheim, perhaps the most significant change was from the perception of ourselves as embedded in spaces of both body and soul to a universe in which the material body alone was important. Some of the claims made for cyberspace revolve around the recognition that if not the soul then at least the perceiving psyche is integral to our conception of the technospaces in which we live.

The emergence of cyberspace

One way to envisage the changes made to the practice of everyday life by cyberspace in all its forms is to compare current technologies to those available immediately after the Second World War. This was the point when many information and computer technologies came into existence, the history of which has been explored by a number of commentators such as Flichy (2002) and Winston (1998).

Fundamental to cyberspace is telecommunications, literally communication over a distance. This itself is nothing new: telegraph, in the mid-nineteenth century, established a vital communications network across the British Empire, replacing or supplementing other long-distance systems

Conceptual Map of Cyberspace

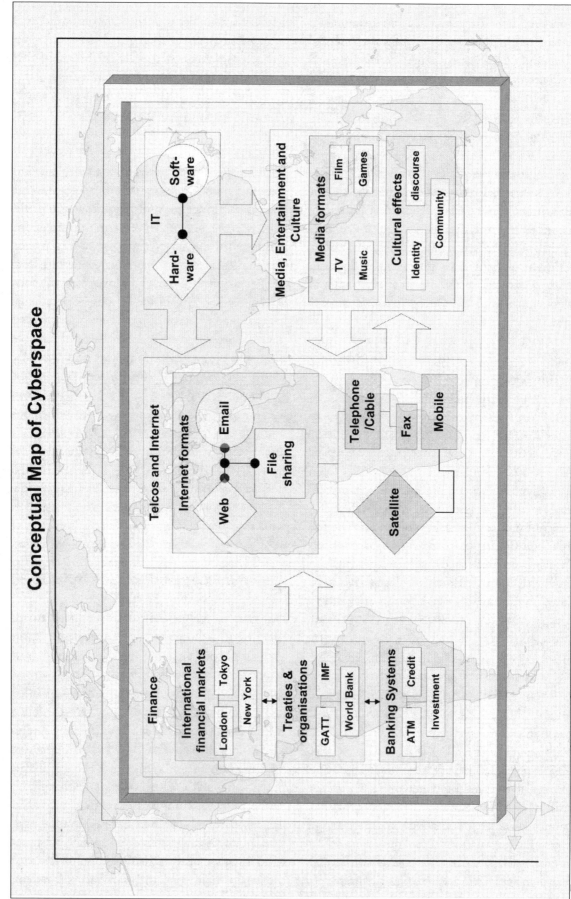

Figure 1.1 A conceptual map of some of the elements of cyberspace.

already in place such as mail and semaphore, while the end of the nineteenth century saw the invention of the telephone. Until the 1960s, however, telephones even in the West were in short supply, extremely expensive, and—more importantly—connections still had to be made manually for anything other than local calls. Ironically, answering machines and even primitive faxes were available by the 1950s, but until automation of telephone exchanges was implemented fully, telecommunications faced a huge bottleneck. Transatlantic communication had long been possible, with Atlantic telegraph cables having been laid during the mid-nineteenth century, but the space race of the 1950s began the mobilisation of a geostationary satellite system that would provide comprehensive contact worldwide.

The post-war entertainment boom was, of course, only just beginning in certain areas such as television: transformations in printing during the inter-war period made colour reproduction of glossy magazines simpler than ever, although wartime rationing represented a retrograde movement. Television was only just starting to emerge as a popular mass medium in the West at this time: at the beginning of 1952, for example, there were only 600,000 television licences in the UK, although a similar number were sold in the months preceding the Queen's coronation that year, an event watched by an estimated 20 million people and which marked the emergence of TV as a popular medium. Radio, long favoured in the home, also shifted from valves to transistors after 1947: in the long term, this enabled more portable sets and reduced their price considerably, although the first to go on sale in 1954 were still extremely expensive.

Throughout the early 1950s, most electronic and communication equipment still used valves: the triode vacuum valve, invented by Lee de Forest in 1906, enabled a signal in one circuit to control the current in another circuit, giving rise to effective electronics. Manufacture was largely a manual process and miniaturisation was restricted, meaning that there was a limit to how cheaply these important components could be reproduced. In addition to being limited in terms of size and cost, each valve also consumed at least two watts on average, so the move from valves to transistors, coupled with the integrated circuit after 1959, meant that components and interconnections could be mass produced as single, relatively cheap items.

Technology is not the only component of cyberspace; indeed, of the three elements we have briefly considered here—computer, telecommunication and entertainment technologies—the latter is probably most important insofar as it represents a shift in social perceptions of ourselves as consumers. Post-war innovations, however, were important for the following, interrelated reasons: miniaturisation (particularly following the invention of the transistor and integrated circuit), coupled with increased automation of electronics and telecommunications, effected huge increases in production capacity coupled with rapidly falling costs. More and more electronics became *consumer* electronics, indicating the ways and means by which cyberspace technologies could infiltrate daily life to an ever-greater degree.

Imagining the future

Just as the term 'cyberspace' was coined by a science fiction writer, so SF in film and literature is often the best place to begin looking for blue-sky thinking on the way that cyberspace will exist in the future.

Future gazing has been a favourite activity of the twentieth century. Jules Verne and H.G. Wells outlined their visions of impending decades and centuries, and—particularly following the Second World War—the information technologies and telecommunication networks that constitute cyberspace have played an important role. Often the vision that is important to the development of narratives is far from the mark: not only was man not travelling to the further reaches of the solar system in 2001, but the superior AI of HAL also has yet to emerge in the near millennium. At the same time, many writers and film-makers have attempted to capture details of the present that may inform the future, such as the integrated computer and entertainment systems used in Ridley Scott's *Blade Runner*, or the miniature communication devices in various *Star Trek* television episodes of the 1960s that look surprisingly similar to the mobile phones and handheld computers of the 1990s and the new century.

Probably the most detailed recent vision, elements of which are more than possible in the next few decades, was the 2002 Steven Spielberg film *Minority Report*, adapted from a book by Philip K. Dick. The potential future shock realism of the film was due to the fact that the film's production designer, Alex McDowell, had consulted a wide range of experts from the worlds of computing, car design, robotics and even advertising (McIntosh and Schofield 2002). Thus, for example, when John Anderton is besieged by advertising screens appealing to him directly as he attempts to evade his former colleagues ('John Anderton: you could use a Guinness right now'), these ideas were drawn from technologies—such as retinal scanning and databases of consumers' preferences—that already exist. Likewise, when Anderton is on a subway train and a fellow passenger's newspaper is updated to show the face of the wanted fugitive, the technology that will make digital paper linked wirelessly to content providers widely available is already underway at Xerox PARC, where developers are working on a project called Gyricon, a flexible plastic containing millions of multi-coloured beads suspended in an oil-filled cavity that can be manipulated by electrical power.

Some elements of the film, such as hundreds of cars traversing buildings vertically, or fully autonomous spider robots, are, for the time being at least, purely the stuff of fantasy. Even technologies such as those listed above, while perfectly possible, do not operate in a social and psychological limbo: thus, for example, while it may be technically possible to provide personalised advertising in the very near future, concerns over privacy and even advertisers' fears that consumers will be repulsed by such tactics are larger obstacles to their widespread adoption. McIntosh and Schofield point to one example in the film where technical feasibility does not automatically lead to usability: Jetpacks, which had their original inspiration in the Buck Rogers comic books of the 1920s, have been designed and engineered, notably the Bell rocket belt designed by Wendell Moore at Bell Aircraft in the 1950s or, more recently, the SoloTek, created by the company Millennium Jet, but have all proved too dangerous or costly to be effective.

Cyberspace and cybernetics

The term 'cyberspace', invented by Gibson, obviously owes much to the term 'cybernetics', coined by Norbert Wiener in 1948. Cybernetics is the science of control theory applied to complex systems, and was defined by Wiener as 'the science of control or communication, in the animal and the machine', from *kubernetes*, the Greek for 'steersman' or 'pilot'. Cybernetics is a theory of machines and systems that treats not things but ways of behaving: any system that is not spiralling out of control or in a state of collapse must be self-regulating to some degree, and it is how such systems are controlled or regulated that is of interest to cybernetics. At its simplest, a cybernetic system works like a thermostat, turning heat on or off when a system falls or rises to a certain point.

Cybernetic theory has been applied far beyond its original application in systems science, for example, in the field of regulation and social phenomena (Dunsire 1993; Beer 1994). Dunsire, for example, has identified three main strategies of control that may be employed by governmental regulators: the first is simple steering, where policy-makers intervene on an ad hoc basis; more complex is homeostasis, where alterations are made to correct a system that deviates from a desired state or range of states; and finally the calibration, or balancing, of opposing forces such as requirements of equal access to information sources versus the demands of the free market. The more complex a system, the more complex the system of regulation is likely to be, so that single controllers are unlikely to be sufficient.

In 1991, Timothy Leary expounded an entertaining—if limited—theory of cyberpunks as 'reality pilots', guiding the rest of us to decentralised self-reliance (returning to the original meaning of the *kubernetes*, as opposed to the Latin *gubernare*, 'to govern'). Leary opposed his vision of cybernetics to refer to selforganisation and self-direction, as opposed to systems of control and governance. The opposition is not as clear as Leary supposes: Wiener's theory of cybernetic systems is that ultimately they are *self*-controlling. The important contribution of cybernetics to notions of cyberspace is that this is a complex system of fields or possibilities that will adapt and change, and redirect in order to continue functioning, the analogy being to a living organism or multifarious social system.

Cyberspace and ICT

While we have already seen that cyberspace is much more than simply information and communication technologies (ICT)—many of which will be examined in greater detail in Chapter 5—its relationship to technology is profound. As Sally Munt (2001: 6) observes:

> Science and technology have had a profound effect on the way humans perceive space and time—think, for example, of the way information technologies such as the telephone have reduced our former perception of the world as inaccessible, unknowable and exotic to a sensibility of nearness, friendliness, fellowship and instantaneity (the so-called 'global village'). Think how the invention of the microchip opened up the 'inner worlds' of the body.

As Lovelock and Ure (2002) point out, the explosion of new media, the Internet and thus cyberspace may be partly explained by three observed factors, popularly labelled 'laws'; that is, Moore's law, Metcalfe's law and Gilder's law. Moore's law, named after one of the co-founders of Intel, Gordon Moore, and first expressed in 1964, stated that the number of transistors that could be etched on to a computer chip would

double every eighteen months; since then (and with some adjustments to the time scale), this has commonly been interpreted to mean that computer power doubles every year to a year and a half.

Significant as it is, Moore's law contributed to the computer boom of the 1980s and 1990s but is perhaps less important overall than Metcalfe's law, so called after Bob Metcalfe, the inventor of Ethernet. Metcalfe observed that the value of a network is proportional to the square of the number of people using it; that is, the rate of return from a network increases exponentially as more and more people connect to it—doubling the number of users from two to four does not merely double its value, but increases it eightfold. Known as the 'network effect', this is often linked to Gilder's law, named after the futurologist George Gilder who has predicted that total bandwidth will triple every year for the next twenty-five years.

These three laws are often treated as technological imperatives, deterministic laws that must be obeyed in a similar manner to Newton's observation that every action has an equal and opposite reaction. This is not so: a number of commentators (Chapman 1994; Kroker and Kroker 1996; Wilson 1997) have warned of the dangers of isolating technology from social and historical conditions. Machines—at least for the moment—do not evolve without human interaction and the requirements of governments, business and other social groups. Munt also points out that there is a much more complex philosophical relationship between the laws of science and human beliefs, that 'the perspectives of science are thought-structures, that is ideologies, which organize the world into sets of believable fictions' (2001: 7). Munt's ideas owe much to Michel Foucault and Thomas Kuhn, that scientific knowledge relies on comprehensible models or 'paradigms' which are partial in their representation of the world and hence ideological: such observations on the nature of scientific knowledge have been criticised, particularly from within the scientific community, but at the very least the discovery of scientific 'truth' is frequently dependent on institutions and practices (universities, grants, a publishing industry) that are demonstrably tied to less pure ideologies.

Cyberspace and society

In addition to technologies and media, any text dealing with cyberspace must devote attention to the effect of new technologies on society and culture, which will be the focus of the following two chapters. What Castells (1997, 2001) refers to as a 'network society' is important not merely because computers and communications networks have been introduced into the home and workplace, but because such commodities as email and ecommerce are also transforming working and living relations. As he observes in *The Internet Galaxy* (2001: 1):

> The Internet is the fabric of our lives. If information technology is the present-day equivalent of electricity in the industrial era, in our age the Internet could be likened to both the electrical grid and the electric engine because of its ability to distribute the power of information throughout the entire realm of human society. Furthermore, as new technologies of energy generation and distribution make possible the factory and the large corporation as the organisational foundations of industrial society, the Internet is the technological basis for the organisational form of the Information Age: the network.

MacKenzie and Wacjman (1999) point out that most assumptions about the relationship between technology and society are driven by 'technological determinism', the notion that contact between the two is one-way and that technology shapes—even causes—social interactions. This, as has already been suggested in this chapter, is extremely simplistic and contributes to a passive approach, that our choice as consumers at most consists of accepting or adapting to new

technologies as they come online. Castells (2001: 36) agrees with this: 'Technological systems are socially produced. Social production is culturally informed. The Internet is no exception.'

One example of the intricacy of social, economic, political and technological relations centres on the powerhouse of the ICT revolution—the microchip. Invented by Intel in 1971, huge improvements in miniaturisation have resulted in vast leaps forward in processing power as more and more components can be built into each chip. The results of this have been a steady decline (in real terms) of the price of computers as their capacity has doubled every eighteen months or so. And yet, as Russell Cowburn of Durham University points out, the apparently technologically deterministic first Moore's law is accompanied by what has become known as Moore's second law: that the cost of a chip-manufacturing/fabrication plant, or fab, doubles every three years, so that the cost of constructing such a fab in a decade's time could cost up to $500 billion (cited in Akass 2003).

One of the consequences of this is that sales of one generation of processors finances research and production of the next. If research and development costs cannot be recouped, technology does not continue its inevitable progress. Something close to this has been seen in the shift from second-generation mobile phones to a third generation (3G): successful attempts by governments such as those in the UK to charge heavy fees for licences resulted in a stalled roll-out of 3G devices—particularly when it became clear that consumers did not wish to pay the excessive prices required of them. In such situations, new technology is affected by economics, government policy and consumer trends.

In their introductory essay to *The Handbook of New Media* (2002), Leah Lievrouw and Sonia Livingstone outline some of the main approaches to the study of new media that include sociology (such as Daniel Bell's arguments around 'post-industrial society'), social psychology, political economy, management and communication theory, and cultural studies as well as more traditional approaches based on systems engineering and analysis. They suggest two broad categories to the study of new media and ICT: researchers interested in technological, economic and behavioural issues have tended to concentrate on systems, industry structures and ownership, or the psychology of users, while researchers from a critical or cultural studies background focus more on new media content and its forms (2002: 5).

Cyberspace and cyberculture

We shall be exploring another important relationship—that between cyberspace and digital or new media—in the following section, but before doing so it is worth pausing for a moment to highlight the significance of cultural studies in this area, what is often referred to as 'cyberculture'. While not coterminous, cultural studies and the concerns of new media have often overlapped and, once the study of ICT moved outside specialist computing and engineering departments, it was often eagerly seized upon by those who had made a study—social, textual and psychological—of other media formats such as television, magazines and films.

Cybercultural concerns recur repeatedly throughout this book, complementing its interest in describing new technologies. Recent significant work in the area includes David Bell and Barbara Kennedy's *Cybercultures Reader* (2000), as well as Bell's *Introduction to Cybercultures* (2001), David Gauntlett's collection of essays on *Web.studies* (2000a), and Andrew Herman and Thomas Swift's *The Worldwide Web and Contemporary Cultural Theory* (2000). Some of the main contributions made by cultural theorists to the study of cyberculture deal with themes around configurations, representations and perceptions of bodies and identities, the significance of social formations such as virtual communities, and the discourses of cyberspace in popular culture and elsewhere.

Stories of cyberspace

One useful way of thinking about cyberspace and cyberculture, proposed by David Bell (2001), is as a series of stories. Bell distinguishes what he sees as three main types of narrative by means of which we attempt to understand cyberspace: material stories, symbolic stories and experiential stories.

Material stories include histories of technology—'the story of *how it came to be what it is*' (2001: 8)—and in this category Bell includes the various histories of the Internet that have proliferated in recent years, as well as accounts of virtual reality and computing itself, of which Paul Edwards' *The Closed World* (1997) is an excellent example. Such histories tend to concentrate on the innovations implemented by scientists and engineers, often due to the intervention of the military. These stories tend to fall into Lievrouw and Livingstone's definitions of technological and economic research, dealing with political economies of technology and its social implications for labour and consumption, as well as counter-cultural aspects associated with the personal computer and Internet. In this chapter, we have seen material stories of cyberspace associated with its emergence, and will deal with a number of other material accounts related to the growth and development of the Internet and cyberspace more generally in Part I of this book.

Symbolic stories include literary and generic accounts, most notably in cyberpunk but also SF and other forms of speculative fiction. Such symbolic retellings are an important source of our myths of cyberspace (to such an extent, suggest some critics, that those myths have obscured the reality of cyberspace), though they are not the only source. Popular culture provides another reference point for our understanding of cyberspace, not merely insofar as the Internet provides the ultimate means for disseminating urban myths, but also because films, television and newspaper stories often provide us with the terminology and frameworks to discuss our shared experiences of new technologies.

This leads on to Bell's third category—experiential stories, where material and symbolic stories are folded into their everyday use. Such experiential descriptions and analyses have become one of the most fruitful areas of the cultural study of cyberspace at the end of the

1990s, concentrating on the more ordinary (but often more profound) aspects of ICT in daily life. Bell provides a fairly extensive account of his own relations with computers, as well as examples of how other users such as Sean Cubitt (1998) come into contact with the human–computer interface. Computer games, the ease with which we transform ourselves into mouse-wielding cyborgs, and our experiences with technologies in areas such as medicine—these and many other areas have important effects on our understanding of ourselves as citizens, consumers and subjects into the twenty-first century.

Digital media and communication

Contemporary notions of cyberspace have been tied up with the development of digital media and communication technologies, a means of quantifying information so that it can be transmitted as a series of bits. In contrast to analog information, which records a continuous stream or spectrum of data, digital descriptions of data store or transmit those data as a sequence of discrete symbols from a finite set. Analog data are best thought of as a wave, or rolling down a hill; digital data break down the wave into finite quantities, similar to walking down steps. Computers do not have to be digital—early computers were analog, measuring fluctuations in a current, and electronic equipment often still makes use of analog systems. Digitisation, however, samples signals and, if such sampling is accurate or closely spaced enough, can be used to re-create an apparently perfect replica of that signal: the virtue of digital over analog systems is that because the digit is a symbol of the signal it can be converted more easily into another format.

An important contribution to computing has been the use of binary code or, more specifically, the binary digit—the bit. This is conventionally represented by the numbers 1 and 0, which in turn represent a current passed through a transistor or circuit: if a charge is present, this is represented by 1, otherwise it is a 0. What is important here is how binary digits can then be used to quantify information, that numbers can be treated as symbols to be manipulated, after the work of George Boole, who used such symbols to define logical statements as true or false. The transition from number-cruncher to symbol-manipulator was recognised by Alan Turing in his essay 'On computable numbers' as the first step to building a general purpose computing machine. In the words of Nicholas Negroponte (1995: 14):

> A bit has no color, size, or weight, and it can travel at the speed of light. It is the smallest atomic element in the DNA of information. It is a state of being: on or off, true or false, up or down, in or out, black or white. For practical purposes we consider a bit to be a 1 or a 0. The meaning of the 1 or 0 is a separate matter.

Because certain problems, or algorithms (sets of rules for defining and solving problems in a finite number of steps) can be represented by such symbols, they can be converted into digital forms; this is, however, not true of all problems.

New media and ICT

Another important aspect of cyberspace is its relationship to media, both media forms, particularly those associated with the loose category, 'new media', and *the* media—the press, television, film and publications online that constitutes what is often referred to as the public sphere. The relationship with the latter is the focus of Chapter 14 on virtual communities and online public spheres, while we deal with a number of new media formats throughout this book—film, video and games as well as the obvious formats associated with the Internet.

Lievrouw and Livingstone (2002) indicate how the phrase 'new media' is used as shorthand for cultural and technological industries associated with multimedia, entertainment and ecommerce, all of which are predicated in some shape or fashion on digital technologies. As Wise points out, the closely associated term 'multimedia' was originally devised as a marketing concept for

Apple's Multimedia Lab (Wise 2002: 46) before expanding into business, entertainment, training and consumer formats such as kiosks, CD-ROM and DVD. Is there anything distinctive about such new media? Since Wilbur Schramm's work in the 1970s, one attempt to classify difference between new media and old is in terms of those which may combine parallel human sensory perception, such as combining visuals and sound, or provide two-way (duplex) as opposed to one-way (simplex) transmission.

The combination of human sensory perception cannot be restricted to new media: while it is rare for inanimate media to combine such effects before the twentieth century (books may mix words and images, but they do not combine audio and visual perception), this was not the case with live performances such as theatre; the same is true of duplex versus simplex transmission. If we leave live performance outside the equation, however, it is extremely rare for truly multimedia media prior to the twentieth century, and the claim often made for computer-based or digital media is that they encourage user participation and interaction. Multimedia, then, may be a feature of twentieth-century phenomena such as cinema and television, but it is mainly with the digital media of the past two to three decades that such multiple sensory experiences have been combined with interactivity.

At the beginning of the twenty-first century, many of the concerns associated with new media appear to be slightly in the doldrums, but this is largely because the expansion of multimedia and new media enterprises was so rapid during the 1980s and 1990s. Key to this expansion, at least for the digital market, was the notion of convergence, that while the output of film, text and photography was very different, the software and hardware required to create them could all be run from the same box. In the early stages of ICT, specialist fields such as video editing required equally specialist hardware to ensure that performance was as effective as possible, but in recent years, as desktop PCs and Macs offer processing power equivalent to the supercomputers of the 1970s and early 1980s, this is no longer the case.

Dissemination and suppression of new technologies

In his history of technology from the telegraph to the Internet, Brian Winston proposes a model for the dissemination of new technologies in which suppression is as important as diffusion. Put simply, it is not enough for novel gadgets, techniques and devices simply to work well—they must also fulfil a social need and not threaten an overtly powerful way of doing things already in practice. 'The most obvious proof of the existence of a "law" of suppression of radical potential, then, is the continuation, despite the bombardments of technology, of all the institutions of our culture in forms subject to alternation but not revolutionary change' (Winston 1998: 13). If technologies were disseminated as soon as they were invented, it is unlikely that there could be social continuity.

Technology has always been important to the economic conditions of communication and media. Thus, for example, the ability to reproduce texts, music, images and films has contributed to the developments of each of these as a viable industry beginning with what McLuhan called the 'Gutenberg galaxy' of print. The first real boom for mass-media technology was in the period 1880 to 1930 which saw, among other developments, the growth of photography, cinema, radio and cheap printing, but which has also been surpassed by the post-Second World War boom, in particular during the 1980s. Combined with deregulation, eight new important technologies entered the mainstream in the 1980s and 1990s—video, CD, DVD, mobile communications, cable, satellite, teletext/videotext and online databases—of which only videotext (familiar to most in the UK via Teletext) did not enjoy widespread global support.

These technologies—in particular cable, satellite and online systems—have three main results in relation to distribution:

1. They reduce the time to diffuse communication of material between producer and distributor
2. They raise the number of units in circulation massively despite initial high set-up costs
3. They reduce the costs related to distribution

Such technology often has contradictory results, resulting in wider decentralisation of information at the same time that ownership becomes more concentrated. Thus, in the 1980s, for example, local TV and radio stations in the USA broke the monopoly of the networks in providing news by using satellite for images and information—at the same time that more and more of these independent stations were being bought up by companies such as Rupert Murdoch's News Corporation. New technology can mean more efficient information gathering and distribution, opening it up to more and more groups, but also making it easier for larger, transnational companies to control their services.

Some of the ways in which new technologies have been adopted can be understood when considering the steps taken with older forms, in this case the first successful digital communications medium: Morse code.

When old technologies were new: Morse code and the telegraph

Morse code was used in maritime communication for over a hundred years, from 1897 when Marconi sent a series of messages between an Italian warship and a shore station until 1999. Morse code was the world's first successful digital communication system, invented by Samuel Morse, the son of a New England Congregationalist minister, in 1844, when he sent his first public message, 'What hath God wrought', across the telegraph line between Washington and Baltimore (Standage 1998; Winston 1998).

The telegraph had been in use for nearly a decade by that time, the claimants for its invention including Baron Pawel Schilling, Sir William Fothergill Cooke and Charles Wheatstone, as well as Edward Davy, who proposed telegraph lines as a means of preserving rail safety. Tom Standage, in his book *The Victorian Internet* (1998), has drawn parallels between the steam age and the electronic age, and certainly Morse code in particular served as a precedent for digitising information that would be useful for encoding cyberspace: operators have been communicating in bits for more than a century and a half.

The basic time interval for sending messages via Morse code is the duration of the dot, with dashes being the equivalent of three units. The letter E, the most common in the English language, is one dot in Morse, with less common letters such as Q or Y consisting of three dashes and one dot in different combinations. Despite its sophistication (evidenced by its long life), Morse code was difficult to automate, and so as electromechanical typewriters were developed in the early 1900s, users began to employ the Baudot code, so-named after its inventor, Emile Baudot, that used fixed character lengths, as did its successor, ASCII.

While Morse code per se was ultimately a dead-end for digital computers, the telegraph itself became 'the model of all electrical signalling systems which follow' (Winston 1998: 29). This was not limited to its technical innovations: investments that had been made in alternative communication systems, such as semaphore, meant that governments were often unwilling to adopt the new technology, while ambiguities over ownership slowed down dissemination of the telegraph. None the less, along with the invention of the telephone in the late nineteenth century, the foundations had been laid for the digitisation of telecommunications and the beginnings of cyberspace.

Policy and regulation

At the time that Morse code was finally phased out for official communication, more pressing matters concerned the distribution and dissemination of digital media technologies that had been introduced in the final decades of the twentieth century. As has been mentioned several times in this introduction, concentrating on new technologies at the expense of social, political and psychological consequences provides only a limited picture of the effects of such technology. In particular, many governments and commercial enterprises have been concerned about the implications of digital media while, at the same time, attempting to benefit as much as possible from them.

Issues around policy, regulation and ethics form the major part of the final section of this book, but it is also worth drawing attention to some of the main factors facing regulators of new media. For producers of content distributed across new media channels, a major concern is protecting intellectual property rights, as the ease with which information in the form of text, music and even video can be digitised and copied has placed copyright rules under considerable strain.

Another area of contention arises due to the friction—by no means unique to digital media—between individual rights and social responsibilities to society. This has become more important in the aftermath of various governments' crackdown on terrorism, as the spread of global telecommunications systems has provided both the means for new, widespread forms of communication (one thinks of satellite transmissions of videos made by Osama bin Laden) as well as tools to track and monitor individuals more closely than before. Some see this as a diminution of the individual's right to privacy and free speech, while others argue that policy makers have social responsibilities to police digital networks more thoroughly, not merely in terms of fighting terrorism but also against other crimes such as fraud and child abuse.

Most if not all media formats have brought with them considerable headaches for a political elite, and few have been as dramatic as the Reformation that was, in part, fuelled by developments in print media. In the twentieth century the dumbing effects of television, video nasties, a press often depicted as out of control have all been depicted as problematic, but few have so easily crossed national boundaries and mores as the Internet.

The Internet and the Web

Thus far, we have said relatively little about the most obvious current incarnation of cyberspace in everyday life: the Internet. The reason for this has been to emphasise that cyberspace and the Net are not synonymous terms; we prefer to use cyberspace to refer to a wider range of cultural, social and political networks in which a particular system of communications, in this case the Internet, can work.

At the same time, it is clear that the Internet in its manifold forms—including the World Wide Web—has provided a radical transformation of the way in which we communicate, work, consume, find information and entertainment and connect to other people around the world. The Internet is typically described as a 'network of networks', a system of hardware (computers, routers, cables or wireless transmitters and receivers) and software (the protocols that provide rules for connecting between different machines) that has resulted in huge changes in the post-war computer industry. If computers, particularly the personal computer, following its invention in the 1970s, made a significant difference to the way people worked with and processed information, it was clear that much of the information supplied to and from computers still needed to be turned from bits into atoms, or vice versa. If you wanted to view the output from a computer, such as a typed message or image, you would typically have to print it out. Transferring information between computers was difficult, extremely so if different machines used different operating systems.

The revolutionary effect of the Internet has been to provide an open system of rules that may be used to transfer information quickly and easily from machine to machine. It is for this reason that Metcalfe's so-called law, that the value of a network is proportional to the square of the number of people using it, will probably be more significant in the twenty-first century than Moore's law, that the number of transistors capable of being fitted onto a microchip will double every one to two years. Throughout large parts of this book, we will consider the impact and influence of Internet technology on cyberspace, but it is important to remember that as the Internet of today is very different to its predecessor from the late 1960s, ARPANET, so the Matrix envisaged by Gibson, and the cyberspace of the future, will be very different to what we experience today.

The development of the Internet

The origins of the Internet lay with the Advanced Research Projects Agency (ARPA), which was founded following the launch of Sputnik to pursue scientific, military and academic research. Between 1963 and 1967, ARPA investigated the feasibility of building computer networks before selecting a number of computer hosts to join ARPANET, as the project was later known, in 1968. Work began in 1969, providing protocols that would connect computers at different sites and would also create a resilient network, capable of rerouting information in the event of failure on any part of the network (Hafner and Lyon 1996; Naughton 1999).

We shall examine the technologies that constitute the Internet in later chapters in this book: throughout the 1970s, however, the prototype of the Internet grew slowly as other networks around the world, such as ALOHAnet in Hawaii and University College London, connected to ARPANET. Alongside official development, other computer users were exploring ways of communicating online, most significantly through the work of Jim Ellis and others at Duke University who developed Usenet, the 'poor man's ARPANET'. At this stage, such computer networks remained the preserve largely of scientists and computer engineers, but the introduction of the personal computer in the late 1970s signalled the potential for those networks to form the backbone of a mass medium.

Throughout the early 1980s, ARPANET remained one network—though an important one—among many, with governments and institutions developing their own information systems, such as Minitel in France. Important work in the 1980s concentrated on the development of an architecture that could be connected to more easily, particularly via the introduction of the Domain Name System (which would eventually mean that every server attached to the Net would not need to carry the address of every other server—something that severely restricted growth). By the end of the decade, the infrastructure for a unified and universal system was in place, but the Net still remained a hostile environment for those who were not computer experts.

The 'killer app' that was eventually to make the Internet essential for many users was probably email, but the eye candy that first caught their attention—and also focused computer engineers' attention on ease of use—was the World Wide Web, developed by Tim Berners-Lee while he was working at the European Centre for Nuclear Research (CERN) in Geneva (Berners-Lee 1999). Berners-Lee developed the language for formatting pages and communicating between web servers (HTML and HTTP respectively) in 1990, and companies such as the National Center for Supercomputer Applications (NCSA) and later Netscape took up his work to popularise the Web for many more users. Equally significantly, Berners-Lee was committed to developing the Web as an open standard that would be adopted as widely as possible as a means for exchanging information, having realised that proprietary systems had severely affected the capabilities of computer-mediated communication until that point.

By the mid-1990s, aided in particular by the Web and email, Internet usage expanded rapidly, fulfilling the conditions of Metcalfe's law as individuals, governments and corporations began making available huge amounts of data in open and immediately accessible forms. The transformation between 1995, when Microsoft launched the Microsoft Network alongside Windows 95 as a superior alternative to the 'over-complicated' Internet, and 2000, when dotcom boom-andbust stories dominated the media and Microsoft was under investigation for allegedly monopolising access to the Internet via its browser, was profound: the Internet was still a primary place of research and communication for scientists and computer engineers—only now they constituted a tiny fraction of the estimated 500 million users connected online.

The Grid

While the Web has often become synonymous with current configurations of cyberspace, new developments such as peer-to-peer networking serve as a warning that this is not always the case. As such, it is worth ending this chapter with a glance at some of the developments that could affect the way we use cyberspace in future years.

In the past decade we have become used to an international computing network, the roots of which were established in the late 1960s and early 1970s and which has expanded as part of a global telecommunications network. The current Internet effectively provides a planet-sized hard drive of constantly updated information, yet this may only be the first step to creating a planet-sized computer.

As we shall see later in this book, current technologies that have been following a variant of what is known as Moore's law cannot do so forever: the technical processes by means of which computers are manufactured are within sight of barriers of physics which means that such development will probably plateau in the first few decades of the twenty-first century. Different technologies (such as quantum computing) will probably have an enormous contribution to make, but there remains a limit to what can be done.

More powerful computers, however, do not merely rely on cramming more components into smaller spaces. Over the past ten years or so, the fastest machines have relied less and less on the sheer computing muscle of one or two processors; instead, supercomputers such as ASCII White work by connecting massively parallel processors, capable of achieving twelve teraflops (twelve trillion calculations per second), some 35,000 times faster than the speediest Athlon computer in 2001. Even IBM's supercomputer, however, was some six times slower than Seti@Home, the program that analyses astronomical data in search of extraterrestrial life by utilising spare processing cycles of volunteers' computers. Throughout 2001, Seti@Home averaged seventy-one teraflops (setiathome. ssl. Berkeley.edu), yet its constituency of 500,000 users represents only a small fraction of the potential computers that could be connected to the Internet. It has been estimated that were all those computers joined up to form a worldwide grid, a global super-processor, as it were, the computing power available would rise to more than 250 petaflops, 20,000 times faster than ASCII White.

Commercial grid-like products, that distribute tasks around networks, are already available from IBM and Sun, but a generic Grid is a long way off, particularly as companies such as Microsoft with .Net are not enthusiastic about an open source alternative. None the less, prototype grids such as the University of Wisconsin's Condor (www.cs.wisc. edu/condor/), DAS, based in the Netherlands (www.cs.vu. nl/~bal/das.html), and the EuroGrid (www.eurogrid.org) have demonstrated how such projects can work on a small scale. Much of the current research into grids is concerned with the economics of such a project, how resources can be pooled in order to encourage users and organisations to share spare processing power, and how data may be distributed across networks. If and when the Grid becomes a reality, the current wired world of cyberspace will appear extremely restricted by comparison.

Bodynets, personal webs and the future

Projects such as the Grid—and indeed the Web and Internet itself—are immense and ambitious, but cyberspace envelops us in ways that are also intensely personal. Theories that move towards a definition of us as a cyborg, particularly in the aftermath of Donna Haraway's (1991) influential essay, are often concerned less with the relationship of biology and invasive technology than with the ways in which we surround ourselves with instrumental extensions of ourselves—pens, watches, mobile phones, personal organisers. The social and psychological effects of such machinic extensions can be immense: Neil Postman (1990), for example, has remarked on the ways in which the invention of the clock, created by Dominican monks to regulate their worship, engineered a complete social transformation as part of the Industrial Revolution.

At present, cyberspace still tends to be something we plug into, an opaque boundary that we generally must make an effort to interface with, such as by sitting in front of a computer and dialling into the Internet. This is not always the case, however, even now: if we accept the wide-ranging definition of cyberspace with which we began this chapter, then withdrawing money from a cash machine or ATM links us to global financial systems where capital functions largely as pure data. Likewise, mobile phones form part of an extended telecommunications network that is measured not merely by its extent but also in terms of its saturation of our daily lives. One technological aim (which was, for example, hinted at in *Minority Report*) is to transform our individual spaces into clouds or nets of personal data that will be able to interface with global networks almost transparently.

12. Making Relationships Work

by J. Dan Rothwell

Interpersonal communication, whether face to face or mediated, is an essential element of day-to-day living. A primary goal of interpersonal exchange is the development, maintenance, and dissolution of relationships. This chapter looks at interpersonal communication in relationships of various sorts. Throughout its pages, the chapter provides both descriptive and proscriptive information that will help any reader better understand the complexities of this essential part of human experience. This chapter also provides valuable insights on how to be a better communicator within a variety of types of relationships.

To make the most of this chapter, readers should apply the concepts covered in it to a variety of their own interpersonal relationships. Of particular interest in this chapter is the application of key communication concepts within the context of social networking. The many relationship-based implications of online communication are explored in a meaningful and informative manner in the latter portion of this chapter.

JESSICA TANDY AND HUME CRONYN were married for 52 years, and the marriage ended only when Tandy died. Their relationship was the more remarkable for its longevity because they stayed happily married even though they were both successful, acclaimed actors. Hollywood is legendary for chewing up marriages. Yet Tandy and Cronyn remained steadfast partners for five decades despite great notoriety and professional success, each of them winning numerous stage and screen awards. They starred, sometimes separately and sometimes together, in a variety of successful movies. Given a choice among models of romance that included several famous relationships, respondents to one survey picked Tandy and Cronyn's relationship as the ideal (Kanner, 1995). Contrary to the enduring success of their relationship, both had been married previously. Why does one marriage last until death and another survive for what seems like the blink of an eye? What makes relationships succeed or fail?

The purpose of this chapter is to discuss why interpersonal relationships at home, at work, at school and at play succeed, struggle, or sink, and what you can do to make them more durable and rewarding.

Main Reasons for Forming Relationships

Our relationships with others can seem so fragile. Marriage rates in the United States have dropped to their lowest level (52% of adults) ever recorded by the U.S. Census Bureau (Mather & Lavery, 2010). According to Pew Research Center, only 43% of married couples in the United States are "very happy" ("Is Marriage Bliss?" 2011). Stephanie Coontz, director of public education for the Council on Contemporary Families, notes that American adults now spend half their lives unmarried (cited in Roberts, 2007).

The flavorful wine of a new marriage may gradually turn into the bitter vinegar of divorce. Rates of divorce dropped slightly during the 1990s but remain high today. About 50% of first marriages, 60% of second marriages, and 75% of third marriages end in divorce (Epstein, 2010). Cohabitations (intimate couples living together but unmarried) are even less stable. A mere 10% of couples who cohabit remain together for more than five years (Crooks & Baur, 2011). High-school sweethearts rarely stay together for life. Gay and lesbian relationships are at least as fragile as heterosexual relationships (Kurdek, 2005).

Despite their apparent fragility, most people crave stable, long-term relationships. The U.S. Census Bureau has consistently shown that in the last three decades more than 95% of the American public want to be married now or in the future. The probability that an adult living in the United States will get married at some time during his or her life is almost 90% (Mather & Lavery, 2010). That figure would be higher if gays and lesbians were granted legal civil marriages.

Sustaining relationships has never been more challenging, and making friendships work is no exception. One study found that American adults, on average, had only two close friends, down from three in 1985 (Hampton et al., 2009; see also "Social Networking Sites," 2011). They may have 5,000 "friends" on Facebook, but truly close friends are few for most people. Fewer close friends mean a weakening social support network in stressful times. In addition, 80% of respondents to a face-to-face survey of 1,467 individuals reported that they discuss important matters in their lives only with family members, up significantly from 57% in 1985 (McPherson et al., 2006). About 10% confide only to a spouse and no other person, almost double compared to 1985. Sustaining friendships during your college experience can be especially challenging given the typical high stress associated with a college education, close proximity of dorm living, and competitive atmosphere that often pervades college life. One key problem is that friendships are often taken for granted (Guerrero & Chavez, 2005). Less effort to sustain friendships is made than occurs with romantic partners and family members (Canary et al., 1993).

Why do we seek close relationships if they often end poorly and they are so challenging to sustain? Generally, most of us don't enter relationships expecting them to fail. Most newlyweds think there is *zero chance* that they would ever get divorced (Baker & Emery, 1993). On average, both singles and married couples put their own probability of divorce at about 10% (Fowers et al., 2001). There are several other more specific reasons, however, that, despite frequent setbacks, we continue to seek meaningful relationships with others. In this section, I briefly discuss the main reasons.

Need to Belong: Like Food and Water

Humans have a deep-seated need to belong, to make social connections with other humans. We are "the social animal" (Aronson, 1999; Brooks, 2011). In Chapter 1, I related the story of Genie who was raised in almost total isolation from other human beings with but brief and abusive interactions with her parents. The results were disastrous. Our need for human connection is an imperative, as necessary to our well-being and development as food and water (Baumeister & Leary, 1995). "We humans are social animals down to our very cells. Nature did not make us noble loners" (Parks, 2007, p. 1), although loners at least get to decide how the toilet paper roll gets placed on the dispenser (over or under).

Nature has provided each of us with an "affiliative neuropeptide" called oxytocin. "The levels of this chemical rise when couples watch romantic movies, hug, or hold hands. . . . Oxytocin is also related to the feelings of closeness and being 'in love' when you have regular sex ..." (Amen, 2007). This "love hormone" also seems to increase feelings of trust. "Oxytocin is nature's way of weaving people together" (Brooks, 2011, p. 64).

These human attachments we make, especially in the early formative stages of our development, are particularly meaningful (Sroufe et al., 2005). Attachment theory argues, "Children born into a web of attuned relationships know how to join in conversations with new people and read social signals. They see the world as a welcoming place. Children born into a web of threatening relationships can be fearful, withdrawn, or overaggressive" (Brooks, 2011, p. 62). Communication forms attachments with others, and the quality of these attachments influences the competence of our communication.

Interpersonal Attraction: What Draws Us Together

There are several basic factors that attract us to other people and make the idea of developing a relationship with them desirable. These include physical attractiveness, similarities, and reciprocal liking.

Physical Attractiveness: Looking Good

In Chapter 2, I discussed the beauty bias. Physically attractive individuals have advantages that those with more average looks often do not. Speed dating necessitates quick decisions based on blink-of-an-eye first impressions. Looks tend to dominate as a criterion for these rush-to-judgment decisions whether to seek further contact. Hundreds of studies show that physical attractiveness is equally significant for men and women (Eagly et al., 1991; Langlois et al., 2000).

One study of online dating preferences found that both men and women had a strong preference for "very good looks" from their online prospects (Hitsch et al., 2010). Evolutionary psychologists argue that physically attractive people are more likely to be physically healthy and have good genes. This makes them a good prospect for a mate to produce healthy children (Buss, 2003). This is a debatable point of view, but physical attractiveness is unquestionably a predominant characteristic of interpersonal attraction, at least initially.

Similarity: Birds of a Feather

There's a well-known adage: "Birds of a feather flock together." Is it true that we are drawn to those who are similar to us, or do "opposites attract"? Research resoundingly supports **similarity attraction theory** (Byrne, 1997). We are drawn to individuals who seem to share our interests, values, attitudes, and personality (McCrae et al., 2008). Our level of communication skill also plays a part in attraction, friendship, and relationship satisfaction. Highly skilled communicators are drawn to other highly skilled communicators, and less skilled communicators are drawn to each other (Burleson & Samter, 1996). In addition, a study of online dating found that both men and women prefer a partner with about the same educational level, same ethnicity, and same or similar religion. Divorced online daters also prefer divorced partners (true mostly for women), and those with children prefer dating someone who also has children (Hitsch et al., 2010).

Why are we attracted to those who are similar to us? First, similarity of values, attitudes, personality, background, and communication skills makes relationships less stressful and easier to manage. There is less likelihood of frustration, bickering, and strife (Duck & Pittman, 1994). Second, individuals who share our attitudes and values validate the correctness of our perceptions (Bryne & Clore, 1970). Their worldviews match.

This *matching effect* based on similarities seems tied to relationship success or failure. Physically mismatched couples (one is attractive and the other is not) usually don't stay together long term. The Boston Couples Study showed that dissimilarity in physical attractiveness between partners was a significant factor in the eventual split-up of the relationship (Hill et al., 1976). The more attractive partner may see opportunities available with more physically attractive prospects—the wandering eye.

The matching effect also applies to language styles. College students engaged in four-minute speed dates were three times as likely to want future contact with their partner when their language style (use of prepositions, pronouns, etc.) matched. A second study of casual online chats between dating partners showed that couples whose language style matched were far more likely to be together three months later than those who didn't match (Ireland et al., 2010). This matching effect seems to apply to nonverbal communication as well. When the hand gestures, eye gazes, and postures of two people match when they first meet, they are more inclined to like each other (Shockley et al., 2009). Finally, a sense of humor is a highly desirable quality in a date or mate, and those who exhibit similar senses of humor will likely discover interpersonal attraction, but attraction is less likely to occur if senses of humor are mismatched—you're telling gross jokes and your date finds that kind of humor repulsive (Cooper, 2008).

The matching effect also appears to apply to same-sex friendships and even roommates (Carli

et al., 1991; Cash & Derlega, 1978). Less attractive friends and roommates are seen as holding back the social lives of more attractive friends and roommates. It can be a cold world out there!

Reciprocal Liking: I Like You If You Like Me

We tend to like those who we perceive like us. The perception that others like us can even compensate for the lack of similarities. In one study, for instance, male participants revealed that they liked a female very much when she communicated interest by maintaining eye contact, listening carefully, and leaning toward them. Even though the male participants knew that the female disagreed with them on significant issues (dissimilarities in attitudes and values), they still liked her because she appeared to like them (Gold et al., 1984).

If we assume that others do not like us, we may create a self-fulfilling prophecy by responding negatively to them. This negative response could easily invite a reciprocal negative response from a person who may have been primed to like us but begins to dislike us because of our unlikable behavior toward them (Curtis & Miller, 1986).

Rewards: Exchange Theory

Sometimes we seek relationships based on exchange theory—a cost-benefits analysis that weighs the benefits of a particular relationship against any costs incurred (Jeffries 2002). We seek rewards, anything that we consider desirable, and these rewards may compensate for any perceived imperfections in our partners and friends. We may not be a perfect fit (some dissimilarities), but certain rewards may compensate. A substantial income may compensate for short stature in men (Hitsch et al., 2010). We tolerate some irritating quirks or even difficult moodiness from our partners because they offer us rewards that are equal to or greater than the costs. Our partner or friend talks too much at parties, laughs too loudly, or tells inappropriate jokes to our boss. Yet close friends and romantic partners can provide social support for us when we are stressed, so we overlook the inappropriate behavior (Rusbult & Van Lange, 2003).

A partner or friend can also offer kindness, sensitivity, and thoughtfulness as compensation for only average looks or a small income (Epstein, 2010). Kindness, in fact, is the most important quality desired in an intimate partner by both men and women across many cultures (Buss, 2003). Although social exchange theory can seem coldly calculating, we do tend to make a cost-benefits analysis of our relationships. When the costs of a relationship (conflict, stress, unhappiness, personal safety) outweigh any benefits (companionship, friendship, sex), we usually look for the door to escape.

Forming Close Relationships

Despite the challenges and disappointments, we are driven to find those lasting, happy relationships that prove to be so rewarding and life affirming. In this section, I discuss intimacy and love and the developmental stages of relationships.

Intimacy and Love: Friends, Family, and Romantic Partners

The previous chapter included a discussion of the "dark side" of personal relationships. Our personal relationships also have a very "bright side." We have many relationships in our lives. Some are casual, some professional, and others are intimate and loving. Intimacy and love are two of the most fulfilling, satisfying experiences humans can enjoy.

Intimacy: Close Connection

An interpersonal relationship is a connection two people have to each other because of kinship (brother-sister), an attraction (lovers and friends), or a power distribution (boss-employee). An intimate relationship is a type of interpersonal relationship that is characterized by strong emotional bonding, closeness, and interdependence, in which individuals meaningfully influence each other.

Although intimacy is sometimes associated with sex ("We were intimate last night"), intimacy occurs in different types of relationships, some nonsexual and non-romantic. One study (Berscheid et al., 1989) of several hundred college students found that respondents' "most intimate relationship" was with a romantic partner (47%), a friend (36%), or a family member (14%). In another study, three-quarters of college students reported that intimacy could occur without sex and romance (Floyd, 1996).

Men and women, however, do not always express and nurture intimacy in the same ways (Wood, 2007). Women typically draw close to one another through talking about personal matters and discussing experiences. When you equate intimacy with only self-disclosure (sharing personal information), it would appear that women are better at establishing intimacy than men. Wood (2007) calls this mistaken notion the male deficit model, and she criticizes it as too narrow in perspective. She notes that men typically talk less about personal matters and share feelings less with other men, but men achieve closeness by sharing meaningful activities and helping each other (Radmacher & Azmitia, 2006; Wood & Inman, 1993). Engaging in building or repair work, watching or playing sports, and getting stuck in mud while off-roading and having to dig out together are all ways to achieve intimacy (Coontz, 2009).

If styles of communicating intimacy differ between men and women, then it is important that the partners recognize this early in the relationship. Otherwise, misunderstandings will emerge. For example, a man fixes an annoying squeak in a door hinge that has bothered his female partner for some time. He assumes that she will recognize this as an act of affection because he perceives it as such. His partner, however, may see this as simple maintenance and not recognize it as an expression of intimacy. Thus, she experiences no act of closeness, and he's probably upset that his act of affection went unrecognized. Men also may think that physical proximity (being in the same room; watching television while sitting on the same couch together) is intimate. Women may see this as the "slouch on the couch." These style differences in communicating intimacy should be discussed.

Love: An Ocean of Emotion

Richard Barnfield described it as "a fire, a heaven, a hell, where pleasure, pain, and sad repentance dwell." Germaine Greer called it "a drug." Then there's the story of a four-year-old whose next-door neighbor had recently lost his wife. The man was crying in his backyard. The little boy came over and sat on the grieving man's lap. Asked later by his mother what he'd said to the man, the little boy replied, "Nothing. I just helped him cry." Love almost defies definition, principally because there is not just one kind of love.

Although we tend to think of love in terms of passion, not all types of love are fever pitched. Robert Sternberg (1986, 1988, 1997) has offered his triangular theory of love to explain the different types. The three elements of love according to this theory are intimacy, passion, and commitment. Intimacy has already been defined as feeling emotionally close to and strongly influenced by another person. Passion refers to both the physiological drives that produce intense physical attraction and sexual responses and psychological desires and needs expressed as the idealization of a loved one and constant thinking about that person (Yela, 2006). Commitment refers to a decision to continue a relationship long term. There are seven types of love related to these three key elements.

1. Liking—intimacy without passion or commitment, such as in some friendships.
2. Infatuated love—passion without intimacy or commitment, such as "puppy love."
3. Empty love—commitment without passion and intimacy, such as in a stagnating, unsatisfying marriage.
4. Romantic love—passion and intimacy without commitment, such as a romantic affair.
5. Companionate love—intimacy and commitment without passion, such as a long-term marriage where partners are more friends than lovers.
6. Fatuous love—passion and commitment without intimacy, such as a "love at first sight" relationship.
7. Consummate love—combines intimacy, passion, and commitment and is the most satisfying adult relationship.

It is not unusual to mistake passion for consummate love. Passion without intimacy or commitment, however, is more a "one-night stand" than a consummate love. In the absence of intimacy and commitment, passion can flame out quickly, leaving emptiness and disappointment. Personal relationships that have the greatest longevity and satisfaction are those in which partners are constantly working on sustaining intimacy and reinforcing commitment to each other. This is the companionate love of friendships that plays an integral part in making our lives rewarding.

Passion does not inevitably disappear as a romantic relationship grows long term, but the giddy levels of passion characteristic of the early stages of romance cannot be realistically sustained (Gonzaga et al., 2006; Tucker & Aron, 1993). In fact, such desperate longing often equated with obsessive passion ("I can't live without you") is detrimental because it controls you, ultimately making the relationship less satisfying than a passionless relationship (Pileggi, 2010, p. 38).

Not to depress anyone, but the average rate of sexual intercourse for married couples declines by half after only a single year of marriage (Hatfield & Rapson, 1996). As romantic relationships mature, passion will be more episodic, appearing sometimes but seeming to disappear at others. When the fires of passion seem to flicker or diminish overall, the warmth of intimacy and the comfort of commitment sustain a long-term relationship (Sprecher & Regan, 1998). Engaging in enjoyable activities can cultivate a healthy passion over the long term when passion becomes more episodic. These activities, however, should not be competitive "because the point of the outing should not be winning but enjoying time together" (Pileggi, 2010, p. 39). Expecting romantic relationships to

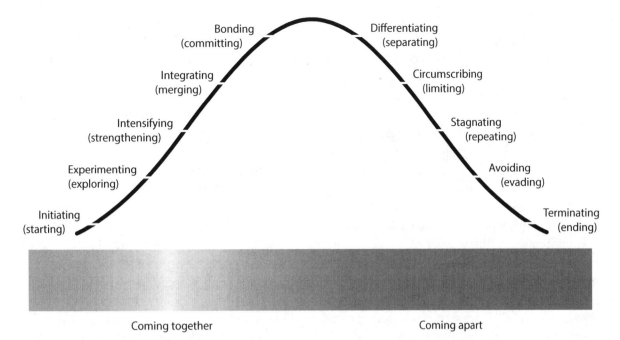

Bonding (committing)		Differentiating (separating)
Integrating (merging)		Circumscribing (limiting)
Intensifying (strengthening)		Stagnating (repeating)
Experimenting (exploring)		Avoiding (evading)
Initiating (starting)		Terminating (ending)

Coming together   Coming apart

remain as they were when passion first ignited sets expectations that doom relationships. We form powerful emotional attachments in committed relationships, but these attachments mature and change over time (Hazan & Shaver, 1994a &b).

Relationship Development: Coming-Together Phases

Knapp and Vangelisti (1992, 2005) examined a large body of research on phases of relationships and communication patterns (see especially Honeycutt et al., 1989; Honeycutt et al., 1992). They synthesized this research into their stages of relationships model that has five "coming-together" and five "coming-apart" phases [see figure above]. The model applies equally well to mixed-sex and same-sex intimate relationships (Haas & Stafford, 1998; Peplau & Spalding, 2000).

Particular patterns of communication occur in each phase; some advance the development of your relationships, and others lead to deterioration. Recognizing the difference can make or break interpersonal relationships. Movement through the phases may be rapid, especially the early phases, or it may be slow when one partner wants to move forward or backward but the other partner resists. There may be substantial overlap between phases as you move in either direction. Movement may not even be sequential because

sometimes phases are skipped. Let's look at each of these phases, recognizing that we're describing intimate relationships. Other relationships, such as those with coworkers, follow different patterns.

Initiating: Taking the Plunge

During the initiating phase, we are surveying the interpersonal terrain. We try to put our best foot forward by appearing friendly, open, and approachable. Communication approaches that seem to work effectively during this phase were revealed in one study (Douglas, 1987). Networking (learning about a person from someone who knows him or her), offering (making yourself available for conversation by sitting in an adjacent seat or being in a place the person usually frequents), approaching (signally an interest verbally or nonverbally with a smile or a self-introduction), and sustaining (keeping the conversation going by asking questions) all work well.

Communication approaches that don't work effectively during this phase of personal relationship development include expressing deep feelings ("I'm afraid to love again"), keeping silent to create an air of mystery (there's no mystery in looking doltish), asking for big favors ("Will you help me move?"), and diminishing oneself (Woody Allen: "My one regret in life is that I am not someone else"). Using a cell phone, talking about an "ex," and not making eye contact are additional "don'ts" during the initiating phase noted in a survey by the dating service It's Just Lunch ("Navigating Today's Complex Dating Scene," 2011).

So what about clever opening lines? A man approaches a woman in a bar and says, "How much does a penguin weigh?" The woman replies, "How much?" The man responds, "Enough to break the ice." Does this work for you? What about this opener: Man says, "Did it hurt?" Woman replies, "What?" Man responds, "When you fell from heaven?" Then there's the man asking a woman, "Was your dad a thief when he stole the stars for your eyes?" (Goldston, 2007). A basic problem with all of these opening lines is that they are not customized for the individual who is of interest to you. Research shows that attempting to find the perfect opening line is wasted effort ("What Social Science Can Tell You about Flirting," 2007). Most openers are awkward, silly, or embarrassingly lame. Some are clever, but the best openers are simple introductions ("Hi, I'm Glen. What's your name?") or conversation starters ("What do you think about this crazy weather we've been having?"). Just K.I.S.S.: Keep It Simple and Straightforward.

This shouldn't discourage you from using humor, however. In the initial stages of relationship formation, humor can have a very large, positive impact on the future prospect of a relationship if the humor is viewed as appropriate (Cooper, 2008). You want a dating prospect to laugh with you, not at you.

Experimenting: Auditioning for the Part

The experimenting phase is when we "audition" for the part of boyfriend or girlfriend. We experiment by engaging in small talk to discover areas of commonality: "What's your major?" or "Do you like ice skating?" We're casually probing, searching for ways to connect with others. All of us have superficial contacts with hundreds of people that never develop to any extent. Most of our transactions do not progress beyond the experimenting phase of development.

Intensifying: Warming to the Relationship

The intensifying phase is when relationships deepen. Individuals use a variety of communication approaches to intensify relationships (Taraban et al., 1998). The top 10 approaches identified in one study are these (Tolhuizen, 1989).

1. Increased contact (39.2%)—seeing or phoning partner more often.
2. Relationship negotiation (29.1%)— openly discussing feelings about the relationship.
3. Social support and assistance (26.1%)— requesting advice from a parent or friend.
4. Increased rewards (17.6%)—doing favors such as doing partner's laundry or fixing partner's car.
5. Direct definitional bid (16.6%)—asking for a commitment from partner.
6. Tokens of affection (16.1 %)—giving gifts, sending flowers, giving cards.
7. Personalized communication (15.1%)— listening to partner or friend.
8. Verbal expressions of affection (14.1%)— saying "You're really sweet"
9. Suggestive actions (13.1%)—flirting.
10. Nonverbal expressions of affection (12.1%)— gazing, touching.

Women use relationship negotiation far more often than men; men use direct definitional bid and verbal expressions of affection more often than women (see also Owen, 1987). Which of these approaches do you use most frequently?

The success of any of these approaches depends on the unique dynamics of a particular relationship. What is effective in one relationship may fail disastrously in another. Be careful not to move too quickly and exuberantly to intensify a relationship. Your partner may knock over furniture in a determined effort to flee the scene.

Trying to intensify a relationship is one thing; determining if the effort is working is quite another. Individuals conduct "secret tests" during the intensifying phase to check out the success of their intensification efforts. Endurance requires a partner to tolerate unpleasant behavior such as criticism and inconvenient requests (taking care of a slobbering, ill-trained dog big enough to saddle and ride). If your partner endures the test, commitment is assumed. Public presentation tests the intensity of the relationship by introducing your partner as "my boyfriend/girlfriend" to see if the partner is comfortable with the label. Separation tests the relationship by keeping the partners away from each other for a period of time to see if the relationship will remain viable. This, of course, is a risky test because, although "absence makes the heart grow fonder," "out of sight out of mind" may occur instead. Third-party questioning occurs when one partner asks a friend to check out the other person's depth of feeling about the relationship and then reports the results to the interested party. Triangle tests involve asking a friend to make the partner jealous by seeming to express interest in the partner concocting the test (Baxter & Wilmot, 1984).

Women are more likely to employ these "secret tests" of a relationship because they monitor relationships more than men (Baxter & Wilmot, 1984). In particular, separation and triangle tests are the most frequent choices. Endurance, separation, and the triangle tests are also the least constructive. The triangle test in particular is the most dangerous. Feeling the need to induce jealousy in a partner is a sign that the relationship is of low quality, and the triangle test is unlikely to be constructive. Secret tests generally are "more common in deteriorating [versus stable] relationships" (Goodboy et al., 2010, p. 74). Nevertheless, public presentation and third-party questioning are relatively harmless ways to test the depth of a relationship.

Integrating: Moving Beyond "Just Friends"

The integrating phase fuses a relationship. Individuals seem to merge into a distinct couple. Social circles of friends mix. Nonverbal markers of intimacy are displayed, such as pictures, pins, or clothing belonging to the other person. Self-disclosure is more revealing and potentially risky. Life goals and aspirations are shared. A sexual relationship often occurs at this stage (sex on a first date or "one-night stands" are not included as examples of this stage). Partners may begin living together, indicating that they have moved beyond the "just friends" phase.

Bonding: Strings, Rings, and Other Things

The public-ritual phase that institutionalizes the relationship is called bonding. We are communicating to the world that we have a committed relationship, not just a "no-strings" attachment. An engagement ring may be worn. There may be a public contract, of which marriage is the most obvious example. Gay couples do not have this option in most states. Nevertheless, any public announcement, ceremony, gesture, or proclamation that the relationship is considered exclusive and binding moves the couple into the bonding phase.

This phase usually signals a turning point. A turning point is "any event or occurrence that is associated with change in a relationship" (Baxter & Bullis, 1986, p. 470). Disclosing a personal secret for the first time or lending your classic car that is in mint condition might be turning points in a relationship. Having sex for the first time, moving in together, or saying "I love you" are typical turning points (Mongeau et al., 2006). Although "I love you" can be a powerful turning point in a relationship, one survey found that the words women most want to hear are "You've lost weight" (see Cameron, 2002).

Interestingly, almost half the time, partners in heterosexual relationships do not identify the same turning points in their relationship (Baxter & Bullis, 1986). For example, having sex may be a momentous turning point for a woman that may suggest a long-term intimate relationship, even marriage, but it may be merely a pleasant but not very significant event for a man (Mongeau et al., 2006). Realizing for the first time that his female partner enjoys watching sports or backpacking in the wilderness, however, may be turning points for a man.

As we all know, reaching the bonding phase does not guarantee that partners will remain bonded. Also, bonding is not an idyllic state. You may not wish to remain bonded with your partner. Nevertheless, this chapter will offer several key ways to improve your chances of remaining bonded with your romantic partner if that is your desire.

Relationship Deterioration: Coming-Apart Phases

Rita Rudner once joked, "My boyfriend and I broke up. He wanted to get married and I didn't want him to." Romantic relationships often don't move in just one direction—from friendly to intimate to happy to blissful. Relationships can move forward (coming together) or backward (coming apart), and the outcome is not inevitable. Couples who were once happy but become dissatisfied don't necessarily end their relationship. The direction of a relationship can turn around in an instant. A sexual affair can provoke a partner to leapfrog from bonding to termination, skipping four phases in between that are typical of a relationship that is coming apart. A friendship that is just beginning to intensify may fall apart suddenly because of an act of violence or a perceived betrayal of trust. Nevertheless, some relationships do dissolve, not in an instant but painfully over what may seem a lifetime. *If you want to prevent the demise of a relationship, recognizing the early phases of relationship deterioration can help.* Once you get too far down the path of deterioration, it may be too late to turn around the relationship.

Differentiating: Disintegrating Begins

The first phase of disengagement is differentiating. What were thought to be similarities are discovered to be differences. The pretense of being alike in most ways begins to erode. Assertions of individuality become more frequent. Conflict occurs, although differentiating can occur without conflict. Differentiating is an expected phase in romantic relationships. In the beginning of an intimate relationship, partners may be inseparable. Later in the relationship, giving each other "some space" may be a welcome way to respond. Excessive differentiating, however, can mean trouble ahead.

Circumscribing: Don't Ask, Don't Tell

When we establish limits and restrictions on communication with our partner, we are circumscribing. Both the breadth and the depth of our communication become constrained. Fewer topics are perceived to be safe to discuss for fear of igniting a conflict, and topics that are addressed are discussed superficially. "Let's not talk about that again" becomes a familiar refrain. Communication interactions become less frequent. You've entered the danger zone in your deteriorating relationship.

Stagnating: Treading Water

Stagnating relationships aren't growing or progressing. The feeling is "nothing changes." Communication becomes even more restricted, narrow, hesitant, and awkward than in the circumscribing stage. Even stabs at discussing relationship problems are likely to provoke yet another conflict with an unhappy outcome. Communication begins resembling interactions with strangers. The relationship is barely above water and in danger of sinking.

Avoiding: The End Is Near

In the avoiding phase, partners keep a distance from each other, hoping not to interact. Separation, not connection, is desired. Partners stay away from home by working late, or they spend more time with friends. If physical separation is not possible because children need to be parented, partners' communication may be impersonal and infrequent.

Terminating: Stick a Fork in It

This is the final pulling-apart phase. The relationship is finished—cooked, ceased, done, dead, kaput! Who initiates the termination of a romantic relationship is about equal between men and women (Akert, 1998). Women, however, typically anticipate the demise of a relationship sooner than men, but men take the termination harder. Men are more depressed, lonelier, and unhappier than women following the end of a personal, romantic relationship (Unger & Crawford, 1996). Whether men initiate the breakup or are dumped, they usually prefer not to remain friends with their ex-partner. Women more often wish to remain friends regardless of who initiated the dumping. When the initiation of the breakup is mutual, men and women are about equally desirous of remaining friends (Akert, 1998).

Relationship termination can be traumatic for one or both parties. One study found that individuals who had been rejected by the person they loved spent more than 85% of their waking hours thinking about the person who jilted them. They became love zombies, lurching through life with only one thing on their minds. In addition, they exhibited lack of emotional control repeatedly for weeks or months.

Examples of such lack of emotional control included inappropriate contact by phoning, emailing, texting, pleading for reconciliation, and by dramatic entrances and exits from the rejecter's home, workplace, or social space. Uncontrollable weeping for hours and drinking excessively are other examples. This is passion gone awry that looks remarkably like withdrawal from addiction (Fisher et al., 2010).

Although there is a tendency to view the coming-together stages of relationships as good and the coming-apart stages as bad, especially given the often dramatic responses to rejection, this is not necessarily true. Some romantic relationships that appear promising initially prove to be less satisfying as we get to know the other person better. Some relationships may even be destructive to one or both parties and should not progress. Terminating abusive relationships is positive, not negative. Sometimes relationship participants have to step back before they can step forward. Stages of relationships merely describe what is, not necessarily what should be.

Sustaining Relationships: Friends, Relatives, Lovers, and Coworkers

Sustaining relationships of all kinds can be an enormous challenge. Competent communication is central to meeting this challenge. Chapter 1 discussed the importance of creating a constructive communication climate of cooperation. In this section, I expand this discussion.

Connecting Bids: Keeping Us Together

You enter your living room after a long day at work. Your partner asks you, "How was your day?" Do you utter a dismissive "Same stuff, different day"? You're having lunch with your father at a local cafe. You attempt several times to engage him in conversation, but invariably, his cell phone rings and he conducts business while you both eat.

These exchanges involve what Gottman terms bids for connection. A connecting bid is any attempt to engage another person in a positive transaction, sometimes at a deep and enduring level and other times at a superficial and fleeting level. It says, "I want to feel connected to you" if only for a brief moment (Gottman & DeClaire, 2001). A bid could be verbal, in the form of a question, statement, or comment whose content includes thoughts, feelings, observations, opinions, or invitations. A bid could also be nonverbal, in the form of a gesture, look, touch, facial expression, or vocalization (grunt, sigh).

Making Bids: Reaching Out to Others

Connecting bids vary in importance. There are the hugely significant bids such as, "Let's move in together" or "Do you want to start a business with me?" Some are seemingly insignificant requests characteristic of day-to-day communication: "Honey, will you get me a beer?" or "Mommy, will you help me tie my shoe?" or "Did you read the email I sent to you?" Some bids are subtle attempts to connect: "You look very nice today," "Good morning," or "How was your vacation?" Others can be very direct: "Do you still love me?" or "Do you think of me as a good friend?" or "May I have your phone number?" A vague bid may protect our vulnerable self-esteem, whereas a direct bid may be too risky. For example, instead of asking directly, "Do you want to see a movie with me on Saturday?" you might ask, "What's your favorite movie?" followed by "Maybe sometime we could check out one of those classic movies you love." The vague bid doesn't risk outright rejection as a more direct bid might.

Everybody makes connecting bids every day because we want to feel as though we are a part of the human experience, not alone and separate. We also want to draw close to those most important in our lives. Not all transactions with others, of course, require us to connect. When a telemarketer calls you in the middle of dinner, you probably want to be disconnected. Obnoxious individuals who harass you for a date are only encouraged by a positive response to their connecting bids. Nevertheless, making bids is a central communication process for establishing and sustaining close relationships (Gottman & DeClaire, 2001). How you respond to those bids markedly influences the communication climate for relationships to blossom or wilt.

Responses: Turning This Way and That

Every bid provokes one of three responses: turning toward, turning away, or turning against the bid (Gottman & DeClaire, 2001). The turning-toward response is a positive reaction to the bid. Your partner tells a joke and you laugh. A parent calls to ask for help moving furniture and you agree without complaint. A friend wants to talk and you engage in conversation. A coworker invites you to lunch and you accept.

Sometimes a response may appear to be negative unless you recognize an understanding that exists between two people. For example, a good male friend and I regularly engage in verbal jousting for fun. We ridicule each other, sometimes with seemingly brutal put-downs. To outsiders, it may appear that we do not like each other until they observe us laughing and amused by our verbal sparring. We perceive this feigned fighting as

friendly banter, and it connects us in friendship. Even though on the surface our put-downs appear to be turning against the other person, we understand that this is merely a friendly verbal game, and our participation is actually a turning-toward response to connecting bids. Such verbal jousting may seem odd, even repellent to some people, especially to women, who do not engage in such banter nearly as much as men do (Tannen, 2010). Nevertheless, it is a reminder that communication is not always what it seems on the surface.

The turning-away response occurs when we ignore a bid or act preoccupied when a bid is offered. You ask your partner if she wants her wash put in the dryer, and she waves dismissively as she focuses intently on her computer screen. You ask a friend at work for advice on a project, and without looking up from reading a report, he mutters, "Can't help you now." These turning-away responses are rarely malicious. The turning-away response, however, communicates, "You're not very important to me right now," at least not as important as my primary focus of attention (which is something other than you).

The turning-against response is an overtly negative rejection of a connecting bid. You ask your partner, "Do you want to watch some TV?" and your partner responds, "All you ever want to do is watch that lobotomy box. Get a life!" You offer to help your roommate clean up the clutter in your dorm room. Your roommate remarks, "Don't get your tights in a twist. I know how psycho you can get about a little mess." You approach a coworker and ask for assistance figuring out how to use a new software program. The coworker responds, "Can't help now. Try reading the manual for a change." Unlike the turning-away response, a turning-against response seems harsh, even malicious. In essence, the turning-against response says "Get lost" or "I'm angry or irritated with you."

Consequences: The Glad, the Bad, the Sad

According to research, husbands heading for divorce turn away from their wives' bids 82% of the time. Wives in similar unhappy circumstances turn away from their husbands' bids 50% of the time. Husbands and wives in strong relationships, however, rarely turn away from their spouse's bids (Gottman & DeClaire, 2001). When we turn away from the connecting bids of others, we dampen further attempts to connect. The bidder easily loses heart when a bid is ignored. In fact, attempts to rebid, to try again after an initial bid has been ignored or rejected, are near zero. This is a classic withdrawal reaction typical of a destructive communication climate (see Chapter I). No one can turn toward every connecting bid, but a pattern of turning away can destroy relationships (Gottman & Levenson, 1999).

Not surprisingly, turning against the bids of others also destroys relationships. Negative responses to connecting bids typically produce hostility or withdrawal. Although turning-against responses may seem to be the worst possible reaction one can make to a bid for connection, the research shows that turning-away and turning-against responses are about equally destructive to relationships (Gottman & DeClaire, 2001).

Emphasize Supportive Communication: How to Talk to Others

"The principle of openness implies that it is better to talk things over. The principle of supportiveness implies that it makes a great deal of difference how you talk things over" (LaFasto & Larson, 2001, p. 17). This section explains "how to talk things over" so we can prevent a defensive, competitive communication climate and establish a supportive, cooperative communication climate, a subject introduced only generally in Chapter 1 (see also Gibb, 1961).

Evaluation Versus Description

A friend of mine was in his townhouse when the 6.9-magnitude Loma Prieta earthquake hit central California. Objects flew across the rooms, kitchen cabinets emptied onto the counters and floor, and glass shattered throughout his home. When those 15 seconds of tumultuous shaking subsided, the timid voice of my friend's four-year- old daughter came from the back room: "Daddy, it wasn't my fault." We are quick to defend ourselves if we even think an evaluation might be offered.

Evaluations are value judgments made about individuals and about their actions. Statements of praise, recognition, admiration, or flattery are positive evaluations. One study found that lack of praise for accomplishments was the number one reason employees left their companies ("Praise Thy Employees," 1994). Praise for significant accomplishments plays an important part in constructing supportive communication climates.

Negative evaluation is the culprit in provoking defensiveness. Interpersonal relationships are strained by even moderate amounts of criticism, contempt, and blame (Gottman & Silver, 1994; Stone et al., 1999). We typically don't respond constructively when we're treated like IRS agents at the ceremony for a state lottery winner. Criticism produces more conflict in the workplace than mistrust, personality clashes, power struggles, or pay (Baron, 1990).

Blame, a close cousin of criticism, is no better (Stone et al., 1999). Blame seeks to pin responsibility for a perceived failure on an individual. Focusing on blame makes what has occurred more important than what should occur to solve problems. It usually leads to self-justification— the creation of excuses that absolve us of blame. "How can I be expected to remember to pick up a wedding gift when I have so much on my mind? You might try helping out more" is an example of self-justification followed by a counterattack. Self-justification "is the prime suspect in the murder of a marriage" (Tavris & Aronson, 2007, p. 172). We're focused on protecting our ego, even at the expense of our relationships.

Relationships, even casual associations with coworkers, supervisors, or distant relatives, are strained by negative evaluations. Gottman's research found that it takes at least five positive communication acts to counterbalance every negative one (Gottman & Gottman, 2006; Gottman & Silver, 1999). Failure to maintain this five-to-one magic ratio leads to relationship failure in almost all cases. Couples headed for divorce communicated fewer than one positive behavior directed toward their partners for every negative one (Gottman & Gottman, 2006). Further research reveals that even twenty acts of kindness toward your partner does not usually anesthetize the pain of a single, extremely negative "zinger" ("I hope you didn't pay for that haircut"; "You're not nearly as good as my previous boyfriend") (Notarius & Markman, 1993). How would you react if someone described you as caring, generous, sensitive, friendly, funny, and DUMB? Would even five glowing descriptors counteract the single zinger? (Remember the negativity bias discussed in Chapter 2.) The antidote to poisonous negative evaluations is not to ignore the troublesome behavior of others and glide through life uttering the cheery nostrum to "think positive." Enacting the magic ratio of positive to negative communication helps prevent negative evaluations from emerging, but when they do emerge (notice the ratio is 5 to 1 not 5 to none), being positive doesn't address the problem. The antidote is to be descriptive. A description is a first-person report of how we feel, what we perceive to be true in specific situations, and what behaviors we desire from others. As Aronson (1999) observes, "Feedback expressed in terms of feelings is a lot easier for the recipient to listen to and deal with than feedback expressed in the form of judgments and evaluations" (p. 423). Four primary steps can help you become more descriptive.

1. **Praise first, then describe.** Begin with praise before describing behavior that is problematic ("This is a well-written paper. I do have a few suggestions, however, for improvement"). This inclines recipients to accept suggestions for change, and the motives of those giving the suggestions are also more likely to be viewed as constructive (Hornsey et al., 2008). There is the risk, of course, that a "praise first" strategy might be perceived as patronizing and manipulative. "By design, humans are exquisite insincerity detectors" (Fredrickson, 2009a). Sincere praise for real accomplishment, however, minimizes defensiveness (Hornsey et al., 2008). If there is nothing worth praising or

if any praise offered would appear lame and superficial, however, then skip this step.

2. **Use I-statements, not You-statements** (Narcisco & Burkett, 1975; Notarius & Markman, 1993). I-statements begin with an identification of the speaker's feeling followed by a description of behavior connected to the feeling. "I feel ignored when my contributions receive no response" is an example. If no significant feelings emerge, simply suggest recommendations for improvement ("I have a few changes I'd like you to consider"). Any suggestion that you change something carries with it the implication that you haven't "measured up" in some way (criticism), but framing your message as an I-statement can appear less like a disapproving edict ("You need to make these changes").

3. **A You-statement of negative evaluation, on the other hand, makes you a target for blame.** "You have ignored me and you make me feel like I don't matter to you" is a statement that blames and criticizes. Expert denial from anyone so accused ("I've never ignored you") or a counterattack ("What do you expert when you act like you're starring in a Jackass movie?"). Eschewing You-statements is not always warranted to minimize defensiveness (e.g., "You might find these suggestions useful"), but try getting into the habit of using I-statements instead.

4. **Make your descriptions specific, not vague.** "I feel sort of weird when you act inappropriately around my boss" is an inexact description. "Sort of weird" and "inappropriately" require more specific description. "I feel awkward and embarrassed when you tell jokes to my boss that ridicule gays and women" makes the description much more concrete.

5. **Eliminate editorial comments.** "I get annoyed when you waste my time by talking about silly side issues" uses the first- person singular form but adds editorial language. "Waste my time" and "silly" are editorial asides that spark defensiveness and may lead to a pointless argument. Instead, say, "I get annoyed when you introduce side issues." Then provide specific

examples of side issues. If the tone of voice used is sarcastic or condescending, facial expressions are contemptuous, or gestures are abusive, of course, the editorial remains.

Control Versus Problem Orientation

"He who agrees against his will, is of the same opinion still," observed English poet Samuel Butler. Most people dislike being controlled by others. Control is communication that seeks to regulate or direct a person's behavior, such as "Get off the phone" or "Bring me food."

Controlling communication can easily lead to a contest of wills brought about by **psychological reactance** (Brehm, 1972). Psychological reactance means that the more someone tries to control our behavior and restrict our choices, the more we are inclined to resist such efforts, especially if we feel entitled to choose. For example, if upon returning to your parked car you realize that another car follows you then waits for your space, are you inclined to leave faster or slower? What if your parking stalker honked you to encourage a faster exit? One study found that most people slow their exit, especially if honked at (Ruback & Jweng, 1997).

If the pressure to restrict becomes intense, we may be strongly attracted to that which is prohibited. As advice columnist Ann Landers (1995) observed: "There are three ways to make sure something gets done: Do it yourself, hire someone to do it, or forbid your kids to do it" (p. D5). When parents oppose romantic relationships, such as a teenage daughter dating an older boy, it often intensifies feelings of romantic love (Driscoll et al., 1972). The more strongly parents admonish their children not to take drugs, smoke, or get their tongue pierced, the more likely the kids are to do those very behaviors to restore their sense of personal freedom (Dowd et al., 1988; Graybar et al., 1989). Parents step into the psychological reactance quicksand when they insist that their children obey them. Nevertheless, parents want to protect children from foolish or dangerous behavior. All controlling communication can't be eliminated, but it

can be kept to a minimum and used only when other choices are not practical.

We can prevent defensiveness from occurring when we collaborate on a problem and seek solutions cooperatively instead of demanding obedience. Parents and children can work together, brainstorming possible solutions to troublesome conflicts instead of engaging in power struggles.

Consider some examples differentiating controlling and problem-solving communication:

Controlling	Problem Orientation
Clean up your room -now!	I've asked you repeatedly to clean your room. You haven't done it. I have a problem with the chores I expect you to perform not getting done. How do you see our situation?
Stop talking on the phone	I need to make an important call. Please let me know when you're finished.
If you don't start pulling your weight. I'll fire you	We need to talk about how to improve your performance.

Manipulation Versus Assertiveness

Imagine that you have just met an interesting person at a party. This person seems very open, honest, and attentive. You are complimented by the attention this person pays you. Then imagine that you hear later from a friend that this same person was using you to gain favor with your older sibling. You were a pawn in a chess game. How would it feel to be manipulated in such a callous and deceptive way? Manipulative communication is an attempt by one person to maneuver another toward the manipulator's goal. Most people resent manipulation, especially if it is based on deception. One study of 6,000 team members in organizations found that playing politics, a particularly cutthroat form of manipulative communication, destroys interpersonal relationships and team effectiveness (LaFasto & Larson, 2001).

One summer, I sold encyclopedias for a brief time door to door, when such things were done, working out of Denver, Colorado,

I dutifully knocked on doors. The first person to invite me in was a young, friendly woman who had no idea I planned to pitch the benefits of owning encyclopedias. I was trained to camouflage what my actual purpose was for knocking on doors. Upon entering the woman's home, I was met by her inebriated husband and his unfriendly German shepherd. "If you're selling something," the unpleasant husband grumbled at me, "I'm sicking my dog on you." I manufactured an excuse and quickly left. I found refuge in the house of an elderly couple from the former Czechoslovakia who served me tea and cake and engaged in friendly conversation about "the old country" for almost three hours. I gave up trying to sell encyclopedias for the evening, having recognized how intensely people resented being disturbed by a stranger attempting to hawk his wares. I've since pondered whether that sweet couple remembered the young man who came to visit them for no apparent reason. I quickly retired from the encyclopedia business.

Assertiveness, a skill discussed at length in Chapter 7, is the antidote to manipulation. Assertiveness requires thought, skill, and concern for others. Assertive communication says, "No games are being played. This is how I feel, and this is what I need from you." It is honest and direct, unlike manipulative communication.

Indifference Versus Empathy

The Fatherhood Project at the Families and Work Institute in New York concluded, "It is presence, not absence, that often lies at the heart of troubled families. It is common for family members to be in the same room and be oblivious to each other's thoughts and feelings" (Coontz, 1997, p. 160). This indifference toward others is a sign of a disintegrating family. It also encourages further family deterioration and conflict.

The lowest self-esteem among teenagers occurs in two-parent families in which the father shows little interest in his children (Clark & Barber, 1994). Children often grow resentful of an indifferent or absent parent. This resentment can turn into outright hostility, making future reconciliation between parent and child difficult.

You counter indifference with empathy. Empathy, as defined in Chapter 1, is "thinking and feeling what you perceive another to be thinking and feeling" (Howell, 1982, p. 108). During "difficult conversations," each party tends to see the disagreement from his or her own perspective (Stone et al., 1999). Consequently, each person thinks that the other person is the problem. You don't defuse defensiveness by attacking or by assuming that all rationality and truth resides with you. Strive for understanding, not retaliation. How might a child feel when a father refuses to pay child support? What message does that send to the child? Can you feel the child's pain and understand why he or she might experience it in such a circumstance? That's empathy.

Part of empathy is promoting the positive in your relationships. You can't be indifferent to your partner while also appreciating your partner for small acts of kindness or special favors. Sustaining relationships requires you to give your partner regular, copious amounts of positive, genuine feedback verbally ("You look great," or "I love you") and non-verbally (don't forget flowers or small acts of kindness) (Pileggi, 2010). Promoting the positive in your relationships strengthens attachments, and expressing gratitude is a particularly meaningful way of emphasizing the positive. Expressing gratitude for acts of kindness or generosity enacted by your partner ("Thanks for doing those dishes when I know you're really tired") is the antithesis of indifference. Expressing gratitude is one of the most powerful communication behaviors for sustaining relationships (Fredrickson, 2009b).

Superiority Versus Equality

The line "No matter what this guy does, he thinks that no one can hold a candle to him, although a lot of people would like to" (Perret, 1994, p. 92)

expresses the typical feeling most people have to expressed superiority. The superiority attitude, which alleges others don't measure up, invites defensiveness. Who likes to be viewed as inferior in anyone's eyes? Research on boastfulness, when we brag about our superiority, reveals that braggarts are generally disliked (Holtgraves & Dulin, 1994). Research in the classroom reveals that teachers who communicate an air of superiority are also generally disliked (Rosenfeld, 1983). Leaders in groups who act superior undermine their credibility and influence with group members (Reicher et al., 2007).

Whatever the differences in our abilities, talents, and intellect, treating people with respect and civility, as equals on a human level, is supportive and encourages harmony and cooperation. Treating people like gum on the bottom of your shoe will invite defensiveness, even retaliation.

Note the difference between these examples of expressed superiority and equality:

Superiority	Equality
That's wrong!	Can you think of why that might be incorrect?
When you get to be a parent then you'll know I'm right!	Can you see why I might not agree with you on this?
I'm the boss and I know what's best	Let's discuss this and see if we can find agreement.

Certainty Versus Provisionalism

Few things in this world are certain. Death, taxes, your dryer will eat your socks, and your computer will crash at the most inopportune moment are a few that come to mind. Because most things are not certain, however, there is room for discussion and disagreement. When people make absolute, unqualified statements of certainty, they close off discussion and disagreement. Those who communicate certainty easily slip into using terms such as always, never, impossible, must, can't, and won't, as in, "You always ignore me and you never listen." The result is often that the other party withdraws from the conversation or counterattacks with an attempt to prove the know-it-all wrong (Leathers, 1970).

Provisionalism is an effective substitute for the certainty attitude. Provisionalism means qualifying your statements by avoiding absolutes (remember the probability model discussed in Chapter 6). It is communicated by using terms such as possibly, probably, perhaps, sometimes, occasionally, maybe, might, seems, and could be. Problems and issues are approached as questions to be investigated and discussed.

Defuse Defensiveness: When a Cooperative Climate Isn't Enough

Supportive communication patterns can prevent defensive, hypercompetitive responses from occurring, but what if your partner, relative, friend, or coworker becomes highly defensive despite your best efforts to create a cooperative environment? You're trying to resolve a difference of viewpoint, for example, but the other person becomes defensive the moment the subject is introduced. What do you do? There are several ways to short-circuit the defensiveness of others.

Avoid Defensive Spirals: I Didn't Do It, and Besides, They Deserved It

Lady Astor, the first female member of the British Parliament, was exasperated by Winston Churchill's opposition to several of the causes she espoused. Frustrated, she acerbically commented, "If I were your wife I would put poison in your coffee." Churchill shot back, "And if I were your husband, I would drink it" (Sherrin, 1996, p. 160). An attack produces a counterattack that can easily spiral out of control. Refuse to be drawn into a defensive spiral in which you begin sounding like two kids arguing: "You did so. You did not. Did so. Did not." This means that you speak and listen nondefensively, even if your partner, friend, relative, or coworker exhibits defensive communication patterns. This takes discipline and patience. You have control over your communication. Try using that control to create a constructive dialogue, not a malignant spiral of defensiveness.

Focus on the Problem, Not the Person: Keep Your Eye on the Prize

Unless the problem is the other person, stick to the agenda for discussion. Do not make turning-against responses even if the connecting bid is provocative. For example, this kind of diverting response is not advisable:

SHASHA: We need to go out more. We don't do anything exciting.

MIKE: Do you have to tap your fingers on the table all the time? It drives me nuts. Maybe we'd go out more if you didn't irritate me so much.

When serious issues get detoured by irrelevant remarks about the person, not the problem, and turning-against responses are made to connecting bids, defensiveness is encouraged (Fisher & Brown, 1988). Mike's response diverts attention from the issue raised and centers the discussion on irritating mannerisms. That shifts the agenda and will likely induce a counterattack. Shasha could respond to the criticism of her finger tapping this way: "We can talk about my finger tapping another time. Let's discuss going out more often, and let's do it without insulting each other." Staying focused on the problem and being constructive can defuse defensiveness.

Address Relationship Deterioration: Beyond Sustaining

As relationships fall apart, the desire to turn the direction around and rebuild the connection is typically stymied by the negative atmosphere that pervades the deteriorating relationship. It is difficult to short-circuit a failing relationship and recapture the "magic" that once existed between people. It is especially difficult if infidelity is an issue. Depending on the survey, about 25% of married men and women will cheat on their spouses sometime during their lifetime (Tafoya & Spitzberg, 2007). *Mate poaching*— "trying to woo an individual away from a committed relationship to begin a relationship with them instead" (Tsapelas et al., 2011)—is even more prevalent,

running at 60% for men and 53% for women (Schmitt & Buss, 2001).

Sometimes we don't recognize threats to our relationships soon enough or see that our relationships are deteriorating. We're too busy to notice, or there's too much going on in our lives to respond effectively and quickly to the erosion of love and intimacy and the infidelity that often ensues. It is critical that you respond quickly to the first signs of deterioration in your relationships. Waiting until you're standing at cliff's edge may be too late to save what once was an important part of your life. All the suggestions for sustaining relationships supported by extensive research must be applied with extra vigor if you want to salvage a relationship in crisis.

1. *Resist the temptation to reciprocate negative communication.* Fighting fire with fire will make toast of your relationship. Remain unconditionally constructive. Negativity bias is especially problematic in a relationship in crisis, so avoid the negative comments.
2. *Seek opportunities to praise; compliment, and bolster your partner.* Supportive communication is critical when a relationship begins to hit the skids. "You sure have been working hard," "You look nice," and "That place couldn't run without you" are examples of the type of communication that can begin to turn around a negative communication climate.
3. *Avoid at all costs turning-away and turning-against responses to connecting bids.* You don't repair relationships by choosing communication responses that tear apart bids that connect two people. Find every opportunity to make turning-toward responses to bids of your partner. Make this your raison d'etre, your vital concern.

Cross-Sex Friendships: Sustaining with Complications

Cross-sex friendships are becoming more common and significant (Monsour, 2002). They also can be especially fragile and challenging to sustain (Werking, 1997). Part of the reason is that we typically make a stronger effort to sustain same-sex friendships than cross-sex friendships (Afifi et al., 1994; Rose, 1985). Cross-sex friendships are complicated by ambiguity regarding romantic and sexual potential (Guerrero & Chavez, 2005). This uncertainty can inhibit maintenance efforts (Dainton, 2003).

There are four types of cross-sex friendships, each requiring different maintenance behaviors to sustain the relationship (Guerrero & Chavez, 2005). They are mutual romance (you believe that both of you want the friendship to become romantic), strictly platonic (you believe that you and your friend both want the relationship to remain nonsexual and nonromantic), desires romance (you want the relationship to become romantic but you believe your friend does not want this), and rejects romance (you do not want the relationship to become romantic but you believe your friend does).

Behaviors aimed at sustaining cross-sex friendships are many and varied. They include being pleasant and complimentary, self-disclosing private information, sharing activities, being supportive, sharing tasks, incorporating circles of friends, flirting, engaging in humor, talking about the relationship, and acting jealous or trying to change the friend in some way (Guerrero & Chavez, 2005). The more uncertainty in the cross-sex relationship, the less routine contact and activities, relational talk, self-disclosure, and humor are used. The avoidance of such activities and conversations attempts to maintain the relationship as it is, not as one partner may wish it to be. If one person wants romance but the other does not, the person rejecting the romance may avoid frequent contact and joint activities to discourage any misunderstandings. The person hoping for romance with a partner who seems uninterested may avoid such contact and activities as well for fear of rejection or to safeguard the friendship (Messman et al., 2000). Disclosing romantic feelings (expressing a desire to move from platonic to romantic) inevitably complicates a friendship if one party doesn't want romance to flower.

Research on sustaining cross-sex friendships is in its infancy. Clearly, most people sense that cross-sex friendships can be complicated by uncertainty and asymmetry (contradictory desires for the friendship such as one person wanting romance and the other not wanting it). If you are in the situation of wanting romance to develop but are uncertain whether your friend shares this, approach carefully. If you offer subtle hints of romantic interest and they are avoided or discouraged by your friend, recognize that continuing along the path of pursuing romance may result in the demise of your friendship. You have to decide whether you can keep the relationship platonic when you desire more.

Technology and Competent Interpersonal Relationships

Communication technologies markedly influence our relationships with others and our lives in general. Whether this influence is positive or negative is a subject of lively debate. Let's examine the interpersonal effects of communication technologies.

Social Contact: The Influence of Technology

In 2010, 240 million Americans were using the Internet, second only to China with 420 million users. That's more than three-quarters of the American population ("Internet World Statistics" 2010). Cell phone use among adults in the United States hit 82% by 2011 ("Cell Phones and American Adults," 2011), making those who don't use a cell phone a rarity (some would say dinosaurs). These two technologies in particular have markedly changed our social lives and our communication with others.

Benefits: Expanding Social Networks

The technological advances provided by the Internet and cell phones offer a number of social benefits (Bargh & McKenna, 2004). Internet sites such as Facebook, which had 600 million users worldwide by 2011, and Twitter, which had 175 million users worldwide by the same year

("Internet," 2011), have provided an opportunity for individuals to expand their social networks beyond anything possible in previous historical periods. An early study of Internet and social media use provoked some concern about social isolation spawned by overuse of social networking and Internet sites. More time spent online may lead to less time spent with family and friends engaged in face-to-face social activities (see Kraut et al., 1998). Concern was also raised about online addiction.

Despite these initial concerns, the great hulk of more recent research shows no such negative effects when the Internet is used in moderation (DiSalvo, 2010; Rainie et al., 2011). An Associated Press-Viacom poll reported that 9 out of 10 high school and college students surveyed saw social networking as a tool to keep in close touch with family and friends ("Social Media," 2011). A Pew Research study concludes: "Although some commentators have expressed fears that technology pulls families apart, this survey finds that couples use their phones to connect and coordinate their lives, especially if they have children at home. American spouses often go their separate ways during the day, but remain connected by cell phones and to some extent by internet communications" (Kennedy et al., 2008). Another Pew Research study found that Facebook users, on average, have more close relationships, receive more social support from others, and are more politically engaged than non-users ("Social Networking Sites," 2011). Cell phones and the Internet have largely been responsible for less television watching, not less connection with others.

Romantic relationships are also affected by the new technologies. One study found that the more the use of voice calls by individuals in romantic relationships "the stronger the love and commitment with their partners" (Jin & Pena, 2010). Mobile voice calls seem to allow couples to experience the feeling of continuous connection. Texting, however, does not appear to have a positive effect on romantic couples. Different channels produce different results (see Chapter 1), and texting may be too restrictive or devoid of emotional complexity to function effectively in romantic contexts.

A three-year study in Sweden, Portugal, Great Britain, and Ireland shows that older people get a psychological boost from online communication (cited in Marcus, 1999). Family therapist Howard Adelman encourages his older patients to use email to counteract loneliness and depression. "Seniors are often depressed, and with depression comes withdrawal. Email brings them back to the world" (Marcus, 1999, p. 62). Although older Americans are the least likely to use the Internet and social networking sites, their numbers are mushrooming rapidly. By 2011, 42% of adults 65 or older were using the Internet, up from 10% a decade earlier (Wolverton, 2011). The age group 50-64 has gone from 11% who used social networking sites in 2008 to 47% who did by mid-2010. Those aged 65 and older went from 5% in 2008 to 26% by mid-2010 (Swift, 2010).

Online support groups can also connect people who face troublesome physical or emotional problems (Barnes, 2001). "These groups are focused on a mutually recognized need for emotional support and feedback. Members offer each other encouragement in dealing with a medical or mental affliction that they share in common with other members of the group" (King, 1995). People with physical limitations that make face-to-face support group participation difficult and individuals who could never get together in person because of geographic distances can meet in virtual support groups. Although online support groups are still not widely used, one study found that those with serious and chronic health conditions used support groups far more than those in better health (Owen et al., 2010).

Business can be more easily conducted with cell phones and the Internet. A study by Plantronics of more than 1,800 business professionals from six countries revealed that 83% consider email "critical" to their work success and productivity, and 81% said the same about cell phones (only 38% said the same about instant messaging and 19% about social networking) ("Plantronics Study," 2010). Telecommuting, what the U.S. Department of Labor defines as "pay for work at an alternate site," has become widespread. In 2011, 34 million adults in the United States telecommuted at least part time. That number is expected to increase to 63 million by 2016 (Winters, 2011). According to the Telework Research Network, however, only a fraction of this number (about 3 million) work exclusively at home ("Statistics," 2011). Telecommuting provides more flexible hours for employees to work (not strictly a 9 to 5 workday), results in significantly less work-life conflict and stress than office-based employees experience (Fon- ner & Roloff, 2010), and typically saves resources (less driving) and can put less wear and tear on one's health (less stress from sitting in traffic jams or traveling long distance to and from a worksite).

Drawbacks: Negative Transactions

Telecommuting definitely has its advantages. Unfortunately, the ease and flexibility often obtained from telecommuting can be offset by workaholism (Amour, 2007). With Smartphones, computer laptops, and notebooks, escape from work responsibilities has become increasingly difficult—at the expense of relationships. As Ken Siegel, president of The Impact Group, a collection of psychologists who consult with management of leading global companies, explains, "Extreme work is real. The technological age has exacerbated this problem beyond belief. You can take work into the shower or bath. There's no escape" (quoted in Amour, 2007).

Sticking with drawbacks in work environments, Nucleus Research in Boston determined that almost half of workforce employees access Facebook during work hours. The average time spent on the site was 15 minutes a day. Avid users averaged two hours per day on the site. Most employees (87%) were not using Facebook for work-related tasks. Most usage was for social networking on the job. This "social notworking" costs companies 1.5% in total lost productivity. This is a small percentage, but it runs into the billions of dollars ("Facebook," 2009).

There are some potential drawbacks on the psychological front as well. Lonely people who access the Internet and social networking sites do not assuage their feeling of social isolation.

Psychologist Laura Freberg notes that "chronic loneliness makes people act in ways that push others away. Social networking isn't equipped to handle that and can actually make it worse" (quoted in DiSalvo, 2010, p. 52). Obsessive-compulsive individuals also may use social networking sites in obsessive ways. "A consistent factor across many of the studies in this realm is that social networking is simply a new forum for bad habits" (DiSalvo, 2010, p. 55).

Cell phones can also be a source of some concern. In an elegant San Antonio, Texas, nightclub, a jazz singer was entertaining the crowd when a cell phone rang. The patron answered the phone, then shushed the singer so the patron could hear the call. In Palo Alto, California, a food fight nearly broke out when one customer complained loudly about eight cell phone calls disrupting his meal. One survey by Harris Interactive for Intel found that 63% of respondents were irked by loud talking on cell phones in a restaurant or other public places (Johnson, 2009). Cell phone users can be seen conducting conversations while walking down the street bouncing off passersby like balls in a pinball machine, seemingly oblivious to their surroundings. Restaurants, theaters, and museums from coast to coast have begun creating "cell phone-free zones" or banning cell phone conversations entirely by posting "No Cell Phones" signs at entrances. Cell phone use while driving has become a legislative issue in most states. Movie theaters routinely flash requests to turn off cell phones during the showing of films. Such requests are often ignored by cell phone junkies who feel compelled to text message every five minutes during the movie, distracting others with their brightly lit phone screens. Teachers at all education levels regularly instruct students to turn off cell phones before classes begin, but it is rare that at least one cell phone doesn't interrupt a class session.

Personal conversations formerly relegated to one's home, private office, or possibly an enclosed phone booth now regularly take place in crowded restaurants, buses, airport waiting areas, even in public bathrooms. "By engaging in a call, mobile phone users are capable of transforming public space into their own private space, often at the expense of others around them" (Campbell, 2008, p. 70). The Harris survey found that 55% of respondents reported that they were bothered by private cell phone discussions in public places. One study found that overhearing someone engaged in conversation on a cell phone is more irksome than overhearing two physically present individuals engaged in conversation because in the latter they hear a dialogue but in the former they hear only a "halfalogue." A **halfalogue**—hearing only half the conversation—is more distracting because your brain tries to figure out the unheard part of the conversation (Emberson et al., 2010). It's more difficult to tune out the cell phone conversation.

Cell phone conversations in public places such as theaters and classrooms are considered particularly intrusive and inappropriate among individualistic Americans ("You're disturbing *me*"). In collectivist countries, public cell phone use is more tolerated because keeping in contact with members of an in-group (family, work, etc.) is considered more important than preventing strangers who are not in a preferred group from becoming irritated (Campbell, 2008). Etiquette, our set of rules for appropriate public communication, has not kept up with technological change.

Online Romance: Cyberlove

Online dating services have become increasingly popular and enormously lucrative. Dating sites such as Match.com and eHarmony were raking in about $4 billion annually by 2011 (Whysall, 2011). The depth of online relationships, however, certainly can be questioned, and since there is no physical proximity, you can hardly separate the truth from fiction (Epstein, 2007). Pictures on profiles can be 20 years old, or may even be photos of other, presumably better-looking people. A study of more than 5,000 online daters reported that there is a fair amount of lying and exaggeration on these sites. Women are inclined to lie about their weight, and men are inclined to lie about their age, income, personality, and interests (Hall et al., 2010). One study asked almost 5,000 online daters to respond to the statement: "People

who I have met online have said they were dating only me when they were also involved with someone else." Thirty-nine percent responded that this happened to them "constantly," and another 19% said it occurred "frequently" or "occasionally" (Albright, 2007).

Despite effusively positive advertising from eHarmony, Match.com, and other dating services extolling the virtues of online dating ("find your soul mate"), independent studies show that satisfaction among the users is low (Thompson et al., 2005). A survey of more than 2,000 online subscribers by Jupiter research reported that barely a quarter were satisfied with online dating services (cited in Epstein, 2007). A Pew Internet and American Life Project survey found that 66% of Internet users consider online dating dangerous ("Pew Internet," 2006). A team of psychologists, in a white paper about online dating services, concluded: "When eHarmony recommends someone as a compatible match, there is a 1 in 500 chance that you'll marry this person. . . . Given that eHarmony delivers about 1.5 matches a month, if you went on a date with all of them, it would take 346 dates and 19 years to reach [a] 50% chance of getting married." The paper goes on to conclude that "there is no evidence that . . . scientific psychology is able to pair individuals who will enjoy happy, lasting marriages" (Thompson et al., 2005; see also Epstein, 2007).

Perhaps enduring, joyful marriages are unlikely to develop from online dating, but what about merely pursuing a good time by dating online? Even this limited pursuit doesn't seem to pan out for most people. Respondents to one study found that participants spent an average of 5.2 hours each week looking through profiles and 6.7 hours responding to emails. On a question asking about enjoyment of online dating, respondents averaged 5.5 on a 10-point scale (10 = very much and 1 = not at all) (Frost et al., 2008). Only 3% of committed relationships typically result from online dating services ("More Think It Is Important," 2006). The effort required to search multitudinous profiles and the high expectations created by inflated profiles often lead to disappointment when in-person dates materialize (Sprecher, 2011).

Conflict: Hurling Electronic Flames

Messages communicated by email, texting, or tweeting can be easily misinterpreted.

Sarcasm, for instance, or teasing without the requisite tone of voice, facial expressions, and physical cues that signal how the message should be interpreted can be mistaken for serious personal attacks. Emoticons, graphic notations that indicate emotional information, can help in this regard. Emoticons for a smile (:)), or a frown (:() can indicate a proper tone for a message. Men, however, especially when conducting business by email, may resist using emoticons because they are more closely associated with female communication patterns, and they may seem unprofessional. Emoticons also don't produce understanding if receivers are unfamiliar with them.

Email also reduces the natural constraints on incivility and hostility that come from facing a person directly (Thompson & Nadler, 2002; Van Kleef et al., 2004). Conflict can turn destructive more easily when mediated by technology than when conducted face to face (Holahan et al. 2008; Zornoza et al., 2002). **Flaming** is a cyber-term for an abusive, attacking written message between Internet users (emailed; text messaged; blog comment; Playstation interplay). Typical attributes of an electronic flame include profanity, the use of all capital letters, and excessive exclamation points or question marks (Turnage, 2007). The absence of normal constraints on incivility and hostility that come with in-person transactions (e.g., implicit rules against ugly public displays of anger) often couple with the ease and swiftness of email to the detriment of relationships (Wallace, 1999). As Brin (1998) explains,

> Electronic conversations seem especially prone to misinterpretation, suddenly and rapidly escalating hostility between participants, or else triggering episodes of sulking silence. When flame wars erupt, normally docile people can behave like mental patients. … Typing furiously, they send impulsive text messages blurting out the first vituperation that comes to mind, abandoning the editing process of common courtesy that civilization took millennia to acquire, (p. 166)

Flaming is competitive, defensive communication. Those given to flaming often experience sender's regret—they wish they hadn't sent the angry, emotionally damaging message in the heat of the moment. Once it is sent, however, the damage is done.

So, what can you do if using communication technologies increases hostile conflict? Here are four suggestions.

1. *Use communication technologies selectively.* The cell phone can be an electronic lasso that binds us to others, or what Shenk (1997) calls "electronic leashes," if we can never escape their intrusiveness. Plan for times during each day when you will have no access to any of these technologies. Shut off the computer, switch off the cell phone, and turn off the television set. Decompress your stress that can trigger flames. Try simple conversation or social activities with no technological distractions.

2. *Delay sending any email message that has strong emotional content.* If you want to avoid sender's regret, delay sending any email or text message written in the heat of the moment. Flaming email messages should always be put aside overnight. Never send an angry response to someone else's flame until you have had time to cool down. If an immediate response is required, simply ask for time to reflect on what was said and the way it was said.

3. *Do not use email to fire or to reprimand an employee, to offer negative work appraisals, or to tender resignations.* These highly personal matters should be conducted face to face (Zornoza et al., 2002).

4. *Exercise etiquette on the Net.*

Intercultural Relationships and Communication Competence

Different cultures have different perspectives on love and intimacy. When individuals from cultures with different perspectives develop friendships or romantic relationships, difficulties inevitably arise.

Intercultural Friendships: Additional Challenges

The very definition of friendship varies among cultures (Martin & Nakayama, 2008). Americans have many types of friendships. Other cultures do not have casual friends and close friends. The "special emotional relationship" that exists in only some close friendships in America is a requirement for any designation of friendship in Germany and India, for example. If you are accorded friendship status, there has to be that special emotional bond.

The initial stages of a developing friendship between individuals from different cultures present three problems (Martin & Nakayama, 2007). First, the differences in values, perceptions, and communication style can be troublesome. These are deep-seated, not superficial, differences (see Chapter 3). Second, anxiety is a common experience in the initial stages of any friendship, but intercultural friendships are likely to induce greater anxiety. We experience greater fear of making mistakes and causing offense when we are unfamiliar with the norms and rules of another culture. Third, overcoming stereotypes about a different culture and resisting the impulse to be ethnocentric can be difficult (see Chapter 3).

A study of American and Japanese students who were friends revealed some interesting ways to nurture intercultural friendships (Sudweeks et al., 1990). First, some similarities that transcend the cultural differences must be discovered, whether they are sports, hobbies, lifestyle, or political attitudes. Bridges must be constructed from common experience. Second, making time for the relationship is critical. It takes more time to develop a friendship with a member of another culture because we are typically drawn to others who are like us, not to those who are unlike us. Third, sharing the same group of friends can be very important. A shared group of friends can lend support to an intercultural relationship. Finally, capitalizing on key turning points (requesting a favor; revealing a personal secret) is especially vital in developing cross-cultural friendships. Reluctance to respond positively to a turning point may be perceived as an insult and might end the relationship.

Ultimately, cross-cultural friendships require more "care and feeding" (Pogrebin, 1987) than do friendships between similar individuals. More explaining and understanding must take place. "Mutual respect, acceptance, tolerance for the faux pas and the occasional closed door, open discussion and patient mutual education, all this gives crossing friendships—when they work at all—a special kind of depth" (Pogrebin quoted in Gudykunst & Kim, 1992, p. 318).

Intercultural Romance: Tougher Than Friendships

Romantic relationships can be even stickier than friendships. Once the difficulties of developing a friendship have been overcome, additional problems can develop when romance flowers. Families may raise a stink about cross-cultural friendships, and romance may intensify this opposition (Kouri & Lasswell, 1993). Opposition from one's family isn't necessarily based on prejudice, although surely bigotry sometimes plays a part. Concerns about child-rearing styles, religious differences, politics, gender roles, power issues, place of residence, and rituals and ceremonies may also increase opposition.

Romano (1988) identifies four strategies that are used in intercultural marriages. Submission is the most common strategy. One partner abandons his or her culture and submits to the partner's culture, adopting the religion, value system, politics, and so forth. This is rarely effective because individuals find it enormously difficult to erase their core cultural values and background. A second strategy, compromise, means giving up only part of one's cultural beliefs, values, and habits. This is also very difficult in most situations. Asking one partner to forego Christmas decorations and celebration while the other partner is asked not to observe the Muslim holy month Ramadan isn't likely to be a smooth compromise. A third strategy, obliteration, is sometimes used. Obliteration occurs when both partners attempt to erase their respective cultures from the relationship. This is difficult to accomplish, and it means avoiding basic support groups such as family and friends. Finally, there is consensus, which seems to work best. Consensus is based on negotiation and cooperation. Learning the partner's language, studying the religion, and learning about the cuisine erect bridges between partners. Consensus is built by emphasizing similarities and commonalities in relationships and by de-emphasizing differences. Consensus is difficult even among culturally similar individuals. It is doubly difficult between culturally dissimilar individuals who plan to marry.

Summary

Developing relationships with others is a human imperative. Nature inclines us toward such connections. We form relationships because we have a need to belong, because we are attracted interpersonally to those who are physically attractive, similar to us, and reciprocate our liking them, and because relationships with others can provide benefits that outweigh costs. Relationships are more challenging than ever. Every relationship travels through specific stages. Recognizing what communication behaviors work best at each stage is important to the development of intimate romantic relationships and close friendships. Keeping a relationship from moving into the coming-apart stages is a principal concern. We sustain relationships in a variety of ways; the most important are by understanding the value of connecting bids and our responses to those bids, avoiding defensive communication patterns, and encouraging supportive communication.

Advances in technology influence our relationships with others in powerful ways. Technology can help sustain relationships, or it can become an electronic leash that adds stress to our lives and threatens the health of our relationships. Intercultural relationships are probably the most challenging of all. Individuals from collectivist cultures have a We-emphasis, but persons from individualist cultures have a Me-emphasis. This fundamental distinction in cultural values can put a strain on an intercultural relationship.

13. An Overview of the TV Industry

by Martie Cook

This chapter begins a series of profession-focused chapters address-ing key elements of a communication-based career field. Television is a pervasive part of modern society and has been for several decades. For students of communication it is important to understand some of the basic components that result in message creation. This chapter focuses on the writing aspect of the television industry, but also provides interest-ing insights into the business of television, the impact of technology on the career, and key terminology unique to the field. Whether a student wants to become a television writer, producer, or simply a more informed consumer of television messages, this chapter is a valuable read.

The one constant about television is that television is constantly changing. The way the business operates today won't be precisely how it works tomorrow.

Understanding what drives television as an industry can be almost as important to your career as writing a solid script. In the same way insurance salesmen stand around the water cooler talking about new state regulations, as a writer you must be in the know about the entertainment industry. You must possess a wealth of knowledge of where television has been in the past, where it stands today, and perhaps most significantly where it is headed in the future. On any given day, topics like what shows are hot, what shows are not, and who the show runners are and where they came from (as in what shows they used to run) must roll off your tongue like a second language.

Staying on top of this ever-changing picture can be more than a challenge. The best and easiest way to stay current is to read the industry trade journals, namely *Variety* and *The Hollywood Reporter*. These daily magazines are delivered to studio and network executives as well as to writers and producers and directors. Nearly everyone in the business from the most seasoned professional to the newest intern reads these papers faithfully every day. So should you. It is here that you will find up-to-date information on the industry in which you plan to become employed. You will discover precious tidbits like recent deals that have been made, TV shows that have been picked up, TV shows that have been canceled, who is suing who and why, TV ratings, who's been hired, who's been fired, and hundreds of other pieces of important information that will help keep you in the know. The last thing you want is to find yourself in the company of industry insiders and you can't join the conversation because you are uninformed.

> "Come to Hollywood. Go to as many parties and events as you can. Stay somewhat sober so that when you speak, people can understand your words. Then rub elbows with as many people as physically possible. Remember … don't go to parties with people who are plumbers and mechanics. They really won't help your writing career. Also get the industry trades: *Variety* or *The Hollywood Reporter*. If you can't afford to buy them, steal them. Read the articles. Know what's going on in the business. Remember the names of people you read. These people will be at these parties and events. Talk to them with the knowledge you get from these trades.

Compliment them. They will love you. They may remember you. They may hire you. Oh, and have a spec script or two in the wings that you can send them in case they ask."

John Frink, co-executive producer,
The Simpsons

If you live in New York or Los Angeles, *Variety* and *The Hollywood Reporter* are relatively easy to get your hands on. If you live outside of these two cities, you can get a subscription either by mail or online. You should also make a habit of reading the *L.A. Times* Entertainment and Business sections. If you don't have time to do this every day, you should at least make a valiant attempt to read them on Sunday. Again, they are loaded with industry news. And since you are in a reading mode, plan to devour the same sections of *The New York Times*—and while you are at it, be sure to make *The Wall Street Journal* part of your routine as well. Knowledge is power. If you are to succeed as a television writer, you can't live in a shell. It is imperative you are up to date with what is going on in your industry, and that includes even the seemingly minor stuff.

At the risk of overwhelming you, while I have recommended certain sections in the above papers, the truth is that you should read at least one major newspaper cover-to-cover every day. If you absolutely don't have time to do that, then make sure that you catch at least one TV newscast per day. Turn on the local news while you are getting ready for school or work. Flip on CNN while you are eating dinner. Television is a reflection of society and the way we live our lives. To succeed as a writer, not only do you need to know what is going on in the big, bad world around you, but you also need to have an opinion about it—and you need to be prepared to put that opinion forward in a clear, concise way at any given moment. Good scripts have definitive points of view. How can you have a point of view on something you know nothing about?

In addition to your writing, you will also need to be up to speed on current events in order to carry on intelligent conversations with people in the industry. There tends to be a huge misconception among young, wannabe writers that those in the entertainment business (Californians in particular) are a bunch of shallow, not-so-bright people who sit around all day waxing their surfboards and bodies. Let me assure you—just the opposite is true. While every industry has its share of morons, I have found the majority of people who work in entertainment to be incredibly smart. They are up to date with what's going on in the world around them. These are people who know the names of their senators and congressmen and how to reach them. Do you? If not, it's time to get on the ball.

It's Called Show Business for a Reason

Most writers will tell you that the entertainment industry today is about 30% "show" and 70% "business." Like every other major corporation around the globe, studios and networks exist for one reason and one reason alone—to make money. The same way Ford profits by selling cars, and Coca-Cola makes money off of its soft drinks, studios and networks make money off of their shows. If a show isn't bringing in revenue, it will be canceled.

Television shows, often along with careers, live and die by what are known as the Nielsen ratings. Nielsen is the primary industry-approved company that gathers important data on what shows America is watching. In analyzing those numbers, it is also easy to see what America isn't watching. The tricky thing about Nielsen ratings is that, while technology tells us what shows people are tuning in to see, there is no real effective way to gauge whether viewers actually like or dislike the programs they choose. Ironically, when all is said and done, this amazingly creative industry is driven by math. The bigger a show's ratings, the more advertising dollars that show generates. This is the reason super bowl ads are notoriously sky high.

> "I have a tremendous respect for the audience. I believe the audience knows what they want, and I believe television

is a reflection of that. If you respect the audience and respect what they want, it's easier to create programming."

> Lucie Salhany, former chairman, FOX Broadcasting Company; founding president and former CEO, United Paramount Network (UPN)

Once upon a time, if a show wasn't doing well in the ratings, but it had critical acclaim—or the network brass believed in it—the network would stand behind it and keep it on the air, giving it a chance to catch on. Today that is simply not the case. With production costs skyrocketing, if a network doesn't see an almost immediate return on its investment, the show is taken off the air. Likewise, letter-writing campaigns were once considered a powerful weapon that television audiences had at their disposal. If viewers were passionate about a particular show, but it had low ratings and the network decided to cancel it, fans could—and would—write letters by the truckload, asking the network to reconsider. Many of these campaigns were successful in saving several shows from certain death, including *Star Trek* (the original series) and *Cagney and Lacey*.

While letter-writing (and now e-mail) campaigns still happen, the punch they pack isn't nearly as powerful as it once was. You may argue that *Family Guy*, which was canceled and then returned to the air, was a result of such a letter-writing campaign. While letters and e-mails from fans may have contributed to the Griffins' return, insiders will tell you that the show's resurrection was more likely a direct result of its popularity in reruns on The Cartoon Network combined with the release of a *Family Guy* DVD, which sold like hotcakes. Thus, FOX realized the show was a potential gold mine. And this is what it all comes down to. In this day and age, shows must perform financially or they go bye-bye.

No one is immune to this rule, including those programs that are backed by powerhouse producers with proven track records. Case in point: *Arrested Development*. Produced by Imagine Entertainment (Oscar-winner Ron Howard's well-respected company), the show had a cult following, won critical acclaim and garnered Emmy awards, including the highly coveted Best Comedy Series. Sadly, *Arrested Development* had big buzz, but lacked acceptable ratings. So FOX pulled the plug.

Technology Is Changing the Face of Television

Technology is quickly altering how and when America watches television. Television is no longer just about the box in the living room that families gather around like they did in the fifties and sixties. Today, in addition to broadcasts, we now have podcasts, which generally require that content be much shorter in length. As I write this, networks and cable companies are scrambling to make deals here, there, and everywhere to get their content distributed through the various means now afforded by technology. Some writers and producers tend to shy away from technology, preferring to focus only on the creative aspects of the industry. If you are one of these people, I say "wake up and smell the coffee cake." Technology is no longer something reserved for pimple-faced geeks and nerds. Rather, it is something everybody in our industry from the high-powered executive to the just-starting-out intern must be aware of and stay on top of in order to be successful.

> "Have a working knowledge of alternative distribution platforms like broadband, PDAs, and cell phones. Increasingly, all programs are being asked to provide different versions to meet the growing demand for alternative delivery systems. It is the near-term future of our business."
>
> Joel Cheatwood, executive director/
> program development, CNN

Product Integration

For decades, networks have relied heavily on Nielsen ratings to set advertising rates. But experts and insiders agree that big changes loom on the horizon. Devices like TiVo, On Demand, iPods, cell phones, and the Internet, which allow viewers to watch programs at their leisure, skipping the very ads that paid for the shows to be made, are all-but-guaranteed to revolutionize the entire television industry.

While no one knows for sure exactly what the future holds in terms of television advertising, product integration—at least in series television and movies of the week—is a good bet. In the past, writing specific products into scripts has been something writers had to stay away from. If a company didn't pay for advertising, networks were not going to promote their product for free. In the future, advertising dollars may well come from product integration, which will work much as it does in feature films. Just as E.T. liked Reese's Pieces, we may soon discover that the TV characters we have come to know and love possess certain commercial tastes as well. As this book goes to press, there is huge debate in the industry as to whether writers will be forced to advertise products within the context of a story. Instead of the generic line, "I'm gonna get a soda," TV characters in the future may proudly announce, "I'm gonna get a Caffeine-free Diet Vanilla Coke, made with Nutra-Sweet"(okay, that might be an exaggeration, but you get the point).

Most writers are resistant to this idea, feeling as though it cramps creativity and forces them to write dialogue that is neither character-specific nor natural. At the same time, despite the opposition, writers understand that the industry is changing, and if they want to survive, they will have to change with it. That doesn't mean they are taking it lying down. Currently, the Writers Guild of America, along with other Hollywood unions, is in talks about codes of conduct and ethical issues involving product integration. Writers are also investigating the possibility of being paid for by incorporating advertisements in their scripts.

The Role of Production Companies, Studios, and Networks

Production companies, studios, and networks work hand in hand. Production companies produce the product. Networks air the product. Think of it this way: without production companies, networks would have little if any programming to broadcast. Without networks, production companies would have a difficult time getting their shows in front of an audience.

No doubt you have heard of the major studios with giant, internationally recognized names such as Warner Bros., Universal, Paramount, and Sony. What you may not realize is that under the umbrella of these large companies are much smaller production entities with names you probably aren't as familiar with, or maybe even heard of at all. These smaller companies produce the shows in conjunction with the name studio. Most, if not all of the networks also have their own in-house production companies. Until recently, studios were completely independent from networks. Now, because of an FCC (Federal Communications Commission) ruling that eased rules on mergers, the relationship between studios and networks is much more incestuous. It's no longer Universal or NBC. Rather, they are one and the same: NBC Universal. The same is true with ABC and Disney, and CBS and Paramount. As if that weren't confusing enough, even though NBC Universal may now be one conglomerate, every television show that is produced at Universal doesn't necessarily air on NBC. And if that doesn't make you dizzy enough, try adding in the numerous other media outlets that fall under a particular banner. For example, it's no surprise that the Disney Channel and ABC Family are part of the Walt Disney Company.

The Difference Between Network And Syndication

In the golden days of television there were three networks—ABC, CBS, and NBC. Today we can add FOX and the CW to that distinguished list.

All networks have affiliates. Affiliates are smaller stations in every market around the country. Some affiliates are known in industry jargon as O&Os—meaning they are owned and operated by the network. Others are privately owned either by companies or individuals.

Affiliates broadcast the programs carried by the network with which they are affiliated. For example, you should be able to find the *Today* show on every NBC affiliate in America, but you would never find it on a CBS affiliate. Affiliates make a commitment to carry network programming. However, they have the right to—and will on occasion—back out of this deal if the network offers programming they feel may be inappropriate or could get them fined by the FCC. Though this rarely happens, it occasionally does. Some ABC affiliates chose not to air the historic *Ellen* coming-out episode. While most considered this to be ground-breaking television, some considered it inappropriate. Likewise, several affiliates refused to air Steven Spielberg's Academy Award-winning film, *Saving Private Ryan*, because of indecency concerns—namely violence and language—things that can get affiliates in hot water with the FCC. Along the same lines, some CBS affiliates refused to air *9/11*, a top-notch documentary about the September 11th terrorist attacks in New York City because some of the firemen muttered obscenities. (In their defense, who wouldn't, with all they must have seen and dealt with that day?) Surprisingly, despite rave revues, some CBS affiliates stuck to their guns with a steadfast refusal to air, deeming the language to be unsatisfactory for their audiences.

There are certain time periods each day during which most affiliates run network programming. The most lucrative is what's known as prime time. Traditionally, prime time is 8:00 p.m. to 11:00 p.m. Eastern and Pacific and 7:00 p.m. to 10:00 p.m. Central and Mountain Monday through Saturday. (Sunday, it starts one hour earlier). With the addition of FOX and the CW, there is "common prime," which is 8:00 p.m. to 10:00 p.m. Eastern and Pacific and 7:00 p.m. to 9:00 p.m. Central and Mountain (again, it begins one hour earlier on Sunday). Affiliates also tend to carry network programming in the morning, with programs such as the *Today* show and *Good Morning America*. Many will then break for a local newscast and pick up network programming again in the afternoon.

Other blocks of time such as early morning, late afternoon, and early evening are set aside for each affiliate to put whatever it chooses on the air. Most, if not all, stations produce their own newscasts. Some may produce other local programming such as a news magazine or a public affairs show. Due to exorbitant production costs, most affiliates can't afford to produce much original programming—in most cases not enough to fill all the local air time. This is where syndication comes in.

Syndicated programs are shows that have been created and produced by another TV entity and then offered up for sale to local affiliates, independents, and cable stations. Think of shows like *Law & Order*, *Seinfeld*, and *Friends*. Depending on where you live, you can probably see at least one of these shows on a daily basis. Once a show has reached at least a hundred or so episodes, local stations can buy the rights to air the reruns for a set period of time.

But syndicated programs aren't always reruns. Shows like *Dr. Phil*, *Oprah*, *Wheel of Fortune*, *Judge Judy*, and *Jeopardy!* are syndicated, but they continue to produce new episodes. This is known as first-run syndication.

Like the networks, local stations make money on these programs by selling advertising. In syndication, shows may be slightly re-edited from their original formats in order to add extra commercial time.

What Are Television Sweeps?

Television Sweeps are the prime rating periods that networks use to set advertising rates. Sweeps months are November, February, May, and July. You may notice that programming is considerably more exciting during these months. Because so much money is at stake, networks do everything they possibly can to pull in viewers. During Sweeps, you will probably see some of the best television of the season, with very few reruns.

Traditionally, it is during Sweeps that most of the so-called big moments occur on TV. Depending on the show, characters may kiss for the first time, get married, have babies, and even get killed off. Financially speaking, the shows that air during Sweeps are so important to the networks and studios that they will almost always be written by one of the staff writers.

Staff Writing vs. Freelance Writing

In series television all shows have writing staffs. These writers come to work Monday through Friday in the same way a lawyer or a stockbroker does. The number of staff writers on each show varies, depending on the show's budget. In addition to staff writers, during the course of a season, most shows will farm out a few scripts to freelance writers. Unlike staff writers, freelance writers are not given offices, nor are they on the studio payroll. Rather, they are paid per script. Most writers start out as freelancers and as they get work produced and build professional writing credits they will then (with any luck) wind up with a staff writing job. While writing on a show is anything but easy, staff writing jobs are considered cushy because of the money and many perks that can come with them. For this reason, staff writing jobs are highly coveted and, unfortunately, there are not nearly enough of them to go around.

> "There's a lot of really fun things about being on staff. You get to sit around all day with really bright, funny people. You make jokes, tell pointless stories, doodle, and there's even people that bring you all of this endless free food. It can be easy to lose sight of the fact that, while this might not be a standard nine-to-five desk job, it's still a job. Executive producers are under a tremendous amount of pressure

to keep a show on track. So while you're having all this fun, you also have to stay focused. You must be professional and never lose sight of the fact that you're there to contribute to the room and help keep everything moving."

Manny Basanese, writer/producer, *The Steve Harvey Show* and *The Wayans Brothers*

Do You Have to Live in L.A.?

If you want to write for series television, you absolutely, positively must live in the Los Angeles area. This is where the TV business is located. If you are to get a staff writing job, your office will be likely be located at a studio or production company in L.A. Writers who resist Los Angeles will ask about New York. Again, most series television is produced in Los Angeles. Even that handful of shows that are actually shot in New York will often come through Los Angeles–based production companies, and those staff writers are generally represented by Los Angeles–based agents. Not to mention that since most of series television is done in L.A., statistically speaking, your odds of finding work as a writer in La-la-land are significantly higher than they are of finding work in the Big Apple.

"Don't think you're going to do it from Lebanon, New Hampshire. Get off your ass and get out here."

Jay Leno, host of *The Tonight Show*

You will also find that most agents won't take on new writers who don't live in Southern California. The reason is that in order to get hired, you have to be available to meet with producers and executives. Often these meetings are set up quite quickly. I see many wannabe writers delude themselves into thinking that they can write television from the farm in Iowa, get an agent from the farm in Iowa, and then hop on a plane when necessary to take meetings. This is not close to being realistic. Once you enter the professional writing world, you are competing not only with newcomers like yourself, but also with those who have produced writing credits. With all of these qualified writers right at their fingertips, why would a studio or production company go through the hassle and inconvenience of waiting for an unproven writer to hop on a plane? The answer is they wouldn't.

If you are serious about writing for series television, you should want to move to Los Angeles as soon as possible. By living close to your industry, you will be able to open doors and make connections that could eventually help you sell your first script. You also might be able to land an entry-level job and start learning firsthand how the business works. This could get your writing career up and running faster.

Writing for Existing Shows Is Your First Step

It's important to understand that no one is going to hire you as a TV writer simply because you want to be one. As with any business, in order to get work, you have to prove that you can actually handle the job. Hollywood is heavily unionized, which makes production outrageously expensive. To cut down on costs, production schedules are usually tight, allowing little, if any, room for error. If a script isn't ready for shooting when it is supposed to be, the cost to delay production can be astronomical. Therefore, most producers will not give out writing assignments to unproven writers without being fairly certain that the writer will not only turn in a decent script, but will turn it in on time. So if you are a new writer without a track record, how do you prove to producers that you can in fact step up to the plate and do a professional job? The answer is you write what is known as a "spec" script. In series television, a spec is the first step to getting work as a writer.

What Is a Spec Script?

Simply put, a spec script is a writing sample. You don't get paid to write it; however, if done well, your spec could open doors and generate work for you down the road. Think of a spec script as your calling card. The same way actors and models send out head shots in hopes of gaining future employment, you will use your spec script to find work as a TV writer.

> "Have knowledge of the medium. Watch everything that's on. Then pick a show that is respected for its creative execution. It may not be the top-rated show, but people in the industry respond to it and respect it. And don't say, 'I don't want to watch television.' That's like a banker saying, 'I don't want to count money.'"
>
> Jeff Eckerle, writer/producer, *Law &Order: Special Victims Unit*

Your first order of business is to come up with a story idea for an existing show. Ideally, your story should use all of that show's main characters, and should utilize as many of the show's regular sets as possible. Once you have the story, you will write a sample teleplay from beginning to end. The goal is to have an end product that mirrors the actual scripts that are produced on that particular show.

Choosing a Spec Script that Will Work for You

When you are deciding which show to spec, there are certain criteria that should be considered in order to choose a show that will work for you. To begin with, the show must be currently on the air in prime time. Don't mix this up with shows that have been canceled and are rerunning in syndication. I can't tell you how many times people have said to me, "The only show I watch is *Seinfeld*. So that's what I want to write." Here is my stock response. First of all, if you want to work as a TV

writer, you have to be constantly watching television—and yes, that means more than one show. Secondly, writing a spec for a canceled show is a colossal waste of time. Once a show goes off the air, it quickly becomes yesterday's news. Producers generally won't read these scripts and agents won't sign you on them. You must write a spec for an existing program to show that you are current with what is on the air today.

> "When it comes to choosing what show to spec, you should pick a show that you relate to … not the most popular show that you have no affinity for. It should be a show that is well-known but not oversaturated … and that's a tough one."
>
> Kate Boutilier, screenwriter, *Rugrats* and *The Wild Thornberrys*

Before you jump into the saddle, it is advisable to take a big-picture look at your long-term career goals. Where and how do you see yourself fitting in within the TV industry? To help establish where your sensibilities lie, you might want to think about who you are as a person. Are you someone who is exceptional at making people laugh—or do you possess more of a flair for drama? You may also want to look at the kind of TV shows you are most attracted to. If you tend to watch more drama than comedy, you will probably be more comfortable scripting a one-hour drama than a joke-heavy sitcom. But what kind of drama do you find most appealing? Rough-and-tough crime shows like *CSI* or softer, more character driven vehicles like *Grey's Anatomy*? By writing the kind of show that you really have an affinity for, you will probably struggle less, and in the end produce a stronger writing sample. Be aware that, whatever kind of spec script you choose, it's no guarantee of the kind of show you will eventually end up writing for. The spec that got me the most attention was a *Married with Children*. It was deliciously raunchy and extremely fun to write. Ironically, in the sitcom arena it only got me work on squeaky-clean family shows.

After you make up your mind about what show you want to spec, you need to research it carefully before you start writing. Look closely at how well it is doing in the ratings. While you won't always know for sure if a show is going to be picked up for another season, you can usually make an educated guess. If its ratings are at all iffy, I would steer clear of it. As you are about to find out, writing a solid spec script takes an enormous amount of time and energy. The last thing you want to have happen is to work as hard as you are going to have to work only to find out that once you have finished the show has been canceled and you have to start all over again at square one. If you can find a show that looks like it will be around for a few years, all the better. As long as a show is on the air, you will have a current spec script that can continue to be sent out. Though it happens infrequently, there are shows—usually those that are doing extremely well in the ratings—that networks make commitments to a year or more in advance. These shows tend to be a good bet to spec because it is likely that by choosing one, you will have a writing sample that is current for at least a few seasons.

> "Write a sample. Make sure every word is exactly what you want it to be. Go over it and over it and over it until each line says and exemplifies exactly what you want to say."
>
> Tom Towler, supervising producer, *JAG*; writer, *BTK Killer*

Writing a spec for a brand new show can also be risky. In the first season, shows often struggle to find their voice and identity. Things change as the writers and producers get a feel for who the characters are and where they are going. Also, if the show isn't an instant mega-hit, there may be some producers on other shows who won't be as familiar with it, which can be problematic when it comes to getting it read. Beware of shows that are too obscure for the same reason. Producers have to have a general idea of what the show is and who the characters are in order to evaluate your writing and your script.

Each season a few breakout shows quickly become hits. I commonly refer to these as "the flavor of the month." They are the shows that every writer wants to spec. While there is technically nothing wrong with writing one of these shows, I think it can put you at a slight disadvantage. Let's say you decide to spec a *Desperate Housewives*, which happens to be one of the specs that everyone is writing. When you send it out to an agent, that agent will likely take it home to read over the weekend with 10 other scripts. If six of the 10 are *Desperate Housewives* specs, how well do you think the agent will remember your script by Monday morning? The answer is probably not that well. If, however, there were six "*Desperate Housewives*" specs, but you wrote a dynamite episode of *Law & Order*, your script would have a much better chance of standing out among the pack.

The same thing is true when your agent sends your spec for producers to read. Producers grow tired of reading specs for the same show over and over again. Often the scripts that aren't "the flavor of the month" end up getting writers noticed.

Studying the Show Before You Write

Before you hunker down to write—or even come up with a story for your spec—it is imperative that you sit down and watch the show over and over again. It is virtually impossible to write a stand-out spec script for a show you have seen only once or twice. If possible, you should tape the show. Then play it back repeatedly. Listen to how the characters talk. What is the rhythm of their dialogue? Who are they as people? What do they value? Also, checkout the sets. Which ones are used every week? Which ones are used most often? You'd be surprised at how much you miss when you see a show only once. These seemingly minor details will all become major points when you write your spec.

> "The key for any new writer is to produce a great spec script. Pick a show you love. Take the time to research it.

Watch it over and over until you get the voice of the characters."

Marc Warren, executive producer, *Full House* and *That's So Raven*

Purchasing a Sample Script of the Show You Want to Write

In addition to taping your show, it is also a smart idea to purchase an actual hard copy of a produced script for the show you intend to write. There are many reasons to do this, the most important being that you are trying to write a script that looks similar to the produced scripts of the actual show. Therefore, you need to get everything right. Having a produced script to refer to will be incredibly helpful. Little things that you may not think about will become key as you write. To give you an example, let's look at the show *Law & Order*. Can you tell me, off the top of your head, how the producers refer to Jack McCoy's office in scripts? Is it "Jack McCoy's office" or "McCoy's office" or "executive ADA's office"? My guess is that you probably don't have a clue. That's okay. However, when it comes to actually writing your spec, you must get it 100% correct. I can all but promise you that as you write, you will come to places that you just aren't sure of. Having a produced script at your fingertips will help ensure that all of your "Ts" are crossed and your "Is" are dotted.

Another reason that it is good to have an actual script is for formatting issues. As you will see once we get going, while there are general rules for formatting a script, each show puts its own, ever-so-slight spin on those rules. By having an actual script, you'll be able to see exactly how the writers of the show handle various issues.

"Read everything and see everything. Then dig deep into who you are as person, as a character, as a human. What unique point of view can you add to a story? Then forget everything you've seen before you and focus on a story/pitch/idea that only you could tell."

Steve Stark, executive producer, *Medium*; president, Grammnet Producers

There are lots of places that you can buy scripts of shows that have been produced. Generally, they aren't that expensive—usually around $10. Personally, I buy scripts over the Internet from a company called Script City (www.scriptcity.com) because they have a fairly large selection of TV scripts. But anywhere you can find them—as long as they are copies of an actual produced show—will be fine.

It may be difficult to find scripts of newer shows—especially those that are in their first season. If you have decided to spec a new show and you absolutely can't get your hands on one of their scripts, then buy a script that is similar to the show you want to write. For example, if you are scripting a one-hour drama that is plot-driven, an episode of something like *Law & Order* or *CSI* would be a better example than an episode of *The Simpsons*.

Steer clear of downloading scripts from random sites on the Internet. You have no way of knowing who typed the material or how meticulous that person was. In my TV Writing classes, I always require my students to buy a script for whatever show they want to spec. I warn them repeatedly about the dangers of downloading scripts. I explain ad nauseam that people who read scripts for a living have extremely trained eyes. Mistakes are spotted in a heartbeat. Without fail, each semester, one or two students don't heed the advice. At the end of the semester, they turn in their spec scripts and I immediately see places where their format is miles off. When I push them, they sheepishly admit to downloading scripts from cyberspace. Don't fall into that trap. Believe me when I say that improperly formatted scripts equal not getting hired.

Why Two (Sigh!) Specs Are Better Than One

I wish I could tell you that once you have finished and polished your first spec script, you can sit back and relax. Unfortunately, you just can't. You now need to write a second spec script. Most agents will want to see at least two writing samples before signing you. Unbelievable as it may sound, there seems to be a tendency among agents to think that if a new writer has one good spec script, it could be a fluke. Before signing you, agents want to be sure that you are someone who can consistently pump out good script after good script. Therefore, they will usually require two samples.

Another reason for needing more than one writing sample is that some producers are more finicky than Morris the Cat. When it comes to television, many have definitive likes and dislikes. You have to give them what they want. If your only sample is a *My Name Is Earl* and the producer who is going to read your work vehemently dislikes *My Name Is Earl*, even if you have written the most brilliant *My Name Is Earl* script in the entire Milky Way, chances are you still won't get hired by that particular producer. Therefore, it's good for your agent to be able to offer up another choice.

When writing a second spec script, it is imperative that you don't spec the same show. You want to be able to demonstrate that you are a writer with huge range. If you are doing comedy and you have written a traditional sitcom like *Two and a Half Men*, it might be wise to try your hand at a single-camera show like *Scrubs* or an animated show like *South Park*. In the same vein, if you are writing drama and your first spec script is a character-driven show like *Grey's Anatomy*, then you might want to try a plot-driven drama like *CSI*. The goal is to prove that you are versatile—put you on any writing staff and you will be able to handle it. That said, if shows like *CSI* are not your cup of tea—and not in the realm of what you feel comfortable writing—then you shouldn't do it because your final product will probably reflect that. In which case, you should choose another character-driven show. Just be sure to look for one that doesn't too closely mirror the spec that you already have under your belt.

Once you have two solid spec scripts, you may want to round off your portfolio with an original sample. This could be a television pilot (see Part IV), a play, or even a short story. At a time when producers and agents are constantly looking for writers with a fresh take on material and a unique point of view, it is quite possible they will ask to see something original before making a commitment to you.

Writing Is Rewriting

The worst disservice you could do yourself is to think that your first draft is your final draft. A spec script is the most important script you will ever write. Everything is riding on it. Therefore, it is hugely important that you take the time to rewrite it and rewrite it and rewrite it. You need to get it as near-perfect as is humanly possible. If you are a brand new writer and you whip out a spec script in a couple of days—or even a couple of weeks for that matter—I can almost promise you that it isn't as good as it can be.

> "You have to have a total myopic devotion. Writing is such a time commitment. Writing is about rewriting. You're never gonna get there through the first draft. We were willing to—and did—throw out entire drafts two days before taping. If it's on the page, it'll be on the stage."
>
> Max Mutchnick, creator, executive producer, *Will and Grace*

The Reason Your Spec Probably Won't Sell

Once a spec script is finally finished, new writers will often be so thrilled with the accomplishment that they will want to shove the script in an envelope and send it off to said show to be produced. Unfortunately, spec scripts almost never get produced and there is a legitimate reason.

If you are Marc Cherry—or anyone on the *Desperate Housewives* writing staff—you know each of the characters intimately. Their voices resonate inside your head day after day, night after night, and even in the wee hours of the morning when you wish they would pipe down so you can get some sleep. You know absolutely every minor detail about their past because you've written it. As a freelance writer, no matter how much you study a show before you write it, you simply won't have the same inside track that the show's writers and producers do. So, if you have written a spec *Desperate Housewives*, it is quite probable that here and there throughout your script you may have things that are slightly off. It could be a minor story or character point or it could be that your dialogue isn't exactly character-specific. When your agent sends your spec script to the writing staff of *Desperate Housewives*, they will no doubt pick up on the flaws in your script instantly, and they will conclude that you don't know their show.

On the other hand, when your agent takes that same *Desperate Housewives* script and sends it to shows like *Lost* or *Grey's Anatomy*, the producers of those shows may not see the flaws. The reason is that they are so busy writing and producing their own shows that, like you, they may watch *Housewives*, but they don't know it like the back of their hand. So any little bumps in your script will generally go unnoticed by the producers of another show.

"You never write a spec script with the idea that it's going to be produced. It's not. That's not what you want your spec script to do. Produced shows suck. Yours has to be better than that. You might also shoot for a show that lasts a few years so you don't have to write another stupid spec script."

John Frink, co-executive producer,
The Simpsons

While most agents will eventually send your spec script to the show you have written, they usually don't expect much. Neither should you. However, there are lots of other shows out there where you or your agent can submit your work. If your spec script is outstanding, there is a chance you will get hired.

Declaring Your Major (And Minor)

In series television, there are comedy writers and there are drama writers. Most writers don't bounce back and forth between the two. Therefore, you must declare yourself as one or the other. This is how your agent will generally sell you.

That said, once you have written two solid spec scripts in either the half-hour format or the hour-long format (and something original), it might be a good idea then to write a spec for the opposite. So if you've decided you want to write comedy and now have two good samples, I suggest that you spec a drama and keep it in your back pocket. The reason is that most of the time, comedy producers won't read drama specs and drama producers won't read comedy specs. As you will soon see, drama and comedy are, in their own ways, extremely different. Thus, it becomes difficult for producers who work in one area to accurately judge the other. In order to keep all of your prospects open, it is wise to have at least one script in the opposite arena. You have to be ready when opportunity knocks, and in Los Angeles that can happen anytime anywhere. You never know who you might meet at a party or even standing in line at the grocery store.

14. Introduction to Film Studies

by Amy Villarejo

This chapter looks at the film industry from an academic perspective. The chapter gives readers an overview of the historical development of film and cinema in much the same way that the "Cyperspace" chapter laid a foundation for understanding emerging communication technologies. Reading the present chapter will not make someone a great filmmaker, but will make any engaged reader more thoughtful and informed about film. By addressing various elements of film, from outlining different genres and their development to explaining the truths behind the myths surrounding film and the movie industry, Villarejo provides readers an opportunity to think about the films they see as well as the industry influences behind them. For potential future filmmakers, she provides a vocabulary for engaging with their future field.

If you've picked up this book to learn something about what it means to study film, you already know in large measure what cinema is: you've been watching movies since you first toddled out to the family television set, or since you braved your first excursion to a multiplex matinee. If you're old enough, you may have witnessed formats come and go. Perhaps you thrilled in your first chance to watch a beloved film at home on video, re-winding the tape over and again to watch Gene Kelly singin' in the rain or Greta Garbo

Amy Villarejo, "Introduction to Film Studies," *Film Studies: The Basics*, pp. 1-23. Copyright © 2007 by Taylor & Francis Group LLC. Reprinted with permission.

unleashing her famous first spoken line in *Anna Christie* (Jacques Feyder, 1931): "Gimme a whiskey, ginger ale on the side, and don't be stingy, baby." DVDs, now repackaged with all of the "extras" that persuade us to replace those VHS tapes, may soon go the way of CDs, consigned right into the dustbin that receives the detritus of digital culture. Who knows? You may be born into a world in which cinema streams in bits onto our computer screens more than it lights up the screens of our neighborhood theaters.

No matter your point of entry into the matrix, welcome. Cinema lives and has always lived in multiple forms, some slowly dying, some newly emerging. In the late nineteenth century, cinema itself emerged from a diverse world of toys and machines that created the illusion of movement. Christened with perversely scientific names, these Phenakistoscopes, Thaumatropes, Zoetropes, and Praxinoscopes (all versions of spinning motion toys) competed with magic lantern projections and panoramas to entertain audiences with dizzying perspectives and steaming locomotives, acrobatic feats and elaborate stories. Forms of magic lanterns collected at the George Eastman House in Rochester (Lampascopes, Kodiopticons, Moviegraphs, and even a contraption dubbed "Le Galerie Gothique") testify to the ingenuity and variety of "pre-cinema." Some project, throwing larger-than-life images from slides onto screens and surfaces. Others invite spectators into more private viewings, into simulacra of theaters or, as with the later Edison Kinetoscopes, into solitary "peep" shows of sequential images that suggest movement. Some exploit the ideas of sequence or series, while others concentrate on the fantastic and imaginary worlds of storytelling. Taken as a whole, they anticipate but don't quite cross the threshold of cinema's illusion of continuous movement.

Enter early photographic studies of motion. Eadweard Muybridge perfected the large-scale photographic panorama of San Francisco in 1878, a sequence of thirteen photographs taken at different moments that together offer the spectator a 360° view of the city from atop Nob Hill. As opposed to the painted panorama, which conceals or renders irrelevant issues of duration, the photographic series creates from many individual instants an illusion of continuity: "many hours of the day masquerading as a single supreme moment, like a film in which segments shot at various times are edited into a believable narrative" (Solnit 2003: 176). But it is Muybridge's later famous analysis of a trotting horse that transforms those possibilities for thinking about time and motion that led to cinema's creation. The story goes like this: California former governor, robber baron, and racing horse aficionado Leland Stanford wanted to know whether, in the course of a trotting horse's stride, all four hooves were ever off the ground at once, and he hired California's best photographer (though he was both an Englishman and a murderer—no causal relationship implied) to find out. Muybridge's feat was not only to string threads across the race track to be tripped by the trotting horse, each triggering a camera's shutter in turn, but actually to create images from these enormously quick exposures. Silhouettes of the horse, to give him his due, named Occident, answered affirmatively to Stanford's question, but the larger accomplishments, practical and philosophical, are his legacy (see Figure 1.1). First, Muybridge had to create what was in essence a film studio at the racetrack; to compensate for slow film speeds, he created a blindingly white environment for the horses to pass through, complete with distance markers and choice framings. Second, Muybridge fused technological development (of the triggers, shutters, chemistry) with the subjects he sought to photograph in order to invent a new medium, much as the cinema was to do in the decade following Muybridge's study for Stanford. But, third, Muybridge returned movement, and movement in a series that anticipates narrative, to photography:

> Muybridge had reduced the narrative to its most basic element: the unfolding of motions in time and space. Most of his sequences depicted the events of a few seconds or less, and he boasted that the individual exposures were as brief

as one two-thousandth of a second. By imposing stillness on its subjects, photography had represented the world as a world of objects. But now, in Muybridge's work, it was a world of processes again, for one picture showed a horse, but six pictures showed an act, a motion, an event. The subject of the pictures was not the images per se but the change from one to another, the change that represented time and motion more vividly, more urgently, than the slow motion of parades passing and buildings rising. It was a fundamental change in the nature of photography and of what could be represented.

(Solnit 2003: 194)

Muybridge was not alone in this exploration, but it was his work, alongside the "chronophotographic" camera of French photographer Etienne-Jules Marey, that suggested a way of thinking about time and motion through successive **frames**. Cameras equipped with a **shutter**, creating an interval of blackness in the exposure of each frame of film coated with a light-sensitive **emulsion**, recorded frame after frame (from ten to forty frames per second, or **fps**) of whatever lay before it; when projected, again with a shutter moving and at the same rate, the human eye perceives the individual frames as continuous motion, due to a still-baffling phenomenon scientists first called "**persistence of vision**" and tend now to call "persistent afterimages." The cinema, then, arises truly from an interface: a technology of continuously moving still images and a process of perception on the part of the human spectator which readies him or her to receive this continuity as motion itself.

Thomas Edison's Kinetograph and the Cinématographe of the Lumière brothers in France soon recorded our first films upon the principles and techniques Muybridge made concrete: more acrobats and strongmen, like the stock images of the "pre-cinema," but also everyday images (the Lumière *actualités* of workers and babies) (see Figure 1.2). It was in the very interval

between meeting Muybridge and meeting Marey, in fact, that Edison transferred his model for sound recording and playback to images:

> He assigned the job of studying two apparatuses—one for the recording of images, baptized the Kinetograph, and the other for viewing them, named the Kinetoscope—to an employee with a passion for photography, the Englishman William Kennedy Laurie Dickson. The two men proceeded cautiously. Arriving in Paris for the Universal Exposition of 1889, Edison met Marey, who told him about the progress of his own work. Eventually, in order to record photographic views, the American inventor abandoned the cylinder for a celluloid roll with perforations (sprocket holes) along each side, through which a toothed sprocket wheel would run; this ensured a uniform feed.

(Toulet 1995: 35)

To feed his Kinetoscopes, machines for peep show or solitary viewing, Edison built a movie studio in what were then the wilds of New Jersey, dubbed the "Black Maria" for its resemblance to the New York paddy wagons called by that name. From here Edison "cranked out" (a phrase derived from the hand-cranking of the camera) film after film: "Horses jumping over hurdles, Niagara Falls with its torrents plunging to rocky depths, trains rushing headlong across the screen, cooch-girls dancing, vaudeville acrobats taking their falls with aplomb, parades, boats, and people hurrying or scurrying along," summarized an early historian (Jacobs 1967 [1939]: 4). In France the Lumière brothers went a step further, perfecting a device that could record *and* project: the Cinématographe. Building upon Edison's invention, the Lumières solved the remaining problem of how to ensure that the film advances at a uniform rate to resynthesize the recorded image. The solution came to Louis Lumière in a dream: "In one night, my brother invented the Cinématographe," recalled Auguste (Toulet 1995:

40). Audiences responded hungrily and immediately to those images of ourselves "hurrying and scurrying" captured by mobile cameras and projected larger than life.

In the mid-1890s, in these first few years of cinema's life, congealed the essence of what we now mean when we refer to cinema. Above all, cinema is dynamic. It animates the world around us; it transports us to worlds we imagine or know only through images. Muybridge's experiments revealed the very idea of the interval: the transformation or mutation of the object from one state to the next, the essence of change itself. The inventor who soon became one of Edison's chief cinematographers, our passionate employee Englishman Dickson, dreamt deliciously of cinema's reach as early as 1895, when he and his wife wrote its first history:

No scene, however animated and extensive, but will eventually be within reproductive power. Martial evolutions, naval exercises, processions and countless kindred exhibitions will be recorded for the leisurely gratification of those who are debarred from attendance, or who desire to recall them. The invalid, the isolated country recluse, and the harassed business man can indulge in needed recreation, without undue expenditure, without fear of weather, without danger to raiment, elbows and toes, and without the sacrifice of health or important engagements. Not only our own resources but those of the entire world will be at our command, nay, we may even anticipate the time when sociable relations will be established between ourselves and the planetary system, and when the latest doings in Mars, Saturn and Venus will be recorded by enterprising kinetographic reporters.
(Dickson and Dickson 2000 [1895]: 51)

This took until 2005, when the first "cinematographer" of the Mars Rover mission received an Emmy Award nomination.

At the same time that we dream of cinema's reach, most of our films are literally dying: **prints** and **negatives** decomposing or bursting into flame, fading or melting into illegibility. Paolo Cherchi Usai, senior curator of the Motion Picture Department at George Eastman House and one of the leading figures in film preservation, elaborates on the philosophical, aesthetic and political consequences of the proliferation of images in the current moment combined with the phenomenon of the ongoing death of cinema, which can result from physical and environmental factors:

In addition to the factors which can prevent its coming into being (malfunction of the apparatus, inadequate processing of the negative or its accidental exposure to light, human interference of various kinds), there is the host of physical and chemical agents affecting the image carrier: scratches or tears on the print caused by the projecting machine or its operator, curling of the film base as a result of a too intense exposure to the light source, colour alterations arising out of the film stock itself, environmental variables such as temperature and humidity. As soon as it is deposited on a matrix, the digital image is subject to a similar destiny; its causes may be different, but the effects are the same. Chronicles [read by Cherchi Usai] also mention catastrophes and extraordinary events such as fires, wars, floods, and destructive interventions from the makers themselves or the people who finance their activities.
(Cherchi Usai 2001: 13)

By his estimate, fully 80 percent of the films made during the silent era (until the mid-1920s) are lost (Cherchi Usai 2001: 122). In Cherchi Usai's view, loss pervades the film experience, too. It is a product of the physical reality of perception, in which we "watch" a black screen each time a shutter passes over the projector, in which we turn away from the image each time we blink (according to the level of humidity in the room), in which we may find ourselves distracted or bored, drawn into reveries other than those onscreen. This physicality of perception alerts us to the fact that each viewing of a film is an evanescent experience, archived in memory, consigned to the realm of the unseen. If preservationists reclaim some of what has been lost, they and we will never be able to assert full or final control over the visible world; we will only catch glimpses of it. Experimental filmmaker Bill Morrison's *Decasia* (2002) is composed entirely of decaying archival footage, recording this process of loss. Seeking out footage filmed on highly flammable nitrate stock, Morrison painstakingly transferred this compilation of fragile images and set them to an original symphonic score: ghost-like figures (camels, dervishes) emerge out of the scratches, discolorations, and static to haunt us briefly before they yield to the texture of the film's surface.

From its birth, then, until the present moment, cinema has assumed multiple guises and forms, circling into and out of sight, from its roots in the early motion of toys and machines: vaudeville style exhibition, the invention of the "talkies" (from the recording of sound on discs to accompany films to today's use of digital Dolby surround sound), various uses of color (from early cinema's hand-tinted frames to Technicolor and beyond), widescreen formats like Cinemascope and VistaVision, different film **gauges** (from 8mm for home movies to the theatrical standard of 35mm and IMAX films in 65mm), and various reproductive, transfer, and storage technologies. And from those early kisses, trains, and trips to the moon? We may have replaced May Irwin, the first kissing lady of the screen, with J-Lo and "Bollywood babe" Udita Goswami, but we're still traveling.

Why Study Film?

Cinema's dynamism, its capacity to arrange and rearrange time and motion, thus reveals its dimensions that are deeply social, historical, industrial, technological, philosophical, political, aesthetic, psychological, personal, and so forth. The aggregate of these multiple dimensions indeed *is* cinema (for individual works I reserve the word "film" or "movie"). For enthusiasts, cinema rewards study like few other objects precisely because its reach is so great that it is never exhausted, its scope so varied that one rarely finds oneself thinking along a single plane of thought. Cinema is about everything and always about itself. About each image, we might ask, as Reynold Humphries does of the films of Jean-Luc Godard, "What values and ideas are already contained in an image from the fact of its mere presence?" (Humphries 1975: 13). If various images presented by cinema delight or thrill, agitate or unnerve, those images further offer themselves for analysis of their combinatory logic, for example. The great Soviet director Sergei Eisenstein, like the British (and later Hollywood) legend Alfred Hitchcock, advocated a science of audience stimulation whereby the director could calibrate, with unfailing precision, the image to the intended audience effect. While Eisenstein called his theory of combination **montage**, seeking to continue cinematically the political agitation of the Bolshevik Revolution, Hitchcock pursued his own ideas toward the end of pure response, what he among many others called "pure cinema," in the genre of the thriller:

> Ernie, do you realize what we are doing in this picture? The audience is like a giant organ that you and I are playing. At one moment we play this note and get this reaction, and then we play that chord and they react that way. And someday we won't even have to make a movie—there'll be electrodes implanted in their brains, and we'll just press different buttons and they'll go 'oooh' and 'aaah' and we'll frighten them, and make them laugh. Won't that be wonderful?
>
> (Spoto 1984: 440)

Likewise, if particular stories emerge from particular socio-historical contexts, those narratives benefit from careful study of their correspondences and divergences with the moment or context, but also of how they *mold* their moments and contexts, sometimes indelibly. Orson Welles' *Citizen Kane* (1941) both studies American isolationism in the first years of the Second World War *and* argues against it through the "fictional" figure of Charles Foster Kane, living a life of self-imposed isolation amidst the relics of memory, himself based upon newspaper and film magnate William Randolph Hearst. The extraordinary Senegalese filmmaker Ousmane Sembene both comments on the politics of foreign aid to African countries in one of his best films, *Guelwaar* (1992), and structures his critique of political violence, religious intolerance, and patriarchal authority around its murderous effects (see Figure 1.3).

The study of cinema, in other words, is emphatically not an attempt to arrest its dynamism, to still it in order to subject it to scrutiny. It is rather the pursuit of cinema as an historical hydra, with tentacles reaching into all aspects of our individual and collective lives. This book traces several of those tentacles in each of its five subsequent chapters. It is not meant to be a comprehensive introductory textbook but rather an engaging and provocative accompaniment to what is for most people a lifelong relationship with the cinema. Toward that end, *Film Studies: The Basics* offers the reader multiple ways in which to situate, to enrich, and to enlarge his/her knowledge and experience of film; it hopes to be a companion as well as a guidebook to adventurous and wondrous viewing.

Chapter 2 offers a quick primer in the language of film analysis or the formal study of film (covering **cinematography**, *mise-en-scène*, **editing**, **sound**, and **narrative**), demonstrating that some specialized terms are essential for understanding how films work and how films solicit our attention and responses. Some historical understanding of cinema is likewise crucial for understanding the medium today: how it not only reflects but shapes history. For the reader seeking a basic knowledge of the field of film studies, then, Chapters 2 and 3 essentially open up the arenas of film analysis and film history, both taught widely, if frequently separately, in many colleges and universities. Toward a second goal of offering a rudimentary introduction to further and more advanced intellectual issues and questions of film study, two chapters on production/exhibition and reception follow. These provide a more subjective assessment of the bread-and-butter issues of film studies as an academic discipline: the relation between art and industry, questions of genre and authorship, film censorship, film labor, technologies of cinema, exhibition histories and practices, stardom and fandom, publicity/marketing/promotion, spectatorship, film theories, and the like. The final chapter treats film in the context of emergent media and new academic configurations: digital culture, new media, visual studies. Together the chapters privilege the "why" of cinema study by surveying the "what" (substance), "when" (history), "who" (makers and viewers), and "how" (mechanisms) of film. My overarching goal is to offer the reader an exposure to the infectious enthusiasm, if not mania, that is cinephilia, while simultaneously providing a grounding in the study of cinema that will make future viewing more rewarding.

What Is Film?

If I've made reference to your experience as first-time popcorn munchers at the multiplex, or as DVD buyers or renters, it has been to enlist you in the conviction that you have already some considerable experience with a variety of different types of films. You are an expert already, with a feel for what you like and don't like: a sense, for example, of when American director Tim Burton's aesthetic vision seems exciting (*Edward Scissorhands*, 1990) or shallow (*Planet of the Apes*, 2001), or a marked (and deserved) preference for Jet Li over Jackie Chan. You find yourself so saturated with the conventions of genre (drum beats signaling threat in suspense films, crescendos of violin strings accompanying romantic unions in melodramas, stock characters in B-westerns, and predictable scenarios in horror spinoffs) that you spend hours delighting in their violations or spoofing on *The Simpsons* or through sophisticated generic revisions in French *noir*. You live amidst cinema, just as a student of economics lives within an economy. Cinema, however, is just as naturalized as is our economy; that is, its dominant rules, its habitual narratives, its general visual styles, its mode of production, its sites of exhibition, its **tie-ins** (product placements, ties to other commodities like Burger King cups or toy dolls), even its running times, tend to be taken as given, as natural, as unquestioned, and as unchanging. The first step, then, in film education is to notice what we take to be given, true, "how things are," in order that we may confirm, revise, or reject those same assumptions when tested against the most expansive understanding of and inquiry into cinema.

"Films Tell Stories"

Many films do tell stories, thanks to the overwhelming dominance of commercial **narrative** (a chain of events in a cause–effect relationship) cinema. Not so for much of early cinema: its musclemen and magic tricks hewed more to what film historian Tom Gunning calls the "cinema of attractions." Aping theatrical presentations, these films settle the camera into the chair of a hypothetical audience member and train it upon a proscenium, upon which unfolds some daredevil feat or anomalous bodily act. In a portrait of contortionist virility, the amazing Sandow (Prussian Schwarzenegger-precursor Eugen Sandow) expands his chest from its normal forty-seven buff inches to an incredible sixty-one, and holds a platform of three horses, weighing about 3,000 pounds, above his head. The goal? Extracting an unadulterated "awesome!" and nothing more. If virility is reserved for the likes of Sandow and Buffalo Bill, flexibility and plasticity characterize other immigrant groups: Chinese acrobats poke heads through crossed legs, while gun juggling and knife tumbling are done by "an illustrious Moor," Dickson tells us (Dickson and Dickson 2000 [1895]: 40). These early films, often a single shot long (a length of continuously exposed film), exploit the capacity of the cinema to *show*, to

dazzle, to capture our attention. In the early years of cinema, Gunning reminds us, the cinema itself was the attraction, and it was linked as much to practices of storytelling as to the kinds of modern conceptions of time and space discovered in Muybridge's motion studies or in visual culture more largely. While narrative films emerged with the first decade of the cinema, then, and while they largely replaced these "attractions," elements of this cinema of attractions nonetheless persist in our day. With breathless enthusiasm and reverence for their technological accomplishments, we call them "special effects." (These, too, are the most frequent occasions for the question "How did they do that?", which we'll explore in Chapter 2.)

A second arena of film that is non-narrative we refer to as "experimental" or *avant-garde* cinema. A film, for example, called *The Flicker* (Tony Conrad, 1965)—a product of perhaps an excessive fondness in that decade for mind alteration and hallucinogens—alternates frames that are entirely white and entirely black for more than thirty minutes. The pulsating result, inducing anything from entrancement to nausea to rare epileptic seizures, inspired a wave of subsequent experimental makers to create non-narrative experiments in perception. Other experimental films reject narrative in favor of other forms of meaning-making, aesthetic effect, or perceptual experience, and many simultaneously reject the idea of recording a latent image from a prior reality. Artists such as Bruce Connor (in his brilliant film on apocalyptic time, *A Movie* [1958]) or, more recently, Craig Baldwin (in his compilation agitprop films, including *Spectres of the Spectrum* [2000]) use **stock** or **found footage** in order to explore the social consequences of technological innovation and to challenge complacency. The late Stan Brakhage, one of the monumental experimental filmmakers of the twentieth century, attached moth wings (and a few bodies and blades of grass) to film leader and ran it through a projector in *Mothlight* (1963); early *avant-garde* makers such as Man Ray (in his "Rayograms" from the 1920s and 1930s) placed objects directly on film stock and exposed it to light, much as children do today with paper clips, photographic paper, and sunshine.

"Most Films Come from Hollywood"

Dubbed the "dream factory" in an early study by anthropologist Hortense Powdermaker, Hollywood has indeed become synonymous with the movies, and for good reason. American film, like other American commodities, floods the world's markets, whether due to discrepancies in copyright law, lack of funds directed toward national film industries or partnerships, the deregulation of markets, or globalized corporate structures. The largest film industry in the world is not, however, that of the United States. That distinction has for many years instead belonged to India, a country which produces 800 to 900 films per year, about a quarter of which, mainly Hindi superproductions involving huge stars and musical numbers, emerge from "Bollywood" (Bombay Hollywood), compared to dwindling numbers of productions in the United States. The regulation of American exports in countries such as China—the Chinese government's attempt to stimulate an indigenous industry—have not bred solutions, only further problems, such as widespread, overwhelming piracy of DVDs. While Anglophone audiences likely see Hong Kong action pictures or Japanese animation (called *anime*), few except city-dwellers with access to first-rate art or repertory theaters seek out "foreign" films in theatrical release, and their dearth contributes to the persistent impression that Hollywood cinema dominates onscreen.

Even the assumption, moreover, that films emanate from "national" industries requires up-ending, and not simply because we find ourselves in an increasingly "globalized" industry, as I shall discuss at further length in Chapter 3. National film industries have never been "pure," even when they have been most forcefully tied to the nation-state, such as when the German or Italian film industries were overtly harnessed to the Nazi and Fascist regimes during the Second World War. Italian cinema under Mussolini produced propaganda, yes, but it also produced scores of melodramas, comedies, and films of social interest involving some of the extraordinarily talented figures, such as Vittorio DeSica, we tend now to associate with the Italian post-war cinematic movement called "neorealism." Later, when the American studio system began to collapse as it competed with television and squandered enormous amounts of money on **blockbusters** (expensive and widely promoted superproductions), the Italian cinema yoked itself to units devoted to American "international" productions. "Spaghetti" westerns were born of the union. Many of those films, especially those directed by Sergio Leone and featuring scores by Ennio Morricone, have become the stuff of film-buff legend; the famous line delivered by James Coburn in *A Fistful of Dynamite* (1971) before spectacularly blowing up his enemies—"Duck, you sucker"—is an anthem of their style, a peculiar amalgam of brazen violence and camp wit. There's much more to these films than style, however: *Fistful*'s plot, centered around the mysterious entrance of an Irish Republican Army (IRA) explosive expert upon the scene of the Mexican Revolution, displays the extent to which ideas of America, that complicated promise of freedom amidst histories of social repression, circulate in fantastic spaces only movies can create. "Which way is America?" asks one of the film's characters, revealing a fusion of Europe and the Americas in which, as film scholar Marcia Landy observes, "most modern discourses of nation are unstable constructions" (Landy 1996: 69). Even "Hollywood" itself wobbles on its national foundation: from the works of émigré directors like Douglas Sirk (né Dietlef Sierck) and Fritz Lang to those of Paul Verhoeven (who directed *Basic Instinct* [1992]) and Jan de Bont (of *Speed* [1994] fame), the American cinema absorbs and cannibalizes, and is absorbed and cannibalized in turn by the rest of the world.

"Films Star, Well, Stars"

(A different assumption from the more complicated, and certainly equally contestable, assertion that stars, well, act.)

Overwhelmed by the mega-salaries commanded by the likes of Julia Roberts and Tom Cruise, we may feel licensed to assume that the institution of stardom in Hollywood (1) is alive and well and (2) has deviated only slightly from the system found there during its heyday, when Mary Pickford and Douglas Fairbanks built their castle called "Pickfair" in the Hollywood Hills, or when the studio Metro-Goldwyn-Mayer (MGM) boasted "more stars than there are in heaven." The story of the emergence of modern stardom offers a palpable index of that institution's pliability and discontinuities: as much as we now attribute early films to their innovative directors (like Thomas Edison, or Edwin S. Porter, or, later, D.W. Griffith), most films before 1910 or thereabouts instead were advertised entirely as products of studios (those complex techno-industrial entities that organized film labor through most of the twentieth century). We owe the idea of the modern female star to Carl Laemmle. He was the head of the Independent Motion Picture (IMP) company who launched an innovative promotional campaign in 1910 for a player named Florence Lawrence, known previously only as "the Biograph girl." One morning, so the story goes, readers of the St. Louis (Missouri) newspapers learned of the death of their beloved "Biograph girl" Florence Lawrence (the first time her name had been used publicly) in an unfortunate streetcar accident. Immediately thereafter, Laemmle responded with a blasting notice that the story (which, it should not surprise you, he himself had planted) was a vicious lie: "Miss Lawrence was not even in a streetcar accident, is in the best of health, will continue to appear in 'Imp' films, and very shortly some of the best work in her career is to be released" (Jacobs 1967 [1939]: 87). He followed up the stories with a visit from Florence Lawrence and the IMP's leading man, King Baggott, to put all doubts to rest, and adoring crowds, delighted that Florence Lawrence was alive, received them.

If Laemmle created America's first star, and perhaps America's first star couple in Lawrence–Baggott, he also gave form to the couple that is more strongly cemented in this story of stardom's birth: the star and the promotion/publicity apparatus upon which he or she rests. For stars, as Robert Sklar notes in his wonderful history of cinema, are mysteries explained by no single variable: "beauty, performance style, or promotional effort" (Sklar 1993: 72). While they may function

as intimates, surrogates, or (to use the language of psychoanalysis that many film scholars have brought to images of stars) "ego-ideals," stars can never be divorced from their screen *personae* and from the myths sustained about them by the industry and its parasites. Just as the cinema *is* the ensemble of its texts and their contexts, stardom is this fusion, and it includes the motor of our desire and pleasure. Stardom is, in other words, a social phenomenon, wherein stars can function as condensations for social anxieties, screens for desire, allegories for transgression, fictions for racial identities, tools for industrial profiteering, models for gender and sexual behavior, and so forth. Promotion and publicity can fuel stars' careers as much as they can destroy them: the greatest star of the silent Chinese (Shanghai) cinema, Ruan Ling-yu, committed suicide at the age of twenty-four, after a tabloid article focusing on her relationships with her estranged husband and lover compared her personal status to that of the "fallen women" she, like Greta Garbo, frequently played. Experimental filmmaker and author Kenneth Anger's chronicle of stars' demises, *Hollywood Babylon* (1975), exemplifies the other side of this kind of tragedy: the pleasure in dirt associated with the fall of stars from the heavens.

If stardom as institution has some historical and social specificity, it does not, however, extend over cinema in its entirety. With regard to narrative film, movements such as Italian neorealism, as well as those cinemas associated with struggles for national liberation (such as "Third Cinema"), feminist cinema, and queer cinema, all depend upon the use of non-professional actors to explore everyday life and the lives of the people constituted in these social and political collectivities. British director Mike Leigh's process combines non-professional with professional actors to inhabit the lives of his frequently working-class characters, which Leigh develops, largely unscripted, over the course of his films' production. Other processes rely upon the dynamics of ensemble casts of actors who know each other well and build improvisationally upon past work: the cycle of films directed by Christopher Guest (*Waiting for Guffman*, 1996; *Best in Show*, 2000; *A Mighty*

Wind, 2003) could not provide better illustration of the hilarious fruits of this sort of collaboration. While a few documentary films may have created stars, such as Michael Moore's notoriety after documenting his pursuit of the General Motors chairman of the board in *Roger and Me* (1989), the practice of documentary tends to exploit stars mostly for their social authority; they can function as "talking heads" or provide "voice of God" narration (such as Morgan Freeman's in *March of the Penguins* [2005]) to convince audiences of a film's worth, thereby bolstering box office receipts. Finally, even those independent productions that have a strong narrative component frequently cannot afford stars whose names and reputations would bring them to distributors' and audiences' attention; many very fine projects founder in development purgatory, waiting for a star's interest, while just as many lousy ones careen through with green lights thanks to an agent's conviction.

"Films are in color." "Films last for about two hours." "Films are the products of directors' visions." "The best films receive Academy Awards." "The costs of films' production exceed the cost of their promotion." "Theater tickets generate movies' profit." "There are no great films from Poland (Mongolia, Ireland, Iran, Burkina Faso, …)." "Films are better now than they were fifty years ago." And so on: whatever your assumptions, film study encourages you to explore them, test them, examine them, compare them, historicize them. Make way, that is, for what you're seeing and hearing and learning, so that you can overcome the alienation factor that results from a film failing to conform to your expectations, however expansive. If you remain open to what a film might be, you are a step further toward thinking about what cinema will have been or might become.

What Is Cinema?

This question is one made famous, and unanswerably so, by the film theorist and *Ur*-cinephile André Bazin. A two-volume study of this title appeared in translation from the French in a 1971 paperback edition; in the hands of students, the well-thumbed, slim pink and lime green volumes were indispensable signifiers of a serious and weighty interest not in films, still less in the movies, but in "The Cinema." The term meant at least the following: a vast knowledge of film history and its canon, a well-honed aesthetic sensibility, an attentiveness to films' formal language and structures, a political understanding of post-war consciousness and the forces condensed in the moment shorthanded as May 1968 in France, a passion for the philosophy of cinema (and/or cinema as philosophy), and a commitment to one or several eccentric critical gestures, such as taking the view (contrary to Bazin's and to every known Truth) that Buster Keaton was a greater physical comedian than Charlie Chaplin, say, or elevating a producer such as Pandro S. Berman (belatedly recognized by the 1977 Irving Thalberg Award from the Academy of Motion Picture Arts and Sciences) to an exalted status, a joke, but not only a joke, Gore Vidal plays out in his novel *Myra Breckenridge*. The Cinema combined a feel for the high and the low, balancing the weightiest questions about how to imagine human freedom with the feeling of frenetic delight in a Mack Sennett chase or the one following upon a funeral in the René Clair short film *Entr'acte* (1924). The Cinema, in the sense of Bazin's query, was not just a way of taking seriously something others dismissed as pabulum or "mere" entertainment (although it was that to be sure), but also a way of asking, more deeply than most before or after him, after the ontology, the essence, of cinema as it relates to our very being. How do certain approaches to life and to social being find cinematic expression? How does cinema help us approach the mystery of the human, the "real," that element of our existence toward which we incline only asymptotically, without ever fully apprehending it?

Bazin's writings, begun during the Second World War and extended through his short life until the 1950s, when he founded the French film magazine *Cahiers du cinéma*, have been read and re-read by generations of film students. His biographer, Dudley Andrew, is right in my view to see his impact as awe-inspiring:

André Bazin's impact on film art, as theorist and critic, is widely considered to be greater than that of any single director, actor, or producer in this history of the cinema. He is credited with almost single-handedly establishing the study of film as an accepted intellectual pursuit.

(Bazin 1997: x)

In fact, Bazin was a kind of guru for those voracious students of cinema who became the leading directors of the French New Wave, such as Jean-Luc Godard and François Truffaut.

There is a danger, however, in simplifying his reflections on realism, which too readily become aligned with his fondness for the movement known as Italian neorealism, about which he wrote as it unfolded in Italy following the war, or his enthusiasm for the work of French director Jean Renoir (son of the Impressionist painter Pierre Auguste Renoir). In neorealism and in Renoir (but also in Orson Welles, William Wyler, and others), Bazin found something massive to push against, to test, to think about, which he called by the slippery and perhaps misleading name "realism." By this name, he referred to what is revealed by a style on a continuum at whose other pole is montage. At realism's end, the cinema is an art and practice of composition and contemplation; the director sets the image before the spectator, often through the **long take** (a shot of a relatively long duration) and **deep space** (the combination of deep focus, or maintaining many planes of action in focus simultaneously, with a set which allows the director to stage action on those many planes), whose active and curious gaze engages it and thereby finds it an avenue toward (not a "representation of") reality. Active, curious, intellectual, committed, open, fluid, engaged: these are the key words of this end of the continuum; but "realism," it must be stressed, does not designate its fulfillment in the "real," only a method for its approach, where "real" continues to stand for that kernel of the mystery of being we never access. At the other end of the continuum lies "montage," associated

as we have seen with the work of Sergei Eisenstein in the (former) Soviet Union but also more generally with **classical Hollywood cinema** (explained at greater length in Chapter 2 and exemplified by D.W. Griffith, from whom Eisenstein learnt the rudiments of "analytical cutting"). Montage directs or restricts the viewer's attention through editing, limiting his/her capacity for contemplation, or for finding gaps or loose associations, by insisting upon meaning, supplying details, and otherwise didactically leading the way. As Bazin explains it in an essay on Wyler:

The technique of analytical cutting tends to destroy in particular the ambiguity inherent in reality. It "subjectivizes" the event to an extreme, since each shot is the product of the director's bias. Analytical cutting implies not only a dramatic, emotional, or moral choice, but also, and more significantly, a judgment on reality itself.

(Bazin 1997: 8)

The problems with the extremes of the continuum become immediately clear, insofar that positioning any given film or filmmaker on this spectrum would lead to a judgment about the director's political/philosophical value: Rossellini (one of the giants of neorealism) good, Hitchcock bad. Or, more perniciously, Rossellini politically progressive *due to his cinematic style*, and Hitchcock politically retrogressive *due to his*. But the kernel of Bazin's insights into the philosophical and political (and social, historical, industrial, technological, aesthetic, psychological, personal—and I need to add here "religious") nature of cinematic expression, how it is able to or unable to seize our collective interest and help it coalesce into deep insight about what one grandly used to call the human condition, should not be lost in continued questions about what cinema *is*. While located quite specifically in the years and works of the post-war period, Bazin's thinking inaugurated an inquiry in the cinema as equal to, and perhaps greater than (given its social power), any serious intellectual and political project.

If Bazin wasn't always quick to complicate his own dichotomizing scheme, his students later continued to follow its strict logic, but with new objects at hand. The contributors to *Cahiers*, avid cinephiles who gorged themselves on American films at the Cinémathèque française as soon as the French government lifted bans on their import following the war, turned attention in the 1950s to those directors who they believed managed to express themselves despite the assembly-line nature of industrial filmmaking. Carrying the seed of Bazin's valuation of agonistic, dialectical approaches toward the ever-elusive "real," they found in the style of some Hollywood genre films a cinematic vision that cut against the grain of standardization, conformity, and routine or rote production. They elevated these directors to the status of authors, or *auteurs* in French, as opposed to those "hacks" (or *metteurs en scène* in French) who were seen merely to be grinding out the already known. *Auteurs* found ways to "sign" their films, or, perhaps more accurately, the *Cahiers* writers found evidence for the Hollywood directors' signatures across bodies of their work, whether through attention to formal **motifs** (particularly those expressed through *mise-en-scène*, in the placement and movement of actors and objects within the frame), or, less frequently, through thematic preoccupations which nonetheless emerge from film style. When American film critics seized upon the French conception of film authorship, or the *politique des auteurs* (the notion that the director is ultimately able to express his—and it was uniformly gendered male—vision through the creative army at his disposal), they did so with a vengeance for taxonomy and hierarchy that dispensed with the care the *Cahiers* critics took to value the contributions of Hollywood to cinema more broadly understood. That is, the *Cahiers* contributors found art when they looked at Hollywood, art as valuable, "signed," and complex as the art cinema that emerged from Europe, Japan, India, and elsewhere in the 1950s from director luminaries such as Ingmar Bergman, Federico Fellini, Satyajit Ray, Michelangelo Antonioni, Luchino Visconti, Andrei Wajda, Akiro Kurosawa, Yasujiro Ozu, Robert Bresson,

Jacques Tati, and so on. And the struggle with the constraints of industrial production only upped the ante; whereas "art cinema" directors enjoyed total freedom and control, by comparison Hollywood directors labored under the boss they all called the Bottom Line. A western like *Stagecoach* (1939) or the later and far more folksy and racist epic *The Searchers* (1956) deserved close analysis and attention, then, for the director's capacity to make style speak through the tried and true formulae and conventions of classical cinema, thereby elevating John Ford to the *Cahiers* inner circle. And Ford especially, since he was the man who was so identified with genre films that when he introduced himself to Cecil B. DeMille (on the occasion of defending fellow director Joseph Mankiewicz against McCarthy-era charges of Communist sympathizing) he merely said, "My name's John Ford. I make Westerns" (Buscombe 1988: 344).

The legacy of the *Cahiers* writings is greater than some acknowledge, for that group insisted in important ways upon the value of commercial cinema, if only some of it, as meaningful and worthy of careful analysis for its contributions to an expressive repertoire and form of collective life. If the tendency of later critical assessments of the *politique des auteurs* has been understandably to bristle at the dichotomizing and dismissive hierarchies of "author/hack," "trash/art," "style/genre" that emerge from these analyses, those who engage with the popular commercial cinema as an object of study nonetheless owe some debt to Bazin and to their writings. It should not surprise us that Truffaut and Godard, like Quentin Tarantino a few decades later, gobbled up as much generic fare as possible, only to adopt it, transmute it, adapt it, revise it toward their own ends in the New Wave, for that group of filmmakers were as interested as Bazin was in a cinema of thought. Indeed, French theorist Gilles Deleuze finds in Godard something akin to Romanticism: "grasping the intolerable or unbearable, the empire of poverty, and thereby becoming visionary, to produce a means of knowledge and action out of pure vision" (Deleuze 1989: 18).

What is cinema, then, if not an opportunity for thought? To discover principles of form, to trace something of its history, to grasp its power to transform: these are the subjects of the following chapters.

Summary

From its inception in the late nineteenth century, film has been a dynamic medium, put to uses other than those of the commercial narrative form. "The Cinema" designates the ensemble of films as they engage with the world of spectators, as we, in other words, respond in the broadest possible sense to what we see and hear. To study film, then, is to test our assumptions about what we take films to be, about what we might expect to see and hear, and to take films seriously as revealing something, again in the broadest possible sense, about who we have been, who we are, and who we might become. Commercial fare, like *Dude, Where's My Car* (2000), and radical documentary, like *This Is What Democracy Looks Like* (from the same year and available to stream online), belong to the cinema, all of which opens itself to study.

15. Journalism

by John Pavlik and Shawn McIntosh

This chapter surveys the history and development of journalism. Venturing from the days of the penny press and yellow journalism to the development of citizen journalists and other impacts of the Internet, this chapter provides readers a useful working knowledge of the industry that pervades much of society. Pavlik and McIntosh effectively address the influences of journalism and journalists on individuals and society as a whole. Readers should note the prominent re-emergence of the discussion of ethics, introduced several chapters ago, in this overview of journalism. A careful reader of this chapter, whether interested in joining the field or simply enhancing his or her media literacy, should finish this chapter with a respect for the historical underpinnings of this industry and a more complete understanding of the potential influence effective journalists wield in society.

Journalism's purpose, according to some journalists, is to "comfort the afflicted and afflict the comfortable." The societal roles and responsibilities of journalism have often been discussed—as government watchdog, as advocate of the common citizen, as panderer to baser tastes among the public, as big business, as influencer of public opinion. Heated discussions on how well journalism is fulfilling its roles continue to this day in letters-to-the-editor pages,

John V. Pavlik & Shawn McIntosh, "Journalism," *Converging Media: A New Introduction to Mass Communication*, pp. 281-316, 4. Copyright © 2011 by Oxford University Press (UK). Reprinted with permission.

call-in talk shows, on the Internet, and in news-rooms. These discussions should not be seen as some inherent failure of journalism; rather, they should be understood as signs of how important journalism continues to be in the modern world.

Journalism plays an important part in three of the four main functions of mass communication: **surveillance**, **correlation**, and **cultural transmission**. It can also play a major role in mobilizing the public. These functions are carried out by the coverage of news. The public learns of events and happenings locally and around the world, and good coverage puts the events in a context that helps people form a picture of what the world is like. Through articles and shows and cultural and artistic figures, culture is transmitted and the public learns the mores of society. To a lesser extent, journalism also serves the entertainment function of mass communication through coverage of entertainment events and news on popular stars.

In order to get a good understanding of journalism, however, it is important to first understand what news is.

What Is News?

The journalist's old adage that news is "when man bites dog" rings true in the sense that news is something that occurs that is out of the ordinary. News usually is about an event that affects the public in some way, or that at least has some element of public interest. It includes coverage of recent events, such as breaking news of a fire or accident, and recent discoveries of events that have already taken place, such as financial wrong-doing by corporate executives or politicians.

Several issues arise on examination of this basic assumption about the definition of news. First is the often-heard complaint by the public that news concentrates too much on negative events—crime, accidents, wrongdoing, etc. Critics say that this overwhelmingly negative coverage gives the public a misleading impression that things are worse than they actually are, such as making it seem that local crime is rising by intense coverage on a spate of robberies when in fact the crime rate has dropped. News organizations do include positive news, such as heartwarming human-interest stories or new store openings, but then they can be accused of acting as a public relations mouthpiece for organizations or individuals and not adequately informing the public of important issues.

Conventional wisdom suggests that news means reporting the unexpected. But the truth is that a large portion of news is largely predictable a day, a week, a month, or sometimes years in advance. Consider the types of news stories about any annual holiday or event, such as advice on shopping for Christmas gifts—a look at the news organization's archives will likely uncover a very similar story the previous year or the year before that.

It is vital that media consumers realize this because news doesn't just happen. It is in many ways manufactured and influenced by a wide variety of people, organizations, and forces—often including advertising and public relations. Historian and Pulitzer Prize–winning author Daniel Boorstin describes what he calls **pseudo events**, such as press conferences or other staged events, like marches and rallies, as an example of how groups can influence what is covered in the news. These events are often known about days or weeks in advance and in the case of press conferences are held specifically to attract media coverage. What kind of news shows up on television or in a newspaper depends on a number of factors, including what other events are happening that day, the type of publication or broadcast organization, and even the political views of the owner, in some cases.

A **soft news day** is when editors feel not much has happened that is news-worthy and therefore will air programming or include articles such as human-interest stories. A flood in India that kills five hundred people may be included as a "World News Brief" on an inside page of a local paper on a slow news day and may not be included at all on a day that has important local news. How do editors decide that a story on a popular local high-school athlete killed in a traffic accident is more important than five hundred killed in India? They try to determine what is of most interest to their readership. In this way, journalists have an important agenda-setting function, which means they can influence by their coverage what is deemed as important by their audience and what is therefore more likely to be discussed by the public.

Although journalism has a strong public service mission, it is nevertheless subject to the realities of the commercial media system. Without significant audiences and typically substantial advertising revenues, most newspapers, news magazines, and news programs on television and radio would cease to exist. Most newspapers and magazines are actually more advertising than news, in terms of the amount of space devoted to each type of content. The Internet has challenged many of journalism's traditional business models, and declines in advertising revenues for traditional media outlets have still not been outweighed by the gain in Internet advertising.

Let's look at two sides of the historical development of journalism—as a profession and as a business—to see how each has influenced the practice of modern journalism.

The Historical Development of Journalism

The advent of the **penny press** and mass distribution of newspapers in the early nineteenth century, discussed in Chapter 4, brought about a sea change in the concept and definition of journalism. Prior to that, editors of newspapers mostly relied on "news" brought to their offices by citizens or gathered by a small staff, as well as liberally copying from other newspapers, often without crediting the sources. Editors' or publishers' (they were often the same person) opinions were often freely mixed with other editorial content, and no thought was given to presenting all sides of an issue fairly. There was also no established practice of putting the most important news first. Articles were usually written chronologically, regardless of the relative importance of the information.

With the penny press and the need to appeal to as wide a readership as possible, however, newspaper publishers often toned down opinions in articles and concentrated more on covering sensational crimes or events. In order to fill their pages, they also had to hire reporters who looked for news to cover rather than passively waiting for news to come to them.

Further fueling the transformation of newspapers were competitors such as **James Gordon Bennett**, who founded the *New York Herald* in 1835. He added a number of features that are now staples in modern journalism, including a financial page, editorial commentary, and public-affairs reporting.

In order to maintain their objective stance throughout the rest of the paper, or at least the public appearance of impartiality, newspaper editors began publishing their points of view exclusively on a special page dubbed the "editorial" page, which is a tradition maintained today by the Western press. Editorials provide a valuable service to the public, helping to guide opinion on matters of public importance, as with endorsements for candidates for public office.

Objectivity and the Associated Press

The notion of what is news continued to evolve and was shaped by the democratization of politics, the expansion of the market economy, and the growing impact of an entrepreneurial middle class. One reason news became more impartial—what is known in journalism as **objectivity**—was the emergence of the newswire service in the 1840s. In 1848, publishers of six New York newspapers organized the **Associated Press** (AP), in large part to take advantage of the capabilities of the telegraph as a high-speed communications medium. Telegraphy was too expensive for any single newspaper to afford, so a consortium, or association of leading press organizations, made economic sense.

Because the AP gathered news for half a dozen newspapers with varying political viewpoints, it needed to publish news reports that were politically neutral and thus acceptable to all its member papers. By the dawn of the twentieth century, AP dispatches had become virtually free of editorial comment.

The Associated Press is still based in New York and is the world's largest news-gathering organization, providing textual, audio, and video news, photos, and graphics to its members. The AP is a not-for-profit members' cooperative including 1,700 newspapers and 5,000 radio and television news operations, that means that the members provide much of the content distributed by the AP, and in turn any member can use the content distributed by the AP. The AP employs 4,100 people (3,000 of whom work as journalists) in 243 news bureaus in 97 countries.

Minority Newspapers

Also important during the 1800s was the rise of various minority or ethnic newspapers. These newspapers served the needs of niche audiences, including Native American, African American, Jewish, and other ethnic groups. Among the earliest minority newspapers was *El Misisipí*, the first Spanish-language newspaper in the United States, which began publication in 1808 in New Orleans.[1] The first Native American newspaper, the *Cherokee Phoenix*, began publication in 1828. The first African American daily, the *New Orleans Daily Creole*, began publication in 1856.

American abolitionist and former slave Frederick Douglass was not only a great statesman but also a journalist, publishing an antislavery paper called the *North Star*. Among the most notable minority newspapers of the day was the *Provincial Freeman*, a newspaper founded and edited by **Mary Shadd Cary**, the first African American woman in North America to edit a weekly newspaper.

Born a free black in 1823 in Wilmington, Delaware, Mary fled with her family to Windsor, Canada, after the Fugitive Slave Act was passed in the United States in 1850. Under this act, free northern blacks and escaped slaves were threatened with a return to slavery. In response to a vigorous campaign to deter runaway slaves from escaping to Canada, Mary wrote a forty-four-page pamphlet, "Notes of Canada West," outlining the opportunities for blacks in Canada. Building on the success of this widely read publication, Mary established her weekly newspaper, the *Provincial Freeman*, targeting blacks, and especially fugitive slaves. Her newspaper reported on a variety of important topics, among them the lies being spread in the United States that African Americans in Canada were starving.

Another important African American woman journalist in the nineteenth century was **Ida B. Wells**. Born a slave in 1862 six months before the signing of the Emancipation Proclamation, Wells spent her adult life fighting racism and especially the lynching of African Americans. Wells wrote for the religious weekly *The Living Way* and for various African American newspapers, including the *Free Speech* and *Headlight*. She was elected secretary of the Afro-American Press Association in 1889.

Pulitzer and Hearst: The Circulation Wars, Sensationalism, and Standards

Although the practice of objective reporting became the norm for the AP, it was well into the twentieth century before most newspapers had adopted this model of reporting for their own staff. Throughout the latter half of the nineteenth and early in the twentieth century another form of reporting became prevalent in many U.S. newspapers. **Sensational journalism**, or news that exaggerated or featured lurid details and depictions, came to dominate much newspaper content of this period. Two of the greatest newspaper publishing titans of this era were **William Randolph Hearst**, publisher of the *San Francisco Examiner* and the *New York Journal*, and **Joseph Pulitzer**, publisher of the *New York World*, the *St. Louis Post-Dispatch*, and other papers.

Joseph Pulitzer

Joseph Pulitzer was born in 1847 in Budapest, Hungary. He emigrated to the United States in 1864, serving in the Union army during the Civil War. In 1868 he moved to St. Louis and went to work as a reporter for a German-language paper. Pulitzer purchased the bankrupt *St. Louis Dispatch* in 1878, later merging it with the *Evening Post*, thus creating the *St. Louis Post-Dispatch*. In 1883 he bought the *New York Post* and later the *New York World*.

He was elected to the Forty-ninth Congress of the United States but resigned after three months because of failing health. His health continued to deteriorate, however, and by 1890 he was almost completely blind and became extremely sensitive to sounds. Despite officially resigning as editor of the *World*, he continued his involvement by communicating through secretaries and assistants while he sought various treatments.

He became embroiled with Hearst in the newspaper circulation wars during the 1890s, using frequent illustrations, a racy style, and colorful headlines to build the circulation of the *World*. Pulitzer wanted his papers to focus on city news and encouraged his reporters to seek out original, dramatic, and compelling stories, especially humorous, odd, romantic, or thrilling ones, and to write accurately and with attention to detail. Pulitzer built the circulation of the *New York World* to three hundred thousand by the early 1890s by mixing good, solid reporting with sensational photographs, comic strips, and "crusades" against corrupt politicians, support for increased taxes, and civil service reform.

After the four-month Spanish-American War in 1898, Pulitzer withdrew from the sensational tools and techniques that had helped build his newspapers' circulations and replaced them with a vision of journalistic excellence, which he outlined in a 1904 article for the *North American Review*.[2] During this time, Pulitzer was instrumental in the passage of antitrust legislation and regulation of the insurance industry because of investigative stories his papers ran. This emphasis on public service journalism and accurate reporting is still a cornerstone of the annual Pulitzer Prizes, which he bequeathed along with an endowment for the Columbia University Graduate School of Journalism after his death in 1911.

One of Pulitzer's most successful undertakings was the introduction of color printing of comics in his Sunday papers. The most notable example was *The Yellow Kid*, a comic strip drawn as busy, single-panel illustrations. Although *The Yellow Kid* was not the first newspaper cartoon, its innovative style contributed much of the comic strip format many today take for granted.[3]

The Yellow Kid was a creation of cartoonist Richard Felton Outcault during the Pulitzer-Hearst news paper circulation war in the 1890s and was characterized by rude, vulgar, and brash behavior on the backstreets of the fictional Hogan's Alley. In some ways, *The Yellow Kid* was a late nineteenth-century precursor to the crude kids of *South Park* created during the cable and broadcast television ratings battles of the late twentieth century.

The Yellow Kid quickly became a central figure in the circulation battles between newspaper giants Pulitzer and Hearst when Hearst hired Outcault away from the *World*. The brashness of *The Yellow Kid* reflected well the journal's overall dramatic style. In reference to the Kid's well-known yellow shirt, critics coined the term **yellow journalism** to describe the sensational style of the newspapers of Pulitzer and his competitor, Hearst.

William Randolph Hearst

William Randolph Hearst was the son of a self-made multimillionaire miner and rancher in northern California. Hearst studied at Harvard and became "proprietor" of his first newspaper, the *San Francisco Examiner*, in 1887 at the age of twenty-three. His father had acquired the paper as payment for a gambling debt. The younger Hearst then acquired in 1895 the *New York Morning Journal* and debuted the *Evening Journal* a year later, hiring away many of Joseph Pulitzer's best reporters and editors by offering them higher pay. He increased his newspaper and periodical chain nationwide to include the *Boston American* and *Chicago Examiner*, as well as magazines *Cosmopolitan* and *Harper's Bazaar*.

Later immortalized in Orson Welles's cinematic triumph, *Citizen Kane*, William Randolph Hearst sensationalized the news by printing colorful banner headlines, adding splashy photography, and some say even inventing the news. Hearst's stories did not always capture the truth, and his readers probably knew it, but they enjoyed reading the accounts and his newspapers' circulation increased tremendously.

Often criticized for his sensational tactics, Hearst nevertheless articulated news standards that resonate even today. Hearst's editorial guidelines from 1933 stated: "Make the news thorough. Print all the news. Condense it if necessary. Frequently it is better when intelligently condensed. But get it in."

One historian has summarized Hearst's actions as inflammatory. Ernest L. Meyer wrote: "Mr. Hearst in his long and not laudable career has inflamed Americans against Spaniards, Americans against Japanese, Americans against Filipinos, Americans against Russians, and in the pursuit of his incendiary campaign he has printed downright lies, forged documents, faked atrocity stories, inflammatory editorials, sensational cartoons and photographs and other devices by which he abetted his jingoistic ends."[4]

Hearst's ornate 130-room mansion, San Simeon, built in the 1920s and nicknamed the Hearst Castle, today stands as a California landmark. In 1945 Hearst established the Hearst Foundation (now the William Randolph Hearst Foundation), which today provides important support for journalism education and other concerns including health and culture. Hearst died at age eighty-eight in 1951 in Beverly Hills, California.

The Muckrakers

Just as the efforts of renowned newspaper publishers Hearst and Pulitzer laid a foundation for many of the practices of contemporary journalism, so did the efforts of a number of very important magazine journalists from the late nineteenth and early twentieth centuries. Among the most important were the **muckrakers**. Journalists such as Ida Minerva Tarbell, Joseph Lincoln Steffens, and Upton Sinclair (author of *The Jungle*) were dubbed "muckrakers" by a disapproving President

Theodore Roosevelt because they pioneered investigative reporting of corrupt practices and problems in government or business. The process was analogous to raking muck, the polite term for the manure, mud, and straw mixture found in stables. Many of the most important muckrakers reported for magazines of the day, in large part because their investigations required considerable time to complete, which fit better with magazine publishing deadlines than with newspapers.

The Rise of Electronic Journalism

The golden age of newspapers started its decline when radio became a medium of mass communication in the 1920s. The public did not have to wait a day or more for news of events like it did with newspapers, and furthermore radio was "free," as it was entirely advertising supported. But television news started the steep decline and eventual eclipse of newspapers as the public's main source of news.

The late 1940s and early 1950s marked the beginning of television news. News was and still is an important part of how broadcast television fulfills its federal mandate to serve in the public interest.

Many of the early news programs were produced by the television network news divisions in New York. In 1947, NBC debuted *Meet the Press*, a made-for-TV news conference, with journalists asking questions of various news makers, often government officials. The program continues today and is the oldest series on network TV. In the 1950s, NBC introduced the *Today* show, the first and still-running early-morning network news show. *Today* had a decidedly entertainment quality back then, with host Dave Garroway joined by chimpanzee sidekick J. Fred Muggs.

Murrow and News in TV's Golden Age

Setting the standard for television news during television's golden age in the late 1940s and the 1950s was the distinguished journalist **Edward R. Murrow**, who first achieved fame by broadcasting dramatic radio news reports from London during

World War II. Murrow produced the popular television programs *See It Now* and *Person to Person* at CBS News.

Murrow's comments on television at the Radio-Television News Directors Association (RTNDA) meeting in 1958 ring equally true today for the Internet: "This instrument can teach, it can illuminate, and yes, it can inspire. But it can do so only to the extent that humans are determined to use it to those ends. Otherwise it is nothing but wires and lights in a box." The same year he also wrote in *TV Guide* that viewers must realize "television in the main is being used to distract, delude, amuse and insulate us."

Changes in Television News Coverage

The introduction of video cameras into the television newsroom brought important changes to television news. **Electronic news-gathering** (ENG) equipment allowed journalists in the field to capture and send videotaped news by satellite to the network, where it could be edited and broadcast much more quickly than film. This has influenced the nature of video storytelling. The late CBS news veteran Bud Benjamin likened it to "NTV" or the video-journalism equivalent of "MTV," or music television, with rapid-paced cuts and entertainment values becoming increasingly paramount in journalism. The growth of cable television has also led to an increasing number of local twenty-four-hour cable news operations.

Foundations of Journalism

Digital technology and the Internet will continue to transform journalism, but professional, mainstream journalism today is still largely practiced as it has been.

Reporters cover events and write stories, editors select what stories get published or aired and where they appear, and how many pages they have for news depends on how many advertisements were sold. Digital technology will not change the fact that reporters need to visit places and interview people. Nor will digital technology replace an experienced editor's judgment on what makes a good story and how to edit that story.

In order to understand what aspects of journalism have changed already and what will likely change some more with convergence, we will first look at basic issues of journalistic responsibility and how journalism is practiced, at least in its ideal form.

The Hutchins Commission and a Free and Responsible Press

In 1947 what became known as the Hutchins Commission published a landmark report titled *A Free and Responsible Press*, offering a critique of the state of the press in the United States. The 133-page report of the Commission on Freedom of the Press was written by Robert Maynard Hutchins and a dozen other leading intellectuals. The report argued that the public has a right to information that affects it and that the press has a responsibility to present that information. Because the press enjoys constitutionally guaranteed freedom, the press carries an additional moral duty to fulfill this responsibility. The commission recommended that the government, the public, and the press could all take steps to improve the functioning of a healthy press. Among these steps, the commission recommended the government recognize that all media have the same constitutional guarantees traditionally enjoyed only by print media.

The commission recommended that the agencies of mass communication assume the responsibility of financing new, experimental activities in their fields. Moreover, the members of the press should engage in vigorous mutual criticism. The commission called on the public to create academic-professional centers of advanced study, research, and publication in the field of communications. Among the first such centers was the Media Studies Center, founded by the Freedom Forum in 1984, nearly forty years after the report. The commission also recommended that existing schools of journalism exploit the total resources of their universities to the end that their students obtain the broadest and most liberal training. Finally, the commission recommended the establishment of a new and independent agency to appraise and report annually on the performance of the press. This has been tried at a national level in the form of a National Press Council but has failed, although a similar idea has had marginal success in some states.

The Separation of Editorial and Business Operations

In newsroom parlance commonly called the "separation of church and state," this is a basic principle in ensuring that news coverage is not influenced by business decisions or advertisers who threaten to stop advertising because they do not like coverage of an issue. This separation is supposed to carry over to the page layout of a newspaper or magazine as well by showing clear differences between advertising and editorial content.

However, many media critics complain that this separation has been breaking down in recent years as publishers or large media corporations that own news organizations increasingly let business decisions influence editorial content. This can happen blatantly, as when the owner of the *Los Angeles Times* used staff reporters and editors to create a special "news" section on the Staples Center that was entirely sponsored (and had content approved by) Staples without explicitly saying so; or it could be more insidious, as when management lays off editorial staff, which has the effect of hampering original local reporting and forces the paper to rely on cheaper but perhaps less relevant wire service news.

Fairness and Balance in News Coverage

Fairness and **balance** in news coverage have replaced the goal of objectivity in journalism. Objectivity, or the principle that news is reported on and presented in a completely unbiased manner, has come under attack in recent years. Critics say that people cannot be completely unbiased and to claim objectivity in a given situation is simply masking the bias of the reporter. In addition, everything from the subsequent editing or placement of a story in a newspaper to the time slot for a news segment can reflect biased coverage, even if the reporter has no strong bias when writing the story. Unintended biases can also show up in the people a journalist decides to interview and the choice of story assignments an editor makes.

The terms "fairness" and "balance" mean that journalists try to present all sides of a topic equally and in a way that does not favor one side. Fairness and balance do not mean that all participants in an issue get equal space for their views, however. A small group of fifty vocal people supporting a minor-party candidate would not get the same amount of coverage as a popular candidate from a major political party simply because they are fielding a candidate in an election or hold nightly protests. Factors such as the relative importance within the context of the story and validity or authority of the news source must be considered when a journalist decides how much coverage to give a person or group.

Framing the News

Traditional news media often decide how they will **frame** a story before the reporting is completed and sometimes before it has even begun. This is one of the biggest problems in journalism today, because frequently the facts of a story are forced to fit into the frame, or angle, regardless of reality. Yet framing cannot be avoided, simply because it makes writing a news story easier and faster. Balance, or fairness, is often not achieved, and often journalists are not even aware that they are framing stories. They see their work as simply reflecting reality.

Perhaps even more problematic, however, is the fact that frequently events in the real world are forced into an existing frame, when reality is in fact more complex and defies framing. The need for journalism often to demonize one side over another can have serious repercussions for reporting on each side and even for what words are used to describe certain actions. Depending on one's loyalties, a "terrorist attack" could also be described as "armed resistance."

Expert Sources

A related issue to framing, also problematic in the media—especially on television—has to do with the use of "expert" sources to give the news more credibility. At the three main television networks, ABC, CBS, and NBC, most speakers selected to give their views during the news or other public-affairs programs are white and male. The Tenth Annual Women, Men and Media Study, conducted by ADT Research in conjunction with the Freedom Forum, shows that during the first six months of 1998, "Nearly nine of ten 'expert' sound bites (87 percent) on the network newscasts were provided by men, and *more* than nine in ten (92 percent) were provided by whites." Women were featured in just 13 percent of expert sound bites and people of color just 6 percent. In contrast, nonexperts on network news programs are much more likely to be of diverse backgrounds.

"Individuals of either sex, any age and all races can be heard from on the network news, as long as they are not wielding power or offering expertise. The networks' 'golden rolodexes' of expert consultants are badly in need of updating," said Andrew Tyndall, director of the study, titled *Who Speaks for America? Sex, Age and Race on the Network News.* Research about other mainstream media, including important print media such as news magazines *Time, Newsweek,* and *U.S. News & World Report,* show similar results.

The News Agenda of Newspapers

An important change in newspaper content has to do with the basic news agenda of newspapers. Research by the Pew Research Center for the People & the Press, an independent opinion research center sponsored by the Pew Charitable Trusts, indicates that in 1980 the front page of the average daily newspaper was quite different in its news agenda than it is today.

One of the most important differences is that, in 1980, one of every three front-page news stories dealt with government or public affairs, compared to just one in every five today. Government and public-affairs matters are traditionally considered the cornerstone of journalism in a democracy. A second important difference is that in 1980, only one in every fifty front-page daily newspaper stories dealt with celebrities, popular entertainment, and other related subjects. Today, one in every fourteen front-page daily newspaper stories deals with celebrities and the like.

There are a number of reasons for this dramatic shift away from public affairs and toward popular entertainment. An increasingly competitive media environment, in which newspapers must compete against electronic entertainment media, is one. Also important is the changing ownership structure and economics of newspapers. Further, technological change is contributing to this transformation, as newspapers struggle to reinvent themselves in an online, digital age.

The News Agenda of Television News

Television news counts on interesting visuals to help tell its stories, and this can often dictate the ordering of stories in a newscast or even whether a story is aired or not. Stories with dramatic video footage, such as fires or accidents, are more likely to air than stories in which stock footage is needed or ones with poor quality video.

Time constraints of less than thirty minutes or an hour to cover local, national, and international news, business news, sports, and weather also place limitations on how long particular stories can be within a newscast. In-depth looks at newsworthy issues must be sacrificed in order to cover a wider range of news stories. The need for scheduled commercial breaks often means that guest experts are asked to explain complex subjects in less than a minute.

Perhaps because of the visual nature of television, television news has always had an eye on the entertainment aspect of media, as demonstrated as far back as the early days of the *Today* show mentioned earlier. The rise of twenty-four-hour news channels also means that there is much more of a **news hole** to fill, which encourages stations to be less discriminating about what they consider newsworthy. Sometimes this is a good thing, as events that would otherwise not reach a televised audience are covered, but other times the material serves mainly a public relations or entertainment purpose. Worse still is that some print publications take their lead from news channels regarding what should be covered.

From Event to Public Eye: How News Is Created

There must always be news to fill the regularly scheduled evening broadcast on television, the morning's paper, or the weekly news magazine. Like an accordion, news can expand or contract as required by the day's events, but only to a limited degree. The fact is, whether anything important happens today or not, the networks will still have at least a thirty-minute newscast (actually, twenty-two minutes, after subtracting the time for commercials). Sometimes, during a major breaking news event such as the September 11 World Trade Center and Pentagon attacks, they will extend the news to an hour or even have continuous coverage.

Techniques of gathering, reporting, and presenting the news to the public have been refined over the years and have changed surprisingly little. There are variations between techniques that print journalists and television journalists must use, of course, but the basic principles are largely the same. We will look at some of the basic steps in the news-gathering process for print and television.

Gathering the News

The Associated Press news service publishes for its members a daily listing of upcoming news events such as important court cases, demonstrations, and press conferences. It's called the AP daybook, and most journalists or their assignment editors refer to it at night to get ideas for stories to cover the next day. The daybook is a pretty good predictor of the next day's news. Some media critics claim that much news is actually manufactured by media organizations, with the help of public relations professionals sending press releases and creating pseudo events such as press conferences,

marches, or awards ceremonies with the sole purpose of getting the attention of the press or public.

Although news covering pseudo events or based on press releases may well be "manufactured," the fact is journalists must largely rely on these sources in order to be informed of what is happening. But journalists also use sources they have developed through experience covering a **beat**, or subject area they specialize in. Initially beats covered geographic areas, much like a police officer's beat. Geographically based beats still exist, but increasingly beats cover specific subject areas, such as education, city hall, the state capital, or science. Through their reporting, journalists become aware of interesting developments that may be newsworthy and can cultivate sources that inform them further. Small newspapers cannot afford to have highly specialized reporters and often simply have general-assignment reporters who cover a range of topics.

Moreover, the media tend to spotlight selected issues and stories. These stories often resonate through the entire media system, whether about the release of a highly anticipated movie, a natural disaster, or a U.S. presidential campaign. An unusual advertising campaign for a movie, for example, may trigger news stories about the campaign and its effect on the success of the movie, which in turn generates more publicity for the movie—which adds to its popularity. Some news filters up through the media network, starting as a story in a local paper that is then covered by a regional television station, where it is seen by a reporter for a national newsweekly, who covers the story and thus brings it to a national audience.

Producing the News

Once a story has been assigned or chosen and the raw material—interviews, background facts, or video footage—has been gathered, the reporter then has to make sense out of it all and shape it into a compelling piece that accurately reflects the facts. Depending on whether the story involves breaking news or not, the reporter sometimes has very little time to write or produce it before a deadline. Few journalists have the luxury of putting a story aside for a week to ponder word choices or polish their prose.

Newspaper editors decide which stories are most important and where they will be placed in the newspaper in meetings several hours before story deadlines, and these spaces are blocked out (advertising space has been blocked out first). Sometimes breaking news or an unexpected event may push planned stories from their slots or from the newspaper entirely.

Editors look for logical weaknesses or errors in stories, often asking reporters to get more information or make more calls to make the story complete. Fact checkers research all facts stated in the story for accuracy and, depending on the media organization and the laziness of the reporter, sometimes have to replace many TKs (used in journalism to mean "to come") in a "finished" story with hard facts based on their research. Copyeditors correct writing errors and make sure everything is written according to the proper style. In larger newspapers, headline and caption writers read the stories and come up with headlines and photo captions that fit within the space allotted. In smaller newspapers, journalists may have more than one role or may be responsible for fact checking or suggesting headlines as well.

Design and page-layout artists put the copy-edited articles and graphics in a digital version of the paper using a page-layout program such as QuarkXpress. Proofreaders check for editorial errors, and after the issue is approved by an editor, it is sent to the printer. This used to be done by taking negative photographs of hard copies of the pages, but now it is mostly done entirely electronically, and the printer receives the pages digitally through a high-speed Internet connection.

In television news, camera crews and reporters usually return to the station to edit footage shot on location and to add voice-overs and graphics to the video. Since time is so critical, news segments are edited and rehearsed down to the second to fit into their selected time slots. With breaking or international news, reporters will report live from location, often broadcasting via satellite.

Television news, because of the amount of equipment needed to shoot video, requires more people to gather and produce a story. A crew of two people, a camera person and a reporter, is usually needed. Digital video technology has helped reduce the number needed to shoot broadcast-quality video to a single camera person and reporter, but there are still many more technical steps involved in assembling a television news package than in writing a print story.

At the station, the producer and reporter decide on what to edit and how the story will be put together, usually working with video editors or other technicians to carry out their instructions. At some stations, news anchors also have a role in editorial decisions, while at other stations they simply present the news.

Distributing the News

The goal of both print and electronic media in distributing the news is the same: to attract as large an audience as possible. The reasoning is simple: a larger audience means a higher advertising rate and more income for the media organization.

Newspapers and magazines use colorful or dramatic photos on their front pages or covers, often with what the editors have decided is the most enticing story. Some magazines may send press releases about what they feel are particularly noteworthy stories coming out in the next issue, with the hope that other media outlets will report on these and generate more sales. Individual stories can be syndicated and appear in other print-media outlets.

Print media are distributed through subscriptions and newsstand sales. Subscribers are more valuable to media organizations because they represent a stable revenue base and provide mailing lists that can be sold or rented to other organizations. Material costs for print media, ranging from paper to ink to delivery trucks, can be quite high.

Television stations have short teasers during commercial breaks throughout the evening, usually asking a provocative question such as, "Could the food you are eating be dangerous? Find out at eleven." Often the stories that have acted as the bait to get viewers to watch the news are not the lead story but appear later in the program, in order to keep people watching. This is also the reason weather forecasts usually come toward the middle or end of a news broadcast. National news shows are transmitted by the network to affiliate stations, sometimes with time slots available for additional local news content. Networks also send video feeds of international and national news coverage to local affiliates so they can use the footage in their news reports.

Types of Journalism

The basic outline of the way news is produced in professional journalism does not show how its tenets have been challenged over the years by other types of journalism that have developed. These other types are a testament to the importance many people put on journalism, making claims of varying severity that mainstream or professional journalism is not living up to its ideals in informing citizens or acting as a watchdog of government.

Much serious questioning of journalism took place during the 1960s, even among established journalists, when social upheavals led many to question norms in established society. Leading reporters such as James "Scottie" Reston of the *New York Times* and Paul Anderson of the *St. Louis Post-Dispatch* perceived the limits of "objective" news reportage that simply stated the facts in a story and developed the beginnings of **interpretive reporting**, which tried to explain the story by placing the facts into broader context.

Critics of interpretive reporting argue that it does no better at adequately representing the complexity of reality than objective reporting. Still, interpretive reporting opened the door to a variety of journalistic styles during the 1960s, including New Journalism, literary journalism, and advocacy journalism.

New journalism developed in the 1960s and 1970s during a time of great social, political, and economic upheaval in the United States, ranging from the Vietnam War to Watergate. Many journalists sought to present a true account of the complexity or spirit of the times. What emerged was a form of reporting that often used literary techniques such as point of view, exploration of characters' emotions, and first-person narrative. Topics included popular social issues and the drug culture. Truman Capote, Tom Wolfe, and Norman Mailer were three prominent writers using new journalism techniques in their books. Critics charged that the literary style often blurred the line between fact and fiction.

Literary journalism in some ways has roots that go back to the muckrakers, although its modern form does not always tackle social problems with the same fervor as the muckrakers. Literary journalism stays closer to true, observable narrative in its storytelling, and its pace may be slow, with frequent lengthy side trips on other topics. Because of the length of articles and variety of topics covered, literary journalism does not generally deal with breaking news events, though news events may be the basis for some literary-journalism stories. One of the finest literary journalists is John McPhee, who combines immersive reporting, solid research, and excellent writing to create engaging stories. Other practitioners of literary journalism include Joan Didion, James Fallows, and Robert Kaplan, all of whom write on a range of issues, including foreign affairs and politics.

Another descendent of muckraking, one that keeps the muckraker's critique of society firmly in focus, is advocacy journalism. It maintains a strong commitment to political and social reform. Leading examples of advocacy journalism are Gloria Steinem (founder of *Ms.* magazine and a leader of the women's movement), Pete Hamill (one-time editor of the *Daily News* in New York), and Nicholas von Hoffman. Much of early environmental journalism was a type of advocacy journalism.

Alternative Journalism

Alternative journalism, often called radical journalism in the past, departed considerably from the traditions of objective reporting and has a much older lineage than some of the types of journalism just mentioned. Its roots go back to some of the radical and socialist newspapers published in the nineteenth century in the UK that were meant to give workers a united voice and sense of injustice. Some radical papers had large circulations in their heyday, comparable to some of the most popular traditional papers of the day, but the advertising-supported model put these newspapers at a disadvantage because advertisers did not want to be associated with radical political movements. In addition, most readers of these papers were working class, so were not considered desirable customers. As a result, such papers tended to struggle to stay afloat or toned down their political rants to be more attractive to advertisers.

Alternative journalism often purposely defied the conventions of professional journalism, both in tone and choice of topics, much as the new journalists did decades later. Despite existing on the fringes throughout most of the twentieth century and never seriously challenging mainstream journalism, it did provide an outlet for stories not seen elsewhere, some of which would then make their way into the mainstream.

Magazines such as *Mother Jones, The Progressive*, and *The Nation* can be seen as inheritors of the radical-journalism tradition and examples of alternative journalism that straddle the gap between radical journalism and mainstream standards of professional quality. And of course the alternative weeklies available in most urban areas, such as the *Boston Phoenix* and the *Houston Press*, are examples of the genre, with their edgy, contrarian coverage of topics that is often geared to a younger audience.

Alternative journalism was given new life in 1999 during the WTO protests in Seattle, when an ad hoc group of protesters created their own media to cover the event because they felt the mainstream press was misreporting or underreporting the events. The independent media movement, called Indymedia for short, was founded and has quickly spread worldwide thanks to the growth of the Internet. Although most Indymedia groups remain small, their decentralized structure and open publishing systems allow people to easily contribute stories, providing outlets for many who would not otherwise get involved in journalism. Some local groups, such as Indymedia NYC, publish professional-quality newspapers along with a robust website.

Public Journalism

Public journalism, sometimes called civic journalism, developed in the early 1990s out of dissatisfaction among some editors and journalists over how poorly mainstream journalism seemed to be covering important social and political issues. They saw the growing cynicism and apathy among the general public in civic affairs, and the increased distrust of journalists, and wondered if perhaps mainstream journalism coverage had an influence on those attitudes.

Public journalism takes a much less radical approach to engaging the public than alternative journalism, mostly because it originated from longtime and respected professional journalists. It expands on the watchdog role of journalism but tries to engage the citizenry more closely with creating and discussing the news. Public journalism also tries to avoid framing the news in terms of conflict and extremes and examines the news in a more nuanced fashion.

Newspapers experimenting with public or civic journalism around the country have reported a higher level of trust toward the press by their readership and some signs of increased civic participation and awareness of social and political issues. Critics of civic journalism charge that it is little more than boosterism or advocacy journalism and weakens the role of the press as a sometimes unpopular but critical voice of a community's conscience. Others criticize it for not going far enough in breaking the barrier between professional journalists and audiences, seeing it as a way for journalists to try to maintain their privileged position as professionals who for some reason can report better on the news than citizens can.

Partly because of the two forces of criticism—that of professional peers and that of citizens—public journalism has waned in recent years. Later studies in communities with papers that followed public-journalism principles noted no significant increase in political awareness or participation among the public, so the results of its success seem to be mixed.

What the debates on public journalism did do was provide a precursor to the challenges professional journalists would face in the early twenty-first century with the rise of citizen journalism.

Citizen Journalism

The Internet and especially social-media tools have allowed the rapid growth of what is called citizen journalism. Although it takes many forms, and is still being defined, it broadly encompasses everything from blogging to Slashdot to more formal ventures such as OhMyNews that emulate professional journalism in important aspects. Some scholars even include product-review sites by consumers as a form of citizen journalism.

Citizen journalism differs from the other types of journalism already mentioned in that it is usually not created with an explicitly political or radical agenda, like advocacy or alternative journalism, and its driving force has been citizens rather than professional journalists, as in public journalism.

It is partly for these reasons that mainstream journalism has been more willing to embrace some citizen-journalism efforts, even if cautiously in many cases. Some news organizations have tried to cultivate its viewers and readers as sources of raw news footage, such as CNN's iReporter. Other news organizations, especially some newspapers, have adopted a more integrated and thorough approach in which citizen journalists post news and stories on a stand-alone website, perhaps partially cobranded with the newspaper, and the best of the stories get published in a weekly edition. Still other organizations have conducted training sessions for citizen journalists, teaching them interviewing, reporting, and writing skills.

Original citizen-journalism sites have had a rougher time of it, some proving wildly successful and others failing miserably. One success is OhMyNews, the South Korea–based

citizen-journalism site that operates much like a traditional news organization, with paid editors and a hierarchy in the editing process before stories are posted. Another is Vancouver-based NowPublic, which launched in 2005 and now has reporters in 140 countries. Citizen-journalism advocate Dan Gillmor launched Bayosphere in 2005, a citizen-journalism site that was intended to cover the San Francisco Bay area. However, after seven difficult months, the project was largely abandoned. Gillmor continues to believe in the potential of citizen journalism, but he learned some hard lessons about the practicality and economics of making it a reality.

One common thread in citizen-journalism sites is the emphasis on conversation and interaction between participants and a blurring of the lines between journalist and audience. Many professional journalists find this development very threatening, as it challenges their privileged position as the arbiters of what is important enough to be considered news. In this way, journalists are losing their gate-keeping function and journalism is evolving into what Australian media scholar Axel Bruns calls a gatewatching function, as discussed in the previous chapter.

Despite the great potential in increasing participation and interaction between citizens who practice citizen journalism, there still is no clear business model to ensure the success of the movement. For most citizen-journalism sites, even ones founded by news organizations, citizen reporters are unpaid volunteers. This can be a barrier to attracting top-quality reporters and editors, and it hampers news gathering, which can be time-consuming and costly.

An International Perspective

There is nothing sacred about the inverted-pyramid style for news stories or the emphasis on fairness and balance in news that is taken for granted in the United States. Most Americans do not realize that there are a number of ways journalism can be practiced because they generally do not see news from other countries—or if they do, it is likely the English-language BBC, which follows the same tenets of fairness and balance in its coverage.

However, a look at news styles, even in other European countries, will often show a surprising variety in how news is written. Reporters' opinions may be more prevalent or obvious in some ostensibly factual news accounts, or reporters may insert their own thoughts or feelings about the news they are covering.

In many countries journalists still face censorship or licensing restrictions, which of course shape the kind of news that appears in print or on TV or radio. In these cases, journalists may act more like government stenographers, simply recording government meetings and events that the state deems important to publicize, with the only editorial voice being that approved by the state.

These examples show how journalism has been shaped by economic, political, and social realities and how what we see today in the newspaper, given different historical developments in the United States, may have turned out very different—and will continue to change.

Journalism in the Digital World

The digital tools available to journalists to help them do their jobs more effectively have been slow to be adopted by mainstream news organizations. Busy work schedules and unwillingness on the part of media corporations to subsidize professional training and development for their journalists play a part in the slow rate of adoption. However, more and more journalists have seen the value in using one tool—the Internet—in making their jobs easier.

The increased power of the audience to communicate with journalists and with each other in a public forum, whether as citizen journalism or simply discussions on blogs or forums, also can be threatening to some journalists who are accustomed to being the gatekeepers of information. Now readers and viewers online can point out, quite publicly, when a journalist errs. News sites have found that if they do not provide a discussion forum for their readers, the readers will simply go elsewhere to discuss stories and point out errors.

As Table 10–1 shows, out of the top ten news sites in 2008 three were based on print publications, four were based on television news networks, and three were essentially news aggregators, such as Yahoo! News and Google News, which use stories from the wire services and other news sources. All of the sites showed substantial growth of online viewers between 2007 and 2008, a trend that was even greater among the top twenty online newspapers.

The growth in online viewers of news sites may seem like a good thing, as it shows people are still engaged with the news, but it has put the news industry under even greater pressure. Not only must news organizations compete with their traditional media counterparts, but they also have to compete with the online versions of their competitors. Furthermore, ad revenues have not counterbalanced the drop in ads from the traditional media product, especially in print.

Advances in technology not only threaten business models, but they can bring about changes in how people use the Internet, thereby changing the role online news may play in the public's overall picture of media use. Even so, there are some trends that perhaps show the way to what role online journalism fills in providing news and information to the public.

The 24/7 News Cycle

Online news is not tied to a printer's schedule or specific broadcast slot, which means that it can be presented twenty-four hours, seven days a week. This can cause the increasingly common situation in which a media organization's website scoops its print newspaper or television news show. Many media companies used to avoid this by putting an **embargo**, or temporary hold, on publishing the news on the Web until the traditional media product had published or aired the story. However, as the chance for getting scooped by the competition rose, the practice became less common, and news organizations have grown accustomed to their websites being the place where news breaks. A non-deadline-driven news cycle wreaks havoc on the way news is usually processed and could add to production costs as more reporting and editing staff are needed to process news around the clock.

Nontraditional News Sources

The public's ability to access nontraditional news sources has two components: getting news from traditional news outlets that are not usually viewed or read by the public and getting news from a wider variety of nonjournalism sites, such as blogs or discussion groups. An example in the former category is viewing an online newspaper from the Middle East to see how a story is covered there or watching an Al Jazeera newscast. Even looking at UK media coverage of international issues can often be a valuable and educational experience for U.S. audiences who receive a fairly narrow range of international news. With non-journalistic, nontraditional outlets, users should have a high degree of media literacy so they can weigh sources of news and any biases the website creator may have.

News sources increasingly view themselves as content providers who can publish without relying on a traditional journalistic publisher or gateway. NBA.com, for example, publishes extensive news about its basketball games and includes video clips. Why would a viewer go to CNN or ESPN when he or she can get sports news straight from the source? Subscribing to follow an influential person's Twitter account or blog can often point people to news that they would not otherwise see, which could come from mainstream media or from other blogs. The danger in nontraditional news sources like these is that they may not have the same commitment to fairness and balance of coverage that a professional news organization would have. It is unlikely a user would find an exposé on NBA.com about financial wrongdoing by the league, for example. On the other hand, many members of the public may not care about such news and simply want to get basketball scores and news on the latest trades. In that case, going to a site like NBA.com may be fine.

Online Users' Media Habits

Online users' media habits differ from traditional media use in a number of ways. First, online users are generally more active in their media use and will easily visit different websites to find the information they are seeking. This shorter attention span for viewing media content means that news stories have to compete harder for the audience's attention. Most people do not like to read large amounts of material online and tend to skim written material. This also encourages producing shorter printed stories or stories with interactive graphics or multimedia.

Users want to quickly understand not only the essential facts in a story but its context as well and will readily use hyperlinks to click to related stories or other websites. However, from a business standpoint, media organizations do not want visitors to leave their website, so there is a natural tension regarding what hyperlinks to provide and how to provide them in a way that allows users to explore further yet encourages them to remain.

On the other hand, with the rise in popularity of blogs, news sites want their stories to be mentioned and linked to in order to drive traffic to their site. Some blogs are so heavily read that a mention in an entry can crash a smaller news site's web server because of the high volume of people visiting the site, something called the **Slashdot effect**. This refers to what has frequently happened when a site is mentioned on the very popular news site Slashdot.

Personalization

The Internet allows users to personalize the content they receive, ranging from localized weather forecasts to choosing news on favorite sports teams or companies in a stock portfolio. Personalization is one of the unique features of online media that traditional media simply cannot compete with, and its development will play a key role in making the Internet an increasingly important source for news. Personalization could lead to changes in the way journalists write or produce stories. For example, a standard version of a story could also include various hyperlinked informational modules, or types of sidebars that can be called up on demand, that would be of interest to users in specific demographics.

Journalists will obviously not be able to write individual stories for each user, but it is likely that elements of stories could be broken up by computer and reconstituted in a personalized format based on demographic data or user characteristics.

Contextualization of News

Despite often being able to access the raw material that a journalist has used to write a story, users will still want some kind of context for the data and some kind of interpretation of it. If anything, the interpreting function will become more important for journalists, as most people will not have the time, ability, or desire to sift through raw data to determine the important points in a story.

For example, a user may click on an interactive crime map when reading an online news story about a certain crime in a different part of town and then select her own zip code to call up an interactive map of her neighborhood. She can see on the map what types of crimes have been committed in the neighborhood within the past year. Ideally, she will also be able to click to get more information on a specific crime, when it occurred, what the rate of occurrence is for that crime, and whether it's increasing or decreasing—with possible explanations from expert sources on why. Hyperlinks to archived news stories of the crime, if there are any, would also help put the interactive map in context. Such **mash-ups** that combine geographic data overlaid with editorial content are becoming increasingly popular and easy to create.

Convergent Journalism

Online video, audio, and interactive graphics are increasingly used with text stories to enhance and supplement them. Likewise, text can be added to primarily video stories to offer different ways of accessing the information and to provide more depth and context than video or audio alone can

do. Journalists will have to become versed in the various tools of online journalism, including video, audio, and writing.

A truly interactive multimedia experience that allows the user to stop or replay segments at will, skip familiar information, and learn background information as needed will help differentiate online journalism from its nondigital counterparts.

Technology can change not only the production and presentation of the news but how it is gathered. Digital cameras and video cameras have made photography and videography much easier for journalists, so much so that a single reporter can videotape interviews or footage that can be used in a multimedia news story. Voice of America radio journalists have received digital-video shooting and editing training and have been able to add video elements to their stories online, and other news organizations such as the BBC are training many of their journalists in video techniques. Journalists will have to be conversant, if not necessarily expert, in a range of digital media tools. Unmanned air vehicles (UAVs), smaller and cheaper versions of what the U. S. military uses, can also be useful news-gathering tools. Already, some local law enforcement uses UAVs for surveillance, and there is no reason news organizations couldn't use them for certain kinds of stories or for covering traffic conditions, for example.

Journalism Ethics

Because of journalism's unique role in society, its protection by the First Amendment, and its public service mission, many ethical dilemmas arise in the course of practicing it. Ethical questions play a role in the entire news-gathering and production process, and many questions do not have easy answers. Ethical issues become even more important as more citizens practice journalism or some form of it.

Editors must consider whether headlines and captions accurately reflect the important points of a story or simply titillate. Privacy issues play a role when private citizens are thrust by circumstance into the media spotlight. Reporters must consider fairness and balance in their choice of interview subjects. Photo editors and designers must avoid the temptation to alter elements of photos to make them more dramatic. Societal mores and cultural values of the audience must be considered when determining what qualifies as news and how it is reported, although newspapers must also sometimes take highly unpopular stands on issues when acting as the public's conscience.

Privacy Rights Versus the Public's Right to Know

Although there is no actual law stating the public has a "right to know," it is often cited as a commonly understood principle when journalists are trying to obtain information that can help the public make better-informed decisions regarding anything from political candidates to corporate wrongdoing to potentially dangerous foods, drugs, or buildings.

Gathering proof of wrongdoing is one of the biggest challenges journalists face. Admissions of guilt are unlikely to come out during an interview-if the subject even agrees to an interview, which is often not the case. Journalists are often barred from the very locations they need to visit in order to gather information. Employees are forbidden by management to speak to journalists or threatened with losing their jobs if they do; police or public officials refuse to see or talk to journalists or are slow in providing requested documentation, even if the documents are public.

New technology such as miniature microphones and cameras, or the old technique of going undercover, may seem easy answers to the journalists' dilemma. But the ethics and legality of these tools and actions must be considered. Sometimes these techniques are the only ones that will give access to people engaged in illegal or unethical behavior, such as selling drugs or arms.

Federal law prohibits the media or anyone else from intentionally intercepting, or attempting to intercept, anyone's communication by wire, oral, or electronic means. Citizens have a reasonable expectation of privacy for oral, or spoken, communications, including via a telephone or over the Internet. However, it is complicated in that states have varying laws on whether only one person or both people in a conversation must give consent to have a conversation recorded.

Regardless of the legality of intercepting communications, is it ethical? There is no easy answer, as it depends on the circumstances. It also depends on whether it is print or broadcast media. The FCC generally prohibits the use of wireless microphones to overhear private conversations unless all parties to the communication have given prior consent. Conversations that occur in a public place, such as a bar, however, would not be subject to the same prohibition, since people in public places cannot expect the same right to privacy. Broadcast television or radio stations may not record telephone conversations without the consent of all parties, and they must notify the parties prior to broadcasting any of the recorded content. Long-distance calls can only be recorded under limited circumstances, including an announcement made at the beginning of the call indicating it will be recorded or possibly broadcast. Violation of these rules can result in the forfeiture of the station's license, fines, or other penalties.

One area of confusion regarding privacy is whether posting material in a blog or on a social-media site like Facebook is public or not. Some claim that it is the same as a public space, but it gets more complex when one considers the shelf life of material online. An offhand comment in a bar disappears once it is said, but an inflammatory blog post written years ago and later deleted may still exist somewhere on the Web.

Going Undercover

The legality and ethics of journalists going undercover are also not settled. It in many ways depends on how ethical or responsible the media professional was in using these techniques. Questions that may be asked in a court of law include the following: Were the media being fair? Does going undercover or using hidden cameras somehow manipulate or distort the situation? Do the undercover techniques help build meaningful information or simply sensationalize the story? If a media professional (or anyone else, for that matter) is convicted of violating the law in going undercover, there are a variety of potential penalties, including substantial prison terms and fines.

The Internet raises new questions about a journalist not announcing her identity. If she engages in a discussion in a child-pornography online discussion group without revealing her identity as a journalist pursuing a story, is it ethical to use others' posts without their permission? Is it ethical to pose as someone other than a journalist in order to get people to talk as they naturally would in an online forum?

Victimizing the Victims

Crime victims can feel doubly victimized when their names are made public by the media, especially with crimes such as rape that still carry a social stigma. Most newspapers and television stations do not make rape victims' names public, although critics of this practice argue that it further stigmatizes rape rather than educating the public about the crime of violence that it is.

Publicizing details of crimes can also contribute to copycat crimes, and journalists must always consider what kinds of information in a story are important and what are simply lurid or titillating details. Needlessly mentioning race, gender, or sexual orientation can often be unethical in framing a subject in a way that may reinforce social stereotypes.

Photographs and video have a power to sometimes tell a story in a way that words alone cannot. Yet, publicly presented dramatic photos or footage are not always justified for their news value alone. In fact, in cases of human tragedy, sadness, or crime, personal grief has been violated by the repeated presentation of pictures or video in newspapers, magazines, or on television.

On Sunday, June 11, 2000, the annual Puerto Rican Day Parade in New York City was marred by a group of fifteen to twenty-five men who assaulted women attending the parade. Amateur video documented many of the assaults, and the footage was used by the police to apprehend suspects. Television also aired much of the video and newspapers published print photos extracted from the video, sometimes revealing the identities of the women who were being assaulted.

This is a typical situation a news director or editor faces when deciding what to print or air as news. There is no doubt that footage and pictures of seminude women would attract a larger audience (along with vociferous complaints from various groups), but the ethics of showing such material must be considered in the effects it would have on the victims and their families.

Society of Professional Journalists Code of Ethics

The Society of Professional Journalists (SPJ) is a large organization of working journalists and student chapters that tries to ensure that journalism is being practiced professionally and ethically and that it is fulfilling its role in society. The SPJ's code of ethics states that journalists should 'seek truth and report it" and that "journalists should be honest, fair and courageous in gathering, reporting and interpreting information." These are some of the other principles in the code:

- Test the accuracy of information from all sources and exercise care to avoid inadvertent error. Deliberate distortion is never permissible.
- Diligently seek out subjects of news stories to give them the opportunity to respond to allegations of wrongdoing.
- Identify sources whenever feasible. The public is entitled to as much information as possible on sources' reliability.
- Make certain that headlines, news teasers, and promotional material, photos, video, audio, graphics, sound bites, and quotations do not misrepresent. They should not oversimplify or highlight incidents out of context.
- Never distort the content of news photos or video. Image enhancement for technical clarity is always permissible. Label montages and photo illustrations.

- Avoid misleading reenactments or staged news events. If reenactment is necessary to tell a story, label it.
- Support the open exchange of views, even views journalists find repugnant.
- Avoid undercover or other surreptitious methods of gathering information except when traditional open methods will not yield information vital to the public. Use of such methods should be explained as part of the story.

The Business of Journalism

The early years of the twenty-first century have been especially challenging for the media business, especially for news organizations. Advertising revenues have been in steady decline for the past several years, especially in print media. Although online advertising is growing, it still makes up a small portion of overall revenues and does not compensate for the reduced revenues in traditional media.

Some media companies that predicted new business opportunities in media convergence, such as the former AOL Time Warner or Bertelsmann, spent large amounts to provide services or media that never made a profit. Other media companies that adopted a more cautious approach with digital media see even fewer reasons to invest in new technologies. However, even the executives who have been burned say the changes will come and that they simply moved too quickly.

The loss in advertising revenues, combined with a recession that began in December 2007, has severely strained news organizations. In 2008, the American Society of News Editors (ASNE) found that the newspaper industry had suffered its largest drop loss in thirty years, with a 4.4 percent workforce decrease compared to 2007.

Not only have layoffs become common, but entire news bureaus are closing down. In 2000, Cox newspapers had thirty correspondents in Washington, D.C., to cover the inauguration of President George Bush. In 2008, Cox announced that it would be closing its Washington bureau early in spring 2009. Some news organizations have taken what are considered even more drastic steps. In 2009, the respected newspaper *Christian Science Monitor* announced that it would stop publishing a print newspaper and only exist online. In March 2009, the 146-year-old *Seattle Post-Intelligencer*, a Hearst paper, ceased publishing its print edition and went to online-only.

In order to cut costs, news organizations may use other methods that affect the quality of the final news product even though staff may not be laid off. It has already been mentioned that using a greater percentage of wire service copy rather than original local reporting saves money, but at the cost of making the news less relevant to a local audience. Investigative journalism is usually scaled back substantially when a news organization is trying to cut costs. Publishers may increase the advertising percentage in a newspaper or raise advertising rates in order to increase revenues, although there is debate whether these practices hurt a newspaper in the long run.

There will always be a tension between the business side and the editorial side in a news organization. The editorial side is looking for stories in line with the adage that journalism should "comfort the afflicted and afflict the comfortable," and often publishers or their corporate parent are "the comfortable." Journalists can sometimes face severe pressures or even get fired if they do not go along with a publisher's wishes in either killing a story on a subject that a powerful advertiser does not want to see or downplaying news that is embarrassing to the publisher's associates or friends. Rare is the media owner who is willing to turn the investigative spotlight on himself as readily and thoroughly as he is on others.

Salaries

Salaries for journalism professionals vary according to several factors, including the type of medium one works in (television is the highest paid, print media the lowest), the location or market (i.e., the larger the market, the higher the pay), the type of position one occupies (farther up in management, ownership, or celebrity status correlates positively with pay), experience, and a variety of other less definite factors, including gender, with men generally being paid more than women, as unfair as that may be. Salaries and overall compensation vary so widely—from fifteen thousand dollars a year to many millions of dollars—that crude averages are relatively meaningless.

In general, network television offers the highest salaries for midlevel jobs as producers. National magazines and newspapers offer fairly good pay, while papers in mid- and small-sized markets offer relatively poor salaries in comparison to jobs of a similar level in public relations, for example. Internet media offer fairly good salaries, and until the dot-com bust their stock option plans made a lucky few journalists instant millionaires when the companies went public. Many more people missed that train than rode it, however, as Internet media companies started going bankrupt.

Diversity in the Newsroom

Circumstances in American newsrooms have been slow to change. In 1950, African American journalist Marvel Cooke (1903–2000) was hired as a reporter and feature writer for the *New York Daily Compass*. She was the only woman and the only black person on the staff of the paper and was among the first blacks to work for any white-owned daily newspaper.

The American Society of News Editors (ASNE) regularly conducts a survey on employment of women and minorities by U. S. daily newspapers. The numbers of minority and women hires have fallen short of mirroring the percentages found in the general population and fall far short when it comes to management. Because of the layoffs and hiring freezes throughout the newspaper industry in recent years, the percentage of minority employees has actually risen slightly, to just over 13 percent.

Industry watchers worry that the persistent dominance of white males in newsrooms skews news coverage toward the type of material that appeals to them, as opposed to stories relevant to underrepresented minority groups.

The employment outlook for journalists in the digital age is generally not good, as it largely reflects how well the overall economy is doing combined with the trends already mentioned among news organizations. After a decade of strong growth in employment and business, the twenty-first century got off to a troubled start, and media and technology companies have been especially hard hit with the downturn in the economy.

However, it is an exciting time to be a journalist. Online journalism is still in its infancy and plays an increasingly important role in the overall journalism picture, and there are still possibilities for journalists in traditional print, radio, and television. And within specialty areas such as financial journalism or science journalism, there is an almost endless number of niches that can be pursued.

Specialized Journalism Types

With an increasingly complex world, not only do reporters often specialize in a subject area in order to better cover that topic, but there are whole branches of specialized journalism, complete with their own support organizations. Working in a small- or medium-sized newspaper or broadcast station means journalists are less likely to be able to focus on one field, but working in bigger publications lets journalists specialize. Following is by no means a complete list, as it does not cover beats like education or local or national politics, but it should give a general idea of the range of specialties.

Business and Financial Journalism

Business news is often read by a highly educated, knowledgeable audience seeking specific information. It can be difficult for journalists to penetrate an organization's public relations office to get access to executives, and when they do it can be hard to get candid information. Understanding business practices (such as accounting procedures) and being able to read and understand various complex forms are important, as is being able to write about complicated issues, such as changes in tax laws, that the general public may find boring. On the other hand, investors are usually very interested in learning the truth about companies, and financial journalists must be able to separate the hype from the reality.

Arts and Entertainment Journalism

As mentioned earlier, entertainment-related stories have become more prominent in the news in recent years. Much of entertainment journalism, especially on television, on programs like *Entertainment Tonight*, is little more than orchestrated interviews and video shoots with artists or stars that essentially help them promote their latest films. "Behind-the-scenes" segments serve this purpose as well and help viewers feel like they are seeing the "real" person behind the star, even though there is little of true informational value in such features.

On the other hand, cultural and art criticism play an important role in helping define public tastes and form cultural trends in everything from fashion to film. Reviews in prestigious magazines like the *New York Times Review of Books* can be the deciding factor for a book's success, Coverage of the entertainment industry as a business can yield important information on corporate changes occurring with media companies.

Sports Journalism

Sports journalism shares many of the characteristics of both arts and entertainment journalism and business journalism. Like popular singers or movie stars, popular athletes can be almost impossible to approach for in-depth interviews, and journalists may mostly get the usual mumbled platitudes in the locker room after the game.

A sports franchise is a business and the owners treat it as such, jealously guarding company secrets just like businesses everywhere, yet sometimes asking for public funds to build facilities like stadiums. In addition, media access is strictly controlled by the various leagues, making it easy

for journalists who pry too closely into touchy issues to be barred from further access to the team or players. This can have a dampening effect on thorough coverage of important issues, such as drug use by players.

Health or Medical Journalism

Health or medical news is almost always of high interest to the public, and journalists in this area have an especially important responsibility to report information accurately and fairly. Claiming that a drug company will have a cure for cancer within three years only gives cancer sufferers and their families false hope, despite what the company may say. Journalists specializing in health and medicine must not only have a good grasp of medical terms and drugs, but they must also be able to read and understand the medical literature and critically analyze statistics and complex studies. They must also know the business side of the health care and pharmaceutical industries, which have tremendous public relations machines to promote their interests, and report this complex information in a way that engages the audience.

Science and Technology Journalism

Science journalists have a double challenge in covering their areas, as the U.S. public generally does not understand basic scientific principles or care about science-related topics compared to other types of news, such as sports or entertainment. The science journalist must interpret and explain complex concepts or findings in an easy-to-understand way and show why the public should care about the topic. Hot-button issues such as cloning or genetically modified foods have many facets that defy quick explanations and are often misreported. Scientists are notoriously hesitant to announce findings with the kind of certainty or sound bites that journalists seek in order to make a good story.

Technology coverage has many of the same issues, in addition to difficulties in accessing executives of technology companies and getting beyond corporate PR hype. Much of the technology press failed miserably in predicting the dot-com collapse in 2000 or pointing out weak companies. Sometimes technology companies were out of business by the time a glowing profile of them appeared in a magazine, such as *Business 2.0*'s positive feature in its June 2000 issue on APBNews. com, which went bankrupt earlier that month.

Environmental Journalism

Like science journalists, environmental journalists often have to explain complex concepts in interesting and clear ways that the general public can understand. As many environmental processes take place slowly and there is often disagreement over what a finding may mean, it is often hard to find a solid angle within the traditional media framework for environmental stories. Environmental catastrophes such as oil spills often become major news events but suffer from the **media spotlight effect**, in which there is intense coverage for a short time and then the media flock moves on to another news item. Environmental journalism started out as a form of advocacy journalism but has shifted in recent years to be more impartial in environmental coverage.

Looking Back and Moving Forward

Journalism plays a crucial role in informing the public of important events taking place domestically and internationally and providing a context that helps people understand the world better. News is the bedrock of journalism, although news is often manufactured by public relations professionals, individuals, or organizations, and the amount of news coverage on any specific topic can change from day to day depending on the perceived importance of other news events.

The challenges that the Internet and digital media have brought to journalism are great, and the industry and profession has for the most part resisted change rather than embracing it. This resistance has had negative effects in that many news organizations, especially newspapers, are

only recently trying to figure out ways to exist in the media system today. For many, it is already too late, as advertisers go elsewhere and they cut back staff, making themselves seem even less relevant to the public.

Despite the bleak employment picture for journalism graduates in the past several years, the rapid changes in the industry mean that there are jobs available for the candidates with the right skills to work in the convergent journalism newsroom of the future. Knowing how to use technology is of course important, but it is not considered the most important factor in being marketable.

Time and time again news organizations lament the poor writing skills of recent hires, and this does not change in an online news environment. If anything, even for Web-based video, writing well becomes even more important than in the nondigital forms of journalism. Practice your writing skills and master the forms of journalism and get some published clips in order to make yourself more marketable.

However, the days of journalists being able to say, "I am a print journalist" or, "I am a radio journalist" are soon coming to an end. Increasingly, print reporters are given a digital video camera or audio recorder and asked to shoot or record footage. Similarly, television journalists are being asked to write text stories to accompany video. The convergent journalist of tomorrow cannot be expected to be an expert in every type of media but should be comfortable using all of them.

Appreciating the power of storytelling is also important, and being able to tell a story using multimedia, hyperlinks, and other forms of interaction in an appropriate way will be what separates good journalists from hacks. Knowing some multimedia tools, such as basic image editing, will be required. But knowing how and why to use various digital tools will be even better.

In some ways, journalism has always been about knowledge creation and knowledge management. Good reporters have extensive files of sources and contacts they can reach out to when they need to get information quickly, and they have developed a sense for differentiating good information from bad. These are exactly the kinds of skills that any citizen will need in the future.

This does not change in the world of convergent journalism and in fact becomes more important as there are more potential sources for information. This is one reason it is good, in college, to focus on a subject area other than journalism. Learning economics, history, sociology, political science, biology—or any number of fields—can provide valuable critical-thinking skills and a base of knowledge to draw from while working as a journalist. Minoring in journalism or, better yet, getting experience as a student journalist at your school's newspaper, radio, or TV station can be an invaluable education in and of itself, even if you do not think you want to be a journalist. The critical-thinking skills you will learn, the practice in writing under deadlines, and the experiences you will gain will be useful in any career.

Notes

1. The Write Site, "Tracing the Story of Journalism in the United States." Retrieved July 5, 2002, from http://www.writesite.org/html/tracing.html.

2. Joseph Pulitzer, "The College of Journalism," *North American Review* (May 1904).

3. Michael G. Robinson, American Culture Studies, "1890s" course, spring 1996. http://ernie.bgsu.edu/~wgrant/i890s/yellowkid/introduction.html.

4. George Seldes, "Farewell: Lord of San Simeon," in *Lords of the Press* (New York: Julian Messner, 1938)..

16. The Practice of Public Relations

by Shannon A. Bowen, Brad Rawlins, and Thomas Martin

This chapter provides readers with a basic understanding of the field of public relations. Examining varying contexts in which public relations practitioners work provides a glimpse into a career field that novices to the study of communication find perplexing. Such a perspective provides a platform for discussing the fundamental skill sets PR professionals use and the duties they perform. The inclusion of specific examples, and even a short case study, gives introductory students a clearer understanding of varying elements of the profession. It is highly likely that any individual entering a communication career field will someday engage with a public relations practitioner, therefore, any student of communication will benefit from a close reading of this chapter.

Public relations is a large discipline that can be subdivided into many types of functions. There are four primary areas of functional responsibility or different locales in which we can categorize the profession of public relations:

1. Corporate public relations

2. Government/public affairs

3. Agency public relations

4. Nonprofit/NGO/activist
   public relations

These primary functional areas differ but also have the commonality of using the strategic management process. In the earlier chapter briefly outlining public relations subfunctions, we promised more specificity on how those functions actually operate within an organization. Now that we have thoroughly discussed the strategic management of public relations, we will relate how they operate in day-to-day corporate and agency settings, and how they relate to government and public affairs as well as nonprofit, NGO, and activist public relations.

Corporate Public Relations

Unlike some corporate functions, such as legal and finance, the communication function does not have as its primary mission fulfilling specific regulatory or compliance requirements. As a result, the function is rarely organized in a uniform fashion from one organization to the next. Similarly sized organizations can vary widely in the resources and number of employees devoted to communication. Reporting relationships and functional responsibilities also differ depending on the nature of the company.

For example, companies that are heavily focused on building and sustaining strong consumer brands may devote far more employees and greater attention to the communication function than organizations that operate exclusively in the business-to-business sector. A company that sells directly to consumers has a greater need for a large media relations team since it can field dozens of calls each day from both mainstream and trade media. When a new product is being launched, the staff will be called upon to plan press conferences, conduct satellite media tours with local television stations, and organize customer events.

Companies that sell their products to other businesses rather than directly to consumers may have similar needs from time to time, but they are usually on a much smaller scale. Some industries, such as fashion, entertainment, packaged goods, and travel, place a greater emphasis on communication than those with longer selling cycles, such as construction, manufacturing, and engineering.

Newer fields, such as computing, also tend to rely more on public relations and social media programs than through traditional advertising channels.

In many organizations, the senior leader of the communication team reports directly to the CEO, whereas in others, that individual may report to the head of legal, marketing, or human resources. Regardless of the specific reporting relationship, in virtually all companies, the function is responsible for communicating with the media and usually has the lead role in developing employee communication as well. Public relations activities, such as the management of corporate events, press conferences, product launches, large employee gatherings, and leadership meetings normally also are managed by the chief communications officer (CCO) and his or her team.

In some companies the function is also charged with managing investor relations—that is, communicating with the company's shareholders and financial analysts who follow and report on the company. In a publicly traded company, the investor relations function must comply with a number of securities regulations regarding the company's disclosure of its financial results. These activities involve the release of quarterly and annual financial results and providing timely information to shareholders regarding any event that meets the definition of **materiality**, an event that could have a positive or negative impact on the company's share price. In fulfilling these requirements, the investor relations function works closely with the finance and legal departments, as well as the company's outside audit firm.

Most CCOs would maintain that there is no such thing as a typical day. Some of the most important qualities of successful CCOs are flexibility, patience, analytical ability, and the ability to remain calm under pressure. All organizations face potentially damaging issues every day. The CCO must monitor these issues on an ongoing basis, much like a chef watching many simmering pots on the stove. The objective in this pursuit is not to let any of these issues boil over into full-fledged crises. This task has been made harder by the ubiquitous presence of the Internet. The Web has provided the means for unhappy customers, disgruntled employees, or disappointed shareholders to voice their concerns in a very public manner with a few computer keystrokes.

Although the corporate public relations function is extremely complex and varied by industry, what follows are a few of the main responsibilities and areas of focus for any CCO.

Responsibilities and Focus of the Chief Communications Officer

Although not every organization is newsworthy or wishes to be, most larger size organizations seek to develop ongoing relationships with local, national, and international media. These relationships facilitate the flow of information to and from the organization to publics outside its boundaries. The size of the **media relations** staff is relative to the amount of press coverage the company receives. For example, a firm with a large headquarters in a major city will probably have a more active relationship with the press than a smaller organization located in a small town. Due to their level of controversy or public interest, some industries generate more media attention than others. Organizations with highly visible chief executive officers (CEOs) also tend to attract more press interest, and many CEOs have a presence on social media forums, such as Facebook or Twitter, to facilitate public interest. The CCO normally has some hand in managing these communications, as well as preparing executives for major media appearances, key industry speeches, employee meetings, testifying before government entities, and participating in community events. This facet includes speechwriting, ghost writing op-eds, and rehearsing key messages for media interviews.

Many CCOs are also responsible for overseeing **internal relations** and conducting research on employee publics. Though sometimes undervalued, a company's communication efforts with its own employees can yield the highest returns. Employees often feel they are the last to hear of major developments within their organizations, but the most successful organizations are now placing greater emphasis on keeping employees well informed, conducting an ongoing *dialogue* with internal publics, and incorporating their views into management policy in a symmetrical manner. Much of the focus in internal communication is now centered on the role of the first line supervisor. When that individual does a good job of communicating about issues, employees are more willing to pay attention to organizationwide initiatives.

Many corporate CCOs spend a great deal of time interacting with the chief marketing officers (CMOs), or marketing heads, of their organizations. Although the marketing function usually has primary responsibility for managing product brands, the corporate communication function normally manages the corporate or organizational brand, as well as the overall reputation of the organization for quality, customer service, and so on. This activity may include corporate advertising that speaks to the attributes and values of the entire organization rather than of a specific product or service. It also includes participation in industry coalitions, thought leadership forums, and academic panels. Recent research by Stacks and Michaelson found parity between public relations messages and advertising messages, meaning that public relations should be equally incorporated into the marketing mix alongside, rather than as subservient to, advertising.[1]

Increasingly, **key messages** must be delivered through Web-based channels since that is the source of information for a growing percentage of the audience. Most organizations also operate internationally, meaning that messages must be tailored for global audiences. The communication strategy must include adequate feedback mechanisms so that the organization knows how effectively key messages have been received and what further steps must be taken to provide informative and useful content to publics.

CCOs have the weighty responsibility of **issues management**, and that may include crisis and risk management in industries that are prone to hazards, risks, or product failure (such as the airline industry, the automotive industry, pharmaceuticals, and so on). The key to issues management is providing wise counsel to the senior team whenever major decisions are debated. Organizations face many choices in the course of business and virtually all the major ones have a communication dimension. As stated earlier, the CCO and the communication team act in many ways as representatives of the many publics who are not in the room when these decisions are made. An effective corporate communication function counsels the organization of potential risks, provides its publics a constant voice that can be heard by decision makers, and helps the organization translate strategy into action. The effective CCO has a thorough understanding of the organization's business objectives and the role of the communication function in helping meet these objectives.

The best counselors are those who take the time to listen carefully to the issues and concerns of the other functions to whom they are providing advice and the publics whose views they represent. In order to understand the position of these publics, the communication team relies on research. This research, which was covered more extensively in a previous chapter, provides the team with a better sense of how employees, customers, shareholders, and others view the organization generally, as well as specific issues that relate to the organization. Indeed, it is research that allows our decisions to be strategic rather than happenstance.

Finally, in a day-to-day environment, much of the time and attention of the CCO is focused on managing the public relations staff. Recruiting and developing the best talent, as in all corporate functions, is fundamental to building credibility within the organization and being positioned to offer the most useful counsel. CCOs are constantly seeking employees who can think critically, write and present articulately, and develop and maintain excellent personal relationships with their internal publics, as well as external publics. They can help their colleagues become better leaders by enhancing their skills in listening empathetically to employees and increasing their focus on workgroup communication.

The overriding mission of the CCO is to enhance the relationships an organization has with its publics by helping the organization make better, more informed decisions that take into account the impact and likely reaction to those decisions. The CCO uses all the tools available to accomplish this goal. In fulfilling this mission, the CCO works with his or her team to develop and distribute key messages that advance the organization's mission. Corporate communicators who understand this mission and can deliver tangible results are highly valued by the organizations they serve.

Agency Public Relations

In addition to in-house departments, most organizations—from small firms to huge global entities—work in partnership with public relations agencies to develop and implement communication programs. These agencies generate billions of dollars in revenue, employ thousands of counselors, and serve as the source of training and development for hundreds of young entrants to the field each year.

Agency Definitions

There are four major types of public relations agencies. They range from full service agencies to specialists who fill a particular organizational or client need. Further, they range from being units of larger, umbrella organizations to individually owned agencies.

Full Service Agencies

Some of the largest agencies offer a full spectrum of services, from traditional media relations and event planning to highly specialized research, training, and social media expertise. Some of these large agencies, such as Ketchum, Burson Marsteller, Weber Shandwick, Porter Novelli, and Fleishman-Hillard are part of large media conglomerates like Omnicom, WPP, and Interpublic. A number of large agencies, most notably Edelman, have remained independent.

Public Affairs Agencies

Agencies such as APCO Worldwide are recognized primarily for their expertise in public affairs. These agencies focus on developing advocacy positions for or against legislative initiatives, organizing grassroots campaigns, lobbying members of Congress and other government leaders or coaching their clients to do so, and participating in and often leading coalitions that link together like-minded members.

Strategic Counsel Services

Kekst, Sard Verbinnen, Abernathy MacGregor, and others focus specifically on what often is referred to as "strategic communication," including mergers and acquisitions, investor relations, and defending hostile takeovers. These agencies are brought in to supplement corporate staff and agencies of record when a company decides to make a major move, such as buying another company or selling a large subsidiary. They are also retained when a company is facing an unwanted takeover by another firm. It is common for both parties in hostile takeover attempts to retain competing strategic agencies. These are often waged in highly publicized battles that command the front pages of major media for days. The strategic counselors develop long-term relationships with a few key mergers and acquisitions (M&A) reporters for *The Wall Street Journal*, *New York Times*, and others, which they try to use as leverage on behalf of their clients.

Corporate Identity Services

Corporate identity specialists—Landor, FutureBrand, InterBrand, and others—develop branding strategies and programs for both organizations and brands. These agencies utilize extensive research to develop brand platforms for their clients that build on the existing perceptions of companies or their products. Their expertise includes graphic design, naming, brand engagement programs for employees, and complete identity systems.

Corporate Social Responsibility

In recent years a number of agencies have chosen to specialize in corporate philanthropy programs. They work with clients to determine areas in which they can match their areas of expertise with global human needs, such as hunger, health, the environment, and poverty. They design programs that help address these needs by utilizing the employees, technical expertise, and financial resources of their clients.

Trends in Agencies

Regardless of their particular area of focus, all of these agencies are being affected by a number of new industry trends.

According to a survey conducted by the Council of Public Relations Firms, the industry's trade association, agencies are finding that their clients are increasing their *outsourcing* practices. With pressures on profit margins intensifying, many companies find that they can better manage the ebbs and flows of communication activity by hiring an outside agency for certain communication activities in lieu of using internal staff.[2] When times are good and the needs multiply, organizations can increase the amount of agency support they receive; when times are lean they can cut back the support of outside firms.

Companies and agencies are also using more *virtual teams*, meaning teams that include the client's employees, the agency's employees, and independent contractors all working on the same project.[3] In many cases, these teams are located in different offices, cities, time zones, even continents, all connected through the Internet.

Most agencies are expected to provide strategic counsel, not just tactical solutions that involve executing programs. In order to do this effectively, the agency team must employ thorough *external research* that identifies pending issues and opportunities for the client. Their recommendations often go beyond the realm of communication, challenging the organization to consider the implications of policy changes or major operational decisions.

Regardless of how the agency-client relationship is structured, clients expect the agency to anticipate issues and provide a fresh perspective that can assist them in making critical decisions and recommendations to their CEOs and internal publics and colleagues. To do this well, the agency team must spend time conducting *internal research*—getting to know the unique aspects of their client's business. These aspects normally include competitive threats, labor relationships, legislative and regulatory constraints, and the global trends that will affect the future of the business.

Most large agencies have a *global reach*, they operate global networks, with major offices in North and South America, Europe, and Asia. Some do this with their own employees and others form partnerships and networks with independent agencies in other countries. Either way, it is increasingly important for multinational clients to be able to call upon an agency that can offer counsel throughout the world.

Agency Life Versus Corporate Life

The resumes of many practitioners often include experience in both agency and corporate positions, and many of the management responsibilities of the corporate CCO are also conducted by agency professionals. Agency professionals oftentimes build an area of expertise with long-term service for a client or within an industry, and work as expert prescribers resolving problems and crises as an outside consultant from the agency, and return to their agencies once the problem is solved.

The agency world offers the opportunity for varied assignments with multiple clients. A career path through the agency can provide opportunities in a wide range of areas, including media relations, issues management, crises management, brand building, event planning, and corporate reputation work. To some, one of the negative aspects of entry-level jobs in agencies is that they are highly focused on conducting events, publicity, and media pitching.

On the corporate side, most employees, especially at the entry level, are focused on a single industry or line of business. Since corporate departments are often smaller, the career path may be more limited, whereas agencies may have a diverse client list and numerous opportunities for travel. On the other hand, corporate communication positions can provide a more strategic focus, depending on the company. From a practical standpoint, the benefits offered in corporations are usually better for new hires, though this is not always the case.

Clearly, the line between corporate and agency roles is becoming less distinct. With the use of virtual teams increasing, clients are more focused on results than on the demarcation between the agency and the corporation. In both worlds, leaders are looking for ways to improve their value to the organization, whether they are serving internal or external clients.

Government Relations and Public Affairs

Government relations and public affairs are the types of public relations that deal with how an organization interacts with the government, with governmental regulators, and the legislative and regulatory arms of government. The government relations and public affairs are discussed together in this section; the two functions are often referred to as synonyms, but there are very minor differences. **Government relations** is the branch of public relations that helps an organization communicate with governmental publics. **Public affairs** is the type of public relations that helps an organization interact with the government, legislators, interest groups, and the media. These two functions often overlap, but government relations is often a more organization-to-government type of communication in which regulatory issues are discussed, communication directed to governmental representatives takes place, lobbying efforts directed at educating legislators are initiated, and so on. A strategic issue is any type of issue that has the potential to impact the organization, how it does business, and how it interacts with and is regulated by the government. Heath contends that "**public policy issues** are those with the potential of maturing into governmental legislation or regulation (international, federal, state, or local)."[4]

Public affairs is the external side of the function that deals more broadly with public policy issues of concern among constituents, activists, or groups who lobby the government on behalf of a certain perspective. Public affairs are often issues of public concern that involve grassroots initiatives, meaning that everyday citizens organize and create a movement in favor of a certain issue or perspective. In that case, public affairs specialists would work to resolve conflict or negotiate on behalf of an organization, working with these groups to create an inclusive solution to problems.

Public affairs specialists act as lobbyists on behalf of their organizations, and they interact with publics who are interested in lobbying the government for legislation regarding particular issues. Public affairs specialists might focus on a particular area of public policy, such as international trade agreements or exchange rates, security and terrorism, equitable wages and working conditions, the regulatory process, safely disposing of production by-products, and so on. The list of public policy issues with which an organization must contend is practically endless.

In some organizations, the governmental relations arm or public affairs unit is coupled with issues management, or it can even be the same public relations executive responsible for both roles. Issues management and public affairs are extremely close in their responsibilities, goals, and activities. Both issues management and public affairs seek to facilitate interaction between organization and the government or governments with whom it must deal, and to incorporate and update organizational policy in accordance with governmental standards. However, issues management is the larger function because it deals not only with governmental and regulatory publics but also many other types of publics. The governmental relations or public affairs function is more narrowly focused on legislative, regulatory, and lobbying issues.

Public affairs can be used in a corporate setting to interact on policy and legislation with the government, interest groups (or, as discussed in the following section, activist publics), and the media. An organization must also use public affairs to communicate about policy and procedures with investors, regulatory publics, employees, and internal publics, as well as communities and customers.[5]

Case: Horse Public Policy

Public affairs issues often center on a conflict of ethical values or rights between organizations and publics, and sometimes organizations, publics, and one or more branches of the government. An example would be the grassroots movement in the United States to protect wild horses from slaughter for human consumption in Europe and Asia. Many animal protection and rights organizations have lobbied officials on behalf of the horses, and those officials introduced legislation to make horse slaughter for human consumption illegal. According to the Associated Press, the U.S. House of Representatives voted 263 to 146 to outlaw the killing of horses for human consumption based on the active public affairs initiatives of the National Thoroughbred Racing Association and grassroots initiatives, such as "Fans of Barbaro."[6]

A sponsor of the slaughter-ban legislation, former Congressman Christopher Shays (R-CT) said, "The way a society treats its animals, particularly horses, speaks to the core values and morals of its citizens." Defenders of horse slaughter, including the meatpacking industry and its public affairs lobbyists as well as the U.S. Department of Agriculture argue that it provides an inexpensive way to dispose of these animals. "These unwanted horses are often sick, unfit or problem animals," said Rep. Collin Peterson (D-MN). Clearly, the two sides of this debate and all the businesses and organizations involved on each side are lobbying their point of view with governmental officials and also using the mass media to build public understanding and support for their position.

At the core of this debate is an ethical divergence over the value of equine life and the role of horses in America's society and history. At contest is the future of both those horses who live free in American herds and former sport or pet horses, and even stolen horses sold to the slaughter industry. Much money is at stake for the ranching and meatpacking industries, the Bureau of Land Management, the Department of Agriculture, and the resources invested in this legislation by the animal rights lobby.

Issues Management and Public Policy

A large part of public affairs is ongoing issues management, and the issues management function is often grouped within the same department or set of responsibilities as public affairs. For example, the public relations function at Johnson & Johnson is divided into several functional departments, the highest level being "public affairs and group issues."[7] In most organizations, especially in corporations, issues management and public affairs are inextricably linked. Organizations must manage public policy issues that they create as a consequence of their doing business. Organizational policy must continually be revised and updated to reflect the current regulatory environment as well as the demands placed on it by publics.

Issues management is the process through which an organization manages its policy, and identifies potential problems, issues, or trends that could impact it in the future. The issues management process is a long-term, problem-solving function placed at the highest level of the organization through which it can adapt organizational policy and engage in the public affairs process. Issues management allows the top professional communicator to interact with government and publics, advising the CEO about the values of publics and how they enhance or detract from the organization's reputation with those publics.

Heath defines the issues management function in the following way: "Issues management is a process for establishing a platform of fact, value, and policy to guide organizational performance while deciding on the content of messages used to communicate with target publics."[8] Those target publics include key executives of the organization, legislators, government regulators, interest groups, and so on. Heath explained, "An issue is a contestable question of fact, value, or policy that affects how stakeholders grant or withhold support and seek changes through public policy."[9]

Why is issues management so important? Grunig and Repper noted that if an organization is unresponsive to the appeals of publics, they will lobby the government to regulate the organization or seek other public policy changes forced onto the organization in the public policy arena.[10] In that case, the organization loses its autonomy, meaning that key decisions are legislated and regulated rather than made by top management, often costing the organization a great deal of money or resources. Ideally, the organization would know how to best allocate its own resources and would manage issues in a more efficient and effective way than having those legislated and standardized across an industry, so maintaining its autonomy is generally the goal of issues management.

In issues management, we not only look for emerging issues that can affect our organization, but we also seek to build long-term, trusting relationships with publics, both governmental and grass roots. Heath explains how communication is used to help in the issues management process by noting that "the more that an organization meets key publics' need for information, the more likely they are to be praised rather than criticized."[11] Of course, managing the organization in a way that is ethical and does not seek to exploit publics or other groups allows the issues management function to truly contribute to organizational effectiveness: "Issues communication is best when it fosters mutual understanding that can foster trust. This communication must be two-way and collaborative."[12]

Issues management should be collaborative, based on the research that the issues manager has conducted. The research is what makes the issues management process "two-way," meaning in that it is based on understanding the view of publics by bringing input into managerial decision making from outside the organization. This research can be used to provide vital information at each stage of the strategic planning process. However, Heath notes that "communication may not suffice to reconcile the differences that lead to the struggle."[13] Thus, issues management cannot resolve all problems with communication or make all decisions mutually beneficial. It can help to incorporate the values of publics into strategic decision making whenever possible so that less resistance from those publics is evidenced, and their lobbying initiatives do not target the organization, which could lead to a loss of decisional autonomy through legislation.

Issues management is normally conducted on a continual, ongoing basis in which the manager is monitoring, researching, advising, and communicating about a number of concurrent issues at any given time. How many issues are managed will depend on the size of the organization and the turbulence of the industry in which it operates. Successful issues managers are those who hold in-depth knowledge of their industry, problem-solving ability, negotiating skill, and

1. Identify public issues and trends in public expectations
   - Scan the environment for trends and issues
   - Track trends in issues that are developing
   - Develop forecasts of trends and issues
   - Identify trends and issues of interest to the corporation
2. Evaluate their impact and set priorities
   - Assess the impacts and probability of recurrence
   - Assess the corporate resources and ability to respond
   - Prepare the issue priorities for further analysis
3. Conduct research and analysis
   - Categorize issues along relevant dimensions
   - Ensure that priority issues receive staff coverage
   - Involve functional areas where appropriate
   - Use outside sources of information
   - Develop and analyze position options
4. Develop strategy
   - Analyze position and strategy options
   - Decide on position and strategy
   - Integrate with overall business strategy
5. Implement strategy
   - Disseminate agreed-upon position and strategy
   - Develop tactics consistent with overall strategy
   - Develop alliances with external organizations
   - Link with internal and external communication networks
6. Evaluate strategy
   - Assess results (staff and management)
   - Modify implementation plans
   - Conduct additional research

Figure 1. The steps of issues management

Source: Buchholz, Evans, and Wagley (1994), p. 41.

the analytical ability to examine the issue from numerous perspectives. Let us take a closer look at the process of conducting issues management.

In the mid-to-late 1970s, Chase posed an early and widely accepted model of issues management. That model included the following steps:

1. Issue identification
2. Issue analysis
3. Change options
4. Action program[14]

The Chase model, though easy to remember, is a bit simplistic, and others have elaborated on the steps in great detail. For example, Renfro's book on issues management summarized the process thus: "1) scanning for emerging issues, 2) researching, analyzing, and forecasting the issues, 3) prioritizing the many issues identified by the scanning and research stages, and 4) developing strategic and issue operation (or action) plans."[15] Although Renfro's model is an excellent one, we believe that Buchholz, Evans, and Wagley offered a slightly more comprehensive, six-step model for managing issues that is directly designed for the public policy needs of management.[16] (See Figure 1)

Arguably, the most important phase of issues management is the **issues scanning, monitoring, and analysis phase**. If an issues manager fails to identify an emerging issue, the hope of creating a proactive plan to manage the issue diminishes. Once an issue emerges into the public policy arena, the organization loses control of defining the issue and time is of the essence in its management. Monitoring for emerging issues and predicting the future importance of issues is called **issues forecasting**. Issues forecasting is a bit like fortune telling; we can never accurately predict the future emergence of an issue with all of its nuances and the dynamic interactions of the issue with publics.

Another argument could be made that the research and analysis of an issue is the most important phase for determining priorities and how to best handle the new issue. The more research an organization can gather, the more informed its

decisions should be. Still, an element of strategy exists within the collection of data, its analysis, and its interpretation into managerial policy. But as Heath cautions, "Data are only as good as the insights of people who analyze them."[17]

A large part of government relations and public affairs is the **lobbying process** in which the research, knowledge, and policies formulated through issues management are communicated to legislative publics. This communication often takes place while educating elected officials on an organization's point of view, contribution to society, regulatory environment, and business practices. The legislative process is one in which organizations can integratively and collaboratively participate, helping to inform legislation. Oftentimes, lobbyists are hired to advocate for or against legislation that would potentially impact the organization.

Regulatory impact, or "constraints imposed by outside groups or interests,"[18] is thought to be costly and is normally argued against by organizations that seek to maintain their autonomy in order to create more effective management.[19]

Nonprofit, NGO, and Activist Public Relations

Nonprofit or not-for-profit groups are those that exist in order to educate, fund research, advocate, or lobby on behalf of a public cause or initiative. Oftentimes, nonprofit groups are those with an educational mission existing on behalf of the public interest. For instance, the Cancer Research Foundation of America educates consumers about what food products to eat to increase healthiness and lessen cancer risk. Public relations efforts on behalf of nonprofits generally involve disseminating public information, persuading publics to adopt the ideas of the organization through the use of press agentry and asymmetrical public relations, and the use of symmetrical public relations to increase donor funding and governmental funding of the initiative.

Nonprofit public relations may exist for educational purposes, to promote an idea or cause, or to raise funds for research on an issue or problem. A well-known example would be the many cancer research foundations that exist to raise awareness about cancer and its risk factors, educate the public about preventive measures, lobby the government for further funding of cancer research, and occasionally provide grants for cancer study. Much of nonprofit public relations includes lobbying the government through educating legislators about the problem, ongoing research initiatives, and how the government can increase support for both funding and preventive measures. Nonprofit public relations often relies heavily on member relations, meaning that it seeks to maintain and develop relationships with supportive publics who can distribute the organization's message, and often pay a membership fee to assist in providing an operational budget for the nonprofit. Member relations is often conducted through the use of Internet Web sites, magazines, newsletters, and special events. **Fund-raising** or **development** is the final, vital part of nonprofit public relations. Development is tasked with raising funds from both large fund donors, writing grants for governmental support, and conducting fund-raising with smaller, private donors.

Nongovernmental organizations, or NGOs, are "soft-power" groups who do not hold the political appointees of governmental agencies, and do not have the profit motivation of corporations. They exist in order to carry out initiatives, such as humanitarian tasks, that governments are not willing to handle. NGOs often form around social issues or causes to act in concert with the government but not to be controlled by it, although their sovereignty is at question in some nations. The employees of NGOs are often former government workers or officials. NGOs often partner with local groups or leaders to accomplish specific initiatives. Gass and Seiter noted that "non-governmental (NGOs) also are particularly good at demonstrating goodwill" and that goodwill is a part of establishing credibility.[20] They explained, "Goodwill is much more likely to be communicated via 'soft power'"[21] such as NGOs. Examples would be groups such as Amnesty International or Human Rights Watch.

Activist groups are special interest groups that arise around an organization in order to establish some type of change around their particular issue of concern. Activist groups normally arise from a "grassroots movement," meaning that it comes from everyday citizens rather than those who work in government. That fact makes it slightly different from an NGO and oftentimes activist groups are less official in the formal structure of their organization and its nonprofit status, compared to nonprofits or NGOs. Activist groups can be small and informal, such as a local group of parents banding together to protest a school board decision, or they can be large and more organized, such as People for the Ethical Treatment of Animals.

Activist groups can differ in their purposes and reasons for existing, and in the amount of action-taking behavior that they undertake. For example, some activist groups are termed "obstructionist" because they obstruct a resolution to the problem in order to gain media notoriety for their issue and new membership. Greenpeace is an example of an obstructionist activist group.[22] Other activist groups might use more collaborative or integrative strategies of problem solving in an attempt to resolve their problems with an organization and have those changes integrated into organizational policy.

Activist groups also differ in the issue with which they are concerned, with some issues being broadly defined (such as "the environment") and other issues being very specific (such as "toxic waste runoff"). Grunig's study on activist groups' issues is informative here; she found that "two out of every three activist groups were concerned with a single issue."[23] That single issue could be as specific as the impending destruction of a local, historic building. Or it could be a larger issue such as the amount of pollutants exuded from a manufacturing process.

Activist groups exert power on organizations in many forms of pressure, such as appearances at "town hall" type meetings, rallies and demonstrations, boycotts, anti-Web sites, e-mail campaigns, letter-writing campaigns, phone calls to legislators, lobbying, and events designed specifically to garner media attention. Activist groups are usually filled with young, educated, and motivated ideologues with a strong devotion to acting on behalf of their cause. These groups are normally quite effective in their efforts to have organizations integrate their values into organizational policy.

How to Respond to Activism

Organizations might attempt to "ignore" activist pressure, but that approach simply does not work because it often prolongs or exacerbates the activist group's campaign. When the organization stonewalls, activist groups normally approach elected officials and ask for the organization to be investigated, fined, and regulated. Activists also employ various forms of media that can both influence legislators and change public opinion, building support for their perspective that can be used in creating turbulence for the organization.

The most effective way that public relations can deal with activist groups is to engage them in a give-and-take or symmetrical dialogue to discover their issues of concern, values, wants, and priorities. Collaborative efforts to resolve conflict normally lessen the damage resulting from conflict for organizations; refusing to deal with activist groups protracts the dispute. The efficacy of activist groups, even very small ones, is well documented in the public relations body of knowledge. The *Excellence Study* contends that "regardless of the link of the dispute, the intensity of the conflict or the media coverage involved … all activist groups studied had disrupted the target organization."[24]

Integrative Decisions

Holding face-to-face meetings with activist leaders and members, brainstorming sessions, or joint "summits" tend to work well in building understanding between the organization and its activist. The activist group must also understand the organization's business model and constraints, and the requirements of the regulatory environment in which it operates. Asking for the opinion of activists on organizational policy is never a popular idea with senior management; however, it can result in novel adaptations of those ideas that provide a win-win solution to issues. Hearing and valuing the concerns of activists sometimes offers enough resolution to their dilemma for them to target less collaborative organizations. The crucial point of your response is that activists must be included rather than ignored. Using conflict resolution, negotiation skill, and symmetrical dialogue to understand the activist group helps the public relations professional incorporate their ideas into strategic decision making. A collaborative approach lessens the damage that activists cause to the reputation of the organization, as well as the amount of resources and time that must be spent on responding to activist pressure.

Activism Case: No Place for Gaddafi to Pitch His Tent

In late 2009, the leader of Libya, Col. Muammar Gaddafi, visited the United States for the purpose of addressing the United Nations (UN) general assembly. His visit to the United States led to citizen activism through which we can see many of the preceding principles of citizens acting on behalf of a cause or belief and pressuring the government to aid in their efforts. First, a brief look at the history of United States–Libya relations and specifically those with Col. Gaddafi provides important context for this case of activism. In 1979, the United States embassy in Libya was attacked by a mob and set on fire, causing the withdrawal of all U.S. government personnel.[25] Col. Gaddafi directly and publicly claimed responsibility for the 1988 terrorist bombing of Pan Am Flight 103 in which 270 people died over Scotland, including many Syracuse University students returning home from a study abroad program.[26] According to the U.S. Department of State, diplomatic relations with Libya were not reopened until 2006.[27] However, much hostility remains over the bombing of Pan Am flight 103 and Libya's other support of terrorist activities.

Col. Gaddafi is known for taking a Bedouin tent with him on foreign visits. A recent occasion in which this tent was problematic was when he requested to erect it on President Sarkozy's grounds in Paris in 2007, a move that caused consternation and reportedly "flummoxed presidential protocol service."[28] Gaddafi did erect this tent when he traveled to Belgium for official talks in 2004, and again when he visited Rome in 2009, using the tent to receive official guests. However, these European nations do not consider themselves as personally affected by the terrorist actions of Gaddafi in Libya. In terms of Grunig's situational theory of publics, discussed in Chapter 7, citizens of these European countries have lower problem recognition with Col. Gaddafi than do Americans. The *level of involvement* that Americans experience is higher than that of Europeans, both from the burning of the U.S. Embassy, severed diplomatic relations, and the Libyan terrorist downing of flight 103. High levels of both *problem recognition* and involvement, coupled with a feeling that one can personally impact the situation (known as low *constraint recognition*) all *predict* the rise of an activist public.

To further complicate matters with America, general outrage ensued when Scotland decided to release from prison the terrorist who was responsible for bombing Pan Am flight 103. The convicted terrorist, Abdelbaset al-Megrahi, was released just weeks before Gaddafi's UN address to the general assembly. Al-Megrahi received a hero's welcome upon return to Libya, while the families of many American victims watched the news stories vented their outrage in television interviews, letters to the editor, tweets, and blogs.

When Gaddafi and his associates began planning his trip to speak at the United Nations, to take place on September 22, 2009, they also began looking for a place to erect the Libyan tent. The Libyan embassy owns property in suburban New Jersey, where Gaddafi planned to stay and erect a tent. However, after public demonstrations outside the property, the town of Englewood, New Jersey, blocked Gaddafi from erecting the tent. Residents protesting Gaddafi's potential stay in the Libyan mission spoke frequently to the news media. Rabbi Boteach said, "I live right next door to the Libyan embassy. We want them to leave our neighborhood," adding that even the area's Muslims were against Gaddafi's visit.[29] Syracuse University alumni also appeared on broadcasts voicing their outrage at Gaddafi visiting the very state of that university.

Gaddafi petitioned to assemble the tent in Central Park, and New York City planning and other governmental officials also rejected that request. One news report led with the headline, "Have you got a permit for that Bedouin tent sir? Col. Gaddafi meets his match … New York planning offcials."[30] Finding no home for the tent, the Libyan delegation resorted to subterfuge, impersonation, and using intermediaries to find a temporary place for Col. Gaddafi in the United States.

At this point, Gaddafi's delegation impersonated Dutch officials and attempted to rent space for Gaddafi's tent on the roof of a Manhattan townhouse, but that deal fell through.[31] Gaddafi used intermediaries to rent a Bedford, New York, estate owned by Donald Trump. Aerial photos taken from helicopters buzzed on the news media as the Bedouin tent was constructed on the 113 acre estate, known as "Seven Springs." As Gaddafi wound up his 90-minute address to the UN general assembly, outrage was growing in Bedford. Citizens and media began to congregate at the front gate of the estate, and media helicopters circled. Bedford town attorney Joel Sachs said a stop work order was issued on the tent just after 5 p.m., because it is illegal to build a temporary residence without a permit. The town official called the tent an "illegal structure."[32] News anchors commented on the power of citizen activists. Helicopters provided visuals of the tent being deconstructed that played across media outlets for the rest of the day.

Clearly, Gaddafi underestimated the power of activist publics operating within a representative government to prevent him from engaging in the normal activities of a dictator. The day following the stop work order on the tent, after it was taken down, work began again to build the tent.[33] However, Gaddafi did not visit the tent, as is his usual custom, to receive state visitors or other official visits. Perhaps Gaddafi had finally understood the message issued by activist publics, and governmental officials at their behest such as Congresswoman Nita Lowey, who said Gaddafi is "unwelcome throughout the New York area."[34] The battle over where Gaddafi could pitch his tent was easily won by civic activists, demonstrators, and governmental officials who acted on behalf of residents in their districts. Perhaps the case of erecting a tent is a small one, especially for a country such as Libya. It must address concerns of terrorism, human rights violations, and weapons of mass destruction, to name but a few. However, if activists can place the issue of Gaddafi's tent onto the media agenda and the agenda of elected officials, they clearly hold the power to impact his official visit to the United States.

Chapter Summary

In this chapter, we explained the typical functions of public relations for an organization. Corporate settings were discussed, along with the importance of access to and advising the dominant coalition of function managers who often sit at the management table, experience and knowledge of one's industry, and navigating the organizational structure to gather information and be able to best advise management. Agency settings were discussed, with regard to teamwork, strategic counsel, the fast-paced environment of consulting for clients, the changing dynamics of the news media in relation to social media applications such as Facebook and Twitter, and current trends affecting agencies. Government relations and public affairs were each defined and discussed for their role in the discussion and management of public policy issues. Issues management was discussed, and the six steps to effective issues management initiative were delineated. Finally, nonprofit, nongovernmental organization (NGO), and activists public relations were discussed in light of both their ability to impact public policy and how research shows that an organization should best respond to pressure from these groups. As case examples, the public policy issue and interest groups surrounding the horse slaughter for human consumption

was discussed. The chapter concluded with a detailed examination of citizen activism and local government response to the United States visit of the Libyan leader Col. Muammar Gaddafi as an illustration of the power of activists to change their environment.

Notes

1. Stacks and Michaelson (2009), pp. 1-22.
2. Council of Public Relations Firms Web site (2009).
3. Council of Public Relations Firms Web site (2009).
4. Heath (1997), p. 45.
5. Lerbinger (2006).
6. The source of information for this case example is "House OKs ban on horse slaughter for meat" (2009).
7. Hoover's Handbook of American Business (1997).
8. Heath (1997), p. 45.
9. Heath (1997), p. 44.
10. Grunig and Repper (1992).
11. Heath (1997), p. 149.
12. Heath (1997), p. 149.
13. Heath (1997), p. ix.
14. Chase (1984).
15. Renfro (1993).
16. Buchholz, Evans, and Wagley (1994).
17. Heath (1997), p. 100.
18. Grunig, Grunig, and Ehling (1992), p. 67.
19. Mintzberg (1983).
20. Gass and Seiter (2009), p. 160.
21. Gass and Seiter (2009), p. 160.
22. Murphy and Dee (1992), pp. 3-20.
23. Grunig (1992a), p. 515.
24. Grunig (1992a), p. 523.
25. Embassy of the United States in Tripoli, Libya (n.d.).
26. Halpern (2006).
27. Embassy of the United States in Tripoli, Libya (n.d.).
28. Sage (2007).
29. Wordsworth (2009).
30. Hazleton (2009).

31. Goldman, Radia, and Berman (2009).

32. Goldman, Radia, and Berman (2009).

33. "Qaddafi Tent Back Up on Trump's N.Y. Estate" (2009).

34. "Qaddafi Tent Back Up on Trump's N.Y. Estate" (2009).

17. What Is Advertising?

by Kathleen Hall Jamieson and Karlyn Kohrs Campbell

In this chapter, Jamieson and Campbell explore the field of advertising. They begin with an overview of different types of advertisements, ranging from traditional to nontraditional and overt to covert. Completing this chapter should enlighten the reader to the vast and varied motivations for advertising that result in a wealth of different genres and specialties within the industry. Additionally, the authors encourage readers to be more media literate regarding advertising by considering the larger social impacts of the vast and varied messages advertisers create. This chapter is an excellent read for individuals who consume advertising messages, and is particularly informative for those who want to be responsible creators of ads.

A nonstop coast-to-coast trip on United Airlines from Philadelphia to San Francisco takes about 6 hours. If a passenger chooses to eat a meal during that time, it arrives on a tray that obscures most of the tray she has pulled down from the back of the seat in front of her. Reading material on one's laptop must be set aside to make way for the meal tray. In February 2004 the meal includes two breadsticks, a small salad, salad dressing, a choice of lasagna or chicken, and a 2- by- 3-inch folder ad not for air travel but for Celebrity Cruises. "What's in your destination?" asks the ad. "Caribbean in Spring? Europe in Summer? Panama Canal in Fall? Let Celebrity take you there." Inset into the appeals is a picture of a large cruise ship afloat on glass-smooth water off an island. If the passenger is interested, she can put the small ad card in her purse or pocket. The moment she reads it, Celebrity Cruises has reached an upper-income traveler with an image of travel more idyllic than that in a crowded plane. "From the moment you step on board," notes the second page of the folding card, "outstanding service awaits you. With one staff member for every two guests, savor a taste of luxury that makes you feel like the only guest onboard." Media Dynamics, Inc. estimates that on an average day, an adult in the United States is exposed to 306 radio, television, newspaper and magazine, and Internet ads.[1]

In 2003 $18.35 billion was spent on magazine ads, $1,117.2 billion on television, $12.3 billion on cable; ad revenue on Spanish-language network television was $2.2 billion.[2] In 2003, total ad spending in the United States rose 6.1% to $128.3 billion.[3] The average cost of a 30-second ad in the broadcast of the 2005 Super Bowl was $2.4 million.[4]

When the woman who edits this book for Wadsworth sits down at her nationally advertised computer, she wears clothes advertised both by local retailers and through national ad campaigns. We have never seen her office, but we would bet that the paint an the walls, the desk on which the computer rests, the lamp on the desk, and the pens in the drawer are as familiar to us as they are to you, although we may live thousands of miles apart. All these products probably have been nationally advertised. This form of standardization in our lives is in part the by-product of global advertising.

In a sense, advertising has given us a world in common. You are familiar with the products we purchase, we are familiar with the products you purchase, and that familiarity transcends large geographic distances. In other words, we live in a world filled with advertised products; often the presence of one of these products rather than another in our lives is determined by the effectiveness of the ad campaigns for competing products.

In this chapter we examine what advertising is and what advertising through the mass media does.

Defining Advertising

The ancient Romans identified three goals of rhetoric: to teach, to delight, and to move to action. Of course, these goals rarely occur in complete isolation from one another. As we argued in our discussion of news, the process of choosing a topic, narrowing it, and selecting evidence in its support gives all messages a persuasive component. Taken at face value, news professes to inform or teach, and ads profess to move to action, to advocate one purchasing decision rather than another. By contrast, most prime-time programming (sitcoms, crime shows) professes to delight.

In contrast to news or other types of programming, advertising is more likely to have a goal of explicit action. Here ads are more akin to editorials, which urge active response, than to the other sorts of content surrounding them. An ad asks us to go somewhere, do something, try something, buy something, accept some single idea, add a new word—generally a product's trade name—to our vocabulary, and associate positive images with that word. To accomplish any of these objectives, the ad contains a simple, highly repetitious message. In the past, we could sort the ad from its surrounding content by its simplicity, by its redundancy, and by the clarity with which it urges adoption, choice, or action.

A broadcast commercial is still to some extent a unit of content that appears in 10-, 15-, 20-, 30-, 60-, or 120-second time units and breaks unapologetically into the narrative line of some other broadcast content. Televised programming usually consists of larger units of 30, 60, or 120 minutes, interrupted by commercials. The smaller, 10- to 120-second units of information appear at regular and predictable intervals within the 30- to 120-minute units of content.

Because, unlike the shows broadcast in the early days of radio and television, television programs today are rarely sponsored by just one advertiser, the subjects discussed in the 30- to 120-minute units may differ drastically from those discussed in the adjacent 10- to 120-second blocks. For example, the evening news may report on the president's trip to Europe and cut to commercials for a shampoo, a laxative, or an automobile, then to a promotional ad for a prime-time program on the same network that evening, and then back to the news, where the anchor introduces a report about a hearing on organized crime. But as we will note in a minute, making ads look like programming is increasingly common.

This segmentation and aggregation of discrete, often incompatible thematic units violates all the rules by which we normally judge communicated content. Suppose you heard a speech discussing the president's trip, an upcoming prime-time program, a hearing on organized crime, the merits of a shampoo, a laxative, and a car. Such a potpourri of topics could not be blended into a coherent speech. As an audience member, you would doubt the speaker's grasp of the rules governing public communication and possibly would question the speaker's sanity as well. After all, the ability to address a subject coherently is one sign of a person's command of the speaking environment.

Yet we do not react negatively when television and radio break our train of thought, disrupt the story line, and introduce a series of unrelated messages. Indeed, we expect it. Consequently, *Sesame Street* built "commercials" into the program: "This part of *Sesame Street* is brought to you by the letter *A*."

Shifting Ad Placement

Traditionally the broadcast media provided programming at no direct cost to viewers. Advertisers paid for the programs by buying ads on them. The medium in effect sold eyeballs. Cable and satellite changed this equation somewhat by requiring pay for access to the channel itself while also drawing revenue from advertisers. For a higher subscription fee, premium channels such as HBO and Showtime offer commercial-free entertainment.

The remote control and then digital video recorders undercut the tie between exposure to programming and viewing ads. DVRs are like VCRs, but instead of storing the content on a tape, a DVR stores it on a computer disk drive. Advertisers responded by increasing their focus on product placement within programming, by identifying ways to ensure that customers would not block their ads in other venues, and by increasing their ability to identify people who might want their services or products.

Product Placement

The dilemma for advertisers is simple. The cost of advertising is rising on shows whose viewership is falling. Viewers' ability to block ads on shows they watch is increasing with access to DVRs. As a result, advertisers are making deals to include their products in the shows themselves. So, for example, it is no accident that Kieffer Sutherland's character in Fox's *24* races around exclusively in Fords. When products become integral to the plot, time on screen increases, as it did in an episode of *Everybody Loves Raymond* in which he knocks down a display of Ragu Express, a pasta meal, while stalking his wife in a supermarket.

Blurring Program and Ad Content

Some viewers resent product placement in programming. Concern that product placement may backfire, advertisers are also exploring "situmercials." By mimicking the look, format, and structure of the programming into which it is set, these ads increase the likelihood that viewers will think the program is still on and as a result pay attention to the ad. Political ads have mimicked news formats for decades, but this is a new phenomenon in product advertising.

In Fox's *24*, Kieffer Sutherland plays agent Jack Bauer. Ford Motors blurred the distinction between that program and its ads by bookending the drama with two long, action-packed ads, shot in the split-screen style that is the hallmark of *24*. Although these ads did not feature Sutherland, their lead character was called "Mr. Bauer." The mini-programs touted Ford Motor's cars.[5]

Incentives to View Ads

With blocking software, Internet users have fought against pop-up ads. In 2002 AOL, for example, added blocking capacity to its software. Google, Yahoo!, and Microsoft MSN followed suit

In March 2004 Google, the most used search engine on the Web, announced that it planned to offer free Web-based e-mail service, called Gmail, with a gigabyte of storage. Because most of us only have 50-megabyte e-mailboxes, those who accepted this free large-capacity service would receive ads tied to the content of their e-mail. Although representatives from Google argued that computers, not people, would search the e-mails and slot the ads, privacy advocates raised concerns. "The proposal is little different from asking people to let their phone companies listen in on their calls and butt in at any time to say, 'This call is brought to you by …,'" argued one critic.[6] Others questioned the limits of such a contract between Google and consumers. Would a person who expressed condolences at the death of a friend receive ads for funeral homes? Would the preferences expressed in e-mail be aggregated and stored in a way that linked the owner of the computer to the preferences? "We have no immediate plans to do so in the future," said a spokesperson for Google.[7]

Unless we plan to spend our lives in a darkened room, wearing earmuffs to block the sound of radio and shunning television, the Internet, magazines, and newspapers, we will be exposed to advertisers' efforts to persuade us. Even those who do not subscribe to a newspaper pass newsstands as they move from place to place and see discarded newspapers and magazines on buses, subways, and planes, in cabs, or on coffee tables in homes they are visiting. Bus shelters, buses, the back seats of taxis, kiosks, public toilets, trash cans, and even sidewalks contain ads. Television viewers trying to watch a game glimpse ads in the background. Log onto the Internet and risk assault by banner ads, as well as pop-ups. Close a file and there is a pop-under.

People who want to avoid radio commercials have to ignore the ads being played over the portable radios carried down the street or at the beach, over car radios when they are carpooling, over the computer of the person at the next desk, or over the public address system at the supermarket or shopping mall. Online, 28 percent report avoiding some sites to duck ads; 15 percent have downloaded ad-blocking software.[8]

People who want to ignore Internet ads have to shun e-mail and stay off-line. So obnoxious was the flood of unwanted solicitations from spammers touting penile extensions and Viagra that Congress took action in fall 2003. In December of that year, President Bush signed legislation restricting commercial e-mail. Violators face fines of $250 per violation with a cap of $2 million and could serve prison time.

Nor can we escape advertising by taking to the air. Because those who fly are affluent, they are a prime target for upscale products. So peruse the magazine in the seat pocket and you find ads, plug in the ear phone to listen to music, and you find the channels sponsored, watch the in-flight entertainment and find promos for television programs, and on some flights look down at your tray table and you'll find advertising there as well. "With an average domestic flight time of 2.5 hours," says SkyMedia's president, "our advertisers will be able to achieve a level of penetration, impact and recall unmatched by virtually any other medium."[9]

The mass media pervade our environment, and with the mass media come the advertisements that underwrite them, A message tailored to persuade an audience to accept a product is not, in itself, advertising. When the people selling the product pay for time or space to enable them to *bring the message in a specific unalterable form to that audience*, however, we call the message *advertising*. An advertiser, within the bounds of taste and the law, controls what the message says, how it says it, and where and how frequently it appears.

The mass media have rules of conduct guaranteeing that the advertisers can communicate what they want at the time or in the space purchased. For example, when a television ad is cut short by a technical malfunction or the programming in which the ad is embedded fails to reach an audience of the size guaranteed by the network, the advertiser is entitled to a "make-good," a rebroadcast of the commercial at a comparable time at no additional charge. Similarly, when a newspaper transposes two prices in an ad, the newspaper will, at no cost to the advertiser, run a correction in the next edition or in the next day's paper.

Some forms of advertising do not fit neatly into this definition, because they reach their audiences without the purchase of time or space. The dividing bar that separates your groceries from the next customer's at the checkout counter of the supermarket, for example, may carry a message from a cigarette manufacturer: "For a light smoke—try X," The cigarette manufacturer has given the dividers to the store free of charge, in the hope or with the agreement that they will be used. Their use functions as advertising. When your groceries are bagged, you may notice a message about the store on the bag. When you carry the groceries away from the store or use the bag as a garbage bag in your home, you have become the carrier of an ad for the store, just as you have become a walking ad for Calvin Klein when you wear jeans with his name stitched onto the hip pocket.

A movie hero may drink a certain soft drink—a form of advertising purchased by the soft drink manufacturer in exchange for supplying cast and crew with the product, or in exchange for what is called a "promotional consideration." Whether promotional considerations were at play or not we do not know, but in the 2003 best-seller *By the Light of the Moon*, by Dean Koontz, the characters drink Sierra Nevada, like Cheez-Its but not Goldfish, and approve of the upscale Peninsula hotel in Beverly Hills. And in *Something's Gotta Give*, the writer played by Diane Keaton types through sorrow and glee on a laptop prominently displaying the Apple logo.

The ability to add images digitally that did not occur in the picture in the first place has enhanced moviemakers' ability to generate special effects such as the balletic fights in the *Matrix* trinity. It has also augmented the advertiser's ability to place products and the ability of those with a digital camera to alter photographs of family and friends. Jamieson did this at the University of Pennsylvania's Annenberg School for Communication, by taking a digital picture of

the other deans and digitizing Winston Churchill into it. Of course, no one believed that Churchill had risen from the dead to administer at Penn. But who will know that the can of Coke shown for a second or so on the coffee table in the sitcom wasn't there when the show aired on network television but appeared only in syndication?

"Tie-in" campaigns are now big business. To enhance one another's markets, in December 2003, MasterCard engaged in cross-promotion of the holiday film *The Cat in the Hat*. Although his face is obscured, Dr. Seuss's famous cat is evident in the print ad showing his white-gloved paws and red- and white-striped hat. The identification is increased by ad lines that mimic the Seuss style: "travel book for friend, Nanook: $29." "bathtub ship for Cousin Chipo: $18." The point of the ad: remind readers to see the film, use MasterCard, and enter the MasterCard Trip-A-Day Giveaway to win a trip to the Universal Orlando Resort. Universal, of course, produced the film. Similarly the third movie in the *Lord of the Rings* trilogy was launched along with merchandise that included a *Lord of the Rings* chess set and a *Shards of Narsil* sword.

The assumption of such tie-ins is that those who like the movie will be disposed toward the products and vice versa. The corollary, of course, is also true. When the producers of *Bad Santa*, the story of a department store Santa who drinks, steals, and despises children, approached the ad agency with the Stolichnaya account about having the lead character drink that brand of vodka in the film, the liquor representatives turned them down on the grounds that the company's marketing principles ban "association with any situation involving abuse of our products."[10]

Sometimes, of course, advertisers have no control over the identification of their product with an undesirable individual. When U.S. troops captured former Iraqi dictator Saddam Hussein in December 2003, they found the canned meat Spam in his hideout. An article in the *New York Times* labeled the result "the product placement from hell." "How do you respond to an unsolicited endorsement from the Butcher of Baghdad?" asked the story, "It's not the most positive association," conceded Jute Craven, a spokeswoman for Hormel Foods. But she pointed to the upside: "It's further evidence of the worldwide appeal of Spam."[11]

Rental videos and DVDs have also become carriers of advertising, often for other movies by the same company or for movies trying to reach the same target audience. Rent a movie with French subtitles, and you are likely to see previews for other foreign language films, for example.

Realizing that movie cassettes and DVDs reach a predictable local audience—those living within a specifiable distance of the rental store—an inventive local marketer began placing local ads on video rentals. People in Wichita, Kansas, who rented *She's Having a Baby* saw ads for a local tire service. Because Paramount had released the film, it sued, charging copyright infringement. A Kansas circuit court judge dismissed the suit, saying, "This court is frankly skeptical that viewers actually care whether Paramount is the source or sponsor of the advertisements." Despite the judge's dismissal, the local marketer lost anyway. Fearful of being taken to court by Paramount, the tire service returned to more traditional advertising channels.[12]

Ads are also included in faxed newspapers, which usually are two- or three-page summaries of the days top stories sent to businesses that cannot get same-day delivery. The *Hartford Courant*, the first newspaper to provide a fax service, started in April 1989. The *Courant* continues to produce its fax paper, which now has a readership of several thousand but has discontinued the sale of its bottom-of-the-page $100 ads. The *New York Times'* "TimesFax," however, which is sent all over the world, to seventy-eight Caribbean resorts and sixty-four cruise ships, considers advertising a big part of its publication and offers various special editions as vehicles for its advertisers.

Some advertising is faxed directly and without invitation to the fax machines of those owning them. Junk mail imposes costs on the recipient and the community in terms of disposal costs and opportunity costs. But the costs of junk mail are largely borne by the sendee. Junk faxes, however, impose involuntary costs on the receiver in a number of costly and direct ways. Not only

does the receiver have to pay for the paper and toner costs, incur the costs of wear and tear on the fax machine, but also expend time and energy on printing, sorting, and reading the multitude of often unwanted messages. In December 1991, President Bush signed legislation to permit those who do not wish to receive junk faxes to enter their names on a list. Advertisers who transmitted to the fax machines on that list would be violating the law.

Telephones have also become conduits of unwanted advertising. We assume that most of our readers have at one time or another rushed to their phone expecting a call from a friend, only to hear a recorded voice telling them that they have won a trip or prize or were eligible to receive a deep discount on magazines. Such intrusive use of the telephone can be life-endangering when the numbers reached are those of the fire station, the police department, or a hospital's emergency line. By tying up the fine, the advertiser blocks the access of those who need to reach the hospital or the fire or police station.

Some people contended that these calls are an invasion of personal privacy, particularly when, through random-digit dialing, such calls reach individuals who had paid to have their phone numbers unlisted. A 1990 U.S. Congress Energy and Commerce Committee report revealed that "more than 180,000 solicitors call[ed] more than 7 million Americans every day with recorded messages sent by automatic dialers, and more than 2 million businesses send more than 30 billion pages of information by fax each year."[13] Legislation in 1992 required telephone solicitors to provide their name, business, and business phone or address. These regulations were applicable to both live and recorded messages.[14] As direct marketers moved toward fully automated systems; the percentage of all telemarketing solicitations that were automated rose 10 percent between 1994 and 1997, reaching 41 percent in 1997.[15] In response to these intrusions, Congress authorized a federal Do Not Call Registry in October 2003.

In other words, television, radio, and newspapers are not the only conduits of advertising, and many forms of advertising do not appear in purchased time or space. This chapter focuses on advertising found in the mass media, however, because without this advertising the mass media as we know them in the United States would not exist.

Mediated Advertising

Before the advent of the mass media, salespeople were often the bearers of their own advertising, repeating the same message and carrying the same products from door to door. With the rise of mass media, such door-to-door advertising has become prohibitively expensive for most nationally sold products. Even with products like Avon cosmetics that are still sold door to door and person to person, television ads are used to predispose residents to open their doors and purchase the product.

When the door-to-door salesperson was replaced by a mediated one, the ability of the salesperson to tailor the message to each individual receiver or adapt the message in response to audience reaction was reduced. The producer of an ad carried by the mass media, rather than in person, must create a message that speaks to what a mass audience shares rather than to the individual differences of the millions who will hear or see the message.

A second major shift occurred when television, radio, and print became the conduits of advertising. None of these media could bring a real product into your home. Instead, each carried a representation of the product. So, although the traveling salesperson could show you that the product worked and could actually sell you the product, the mass-mediated ad was forced to add another step in the persuasive process. The ad needed to persuade you to go where the product could be found and to buy the product. First, the ad often attempted to give you a vicarious experience of using the product satisfactorily, so the next time you had the option to buy the product, it would already seem comfortable and familiar. Thus, the seller who would throw dirt onto a cloth

stretched out on your carpet to demonstrate that the vacuum cleaner would efficiently pick it up was replaced with a mediated salesperson in an ad who showed you something the producer hoped would be comparable. But in your home you could see the dirt, see the vacuum, and testify that there were no tricks. The door-to-door salesperson offered firsthand experience of the performance of the product. In the ad, all sorts of tricks could be employed to make it appear that the vacuum was more effective than it really was. Consequently, a need arose for rules governing what an advertiser could and could not do in ads.

A third shift occurred with the arrival of Internet advertising, According to Nielsen/Netratings, nearly three quarters or 204.3 million homes had access to the Internet in February 2004, up 9 percent from 2003. Websites with the largest numbers of users were: Microsoft's MSN (95.2 million), Yahoo! (92.2 million), and Time Warner (71.9 million).[16] In 1998, $2 billion was spent advertising on the Internet.[17]

Internet ad spending peaked during the dot.com boom in 2000 at $8.1 billion.[18] Online ads dropped 12 percent from 2000 to 2001 and another 15 percent in the following year. In 2003 the revival began.

The convergence between the television and the personal computer is opening new opportunities for advertisers. WebTV, ACTV, Source Media, and World Gate are interactive software firms that enable people watching an ad in a television program to click on a link and be sent to the relevant website for additional information. A viewer can also link to a chat room to talk about the product. Although the advertiser isn't physically in your living room, you and he or she are now closer to the relationship of salesperson and client that characterized house-to-house selling, Meanwhile, of course, you are not watching the program that has returned to the screen after the ads. And you are paying no attention to any of the ads that followed the one that enticed you into hyperspace.

Early in the history of the Internet, programmers foresaw "some real problems with the prospect of giving television viewers one more reason to leave the tube and surf the Web," notes an article in *Electronic Media*.[19] Evidence that the decline in television viewing was accompanied by a rise in web use justified those fears.

Kinds of Traditional Mass Media Advertising

All advertising identifies a product, service, or idea; differentiates it from related products, services, or ideas; associates it with things we value; induces us to participate in the creation of its claims; and repeats its key concepts. Most ads also are part of a campaign, and all employ slogans in some form. Yet despite these similarities, ads can be divided by type.

The regulations governing some ads (for example, political) differ from others (commercial and PSAs—public service announcements); the space or time to air some ads must be purchased (commercial, political, and advocacy or issue ads), but others (PSAs) are aired at no cost to the producer; and the objectives of different types of ads range from marketing a corporate image to electing a candidate. Therefore, we differentiate here in general terms the different kinds of advertising.

Obviously, some of these types overlap. Some ads sell both a product and a service, for example, and some PSAs urge us to vote, an appeal that may benefit one candidate or party more than another. Distinctions are also complicated by advertisers' deliberate blurring of image-building ads and PSAs. Similarly, product ads occasionally incorporate actors playing politicians whose reelection is ensured by judicious use of a certain brand of toothpaste or mouthwash. In general, however, categories are a useful way of understanding the special forms an ad can take.

Ads can be classified by the product they sell (service, goodwill, or special product ads); whether the time or space in which they run is purchased (commercials) or provided by the outlet as a community service (public service announcements); or the type of information they provide, the types of appeals they make, and the types of regulations that govern them (advocacy and political ads).

Product Ads

Some ads market a product or a product line. Ads for Dairy Queen, for example, create a world filled with Dairy Queen products and their ingredients. Mountains of chocolate and fields of fresh strawberries, pineapple, and bananas are all part of this world. Some of the ads argue that we ought to participate in this world without identifying specific products. Others tell us about a special kind of sundae or a banana split.

The televised ads for Dairy Queen illustrate well the purpose of an ad for a product or product line. By showing us the texture of the fresh fruit, the vibrant colors of the strawberries, and the rich "rivers" of chocolate, the ads preview the product, familiarize us with the product's name, and induce us to experience the sensations of eating the product. Although the world is a miniature one, the close-up shots create the illusion that there is actually a tropical retreat with larger-than-life fruit and mountains of chocolate. The world in close-up is the size of our television screen.

A food is a consumable commodity with which we've all had experience. The function of food is clear. Consequently, the strategy of an ad for food is generally to make the food appear as delectable as possible. But what is the function of a camera? Ads for digital cameras sell us the capacity to preserve the moment. They tell us that we can relive the best of now, unlike the ancient world of film; we can see what we will relive in time to correct the memory. Were Mom's eyes closed in the shot? Erase and reshoot.

The Product as Ad

When a small box of cereal, deodorant, or laundry detergent appears in your mailbox along with a coupon toward purchasing more of the product, the product itself is functioning as an ad. The product also becomes its own ad when a person behind a small table at the supermarket offers shoppers a free taste of a product and a discount coupon. The free sample has been a staple of product advertising since the inception of the profession.

When the product can be hazardous, such promotions provoke controversy. Under threat of government action barring advertising to children, a major cigarette advertiser in summer 1995 announced an end to the sample as ad. Philip Morris "said it will no longer send out 4 million to 5 million packs of cigarettes by mail nor will it give away 15 million to 20 million at events annually." The company indicated, however, that it would continue distributing coupons that could be redeemed for free packs.[20] Because nicotine is potentially addictive, providing the pack of cigarettes as a sample is a particularly insidious practice.

Service Ads

An ad for First Bank positions a bank official on camera looking at us, the banking customers. As the bank officer entangles himself in the esoteric jargon of his profession, his image is blurred on the screen, and his voice is muted. Everyone in the audience who has experienced institutional double-talk has a frame of reference for this type of institutional officer. The camera is reacting for us; we make little sense of such presentations. The audio track becomes our ears as we tune the message out. The ad has induced us to re-create a familiar experience. The announcer now can tell us that First Bank has simplified the banking process; the simplification brings the bank official back into focus. The ad has told us that this bank provides a service. Our past experience is used to help us make that service seem desirable.

Ads for a service often show us what it is like without, and then with, the service. An ad for an airline, for example, shows a large person crammed into a small seat being elbowed by the passengers on either side. The service? Wider seats, fewer people per row. In the second scene the same person is in an uncrowded seat with ample room.

Goodwill Ads

The ads we have described are clearly intent on selling something—a product, a product line, or a service. One type of ad is noteworthy for the absence of a specific sales pitch for a tangible profit-making item. This is the goodwill ad.

In the late 1970s, it was difficult to find an ad for a gas company that was selling gasoline or the services a gas station provides. Instead, oil companies were selling their concern for the environment, their conviction that we ought to conserve energy, or their safe driving tips. These goodwill ads were an attempt to alter the public image of the oil companies in the wake of rising gasoline prices, the long lines at the pumps, the oil spills that had endangered wildlife in the United States and abroad, and accusations of influence peddling that had pervaded the political climate during the Watergate investigations.

This type of ad falls under the general heading of "image advertising." Related forms are more specific in connecting their appeals to a product. IBM, for example, does not want to be associated with the notion that computers are dehumanizing and threatening. Consequently, ads for IBM show the humane uses of computers. IBM computers are instrumental in saving lives, argues one ad. Weyerhauser Lumber Company, "the tree-growing people," shows planned tree planting that, the ads argue, will make it possible for today's children to build houses tomorrow.

Such image advertising can produce substantial results. After sponsoring the 1994 coast-to-coast Olympic torch relay, AT&T conducted a survey to assess the relay's results. Every potential long-distance customer in this crucial time of divestiture was aware of the relay. Half were aware of AT&T's sponsorship. More important for the phone company, those who recognized that AT&T had sponsored the event were, by a statistically significant margin, more disposed to choose AT&T as their long-distance phone company.[21] In 1986, the growing awareness of such potential rewards prompted major companies, from Eastman Kodak to American Express, to tie their corporate identities to the reconstruction of the Statue of Liberty.

At the turn of the century, the images with which products tended to be identified were environmental. Crest toothpaste's print ad read,

"Turn this page back into a tree. Simply send in this certificate with proofs-of-purchase from two Crest cartons. And, together with The National Arbor Day Foundation, well plant a seedling in a Yellowstone-area National Forest on your behalf." An IBM spot emphasized the ways that the corporation was working with the United Nations to solve environmental problems. The spot contrasted gridlocked traffic with a swarm of beetles. Pictures of nature were intercut with topographic maps on computer screens. We saw nature, then nature through the computer. IBM and nature were conjoined.

The causes to which goodwill advertising are tied are noncontroversial. No one opposes use of a designated driver to reduce traffic fatalities. Accordingly, Coca-Cola distributes free products to those identified as designated drivers who attend the home games of the Milwaukee Brewers. And because beer companies do not want to be associated with traffic fatalities, it is not surprising that one of the corporate sponsors of the baseball team's designated driver program is the Miller Brewing Company of Milwaukee. Image advertising is designed to identify a company and its products with a positive image and to dissociate them from any negative images that may have been created in news channels.

Companies that sponsor programming on Public Broadcasting Service stations are also engaging in image advertising, Instead of linking the company's name with some socially approved idea (conservation, for example), sponsorship links the company with bringing culture or quality programming at no direct cost to U.S. homes. Such sponsorship argues that the company is a good citizen of the community. We are less likely to believe evil of a good citizen. Consequently, such sponsorship insulates the company from criticism and creates positive associations for the company's products.

The benefits of event sponsorship were dramatically illustrated by the results of a survey conducted in summer 1995 on the 1996 Summer Olympics, held in Atlanta. The surveyors found that "23% of consumers would definitely or probably switch from their current brand to a brand offered by an Olympic Sponsor. And of the 64% who will be following the Olympic Games, 29% said they would definitely or probably switch to an Olympic-sponsored brand."[22]

Advocacy Ads

When the company as good citizen takes a position on a public policy in an ad, the ad becomes an advocacy ad. Many stations refuse advocacy ads out of fear that they will then be bound to air the other side's position as well. Determining what is and is not an advocacy ad is difficult. In 1981, ABC became the first of the networks to agree to air advocacy ads, but the network stipulated that the ads could run only on late-night television, a less than desirable time for most advertisers and a time when advertising space is more difficult to sell. By October 1990, stations owned and operated by NBC, CBS,and ABC were all being permitted to determine whether, or not to accept such ads. The change in policy was prompted by the willingness of the stations' cable competitors to accept advocacy ads and by the demise of the Fairness Doctrine. Airing such an ad no longer carries an obligation to provide free airtime for opposing points of view.

In summer 1990, Anheuser-Busch aired a 30-second advocacy ad that opened by showing workers at lunch and farmers in their fields. The announcer said that America was built by individuals willing to give their fair share. The ad then said that Congress now wanted Americans (note, not Anheuser-Busch), who already were paying about $3 billion in excise taxes on beer, to pay more than their fair share. As a foaming stein of beer appeared on the screen, the tag said, "Can the Beer Tax. 1-800-33-Taxes." When viewers called, they were asked if they would like to have a letter protesting a proposed hike in the excise tax sent for them to their congressional representative. In the campaign's first month, 110,000 callers asked to have the letters sent.

To magnify the power of the campaign, beer industry officials hinted that if the tax were increased, their companies might reduce sponsorship of sporting events and decrease spending on television advertising. Increasing the economic impact should have increased the number of groups supporting the beer industry's position. However, critics noted that reduction of advertising was unlikely because that was the industry's major means of sustaining sales and introducing such new products as ice beer.[23]

There have been occasional controversies over advocacy ads. In spring 1986, J. Peter Grace, chairman of W.R. Grace and Company, protested to the press and public that one of his ads had been rejected by the networks. Set in the year 2017, the ad showed an elderly man in a witness cage. The man is being cross-examined by a child who wants to know how the man could have let federal deficits reach $2 trillion. The networks refused to show the ad. In so doing, they were within their rights. In *Democratic National Committee v. CBS*, the U.S. Supreme Court held that the editorial judgment about what to air and what not to air belongs to the broadcaster.

Maintaining their ban on advocacy ads, in the 1993–94 season, the three major broadcast networks all rejected advocacy ads on health care reform. As a result, the only "national" ads that aired for and against the Clinton reform plan appeared on CNN, an outlet available in 1995 in about two out of three homes in the United States. During the health care reform debate of 1993–94, more money was spent on advocacy ads than had been spent to elect Bill Clinton president in 1992. We will discuss issue advocacy at greater length in the chapter on political ads.

Direct-Response Ads (Infomercials)

Infomercials, also known as direct response ads, ask you to call in to order the product. In form they resemble a program but are instead selling a product. Throughout the program, a toll-free number appears. By calling it, viewers can order the product. On January 1, 1990, when the Federal Communications Commission's regulation called Syndex (for "syndication exclusivity") went into

effect, use of infomercials by cable stations rose. Syndex stipulates that cable stations cannot show syndicated programs if the same programs are being shown on local television in the same market. During the time that is now blocked out by Syndex, cable stations can, if they choose, pick up infomercals beamed to them 24 hours a day at no charge via satellite. In 2003, $154.1 billion in revenue was produced by direct-response television, up from $85.3 billion in 1997.[24]

Infomercials selling music often assume the look of a rock 'n' roll or country special. For one, a producer gathered the rights to 150 past hits and packaged them on twenty cassettes. He then paid disc jockey Wolfman Jack to endorse the product as "Wolfman Jack's favorite all time hits"; $200,000 in production costs later, the infomercial offering the cassettes was ready to air. Another infomercial featuring chef Arnold Morris resembles a Julia Child cooking show. Its title is "Arnold's Gourmet Kitchen."[25]

In April 2004, the Electronic Retailing Association, to which many infomercial makers belong, announced "a new self-regulatory program … to throw out companies that make false claims and send their names to the Federal Trade Commission for investigation." Under the new process "complaints about misleading infomercials, online ads and other direct response vehicles will be referred to an independent review board of the National Advertising Review Council, a partnership of advertising trade associations and the Council of Better Business Bureaus." The announcement came after a series of large settlements against driect response marketers. These included Fast Abs, which promised "six-pack" abs without exercise, Other products that didn't deliver as promised included the Rio Hair Naturalizer System, which caused hair loss and scalp irritation.[26]

Public Service Announcements

Unlike the advertising we have discussed so far, public service announcements (PSAs) are not aired in purchased time or space. Television stations meet part of their FCC-stipulated obligation to be responsive to the needs of the community by airing public service ads. A public service ad is generally created and sponsored by a nonprofit organization to convey noncontroversial information to the public.

Ads for charities such as United Way and the Children's Hospital of Washington are PSAs. The National Institutes of Health sponsors PSAs to remind people with hypertension to take their medicine, to warn us to watch for cancer's early warning signals, and to discourage us from smoking. During election years, the League of Women Voters, the networks themselves, and specially created committees use PSAs to urge us to register and vote.

The PSAs most likely to be aired are sponsored either by an agency of the government or by the Advertising Council, The Advertising Council, which accepts a limited number of campaign assignments each year, is sponsored by ad agencies. It costs a non-profit agency upward from $100,000 to pay the production costs for an Ad Council campaign. Ad Council campaigns have been criticized for their pro-industry bias. In one often-run ad, for example, a Native American man is shown paddling his canoe down a polluted stream. As he steps to the shore, someone throws a bag of garbage from a passing car, and a tear runs down his cheek. Critics of this ad argue that littering is a minor form of pollution. Significant air and water pollution is caused by industry. Littering could be reduced by banning nonreturnable bottles—a proposal industries have fought bitterly. This Ad Council campaign provides some support for the contention that the council deflects criticism from industry and shifts blame and responsibility to individuals, who are often powerless to correct the problems isolated in the ads.

The major advantage of an Ad Council campaign is the ability of the ad industry to place its PSAs in desirable free time. Not all effective PSAs are sponsored by the Ad Council. A Clio award–winning ad for the Humane Society shows in slow motion the violence that occurs at rodeos, while a Strauss waltz plays in the background. The ad focuses our attention on an often-ignored facet of the rodeo. The ad argues persuasively that rodeos are inhumane. Similarly, Mothers Against Drunk Driving (MADD) sponsored a series of PSAs encouraging youths and the public at large to consider the cost in human life that is exacted by people who drive while intoxicated.

One $2-million PSA radio campaign was privately funded. Martin Himmel, former president of Jeffrey Martin, Inc., commissioned media guru Tony Schwartz to produce an antismoking campaign. In one of Schwartz's spots, Patrick Reynolds, grandson of the founder of the R.J. Reynolds Tobacco Company, reveals that his grandfather, a tobacco chewer, died of cancer, as did his heavy-smoking father. His mother and three brothers all have emphysema, says Reynolds. "Now tell me," the ad concludes, "do you think the cigarette companies are truthful when they tell you that smoking isn't harmful? What do you think?"

Because its producers do not pay for the time in which the PSA is aired, they cannot control its placement. Stations tend to place PSAs in times no one has purchased. Consequently, PSAs often air early in the morning or late at night, when few viewers are watching, or in documentaries for which the network could not find enough sponsors.

In 1999 a federally sponsored antidrug campaign blurred the traditional distinction between the PSA and the paid ad. Concerned that antidrug PSAs produced by such nonprofit groups as the Partnership for a Drug Free America were not being given the airtime that would reach the targeted adolescent audience, Congress appropriated $170 million dollars for a televised advertising campaign based on purchased time.

The Internet increased the ability of PSAs to deliver audiences to messages. The "Face the Issue" campaign, which focuses on domestic violence, eating disorders and drug abuse, illustrates the way in which PSAs can drive viewers to help sites. Created by Jane Semel and Melanie Hall, who head a nonprofit production company, the campaign ties visually riveting ads to the www.facetheissue.com site. In one ad a young woman kneels on the floor over the toilet. "Sound familiar?" asks a female voice. "If so, you may have bulimia. You cannot flush away your problems. It won't go away until you stop gagging your pain and give it a voice." Run on channels such as MTV the ads direct viewers to the website where they can discuss their problems. In its first two months of operation, the site generated two million hits.

Political Ads

Some ads argue that we should elect one person rather than another or urge us to vote a specific way on a resolution or referendum. These ads, which differ in some important ways from other types of ads, will be discussed in Chapter 10.[27]

Issue Advocacy Ads

Some ads argue for or against a piece of legislation, while others make a case that a politician is or is not doing a good job without using such terms as "vote for" or "vote against." These issue advocacy ads are discussed in Chapter 10 as well.

Nontraditional Advertising

In-store advertising and adaptive billboards are among the areas in which technology has increased the capacity of advertisers to bring their ads to receptive audiences.

In-Store Advertising

In-store televised advertising is increasing because the fragmentation of mass media has made it more difficult for advertisers to reach the mass audience. A customer in the "health and beauty" aisle is more likely to buy a deodorant than if he or she is wandering the electronics aisle. Advertisers customize ads for play in specific sections of stores: Health ads in the health aisle, ads for DVRs in the electronics aisle. This sort of placement tries to increase impulse buying. The executive vice president of sales for Premier Retail Networks, which places ads in stores, reports that "ads that communicate specific information

about a product or an offer work better than the more emotional, slice-of-life advertising that dominates regular television."[28]

Digital Billboards

Digital technology now exists to permit advertisers to change the messages on billboards as often as they'd like. If a supermarket chain brings in a truckload of great peaches, the billboards on the routes to the store can tout the special on very short notice. Digital billboards also can adjust digital billboards according to the radio stations playing inside passenger cars. "Based on survey data of station demographics, Smart Sign calculates the average income of passersby based on what they are listening to, and then changes the message to target the biggest cluster of people driving by. The company [Smart Sign Media] operates 10 digital billboards in California."[29]

Search Advertising

Search a product, concept or service on sites such as Yahoo! and Google, and you receive a search-result page complete with links to an enterprise offering the product. The process works by using an algorithmic engine to scan the text of web pages and match the search to the keywords on which advertisers have bid. Companies bid to ensure that their ads are placed high on the search results page and then pay when a user clicks to their site. At up to $100 per lead, the highest-paying keyword in spring 2004, is *mesothelioma*, a rare asbestos-related cancer. This word ties victims to lawyers who advance cases that produce average settlements of about $6 million.

As the *Wall Street Journal* explains, "These Web searches by patients provide fertile advertising ground for lawyers. Paid-search ads typically run at the top of the side of main search results, so if people search for mesothelioma, they get nonpaid results framed by the ad. ... When viewers click on the ads, they are sent to lawyer sites with a mixture of information, links to other cancer Websites—and a phone number, online form or e-mail address to contact an attorney."[30]

The search, in other words, provides leads for attorneys in a high-yield area of litigation.

Complicating the search advertising process is the fact that ads can attach a product to a negative context. This occurred when an ad for luggage stores was placed on a news website about a murderer who "carried away his victims in a suitcase."[31] Nor was the sponsor pleased when an ad for steroids was tied to a news report on steroid abuse.[32]

Sponsored Links

Three services that are in effect media buyers on the web, place ads on websites, and tally and track the results are DoubleClick Inc., Advertising.com Inc., and Google. Called *contextual advertising*, this process automatically tags a client's ads to pages likely to attract the prospective purchaser of the client's product. The owners of the site receive a payment for placement on the site. The service scans websites for words that indicate relevance to a client. As the *Wall Street Journal* explains, "Google uses an auction system of selling key words and placement to the highest-bidding advertiser—much as it auctions off the nicest spots on search results through its own Website, though 'relevance,' or the click-through rate of the ad, is also factored into placement. Google charges advertisers a wide range of prices for such placements, starting at five cents and going up. Its technology can deliver advertisers' promotions on both search Web pages and content Web sites."[33]

Spam

In December 2003 Congress passed the Can-SPAM Act, a law that took effect January 2004 regulating unsolicited commercial e-mail. Under that law, there must be an existing relationship between sender and receiver; senders must have a valid U.S. postal address, and there must be a way for receivers to block future mailings from the sender. Until February 2004, spam made up 62% of e-mail traffic, up from 58% in December. In March 2004 a Pew Center for the People and the Press survey found that 53 percent of adult e-mail users hadn't noticed a change in the amount of spam since January 1; 24 percent said the percentage had increased at home and 19 percent reported an increase at work. Five percent reported ordering a product or service as a result of an unsolicited e-mail.[34] In the first major legal action under the act, four large internet providers filed civil suits against hundreds of alleged spam producers in March 2004.

How To Determine Whether It's an Ad

Advertising can also be defined by distinguishing it from the content that surrounds it. In the mass media, advertisers pay for access to the audiences attracted by programming. How does the ad itself differ from that programming?

How Ads Reveal the Advertiser

What distinguishes a televised soft news story about Jamaica, presented from a human interest angle, from a televised commercial brought to you by the Tourist Bureau of Jamaica? The commercial will identify itself as a commercial by disclosing its source. This disclosure, called a "tag," generally takes a visual form and usually is placed at the end of the commercial.

What distinguishes a televised view of a candidate's day, broadcast as a news segment on the evening news, from a slice-of-life commercial paid for by the candidate's campaign committee? The commercial is required to contain a tag identifying the committee paying for the ad. Again, the tag generally occurs at the end.

Because we are less likely to be manipulated by a message that warns us that it is manipulating us, as a commercial warns us by identifying itself as a commercial, producers of commercials try to incorporate the identifying tag in an inconspicuous way. Political committees, for example, are often legally incorporated under such titles as "Friends of Reuben Spellman," precisely because the commercial can then legally be tagged thus: "and that's why this message was paid for by Friends of Reuben Spellman." Such a tag is called a "no-tag."

How Ads Reveal the Intended Audience

The biblical injunction "Seek and you shall find" takes on a new meaning when we are in the market for a product or have a problem that could potentially be remedied by a product. Have you ever noticed that when you have a cold, television and radio are filled with ads for cold remedies? And when you are trying to determine which car to buy, the number of automobile ads seems to increase? When we are troubled by a problem or an unmet need, we become information seekers about that problem or need. Communication that was always in our environment suddenly becomes relevant, and we recognize it and attend to it. We seek information to help us make a decision. At the same time, the presence of the information assures us that our problem is not an imaginary one and that the problem is important. Ads about our problem tell us it is a real one, it is significant, and we are justified in being concerned about it.

We also seek information once the decision to purchase has been made. After the decision, however, the reasons for seeking the information change. Before the decision, we seek information comparing products, arguing the unique benefits of one over the other. After we have purchased the product, we seek information to assure ourselves that the decision was a wise one. In these two instances, we function as active communication participants: We seek information.

Often, however, we are passive receivers of information. We are frequently receptive to information and willing to become involved in the creation of messages about products when we are not deliberately seeking certain types of information. How do advertisers alert the passive receivers that a product is designed for them?

In some cases, the identification is visual. In 1995, Dominos tried to increase its share of the $18.6-billion-a-year pizza market with ads featuring three 30-ish male football fanatics. At the center of the ads is Gus, his baseball cap turned backward on his head, who is both a wiseguy football expert and an expert at ordering and eating pizza. The ad indicates not only that it is seeking 30-something male customers but that it is trying to increase the number of orders it gets during football games. The ads were slated as part of the chain's sponsorship of the *NFL Live* "Halftime Report."[35]

Other ads telegraph their audience both visually and verbally. If an ad says, "Trabo, the fun game for the whole family," and shows a mother, a father, a boy, and a girl playing a board game, that ad is not soliciting the attention of single adults. Although single adults might buy the product, the ad is picturing youngsters and their parents as its prime audience. The tone of the ad—the laughter, the upbeat music, the good-natured comments among participants—may also be speaking to those in the audience who view recreation as a social rather than solitary activity, whether they identify themselves with the family in the ad or not. But the ad is clearly not speaking to the single adult whose idea of an enjoyable evening is dancing into the wee hours of the morning at the hottest nightspot.

By showing the game being played by children with adults, the advertiser is also establishing that this is a game better suited for both children and adults than for adults alone. It is not a game too difficult for children; moreover, it is not X-rated. Yet it can be played with satisfaction by adults and children. Many products, from toothpaste to breakfast cereal, can be used both by children and adults.

A major sports figure, such as basketball star Michael Jordan, appeals to sports fans in general and the market of young males in particular. The products endorsed by Jordan have included those manufactured by Gatorade, Nike, McDonald's Corporation, Rayovac, and Sara Lee Corporation. These products, unsurprisingly, were featured in Jordan's first film, titled *Space Jam*, released in 1996.

When Pepsi-Cola signed Grammy winner M. C. Hammer to promote its "cool cans" in rap's rhythmic chants, it was targeting the younger market. Similarly, Coca-Cola hired Heavy D & the Boyz to turn Sprite's "I like the Sprite in you" into rap ads for radio and television. In addition to its clear attraction to younger viewers and listeners, rap has a number of persuasive advantages. Rhyme is memorable. Moreover, as the senior vice president group creative director of J. Walter Thompson USA notes, "You can, without being untrue to the form of rap, get more lyrics per 30 seconds than with any other form of music."[36] In summer 1990, four of the country's top albums were by rap groups, and one of MTV's top-rated shows was *Yo! MTV Raps*.

Comparatively few products dictate use exclusively by either adults or children, as diapers and aftershave do. Yet many products are marketed to the whole family with the argument that the product is good for the children. One toothpaste, for example, is advertised with the appeal that if this product is used, the children will brush longer because they will like the taste of the toothpaste. The assumption, of course, is that Mom or Dad will buy the same brand for the whole family. Another toothpaste promises that it gives your mouth sex appeal—a claim that reveals that its target audience is very different from the audience for the ad featuring 6-year-old Johnny, who brushes longer with the better-tasting toothpaste.

Indeed, if the advertiser used children as spokespeople to claim that the toothpaste gives your mouth sex appeal, the ad would be offensive. Both of these ads identify an intended audience implicitly. An explicit identification of intended audience is made in ads for Ma Jolie that show a 20-something woman over the tag "Ma Jolie clothes for women."

Ads reveal not only the likely age of those targeted by the advertiser but also whether the ad is designed to reach men or women or both. Again, some ads do this explicitly. One deodorant ad, for example, tells us that the product was specially formulated for women. In another ad for a deodorant soap, a male character tells us that the product is strong enough for a man. Then an attractive woman adds that she likes it, too.

The ways in which ads signal the gender of the intended purchaser can be seen by turning off the sound on the television set and comparing the visual texts of ads for aftershaves and for perfumes. Without hearing the verbal pitch, we can tell whether the product is being sold to men or women by determining whether a man or a woman is the visual focus of the ad. Is she turning to look at him, or is he turning to look at her? Are several men in pursuit of one woman, or several women in pursuit of one man?

An ad can also solicit the attention of the intended audience by recreating the lifestyle that the audience member either has or desires. Why do ads for beer show groups of people rather than individuals? Why are men rather than women shown in most beer ads? In what sorts of environments are the people in beer ads shown? How are the people in ads for beer dressed—formally or casually? Are the people in beer ads middle class or upper class?

Now consider the same questions about an expensive scotch (Chivas Regal) or gin. The lifestyle created in beer ads is different from the lifestyle portrayed in ads for more expensive hard liquor. The ads tell us that beer is an outdoor as well as an indoor drink, that beer drinkers are active, often in sports, and that beer is a drink for people who are comfortable in casual clothes with groups of friends; it is not a drink for the solitary drinker or for the man in the tuxedo. The advertisers single out their market by customers' preference for certain sorts of activities. One beer urges us to grab all the gusto we can get; the appeal is assertive and rugged. Another beer tells us that it is the beer for "when it's time to relax."

The mood of the two ads will be different, because the basic appeal is different. One is more active than the other, and one is more individualistic than the other. Beer ads also single out their audience by the types of environments in which the ad situates the product. Some ads place the beer drinkers in a bar; others place the beer drinkers outdoors. One beer's advertising tactic has been to show appropriate and inappropriate times for enjoying a beer, with the slogan "It's the right beer now."

Many beer ads appeal to sports enthusiasts by including famous hockey, baseball, or football professionals in the ads. Some beer advertisers set themselves apart by appealing to an upper-class market. They do this by adopting an exotic name (Michelob rather than Pabst, Schlitz, or Budweiser), by packaging the beer in a bottle with foil wrap, by implying that the beer is made by more expensive processes than other beers, by charging more for the product, by labeling the product "premium" beer, and by stressing that the beer or its recipe is imported. Thus, ads themselves provide some of the clues about the identity of the intended audience.

The place in which we find the ad also provides clues. Ads targeted to children appear during certain types of television programming, such as children's specials or cartoons, and at the hours when children's programming occurs—early morning, especially Saturday. They also appear in magazines such as *Ranger Rick*. Ads designed for homemakers are seen at all hours, particularly during soap operas in the afternoon and during morning talk shows; they appear in so-called women's magazines such as *Better Homes and Gardens*. Ads for older people appear more often during news and public affairs programming, the types of programming older adults are most likely to watch. Ads for men appear during sports events or in so-called men's magazines; ads for adults appear during prime time. An image-building ad for a corporation will appear adjacent to a prestigious public affairs program such as *Meet the Press* because highly educated people, opinion leaders, and those who control the other media are more likely to attend to such programs.

Some targeting is controversial. When R.J. Reynolds announced that it was introducing a new cigarette called Uptown, directed primarily at African Americans, protests from the African American community and from Louis Sullivan, then U.S. Health and Human Services secretary, followed. The cigarette, which was to have been test-marketed in Philadelphia in December 1989, was withdrawn.

Advertising and Reality: Stereotypes

Stereotypes are simplified, inaccurate conceptions or images that have become standardized and are widely held. A stereotype can idealize or demean the group it types. If a depiction of a group reflects reality, we do not consider that depiction a stereotype.

Stereotypes make it possible for us to form generalizations about a person or advertised character without requiring a great deal of information or evidence. The less time we have to process information, the more likely we are to rely on stereotypes in drawing conclusions. The less time television producers have to communicate a message, the more likely they are to rely on stereotypes.

For example, in a 30-second commercial a writer cannot create three-dimensional characters but must instead deal in the shorthand of stereotypes. The Harried Housewife, the Bumbling Husband in the Kitchen, the Archetypal Grandmother, and the Nosy Neighbor are stock characters in commercials whose type we recognize immediately. Consequently, the writer can introduce a limited number of cues about them in a few seconds and proceed to deliver the message through them because we fill in the appropriate characteristics for this type of character.

Often the stereotypes found in commercials are so ridiculous or so harmless that they provoke no protest. Mr. Whipple, the storekeeper who lurked behind the display cases waiting to ensnare shoppers for squeezing the Charmin, and Aunt Bluebell, who arrived at the homes of relatives with toilet paper hidden in her purse, were two such eccentrics. These characters were so implausible that if we identified with them at all, it was as comic foils.

By contrast, when a lazy, greasy, conniving thief in a sombrero and gun belt speaking in a parody of a Mexican dialect was chosen as the trade character for Frito's corn chips, Latino groups protested. The Frito Bandito embodied and consequently reinforced negative stereotypes about Latin Americans in general and Mexicans in particular. By drawing public attention to the stereotypes on which the Frito Bandito was based, the protest made it more difficult for the ads to use the stereotype to convey a commercial message. The protests also demonstrated that the Bandito offended a large, vocal group of potential customers, a result no advertiser desires. Consequently, the Frito Bandito disappeared from ads.

Stereotypes that are nearly universally held rarely draw protests because we are unable to see them as stereotypes. For decades the public tolerated ads in which older people were portrayed as fools or comic foils. When the gray rights movement focused attention on these ads, the number of ads decreased in which older characters' seeming inability to hear, understand, or recall a product's name provided an excuse for repetition of that name.

Stereotypes are powerful means of reinforcing societal attitudes about groups of people because the process of stereotyping involves the receiver in creating the message. When the negative attitude that is reinforced is about a large, politically and economically important group such as Latinos, African Americans, women, or elders and is recognized by spokespeople for that group as destructive (messages, for example, that a woman's life is fulfilled if her floors shine, that older people are senile, or that Latinos are lazy and dishonest), then protest will follow because representatives of the stereotyped group fear that the stereotype will reinforce undesirable role models and will perpetuate discrimination against the group. Some groups have used the media to change the way in which they are portrayed by the media, as we will show in Chapter 9.

Advertising Values

Often we are unaware that advertising embeds assumptions not directly related to the products being advertised. These assumptions are depicted in Figure 6–1.

Television transports people to a middle-, upper-middle, and upper-class world. In the process it creates expectations in us all, expectations based on the assumption that the norm or standard in this country is a middle-class existence—or better. People in ads have spacious kitchens, large lawns, expensive appliances, and cars; they travel worldwide. Ads take for granted that the audience routinely buys soaps, deodorants, makeup, and cologne and that the audience is not making a decision about whether to buy the product but rather is deciding *which* brand to buy. The Television Bureau of Advertising reports that in 2001, 4,901 brands were advertised on network television.

The World According to Commercials

In the process of being urged to purchase the multitude of products that ads advocate, we are also being persuaded to a certain style of living. Contrast, for example, out standards of personal hygiene with those of our great-grandparents at the turn of the twentieth century, Underarm deodorants, in the forms we know them, did not exist, and no one seemed to mind. Advertising and changing expectations about personal hygiene have persuaded us that certain types of body odors are offensive and ought to be camouflaged or altered. Embedded in the argument that we ought to use a specific mouthwash is the assumption that we ought to use a mouthwash.

Similarly, the argument that we ought to use a specific floor wax assumes that we ought to wax our floors. Embedded in the argument that we ought to use a specific room deodorant is the assumption that we ought to use one.

Reliance on packaged products has contributed to the growing problem of waste disposal in the United States. If we didn't use so many packaged products and such heavily packaged products, the problem would be smaller. Because advertisers want us to continue to use their products, they reassure us that doing so is environmentally responsible. This notion of responsibility was newly found in a climate in which the public began expressing concerns about the vulnerabilities of the planet.

Accordingly, in 1990, a number of companies be an using and touting their use of recycled materials in their packaging. Lever Brothers announced in July 1990 that the plastic bottles containing Wisk, All, and Snuggle would contain "up to" (note the careful use of language) 35 percent recycled resins. Procter & Gamble announced that it would include at least 25 percent recycled high-density polyethylene in bottles of Tide, Cheer, Era, Dash, and Downy. Bottles containing Spic and Span liquid cleaner would be made entirely of recycled materials. The scope of the industry's contribution to the landfill problem is evident in its claim that "in the first year of P&G's bottle recycling program, the company will produce 110 million containers that use the recycled plastics, keeping about 80 million bottles out of the nation's waste stream."[37] By Earth Day in April 1995, Procter & Gamble could claim to have reduced the amount of waste it produced by 1 billion pounds.[38] However, in 2002 *On Earth* magazine reported, "After several years of post–Earth Day '90 progress, P&G's efforts are flagging. Its use of recycled material in its products has fallen by more than half, and, in its annual sustainability report, the company has stopped reporting the recycled content of its packaging altogether."[39]

In the process of embedding assumptions about the kinds of products we should use, advertising has created norms governing our sense of the acceptable home: a home in which the faucets, floors, furniture, mirrors, and dishes (but not the faces of the women) shine; a home that is odor-free (no smell of cat, fish, cigars, feet) and filled with artificial, chemically created outdoor scents (lilac, rose, herbs, evergreen). This home is filled with subtle deceptions. Spouses marvel at the cleanliness, unaware of how little effort it took with the new product to achieve that effect; and they assume that foods created from chemically enhanced mixes are homemade.

In the world of commercials, avenging guardians of the social order exist to ferret out those who fail to use the sanctioned products. Nosy neighbors and socially superior guests are ever alert to spot the smell of a cat or a cigar, or to comment snidely about spots on glasses, dull dishes, or dust on the furniture.

The characters who live out their lives in the 30- to 60-second world of the broadcast ads and in the pages of print ads seek and obtain almost instant gratification. Problems arise and are met. Promises of product performance are made and kept. All this occurs in a very brief time span. The answer to all the problems, needs, and expectations in the ads is ultimately found in the purchase of some product. The link between problem and solution is clear and unequivocal. Not only is the gratification instant, but it also occurs as a result of the product advertised. In contrast, our lives are more complicated and more ambiguous than the lives of advertising's population.

Characters in ads are also what psychologists would describe as "other-directed." Characters seek the approval of others in ads. When that approval is withheld, crises ensue. Neighbors detect odors in the house, and a crisis erupts; an air freshener is the answer. Parents detect spots on drinking glasses, and a crisis occurs; a new dishwashing product eases the tension. Acquaintances spot "ring around the collar," and the family is thrown into turmoil. A clothes-washing product resolves the crisis. In each of these instances, the others disapprove not only of the condition (the ring, the odor, the spots) but also implicitly, if not explicitly, of the ad's protagonist *because* of the condition. It is not only the product that ultimately wins approval in the ad but also the person who uses the product.

The need for social approval is strongly felt by all of us. It is a need that advertising exploits. In the process of exploiting the need, advertising reinforces, legitimizes, and enhances it.

In one sense, advertising is powerfully conservative—it is loath to offend; it reinforces institutional values. In another sense, advertising is radical because it holds out a world full of products and promises the good life to those who buy them. Yet the mass media reach many who lack the money to buy the products. Ads are materialistic. Purchase and consumption of material goods are glorified in commercial ads. Our assumptions that ads are created to sell products are so deeply ingrained that we distrust ads created to enhance the image of a corporation, which claim that "this corporation is a good citizen of the community." The notion that a manufacturer might pay to bring us a noncommercial message is suspect because until recently we had seen few such ads. In fact, the manufacturer is still selling a product. The product here is the company's good name, and when we respect it, the advertiser can link it to the product line and urge us to buy.

The acquisition of material goods brings happiness in the ads; material goods are satisfying. Because the ads simplify, we do not see other factors that make a happy ending possible; we do not see those factors that make the happy ending impossible even with the product or see the unhappiness that may be caused by the product.

Seeing the Other Side

Although it is generally true that ads reinforce the assumption that consumption of products is good, there is at least one major exception. In the name of fairness, the Federal Communications Commission required stations that broadcast cigarette ads also to run a certain number of antismoking ads free of charge. During the period in which both pro-cigarette and anticigarette ads were aired, audiences were exposed to messages arguing that consumption of a product (cigarettes) was not only not good (as the pro-cigarette ads claimed) but also harmful and that it should be avoided or stopped. The antismoking campaign challenged an unspoken premise in commercial advertising—the premise that consumption of products is good. By challenging the premise, the antismoking ads made us aware of it. In a sense, the counterads were not merely countering smoking but also countering advertising.

The Interplay of News and Advertising

We live in a complex world in which messages interact with one another to form impressions. Because people pay attention to information on topics of importance to them, public recall of news about health is high. When scientific studies seemed to confirm that oat bran had the potential to lower cholesterol, advertisers hurried to capitalize on this finding, introducing new products such as Ralston Purina's Oat Bran Option, and making new claims for old products, such as General Mills's Cheerios and Quaker Oats.

The legitimacy that news can endow, however, news also can take away. In mid-January 1990, the prestigious *New England Journal of Medicine* published a major study downplaying the ability of oat bran to reduce cholesterol. The study was carried in print and broadcast media reports. In March, Arbitron/SAMI scanner reports showed that oat bran cereals, which had peaked at 4.9 percent of the cereals market in January, had plunged to a 3.18 market share. Note the claims that survive on the boxes of Post Raisin Bran and General Mills' Cheerios in 2004:

- Raisin Bran: Studies show high-fiber foods like Post Raisin Bran may actually help lower your risk of heart disease.
- Cheerios: As part of a heart-healthy diet, the soluble fiber in Cheerios can reduce your cholesterol.

To Sum Up

It is common to see the premises underlying a given ad campaign challenged in news and public affairs programming. News programs carry word of recalls, of Federal Trade Commission investigations, and of court cases in which advertisers' claims are challenged; consumer advocates in newspapers and on television investigate harmful effects of products. These exposés constitute a form of counteradvertising. They make us aware that ads do not tell the "whole truth" about a product and that they ought to be evaluated critically. In the next chapter we focus on the critical evaluation of advertising's claims and evidence.

Use InfoTrac College Edition to access information on topics in this chapter from hundreds of periodicals and scholarly journals. Enter keyword and subject searches: *advertising, mediated advertising, infomercials, public service announcements.*

Selected Reading

Turow, Joseph. *Breaking Up America: Advertisers and the New Media World.* Chicago: University of Chicago Press, 1997.

Notes

1. Media Dynamics Incorporated, "Ask the Experts," http://www.meaiadynamicsinc.com/askexpert.htm.
2. Janet Whitman, "Magazine Trade Group Reviews How It Tallies Ad-Page Revenue," *Wall Street Journal*, 21 January 2004, p. B7.
3. Suzanne Vranica, "U.S. Ad Spending Rose 6.1% in 2003," *Wall Street Journal*, 9 March 2004, p. B6.
4. Stuart Elliott, "Ad Reaction Claims Superbowl Casualty," *New York Times*, 3 February 2005, p. CI.
5. Brian Steinberg, "Advertising," *Wall Street Journal* March 2, 2004, p. Bll.
6. "Senator Blasts Google Plan," *Palo Alto Daily News*, 10 April 2004, p. 4.
7. Katie Hafner, "In Google We Trust?" *New York Times*, 8 April 2004, p. E6.
8. "Trends (A Special Report): The Net—Safety, Blogs and Protocols," *Wall Street Journal*, 9 February 2004, p. R3.
9. Joe Sharkey, "High-Altitude Advertising for a Captive Audience," *New York Times*, 23 December 2003, p. C6.
10. John Lippman, "Hollywood Report," *Wall Street Journal*, 21 November 2003, p. W12.
11. John Tierney, "Political Points," *New York Times*, 21 December 2003, p. 30.
12. Joanne Lipman, "Local Video-Ad Business Goes on Blink," *Wall Street Journal*, 23 August 1990, p. B6.
13. "House Considers Restriction on Advertising by Telephone and Fax," *New York Times*, 31 July 1990, p. A13.
14. N. Paradis, "Reducing Telephone Solicitations," *St. Petersburg Times* (Florida), 15 March 1998, p. 2F.
15. "Degrees of Telemarketing Automation," *The Direct Marketing Association Statistical Fact Book* (New York: Direct Marketing Association, 1998), p. 152.
16. "Home Access to Web Rises to Nearly 75% in U.S.," *Wall Street Journal*, 18 March 2004, p. B5.
17. "Everything You Always Wanted to Know about Advertising," *Advertising Age*, 3 May 1999, p. 32.
18. Mylene Mangalindan. "Starting to Click: After Wave of Disappointments, The Web Lures Back Advertisers—New Generation of Pitches Nets Data on Consumer; Not a Mass Audience—Getting Drivers to Showroom," *Wall Street Journal*, 25 February 2004, p. Al.
19. Lee Hall, "Convergence," *Electronic Media*, 5 April 1999, p. 11.
20. Ira Teinowitz, "Philip Morris Hits Youth Smoking," *Advertising Age*, 10 July 1995, p. 31.
21. Martin Gottlieb, "Cashing in on Higher Cause," *New York Times*, 6 July 1996, p. E6.
22. Leah Rickard," '96 Olympics Capture Consumer Awareness," *Advertising Age*, 10 July 1995, p. 21.
23. Kim Foltz, "Busch Spots Fight Rise in Beer Tax," *New York Times*, 30 July 1990, p. Dll.
24. Nat Ives, "Infomercials Clean Up their Pitch (But Wait, There's More)," *New York Times*, 12 April 2004, p. C12.
25. Anthony Gnoffo Jr., "The Ad That Looks Like a Show," *Philadelphia Inquirer*, 27 November 1989, p. El.
26. Ibid., p. 22.
27. Shaila K. Dewan, "The New Public Service Ad: Just Says 'Deal with It,'" *New York Times*, 11 January 2004, p. 4:5.
28. Erin White, "Advertising," *Wall Street Journal*, 23 March 2004, p. Bll.
29. Kimberly Palmer, "Highway Ads Take High-Tech Turn," *Wall Street Journal*, 12 September 2003, p. B5.
30. Carl Bialik, "Lawyers Bid Up Value of Web-Search Ads," *Wall Street Journal*, 8 April 2004, pp. B1-B7.
31. Saul, Hansell, "Internet Advertising Thrives on Targeted Ads," *New York Times*, 29 December 2003, p. 6.
32. Ann M. Mack, "Meet the New Black: Contextual Advertising," *Adweek*, 12 April 2004, p. 9.

33. Mylene Mangalindan, "Seeking Growth, Search Engine Google Acts Like an Ad Agency," *Wall Street Journal*, 16 October 2003, p. B2.

34. "No Spam Relief," *Wall Street Journal*, 18 March 2004, p. B4.

35. Melanie Wells, "Domino's Ads Play on Football," *USA Today*, 4 August 1995, p. 10B.

36. Patricia Winters, "A Trend, Friend: Is Rap 4 U, 2?" *Advertising Age*, 25 June 1990, p. 22.

37. Laurie Freeman, "Lever, P&G Green Plans Differ," *Advertising Age*, 23 July 1990. p. 46.

38. Don Hopey, "Earth Day Message Is Clear," *Pittsburgh Post-Gazette*, 22 April 1995, p. A3.

39. Jason Best, "Spin Machine: Briefings; Proctor & Gamble and Recycled Plastics," *OnEarth*, 2 September 2002, vol. 24, no. 3, p. 10.

Chapter 16: Discussion Questions

1. Name two differences between corporate and agency public relations.

   _____

   _____

   _____

   _____

2. What do non-profit PR practitioners do?

   _____

   _____

   _____

   _____

3. What are the six steps of issue management for a PR professional?.

   _____

   _____

   _____

   _____

4. What is the most important phase of issue management? Why?

   _____

   _____

   _____

   _____

5. What is issues forecasting?

   _____

   _____

   _____

   _____

6. Name an advantage and a disadvantage a non-profit PR professional may have relative to a corporate PR professional.

_____

_____

_____

_____

7. Provide an example (other than the case study in the chapter) of government relations or public affairs PR.

_____

_____

_____

_____

8. What is the main difference between a corporate PR professional and an agency PR professional?

_____

_____

_____

_____

9. Name three responsibilities of a corporate CCO.

_____

_____

_____

_____

10. What are "integrative decisions"?

_____

_____

_____

_____

Chapter 15: Discussion Questions

1. What is news?

   _____

   _____

   _____

   _____

2. How did the "penny press" impact journalism?

   _____

   _____

   _____

   _____

3. What is yellow journalism?

   _____

   _____

   _____

   _____

4. "Muckracking" refers to what type of journalism?

   _____

   _____

   _____

   _____

5. Name one positive and one negative effect electronic media had on journalism.

   _____

   _____

   _____

   _____

6. Why were the editorial and business operations in a newspaper separated?

_____

_____

_____

_____

7. What is the difference between "objective" news coverage and "fair and balanced" news coverage?

_____

_____

_____

_____

8. What does it mean to "frame" a news story?

_____

_____

_____

_____

9. Explain agenda setting in relation to journalism.

_____

_____

_____

_____

10. What is the impact of converging communication technologies on journalism?

_____

_____

_____

_____

Chapter 14: Discussion Questions

1. According to the author, what is the aim of film studies?

    _____

    _____

    _____

    _____

2. What is the effect of "persistent afterimages" as it relates to film?

    _____

    _____

    _____

    _____

3. How is Edison's Kinetoscope related to modern movies?

    _____

    _____

    _____

    _____

4. What is responsible for the loss of over 80% of all silent films ever produced?

    _____

    _____

    _____

    _____

5. According to this author, what is the difference between "cinema" and "movie"?

    _____

    _____

    _____

    _____

6. What can we learn about a society by studying its films?

_____

_____

_____

_____

7. Have films always told stories? Explain.

_____

_____

_____

_____

8. What is wrong with the assumption that Hollywood is the film capital of the world?

_____

_____

_____

_____

9. According to the author, what role did publicity play in the development of the first female film star?

_____

_____

_____

_____

10. Why is it beneficial for both consumers and producers of cinema to study films?

_____

_____

_____

_____

Chapter 13: Discussion Questions

1. How is technology changing the face of the television industry?

    _____

    _____

    _____

    _____

2. Networking is a key to industry success. What have you learned about from the other chapters that may help you develop networking skills?

    _____

    _____

    _____

    _____

3. What allowed networks and major studios to merge?

    _____

    _____

    _____

    _____

4. What is the role of syndication in the television industry?

    _____

    _____

    _____

    _____

5. What is a "spec script"?

    _____

    _____

    _____

    _____

6. What is the benefit of writing a spec script based on an existing television show?

_____

_____

_____

_____

7. Why might someone going into production want to know about screenwriting?

_____

_____

_____

_____

8. Screenwriters, producers and directors can benefit from researching past television shows. How?

_____

_____

_____

_____

9. Why do television industry professionals care about advertising?

_____

_____

_____

_____

10. What are the benefits and drawbacks of relying on Nielsen Ratings in an era of media convergence?

_____

_____

_____

_____

Name: _____

Chapter 12: Discussion Questions

1. Why do we form relationships?

   _____

   _____

   _____

   _____

2. What is the connection between communication and attachment theory?

   _____

   _____

   _____

   _____

3. List the four factors of interpersonal attraction that the chapter explains.

   _____

   _____

   _____

   _____

4. Provide an example of non-sexual, non-romantic intimacy in a relationship.

   _____

   _____

   _____

   _____

5. Which of the seven types of love does the chapter argue is the most satisfying in an adult relationship?

   _____

   _____

   _____

   _____

6. List the "coming-together" phases of relational development.

_____

_____

_____

_____

7. What are the five "secret tests" individuals conduct during the intensifying stage of relationship development?

_____

_____

_____

_____

8. What is a connecting bid?

_____

_____

_____

_____

9. Explain one postive and one negative effect of social networking on relationships.

_____

_____

_____

_____

10. What are the three pieces of advice the chapter provides for salvaging a relationship that is at risk?

_____

_____

_____

_____

Chapter 11: Discussion Questions

1. What is cyberspace?

   _____

   _____

   _____

   _____

2. What technologies provided the historical roots of telecommunications?

   _____

   _____

   _____

   _____

3. Briefly explain the relationship between science fiction and cyberspace.

   _____

   _____

   _____

   _____

4. What is cybernetics?

   _____

   _____

   _____

   _____

5. Explain one influence cyberspace has on society.

   _____

   _____

   _____

   _____

6. What are Bell's three types of narratives for understanding cyberspace?

_____

_____

_____

_____

7. What is one benefit of digital systems over analog systems?

_____

_____

_____

_____

8. What does the chapter identify as "the world's first successful digital communication system"?

_____

_____

_____

_____

9. What is the difference between "cyberspace" and "the Internet"?

_____

_____

_____

_____

10. What is the most surprising piece of information you learned from this chapter?

_____

_____

_____

_____

Chapter 10: Discussion Questions

1. What is convergence?

    _____

    _____

    _____

    _____

2. Why should communication students care about convergence?

    _____

    _____

    _____

    _____

3. What difference do you see in this chapter's definition of communication and the definition provided in Chapter One of this text?

    _____

    _____

    _____

    _____

4. What are the four differences media make in the transactional model of communication?

    _____

    _____

    _____

    _____

5. Provide an example of how you use mass media, using one of the four ways outlined in this chapter.

    _____

    _____

    _____

    _____

6. Why is the ability to simultaneously share the same information with millions of people important?

_____

_____

_____

_____

7. What are the three impacts of mass communication on culture?

_____

_____

_____

_____

8. What is media literacy?

_____

_____

_____

_____

9. Based on the media literacy skills outlined, how does reading this chapter enhance your media literacy?

_____

_____

_____

_____

10. Summarize the relationship between mass communication and the information provided in previous chapters of this book.

_____

_____

_____

_____

Chapter 9: Discussion Questions

1. How do basic cultural values influence differences in mass media?

   _____

   _____

   _____

   _____

2. Explain how the relationship between media and society is reciprocal.

   _____

   _____

   _____

   _____

3. What were the four key influences of the early period?

   _____

   _____

   _____

   _____

4. What were the three key influences of the colonial period?

   _____

   _____

   _____

   _____

5. During which time period does DeFleur argue America experienced the most dramatic techno-logical and social change?

   _____

   _____

   _____

   _____

6. Why was steam important in the development of mass communication?

    _____

    _____

    _____

    _____

7. Provide three examples of how the U.S. became a "Mass Communication Society."

    _____

    _____

    _____

    _____

8. How did the move from and agriculture-based society to an industrial-based society impact media?

    _____

    _____

    _____

    _____

9. Which of the six predictions for the future do you most agree with? Which do you least agree with?

    _____

    _____

    _____

    _____

10. What historical connection did you find most interesting? Why?

    _____

    _____

    _____

    _____

Chapter 8: Discussion Questions

Define, in your own words, the following concepts:

1. First Amendment

    _____

    _____

2. Chilling Effect

    _____

    _____

3. Clear and present danger test

    _____

    _____

4. Prior Restraint

    _____

    _____

5. Libel

    _____

    _____

6. Slander

    _____

    _____

7. Shield Laws

    _____

    _____

8. Censorship

    _____

    _____

9. Obscenity

    _____

    _____

10. Fair Use

_____

_____

11. Fairness Doctrine

_____

_____

12. False Advertising

_____

_____

13. Children's Television Act

_____

_____

14. Intellectual Property

_____

_____

15. Copyright

_____

_____

16. Cybersquatting

_____

_____

17. Digital rights management

_____

_____

18. FCC

_____

_____

Chapter 7: Discussion Questions

1. Define "ethics" in your own words.

_____

_____

_____

_____

2. According to Kenneth Andrews, what are the three qualities required for a decision to be ethical?

_____

_____

_____

_____

3. Define the following three concepts: meta-ethics, normative ethics, and applied ethics.

_____

_____

_____

_____

4. According to the author, what is one major challenge individuals face if ethics is learned from observing others?

_____

_____

_____

_____

5. What is the categorical imperative as it pertains to communication ethics?

_____

_____

_____

_____

6. List three ethical considerations that may arise in a particular communication profession.

_____

_____

_____

_____

7. What are the benefits of communication professional associations delineating ethical rules or codes?

_____

_____

_____

_____

8. What are the drawbacks of communication professional associations delineating ethical rules or codes?

_____

_____

_____

_____

9. What is the difference between "good & bad" and "right & wrong"?

_____

_____

_____

_____

10. What classical approach to communication ethics best fits your perceptions of ethics? Explain..

_____

_____

_____

_____

Chapter 6: Discussion Questions

1. What are the two main perspectives to studying communication covered by this chapter?

    _____

    _____

    _____

    _____

2. What fact about the study of communication did you find most surprising/interesting?

    _____

    _____

    _____

    _____

3. What are the three primary means of persuasion, according to Aristotle?

    _____

    _____

    _____

    _____

4. Where were the first series of lectures on communication from a classical Aristotelian perspective held?

    _____

    _____

    _____

    _____

5. In your own words, briefly explain the relational perspective.

    _____

    _____

    _____

    _____

6. Why was the classic Greco-Roman approach to communication particularly well-suited to American perspectives?

_____

_____

_____

_____

7. Name three areas of communication studies/research now in existence.

_____

_____

_____

_____

8. What is "communibiology"?

_____

_____

_____

_____

9. According to the author, why did the relational perspective grow in prominence during the 1960s and 1970s?

_____

_____

_____

_____

10. How might the content of this chapter be helpful to a person in a communication profession?

_____

_____

_____

_____

Chapter 5: Discussion Questions

1. What are the five attributes of a book?

2. How do online written artifacts differ from books?

3. What lessons from Ptolmey I's 286 b.c. "problem" are applicable today?

4. List the fundamentals of good writing (the "be" statements).

5. What is reverse outlining?

6. What are the four steps in the writing process?

    _____

    _____

    _____

    _____

7. Do you see any evidence of the "online effect" in your writing? Explain.

    _____

    _____

    _____

    _____

8. Why aren't "be concise" and "be imaginative" as contradictory as they may sound? (Or, how can one be both concise and imaginative in writing?)

    _____

    _____

    _____

    _____

9. Why did Plato and Socrates argue against writing?

    _____

    _____

    _____

    _____

10. Although moveable type was actually invented in China in 11th century, who usually gets credit for the invention and when did he make his invention?

    _____

    _____

    _____

    _____

Chapter 4: Discussion Questions

1. In your own words, what does "interpellation" mean in this context?

    _____

    _____

    _____

    _____

2. What is the "producer function" referred to in this chapter?

    _____

    _____

    _____

    _____

3. The authors of this chapter argue that producers of visual images are only partially responsible for their meaning. Who else is responsible? Briefly explain why/how.

    _____

    _____

    _____

    _____

4. What is the impact of context on the way someone interprets a visual message?

    _____

    _____

    _____

    _____

5. What are the two "fundamental concepts of value" in all viewer interpretations?

    _____

    _____

    _____

    _____

6. What is the difference between aesthetic judgment and taste?

_____

_____

_____

_____

7. Briefly explain the idea of "institutional critique" as it relataes to visual artifacts.

_____

_____

_____

_____

8. Summarize, in your own words, Marx's critique as it applies to communication.

_____

_____

_____

_____

9. What are the three positions a "decoder" might take in reading a visual message?

_____

_____

_____

_____

10. How might someone in a communication profession use the information in this chapter in order to be more effective? Select one profession and provide an example of how this information might be used.

_____

_____

_____

_____

Chapter 3: Discussion Questions

1. Name the 5 types of gestures explained in this chapter.

   ~~Kinesics~~, ~~Proxemics~~, ~~Gestures~~, ~~haptics~~
   Emblems, illustrators, regulators, affect displays,
   and adaptors

2. What does the term "haptic" refer to?

   The term "haptic" refers to of or relating
   to sense of touch

3. What are the six functions of nonverbal communication, according to this chapter?

   The six functions of non-verbal communication
   are: Structuring and relating interaction, Creating and
   managing identities and impressions, Communicating emotion,
   defining and managing relationships, Influencing others, Deceiving others

4. Paraphrase in your own words the meaning of "display rules."

   Display rules are culturally and socially acceptable
   codes of displaying context-based emotions
   at the appropriate time.

5. Give an example of one way in which a communication professional might use the knowledge from this chapter in a professional environment.

   A communication professor might use vocalics to
   keep a class engaged in topics, use appropriate
   proxemics to non-verbally communicate a student-
   teacher relationship

6. Give a brief example of how nonverbal codes help manage relationships.

Non-verbal codes help manage relationships more subtley than direct verbal communication through things like body language and ~~gestures~~ physical appearance to display dominance (~~handshake~~ to ~~physical contact~~ eye contact and formal action)

7. What are some advantages of a functional approach to understanding nonverbal communication codes?

Some advantages of a functional approach to understanding nonverbal communication are the ability to have an influence over other people through physical attractiveness, credibility and perception of power.

8. Give an example (not from the book) of using nonverbal cues to generate group identity.

Some people create a group identity through intricate haptic rituals, such as a secret handshake or celebratory gestures to others to display a group identity.

9. Do you consider yourself more monchronemic or polychronemic? Provide an example to demonstrate why you chose as you did.

Given the culture that I grew up in (north America) I would classify myself as relatively monchronemic as I have difficulty thinking about multiple things at once and often consult a calendar so I can tackle projects one day at a time.

10. If you were trying to convince your professor to give you an extension on a paper, how might you use nonverbal cues to enhance your message? Give specific examples. (Hint: think about the final paragraph of the chapter conclusion.)

I would use kinesics and proxemics, maintaining eye contact as well as a close/but acceptable distance to show i'm concerned ~~and~~, but no haptics to display recognition of power in relationship. Hopefully I have an artifact such as a doctors note that corroborates with my story.

Name: Paul Visshly

Chapter 2: Discussion Questions

1. What is the characteristic of language all dialects share (i.e., the definition of language)?

   All dialects of language share the fact that they use symbols governed by rules to convey messages between individuals.

2. Name the four types of rules related to language.

   Phonological, Syntactic, Semantic and Pragmatic.

3. Provide an example of the power of language to shape attitudes (something not used as an example in the chapter).

   The use of the label "hipster" has recently been used to, often to marginalize or stigmatize groups or individuals participating in recent cultural fads in the US

4. Should the "generic he" be acceptable language use in our current society?

   I think that as society progresses and we understand and become more self-aware about the underlying sexism, we shouldn't abandon practical language for politically correct language in the same cases.

5. What is the danger in a young, female professor using an overly polite speaking style with graduate students in her class?

   Her politeness and use of powerless language could be misinterpreted as weakness and the potentially be taken advantage of.

6. Provide one example of convergence and one example of divergence in speech accommodation.

An example of convergence could be for example, a parent using slang to relate to their child, an example of divergent language would be a politician using political jargon to appear more knowledgeable about issues than his opponent.

7. Give three "regionalisms" from your home (state, town, region).

(NY) State : "Hero" = large sandwich

(Mamaroneck) Town : "Mamdo" = Hometown

(Northeast / Mid Atlantic) Region : "Youse" = Plural for you

8. According to the authors, what type of description solves the problem of abstract language?

The authors say behavioral description solve the problem of abstract language.

9. Do you agree that men and women communicate differently? Why or why not?

Although a huge generalization, I agree that men and women communicate differently and for different reasons. I also agree that most use communication as a primary way of building and maintaining relationships

10. In your own words, define linguistic relativism.

Linguistic relativism reflects a cultures implicit or outlook on the world that it inhabits

Name: Paul Mellaly

Chapter 1: Discussion Questions

1. List the characteristics of communication competence.

    The characteristics of Communication Competence are: that there is no ideal way of properly Communicating, it depends on the situation, it involves relationships, and it can be learned.

2. Use the transactional model of communication to briefly describe an interaction you had with someone this week.

    During a meeting with my professor office hours, I noticed that he stopped checking his email when I spoke to him, and when he spoke he would then go back to the computer.

3. Briefly assess your level of communication competence using the concepts outlined in the chapter.

    Although I am often aware of the number of behaviors available to me, I don't always choose the most appropriate one or skillfully conduct it.

4. What are the different categories of communication, according to the chapter?

    Interpersonal, dyadic, Small group and mass

5. List the different needs communication fulfills.

    Physical, Identity, Social and Practical needs.

6. Give an example of how you understand your identity through communication.

   I understand my identity through conversations about interests or politics with people by recognizing either that I agree with what they are saying or I don't.

7. Why is the transactional model of communication more accurate than the linear model of communication?

   It is more accurate, because we are simultaneously receiving and sending messages and working with prior data.

8. What are the limitations of the transactional model?

   Some limitations involve receiving nonverbal symbols that are not intentional and factoring in what is effectively false communication.

9. List the key components to the transactional model of communication.

   Some key components to the transactional model of communication involve feedback and the two or many channels that both decode and respond.

10. Select the "misconception" about communication you found most revealing or interesting. Paraphrase the misconception in your own words and provide a brief example of it (not an example provided in the chapter).

    "Communication will solve all problems?" I find that sometimes people place too high a regard for communication and it often ends up complicating or making things worse